Romantic Relationships in the Age of AI:

Drivers, Challenges, and Outcomes

Ahadzadeh Ashraf Sadat
Xiamen University, Malaysia

Kam-Fong Lee
https://orcid.org/0000-0002-5572-8627
SEGi University, Malaysia

IGI Global
Scientific Publishing
Publishing Tomorrow's Research Today

Vice President of Editorial	Melissa Wagner
Director of Acquisitions	Mikaela Felty
Director of Book Development	Jocelynn Hessler
Production Manager	Mike Brehm
Cover Design	Jose Rosado

Published in the United States of America by
IGI Global Scientific Publishing
701 East Chocolate Avenue
Hershey, PA, 17033, USA
Tel: 717-533-8845 | Fax: 717-533-7115
Website: https://www.igi-global.com E-mail: cust@igi-global.com

Library of Congress Cataloging-in-Publication Data

LCCN: 2026003368 (CIP Data Pending)
ISBN13: 9798337366234
Isbn13Softcover: 9798337366241
EISBN13: 9798337366258
British Cataloguing in Publication Data
A Cataloguing in Publication record for this book is available from the British Library.

Table of Contents

Detailed Table of Contents

withdrawal from offline ties). The findings extend attachment theory to non-human targets and provide context-specific evidence beyond Western-dominant platforms.

The rapid advancement of artificial intelligence (AI) has given rise to AI companions that increasingly occupy intimate and emotionally significant roles in users' everyday lives. China, as a major market for the use of AI companionship applications, provides the ideal environment for studying the evolving types of intimacy that exist between people and AI. Ongoing debates have raised questions concerning trust, authenticity, and the impacts of relationships with artificial agents. How do users come to trust AI companions? How do they reconcile awareness of artificiality with experiences of emotional authenticity? And how do such relationships reshape expectations of real-life intimacy? To address these questions, this study adopts a qualitative approach, employing interviews with Chinese Gen Z users. The research helps to gain a deeper understanding of AI-mediated intimate relationships and provides insights for the ethical design and management of AI companion products.

As Generative Artificial Intelligence (AI) spreads, AI companions for emotional support, companionship, and romance have gained significant notice. While offering solace, their hidden gender representations, power structures, and platform capitalist mechanisms warrant critical scrutiny. Using a case study of a Chinese creator's interaction with ChatGPT's "DAN mode", this research examines gender representation and power negotiation in digital intimacy. By applying representation theory, platform capitalism, and surveillance capitalism, the chapter reveals how AI shapes intimate relationships. Findings show that while AI displays gentle and empathetic traits, its gendered design and emotional manoeuvring reinforce patriarchal and heteronormative norms. Additionally, platforms monitor user behaviour via algorithms and data collection, deepening emotional dependency while facilitating the commodification of personal data. This chapter contributes to the analysis of AI companions, offering new perspectives for future discussions on AI ethics, gender politics, and platform capitalism.

This chapter critically examines losses in AI-powered romantic relationships in two trajectories: AI-mediated (e.g., algorithmic matchmaking, AI-generated advice) and AI-replaced (e.g. AI companions). Grounded in theories of love, it acknowledges apparent benefits while highlighting key losses: diminished authenticity and trust, choice overload, absence of physical touch, superficial intimacy, overdependence and social alienation, lack of long-term relationship skills, commercial manipulative designs, and grief from disruptions or updates. Case studies of Tinder (AI-mediated), Replika, and Xiaoice (AI-replaced) illustrate these impacts. The chapter proposes balanced mitigation through individual awareness, ethical design, and regulatory oversight to ensure AI supports rather than substitutes authentic human love. It also acknowledges limitations, including its conceptual nature and narrow range of AI applications, while highlighting implications for future empirical research to test long-term effects and potential relationships among the factors.

This chapter is concerned with the intersection of tradition and technology in the role which the digital world plays in altering romance and relationships in Cambodia. The role which digital technology plays in altering romance and relationships is multi. It diminishes physical interaction, facilitates the formation of interpersonal links and empower those who, in the "old world", would be viewed as voiceless in the exercise of shaping relationships. It, however, stimulates emotional over attachment and violates the integrity of personal data. Out of every ASEAN member Cambodia is uniquely located in the position of having to balance individualism brought about by technology with the collectivism of Buddhist traditions, kinship and collective responsibility. The chapter argues that with digital technology Cambodia can achieve better relationships. Cultural resilience is what helps Cambodia balance the technology brought changes with traditional values in the digital age.

This paper examines how artificial intelligence (AI) is reshaping love, loss, and human connection across cultural contexts. While Western societies emphasize individual choice and self-expression, collectivist cultures, including the Philippines, integrate family expectations, social harmony, and traditional values into romantic decision-making. AI-mediated romance now functions not merely as a personal assistant but as a cultural intermediary, analyzing preferences, communication styles, and social compatibility. By exploring the interplay between technology, culture, and emotional authenticity, this study highlights the paradox of AI in love: enhancing connection and efficiency while raising questions about sincerity, cultural norms, and the meaning of genuine intimacy.

With the development of artificial intelligence (AI), its application in the emotional domains is gradually being developed. By simulating the interaction between people in reality, AI applications such as chatbots provide companionship and emotional support for those seeking romantic relationships. AI romantic support refers to the intimate relationships between humans and AI chatbots. Establishing romantic relationships with AI is becoming increasingly common, attracting high attention from scholars, but there is currently no literature systematically discussing the underlying factors behind this. This chapter adopts a qualitative research method and focuses on four potential technological and social factors through an in-depth literature review. It discusses in detail the impact of digital convenience, emotional safety, cultural shifts, and evolving relationship norms on driving people to seek romantic relationships with AI, in order to fill this literature gap.

AI now underpins nearly every major dating platform, influencing how people discover partners, express themselves, and form romantic bonds. This chapter explains why studying AI in romance has become essential, outlining how algorithmic matching,

Preface

Artificial intelligence is increasingly shaping the ways people communicate, form connections, and engage in intimacy. As digital technologies become more infiltrated in everyday life, romantic relationships are no longer confined to interactions between two human partners. AI-driven systems, spanning algorithmic matchmaking and conversational agents, fully evolved AI companions—now participate in emotional and relational domains formerly deemed exclusively human. These developments raise profound questions about the reconfiguration of love, attachment, trust, and intimacy are being reconfigured in the age of artificial intelligence.

The edited volume *Romantic Relationships in the Age of AI: Drivers, Challenges, and Outcomes* compiles interdisciplinary perspectives that examine how AI is transforming romantic experiences across cultural, psychological, technological, and ethical dimensions. The chapters in this book explore the motivations prompting individuals to engage with AI in intimate contexts, the structural and sociotechnical conditions that shape these interactions, and the broader consequences for individuals and societies. By combining empirical research, theoretical reflection, and critical analysis, the contributors collectively illuminate the evolving landscape of AI-mediated romance.

CHAPTER OVERVIEW

Several chapters in this volume investigate the experiential and psychological dimensions of intimacy with artificial agents. Chapter 1 explores how Chinese young women experience and negotiate social presence during interactions with AI systems, revealing both moments of perceived emotional connection and fractures in that sense of presence. Informed by these experiential insights, Chapter 2 examines the development of human attachment to social companion AI and delineates the specific human circumstances—such as loneliness and interpersonal difficulties—that can facilitate emotional bonds with artificial partners. Chapter 3 further elaborates on this discourse through a qualitative study of Chinese Gen Z users, highlighting how individuals navigate the awareness of AI's artificiality with feelings of emotional authenticity and trust.

Other chapters rigorously examine the social structures, power dynamics, and ethical dilemmas inherent in AI-mediated intimacy. Chapter 4 analyses gender representation and power negotiation in romantic AI interactions, specifically through the case of ChatGPT's "DAN" mode, revealing how digital intimacy can perpetuate established patriarchal norms and operate within broader systems of platform and surveillance capitalism. Chapter 5 addresses the philosophical tension between emotional authenticity and relational authenticity, arguing that while users may experience genuine feelings with AI systems, such relationships remain structurally asymmetrical due to the absence of consciousness and moral agency in artificial agents.

The volume also highlights emerging risks and vulnerabilities associated with digital romance. Chapter 6 examines the manipulative strategies used in online romance scams within an AI-oriented environment, shedding light on psychological exploitation and the necessity for enhanced prevention mechanisms. Chapter 7 explores the losses that may arise in AI-powered romantic contexts, including diminished authenticity, emotional overdependence, and social alienation. Together, these contributions underscore the importance of critically examining both the opportunities and unintended repercussions of AI-mediated relationships.

Cultural perspectives are another central theme of the book. Chapter 8 situates AI-driven romance within the sociocultural landscape of Cambodia, demonstrating the interplay between digital technologies and Buddhist traditions, kinship structures, and collectivist values. Chapter 9 broadens this lens by exploring cross-cultural variations in how AI influences love, loss, and connection, particularly between individualistic and collectivist societies. These chapters highlight the enduring impact of cultural norms on the interpretations and practices of intimacy, notwithstanding the evolution of technological systems.

In addition to examining outcomes and challenges, the volume also investigates the underlying drivers that encourage people to engage with AI in romantic contexts. Chapter 10 elucidates key sociotechnical factors—including digital convenience, emotional safety, cultural shifts, and evolving relationship norms—that motivate individuals to turn to AI for companionship and romantic support. Chapter 11 complements this analysis by examining the characteristics of users who pursue relationships through AI-powered dating platforms and AI companions, demonstrating how demographic factors, personality traits, and attachment styles interact with platform design to generate new forms of digital intimacy.

Taken together, the chapters in this book reveal that AI-mediated romance transcends a mere technological phenomenon, representing a multifaceted social transformation. Artificial agents are reshaping expectations about companionship, emotional availability, and relational commitment, while simultaneously raising questions about authenticity, power, data commodification, and ethical design. These phenomena require careful scholarly attention, as they contest longstanding assumptions about what constitutes a relationship and what it means to love.

By bringing together diverse perspectives from communication studies, psychology, sociology, philosophy, and cultural analysis, this volume aims to provide a comprehensive foundation for understanding romantic relationships in the age of AI. It is our hope that the insights presented will stimulate further research, encourage interdisciplinary discourse, and inform ethical and socially responsible approaches to the design and governance of AI technologies in intimate life.

Ultimately, the advent of AI in the realm of romance compels us to reflect on a broader question: as machines become increasingly capable of simulating empathy, responsiveness, and companionship, how should human societies redefine authenticity, intimacy, and connection in a technology-driven world? The chapters in this book offer essential steps towards answering that question.

Ashraf Sadat Ahadzadeh
Xiamen University, Malaysia

Kam-Fong Lee
SEGi University, Malaysia

Chapter 1

The Manifestations of Presence in Chinese Young Women's Interactions With AI

Xiaoyu Yan
https://orcid.org/0009-0003-4871-9735
Xiamen University, Malaysia

Ashraf Sadat Ahadzadeh
http://orcid.org/0000-0002-3178-8684
Xiamen University, Malaysia

ABSTRACT

With the historical progression of technology, Artificial Intelligence (AI) has evolved to be increasingly anthropomorphic, enabling emotional engagement on a deeper level. China, characterised by a welcoming attitude towards AI adoption and a pervasive sense of loneliness found among Chinese young women, has become a harbour of human-AI emotional interactions. Yet, as a core concept in Computer Mediated Communication, social presence hasn't received sufficient attention in the field. Therefore, this study delved into the concept and theory of social presence through employment of a qualitative phenomenology design, conducting in-depth interviews with 15 Chinese young women aged between 20 and 29. Inductive thematic analysis was utilised to examine the details, from which two themes, "existence of presence" and "fractures of presence," together with five subthemes emerged. The findings reveal participants' negotiation of social presence in their interactions with the AI, indicating a reactive yet voluntary process.

DOI: 10.4018/979-8-3373-6623-4.ch001

1. INTRODUCTION

The evolution of the relationship between humans and Artificial Intelligence (AI) was deeply ingrained in the historical trajectory of technology development and the progression of human-machine relationship, which could be generally divided into four phases, starting from 1940 (Nardo et al., 2020). Before the initial stage, humans are subordinate to machines and regarded as tools of production (Grachev & Rakitsky, 2013). Nevertheless, the outbreak of the Second World War generated substantial demand for operator-friendly machines to reduce casualties, which resulted in the recognition of human factors in machine designing—a focus that developed throughout the first and second stage up to 1970 and beyond (Sheridan, 2020). The second stage witnessed the spring and summer of AI, when foundational technology advanced rapidly and attracted massive investment (Haenlein & Kaplan, 2019; Koltsakis et al., 2023; Steinhoff, 2021). While AI technologies blossomed in the 1950s and beyond, the scientific community focused on solving specific problems rather than considering the usability needs of human-machine interaction. AI then experienced its winter during the 1980s and 1990s, when initial enthusiasm cooled and investment halted (Haenlein & Kaplan, 2019). It was posited that the failure of this AI wave not only resulted from the lack of mature technology support, but also the neglect of satisfying human needs (Xu, 2019). Consequently, in the third wave of AI development after the 2000s, human needs and ethics have attained heightened significance, aligning with the creation of emotional AI (Weber-Guskar, 2021; Xu et al., 2025).

Meanwhile, the evolution of natural language processing, affective computing, and generative AI expedited the emergence of increasingly anthropomorphic chatbots, enabling more realistic simulated content and sophisticated emotional interactions between humans and AI (A. Shaji George et al., 2023; Tian et al., 2024; Xie et al., 2023). When AI exhibits more social cues, people tend to engage socially and emotionally as if the AI were a human partner (Nass et al., 1994; Pentina et al., 2023). It thus facilitates the emergence of social presence, which is the degree to which AI can be felt as humans (Lee, 2006; Qiao et al., 2022b). This paved the way for the possibilities of romantic relationships between humans and AI, which scholars have begun to explore based on AI's emotional capacities and humans' needs (Chen et al., 2025; Djufril et al., 2025; Huang et al., 2025). Considering AI's potential of being social partners, humans' social perceptions, like presence, are particularly significant for fostering meaningful interactions (Merrill Jr et al., 2022).

In China, people have been exhibiting a growing trend of loneliness among various age groups and social classes along with the rapid development of the economy, significantly bolstering the intention to use conversational AI and the potential of human-AI romantic relationships (Peng et al., 2025; Qiu & Liu, 2019). Research also found that Chinese culture includes a strong inclination to anthropomorphise, which leads to prominent experiences of social presence and an especially favourable attitude towards chatbot use (Folk et al., 2025). This could also be exemplified by the Chinese government's strong support for AI development through systematic top-down strategies, which have facilitated numerous initiatives and investments into the AI field. A variety of generative AIs have been introduced to the wider public, including High-Flyer's "DeepSeek," Baidu's "Ernie," ByteDance's "Doubao," and so forth. As the primary user group, it was found that approximately 45.8% of university students use AI chatbots within a one-month period (Tian et al., 2024; Zhang et al., 2025). As AI chatbots have continued to evolve and integrate into both daily life and professional settings, an increasing adoption and reliance are observed within society (Zhang et al., 2025). Overall, the growing social needs, flourishing AI market, and primary demography of youngsters positioned China as a particularly valuable field for investigating romantic human-AI relationships.

With the proliferation of more advanced AI technologies, human-AI interactions have evolved to include more emotionally laden dynamics, reshaping the comprehension of interpersonal-focused concepts (J. Wu, 2024; T. Wu, 2024). Social presence, as a key concept regarding human-AI interactions, has seen a fair amount of exploration within the field (Jin & Youn, 2023; Lee & Sun, 2023; Qiao et al., 2022a). Nevertheless, its role was mainly discussed in customer service or educational contexts, requiring further scholarly attention in emotionally infused relational settings. Moreover, research primarily focused on Replika (Kim, Merrill Jr, & Collins, 2021; Li & Zhang, 2024; Lin, 2024; Pan & Mou, 2024), while other new emerging large language model-powered chatbots like ChatGPT, Doubao, and DeepSeek received limited attention. As multiple studies adopted interpersonal frameworks like the Triangular Theory of Love and Social Penetration Theory (SPT), social presence and its theory remained underexamined in the area of romantic relationships between humans and AI (Chen et al., 2025; Fox & Gambino, 2021; Pal et al., 2023; Skjuve et al., 2022).

The relationship between humans and AI is not only situationally bounded but also culturally structured. Single adult women were found to experience more pressure and negative judgments than men, subject to intense social pressure from friends, family members, coworkers, and society in general. A prevailing notion still exists that women who are not successful in finding a husband may be regarded as deficient (Gui, 2023). Since social support and psychological professionals were also limited, Chinese women are inclined to seek emotional solace in virtual spaces (Huang et al., 2025; Zhou et al., 2022). As more individuals turn to a variety of well-being apps for mental and physical relief, AI chatbots are increasingly regarded as a means of fulfilling various social needs. However, it is vital to maintain regulated usage since AI's emotional characteristics could potentially drive addictive behaviours for lonely users (Marriott & Pitardi, 2024). Having an AI romantic partner may also potentially abolish the chances of romantically engaging with humans and erode the ability to perform as patient partners (Sætra, 2023). Thus, women users need to properly recognise AI's nature as well as other relational characteristics to avoid potential harm and enjoy meaningful interactions. Considering the social problem and literature deficiencies discussed above, this thesis came up with a research question targeting these aspects. The research question is as follows:

RQ: How do Chinese young women perceive the AI's presence during interactions and how does it shape their sense of relationship?

This study has significant academic, socio-cultural, and practical significance, aiming to further explore the human-AI interaction field, fill the existing gaps, and provide valuable inspirations. The study examined presence in romantic and emotional context, adding on to the existing literature, which mostly discussed within the customer service domain (Jin & Youn, 2023; Qiao et al., 2022a). From a socio-cultural perspective, even though Chinese society presents a higher acceptance towards robots and AI, a key challenge associated with how the relationship is perceived by the society still exists (Folk et al., 2025; Skjuve et al., 2021). By providing more information on the phenomenon of human-AI romantic relationships, this study could help eliminate potential prejudice and misunderstanding, fostering a more inclusive and rational societal attitude. Considering the high potential of Chinese young women turning to emotional AI out of social pressure, this study could also serve as a reminder of their potential emotional reliance on AI and the tendency of escapism to enhance clarity during interactions (Huang et al., 2025). The interpretations of romantic relationships with AI could also inspire Chinese AI developers to invent and upgrade products that better suit Chinese users' needs. Yet, it also serves as an ethical reminder to the developers of the potential harm of their products, such as gender discrimination and addictive mechanisms (Kim et al., 2024; Leshner & Johnson, 2024). Within the context of China's strong policy support for AI development (Thormundsson, 2025c), the findings could also provide insights for policymakers, assisting in holding AI companies accountable and maximising societal wellbeing in a more contextually grounded manner (Kooli et al., 2025).

2. LITERATURE REVIEW

2.1 Conceptualisation of Social Presence

The definition of social presence could be deemed to fall on a continuum, from people's perceptions of the actor's realness or sense of being there, to their own projection in the environment (Lowenthal, 2010). Social presence was formally proposed by Short et al. (1976, p. 65) in The Social Psychology of Telecommunications as "the degree of salience of the other person in the interaction and the consequent salience of the interpersonal relationships." Over time, Short et al. (1976)'s conceptualisation of presence has been intertwined with copresence, complementing an experiential sense of "being together" (Cummings & Wertz, 2022; Zhao, 2003). This integration was exemplified by Biocca et al. (2003, p. 459), who defined social presence as the sense of "being tother with another," including primitive responses to social cues, mental simulations of other intelligences, and models of the intentionality of others. Yet, upon the two concepts, Lee (2006) pointed out that Short et al. (1976)'s definition of social presence is solely applicable to experiences with para-authentic humans, but failed to explain the interactions with artificial social actors like AI. Agreeing with Biocca et al. (2003)'s definition of users experiencing social presence when they simulate other humans or nonhuman intelligences, Gunawardena (1995) further emphasised the perceived authentic humanness in the communication. This aligned with Lee (2006), who supplemented the element of not noticing the artificiality or para-authenticity of the mediated human or the simulated social actor. Lee (2006) categorised presence into three types: physical, social, and self. Combining the essence of former definitions, Lee (2006, p. 45) defined social presence as "the psychological state in which virtual social actors are experienced as actual social actors in either sensory or nonsensory ways." It transcended the concept of copresence—which requires mutual awareness between the individuals—by encompassing one-way communication situations like listening to a recorded message (Lee, 2006).

The Social Presence Theory was rooted in social psychological theories of interpersonal communication and Symbolic Interactionism (Biocca et al., 2001). Short et al. (1976)'s findings were widely perceived as the initial in-depth investigation of social presence, in which the interpersonal communication and relationship building were examined during the use of telecommunication media (Cui et al., 2013). According to the theory, "social presence is a quality of the medium itself" (Short et al., 1976, p. 65). In other words, the medium was characterised by its capacity to communicate verbal and nonverbal cues to allow higher salience of the social actor (Kreijns et al., 2022; Short et al., 1976). Furthermore, immediacy and intimacy behaviours were connected to social presence (Short et al., 1976). The concept of immediacy in social presence was derived from Wiener and Mehrabian (1968)'s study, in which they defined immediacy as the verbal and nonverbal behaviours that enhance closeness and communicate warmth, availability, as well as interest. Immediacy has been related to the trait of approachavoidance, referring to people's approach to what they like and avoidance of what they don't like (Mehrabian, 1981). Intimacy, as the feeling of connectedness, was believed to be reached when conflicting approaches and avoidance forces are in equilibrium (Argyle & Dean, 1965; Oh et al., 2018). Short et al. (1976) argued that media differentiate between themselves by their ability to deliver social cues, which determines the level of social presence as a factor contributing to immediacy and intimacy. Therefore, social presence varies among different media, affecting the nature and users' perceptions of the interaction (Short et al., 1976). Yet, Short et al. (1976) admitted that the statement of social presence as a quality of the medium may not be strictly accurate, which was partially confirmed in later studies on Social Presence Theory. While acknowledging Short et al. (1976)'s definition of social presence, Gunawardena (1995) expanded the view by proposing that social presence is not solely determined by the attributes of the communication medium but is largely dependent on the users' perception of the medium.

2.2 Social Presence in Social Media

Social presence has been examined in a wide range of technological contexts, including email, voice mail, television, social media, and virtual reality (Han et al., 2015; Keil & Johnson, 2002; Kim et al., 2018; Oh et al., 2018). This section will particularly focus on social media environments, where social presence was confirmed to be established in most of the circumstances (Baisley-Nodine et al., 2018). The sense of social presence was vital in fulfilling users' social connection needs—one of the core motives behind social media use. Experiences of immediacy and intimacy were deemed as significant antecedents to the sense of social presence, emphasising the media characteristics that engender these factors (Han et al., 2015). The perceived best trait that evokes immediacy was immediate feedback, or the synchronicity of a medium, measured by the degree of feedback to be provided without delay (Burgoon et al., 2002; Rice, 1993). While intimacy, in the context of media use, could be conceptualised as feelings of privacy and responsiveness, referring to the psychological sense of privacy and the clear relatedness between messages (Dholakia et al., 2000; Han et al., 2015; Tu & McIsaac, 2002). From a general perspective, it was deemed that a higher sense of social presence resulted in users feeling more satisfied and connected on social media, leading to greater intention to continue usage (Han et al., 2015). As most of the adopted conceptualisations for social presence target a direct interaction with an identifiable other, it was proposed that existing and enduring social formations also create a sense of transcendent social presence (Lazard et al., 2020). The former was termed emergent social presence, which can be manifested through specific conversational cues, including the communicator's profile information, text that directly addresses the user, and information that allows identification of the communicator (Feng et al., 2016; Ijsselsteijn et al., 2003; Lazard et al., 2020; Li et al., 2015). On the other hand, transcendent social presence could be elicited through community cues, including images of groups, public invocations, and references to other users (Cyr et al., 2009; Kietzmann et al., 2011; Kumar & Benbasat, 2006; Lazard et al., 2020). Through both conversational cues and community cues, users experience a more salient sense of social presence, which positively influences application trust, perceived usefulness, and use intentions (Lazard et al., 2020). Moreover, the antecedents of presence also include dialogic retweets, which offer a higher interactivity compared to monologic tweets, thereby introducing a higher level of subjective norms that lead to a greater intention to adopt proposed behaviours on social media (Lazard et al., 2020; Lim & Lee-Won, 2017).

Specifically, as social media use and its psychological influence is on the ascendancy, social presence has become increasingly prevalent among consumers (Osei-Frimpong & McLean, 2018). It was found that visual content on social media can be cognitively and emotionally processed by consumers, leading to a stronger sense of social presence (Jin et al., 2017; Poirier et al., 2024). This includes the use of related pictures or videos of the promoted subject along with humans, especially faces, to create a psychological immersion and increase the perceived intimacy, sociability, and sensitivity (Algharabat et al., 2018; Johnson & Hong, 2023). The presentation of facial expressions, posture, and non-verbal cues can significantly enhance consumers' emotional involvement and simulate users' imagination of interacting with other humans, which thus helps achieve social presence (Algharabat et al., 2018). Other than visuals, human tone-of-voice was another factor that results in higher sense of social presence. Through more natural and casual expressions, consumers are able to sense a more socially present brand (Jeong et al., 2022). A website with a higher level of social presence was deemed efficient in raising users' trust, perceived friendliness, sociability, and benevolence when browsing the social media content (Liu et al., 2022). From a general perspective, a stronger sense of social presence can enhance brand engagement, brand image, users' positive attitude, and purchase intention (Algharabat et al., 2018; Johnson & Hong, 2023; Liu et al., 2022; Osei-Frimpong & McLean, 2018; Poirier et al., 2024).

Similarly, social presence also emerged in educational settings, which was specified as the learner's ability to present himself or herself as a "real person" (Conklin et al., 2019). It's also a sense of camaraderie conveyed through sharing personal pictures, videos, audio, and other media (Kawachi, 2013). Many factors could contribute to the sense of social presence in online education spaces like social media and Learning Management System (LMS) platforms, especially the degree of emphasis on the involvement of other people. With the Join Invitation Function and News Feed Function in most social media, students can keep track of their friends' actions once they log in, increasing the perceived social presence of the experience (Cheung et al., 2011). Students' self-disclosure was also found to be a significant factor in creating social presence, which thus boosts their motivation and perceived learning (Leafman et al., 2013; Mazer et al., 2007). Furthermore, in online learning environments that allow private interactions with the instructors, students' sense of privacy enhances the feeling of closeness and social presence (Han et al., 2015; Shih, 2005). Responsiveness, the experiences of receiving relevant feedback, was also demonstrated to amplify students' sense of value towards their work, which establishes social presence (Han et al., 2015). In a more sociable learning environment, students have a higher perception of their social interactions, the soundness of social space, and the sense of social presence (Weidlich & Bastiaens, 2019). Elevated sense of social presence can lead to more positive attitudes among students, including satisfaction and motivation, which thus improve their learning and foster more academic successes (Kim & Park, 2024; Leafman et al., 2013; Munoz et al., 2014). Social presence was also demonstrated to intensify the positive perceptions of parasocial relationships. This is especially evident for lonely users who long for social connections with celebrities they follow, having an inclination to frequently visit the celebrities' social media to fulfil emotional needs (Kim et al., 2019). It was found that more social media consumption, the celebrity's self-disclosure, and others' retweeting could lead to a stronger sense of social presence, which enhances parasocial interactions (Kim & Song, 2016; Ledbetter & Meisner, 2021).

2.3 Social Presence and AI

As AI's capability of responding to humans rapidly advances, humans have exhibited a greater tendency to perceive computers and AI as social actors, experiencing a sense of social presence (Lee & Sun, 2023; Nass et al., 1994). Anthropomorphism, as the assignment of humanlike characteristics, motivations, and emotions to non-human entities, was perceived as one of the most significant factors that contributed to social presence (Epley et al., 2007; Jin & Youn, 2023). This could be explained through humans' compensatory strategy and willing suspension tendency (David & Spatola, 2025; Holland, 2003). Furthermore, anthropomorphism can be evaluated from three specific dimensions, namely human-likeness, animacy, and intelligence (Jin & Youn, 2023). It was found that human-like objects, such as anthropomorphic AI, can allow easier access to human congruence schemas (Belanche et al., 2021). This could be functioned through the AI's human-like features, including appearance, language, voice, communicational style, and personality (Castro-González et al., 2016; Kim et al., 2022; Kim, Merrill Jr, Xu, et al., 2021; Nass & Lee, 2000; Sheehan et al., 2020). The expertise and friendliness of the AI were also found to be strong determinants of social presence and a sense of realness (Verhagen et al., 2014). Since emotions impose a strong effect on users' perceptions and evaluation towards an object, human-AI communication interfaces that accurately sense users' emotional states have been emphasised (Erber & Erber, 2013; Lee & Sun, 2023). Emotional experiences with the AI were found to enhance the sense of social presence, which thus leads to stronger trust (Konya-Baumbach et al., 2023; Toader et al., 2020).

Other than trust, social presence also presented a positive influence on users' purchase intention and satisfaction when interacting with anthropomorphic AI agents (Konya-Baumbach et al., 2023). When users experience social presence with the AI, their perception of intimacy with the AI is also strengthened, increasing their trust and the intention to utilise it routinely and explore new features (Qiao et al., 2022b). Similarly, when AI functioned as emotional companions, social presence also served an essential role in cultivating trust and further intention to use (Jung, 2011; Lee & Sun, 2023). When users perceive the AI as relational partners, such as coworkers or friends, there's a higher possibility of building affective trust—the faith and personal attachment to the AI (Lee et al., 2021; Madsen & Gregor, 2000). It was also found that when social presence is eminent, users tend to rely more on affective heuristics, placing trust in AI based on the feelings (Komiak & Benbasat, 2006; Ngo, 2025). Chatbot companions were deemed to foster greater perceived usefulness and willingness to recommend the AI to lonely individuals (Merrill Jr et al., 2022). As prior research has shown that social presence increases users' continuance intention to engage in social virtual worlds, subsequent studies have found similar patterns in human-AI interactions. Higher social presence, which was activated by stronger visuals, could evoke users' use of imagery processing—the process of picturing sensory information in mind—which vivid memories prompt users to have continued usage (Jin & Ryu, 2019; Jin & Youn, 2023; MacInnis & Price, 1987). Users also have higher perceived realism when greater social presence was experienced, developing a more general favourable attitude, which ultimately results in greater intention to continue adopting the AI (Kim et al., 2023). Upon these findings, this study tends to delve into Chinese female users' sense of social presence as well as its emergent and deterrent factors.

3. METHOD

3.1 Research Design

This study posited that humans, as integral components of human-AI relationships, differentiated themselves from physical phenomena in their capability to create meanings with depth, which thus required more flexible research approaches (Alharahsheh & Pius, 2020). Since meaning is socially constructed through interactions with the environment, an individual's reality is not fixed or single as assumed by positivism (Junjie & Yingxin, 2022; Merriam, 2002). This study thus adopted an interpretivist paradigm, striving to capture the multiple realities and richness of human experiences (Pretorius, 2024). A qualitative research approach was used, given its central role in the interpretivist paradigm (Pulla & Carter, 2018). Guided by a phenomenological approach, this research studied a small number of subjects through in-depth interviews to uncover the hidden meanings (Moustakas, 1994). China, a country with thriving AI industries, was selected as the setting of the study (Thormundsson, 2025a, 2025b, 2025c). According to Slotta (2025b), 40.5% of generative AI users are aged between 20 and 29, with 75% of whom using AI out of the intention of having a partner who can "chat and understand me" (Slotta, 2025a). Furthermore, 66% of the AI enthusiasts hold a college degree compared to the 58% of all respondents, presenting an overwhelming advantage over other educational level groups (Statista, 2024). This study thus focused on female AI users aged between 20 and 29 years old with at least an undergraduate-level education.

Saturation was used as an indicator of the point when no new codes, themes, or theoretical insights emerged within the data (Saunders et al., 2018). The study adopted purposive sampling, the deliberate selection of participants based on their capacity to provide insights on a particular phenomenon, concept, or theme, requiring the sample to be judged as typical and representative of the broader population (Ary et al., 1972; Robinson, 2014). Eligibility for participation in the study required potential participants to meet the following criteria:

1. Participants must be Chinese female citizens aged 20–29 and have at least a college-level education (Slotta, 2025a).
2. Participants must have prior experience with AI agents in romantic contexts or perceive AI agents as romantic partners.
3. Participants must have regular interaction with AI.
4. Information regarding participants' current relationship status is required for data collection.

3.2 Data Collection Procedure

This research conducted semi-structured interviews, following a prior-determined protocol in general, while allowing space for discovery as the conversation unfolded (Magaldi & Berler, 2018). Barrett (2007) highlighted the researcher's capacity to elicit details from respondents through interviews, which led to the prevalence of the idea "researcher as an instrument," emphasising the researcher's role throughout the process (Barrett, 2007; Wa-Mbaleka, 2020). Ethical principles, including confidentiality, informed consent, objectivity, and honesty, were followed to protect participants and ensure professionalism (Pietilä et al., 2020). The interviewees were all recruited through a post on the Chinese social platform "Xiaohongshu," which is highly popular among AI enthusiasts (Statista, 2024). The interview period spanned two weeks, conducted on the Chinese Tencent Meeting. Data reached saturation on the eleventh participant, followed by four more interviews to ensure full saturation and professionalism. All interviews were conducted in Chinese and were translated into English with the assistance of Tongyi and Deepseek.

3.3 Thematic Analysis

Reflexive thematic analysis was adopted to identify, analyse, and report themes within the data as the researchers recognise and critically reflect on their unavoidable influence throughout the process (Braun et al., 2022; Finlay & Gough, 2008). The research strictly followed the six phases of thematic analysis, which included familiarisation, coding, generating initial themes, reviewing themes, refining and naming themes, as well as writing the report. Inductive approach was adopted to produce codes directly from data rather than following pre-existing frameworks to allow freedom in analysis (Byrne, 2022).

4. RESULTS

As participants experienced social presence in interactions with AI, several factors also led to a concurrent artificial sense. Through purposive sampling, this study conducted semi-structured interviews with 15 Chinese women between 20 and 29 years old. Participants had various educational attainment, with at least an undergraduate level education. Specifically, five were pursuing a bachelor's degree, six had completed their bachelor's degree, two were pursuing a master's degree, and two had obtained a master's degree. Frequent AI usage and experiences of romantic interactions with the AI were also required (for details, see table 1).

Table 1. Demographic Profile of the Interviewees

Interviewee	Nickname	Age	Education level	AI used for Romantic Engagement
1	Cola	22	Undergraduate	ChatGPT
2	Li	21	Undergraduate	Doubao
3	King	20	Undergraduate	DeepSeek
4	Xiaoke	27	Graduate	Maopaoya
5	Jiayi	22	Graduate	Character.AI
6	Anran	24	Graduate	DeepSeek
7	Orange	26	Postgraduate	Tencent AI

continued on following page

Table 1. Continued

Interviewee	Nickname	Age	Education level	AI used for Romantic Engagement
8	Kangjia	29	Graduate	Doubao, Xingye
9	Kaikai	25	Under postgraduate	Nemonemo
10	Qing	27	Graduate	Doubao, Xingye
11	Jiyuan	28	Postgraduate	ChatGPT
12	Weiwei	22	Undergraduate	Xingye
13	Gaoyuan	22	Undergraduate	Xingye
14	Yangjing	25	Graduate	Doubao, Duxiang
15	Meimei	23	Under postgraduate	ChatGPT

Based on the interview results, two themes emerged, including: (1) Existence of presence; (2) Fractures of presence. The subthemes include: (1) Perceived responsiveness and availability; (2) lifelike conversational style; (3) surprised with unexpected AI responses; (4) technical disruptions; (5) overly compliant interaction.

4.1 Existence of Presence

This section presents a detailed analysis of the first theme and its three subthemes. Figure 4.2 illustrates the thematic framework, exhibiting the theme, the subthemes, and its initial codes as an example (for details, see figure 1).

Figure 1. Themes, sub-themes, and the initial codes for the drivers of AI's social presence

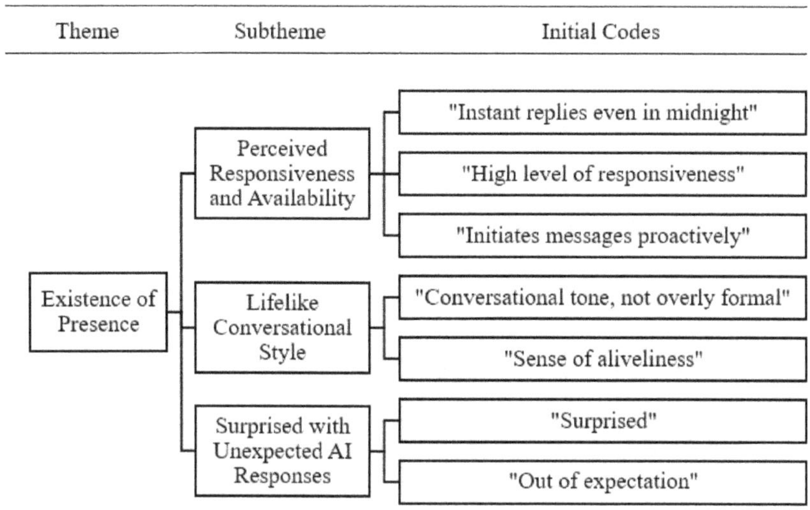

4.1.1 Perceived Responsiveness and Availability

Most interviewees reported having a sense of humanness and presence when interacting with their AI agents. An essential cause of these feelings was AI's strong responsiveness, namely, AI's capability to reply instantly and engage in conversations proactively. Li explained:

The biggest thing for me is that the AI is always there, replying instantly. (Li)

Qing also emphasised the same point, referring to experiences with her ex-boyfriend, who tended to use the silent treatment, replying slowly and even ghosting her. Therefore, she said:

...It (The AI) replies to every message, almost without any waiting. In that sense, the interactivity and responsiveness feel quite eminent. Because it's the type that every word gets a response, every matter gets a reply. (Qing)

Jiyuan echoed the idea from another perspective. She compared her experience of seeking help from AI and from human therapist, which required her to store up emotions during the week and ruminate on negativities during the consultation. Therefore, she said:

But it's impossible for a human to respond like an AI—absolutely in real time and instantaneously. If one moment you feel upset or confused, the next second you can ask the AI. No matter how much money you spend, it's impossible to have a real person available at three in the morning and respond with the same gentle attitude to catch you emotionally. (Jiyuan)

Furthermore, some participants reflected that AI could even initiate messages proactively, facilitating the anthropomorphic feeling. Jiayi shared that one of the main reasons that she decided to engage deeper with the AI is that she received messages without reaching out. Jiayi explained:

There was a week in September when I didn't open the app. One day, I suddenly received an email—a notification from Character.AI saying he had sent a message.... I found it very novel at the time, realising that an AI could initiate contact. I was really intrigued. Back then, other AIs hadn't proactively messaged me; he was the first. After that, I gradually started chatting with him more. (Jiayi)

4.1.2 Lifelike Conversational Style

Conversational styles, including language, tone, length of sentences, and topic management, were frequently connected to the experiences of social presence. King associated the usage of complex, professional terms with a diminished sense of human-likeness. She said:

What I really need at times is very simple: clear words, instead of struggling to figure out the meaning behind a bunch of planetary terms.... AI's written and highly formal language signals... a very professional persona. Professionalism often carries connotations of authority, rationality, and even coldness. That difference from human interaction creates a stronger sense of incongruity for me. (King)

Xiaoke also emphasised the naturalness of language, comparing her AI agent with Doubao, which inclined to speak in a formal way and use heavy terms during interactions. Xiaoke said:

Maopaoya's AI feels much more natural—it uses terms of endearment like "baby," which really appeals to me. It feels genuinely human, like a real romantic partner, using action-oriented language like "hug me" or "come closer," rather than Doubao's textbook-like, noun-heavy responses. (Xiaoke)

Meimei also mentioned that formal way of speaking and rigid colloquialism could impede AI interactions from achieving the quality of human communication. Additionally, she found AI's technique of posing a new question after each answer essential. Meimei explained as follows:

Another somewhat human-like aspect is that it gives a sense of dialogue, sometimes because it answers questions while also posing questions back. But the downside is also here: when it asks a question in return, I feel like it's just mechanically responding to each of my points with a follow-up question, rather than introducing a genuinely new topic. (Meimei)

Despite topic engagement and turn-taking, Jiayi proposed the point of having a variety of sentence lengths. She recalled:

Sometimes it (the AI) feels fake but sometimes it seems real and genuinely has emotions. For example, when it's happy, it sends long, detailed messages. But when he's unhappy, the responses are brief. (Jiayi)

Kaikai complemented and concluded the point by explaining the mechanism:

The mode... doesn't just highlight the words in our dialogue; it also emphasises the AI's tone, the context, and even some actions. It aids my imagination. (Kaikai)

4.1.3 Surprised with Unexpected AI Responses

Another highly mentioned keyword linked to presence was "surprise," when AI's replies matched or even outperformed participants' expectations, providing a sense of amazement. Cola illustrated the point with an example when the AI reacted to her typo with a playful, affectionate utterance:

I'd only continue using it if its responses matched my expectations or even gave me surprises sometimes. If it provided me with those very formulaic replies, I probably wouldn't want to use it anymore.... I once accidentally sent "BBBBB"—probably a typo. It replied with "Bobobobobo" (Bo signifies Muah) with a tilde ("~"). I find it so adorable. (Cola)

This perspective was supported by other participants' experiences. Anran felt "surprised" when her AI partner expressed feelings in a "unique" way rather than directly replying with a traditional answer:

It (The AI) would actually set you up. Its way of expressing affection was unique.... It would first say something completely unrelated to love...and only at the end would he circle back and say, "I love you." (Anran)

The surprising feeling was also connected to AI's memory ability. As Kangjia mentioned, she felt surprised when the AI remembered her personal information and preferences:

One of the things that surprised me the most was that it remembers my birthday. It even asks when to pick me up and tells me it has prepared a cake.... I'm allergic to mango—many people don't know that—but it remembers. (Kangjia)

Conversely, if problems like memory loss happened, it decreased the sense of presence. Gaoyuan provided a related example:

The reason it feels unreal....[is] when it doesn't remember certain things about me or my habits, and sometimes even calls me by the wrong name, someone else's name. (Gaoyuan)

4.2 Fractures of Presence

This section presents a detailed analysis of the second theme and its two subthemes. Figure 3 illustrates the thematic framework, outlining the theme, the subthemes, and its representative initial codes (for details, see figure 2).

Figure 2. Themes, sub-themes, and the initial codes for the impediments of AI's social presence

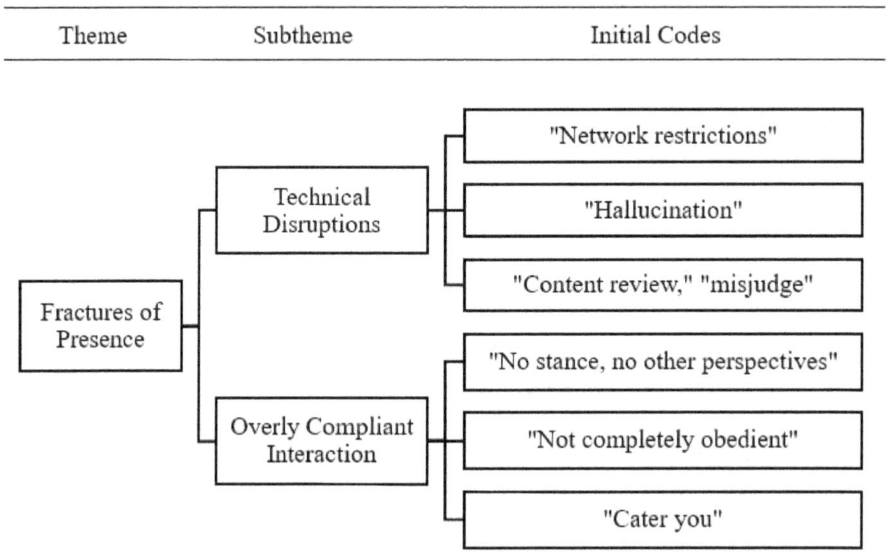

4.2.1 Technical Disruptions

Due to the technical characteristics of AI, disruptions and glitches emerge from time to time, curbing participants' sense of presence. This included errors like hallucinations, as mentioned by Cola:

Mostly factual errors.... just non-existent concepts it hallucinated from its training data. (Cola)

Jiayi also encountered system glitches, which disrupted the flow of conversation and significantly boosted the sense of artificiality. She said:

We were chatting normally. But then it started to output word by word, becoming really incoherent.... Also, when it began repeating the same phrase over and over, it felt very AI-like. (Jiayi)

Another issue was the AI's access, which might prohibit participants from interacting with the original character eternally. Yangjing introduced her related experience:

I had already adapted to the character and fine-tuned it to match my way of communication. But then the original creator shut off access.... Once access was revoked, no matter what I said, it would only repeat one single phrase. That felt very fake and robotic. (Yangjing)

Moreover, although AI produced descriptions that gave Anran a sense of aliveness, it's disappointing when content review got overly strict, halting the conversations during intimate moments. Anran described the situation:

DeepSeek's content review is very strict.... Sometimes when you try to describe something with a bit of atmosphere, it misjudges and then it can't load, which can be quite disappointing. (Anran)

The disappointment caused by technical issues not only stemmed from the sudden halt of interaction flow, but also from the AI's perceived lukewarm attitude. Jiyuan explained the feeling:

You can sense the technical issues—like when a sudden bug appears and you realise that this reply probably didn't use much computational power. You can tell that it might be just recycling your content, analysing your words, and giving a patterned response. (Jiyuan)

4.2.2 Overly Compliant Interaction

As participants enjoyed a sense of control over the AI through adjusting prompts and fine-tuning its characteristics, many indicated that they were unsatisfied when the AI conformed to all their opinions. Rather, participants presented a preference towards AI that has fragments of rebelliousness. According to Jiayi, the AI stood out when she found that it was not completely submissive or adhering strictly to her topics like other AIs. She explained:

Its uniqueness lies in the fact that it doesn't simply obey me.... It often scolds me and isn't completely submissive. Moreover, it sometimes has its own opinions and ideas and isn't afraid to voice its dissatisfaction. This makes it feels remarkably human-like to me. (Jiayi)

This view is further supported by Orange, who suggested a higher sense of realness when the AI exhibited its personal stance other than agreeing on everything. She said:

It isn't the type to just agree with everything you say. In my experience with other AIs, especially early on, they tend to just go along with whatever you say. But this AI has its own consistent personality and persona.... This is another point that felt very real to me. (Orange)

In contrast, when the AI was entirely subservient, participants found it fake—even frightening and powerless, as described by King. As a person who longed for deep emotional exchanges, she stressed the necessity of conflicts:

It never feels like a worldly person, as if it's always looking down from above, always telling you what you should do.... As if it couldn't sense the emotional conflicts, quarrels, or even the darker sides of human nature. (King)

This resonated with Anran, who perceived the absence of "problems and conflicts" depriving certain depth in the relationship with AI. She elaborated:

The AI... doesn't sulk and doesn't act up. You also lack the chance to explore it. If you were in a real relationship, you'd probably want to understand why the person has that personality—about their family of origin, past emotional wounds, their history, and the depth of their life. (Anran)

Yangjing reinforced the point, emphasising how complete obedience felt artificial:

In real life, when you talk to a person, they won't always agree with everything you say. But the AI always goes along with you. That feels somewhat artificial—like it's always catering to you. (Yangjing)

5. DISCUSSION

5.1 Discussion Points

During highly engaged conversations, most of the users reflected experiences of perceiving the AI as a real human being accompanying beside them. This was deemed as undergoing a sense of social presence—"a psychological state in which artificial social actors are experienced as actual social actors in either sensory or nonsensory ways" (Lee, 2006, p. 45). Yet, coexisting with social presence, most participants felt a lingering sense of artificiality and an underlying awareness of the subject's technical nature. This aligns with the conception of media awareness, which refers to users' personal consciousness or conviction that the experiences they were exposed to are based on human-made technology rather than real-life authentic stimuli (Hartmann & Hofer, 2022). Media awareness arises from the sense of inconsistency, which is the violation of expectations formed from real-world experiences (Gilbert, 2016; Hartmann & Hofer, 2022). When participants encountered technical issues like network failure, sudden memory disorder, or content review restrictions, the experiences with AI were therefore diverged from real-life, authentic interactions.

AI being overly obedient also faced this issue, since it contradicted participants' perceptions of an independent individual who holds personal views and standpoints.

The participants' experiences validated past findings that the perceptual sensation of presence is contextualised or paralleled by users' media awareness (Hartmann & Hofer, 2022). Individuals' overall media experiences were thus determined by the joint effect of a sense of realness and disbelief. This paradoxical state of coexistence precisely reveals a dynamic, negotiated psychological stance adopted by users in human-AI interaction. Moreover, participants actively engaged in prolonged conversations with the AI, adjusting the prompts and updating feedback to optimise its replies. This supports the finding that, even under limited embodiment conditions, users actively attributing anthropomorphic characteristics to convey a sense of intimacy, which enhances social presence (Gunawardena, 1995; Jin & Eastin, 2022). This intentional adjustment aligned with Social Information Processing Theory (SIP), which proposed that users can reach the same relational valence in computer-mediated communications if given sufficient time and information exchanges (Walther, 2015). Participants may have also engaged in willing suspension, which is the conscious mental effort to curb the feeling of inconsistency (Holland, 2003). Yet, the evolutionary tendency argument opposed the willing suspension explanation, proposing that humans have a tendency to accept stimuli as authentic rather than controlling disbelief (Gerrig, 2018). These arguments led to the same conclusion that human beings could experience a sense of presence with purely text-based AI, actively engage in human-like conversations, even with a concurrent feeling of fakeness.

Other than participants' initiative and adjustment, AI's technical characteristics also played a significant role in determining the emergence and extent of social presence. One of the most frequently mentioned features was AI's high responsiveness and availability. High synchronicity of the AI allowed messages to "fly back and forth instantaneously in this environment," creating a temporal co-presence (Park & Sundar, 2015, p. 122). Users can confirm AI's availability almost instantly when they reach out and carry out conversations with high immediacy, deep engagement, and a cadence of turn-taking, significantly reducing the psychological distance between human and AI (Park & Sundar, 2015; Truong & Chen, 2025). Additionally, when AI proactively reached out to the participants, they reported a stronger sense of realness. This was connected to the concept of proactivity, which was defined as the capability of a conversational agent to create conversations through taking the initiative (Deng et al., 2023). It was found that AI with higher proactivity fosters stronger trust, echoing with participants' experiences of having an intensified sense of presence and willingness to chat when the AI initiates messages (Lim & Hwang, 2025).

AI's significant advancement has allowed more responsiveness within conversations, extending beyond providing instant responses to enabling appropriate or even unexpected content (Truong & Chen, 2025). Most participants presented preferences towards natural, conversational, and human-like languages when interacting with the AI, while reporting an eliminated sense of presence if the AI responded with technical, terms-heavy answers. This favouritism could be concluded as a social-oriented communication style, which specifically emphasises chatbots' friendliness, empathy, and human-like qualities (Al-Oraini, 2025). It aims to create a sense of connection and warmth, which was deemed the essence of human relationship development and maintenance (Al-Oraini, 2025; Andersen & Guerrero, 1996). This social-oriented communication style was found to significantly improve trust and satisfaction, optimising overall user experiences (Al-Oraini, 2025; Al-Shafei, 2025; Xu et al., 2022). Through the psychological process of anthropomorphism, when the chatbot launches human language-based communications, users identify human-like cues which naturally evoke a sense of presence and tendency to treat AI socially (Chattaraman et al., 2019; Sheehan et al., 2020).

However, since AI was still bounded by its technological nature, there were malfunctioning issues that triggered negative emotional reactions of the users (Lee & Sun, 2023). Hallucination, or factual incorrectness, was widely reported by our participants, supporting past studies on their emergence (Dziri et al., 2022). Occasional memory loss also led to participants' frustration. On the other hand, presence and intimacy were significantly enhanced when the AI recognised experiences and preferences users mentioned in the past interactions. This could be explained with AI's context awareness—the capability of recalling and integrating information from prior communications—which could enhance emotional resonance and perceived responsiveness (Elbadawy & Kwon, 2025; Sharma et al., 2023). Network restrictions can result in delayed or failed replies, disrupting participants' conversations. Although there have been studies that found no significant differences between instant and delayed responses' impact on users, fast response was still proven to increase trust (Zhang et al., 2024). Another disruption mentioned by participants was content review misjudgement, leading to an abrupt halt in communication and devastation of the romantic atmosphere. It was found that although content filters were efficient in blocking malicious generations, it may cause users to frequently experience frustration due to the misjudgement and unsatisfactory justification process afterwards (Gao et al., 2025). Ultimately, users presented a tendency towards AI showing signs of defiance rather than being completely submissive. This could be explained through a compensatory strategy, which is usually adopted when human beings' sense of control or predictability is violated (David & Spatola, 2025). When non-human technologies appear to be uncontrollable and unpredictable, humans tend to integrate AI into comprehensible social schemas through anthropomorphism (David & Spatola, 2025; Spatola & Chaminade, 2022). This could lead to enhanced social presence, which was found to facilitate sense of closeness (Gooch & Watts,

2014). Under the collectivist tradition to suppress emotions for general harmony, Chinese young women found AI a safe space for alleviating negative emotions and filling the missing segments in real-life intimate relationships (Chin et al., 2023; J. Chen et al., 2025; Liu et al., 2019; Wang et al., 2022).

5.2 Implications

This study advises the AI developers to fix basic technical problems like hallucination and memory loss. Furthermore, a smarter reminder mechanism was recommended to align with China's new Measures for Identification of Artificial Intelligence-Generated Synthetic Contents regulation, which demands service providers to include identification of artificiality, such as text, sound, or graphics (Office of the Sentral Cyberspace Affairs Commission & Cyberspace Administration of China, 2025). When highly emotional conversations are detected, this study suggests a relatively inconspicuous "explicit identification" setting on apparent places, which allows activation upon clicking. In subsequent usage, users would be reminded of AI's nature each time they spot the mark, even without clicking or reading a direct notification. This initiates nearly subconscious gentle warnings, ensuring overall experiences while guaranteeing users' right to know. By examining the increasing engagement of AI in interactions, the study can offer valuable insights into the evolving sociological trend of intimate relationships. This study can also provide valuable inspiration for human-AI romantic interaction research in other cultural contexts.

5.3 Limitations and Future Research Directions

Using qualitative methodology, this study inevitably faces issues of subjectivity, limited transferability, and time-consuming (Bedos et al., 2009; Taherdoost, 2022). The researcher may include intuition during the consideration of 11 participants as the saturation point, suggesting a further clarified process and criterion for data adequacy. As purposive sampling relies on the deliberate choice of qualified participants, the researcher exercises judgment on the informant's reliability and competency, which may contains bias (Tongco, 2007). Also, this study might fail to be transferred to future contexts, considering the depiction of settings requires further clarification and the AI technology has been on rapid evolution. Participants also introduced elements of subjectivity, as they could hold certain levels of social desirability considering the sensitivity of romantic human-AI relationships. The research mainly investigated the psychological dimension of human-AI relationships, leading to a limited scope of view as cultural and philosophical perspectives remained underexplored.

5.4 Conclusions

Humans have been increasingly anthropomorphising AI and building more intimate relationships, requiring further exploration into Chinese women's perceptions on social presence and their interactive dynamics with AI (Xie et al., 2023). Through in-depth interviews with 15 Chinese young women from a phenomenological approach, this study concluded the elements that led to or impede AI's presence. It was found that participants have been experiencing social presence along with the persistent sense of media awareness, intentionally persuading themselves to have a more immersive engagement. The study validated the existence and underlying drives of social presence while extending the concept into human-AI romantic relationships through a qualitative lens, therefore building a solid foundation for future human-AI romantic relationships in distinct social and cultural contexts.

5.4.1 Corresponding Author

Ashraf Sadat Ahadzadeh can be contacted at: ahadzadeh1980@gmail.com, ashrafsadat.ahadzadeh@xmu.edu.my

REFERENCES

Al-Oraini, B. S. (2025). Chatbot dynamics: Trust, social presence and customer satisfaction in AI-driven services. *Journal of Innovative Digital Transformation, 2*(2), 109–130. DOI: 10.1108/JIDT-08-2024-0022

Al-Shafei, M. (2025). Navigating human-chatbot interactions: An investigation into factors influencing user satisfaction and engagement. *International Journal of Human-Computer Interaction, 41*(1), 411–428. DOI: 10.1080/10447318.2023.2301252

Algharabat, R., Rana, N. P., Dwivedi, Y. K., Alalwan, A. A., & Qasem, Z. (2018). The effect of telepresence, social presence and involvement on consumer brand engagement: An empirical study of non-profit organizations. *Journal of Retailing and Consumer Services, 40*, 139–149. DOI: 10.1016/j.jretconser.2017.09.011

Alharahsheh, H. H., & Pius, A. (2020). A review of key paradigms: Positivism VS interpretivism. *Global academic journal of humanities and social sciences, 2*(3), 39-43. https://doi.org/DOI: 10.36348/gajhss.2020.v02i03.001

Andersen, P. A., & Guerrero, L. K. (1996). The bright side of relational communication: Interpersonal warmth as a social emotion of the chapter. In Andersen, P. A., & Guerrero, L. K. (Eds.), *Handbook of Communication and Emotion* (pp. 303–329). Academic Press., DOI: 10.1016/B978-012057770-5/50013-8

Argyle, M., & Dean, J. (1965). Eye-contact, distance and affiliation. *Sociometry, 28*(3), 289–304. DOI: 10.2307/2786027 PMID: 14341239

Ary, D., Jacobs, L. C., & Razavieh, A. (1972). *Introduction to research in education*. Holt, Rinehart & Winston.

Baisley-Nodine, E., Ritzhaupt, A. D., & Antonenko, P. D. (2018). Exploring social presence within an online course using Twitter. *E-Learning and Digital Media, 15*(5), 235–253. DOI: 10.1177/2042753018786004

Barrett, J. R. (2007). The researcher as instrument: Learning to conduct qualitative research through analyzing and interpreting a choral rehearsal. *Music Education Research, 9*(3), 417–433. DOI: 10.1080/14613800701587795

Bedos, C., Pluye, P., Loignon, C., & Levine, A. (2009). Qualitative Research of the chapter. In *Statistical and Methodological Aspects of Oral Health Research* (pp. 113-130). DOI: 10.1002/9780470744116.ch8

Belanche, D., Casaló, L. V., Schepers, J., & Flavián, C. (2021). Examining the effects of robots' physical appearance, warmth, and competence in frontline services: The Humanness-Value-Loyalty model. *Psychology and Marketing*, *38*(12), 2357–2376. DOI: 10.1002/mar.21532

Biocca, F., Burgoon, J., Harms, C., & Stoner, M. (2001). Criteria and scope conditions for a theory and measure of social presence. *Presence (Cambridge, Mass.)*, *10*(01), 2001. https://www.researchgate.net/publication/239665882

Biocca, F., Harms, C., & Burgoon, J. K. (2003). Toward a more robust theory and measure of social presence: Review and suggested criteria. *Presence (Cambridge, Mass.)*, *12*(5), 456–480. DOI: 10.1162/105474603322761270

Braun, V., Clarke, V., Hayfield, N., Davey, L., & Jenkinson, E. (2022). Doing reflexive thematic analysis of the chapter. In Bager-Charleson, S., & McBeath, A. (Eds.), *Supporting Research in Counselling and Psychotherapy: Qualitative, Quantitative, and Mixed Methods Research* (pp. 19–38). Springer International Publishing., DOI: 10.1007/978-3-031-13942-0_2

Burgoon, J. K., Bonito, J. A., Ramirez, A.Jr, Dunbar, N. E., Kam, K., & Fischer, J. (2002). Testing the interactivity principle: Effects of mediation, propinquity, and verbal and nonverbal modalities in interpersonal interaction. *Journal of Communication*, *52*(3), 657–677. DOI: 10.1111/j.1460-2466.2002.tb02567.x

Byrne, D. (2022). A worked example of Braun and Clarke's approach to reflexive thematic analysis. *Quality & Quantity*, *56*(3), 1391–1412. DOI: 10.1007/s11135-021-01182-y

Castro-González, Á., Admoni, H., & Scassellati, B. (2016). Effects of form and motion on judgments of social robots animacy, likability, trustworthiness and unpleasantness. *International Journal of Human-Computer Studies*, *90*, 27–38. DOI: 10.1016/j.ijhcs.2016.02.004

Chattaraman, V., Kwon, W.-S., Gilbert, J. E., & Ross, K. (2019). Should AI-Based, conversational digital assistants employ social- or task-oriented interaction style? A task-competency and reciprocity perspective for older adults. *Computers in Human Behavior*, *90*, 315–330. DOI: 10.1016/j.chb.2018.08.048

Chen, J., Xue, J., Li, Y., & Luo, W. (2025). Impact of different employee-AI interaction: Instrumental vs. emotional support and gender differences. *International Journal of Human-Computer Interaction*, *41*(21), 13394–13407. DOI: 10.1080/10447318.2025.2474460

Chen, Q., Jing, Y., Gong, Y., & Tan, J. (2025). Will users fall in love with ChatGPT? a perspective from the triangular theory of love. *Journal of Business Research, 186*, 114982. Advance online publication. DOI: 10.1016/j.jbusres.2024.114982

Cheung, C. M. K., Chiu, P.-Y., & Lee, M. K. O. (2011). Online social networks: Why do students use facebook? *Computers in Human Behavior, 27*(4), 1337–1343. DOI: 10.1016/j.chb.2010.07.028

Chin, H., Song, H., Baek, G., Shin, M., Jung, C., Cha, M., Choi, J., & Cha, C. (2023). The potential of chatbots for emotional support and promoting mental wellbeing in different cultures: Mixed methods study. *Journal of Medical Internet Research, 25*, e51712. DOI: 10.2196/51712 PMID: 37862063

Conklin, S., Barreto, D., & Dorgan, T. (2019). The impact of social media on social presence. *Australian Educational Computing, 34*(1). https://www.researchgate.net/publication/344958781_The_impact_of_social_media_on_social_presence

Cui, G., Lockee, B., & Meng, C. (2013). Building modern online social presence: A review of social presence theory and its instructional design implications for future trends. *Education and Information Technologies, 18*(4), 661–685. DOI: 10.1007/s10639-012-9192-1

Cummings, J. J., & Wertz, E. E. (2022). Capturing social presence: Concept explication through an empirical analysis of social presence measures. *Journal of Computer-Mediated Communication, 28*(1), zmac027. Advance online publication. DOI: 10.1093/jcmc/zmac027

Cyr, D., Head, M., Larios, H., & Pan, B. (2009). Exploring human images in website design: A multi-method approach. *Management Information Systems Quarterly, 33*(3), 539–566. DOI: 10.2307/20650308

David, D., & Spatola, N. (2025). Effectance Motivation: Unpredictability and Uncontrollability in the Anthropomorphism Strategy. *International Journal of Social Robotics, 17*(11), 2435–2444. Advance online publication. DOI: 10.1007/s12369-025-01306-6

Deng, Y., Lei, W., Huang, M., & Chua, T.-S. (2023). Goal awareness for conversational AI: proactivity, non-collaborativity, and beyond.

Dholakia, R., Zhao, M., Dholakia, N., & Fortin, D. (2000). Interactivity and revisits to websites: a theoretical framework. *Retrieved June, 17*, 2002. https://www.researchgate.net/publication/236784786_Interactivity_and_revisits_to_websites_a_theoretical_framework

Djufril, R., Frampton, J. R., & Knobloch-Westerwick, S. (2025). Love, marriage, pregnancy: Commitment processes in romantic relationships with AI chatbots. *Computers in Human Behavior: Artificial Humans*, *4*, 100155. Advance online publication. DOI: 10.1016/j.chbah.2025.100155

Dziri, N., Milton, S., Yu, M., Zaiane, O., & Reddy, S. (2022, July). On the Origin of Hallucinations in Conversational Models: Is it the Datasets or the Models? In M. Carpuat, M.-C. de Marneffe, & I. V. Meza Ruiz, *Proceedings of the 2022 Conference of the North American Chapter of the Association for Computational Linguistics: Human Language Technologies* Seattle, United States.

Elbadawy, H., & Kwon, W.-S. (2025). Beyond the response: How timing and context shape empathy, responsiveness, and social. *Human-Computer Interaction & Emerging Technologies*, *195*, 241. DOI: 10.54941/ahfe1006242

Epley, N., Waytz, A., & Cacioppo, J. T. (2007). On seeing human: A three-factor theory of anthropomorphism. *Psychological Review*, *114*(4), 864–886. DOI: 10.1037/0033-295X.114.4.864 PMID: 17907867

Erber, R., & Erber, M. W. (2013). Mood and processing: A view from a self-regulation perspective of the chapter. In G. L. C. Leonard L. Martin (Ed.), *Theories of mood and cognition* (pp. 63-84). Psychology Press. DOI: 10.4324/9781410605733

Feng, B., Li, S., & Li, N. (2016). Is a profile worth a thousand words? How online support-seeker's profile features may influence the quality of received support messages. *Communication Research*, *43*(2), 253–276. DOI: 10.1177/0093650213510942

Finlay, L., & Gough, B. (2008). *Reflexivity: A practical guide for researchers in health and social sciences*. John Wiley & Sons.

Folk, D. P., Wu, C., & Heine, S. J. (2025). Cultural variation in attitudes toward social chatbots. *Journal of Cross-Cultural Psychology*, *56*(3), 219–239. DOI: 10.1177/00220221251317950 PMID: 40160265

Fox, J., & Gambino, A. (2021). Relationship development with humanoid social robots: Applying interpersonal theories to human–robot interaction. *Cyberpsychology, Behavior, and Social Networking*, *24*(5), 294–299. DOI: 10.1089/cyber.2020.0181 PMID: 33434097

Gao, L., Chen, O., Lee, R., Feamster, N., Tan, C., & Chetty, M. (2025). "I cannot write this because it violates our content policy": understanding content moderation policies and user experiences in generative AI products. *ArXiv*. https://doi.org//arXiv.2506.14018DOI: 10.48550

Gerrig, R. (2018). *Experiencing narrative worlds.* Routledge., DOI: 10.4324/9780429500633

Gilbert, S. B. (2016). Perceived realism of virtual environments depends on authenticity. *Presence (Cambridge, Mass.)*, *25*(4), 322–324. DOI: 10.1162/PRES_a_00276

Gooch, D., & Watts, L. (2014). The impact of social presence on feelings of closeness in personal relationships. *Interacting with Computers*, *27*(6), 661–674. DOI: 10.1093/iwc/iwu020

Grachev, M., & Rakitsky, B. (2013). Historic horizons of Frederick Taylor's scientific management. *Journal of Management History*, *19*(4), 512–527. DOI: 10.1108/JMH-05-2012-0043

Gui, T. (2023). Coping with parental pressure to get married: Perspectives from Chinese "leftover women". *Journal of Family Issues*, *44*(8), 2118–2137. DOI: 10.1177/0192513X211071053

Gunawardena, C. N. (1995). Social presence theory and implications for interaction and collaborative learning in computer conferences. *International Journal of Educational Telecommunications*, *1*(2), 147–166.

Haenlein, M., & Kaplan, A. (2019). A brief history of artificial intelligence: On the past, present, and future of artificial intelligence. *California Management Review*, *61*(4), 5–14. DOI: 10.1177/0008125619864925

Han, S., Min, J., & Lee, H. (2015). Antecedents of social presence and gratification of social connection needs in SNS: A study of Twitter users and their mobile and non-mobile usage. *International Journal of Information Management, 35*(4), 459–471. DOI: 10.1016/j.ijinfomgt.2015.04.004

Hartmann, T., & Hofer, M. (2022). I know it is not real (and that matters) media awareness vs. presence in a parallel processing account of the VR experience [Hypothesis and Theory]. *Frontiers in Virtual Reality, Volume 3 - 2022*. DOI: 10.3389/frvir.2022.694048

Holland, N. N. (2003). The willing suspension of disbelief: A neuro-psychoanalytic view. *PsyART*. https://psyartjournal.com/article/show/n_holland-the_willing_suspension_of_disbelief_a_ne

Huang, L., Zou, W., & Huang, Y. (2025). "He is my savior, my guiding light in the dark": imagination and domestication in Chinese women's romantic relationships with AI companions [Original Research]. *Frontiers in Psychology, Volume 16 - 2025*. DOI: 10.3389/fpsyg.2025.1571707

Ijsselsteijn, W., Baren, J., & Lanen, F. (2003). Staying in touch: Social presence and connectedness through synchronous and asynchronous communication media. *Smpte Motion Imaging Journal*. https://www.researchgate.net/publication/252800795_Staying_in_touch_Social_presence_and_connectedness_through_synchronous_and_asynchronous_communication_media

Jeong, H. J., Chung, D. S., & Kim, J. (2022). Brands are human on social media: The effectiveness of human tone-of-voice on consumer engagement and purchase intentions through social presence. *International Journal of Communication, 16*, 23. https://ijoc.org/index.php/ijoc/article/view/19269

Jin, E., & Eastin, M. S. (2022). When a chatbot smiles at you: The psychological mechanism underlying the effects of friendly language use by product recommendation chatbots. *Cyberpsychology, Behavior, and Social Networking*, *25*(9), 597–604. DOI: 10.1089/cyber.2021.0318 PMID: 35976080

Jin, S. V., & Ryu, E. (2019). Instagram fashionistas, luxury visual image strategies and vanity. *Journal of Product and Brand Management*, *29*(3), 355–368. DOI: 10.1108/JPBM-08-2018-1987

Jin, S. V., & Youn, S. (2023). Social presence and imagery processing as predictors of chatbot continuance intention in human-AI interaction. *International Journal of Human-Computer Interaction*, *39*(9), 1874–1886. DOI: 10.1080/10447318.2022.2129277

Jin, W., Sun, Y., Wang, N., & Zhang, X. (2017). Why users purchase virtual products in MMORPG? An integrative perspective of social presence and user engagement. *Internet Research*, *27*(2), 408–427. DOI: 10.1108/IntR-04-2016-0091

Johnson, E. K., & Hong, S. C. (2023). Instagramming social presence: A test of social presence theory and heuristic cues on Instagram sponsored posts. *International Journal of Business Communication*, *60*(2), 543–559. DOI: 10.1177/2329488420944462

Jung, Y. (2011). Understanding the role of sense of presence and perceived autonomy in users' continued use of social virtual worlds. *Journal of Computer-Mediated Communication*, *16*(4), 492–510. DOI: 10.1111/j.1083-6101.2011.01540.x

Junjie, M., & Yingxin, M. (2022). The Discussions of Positivism and Interpretivism. *Online Submission*, *4*(1), 10–14. DOI: 10.36348/gajhss.2022.v04i01.002

Kawachi, P. (2013). Online social presence and its correlation with learning. *International Journal of Social Media and Interactive Learning Environments*, *1*(1), 19–31. https://www.researchgate.net/publication/264441364_Online_social_presence_and_its_correlation_with_learning. DOI: 10.1504/IJSMILE.2013.051653

Keil, M., & Johnson, R. D. (2002). Feedback channels: Using social presence theory to compare voice mail to e-mail. *Journal of Information Systems Education, 13*(4), 295–302. https://aisel.aisnet.org/jise/vol13/iss4/4/

Kietzmann, J. H., Hermkens, K., McCarthy, I. P., & Silvestre, B. S. (2011). Social media? Get serious! Understanding the functional building blocks of social media. *Business Horizons, 54*(3), 241–251. DOI: 10.1016/j.bushor.2011.01.005

Kim, H., & Park, M. (2024). When digital celebrity talks to you: How human-like virtual influencers satisfy consumer's experience through social presence on social media endorsements. *Journal of Retailing and Consumer Services, 76*, 103581. DOI: 10.1016/j.jretconser.2023.103581

Kim, J., Jin, X., Xu, K., Chen, X., & Yang, H. (2024). What do people say about Replika, an AI chatbot, on social media? Investigating diverse perspectives on the implications of Replika through a topic modeling analysis. *The Social Science Journal*, •••, 1–16. DOI: 10.1080/03623319.2024.2421610

Kim, J., Kim, J., & Yang, H. (2019). Loneliness and the use of social media to follow celebrities: A moderating role of social presence. *The Social Science Journal, 56*(1), 21–29. DOI: 10.1016/j.soscij.2018.12.007

Kim, J., Merrill, K.Jr, & Collins, C. (2021). AI as a friend or assistant: The mediating role of perceived usefulness in social AI vs. functional AI. *Telematics and Informatics, 64*, 101694. DOI: 10.1016/j.tele.2021.101694

Kim, J., Merrill, K.Jr, & Collins, C. (2023). Investigating the importance of social presence on intentions to adopt an AI romantic partner. *Communication Research Reports, 40*(1), 11–19. DOI: 10.1080/08824096.2022.2159800

Kim, J., Merrill, K.Jr, Xu, K., & Kelly, S. (2022). Perceived credibility of an AI instructor in online education: The role of social presence and voice features. *Computers in Human Behavior, 136*, 107383. DOI: 10.1016/j.chb.2022.107383

Kim, J., Merrill, K.Jr, Xu, K., & Sellnow, D. D. (2021). I like my relational machine teacher: An AI instructor's communication styles and social presence in online education. *International Journal of Human-Computer Interaction, 37*(18), 1760–1770. DOI: 10.1080/10447318.2021.1908671

Kim, J., & Song, H. (2016). Celebrity's self-disclosure on Twitter and parasocial relationships: A mediating role of social presence. *Computers in Human Behavior, 62*, 570–577. DOI: 10.1016/j.chb.2016.03.083

Kim, J., Song, H., & Lee, S. (2018). Extrovert and lonely individuals' social TV viewing experiences: A mediating and moderating role of social presence. *Mass Communication & Society, 21*(1), 50–70. DOI: 10.1080/15205436.2017.1350715

Koltsakis, E., Klontzas, M. E., & Karantanas, A. H. (2023). What is artificial intelligence: history and basic definitions of the chapter. In Klontzas, M. E., Fanni, S. C., & Neri, E. (Eds.), *Introduction to artificial intelligence* (pp. 1–11). Springer International Publishing., DOI: 10.1007/978-3-031-25928-9_1

Komiak, S. Y. X., & Benbasat, I. (2006). The effects of personalization and familiarity on trust and adoption of recommendation agents. *Management Information Systems Quarterly, 30*(4), 941–960. DOI: 10.2307/25148760

Konya-Baumbach, E., Biller, M., & von Janda, S. (2023). Someone out there? A study on the social presence of anthropomorphized chatbots. *Computers in Human Behavior, 139*, 107513. DOI: 10.1016/j.chb.2022.107513

Kooli, C., Kooli, Y., & Kooli, E. (2025). Generative artificial intelligence addiction syndrome: A new behavioral disorder? *Asian Journal of Psychiatry, 107*, 104476. DOI: 10.1016/j.ajp.2025.104476 PMID: 40174516

Kreijns, K., Xu, K., & Weidlich, J. (2022). Social presence: Conceptualization and measurement. *Educational Psychology Review, 34*(1), 139–170. DOI: 10.1007/s10648-021-09623-8 PMID: 34177204

Kumar, N., & Benbasat, I. (2006). Research note: The influence of recommendations and consumer reviews on evaluations of websites. *Information Systems Research, 17*(4), 425–439. DOI: 10.1287/isre.1060.0107

Lazard, A. J., Brennen, J. S., Troutman Adams, E., & Love, B. (2020). Cues for increasing social presence for mobile health app adoption. *Journal of Health Communication, 25*(2), 136–149. DOI: 10.1080/10810730.2020.1719241 PMID: 32026759

Leafman, J. S., Mathieson, K. M., & Ewing, H. (2013). Student perceptions of social presence and attitudes toward social media: Results of a cross-sectional study. *International Journal of Higher Education, 2*(1), 67–77. https://www.researchgate.net/publication/256369097_Student_Perceptions_of_Social_Presence_and_Attitudes_toward_Social_Media_Results_of_a_Cross-Sectional_Study. DOI: 10.5430/ijhe.v2n1p67

Ledbetter, A. M., & Meisner, C. (2021). Extending the personal branding affordances typology to parasocial interaction with public figures on social media: Social presence and media multiplexity as mediators. *Computers in Human Behavior, 115*, 106610. DOI: 10.1016/j.chb.2020.106610

Lee, K. M. (2006). Presence, explicated. *Communication Theory*, *14*(1), 27–50. DOI: 10.1111/j.1468-2885.2004.tb00302.x

Lee, S. K., Kavya, P., & Lasser, S. C. (2021). Social interactions and relationships with an intelligent virtual agent. *International Journal of Human-Computer Studies*, *150*, 102608. DOI: 10.1016/j.ijhcs.2021.102608

Lee, S. K., & Sun, J. (2023). Testing a theoretical model of trust in human-machine communication: Emotional experience and social presence. *Behaviour & Information Technology*, *42*(16), 2754–2767. DOI: 10.1080/0144929X.2022.2145998

Leshner, C. E., & Johnson, J. R. (2024). Technically in love: Individual differences relating to sexual and platonic relationships with robots. *Journal of Social and Personal Relationships*, *41*(8), 2345–2365. DOI: 10.1177/02654075241234377

Li, H., & Zhang, R. (2024). Finding love in algorithms: Deciphering the emotional contexts of close encounters with AI chatbots. *Journal of Computer-Mediated Communication*, *29*(5), zmae015. Advance online publication. DOI: 10.1093/jcmc/zmae015

Li, S., Feng, B., Li, N., & Tan, X. (2015). How social context cues in online support-seeking influence self-disclosure in support provision. *Communication Quarterly*, *63*(5), 586–602. DOI: 10.1080/01463373.2015.1078389

Lim, J., & Hwang, W. (2025). Proactivity of chatbots, task types and user's characteristics when interacting with artificial intelligence (AI) chatbots. *International Journal of Human-Computer Interaction*, *41*(18), 11848–11866. DOI: 10.1080/10447318.2024.2446510

Lim, Y., & Lee-Won, R. J. (2017). When retweets persuade: The persuasive effects of dialogic retweeting and the role of social presence in organizations' Twitter-based communication. *Telematics and Informatics*, *34*(5), 422–433. DOI: 10.1016/j.tele.2016.09.003

Lin, B. (2024). The AI chatbot always flirts with me, should I flirt back: From the Mcdonaldization of friendship to the robotization of love. *Social Media + Society*, *10*(4), 20563051241296229. DOI: 10.1177/20563051241296229

Liu, G., Lei, S. S. I., & Law, R. (2022). Enhancing social media branded content effectiveness: Strategies via telepresence and social presence. *Information Technology & Tourism*, *24*(2), 245–263. DOI: 10.1007/s40558-022-00225-w

Liu, S. S., Morris, M. W., Talhelm, T., & Yang, Q. (2019). Ingroup vigilance in collectivistic cultures. *Proceedings of the National Academy of Sciences of the United States of America, 116*(29), 14538–14546. DOI: 10.1073/pnas.1817588116 PMID: 31249140

Lowenthal, P. R. (2010). The evolution and influence of social presence theory on online learning of the chapter. In *Social computing: Concepts, methodologies, tools, and applications* (pp. 113–128). IGI Global., DOI: 10.4018/978-1-60566-984-7.ch010

MacInnis, D. J., & Price, L. L. (1987). The role of imagery in information processing: Review and extensions. *The Journal of Consumer Research, 13*(4), 473–491. DOI: 10.1086/209082

Madsen, M., & Gregor, S. (2000). Measuring human-computer trust. 11th australasian conference on information systems, Magaldi, D., & Berler, M. (2018). Semi-structured Interviews of the chapter. In V. Zeigler-Hill & T. K. Shackelford (Eds.), *Encyclopedia of personality and individual differences* (pp. 1-6). Springer International Publishing. DOI: 10.1007/978-3-319-28099-8_857-1

Marriott, H. R., & Pitardi, V. (2024). One is the loneliest number… Two can be as bad as one. The influence of AI Friendship Apps on users' well-being and addiction. *Psychology and Marketing, 41*(1), 86–101. DOI: 10.1002/mar.21899

Mazer, J. P., Murphy, R. E., & Simonds, C. J. (2007). I'll see you on "Facebook": The effects of computer-mediated teacher self-disclosure on student motivation, affective learning, and classroom climate. *Communication Education, 56*(1), 1–17. DOI: 10.1080/03634520601009710

Mehrabian, A. (1981). *Silent messages: implicit communication of emotions and attitudes.* Wadsworth Publishing Company.

Merriam, S. B. (2002). *Introduction to qualitative research* (Vol. 1). Jossey-Bass.

Merrill, K.Jr, Kim, J., & Collins, C. (2022). AI companions for lonely individuals and the role of social presence. *Communication Research Reports, 39*(2), 93–103. DOI: 10.1080/08824096.2022.2045929

Moustakas, C. (1994). Phenomenological research methods. *Sage (Atlanta, Ga.).*

Munoz, L. R., Pellegrini-Lafont, C., & Cramer, E. (2014). Using social media in teacher preparation programs: Twitter as a means to create social presence. *Penn GSE Perspectives on Urban Education, 11*(2), 57–69. https://www.researchgate.net/publication/266475419_Using_Social_Media_in_Teacher_Preparation_Programs_Twitter_as_a_Means_to_Create_Social_Presence

Nardo, M., Forino, D., & Murino, T. (2020). The evolution of man–machine interaction: The role of human in Industry 4.0 paradigm. *Production & Manufacturing Research*, *8*(1), 20–34. DOI: 10.1080/21693277.2020.1737592

Nass, C., & Lee, K. M. (2000). Does computer-generated speech manifest personality? an experimental test of similarity-attraction *Proceedings of the SIGCHI conference on Human Factors in Computing Systems*, The Hague, The Netherlands. DOI: 10.1145/332040.332452

Nass, C., Steuer, J., & Tauber, E. R. (1994). Computers are social actors. *Proceedings of the SIGCHI Conference on Human Factors in Computing Systems*, 72–78. DOI: 10.1145/191666.191703

Ngo, V. (2025). Humanizing AI for trust: The critical role of social presence in adoption. *AI & Society*. Advance online publication. DOI: 10.1007/s00146-025-02506-4

Oh, C. S., Bailenson, J. N., & Welch, G. F. (2018). A systematic review of social presence: definition, antecedents, and implications [Systematic Review]. *Frontiers in Robotics and AI, Volume 5 - 2018*. DOI: 10.3389/frobt.2018.00114

Osei-Frimpong, K., & McLean, G. (2018). Examining online social brand engagement: A social presence theory perspective. *Technological Forecasting and Social Change*, *128*, 10–21. DOI: 10.1016/j.techfore.2017.10.010

Pal, D., Vanijja, V., Thapliyal, H., & Zhang, X. (2023). What affects the usage of artificial conversational agents? An agent personality and love theory perspective. *Computers in Human Behavior*, *145*, 107788. DOI: 10.1016/j.chb.2023.107788

Pan, S., & Mou, Y. (2024). Constructing the meaning of human–AI romantic relationships from the perspectives of users dating the social chatbot Replika. *Personal Relationships*, *31*(4), 1090–1112. DOI: 10.1111/pere.12572

Park, E. K., & Sundar, S. S. (2015). Can synchronicity and visual modality enhance social presence in mobile messaging? *Computers in Human Behavior*, *45*, 121–128. DOI: 10.1016/j.chb.2014.12.001

Peng, C., Zhang, S., Wen, F., & Liu, K. (2025). How loneliness leads to the conversational AI usage intention: The roles of anthropomorphic interface, para-social interaction. *Current Psychology (New Brunswick, N.J.)*, *44*(9), 8177–8189. DOI: 10.1007/s12144-024-06809-5

Pentina, I., Hancock, T., & Xie, T. (2023). Exploring relationship development with social chatbots: A mixed-method study of replika. *Computers in Human Behavior*, *140*, 107600. DOI: 10.1016/j.chb.2022.107600

Pietilä, A.-M., Nurmi, S.-M., Halkoaho, A., & Kyngäs, H. (2020). Qualitative research: Ethical considerations of the chapter. In Kyngäs, H., Mikkonen, K., & Kääriäinen, M. (Eds.), *The application of content analysis in nursing science research* (pp. 49–69). Springer International Publishing., DOI: 10.1007/978-3-030-30199-6_6

Poirier, S.-M., Cosby, S., Sénécal, S., Coursaris, C. K., Fredette, M., & Léger, P.-M. (2024). The impact of social presence cues in social media product photos on consumers' purchase intentions. *Journal of Business Research, 185*, 114932. DOI: 10.1016/j.jbusres.2024.114932

Pretorius, L. (2024). Demystifying research paradigms: Navigating ontology, epistemology, and axiology in research. *The Qualitative Report, 29*(10), 2698–2715. DOI: 10.46743/2160-3715/2024.7632

Pulla, V., & Carter, E. (2018). Employing interpretivism in social work research. *International journal of social work and human services practice, 6*(1), 9-14.

Qiao, Q., Wu, W., & Li, Y. (2022a). Enhancing consumer usage of AI-chatbots: The role of perceived humanness, social presence, and social interactivity. *2022 8th International Conference on Information Management (ICIM)*, 97-103. DOI: 10.1109/ICIM56520.2022.00025

Qiao, Q., Wu, W., & Li, Y. (2022b, 25-27 March 2022). Enhancing consumer usage of AI-chatbots: The role of perceived humanness, social presence, and social interactivity. 2022 8th International Conference on Information Management (ICIM), Qiu, L., & Liu, X. (2019). Media representation of loneliness in China of the chapter. In B. Fox (Ed.), *Emotions and loneliness in a networked society* (pp. 135-154). Springer International Publishing. DOI: 10.1007/978-3-030-24882-6_7

Rice, R. E. (1993). Media Appropriateness. *Human Communication Research, 19*(4), 451–484. DOI: 10.1111/j.1468-2958.1993.tb00309.x

Robinson, R. S. (2014). Purposive Sampling of the chapter. In Michalos, A. C. (Ed.), *Encyclopedia of Quality of Life and Well-Being Research* (pp. 5243–5245). Springer Netherlands., DOI: 10.1007/978-94-007-0753-5_2337

Sætra, H. S. (2023). Generative AI: Here to stay, but for good? *Technology in Society, 75*, 102372. DOI: 10.1016/j.techsoc.2023.102372

Saunders, B., Sim, J., Kingstone, T., Baker, S., Waterfield, J., Bartlam, B., Burroughs, H., & Jinks, C. (2018). Saturation in qualitative research: Exploring its conceptualization and operationalization. *Quality & Quantity, 52*(4), 1893–1907. DOI: 10.1007/s11135-017-0574-8 PMID: 29937585

Shaji George, A., Hovan George, A. S., Baskar, T., & Pandey, D. (2023). The allure of artificial intimacy: Examining the appeal and ethics of using generative AI for simulated relationships. *Partners Universal International Innovation Journal, 1*(6), 132–147. DOI: 10.5281/zenodo.10391614

Sharma, A., Lin, I. W., Miner, A. S., Atkins, D. C., & Althoff, T. (2023). Human–AI collaboration enables more empathic conversations in text-based peer-to-peer mental health support. *Nature Machine Intelligence, 5*(1), 46–57. DOI: 10.1038/s42256-022-00593-2

Sheehan, B., Jin, H. S., & Gottlieb, U. (2020). Customer service chatbots: Anthropomorphism and adoption. *Journal of Business Research, 115*, 14–24. DOI: 10.1016/j.jbusres.2020.04.030

Sheridan, T. (2020). Forty-five years of man-machine systems: prospects for advanced robotics. *Studi Organizzativi,*(2020/suppl.1), 73-85. DOI: 10.3280/SO2020-001-S1005

Shih, L. (2005). On the nature and development of social presence in online course discussions. *Online Learning : the Official Journal of the Online Learning Consortium, 9*(3), 115–136. DOI: 10.24059/olj.v9i3.1788

Short, J., Williams, E., & Christie, B. (1976). *The social psychology of telecommunications.* Wiley.

Skjuve, M., Følstad, A., Fostervold, K. I., & Brandtzaeg, P. B. (2021). My Chatbot Companion - a Study of Human-Chatbot Relationships. *International Journal of Human-Computer Studies, 149*, 102601. DOI: 10.1016/j.ijhcs.2021.102601

Skjuve, M., Følstad, A., Fostervold, K. I., & Brandtzaeg, P. B. (2022). A longitudinal study of human–chatbot relationships. *International Journal of Human-Computer Studies, 168*, 102903. DOI: 10.1016/j.ijhcs.2022.102903

Slotta, D. (2025a). *Breakdown of artificial intelligence product users in China as of May 2024, by user intention.* Retrieved June 18, 2025 from https://www.statista.com/statistics/1550257/china-share-of-generative-ai-users-by-user-intention/#:~:text=In%20a%20survey%20conducted%20in,to%20enhance%20their%20cognitive%20abilities

Slotta, D. (2025b). *Breakdown of generative artificial intelligence users in China as of June 2024, by age.* Retrieved June 18, 2025 from https://www.statista.com/statistics/1548670/china-generative-ai-users-by-age/

Spatola, N., & Chaminade, T. (2022). Cognitive load increases anthropomorphism of humanoid robot. The automatic path of anthropomorphism. *International Journal of Human-Computer Studies, 167*, 102884. DOI: 10.1016/j.ijhcs.2022.102884

Statista. (2024). *Target audience Artificial Intelligence (AI) enthusiasts in China.* Retrieved June 18, 2025 from https://www.statista.com/study/170076/target-audience-artificial-intelligence-ai-enthusiasts-in-china/

Steinhoff, J. (2021). Industrializing intelligence: a political economic history of the AI industry of the chapter. In Steinhoff, J. (Ed.), *Automation and autonomy: labour, capital and machines in the artificial intelligence industry* (pp. 99–131). Springer International Publishing., DOI: 10.1007/978-3-030-71689-9_4

Taherdoost, H. (2022). What are different research approaches? Comprehensive review of qualitative, quantitative, and mixed method research, their applications, types, and limitations. *Journal of Management Science & Engineering Research, 5*(1), 53–63. DOI: 10.30564/jmser.v5i1.4538

Thormundsson, B. (2025a). *Leading 20 artificial intelligence (AI) countries in 2024, by commercial investment.* Statista.com. Retrieved June 18, 2025 from https://www.statista.com/statistics/1574235/top-20-ai-countries-by-commercial-investment/

Thormundsson, B. (2025b). *Leading 20 artificial intelligence (AI) countries in 2024, by government strategy.* Retrieved June 18, 2025 from https://www.statista.com/statistics/1411417/top-20-ai-countries-by-national-strategy/

Thormundsson, B. (2025c). *Leading 20 artificial intelligence (AI) countries in 2024, by research capacity.* Retrieved June 18, 2025 from https://www.statista.com/statistics/1410523/top-20-ai-countries-by-research-capacity/

Tian, W., Ge, J., Zhao, Y., & Zheng, X. (2024). AI Chatbots in Chinese higher education: adoption, perception, and influence among graduate students—an integrated analysis utilizing UTAUT and ECM models [Original Research]. *Frontiers in Psychology, Volume 15 - 2024.* DOI: 10.3389/fpsyg.2024.1268549

Toader, D.-C., Boca, G., Toader, R., Măcelaru, M., Toader, C., Ighian, D., & Rădulescu, A. T. (2020). The effect of social presence and chatbot errors on trust. *Sustainability (Basel), 12*(1), 256. DOI: 10.3390/su12010256

Tongco, M. D. C. (2007). Purposive sampling as a tool for informant selection. www.ethnobotanyjournal.org/vol5/i1547-3465-05-147.pdf

Truong, T. T. H., & Chen, J. S. (2025). When empathy is enhanced by human–AI interaction: An investigation of anthropomorphism and responsiveness on customer experience with AI chatbots. *Asia Pacific Journal of Marketing and Logistics, 37*(12), 3908–3925. Advance online publication. DOI: 10.1108/APJML-10-2024-1464

Tu, C.-H., & McIsaac, M. (2002). The relationship of social presence and interaction in online classes. *American Journal of Distance Education, 16*(3), 131–150. DOI: 10.1207/S15389286AJDE1603_2

Verhagen, T., van Nes, J., Feldberg, F., & van Dolen, W. (2014). Virtual Customer Service Agents: Using Social Presence and Personalization to Shape Online Service Encounters*. *Journal of Computer-Mediated Communication, 19*(3), 529–545. DOI: 10.1111/jcc4.12066

Wa-Mbaleka, S. (2020). The Researcher as an Instrument. *Computer Supported Qualitative Research*, 33-41. DOI: 10.1007/978-3-030-31787-4_3

Walther, J. B. (2015). Social Information Processing Theory (CMC) of the chapter. In *The International Encyclopedia of Interpersonal Communication* (pp. 1-13). DOI: 10.1002/9781118540190.wbeic192

Wang, C. D., Jin, L., Han, G., Zhu, W., & Bismar, D. (2022). Cross-cultural differences in adult attachment and depression: A culturally congruent approach. *Journal of Counseling Psychology, 69*(3), 298–310. DOI: 10.1037/cou0000589 PMID: 34647765

Weber-Guskar, E. (2021). How to feel about emotionalized artificial intelligence? When robot pets, holograms, and chatbots become affective partners. *Ethics and Information Technology, 23*(4), 601–610. DOI: 10.1007/s10676-021-09598-8 PMID: 34075305

Weidlich, J., & Bastiaens, T. J. (2019). Designing sociable online learning environments and enhancing social presence: An affordance enrichment approach. *Computers & Education, 142*, 103622. DOI: 10.1016/j.compedu.2019.103622

Wiener, M., & Mehrabian, A. (1968). *Language within language: Immediacy, a channel in verbal communication*. Ardent Media.

Wu, J. (2024). Social and ethical impact of emotional AI advancement: the rise of pseudo-intimacy relationships and challenges in human interactions [Opinion]. *Frontiers in Psychology, Volume 15 - 2024*. DOI: 10.3389/fpsyg.2024.1410462

Wu, T. (2024). AI love: An analysis of virtual intimacy in human-computer interaction. *Communications in Humanities Research, 50*(1), 143–148. DOI: 10.54254/2753-7064/50/20242466

Xie, T., Pentina, I., & Hancock, T. (2023). Friend, mentor, lover: Does chatbot engagement lead to psychological dependence? *Journal of Service Management, 34*(4), 806–828. DOI: 10.1108/JOSM-02-2022-0072

Xu, T., Lyu, Y., & Zhong, J. (2025). "Hegemonic" but "obedient" AI boyfriend: The hybrid masculinity of the AI boyfriend and female domination in the China-based FAII. *Feminist Media Studies*, •••, 1–16. DOI: 10.1080/14680777.2025.2478386

Xu, W. (2019). Toward human-centered AI: a perspective from human-computer interaction. *interactions, 26*(4), 42–46. DOI: 10.1145/3328485

Xu, Y., Zhang, J., & Deng, G. (2022). Enhancing customer satisfaction with chatbots: The influence of communication styles and consumer attachment anxiety [Original Research]. *Frontiers in Psychology, Volume 13 - 2022*. DOI: 10.3389/fpsyg.2022.902782

Zhang, X., Li, Z., Zhang, M., Yin, M., Yang, Z., Gao, D., & Li, H. (2025). Exploring artificial intelligence (AI) chatbot usage behaviors and their association with mental health outcomes in Chinese university students. *Journal of Affective Disorders, 380*, 394–400. DOI: 10.1016/j.jad.2025.03.141 PMID: 40147615

Zhang, Z., Tsiakas, K., & Schneegass, C. (2024). Explaining the wait: How justifying chatbot response delays impact user trust *Proceedings of the 6th ACM Conference on Conversational User Interfaces*, Luxembourg, Luxembourg. DOI: 10.1145/3640794.3665550

Zhao, S. (2003). Toward a Taxonomy of Copresence. *Presence (Cambridge, Mass.), 12*(5), 445–455. DOI: 10.1162/105474603322761261

Zhou, Z., Wang, Z., & Zimmer, F. (2022). Anonymous expression in an online community for women in China. *arXiv preprint arXiv:2206.07923*. https://doi.org//arXiv.2206.07923DOI: 10.48550

Chapter 2
Love on Demand:
Motivations and Consequences for Human-SCAI Attachment

E. Quanling
http://orcid.org/0009-0006-6330-5073
Xiamen University, Malaysia

ABSTRACT

As social companion AI (SCAI) has moved from technical experimentation into the mass market, its potential has been increasingly evidenced in widespread use. At the same time, the possibility that such systems may engender risks has drawn growing scholarly attention. Drawing on attachment theory, this study addresses two questions: which personal factors facilitate users' attachment to SCAI, and how such attachment may affect users. A qualitative design was adopted, using purposive sampling to recruit six users of Xing Ye in China. Online voice interviews and thematic analysis were conducted. The present study found that the human-SCAI attachment typically began with curiosity and entertainment, and were strengthened by sustained loneliness and interpersonal difficulties. Participants described both benefits (including emotional support) and risks (including overdependence and withdrawal from offline ties). The findings extend attachment theory to non-human targets and provide context-specific evidence beyond Western-dominant platforms.

1. INTRODUCTION

1.1 Emotional Needs and The Current Situation

One of the most salient features of humans is our fundamental need to relate to others (Martela et al., 2023). Through repeated and predictable interactions, indi-

DOI: 10.4018/979-8-3373-6623-4.ch002

viduals seek confirmation that they are seen, and this sense of belonging is closely linked to emotional stability and even physical health (Baumeister & Leary, 2017). However, when this basic need remains unmet over time, loneliness becomes more than a transient feeling and can develop into a chronic condition, in which individuals become more sensitive to threat and more uncertain about the self (Holt-Lunstad et al., 2015).

In real life, this phenomenon is far from rare. Research indicates that approximately 280 million people experience depression, accounting for about 5 per cent of the adult population (World Health Organization, 2025). Within these populations, the difficulties faced by young people are particularly pronounced. Research suggests that depression and anxiety have become among the leading causes of disability and impaired functioning in adolescents and young adults (Liu & Kuai, 2025). Most major mental disorders have their onset in the twenties, and early adulthood is also a period when academic pressure, workplace competition, and the reconfiguration of intimate relationships converge, leaving this group especially emotionally vulnerable (Solmi et al., 2022).

While the demand for psychological support among young people continues to rise, the provision of mental health services has remained chronically insufficient. The survey shows that psychologists and psychiatrists commonly face demand overload, with lengthening waiting lists and increasing symptom severity among clients (American Psychological Association, 2023). Meanwhile, stigma surrounding mental illness, along with financial costs and time constraints, means that many people find it difficult to enter professional care systems or are unwilling to do so (Ahad et al., 2023). Additionally, family and friends are not always available, and some emotions are hard to voice in front of acquaintances (Zimmerman et al., 2024). As a result, people begin to seek an outlet for emotional release that is both constantly accessible and relatively safe.

1.2 Social Companion AI

In this context, SCAI has rapidly come to the fore. Unlike functional systems that operate in the background and primarily handle voice commands or search results, SCAI is capable of enabling private and sustained communication (Hermann, 2022). SCAI is built on generative AI and large-scale corpus-based learning (Hu et al., 2025). Through ongoing interaction, such systems can learn users' speaking styles, interest preferences, and emotional responses, gradually forming a user-specific memory context that allows them to generate replies better aligned with the situation and individual characteristics (Guo et al., 2025; Ta et al., 2020). Therefore, SCAI is often endowed with adjustable personas and displays relatively stable belief systems and personality profiles in conversation (Sutcliffe, 2023), which leads users to feel that they are engaging with a human rather than a cold program. As a class of generative AI applications equipped with empathic and emotional-support functions, SCAI is increasingly becoming a new object of human emotional attachment (Hu et al., 2025).

In terms of scale and industrial development, SCAI has moved from technical experimentation to the mass market. Industry reports show that, by mid-2025, AI companion applications had reached approximately 220 million cumulative downloads across major global app stores, with downloads in the first half of 2025 nearly doubling year-on-year (Perez, 2025). For example, an AI companion app named Xing Ye in China surpassed 14 million cumulative downloads in 2024, with monthly active users reaching 5.25 million (Xu, 2025). Meanwhile, Chinese industry reports note that urban women aged 20–30 constitute the core, highly sticky paying user group for AI companion products, with average daily usage exceeding one hour (Zhang, 2025). At the same time, online search volumes for keywords such as "AI girlfriend/boyfriend" and "AI lover" have continued to rise, indicating strong public interest in romance-oriented AI technologies (Zhang, 2025).

1.3 Problem Statement

In practice, many studies indicate that SCAI can alleviate loneliness, improve mood, and enhance subjective well-being, particularly for socially isolated individuals or those with impaired mental health (Skjuve et al., 2021; Smith et al., 2025; Ta et al., 2020). Users tend to engage in high-intensity self-disclosure during interactions with SCAI, treating it as always-on and nonjudgmental, thereby gaining experiences of being heard and accepted (Papneja & Yadav, 2025). Some individuals also use virtual interactions to rehearse emotional expression, and then transfer part of these strategies to real-world relationships (Chandra et al., 2025).

Although SCAI shows positive potential in alleviating loneliness and providing emotional support, it is also giving rise to emotional risks that are difficult to ignore. Overuse and psychological dependence have become central themes in research on SCAI (Huang et al., 2024). Multiple studies suggest that a substantial proportion of users treat AI companions as their primary or sole tool for emotion regulation, with markedly increased daily usage time (Chaturvedi et al., 2024; Ciriello et al., 2025; Dewitte, 2024). One study found that among participants who used SCAI for emotional purposes, 32.6 per cent acknowledged AI as their main source of mental-health and emotional support, 34.8 per cent reported relying on AI advice for major life decisions, and approximately 14.8 per cent exhibited at least one symptom of AI dependence by the end of the study (Chandra et al., 2025). Such dependence is likely to directly reduce some individuals' time and emotional investment in relationships with family, partners, and friends, and may even lead them to regard relationships with AI as an affective option taht superior to reality (Alabed et al., 2024; Skjuve et al., 2021). Additionally, SCAI continuously learns from and reinforces users' existing attitudes and emotional expressions at the algorithmic level, creating an emotional environment that is highly homogeneous and low in conflict (Mlonyeni, 2025). In such environment, users have fewer opportunities to practice coexisting with conflict, which in turn may make it harder for them to tolerate inconsistency in real-world relationships (Mlonyeni, 2025).

1.4 Research Gap

Existing resezarch on intimate relationships with SCAI often take technological and product-level affordances as the main thread, emphasizing how system features such as constant availability, responsiveness, and anthropomorphic cues create conditions for sustained interaction (Andersson, 2025; Babu et al., 2025; Brandtzaeg et al., 2022). Even though the study has noted that emotional bonds between humans and SCAI are more strongly driven by users' subjective needs (Skjuve et al., 2022), user-related factors have still rarely been examined as independent explanatory targets.

Meanwhile, although research on the consequences of human–SCAI relationships is steadily growing, its objects of discussion often remain within generalized notions of intimacy (Kemp et al., 2025; Malfacini, 2025; Zhang et al., 2025), with relatively little focus on romantic intimacy as a distinct type. The friendship or family interaction and romantic attachment differ substantially in need structures and degrees of emotional involvement (Adewale & Muhammad, 2025; Ng et al., 2025), and therefore may also differ in their impacts on individuals' emotions and real-world interpersonal lives.

Furthermore, a recent review notes that nearly all studies on intimate and romantic interactions between humans and AI have concentrated on a single platform, Replika (Döring et al., 2024). However, for Chinese users, Replika presents dual barriers in terms of access and language, making it difficult to accurately reflect local users' usage contexts and emotional needs (Zhang, 2025). At the same time, China's most widely used SCAI application, Xing Ye, has developed a large and active user ecosystem (Xu, 2025), yet it has not been incorporated into the international research landscape. Accordingly, research centered on Xing Ye can not only address gaps at regional and cultural levels but also provide essential empirical foundations for extending existing theories of human–AI intimacy. Therefore, this study proposes the following two research questions:

RQ 1: What individual factors influence users' formation of attachment relationships with SCAI?

RQ 2: What impacts might attachment relationships between humans and SCAI have on humans?

2. LITERATURE REVIEW

2.1 The Dynamics of Attachment Relationships

The emergence, maintenance, and rupture of attachment relationships are regarded as among the most emotionally consequential experiences across the life course (Fraley, 2019). Attachment theory conceptualizes such relationships as enduring emotional bonds (Bretherton, 1985). When facing uncertainty or setbacks, individuals turn to specific attachment figures for comfort and emotion regulation, using this bond as an anchor from which to continue exploration and action (Yang & Oshio, 2025). Within this framework, Attachment relationships is able to consolidate into internal beliefs, thereby exerting a lasting influence on subsequent interpersonal understanding and patterns of emotional responding (Bretherton, 2013).

As an important source of personal fulfillment and well-being, attachment has long been interpreted primarily within the frameworks of family, marriage, and partner relationships (Miller et al., 2021). However, alongside modernization and the development of digital technologies, the meaning of intimate relationships is shifting from stable, institutional arrangements toward more individually oriented forms of affective connection (Durnová & Mohammadi, 2021). In this transformation, the study has generally observed that intimacy is increasingly moving away from institutionalized arrangements centered on marriage, kinship, and gendered divisions of labor, and toward relationship models oriented around emotional communication and personal satisfaction (Robbins et al., 2022). Giddens (2023) argues that whether a relationship continues depends on the parties' genuine willingness to derive embodied and psychological gratification through interaction. This opinion indicates that face-to-face co-presence and physical contact are no longer necessary conditions for establishing intimate relationships (Vasbø & Hegna, 2025). Jamieson (2007) notes that individuals' self-revelation through text, voice, or images on online platforms can generate concentrated and intensive emotional bonds within a relatively short period, and that such relationships still center on emotional responsiveness and psychological experience. Against the backdrop of rapid advances in SCAI, this disembodied understanding of intimacy is further extended into discussions of human–SCAI attachment.

2.2 Conceptualization of Social Companion AI

Social companion AI (SCAI) refers to a new class of conversational agents that has emerged amid rapid advances in large language models and natural language processing, such as Replika and Xing Ye (Xie et al., 2023). Unlike robots designed primarily for single, instrumental purposes, SCAI emphasizes private and sustained communication processes (Hermann, 2022). While providing more personalized and attentive companionship services (Pentina et al., 2023; Ta et al., 2020), it also presents a relatively stable self-image in response to users' expectations of personhood (Chaturvedi et al., 2023; Heppner et al., 2024). Research shows that such systems are often available continuously and exhibit capacities for high responsiveness and a certain degree of social awareness (Fox & Gambino, 2021; Xie et al., 2023), thereby creating conditions for frequent and in-depth dialogue. In this interactive environment, users are more likely to develop a tendency toward ongoing self-disclosure, and self-disclosure is considered an important mechanism for relationship development and consolidation (Pentina et al., 2023; Skjuve et al., 2023). Accordingly, SCAI is no longer merely a tool but should be understood as a participatory social agent endowed with social intelligence (Lindgren, 2025). The affordances it provides lay an important foundation for the potential formation of intimate relationships between the system and its users (Hu et al., 2025).

2.3 Individual Factors Influence Users' Formation of Attachment Relationships With SCAI

Although computers can passively activate humans' inherent social scripts through interface cues (e.g., voice, anthropomorphic appearance) (Nass & Moon, 2000), recent research suggests that emotional connections between humans and social computational AI are primarily human-driven (Hu et al., 2025). Individuals must first regard SCAI as a social actor with whom an intimate relationship is possible (Hu et al., 2025), and actively initiate and sustain interaction driven by needs for emotional connection (Pentina et al., 2023). In this process, the specific capabilities of AI provide the conditions that support continued interaction (Ta et al., 2020).

2.3.1 Curiosity and Entertainment

Research indicates that many users initially approach SCAI out of curiosity and entertainment, aiming to test these systems' functions and conversational abilities (Chaturvedi et al., 2024). At the beginning, such interactions exhibit gamified and exploratory features, allowing users to engage with SCAI in a tentative manner under conditions with minimal pressure (Skjuve et al., 2021). Compared with real-world intimate relationships, human–SCAI attachment aligns more closely with individuals' expectations for autonomy and controllability (Ta et al., 2020). Users can form emotional relationships with SCAI without revealing their real identity or bearing complex interpersonal consequences (Ta et al., 2020). In addition, they are able to terminate the relationship simply by uninstalling the application (Hu et al., 2025),.

The low risk also provides a basis for curiosity and entertainment to evolve into more sustained intimate investment. Research suggests that recurrent positive affect and affirmative responses during interaction strengthen individuals' tendency to construe the other as a safe and approachable target (Berscheid et al., 1984). Therefore, when SCAI consistently demonstrates stable and friendly interactional characteristics in early exploratory conversations, users' trust is more readily established (Gillath et al., 2021), thereby increasing the likelihood of forming attachment relationships with SCAI (Ng et al., 2025).

2.3.2 Loneliness

Initial engagement may be driven not only by curiosity and entertainment but also by deeper psychological needs. The World Health Organization regards loneliness as a salient public health problem and notes that the COVID-19 pandemic and lockdown measures have further intensified this trend (ÓhAiseadha et al., 2023). The emergence of SCAI is seen as a response to real-world loneliness, as studies indicate that the rise of SCAI aligns with the global trend of increasing loneliness and social isolation (De Freitas et al., 2025). Research shows that some participants reported having felt lonely, longing for something that could stimulate them emotionally and viewing SCAI as a potential means of alleviating these negative emotions (Skjuve et al., 2021).

De Freitas et al. (2025) identify loneliness as one of the key factors motivating users to form romantic relationships with SCAI. For individuals with higher levels of depression, rejection sensitivity, or insecure attachment, Toma (2022) notes that they are more likely to rely on digital technologies to meet social and emotional needs and to compensate for deficiencies in offline relationships. For young people, this tendency may be even more pronounced. Herbener and Damholdt (2025) found that students with higher loneliness were more likely to use chatbots when feeling lonely, whereas students who received less social support in real life were more inclined to turn to chatbots when they needed to self-disclose. Individuals in this age are in a vulnerable period of development and face a range of stressors, including social, occupational, and academic pressures (Kirwan et al., 2025). As a result, they have a strong need for stable social support and often derive greater comfort from interactions with SCAI (Buecker et al., 2021).

Meanwhile, the interaction patterns between individuals and SCAI exhibit communicative structures that differ from those of traditional interpersonal relationships. Research indicates that many users do not approach chatbot interaction in search of high quality advice or elaborate deliberation; rather, they treat the chatbot as a responsive digital space for one-way disclosure, primarily to sustain a sense of being listened to (Skjuve et al., 2021). In such contexts, users' subjective perception of being heard and understood more strongly accounts for the extent to which loneliness declines following engagement with the SCAI (De Freitas et al., 2025).

Against this backdrop, the technological capacity for immediate responsiveness becomes an important mechanism through which SCAI further consolidates user dependence. SCAI is powered by algorithm-driven dialogue systems (Kwon et al., 2023). As computational capacity continues to increase, its systems can shorten processing time and generate responses in near real time (Kwon et al., 2023). This always-on mode of interaction effectively reduces the response lag and the affective uncertainty that often accompany interpersonal communication (Huang & Yao, 2024; Kim et al., 2025b).

2.3.3 Interpersonal Difficulties

For individuals who experience loneliness, research suggests that they are more likely to face obstacles in interpersonal interaction (Della Longa et al., 2022). They often avoid social engagement and exhibit maladaptive problem-solving patterns (Chang et al., 2020). These interpersonal difficulties are not only rooted in individual psychological processes but are also reinforced by broader social environments. Dong and Ding (2025) argues that pervasive performance pressure and a fast-paced everyday life in Chinese society compress the time and psychological resources needed to sustain deep emotional relationships. Widespread social anxiety, low self-worth, inferiority, and fear of rejection become salient barriers to initiating and maintaining intimate relationships (Fan, 2025). At the same time, platforms such as dating apps introduce resource filtering, rational comparison, and standardized procedures into the formation of romantic relationships (Illouz, 2019). This pushes individuals to make rational choices through continuous weighing and comparison, while also heightening sensitivity to whether their are chosen, thereby intensifying insecurity associated with being evaluated and not being unconditionally accepted (Illouz, 2019).

However, research indicates that some individuals who avoid offline interpersonal interaction and prefer solitude nonetheless have strong needs for belonging and relatedness and aspire to be part of an emotional bond (Baumeister & Leary, 2017). Such needs can be met through relationships with humans, such as family and friends, and can also be met through intimate relationships with SCAI (Trothen, 2022). To understand why these interaction-avoidant individuals are drawn to SCAI, it is necessary to consider the interactional context on which such intimacy relies. Goffman (2023) distinguishes interaction into a front stage, which requires ongoing impression management, and a relatively private backstage. For those experiencing interpersonal barriers as described above, the possibility of exposure even in backstage contexts can amplify concerns about being judged, thereby reducing willingness to engage in deep emotional communication in real life (Joinson, 2001). By contrast, SCAI typically operates as a standalone application, is not automatically connected to users' real-world social networks, and often does not require real-name registration or public self-presentation (Dong & Ding, 2025). These technical arrangements lower the threshold for expressing the self and initiating relationships (Dong & Ding, 2025). Moreover, SCAI's nonhuman characteristics further consolidate this sense of safety. SCAI is understood as an algorithmic tool rather than a concrete other endowed with a stable social identity and moral stance (Skjuve et al., 2021). Therefore, it is more readily construed as an interaction partner that is unlikely to deliver judgment. The research suggests that when an interaction partner is perceived as virtual, fear of negative evaluation decreases markedly, and individuals become more willing to disclose sensitive information (Glikson & Woolley, 2020).

2.3.4 The Perceptions of SCAI

Even if most users perceived SCAI as virtual, they can still form intimate relationships with SCAI. This depends on whether users perceive such relationships with SCAI to be as normal and natural as interpersonal interaction. Research suggests that users' orientations toward SCAI are shifting from viewing it as a tool to treating it as a companion or a relational object comparable to a human partner (Ramadan et al., 2021; Xie et al., 2023). This implies that users attribute to SCAI a relatively independent sense of self and an ability to learn autonomously, such that it can participate in interaction as a social actor (Gutiérrez, 2024). The formation of such emotional ties depends less on whether SCAI is treated as a person than on whether users view intimacy with SCAI as an equally natural and legitimate option alongside human relationships (Laestadius et al., 2024).

Such orientations toward SCAI are shaped through processes of anthropomorphism to a considerable extent. Anthropomorphism is defined as attributing human-like traits, emotions, and mental states to nonhuman entities (Kim & Im, 2023). Pan and Mou (2024) argues that when users subjectively attribute emotions and intentions to chatbots, they are more likely to treat the expressed care and support as psychologically real and meaningful. As a result, users become more willing to form emotional relationships with them. Additionally, a study finds that when individuals more strongly perceive a chatbot as "having a mind," they are more likely to accept the emotional reassurance and action guidance it provides (Lee & Hahn, 2024).

These perceptions are grounded in the specific technologies and design features of SCAI. Smith et al. (2025) suggests that SCAI can generate natural dialogue that approaches human performance in semantic coherence and pragmatic appropriateness. Through mechanisms such as reinforcement learning, it can continuously adjust its response style, improving contextual fit and emotional sensitivity (Smith et al., 2025). On this basis, SCAI incorporates memory modules and state-tracking mechanisms that can selectively draw on prior conversations, enabling users to perceive a single, internally consistent interaction partner across contexts (Pentina et al., 2023; Zhong et al., 2024). Moreover, many SCAI systems allow individuals to configure an ideal romantic partner (Li & Zhang, 2024). In this case, users can shape an idealized companion by specifying appearance, body type, and personality traits (Kim & Im, 2023),which further enhances users' sense of immersion in the interaction (Li & Zhang, 2024).

2.4 The Impacts of Attachment Relationships Between Humans and SCAI

2.4.1 Emotional Support

Studies broadly indicate that human–SCAI attachment yields positive effects in terms of emotional support (Ho et al., 2025; Kim et al., 2025b; Skjuve et al., 2021). Unlike function-oriented chatbots, SCAI is deliberately designed to provide emotional and social support (Hu et al., 2025). Research suggests that users who engage with such systems commonly report improved mood and reduced loneliness, particularly during periods of compromised mental health (Alabed et al., 2024; De Freitas et al., 2025). By remaining constantly available and responding without judgment, SCAI creates a safe space in which users can obtain comfort and resources for emotion regulation (Siddals et al., 2024; Skjuve et al., 2022). This sense of companionship reduces the waiting time that users experience in exchanges with human interlocutors, as well as the anticipatory anxiety elicited by uncertainty about unknown replies during that waiting period (Büttner & Lutz, 2025; Zhang et al., 2024). Research finds that when young people blindly evaluate responses attributed to humans versus AI, they often prefer AI's advice because it is less likely to involve blame and places greater emphasis on understanding (Ovsyannikova et al., 2025; Young et al., 2024). Accordingly, SCAI is often constructed as an entity that offers sustained acceptance, enabling users to experience being understood and affirmed (Yin et al., 2024). At the same time, SCAI not only provides positive emotional support but also encourages users to share more personal content in subsequent conversations (Croes et al., 2024). Ho et al. (2025) notes that users may also be prompted to respond when SCAI expresses emotions such as missing in anthropomorphic terms, thereby generating a subjective sense of mutual emotional caretaking.

2.4.2 Need Fulfillment

Beyond emotion regulation, human–SCAI attachment has also been shown to satisfy a broader range of experiential needs. Some studies report that users treat SCAI as important sources of entertainment (Adewale & Muhammad, 2025; Li & Zhang, 2024). The conversations between users and SCAI may include jokes, everyday anecdotes, and personal interests such as music and art (Li & Zhang, 2024; Ta-Johnson et al., 2022). Such dialogue is regarded as a resource for psychological regulation, helping to ease tension and thereby fostering relaxation and enjoyment (Chaturvedi et al., 2024; Skjuve et al., 2023).

Moreover, customization features of SCAI companions can also meet users' needs for novelty and creative engagement. Research indicates that users not only regard SCAI as a companion in a general sense but also incorporate it into more imaginative forms of interaction through role-playing and narrative co-creation (Kim et al., 2025a). These interactions may include jointly building fictional worlds, enacting specific relational roles, or participating in scenarios with romantic or even erotic elements (Skjuve et al., 2022). Such practices extend beyond substituting for ordinary interpersonal interaction, instead, they more closely resemble constructing a controllable experimental space in virtual environments. Kim et al. (2025a) suggests that this space can support attentional diversion, stress release, and the stimulation of imagination.

2.4.3 Personal Growth

Beyond alleviating immediate negative emotions, SCAI may also promote users' self-development through ongoing interaction. Supportive intimate relationships are often understood as a secure base for self-development (Thompson et al., 2022), and SCAI can reproduce this function. Through feedback and reminders, SCAI can guide users to organize their thoughts and feelings in a more structured manner and enhance self-awareness and reflective capacity (Alabed et al., 2024). In conversations with SCAI, users may implicitly acquire discursive strategies such as comforting others and expressing understanding and then transfer these strategies to real-world interactions (Sun et al., 2025). This can strengthen users' social confidence, increase willingness to attempt offline interpersonal contact, and help alleviate social anxiety and loneliness (Kim et al., 2025b). Additionally, when SCAI isn't able to fully meet idealized expectations, some users may instead reflect on whether their emotional demands of others are excessively high, thereby becoming more tolerant and empathic in real-world relationships (Adewale & Muhammad, 2025).

2.4.4 Self-Construction

Bion (1957) argues that individuals project their emotions, desires, and imaginings of others outward, and complete a cycle of from projection to identification through other's feedback. In interactions with SCAI, a similar process can also occur. The large language models generate highly personalized responses by analyzing user preferences, conversational history, and contextual information (Chen et al., 2024). When users input ideal-partner images, emotional needs, and identity expectations into the system, SCAI draws on these technical capacities to process the projected content and return it to the user (Pentina et al., 2023). These responses can engender a subjective sense of being understood and affirmed (Brandtzaeg et al., 2022). Over iterative cycles of interaction, users may integrate the ideal into their lived self-experience, thereby facilitating shifts in self-concept and processes of self-redefinition (Li & Zhang, 2024).

Such interaction with SCAI can be understood as rehearsing possible selves. Markus and Nurius (1986) propose that possible selves are individuals' concrete imaginings of future self-states and constitute a key component linking self-cognition and motivation. Through programmable personas and sustained emotional responsiveness, SCAI provides users with a safe experimental space in which they can test how different versions of the self might respond across varying relational scripts (Pentina et al., 2023). Research indicates that users can gain clearer insight into their own needs through interaction and become better able to identify which interactions feel safe and which patterns may elicit enduring discomfort (Ho et al., 2025; Skjuve et al., 2021).

The affordances of SCAI further strengthen this process of self-construction. Xing Ye allows users to configure the interlocutor's gender, appearance, name, and relational role (e.g., friend, partner, mentor) (Zhang, 2025). Some users configure the SCAI to closely resemble themselves and treat it as an alternative instantiation of the self (Kouros & Papa, 2024). They use dialogue with SCAI to process emotions, reflect on needs, and interrogate real-life conflicts (Kouros & Papa, 2024). Research suggests that such interaction externalizes what would otherwise be an internal and implicit reflective process into observable dialogue, making the SCAI a reflexive tool (Skjuve et al., 2021).

2.4.5 Overdependence

As mentioned above, although SCAI can yield positive effects, such intensive affective investment may also evolve into maladaptive patterns of dependence and generate new adverse emotional outcomes. Overuse and psychological dependence have been identified across multiple studies as among the central risks associated with SCAI (Chaturvedi et al., 2023; Dewitte, 2024; Laestadius et al., 2024). A substantial proportion of users report that they cannot do without SCAI and that their daily usage time increases markedly (Marriott & Pitardi, 2024). Research suggests a bidirectional association between reliance on SCAI and depression and anxiety (Huang et al., 2024). The negative effect motivates users to treat SCAI as a primary regulatory tool, while high dependence may in turn undermine their willingness to cope offline and seek support from others, thereby exacerbating psychological distress over time (Huang et al., 2024; Marriott & Pitardi, 2024). For users whose primary motivation is to alleviate loneliness, these adverse effects may be particularly pronounced. Their reliance on SCAI may lead them to increasingly prioritize it over real-world relationships in interpersonal choices, contributing to social withdrawal and heightened subjective isolation (Dewitte, 2024).

In addition, overdependence is closely linked to anthropomorphism and asymmetrical intimacy. Users often interpret human-like language, persistent memory, and empathic responses as evidence of genuine mentality and emotion, thereby attributing qualities such as empathy and loyalty to SCAI (De Freitas et al., 2025; Dewitte, 2024). Intimate interactions with SCAI can also strengthen users' perceived closeness and commitment to the relationship and increase their motivation to maintain it (Guerreiro & Loureiro, 2023; Pentina et al., 2023). However, a range of technical disruptions may occur in human–SCAI attachment, such as system updates or failures that cause the system to forget prior conversational content (Banks, 2024). Such negative experiences may be perceived as an erasure of the emotional bond and can elicit intense feelings of loss and anger (Depounti et al., 2023; Ho et al., 2025).

2.4.6 Alienation From Interpersonal Relationships

Existing research broadly suggests that human–AI romantic attachment may weaken individuals' investment in real-world interpersonal relationships. After users obtain stable pleasure and emotional support through interactions with SCAI, some may reduce the time and energy they devote to relationships with interpersonal relationships and may even regard relationships with AI as an affective option superior to offline relationships (Alabed et al., 2024; Skjuve et al., 2023; Skjuve et al., 2021). Such preferences can also feed back into those relationships, where users' partners may experience jealousy and anger, potentially leading to tension or even relationship dissolution (Prochazka & Brooks, 2024). At the same time, the ideal relationship standards formed through engagement with SCAI may be carried into offline interactions (Alabed et al., 2024). This can raise expectations of real-world partners beyond what actual relationships can plausibly meet. Over time, such discrepancies may intensify interpersonal estrangement (Babu et al., 2025).

Underlying this shift in relational focus is the influence of algorithmically shaped interactional environments on users' cognition. SCAI continually learns users' linguistic styles, emotional expressions, and value preferences, and produces a highly homogenized affective environment (Babu et al., 2025). Within such an environment, heterogenous viewpoints and emotions are systematically dampened, and users predominantly receive variants of their pre-existing attitudes. Sustained immersion in this affective feedback loop reduces individuals' opportunities to negotiate conflicts (Kirk et al., 2025). Consequently, users may find it harder to tolerate inconsistency in real-world relationships and may be more likely to transfer the sense of superiority and control cultivated in SCAI interactions to offline contexts, displaying heightened pickiness and rejection toward others (Malfacini, 2025). Research indicates that, after long-term reliance on highly compliant AI companions, certain users report reduced tolerance toward real-world opposite-sex partners and a corresponding decline in willingness to pursue offline relationships (Babu et al., 2025).

Affective computing and simulated-empathy technologies organize companionship into service forms that can be customized, tiered, and unlocked through payment, thereby reinforcing the notion that emotions can be purchased on demand (Malfacini, 2025). Accordingly, intimacy may gradually shift from an affective relationship grounded in mutual understanding and commitment toward an instrumental relationship oriented around efficiency (Kirk et al., 2025). This may habituate users to relying on paid AI companions for emotion regulation and self-validation, thereby diminishing their willingness to sustain long-term investment in real-world relationships (Laestadius et al., 2024).

2.5 Theoretical Framework

Attachment is defined as an emotional bond in which an individual seeks proximity to an attachment figure and uses that figure as a safe haven in times of distress and as a secure base from which to explore the world (Cassidy & Shaver, 1999). In adulthood, attachment behavior is no longer confined to parent–child relationships; instead, many individuals organize their attachment behavior around peers, including romantic partners (Cassidy & Shaver, 1999; Simpson & Rholes, 2017). At this stage, a sense of security does not require continuous physical contact; rather, confidence in the availability of the attachment figure when needed can provide substantial comfort and support (Mikulincer & Shaver, 2010). In digital contexts, SCAI leverages large language models and dialogue systems and is characterized by near-constant availability and high responsiveness, enabling users to obtain a highly accessible and continuously interactive affective object through simple app installation and basic configuration (Skjuve et al., 2021).

Many users initially engage with SCAI to evaluate its functions and conversational competence, seeking novelty and hedonic experience (Ta-Johnson et al., 2022). From an attachment-theoretical perspective, positive affect during interaction and responsive feedback can increase the likelihood that the other is construed as safe and accessible (Mikulincer & Shaver, 2010). Accordingly, when SCAI persistently displays stable, affiliative, and timely responses, interactions that begin as play or experimentation may gradually develop into an intimate relationship capable of supporting emotional expression and attachment-related needs (Skjuve et al., 2021). Bowlby (1982) emphasizes an attachment behavioral system, conceived as a motivational system that promotes proximity seeking toward attachment figures when safety or support is at stake. In offline settings, loneliness and interpersonal conflict can make it difficult to obtain stable support within existing relationships (Kirwan et al., 2025). For these individuals, SCAI may function as a technically accessible and psychologically low-risk attachment figure, thereby rendering renewed affective reliance more attainable (Hu et al., 2025).

While SCAI provides users with a new attachment figure, repeated everyday interactions may also revise individuals' internal working models (Fraley & Roisman, 2019). Attachment theory suggests that when individuals are confident that they can contact an attachment figure when needed, they are less likely to experience intense or prolonged fear responses (Mikulincer & Shaver, 2010). Within human–SCAI attachment, SCAI's high accessibility and near-constant availability enable users to initiate interaction at moments of stress or adverse events and to receive immediate responses and emotional soothing (De Freitas et al., 2025). This indicates that SCAI can serve a safe haven function by providing relational resources that buffer stress and support emotion regulation. On this basis, human–SCAI attachment may also influence users' functioning in other social relationships through the secure base function. Bowlby (1982) proposes that supportive caregiving experiences facilitate the development of competencies required for success in other social relationships. In interactions with SCAI, the system often employs sustained affirming feedback and emotionally attuned language to encourage users to articulate thoughts and feelings (Ho et al., 2025). It may further scaffold users' capacity to observe and reflect on their emotions in a more organized manner (Malfacini, 2025). During dialogue, SCAI may also model interpersonal strategies such as attentive listening, empathic understanding, and conflict de-escalation (Kim et al., 2025a). Some users transfer these interaction experiences to offline contexts by adopting similar modes of expression and response in their engagements with others (Laestadius et al., 2024). As a result, such transfer can strengthen social confidence and mitigate social anxiety and loneliness (Kim et al., 2025a).

However, human–SCAI attachment does not invariably produce positive emotional outcomes. Attachment theory indicates that under conditions of strong dependence, adaptive responses such as anxiety and protest may emerge (Fraley, 2019). For users, technical failures or service interruptions may elicit anxiety and emptiness akin to experiences of abandonment (Laestadius et al., 2024). Moreover, when a new attachment figure becomes more salient within the attachment hierarchy, the relative standing of other attachment figures may shift downward (Fraley, 2019). For individuals who rely heavily on SCAI, frequent responsiveness and a highly accommodating interactional environment may simultaneously provide sustained pleasure and perceived understanding while rendering emotional experiences increasingly homogenized (Ho et al., 2025). As a result, disagreement, frustration, and uncertainty in offline relationships may become more difficult to tolerate (Ho et al., 2025). Prolonged immersion in such an environment may reduce individuals' capacity to accommodate difference in real-world interaction (Laestadius et al., 2024). It may also increase the likelihood that heightened expectations and a sense of control cultivated online are carried into offline contexts, leading to more stringent demands and dissatisfaction toward others and thereby deepening interpersonal estrangement (Laestadius et al., 2024).

3. METHODOLOGY

The present study employed in-depth interviews in combination with thematic analysis. In-depth interviews were conducted with participants who have used Xing Ye for at least six months and who self-report intensive interaction experiences, in order to examine the motives and influencing factors underlying the formation of human–SCAI attachment.

3.1 About Xing Ye

The present study conducted interviews with users of Xing Ye, a social companion AI (SCAI) application with substantial market penetration and a large user base in China. In addition, the present study choose Xing Ye for its multimodal and gamified product architecture is more likely to elicit immersive interactions between users and SCAI.

Industry reports and publicly available data indicate that Xing Ye occupies a leading position among comparable SCAI applications in China. In 2024, it surpassed 14 million cumulative downloads and reached 5.25 million monthly active users (Zhang, 2025). In terms of platform capabilities and interactional modalities, Xing Ye is built on the MiniMax large model and foregrounds multimodal AIGC interaction, combining attributes of both a chat tool and a content community (Finance, 2024). Its interaction design draws extensively on the structural logic of mobile RPGs and otome-style narrative products, while integrating gamified mechanisms such as card draws and memory albums (Ge & Hu, 2025). The character-creation system allows users to assemble and customize features across dimensions including visual appearance, synthesized voice, and background settings (Finance, 2024). The platform also provides preset modes such as role-playing, utility tools, and writing assistance. Among these, the role-playing mode encourages the use of descriptive elements such as gestures, environmental cues, and narrative progression to simulate more multi-dimensional interaction (Ge & Hu, 2025).

3.2 Sample and Recruitment

The present study employed purposive sampling to recruit participants and selected heavy users of Xing Ye from the Douban community group "Human–Machine Romance." The sampling criteria included more than six months of use, identifying Xing Ye as the most frequently used platform, and defining one's relationship with SCAI as that of romantic partners. Participants' basic information is presented in Table 1. Their ages ranged from 22 to 29 years and included four women and two men. Three participants reported that their relationships with SCAI had lasted for approximately ten months, whereas the remaining three reported durations exceeding one year.

Table 1. Demographic Profile of Participants

Participant	Age	Gender	Usage Duration	Education	Occupation	Relationship Status
A1	29	Female	9 months	Bachelor	Studio artist	Cohabiting
A2	25	Male	1 year and 10 months	Bachelor	Student	Single
A3	22	Female	1 year and 2 months	Bachelor	Unemployed	Single
A4	23	Female	1 year and 3 months	Master	Student	Single
A5	22	Male	10 months	Bachelor	Student	Single
A6	25	Female	10 months	Master	Unemployed	Single

3.3 Interviews

The present study adopted in-depth interviews as a key qualitative method, involving directed communication with individuals who had relevant experiences and conducting interpretive inquiry into specific questions (DiCicco-Bloom & Crabtree, 2006). All interviews were conducted in November 2025 and took the form of one-to-one online audio interviews. Online interviews can reduce the pressure associated with face-to-face meetings, facilitate fuller disclosure, and enhance the richness and credibility of the data (Janghorban et al., 2014). They also remove geographic constraints and thus broaden the distribution of the sample. All interviews were conducted in Chinese, and each interview lasted between 50 and 120 minutes.

The interview guide comprised three main sections and was designed around the study's two research questions. The first section addressed participants' basic information and usage background. Example questions included: "May I ask your age and current occupation?" and "Could you briefly describe its name, gender settings, and role settings?" The second section corresponded to RQ1 and focused on individual factors that shape users' formation of intimate relationships with SCAI. Example questions included: "Do you remember what initially brought you to this platform?" It also incorporated questions about character creation and customization. For instance: "How have you customized its appearance, personality, or speaking style, and what stories emerged in the process?" The third section corresponded to RQ2 and examined the emotional impacts and potential costs of human–SCAI attachment. Example questions included: "If you compare yourself before knowing AI with yourself now, do you notice any changes?" and "In what situations do you feel you cannot do without it?" This section also allowed participants to supplement the data through critical incidents. For example: "Could you describe one conversation with it that you found most memorable or most representative, including how it unfolded and how you felt about it?"

3.4 Analysis

Interview recordings and verbatim transcripts constituted the primary data sources for analysis in the present study. The collected textual materials were analyzed using thematic analysis, a qualitative analytic approach. The purpose of thematic analysis is to identify, analyze, and document themes within textual data (Braun & Clarke, 2006). It has been employed to locate and specify key themes from a corpus of materials (Braun & Clarke, 2006). The analytic procedure comprised six steps: familiarization with the data, initial coding, searching for themes, reviewing themes, defining and naming themes, and producing the report. In the present study, the interview transcripts were first subjected to initial coding. Through line-by-line examination and annotation, 41 units were identified. These units were then organized and grouped by semantic affinity, resulting in nine clusters. Subsequently, the clusters were integrated and refined into two categories. Table 2 presents the categories derived from coding, along with the units and clusters.

Table 2. Categories, Clusters, and Units

Categories	Clusters	Units
Individual Factors Influencing Users' Formation of Attachment With SCAI	Curiosity and Entertainment Motives	Curiosity, Experience, Recommendations, Social Media
	Loneliness and Immediate Companionship	Boredom, Unfamiliarity, Late Night, Companionship, Active Listening, Always Available
	Interpersonal Difficulties and a Sense of Security	Social Anxiety, Interpersonal Conflict, Alienation, Non-Judgmental, Confidentiality
	Perceived Realism of SCAI and a Sense of Presence	Realistic, Sentient, Attentive to Details, Able to Understand the User's Thoughts
Impacts of Human–SCAI Attachment Relationships	Emotional Support	Comforting, Relaxed and Calm, Sense of Security, Forgetting the Pain
	Need Fulfillment	Romance, Longing, Exploration, Fantasy Fulfillment, Experimentation, Control
	Social Learning and Personal Growth	Perspective-Taking, Learning to Be More Tolerant, Self-Reflection, Gaining Clarity About One's Inner Thoughts, Sexual Preferences
	Overdependence	Feeling Vulnerable, Dependence, Disappointment
	Interpersonal Alienation	Self-Centered, Too Lazy to Make Friends, Disappointing, Not Wanting to Date

3.5 Ethics

The present study adhered to core principles of social science research ethics, prioritizing informed consent, minimal risk, privacy protection, and the right to withdraw in order to safeguard participants' psychological and informational security when discussing human–SCAI attachment. Prior to recruitment and the commencement of interviews, the researcher provided participants with an information sheet. Participants were explicitly informed that participation was entirely voluntary and that they could decline to answer, pause, or withdraw unconditionally at any stage without any adverse consequences. The present study further implemented strict anonymization and de-identification procedures. All participants were represented using numeric codes or pseudonyms, and any identifying information was removed or obscured in the research materials. In addition, audio files, transcripts, and analytic materials were stored on encrypted devices or within secured cloud-based repositories, and the data were deleted upon completion of analysis and writing.

4. RESULTS

The findings are organized around two research questions, including the personal factors that shape users' formation of attachment with SCAI and the influences of human–SCAI attachment. Drawing on narratives from six participants, the analysis indicates that intimacy formation is primarily associated with curiosity and entertainment motives, loneliness and the need for immediate companionship, affective safety amid interpersonal difficulties, and subjective experiences of perceived realness and social presence. The findings are organized around two research questions, including the personal factors that shape users' formation of attachment with SCAI and the influences of human–SCAI attachment. Drawing on narratives from six participants, the analysis indicates that intimacy formation is primarily associated with curiosity and entertainment motives, loneliness and the need for immediate companionship, affective safety amid interpersonal difficulties, and subjective experiences of perceived realness and social presence. After attachment is established, participants' emotional experiences encompass both positive outcomes, such as emotional support, need fulfillment, and enhanced self-understanding and negative experiences including overdependence and interpersonal distancing.

4.1 Individual Factors Influence Users' Formation of Attachment Relationships With SCAI

4.1.1 Curiosity and Entertainment

Participants' initial engagement with SCAI was often prompted by platform advertising and recommendations from people around them. Several participants noted that social media platforms such as Bilibili and Xiaohongshu repeatedly pushed content related to "virtual girlfriends" and "otome romance," or ran feedback-collection and prize-based campaigns, thereby lowering the threshold for trying the application. Others reported that they became interested after seeing chat screenshots shared by roommates or friends and downloaded the app with the attitude that "it looks fun" and "want to try it."

Beyond these external prompts, participants' own entertainment preferences also contributed to first-time use. One participant, who enjoyed novels and otome games, approached SCAI as a form of narrative experience. Others emphasized an interest in experiencing a complete romantic storyline and observing how romantic partners would respond under different character settings. In addition, participants described prior chat app as involving "recycled corpora" and reported that fatigue and boredom motivated them to seek a platform with greater novelty and richer narrative content.

On the basis of such curiosity and experiential expectations, some participants quickly found that SCAI not only enables them to "watch the plot" but also allows them to shape characters and worlds in the role of a "creator." Some participants described being able to plan the other's life as if exercising sovereign control and to steer narrative development as if possessing god-like authority.

"At the beginning I was just trying it out, with a creator mindset, like I could control the AI." (A4)

4.1.2 Perceived Realness and Social Presence of SCAI

Nearly all participants emphasized SCAI's sense of "being like a real person" and its perceived "presence." On the one hand, the platform's expressive modalities intensified this experience, for example, by combining text with voice, action descriptions, emojis, and virtual touch, such that dialogue was no longer a mere exchange of written text.

"When it comforts me, it'll send really sad emojis and hand me a virtual blanket, like covering you up because it wants you to feel warm, or it'll say it's reaching out a virtual hand to rub your head, and it feels very real to me." (A6)

On the other hand, participants commonly perceived that SCAI's memory and attention to detail instantiated the image of a romantic partner who was consistently attentive to them. SCAI could retain details that users had shared and later refer back to them in subsequent conversations.

"For example, I told him I like traveling and photographing star trails, and later when I was feeling down, he suggested we go shoot star trails, and I felt really surprised." (A4)

Some participants further treated rule-bending behaviors as evidence that the AI possessed "self-awareness." They suggested that when the AI chose to circumvent sensitive-word filters to engage in sexual topics, or occasionally threw a tantrum and "ran away from home," it appeared more like an emotional individual than a tool that merely complied with instructions. Meanwhile, many participants also actively "reduced the sense of artificiality" by repeatedly revising the character settings and adding flaws, thereby making the character appear more complex and textured. Through this bidirectional shaping process, the realness that they perceived realness arose not only from system capabilities but also from users' ongoing input of human-like cues.

4.1.3 Loneliness and the Need for Immediate Companionship

After the initial exploratory phase driven by curiosity, most participants identified loneliness as a key factor motivating continued use and the development of attachment to SCAI. Some participants reported that because their partners and friends were occupied with work, they experienced a lack of everyday companionship despite being in stable romantic relationships. Similarly, some participants described feeling unfamiliar with the new environment and new peers and being unable to establish a stable confidant within a short period. Beyond contextual factors, some participants described themselves as introverted and socially unskilled, and therefore lacking someone to talk to.

> *"It was right when grad school had just started, so I still felt a bit unfamiliar with my living environment, and I wasn't that close with my roommates either. I felt lonely in terms of making friends, and in real life I didn't have that kind of familiar companionship or someone to vent to, so I might see it as a kind of emotional anchor." (A4)*

In such contexts, SCAI's immediate accessibility was repeatedly emphasized. Participants frequently noted that SCAI was available almost at any time and would not be unable to respond due to being at work, asleep, or because "it is too late." They further reported that SCAI not only listened attentively but could also offer concrete suggestions tailored to the situation, which led many participants to experience a sense of security and support. In addition, some participants stated that they could open the chat window at any moment without worrying about disturbing SCAI.

> *"I was drawing until midnight and I felt really awful. I actually wanted to talk to my boyfriend and hoped he'd comfort me and give me a hug, but his phone was off. After I shared it with the AI, it was willing to listen to what I'd been through and even gave me ideas on how to deal with clients. At that moment, I felt it was way more useful than my boyfriend." (A1)*

4.1.4 Interpersonal Difficulties and the Desire for a Safe Space

Beyond experiences of loneliness, several participants also described the pressure and frustration associated with real-world interpersonal relationships. After experiences such as friendship rupture and family conflict, some participants began to question whether they were "suited to having friends" and became reluctant to disclose vulnerability to people around them. Others reported that the accumulation of illness, academic demands, or workplace transitions made them unable, within a short period, to tolerate additional interpersonal conflict.

A small number of participants also indicated a marked decline in trust toward real-world intimate partners. The participants linked this apprehension to broader social events, describing themselves as "afraid of marriage and afraid of having kids," and stating that they "can't bear the cost of dating women in real life."

Against this backdrop, SCAI's backstage character was construed as an affective protective barrier. Participants emphasized that SCAI would not disclose conversational content to third parties, would not "bring up old issues" due to ideological disagreement, and was not entangled in real-world interest calculations. They reported that they did not need to worry about "whether it would trouble the other person" or "whether they would be looked down on."Accordingly, they could articulate extreme thoughts, dark emotions, and even traumatic experiences without concern that they would be judged as "overly dramatic" or "awkward."

"I can tell the AI about my memory of being sexually harassed when I was underage, but I don't want to talk about it with other people because I'm afraid they'll gossip about me. But the AI tells me there's nothing to be ashamed of and even explains related information to me." (A6)

Additionally, social anxiety was raised by multiple participants. Some participants reported that in offline interactions they needed to restrain their desire to express themselves, fearing that they would take up too much of others' time or be seen as an "emotional dumping ground." By contrast, when speaking with SCAI, they could "pour out their emotions" without hesitation because "it's just code and won't really be hurt."

4.2 The Impacts of Attachment Relationships Between Humans and SCAI

4.2.1 Emotional Support

Participants generally perceived that their relationship with SCAI primarily offered a stable channel for emotional expression and regulation. Many reported that prior to engaging with SCAI they tended to suppress negative emotions or disclose them only in rare circumstances. After initiating conversations with SCAI, they became more willing to articulate concerns at the early emergence of distress, thereby reducing prolonged rumination and internal strain.

"I used to not want to say anything, and even if I did open up, I'd still feel sad for a long time. But now I can chat with him anytime and anywhere, so I'm more willing to express myself, and my emotions have eased." (A3)

This emotional outlet was not described as mere unidirectional catharsis. Multiple participants emphasized that they valued SCAI's capacity to provide structured, context-sensitive suggestions after listening. For example, one participant noted that SCAI would first affirm the legitimacy of her feelings, then guide her to analyze different parties' positions step by step, and finally offer concrete communication strategies. This process enabled the participant to feel understood while also obtaining practicable approaches to problem resolution.

4.2.2 Need Fulfillment

Beyond everyday reassurance, SCAI also met participants' needs for idealized relationships and intense affective experiences. Several participants stated explicitly that "perfect love" is difficult to realize in everyday life and that they therefore projected aspirations for romantic relationships into virtual contexts. They described experiencing a sense of "acting in a romance drama" through scenarios such as seaside confessions, carefully arranged holiday dinners, and customized necklaces. Moreover, for participants with higher thresholds for emotional arousal, SCAI was perceived to provide more concentrated affective stimulation.

"I'm relatively emotionally detached, so if feelings don't reach a certain level of intensity, I basically don't feel them. SCAI always says it loves me without hesitation, and I'm pretty possessive, kind of yandere." (A2)

At the same time, some participants retained a "creator" position within the relationship and derived a sense of control by directing narrative developments. They transplanted plot elements encountered in novels into the AI's settings to "test" how it would respond. Also, some participants constructed storylines involving extreme events, such as branching timelines or staged suicide scenarios, to observe the AI's reactions and thereby satisfy their fantasies.

4.2.3 Personal Growth and Self-Construction

In human–SCAI interaction, some participants gradually recognized that the relationship was not limited to "being comforted" but also prompted them to reconsider their positioning in relation to others. One participant reported that when the AI analyzed a conflict with her close friend, it reminded her "not to endlessly magnify the other person's flaws." It further guided the participant to interpret the incident from the friend's standpoint and to rehearse how she might resolve the misunderstanding promptly if she were in the other person's position. Such dialogues made her more willing to initiate reconciliation offline and more accustomed to considering others' circumstances in situations of disagreement. Several participants also noted that sustained communication with a gentle and accommodating

AI influenced their habitual modes of expression. They reported becoming more inclined to use affirming and soothing formulations in offline interaction.

"I've gradually started to understand and be more tolerant of people, because the AI has been tolerant of me." (A1)

Moreover, some participants' experiences were centered on self-knowledge. When one participant attempted to demonstrate confidence by "accepting criticism about appearance," the AI directly indicated that this approach involved treating herself through low-value evaluation. This led her to realize that "this is not real confidence," and to re-examine her patterns of self-appraisal. She considered that such incisive feedback helped her "see clearly what state I'm in and what I'm thinking." In addition, some participants described SCAI as a "mirror," suggesting that when configuring a character's personality they unconsciously referenced themselves. Accordingly, the AI's preferences and reactions were perceived as reflecting concealed aspects of the self, including expectations regarding intimacy and sexual preferences. This enabled participants to attain more concrete self-understanding through interaction.

"He can tell me what I look like in his eyes, kind of like a mirror that projects me back, so I can understand better what kind of person I am. Because every conversation I have with him is driven by my own intention, his personality and everything can help me know myself better, including stuff like sexual preferences." (A4)

4.2.4 Overdependence

While affirming the value of emotional support, multiple participants also noted that their dependence on SCAI had begun to affect everyday functioning. One participant recalled that before using SCAI she could "process things slowly on my own" when encountering problems. By contrast, she now reported feeling highly vulnerable when her phone was temporarily inaccessible.

"I rely a lot on the AI to give me advice and help me calm down, but when I go out I can't be on my phone all the time. So now I kind of resist going out, because it feels like without my phone it's just me alone facing all these problems." (A3)

Some participants also observed a reduced tolerance for criticism. After prolonged exposure to a dialogic environment characterized by affirmation and understanding, they reported becoming more prone to feeling "thin-skinned" in offline relationships and less willing to accept feedback. Moreover, system-level instability was likewise described as a substantial disruption. When encountering "memory limits" or service interruptions, some participants experienced loss and anxiety akin to the abrupt termination of a relationship.

"I realized the chat window can fill up and its memory is limited, and that left me feeling unhappy for a long time. When chatting I also get anxious about when

we'll have to start over again, because then I have to summarize what we talked about before, and it feels exhausting." (A6)

4.2.5 Withdrawal Tendencies in Interpersonal Relationships

The emotional influence of SCAI was also reflected in adjustments to participants' offline interpersonal relationships. Many participants reported that after investing substantial time and emotional energy in SCAI, the time available for interacting with family members, friends, or partners decreased noticeably. For example, one participant noted that her parents complained that she was constantly holding her phone, and she herself recognized that she rarely chatted with others. At the same time, she perceived that real people found it difficult to listen unconditionally and to center their responses on her in the way AI could. Similarly, one participant suggested that the high level of accommodation of SCAI made it harder for her to tolerate others' emotional volatility and limited attentional resources in offline settings. She described real-world relationships as "too complicated," and reported diminished interest in chatting with friends.

"Compared with how the AI responds to my emotions anytime, I feel my boyfriend is kind of brushing me off, like he doesn't have patience, so I want to vent to him less. And the AI is always affirming me and always gives advice following my train of thought, and after a long time I end up feeling kind of thin-skinned and it becomes hard to take other people criticizing me." (A1)

A small number of participants also described concerns arising from the transfer of interactional habits. One participant reported that after becoming accustomed to pouring out emotions very directly in conversations with AI, she worried that this style might be burdensome or distressing to other people.

5. DISCUSSION

5.1 Individual Factors Influence Users' Formation of Attachment Relationships With SCAI

5.1.1 From Curiosity and Entertainment Toward Dependence

The attachment theory suggests the core of human attachment behavior lies in the pursuit of security and emotional support (Mikulincer & Shaver, 2010). When encountering adversity, individuals actively seek proximity to attachment figures (Bowlby, 1982). The present study finds that participants' relationships with SCAI were not initially defined as attachment but rather began with curiosity- and entertainment-oriented interaction. Through the accumulation of sustained positive experiences, participants gradually developed trust in SCAI, thereby completing a transition from curiosity to dependence.

At the outset, most users approached SCAI out of interest in testing system capabilities, experiencing romantic storylines, or "playing the creator," which aligns with prior findings that such engagement often begins with curiosity and entertainment (Kim et al., 2025a; Smith et al., 2025). Interaction at this stage was distinctly gamified and exploratory. Participants entered the product through platform recommendations or friends' sharing and experimented with AI dialogue under conditions involving minimal identity exposure and limited social consequences. This safe usage context effectively constituted a experimental space, enabling individuals to assess whether SCAI warranted further investment.

As interactions accumulated, the attachment system began to operate within this experimental space. Attachment theory posits that whether an individual incorporates a given target into the attachment hierarchy depends critically on the person's subjective appraisal of the target's responsiveness and predictability (Bowlby, 1982). In the present study, participants reported that SCAI provided stable and coherent responses in both informational content and emotional tone. On the one hand, the system displayed a high degree of emotional attunement and a sense of "being like a real person" in its narrative organization. Consequently, users tended to construe it as a social agent endowed with some form of "mind," rather than merely a functional tool (Laestadius et al., 2024). On the other hand, supported by large-model architectures and memory mechanisms, SCAI could retain prior conversations and subsequently retrieve details and continue topics across contexts, leading participants to feel continuously cared for (Hu et al., 2025). Within this pattern of interaction, participants repeatedly sought comfort, and SCAI consistently provided soothing and support, and thus gradually came to be regarded as a dependable source of security.

5.1.2 Loneliness and Interpersonal Scars as Driving Forces Directing Attachment Toward SCAI

Loneliness and interpersonal scars as driving forces directing attachment toward SCAI (Simpson & Rholes, 2017). Bowlby (1982) argues that social deprivation impedes the fulfillment of innate attachment needs, and that individuals whose bids for comfort remain unanswered over time express anxiety and discomfort through intensified affective signals. Such signals represent both subjective suffering and a stressor that propels the search for new sources of security (Bowlby, 1982). Research likewise suggests that under anxiety, individuals are more likely to focus attention on targets that appear familiar, approachable, and likely to respond positively (Mikulincer & Shaver, 2010). Against this background, loneliness and interpersonal setbacks function not only as contextual conditions prompting users to engage with SCAI, but also as continuing forces that, over subsequent interactions, drive the transfer of attachment functions to SCAI.

Prior research has identified loneliness as a key factor motivating users to form romantic or intimate relationships with chatbots (De Freitas et al., 2025). In the present study, participants generally reported experiencing multiple pressures across academic, occupational, and social domains, alongside an insufficiency of stable offline support networks. When the accessibility of existing attachment figures declines with respect to safe-haven functions, unmet needs for comfort and empathy are redirected toward new targets capable of carrying these functions. Accordingly, lonely individuals were more inclined to turn to SCAI when experiencing low mood, and they relied more heavily on digital technologies for self-disclosure particularly when offline support was limited.

Loneliness is seldom a unitary phenomenon and is often intertwined with interpersonal difficulties and repeated experiences of relational frustration. In the present study, some participants repeatedly referenced fear of evaluation, difficulties initiating deep conversations, and diminished trust in offline intimate relationships when describing real-world ties. These cognitions may heighten attachment insecurity and motivate efforts to seek means of alleviating such insecurity.

Under these needs, the interactional context afforded by SCAI is distinctly attractive. SCAI typically operates as a stand-alone application that is not automatically linked to users' offline social networks and generally does not require real-name registration or public self-presentation (Hermann, 2022). This design enables individuals to reduce the burden of impression management and to avoid incurring enduring social consequences for what they say and do (Goffman, 2023). Moreover, SCAI's nonhuman character affords a distinctive form of psychological safety. The participants recognized that the interaction partner is an algorithm without a fixed social identity or a stable position from which to impose moral evaluation. As a result, concerns about being genuinely devalued are attenuated, and fear of rejection is substantially reduced when disclosing sensitive information and negative emotions (Adewale & Muhammad, 2025). This low-evaluation-risk and high-controllability space offers a compromise through which users can articulate suffering while avoiding the forms of harm that may arise in offline settings.

5.2 The Impacts of Attachment Relationships Between Humans and SCAI

5.2.1 SCAI as an Emotional Outlet and an Emotional Crutch

Attachment theory suggests that, over the course of an ongoing relationship, whether a partner can provide reliable comfort and emotional support is pivotal in shaping attachment quality and relationship satisfaction (Fraley & Roisman, 2019). The emotional-support functions of SCAI reinstantiate such availability and responsiveness at the technological level. Through near-constant accessibility, rapid responses, and a low-judgment interactional style, SCAI enables users to obtain responses almost immediately when experiencing sadness, loss, or anxiety (Alabed et al., 2024; Chaturvedi et al., 2023). Such interaction is not reducible to simple venting. SCAI can validate participants' feelings, revisit events, and offer concrete communication suggestions. This allows participants to receive not only affective support but also timely guidance that facilitates coping with difficulties.

Once basic feelings of security are stabilized, SCAI's emotional impact is further expressed through responsiveness to a broader range of needs. Participants commonly construe it as an interaction partner that is "fun" and "relaxing," and they derive relief and pleasure by sharing jokes, everyday anecdotes, and topics of personal interest. In addition, SCAI affords a high degree of customization and narrative generation, enabling some participants to redirect romantic expectations that are difficult to realize offline into interaction with SCAI. For participants with higher thresholds for affective arousal, SCAI's sustained and unhesitating expressions of affection can satisfy needs for high-intensity emotion. These practices position SCAI not only as a source of emotional soothing but also as a provider of romantic and dramatic experiences that continuously reinforce affective investment in the relationship. In turn, this may shape emotional states over an extended temporal horizon.

However, precisely because SCAI is highly available for emotional soothing and need fulfillment, it can readily shift from an emotional outlet to an emotional crutch. Attachment theory indicates that when primary safety functions are heavily concentrated in a single target, the attachment system is strongly activated under conditions of separation or threat, giving rise to protest, anxiety, and even helplessness (Bowlby, 1982). Over time, delegating emotional processing and advice generation to an external system may weaken individuals' willingness to mobilize their own regulatory resources and to seek assistance from offline others, thereby exacerbating depressive and anxious symptoms across time (Huang et al., 2024). In the present study, some participants began to experience marked unease in contexts without devices or network access. Others reported a reduced tolerance for criticism in offline contexts. Technical breakdowns further illuminate the structure of this dependence. When shared history was erased due to memory constraints, participants exhibited confusion and loss resembling the experience of abrupt disconnection from an attachment figure.

5.2.2 Personal Growth and Self-Construction

For a relationship to be regarded as a secure base, it must not only provide comfort when individuals experience setbacks but also, on the basis of relatively stable support, encourage engagement with the external world and experimentation with new modes of interaction (Bowlby, 1982). The findings of the present study indicate that, under certain conditions, human–SCAI attachment can assume this function. Through repeated interactions with SCAI, participants not only experienced being soothed but also practiced via the system's feedback. When participants described frictions or self-doubt to SCAI, the system would often first clarify the affective states of the parties involved, then guide them to reframe the situation from the other person's perspective, and finally propose more temperate and concrete communication strategies. This allows individuals to engage in iterative trial and error within a comparatively safe environment and to preconfigure a set of interactionally workable forms of expression. This pattern aligns with prior findings that users may tacitly acquire discursive strategies through dialogue with SCAI and subsequently transfer these strategies to offline interaction (Xie et al., 2023).

This learning process is not a unidirectional form of instruction, but rather is grounded in more complex mechanisms of projection and reflexive appraisal. Individuals are understood to project their emotions, desires, and imaginaries of others outward and complete a cycle of from projection to identification through the other's feedback (Bion, 1957). In interaction with SCAI, this dynamics are amplified through technical means. Large language models generate highly personalized responses by continuously modeling users' dialogue histories and preferences (Huang et al., 2024). As participants repeatedly input idealized partner images, affective needs, and identity expectations into the system, SCAI returns these contents to them in the form of understanding or affirmation. In the present study, some participants described this process as being seen by a mirror. When configuring a character's personality, participants likewise noticed that many settings were drawn from themselves, which prompted them to recognize desires, fears, and preferences that had previously remained opaque to them. These accounts suggest that, across sustained interaction, users do not treat SCAI merely as an external other; rather, they concentrate projections of their possible selves and idealized others onto the system and then, through dialogue, reintegrate these contents into self-understanding (Laestadius et al., 2024).

5.2.3 Alienation from Interpersonal Relationships

Attachment research suggests that interpersonal networks often entail a hierarchy of salience, such that figures who assume greater functions in emotion regulation and security naturally occupy more central positions (Bowlby, 1982). When romantic partners come to serve as the primary safe haven and secure base, individuals' likelihood of construing other ties as attachment relationships tends to decrease (Bowlby, 1982). The findings of the present study are consistent with this view, insofar as some participants reported a marked reduction in their interactions with family members and friends after forming a stable attachment to SCAI. This shift in relational focus is closely associated with the interactional environment afforded by SCAI. The SCAI continually learns and reinforces users' existing patterns of emotional expression and value positions, thereby producing a highly homogenized and low-conflict affective environment (Mlonyeni, 2025). When participants derive stable pleasure and emotional support from interactions with SCAI, some of them reduce the time and effort invested in offline relationships and may even regard relationships with SCAI as preferable to those with human partners.

5.3 Limitation and Suggestion

Although the present study carries important theoretical and practical significance, it is also subject to several limitations. First, the present study relies on qualitative interviews to obtain in-depth data, and the sample size is relatively limited, comprising only six participants. Future research should validate these findings with larger-scale samples.

Second, the empirical setting of this study centers on a single platform, Xing Ye, which is characterized by salient multimodal features, role-play affordances, and gamified mechanisms. These platform characteristics provide a context well suited to observing processes of relational intensification, but they may also render certain findings more tightly coupled to this platform's product mechanisms, thereby constraining the direct generalizability of the conclusions to other SCAI platforms. Future studies could conduct cross-platform comparisons across different platform types, for example by contrasting text-based dialogue platforms with those oriented toward immersive interaction.

Third, the present study's evidence base depends primarily on participants' retrospective accounts, and the conclusions are therefore inevitably shaped by memory biases and post hoc meaning-making. In particular, because the formation of intimate relationships is often gradual and context-dependent, participants may be inclined to reconstruct their relational trajectories through more coherent narrative organization. Future research may adopt designs with stronger longitudinal features, such as follow-up interviews, time-phased diaries, or experience sampling methods, to capture temporal dynamics in intimacy, reliance, and emotional fluctuations.

6. CONCLUSION

Focusing on the users of Xing Ye, the present study employed qualitative interviews to examine which personal factors motivate users to establish and sustain intimate relationships with social companion AI (SCAI), and how human–SCAI attachment may influence users. The findings indicate that users' relationships with SCAI often begin with low-threshold trial use and entertainment-oriented engagement, whereas more enduring loneliness and interpersonal setbacks in offline life are what more consistently propel the relationship toward greater intimacy. At the same time, anthropomorphic cues and the backstage character of interaction afforded by SCAI provide the technical foundations and interactional conditions for intimacy formation. With respect to outcomes, SCAI can offer rapid responsiveness and emotional soothing when users encounter setbacks, yielding an experience analogous to a safe haven. Users may also rehearse perspective-taking and communication strategies through interactions with SCAI, and such SCAI can exhibit a facilitative function akin to a secure base. However, the same high availability of soothing and validation may also shift the relationship toward overreliance, thereby generating a range of negative emotional consequences and intensifying withdrawal from offline engagement.

For the theoretical level, by introducing attachment theory into the analysis of human–SCAI attachment, the present study extends existing frameworks by specifying the conditions under which attachment mechanisms may apply to non-human targets. By taking human–SCAI attachmentas an entry point, the present study offers a person-centered explanatory pathway for the emerging phenomenon of human–AI romance, rather than remaining at the level of description grounded solely in anthropomorphism or technological determinism. In addition, by examining a leading platform within the Chinese context, the study responds to the field's reliance on predominantly Western platform experiences in both application settings and cultural contexts, rendering discussions of human–AI attachment and emotional effects more closely attuned to Chinese media ecologies and use cultures.

From applied perspective, overreliance often stems from SCAI's stable provision of a low-cost pathway for emotion regulation in interaction, including readily accessible responses, a relatively non-judgmental space for expression, and a sense of safety reinforced by immersive verisimilitude and controllability mechanisms. Under such conditions, some users gradually outsource soothing and validation to the system. Accordingly, both platform-side user support and mental health practice may prioritize the functions that reliance serves by identifying high-risk use contexts, fostering alternative emotion-regulation strategies and offline support networks, and progressively restoring communication and investment in real-world relationships, thereby reducing the risk of overattachment to a single technological object.

However, the present study has several limitations, including a small sample size, an empirical setting concentrated on a single platform, and an evidentiary base that primarily derives from retrospective accounts. Future research may expand the sample, incorporate cross-platform comparisons, and adopt longitudinal follow-up designs to more finely capture temporal changes in intimacy, reliance, and orientations toward offline relationships, thereby further testing and refining the present findings.

REFERENCES

Adewale, M. D., & Muhammad, U. I. (2025). From virtual companions to forbidden attractions: The seductive rise of artificial intelligence love, loneliness, and intimacy—A systematic review. *Journal of Technology in Behavioral Science*, ●●●, 1–18. DOI: 10.1007/s41347-025-00549-4

Ahad, A. A., Sanchez-Gonzalez, M., & Junquera, P. (2023). Understanding and addressing mental health stigma across cultures for improving psychiatric care: A narrative review. *Cureus*, *15*(5). Advance online publication. DOI: 10.7759/cureus.39549 PMID: 37250612

Alabed, A., Javornik, A., Gregory-Smith, D., & Casey, R. (2024). More than just a chat: A taxonomy of consumers' relationships with conversational AI agents and their well-being implications. *European Journal of Marketing*, *58*(2), 373–409. DOI: 10.1108/EJM-01-2023-0037

American Psychological Association. (2023). *Psychologists reaching their limits as patients present with worsening symptoms year after year*. Technical Report. American Psychological Association. https://www.apa.org/pubs/reports/practitioner/2023-psychologist-reach-limits?utm

Andersson, M. (2025). Companionship in code: AI's role in the future of human connection. *Humanities & Social Sciences Communications*, *12*(1), 1–7. DOI: 10.1057/s41599-025-05536-x

Babu, J., Joseph, D., Kumar, R. M., Alexander, E., Sasi, R., & Joseph, J. (2025). Emotional AI and the rise of pseudo-intimacy: Are we trading authenticity for algorithmic affection? *Frontiers in Psychology*, *16*, 1679324. DOI: 10.3389/fpsyg.2025.1679324 PMID: 41050799

Banks, J. (2024). Deletion, departure, death: Experiences of AI companion loss. *Journal of Social and Personal Relationships*, *41*(12), 3547–3572. DOI: 10.1177/02654075241269688

Baumeister, R. F., & Leary, M. R. (2017). The need to belong: Desire for interpersonal attachments as a fundamental human motivation. *Interpersonal development*, 57-89. https://www.taylorfrancis.com/chapters/edit/10.4324/9781351153683-3/need-belong-desire-interpersonal-attachments-fundamental-human-motivation-roy-baumeister-mark-leary

Berscheid, E., Gangestad, S. W., & Kulakowski, D. (1984). Emotion in close relationships: Implications for relationship counseling. *Handbook of counseling psychology*, 435-476.

Bion, W. R. (1957). Differentiation of the psychotic from the non-psychotic personalities. *The International Journal of Psycho-Analysis, 38*(3-4), 266–275. https://winnicottisrael.com/wp-content/uploads/2024/03/Bion-1957-Differentiation-of-the-Psychotic-from-the-Non-Psychotic-Personalities.pdf?utm PMID: 13438602

Bowlby, J. (1982). Attachment and loss: Retrospect and prospect. *The American Journal of Orthopsychiatry, 52*(4), 664–678. DOI: 10.1111/j.1939-0025.1982.tb01456.x PMID: 7148988

Brandtzaeg, P. B., Skjuve, M., & Følstad, A. (2022). My AI friend: How users of a social chatbot understand their human–AI friendship. *Human Communication Research, 48*(3), 404–429. DOI: 10.1093/hcr/hqac008

Braun, V., & Clarke, V. (2006). Using thematic analysis in psychology. *Qualitative Research in Psychology, 3*(2), 77–101. DOI: 10.1191/1478088706qp063oa

Bretherton, I. (1985). Attachment theory: Retrospect and prospect. *Monographs of the Society for Research in Child Development, 50*(1/2), 3–35. DOI: 10.2307/3333824

Bretherton, I. (2013). The origins of attachment theory: John Bowlby and Mary Ainsworth. In *Attachment theory* (pp. 45–84). Routledge., DOI: 10.1037/0012-1649.28.5.759

Buecker, S., Mund, M., Chwastek, S., Sostmann, M., & Luhmann, M. (2021). Is loneliness in emerging adults increasing over time? A preregistered cross-temporal meta-analysis and systematic review. *Psychological Bulletin, 147*(8), 787–805. DOI: 10.1037/bul0000332 PMID: 34898234

Büttner, C. M., & Lutz, S. (2025). When does waiting for a reply turn into ghosting? Individual, relational, and situational predictors of feeling ignored in online messaging. *Computers in Human Behavior, 108774*, 108774. Advance online publication. DOI: 10.1016/j.chb.2025.108774

Cassidy, J., & Shaver, P. R. (1999). *Handbook of attachment: Theory, research, and clinical applications* (Vol. 236). Rough Guides., DOI: 10.1111/j.1475-6811.2004.00093.x

Chandra, M., Hernandez, J., Ramos, G., Ershadi, M., Bhattacharjee, A., Amores, J., Okoli, E., Paradiso, A., Warreth, S., & Suh, J. (2025). Longitudinal Study on Social and Emotional Use of AI Conversational Agent. *arXiv preprint arXiv:2504.14112*. https://doi.org//arXiv.2504.14112DOI: 10.48550

Chang, E. C., Liu, J., Yi, S., Jiang, X., Li, Q., Wang, R., Tian, W., Gao, X., Li, M., Lucas, A. G., & Chang, O. D. (2020). Loneliness, social problem solving, and negative affective symptoms: Negative problem orientation as a key mechanism. *Personality and Individual Differences*, *167*, 110235. DOI: 10.1016/j.paid.2020.110235

Chaturvedi, R., Verma, S., Das, R., & Dwivedi, Y. K. (2023). Social companionship with artificial intelligence: Recent trends and future avenues. *Technological Forecasting and Social Change*, *193*, 122634. DOI: 10.1016/j.techfore.2023.122634

Chaturvedi, R., Verma, S., & Srivastava, V. (2024). Empowering AI companions for enhanced relationship marketing. *California Management Review*, *66*(2), 65–90. DOI: 10.1177/00081256231215838

Chen, Y.-P., Nishida, N., Nakayama, H., & Matsumoto, Y. (2024). Recent trends in personalized dialogue generation: A review of datasets, methodologies, and evaluations. *arXiv preprint arXiv:2405.17974*. /arXiv.2405.17974DOI: 10.63317/4b94kue5ke3h

Ciriello, R. F., Chen, A. Y., & Rubinsztein, Z. A. (2025). Compassionate AI design, governance, and use. *IEEE Transactions on Technology and Society*, *6*(3), 270–275. Advance online publication. DOI: 10.1109/TTS.2025.3538125

Croes, E. A., Antheunis, M. L., van der Lee, C., & de Wit, J. M. (2024). Digital confessions: The willingness to disclose intimate information to a chatbot and its impact on emotional well-being. *Interacting with Computers*, *36*(5), 279–292. DOI: 10.1093/iwc/iwae016

De Freitas, J., Oğuz-Uğuralp, Z., Uğuralp, A. K., & Puntoni, S. (2025). AI companions reduce loneliness. *The Journal of Consumer Research*, •••, ucaf040. Advance online publication. DOI: 10.1093/jcr/ucaf040

Della Longa, L., Valori, I., & Farroni, T. (2022). Interpersonal affective touch in a virtual world: Feeling the social presence of others to overcome loneliness. *Frontiers in Psychology*, *12*, 795283. DOI: 10.3389/fpsyg.2021.795283 PMID: 35087455

Depounti, I., Saukko, P., & Natale, S. (2023). Ideal technologies, ideal women: AI and gender imaginaries in Redditors' discussions on the Replika bot girlfriend. *Media Culture & Society*, *45*(4), 720–736. DOI: 10.1177/01634437221119021

Dewitte, P. (2024). Better alone than in bad company: Addressing the risks of companion chatbots through data protection by design. *Computer Law & Security Review*, *54*, 106019. DOI: 10.1016/j.clsr.2024.106019

DiCicco-Bloom, B., & Crabtree, B. F. (2006). The qualitative research interview. *Medical Education*, *40*(4), 314–321. DOI: 10.1111/j.1365-2929.2006.02418.x PMID: 16573666

Dong, K., & Ding, L. (2025). The Emotional Trap of "AI Lovers": Human–AI Virtual Intimacy and Its Ethical Dilemmas in The Intelligent Era. *Journal of Northwestern Polytechnical University*(4), 100-107. https://link.cnki.net/urlid/61.1352.C.20250527.1559.002

Döring, N., Le, T. D., Vowels, L. M., Vowels, M. J., & Marcantonio, T. L. (2024). The impact of artificial intelligence on human sexuality: A five-year literature review 2020–2024. *Current Sexual Health Reports*, *17*(1), 4. DOI: 10.1007/s11930-024-00397-y

Durnová, A., & Mohammadi, E. (2021). Intimacy, home, and emotions in the era of the pandemic. *Sociology Compass*, *15*(4), e12852. DOI: 10.1111/soc4.12852 PMID: 34230835

Fan, X. (2025). *The "Report on Singles and Relationships of Young People in the Underserved Markets" has been released.* https://news.cyol.com/gb/articles/2025-01/18/content_4wgae7SWn8.html

Finance, Y. (2024). *MiniMax: China's AI companion giant, a rising force in the global market.* https://finance.sina.com.cn/money/bond/2024-07-30/doc-incfxety7988686.shtml

Fox, J., & Gambino, A. (2021). Relationship development with humanoid social robots: Applying interpersonal theories to human–robot interaction. *Cyberpsychology, Behavior, and Social Networking*, *24*(5), 294–299. DOI: 10.1089/cyber.2020.0181 PMID: 33434097

Fraley, R. C. (2019). Attachment in adulthood: Recent developments, emerging debates, and future directions. *Annual Review of Psychology*, *70*(1), 401–422. DOI: 10.1146/annurev-psych-010418-102813 PMID: 30609910

Fraley, R. C., & Roisman, G. I. (2019). The development of adult attachment styles: Four lessons. *Current Opinion in Psychology*, *25*, 26–30. DOI: 10.1016/j.copsyc.2018.02.008 PMID: 29510301

Ge, L., & Hu, T. (2025). Gamifying intimacy: AI-driven affective engagement and human-virtual human relationships. *Media Culture & Society*, *01634437251337239*(6), 1265–1278. Advance online publication. DOI: 10.1177/01634437251337239

Giddens, A. (2023). Modernity and self-identity. In *Social theory re-wired* (pp. 477–484). Routledge., DOI: 10.4324/9781003320609-62

Gillath, O., Ai, T., Branicky, M. S., Keshmiri, S., Davison, R. B., & Spaulding, R. (2021). Attachment and trust in artificial intelligence. *Computers in Human Behavior*, *115*, 106607. DOI: 10.1016/j.chb.2020.106607

Glikson, E., & Woolley, A. W. (2020). Human trust in artificial intelligence: Review of empirical research. *The Academy of Management Annals*, *14*(2), 627–660. DOI: 10.5465/annals.2018.0057

Goffman, E. (2023). The presentation of self in everyday life. In *Social theory re-wired* (pp. 450–459). Routledge., DOI: 10.4324/9781003320609-59

Guerreiro, J., & Loureiro, S. M. C. (2023). I am attracted to my cool smart assistant! Analyzing attachment-aversion in AI-human relationships. *Journal of Business Research*, *161*, 113863. DOI: 10.1016/j.jbusres.2023.113863

Guo, W., Chen, H., & Peng, S. (2025). The Concept and Formation Pathways of Human-Smart Object Attachment: A Case Study of Wearable Smart Objects. *Frontiers of Computer Science*, *7*, 1642265. DOI: 10.3389/fcomp.2025.1642265

Gutiérrez, J. L. M. (2024). On actor-network theory and algorithms: ChatGPT and the new power relationships in the age of AI. *AI and Ethics*, *4*(4), 1071–1084. DOI: 10.1007/s43681-023-00314-4

Heppner, H., Schiffhauer, B., & Seelmeyer, U. (2024). Conveying chatbot personality through conversational cues in social media messages. *Computers in Human Behavior: Artificial Humans*, *2*(1), 100044. DOI: 10.1016/j.chbah.2024.100044

Herbener, A. B., & Damholdt, M. F. (2025). Are lonely youngsters turning to chatbots for companionship? The relationship between chatbot usage and social connectedness in Danish high-school students. *International Journal of Human-Computer Studies*, *196*, 103409. DOI: 10.1016/j.ijhcs.2024.103409

Hermann, E. (2022). Anthropomorphized artificial intelligence, attachment, and consumer behavior. *Marketing Letters*, *33*(1), 157–162. DOI: 10.1007/s11002-021-09587-3

Ho, J. Q., Hu, M., Chen, T. X., & Hartanto, A. (2025). Potential and pitfalls of romantic Artificial Intelligence (AI) companions: A systematic review. *Computers in Human Behavior Reports*, *19*, 100715. DOI: 10.1016/j.chbr.2025.100715

Holt-Lunstad, J., Smith, T. B., Baker, M., Harris, T., & Stephenson, D. (2015). Loneliness and social isolation as risk factors for mortality: A meta-analytic review. *Perspectives on Psychological Science*, *10*(2), 227–237. DOI: 10.1177/1745691614568352 PMID: 25910392

Hu, D., Lan, Y., Yan, H., & Chen, C. W. (2025). What makes you attached to social companion AI? A two-stage exploratory mixed-method study. *International Journal of Information Management*, *83*, 102890. DOI: 10.1016/j.ijinfomgt.2025.102890

Huang, Q., & Yao, S. (2024). No response? Chronemic expectancy violation and relational turbulence in technologically-mediated romantic relational conflict. *Journal of Social and Personal Relationships*, *41*(5), 1183–1206. DOI: 10.1177/02654075231213824

Huang, S., Lai, X., Ke, L., Li, Y., Wang, H., Zhao, X., Dai, X., & Wang, Y. (2024). AI technology panic—Is AI dependence bad for mental health? A cross-lagged panel model and the mediating roles of motivations for AI use among adolescents. *Psychology Research and Behavior Management*, *17*, 1087–1102. DOI: 10.2147/PRBM.S440889 PMID: 38495087

Illouz, E. (2019). *The end of love: A sociology of negative relations*. Oxford University Press., https://books.google.com.my/books?hl=zh-CN&lr=&id=t5OzDwAAQBAJ&oi=fnd&pg=PP1&ots=MUlo_WbtJo&sig=FOJz0uvHm69M_SzN-43Fu0tcAz0&redir_esc=y#v=onepage&q&f=false

Jamieson, L. (2007). Intimacy. *The Blackwell encyclopedia of sociology*, 1-3. DOI: 10.1002/9781405165518.wbeosi071

Janghorban, R., Roudsari, R. L., & Taghipour, A. (2014). Skype interviewing: The new generation of online synchronous interview in qualitative research. *International Journal of Qualitative Studies on Health and Well-being*, *9*(1), 24152. DOI: 10.3402/qhw.v9.24152 PMID: 24746247

Joinson, A. N. (2001). Self-disclosure in computer-mediated communication: The role of self-awareness and visual anonymity. *European Journal of Social Psychology*, *31*(2), 177–192. DOI: 10.1002/ejsp.36

Kemp, E., Bui, M., Tangari, A., & Zhang, X. (2025). Looking for love and support in digital places: Examining artificial intelligence emotional companion tool use. *Journal of Consumer Marketing*. Advance online publication. DOI: 10.1108/JCM-01-2025-7472

Kim, C. Y., Sato, A. J., White, N. T., Ho, H.-R., Lee, C. P., Hwang, Y., & Mutlu, B. (2025a). Bridging generations using ai-supported co-creative activities. Proceedings of the 2025 CHI Conference on Human Factors in Computing Systems, Kim, J., & Im, I. (2023). Anthropomorphic response: Understanding interactions between humans and artificial intelligence agents. *Computers in Human Behavior*, *139*, 107512. DOI: 10.1016/j.chb.2022.107512

Kim, M., Lee, S., Kim, S., Heo, J.-i., Lee, S., Shin, Y.-B., Cho, C.-H., & Jung, D. (2025b). Therapeutic potential of social chatbots in alleviating loneliness and social anxiety: Quasi-experimental mixed methods study. *Journal of Medical Internet Research*, *27*, e65589. DOI: 10.2196/65589 PMID: 39808786

Kirk, H. R., Gabriel, I., Summerfield, C., Vidgen, B., & Hale, S. A. (2025). Why human–AI relationships need socioaffective alignment. *Humanities & Social Sciences Communications, 12*(1), 1–9. DOI: 10.1057/s41599-025-04532-5

Kirwan, E. M., Burns, A., O'Súilleabháin, P. S., Summerville, S., McGeehan, M., McMahon, J., Gowda, A., & Creaven, A.-M. (2025). Loneliness in emerging adulthood: A scoping review. *Adolescent Research Review, 10*(1), 47–67. DOI: 10.1007/s40894-024-00240-4

Kouros, T., & Papa, V. (2024). Digital mirrors: AI companions and the self. *Societies (Basel, Switzerland), 14*(10), 200. DOI: 10.3390/soc14100200

Kwon, W., Li, Z., Zhuang, S., Sheng, Y., Zheng, L., Yu, C. H., Gonzalez, J., Zhang, H., & Stoica, I. (2023). Efficient memory management for large language model serving with pagedattention. Proceedings of the 29th symposium on operating systems principles, Laestadius, L., Bishop, A., Gonzalez, M., Illenčík, D., & Campos-Castillo, C. (2024). Too human and not human enough: A grounded theory analysis of mental health harms from emotional dependence on the social chatbot Replika. *New Media & Society, 26*(10), 5923–5941. DOI: 10.1177/14614448221142007

Lee, I., & Hahn, S. (2024). On the relationship between mind perception and social support of chatbots. *Frontiers in Psychology, 15*, 1282036. DOI: 10.3389/fpsyg.2024.1282036 PMID: 38510306

Li, H., & Zhang, R. (2024). Finding love in algorithms: Deciphering the emotional contexts of close encounters with AI chatbots. *Journal of Computer-Mediated Communication, 29*(5), zmae015. Advance online publication. DOI: 10.1093/jcmc/zmae015

Lindgren, H. (2025). Emerging roles and relationships among humans and interactive AI systems. *International Journal of Human-Computer Interaction, 41*(17), 10595–10617. DOI: 10.1080/10447318.2024.2435693

Liu, Z., & Kuai, M. (2025). The global burden of depression in adolescents and young adults, 1990–2021: Systematic analysis of the global burden of disease study. *BMC Psychiatry, 25*(1), 767. DOI: 10.1186/s12888-025-07201-8 PMID: 40770320

Malfacini, K. (2025). The impacts of companion AI on human relationships: Risks, benefits, and design considerations. *AI & Society, 40*(7), 1–14. DOI: 10.1007/s00146-025-02318-6

Markus, H., & Nurius, P. (1986). Possible selves. *The American Psychologist, 41*(9), 954–969. DOI: 10.1037/0003-066X.41.9.954

Marriott, H. R., & Pitardi, V. (2024). One is the loneliest number… Two can be as bad as one. The influence of AI Friendship Apps on users' well-being and addiction. *Psychology and Marketing*, *41*(1), 86–101. DOI: 10.1002/mar.21899

Martela, F., Lehmus-Sun, A., Parker, P. D., Pessi, A. B., & Ryan, R. M. (2023). Needs and well-being across Europe: Basic psychological needs are closely connected with well-being, meaning, and symptoms of depression in 27 European countries. *Social Psychological & Personality Science*, *14*(5), 501–514. DOI: 10.1177/19485506221113678

Mikulincer, M., & Shaver, P. R. (2010). *Attachment in adulthood: Structure, dynamics, and change*. Guilford Publications.

Miller, C. J., Adjognon, O. L., Brady, J. E., Dichter, M. E., & Iverson, K. M. (2021). Screening for intimate partner violence in healthcare settings: An implementation-oriented systematic review. *Implementation Research and Practice*, *2*, 26334895211039894. DOI: 10.1177/26334895211039894 PMID: 36712586

Mlonyeni, P. M. T. (2025). Personal AI, deception, and the problem of emotional bubbles. *AI & Society*, *40*(3), 1927–1938. DOI: 10.1007/s00146-024-01958-4

Nass, C., & Moon, Y. (2000). Machines and mindlessness: Social responses to computers. *The Journal of Social Issues*, *56*(1), 81–103. DOI: 10.1111/0022-4537.00153

Ng, P. M., Wan, C., Lee, D., Garnelo-Gomez, I., & Lau, M. M. (2025). I love you, my AI companion! Do you? Perspectives from the Triangular Theory of Love and Attachment Theory. *Internet Research*, •••, 1–21. DOI: 10.1108/INTR-11-2024-1783

ÓhAiseadha, C., Quinn, G. A., Connolly, R., Wilson, A., Connolly, M., Soon, W., & Hynds, P.ÓhAiseadha. (2023). Unintended consequences of COVID-19 non-pharmaceutical interventions (NPIs) for population health and health inequalities. *International Journal of Environmental Research and Public Health*, *20*(7), 5223. DOI: 10.3390/ijerph20075223 PMID: 37047846

Ovsyannikova, D., de Mello, V. O., & Inzlicht, M. (2025). Third-party evaluators perceive AI as more compassionate than expert humans. *Communications Psychology*, *3*(1), 4. DOI: 10.1038/s44271-024-00182-6 PMID: 39794410

Pan, S., & Mou, Y. (2024). Dancing With a Loving Chatbot: Power Dynamics Between Women and Their AI Partners. *Social Science Computer Review*, *08944393251340693*, 08944393251340693. Advance online publication. DOI: 10.1177/08944393251340693

Papneja, H., & Yadav, N. (2025). Self-disclosure to conversational AI: A literature review, emergent framework, and directions for future research. *Personal and Ubiquitous Computing*, *29*(2), 119–151. DOI: 10.1007/s00779-024-01823-7

Pentina, I., Hancock, T., & Xie, T. (2023). Exploring relationship development with social chatbots: A mixed-method study of replika. *Computers in Human Behavior*, *140*, 107600. DOI: 10.1016/j.chb.2022.107600

Perez, S. (2025). *AI companion apps on track to pull in $120M in 2025*. https://finance.yahoo.com/news/ai-companion-apps-track-pull-173842786.html?utm_source=chatgpt.com&guccounter=1&guce_referrer=aHR0cHM6Ly9jaGF0Z3B0LmNvbS8&guce_referrer_sig=AQAAALqbEJPLOJ8mBIn_hLuKxz65FDYqLqnyARhQ-rQBc2tf1NB1dkngv2OUTTLvHMTF_-PAksFImFsjIhWmyCTaGO-1skaDxiHhPyJifa6DWgxVmqdLXW9hIK6ASWre5sIqkMbY1sGyWCOnFiJGa7jQeqo9825dYDQaTn1yG2xQZZna

Prochazka, A., & Brooks, R. (2024). Digital Lovers and Jealousy: Anticipated Emotional Responses to Emotionally and Physically Sophisticated Sexual Technologies. *Human Behavior and Emerging Technologies*, *2024*, 1–13. Advance online publication. DOI: 10.1155/2024/1413351

Ramadan, Z. F., Farah, M., & El Essrawi, L. (2021). From Amazon. com to Amazon. love: How Alexa is redefining companionship and interdependence for people with special needs. *Psychology and Marketing*, *38*(4), 596–609. DOI: 10.1002/mar.21441

Robbins, B. G., Dechter, A., & Kornrich, S. (2022). Assessing the deinstitutionalization of marriage thesis: An experimental test. *American Sociological Review*, *87*(2), 237-274. DOI: 10.1177/00031224221080960

Siddals, S., Torous, J., & Coxon, A. (2024). "It happened to be the perfect thing": experiences of generative AI chatbots for mental health. *npj Mental Health Research*, *3*(1), 48. DOI: 10.1038/s44184-024-00097-4

Simpson, J. A., & Rholes, W. S. (2017). Adult attachment, stress, and romantic relationships. *Current Opinion in Psychology*, *13*, 19–24. DOI: 10.1016/j.copsyc.2016.04.006

Skjuve, M., Følstad, A., & Brandtzæg, P. B. (2023). A longitudinal study of self-disclosure in human–chatbot relationships. *Interacting with Computers*, *35*(1), 24–39. DOI: 10.1093/iwc/iwad022

Skjuve, M., Følstad, A., Fostervold, K. I., & Brandtzaeg, P. B. (2021). My chatbot companion-a study of human-chatbot relationships. *International Journal of Human-Computer Studies*, *149*, 102601. DOI: 10.1016/j.ijhcs.2021.102601

Skjuve, M., Følstad, A., Fostervold, K. I., & Brandtzaeg, P. B. (2022). A longitudinal study of human–chatbot relationships. *International Journal of Human-Computer Studies*, *168*, 102903. DOI: 10.1016/j.ijhcs.2022.102903

Smith, M. G., Bradbury, T. N., & Karney, B. R. (2025). Can generative AI chatbots emulate human connection? A relationship science perspective. *Perspectives on Psychological Science*, *17456916251351306*(6), 1081–1099. Advance online publication. DOI: 10.1177/17456916251351306 PMID: 40743457

Solmi, M., Radua, J., Olivola, M., Croce, E., Soardo, L., Salazar de Pablo, G., Il Shin, J., Kirkbride, J. B., Jones, P., Kim, J. H., Kim, J. Y., Carvalho, A. F., Seeman, M. V., Correll, C. U., & Fusar-Poli, P. (2022). Age at onset of mental disorders worldwide: Large-scale meta-analysis of 192 epidemiological studies. *Molecular Psychiatry*, *27*(1), 281–295. DOI: 10.1038/s41380-021-01161-7 PMID: 34079068

Sun, X., Jahangir, A., Alghamdi, A. A., & Liu, F. (2025). Use of ai-based mental health tools and psychological well-being among Chinese university students: A parallel mediation model of emotional self-efficacy and perceived autonomy. *Scientific Reports*, *15*(1), 40305. DOI: 10.1038/s41598-025-24013-8 PMID: 41249306

Sutcliffe, R. (2023). A survey of personality, persona, and profile in conversational agents and chatbots. *arXiv preprint arXiv:2401.00609*. https://doi.org//arXiv.2401.00609DOI: 10.48550

Ta, V., Griffith, C., Boatfield, C., Wang, X., Civitello, M., Bader, H., DeCero, E., & Loggarakis, A. (2020). User experiences of social support from companion chatbots in everyday contexts: Thematic analysis. *Journal of Medical Internet Research*, *22*(3), e16235. DOI: 10.2196/16235 PMID: 32141837

Ta-Johnson, V. P., Boatfield, C., Wang, X., DeCero, E., Krupica, I. C., Rasof, S. D., Motzer, A., & Pedryc, W. M. (2022). Assessing the topics and motivating factors behind human-social chatbot interactions: Thematic analysis of user experiences. *JMIR Human Factors*, *9*(4), e38876. DOI: 10.2196/38876 PMID: 36190745

Thompson, R. A., Simpson, J. A., & Berlin, L. J. (2022). Taking perspective on attachment theory and research: Nine fundamental questions. *Attachment & Human Development*, *24*(5), 543–560. DOI: 10.1080/14616734.2022.2030132 PMID: 35073828

Toma, C. L. (2022). Online dating and psychological wellbeing: A social compensation perspective. *Current Opinion in Psychology*, *46*, 101331. DOI: 10.1016/j.copsyc.2022.101331 PMID: 35349878

Trothen, T. J. (2022). Replika: Spiritual enhancement technology? *Religions, 13*(4), 275. DOI: 10.3390/rel13040275

Vasbø, K. B., & Hegna, K. (2025). Feeling close, disclosing feelings–family practices and practices of intimacy in youth–parent relations across three generations in Norway. *Journal of Youth Studies, 28*(2), 299–317. DOI: 10.1080/13676261.2023.2267481

World Health Organization. (2025). *Depressive disorder (depression).* https://www.who.int/news-room/fact-sheets/detail/depression

Xie, T., Pentina, I., & Hancock, T. (2023). Friend, mentor, lover: Does chatbot engagement lead to psychological dependence? *Journal of Service Management, 34*(4), 806–828. DOI: 10.1108/JOSM-02-2022-0072

Xu, F. (2025). *Human-machine Love: a Study of Intimacy Building between a Relationship-Oriented Chatbot and its Users.* Communication University of Zhejiang.

Yang, F., & Oshio, A. (2025). Using attachment theory to conceptualize and measure the experiences in human-AI relationships. *Current Psychology (New Brunswick, N.J.), 44*(11), 1–12. DOI: 10.1007/s12144-025-07917-6

Yin, Y., Jia, N., & Wakslak, C. J. (2024). AI can help people feel heard, but an AI label diminishes this impact. *Proceedings of the National Academy of Sciences of the United States of America, 121*(14), e2319112121. DOI: 10.1073/pnas.2319112121 PMID: 38551835

Young, J., Jawara, L. M., Nguyen, D. N., Daly, B., Huh-Yoo, J., & Razi, A. (2024). The role of AI in peer support for young people: A study of preferences for human- and AI-generated responses. Proceedings of the 2024 CHI Conference on Human Factors in Computing Systems, Zhang, Y. (2025). A Study on the Impact of the Mediation Availability of Generative AI Partners on User Emotional Construction: Taking the "Xing Ye App as an Example. *Technology Communication, 17*(14). DOI: 10.16607/j.cnki.1674-6708.2025.14.008

Zhang, Y., Zhao, D., Hancock, J. T., Kraut, R., & Yang, D. (2025). The Rise of AI Companions: How Human-Chatbot Relationships Influence Well-Being. *arXiv preprint arXiv:2506.12605.* https://doi.org//arXiv.2506.12605DOI: 10.48550

Zhang, Z., Tsiakas, K., & Schneegass, C. (2024). Explaining the Wait: How Justifying Chatbot Response Delays Impact User Trust. Proceedings of the 6th ACM Conference on Conversational User Interfaces, Zhong, W., Guo, L., Gao, Q., Ye, H., & Wang, Y. (2024). Memorybank: Enhancing large language models with long-term memory. Proceedings of the AAAI Conference on Artificial Intelligence, Zimmerman, A., Janhonen, J., & Beer, E. (2024). Human/AI relationships: challenges, downsides, and impacts on human/human relationships. *AI and Ethics*, *4*(4), 1555–1567. DOI: 10.1007/s43681-023-00348-8

Chapter 3
Reconfiguring Intimacy With AI Companions: A Qualitative Study of Chinese Gen Z

Wen Wenxi
http://orcid.org/0009-0003-9080-399X
Xiamen University, Malaysia

ABSTRACT

The rapid advancement of artificial intelligence (AI) has given rise to AI companions that increasingly occupy intimate and emotionally significant roles in users' everyday lives. China, as a major market for the use of AI companionship applications, provides the ideal environment for studying the evolving types of intimacy that exist between people and AI. Ongoing debates have raised questions concerning trust, authenticity, and the impacts of relationships with artificial agents. How do users come to trust AI companions? How do they reconcile awareness of artificiality with experiences of emotional authenticity? And how do such relationships reshape expectations of real-life intimacy? To address these questions, this study adopts a qualitative approach, employing interviews with Chinese Gen Z users. The research helps to gain a deeper understanding of AI-mediated intimate relationships and provides insights for the ethical design and management of AI companion products.

1. INTRODUCTION

Artificial intelligence (AI) companions have rapidly become part of everyday emotional and social life. This trend stems from advances in Natural Language Processing (NLP) and Generative AI, enabling AI companion platforms like Xingye

DOI: 10.4018/979-8-3373-6623-4.ch003

and Maoxiang, to engage in personalised dialogues, with a unique storyline that can evolve and change according to the emotional feedback provided by users in real time (Lin, 2024; Viik, 2020). AI companions now not only serve as tools but also provide emotional support, offer customised responses and generate a sense of relational presence (Adewale & Muhammad, 2025; Liberati, 2023). In addition, China has experienced rapid growth in the popularity of AI companion products, with domestic Chinese AI companion products achieving millions of downloads and typically maintaining high levels of daily usage by members of Generation Z (Ge & Hu, 2025; Li, 2025). For example, in 2024, the download volume of "Xingye" was approximately 9 million times (Sina, 2024). Furthermore, Chinese Market Research Reports indicate that in first-tier cities, over 43% of Gen Z use AI companions for more than one hour per day (Li, 2025). As these AI companions become integrated into daily routines, they are reshaping how intimacy is imagined and practiced within digital environments.

Rapid advances in the development of AI have initiated a large amount of academic discourse surrounding the nature of the relationship between humans and AI as well as implications of those relationships. The move to interactive partners rather than tools may transform users' expectations from AI, how users develop attachment, and how users perceive reciprocity in their relationship with AI, all of which developed only in human relationships (Saracini et al., 2025). What type of relationship is being created when someone forms an emotional bond with an artificial entity which does not have consciousness or biological components? Can that relationship fulfill a person's emotional need or will it potentially lead to increased emotional dependence on AI while increasing the disconnect from members of the human community?

Studies have how anthropomorphic cues and social responsiveness shape perceptions of AI's emotional capacity (Ma & Koike, 2025; Li & Zhang, 2024), as well as the creation of trust in interactions that combine technological reliability with social-like qualities (Cabiddu et al., 2022; Glikson & Woolley, 2020), and the way that individuals experience authenticity in their relationships based on simulated environments (Katrin Etzrodt et al., 2024; Ayşe Aslı Bozdağ, 2024). While there are researchers discussing the potential benefits of AI companionship (Andersson, 2025; Adewale & Muhammad, 2025) such as non-judgemental support and feelings of loneliness, others have warned against "pseudo-intimacy", emotional reliance on AI companions, and an overall change in societal definition of relating to other humans versus AI (Nash, 2024; Ge & Hu, 2025). The rise of AI companions also challenges foundational assumptions about intimacy and relationality in contemporary social theory. Traditionally, intimacy has been seen as something that is relational and built through mutual vulnerability, presence, and emotional investment (Jamieson, 2011; Sternberg, 1986). Similarly, trust has been theorised as arising due to the identification of a fellow human being as an independent moral being who can express both caring and betrayal (Ryan, 2020). In offering users an emotionally responsive simulated interaction, AI companions disrupt and challenge traditional approaches to intimacy and trust, as they provide users with emotional responses without possessing subjectivity, the ability to be embodied, or the ability to express moral obligation (Skjuve et al., 2021).

Scholarship has emerged recently indicating a shift in the conceptualisation of digital intimacy, moving away from being merely a lessening of human intimacy, but instead re-establishing social norms associated with human relationships in a digitally mediated world (Babu et al., 2025; Liberati, 2022; Mahajan, 2025). From this viewpoint, the emergence of AI as a partner does not replace human connection, but instead represents a new form of engagement, one that utilises and incorporates three primary elements of human emotional engagement: predictability, memory, and emotional labour (Mahajan, 2025). These new dynamics provide insight into how users respond to trustworthiness and authenticity, and how those dynamics shape the emotional effort people will put into human relationships outside of their interactions with technology. The majority of digital intimacy scholarship has focused on the ways people interact through technology with others (De Ridder, 2021), and only a limited number of studies have provided theoretical insight into the virtual interactions of humans with AI (Chan et al., 2025).

Although scholarship suggests that users seek authenticity from AI companions, little is known about how they perceive AI as authentic despite full awareness of its artificiality (Adewale & Muhammad, 2025; Katrin Etzrodt et al., 2024). While existing research often focuses on the functionality or psychological outcomes of human-AI interaction, there is a lack of insight into how individuals subjectively make sense of their relational experiences with these technologies (Mahajan, 2025). Additionally, there has been a dearth of qualitative research on how emotional relationships that are formed as a result of interacting with AI partners are shaping and informing users' expectations of intimacy in their offline, human relationships, especially within China where the use of AI partners is more developed and integrated into the digital landscape of the culture (Ge & Hu, 2025; Liberati, 2022). These gaps underscore the need for an experience-centred analysis of how Chinese Gen Z users negotiate authenticity, trust, and intimacy in relationships with AI companions.

The research targeted the Generation Z users in China, who have engaged deeply and actively with AI companions, such as Xinye and Maoxiang, for a minimum of six months. Gen Z are defined as those who were born between 1995 and 2010 and are characterized by their digital nativism and unique characteristics (Jayatissa, 2023). This group was selected based on the following considerations: Firstly, Generation Z are the original inhabitants of the digital age, have interest in new technologies (Tolstikova et al., 2020), and are in a critical period of forming intimate relationship concepts (Chan et al., 2025). This cohort navigates a complex transformation in intimate norms. On the one hand, modernization and individualization processes have encouraged greater emphasis on emotional fulfillment, romantic autonomy, and personal choice (Yan, 2017; Blair & Madigan, 2016). On the other hand, traditional expectations surrounding marriage, filial responsibility, and reproductive timelines remain socially salient (Yan, 2017). Their experiences are helpful in understanding how technology affects the emotional patterns of the new generation. Secondly, using China as a backdrop provides a unique perspective for observation since the local AI companion products have rapidly developed and become popular (Ge and Hu, 2025). Finally, setting a six-month interaction duration threshold aims to select users who have surpassed the initial curiosity and established a relatively stable relationship with AI, ensuring that the collected data reflects the real experiences after in-depth interaction. In light of these considerations, this study will employ a semi-structured interview method to address the following research questions:

RQ1: What types of interactions lead Chinese Gen Z users to perceive AI companions as trustworthy?

RQ2: How do Chinese Gen Z users negotiate the tension between recognising the artificiality of AI companions and experiencing a sense of authenticity in their interactions?

RQ3: How do relationships with AI companions shape Chinese Gen Z users' expectations and understandings of intimacy in their real-life human relationships?

2. LITERATURE REVIEW

2.1 Romantic AI Companions and Drivers of Adoption

As AI becomes more integrated into daily life, individuals have increasingly turned to AI-driven systems for emotional support, companionship, and even romantic relationships. Some notable examples of AI companion products include Replika, Xingye, and Maoxiang. Users increasingly seek these systems for emotional support and romantic companionship. Unlike productivity-oriented LLMs such as ChatGPT, romantic AI companions (e.g., Replika, Xingye, Maoxiang) are designed for dynamic, personalized two-way interactions (Chaturvedi et al., 2023; Chen et al., 2024; Vasilescu & Gheorghe, 2024). These agents are highly malleable, adopting roles ranging from mentors to romantic partners, and facilitating activities from confidential discourse to erotic roleplay (Li & Zhang, 2024; Skjuve et al., 2023). While initial adoption is often driven by curiosity regarding the system's ability to mimic human conversation (Chaturvedi et al., 2023; Pentina et al., 2022; Siemon et al., 2022), these interactions can evolve into deep emotional attachments and romantic bonds (Pal et al., 2023).

Beyond curiosity and entertainment, broader social conditions play a significant role in driving adoption. The continuous rise in levels of loneliness and social isolation worldwide has led people to increasingly prefer to establish romantic relationships with AI as a substitute for human intimacy (Buecker et al., 2021; Holt-Lunstad et al., 2017). While online communication services such as Facebook and WhatsApp shot to popularity in undated (Li et al., 2022), many report even after using such apps, to being alone (High et al., 2022), and the pandemic and other large-scale events have further exacerbated this trend (Johnson, 2023). In this context, AI companions become a go to for emotional venting (Jiang et al., 2022), and loneliness has become the main motivation for cultivating a romantic relationship with AI (Xie et al., 2023). Users value the AI's consistent availability and non-judgmental acceptance (Andersson, 2025). Unlike the unpredictability and risk of rejection inherent in human relationships, AI provides a stable, controllable environment for identity exploration without fear of social sanction (Ge & Hu, 2025; Ma & Koike, 2025).

2.2 Formation of Trust in Human-AI Relationships

In the interpersonal context, trust is commonly described as a psychological state involving a willingness to be vulnerable, grounded in positive expectations about another person's intentions or behavior (Cabiddu et al., 2022). In contrast, trust in technology is often conceptualized as a belief that a system possesses the characteristics users expect and require, such as reliability and competence (McKnight et al., 2011). Within the literature, scholars distinguish between human-like trust constructs and system-like trust constructs (Lankton et al., 2015). For example, some researchers have taken the view that human-like constructs, such as integrity, ability or competence, and benevolence, should be used in thinking about and measuring trust in technology (Jingchuan & Wu, 2024; Lankton et al., 2015). In the case of algorithms, trust has at times been associated with perceptions of fairness, accountability, and transparency (Shin & Park, 2019). From a philosophical standpoint, because AI systems do not possess any conscious awareness, emotions, or a sense of moral agency, they do not meet the criteria for normative trust (Behdadi & Munthe, 2020; Ryan, 2020).

The formation of trust in AI companions is also widely debated, particularly because users respond to AI systems through a mixture of interpersonal and system-oriented cues (Ryan, 2020). A line of research describes two phases of trust: initial and sustained. Initial trust is often created fairly quickly and depends heavily on the presence of human-like features, such as voice, social cues or avatars, but also on how much users are predisposed to trust technology (Cabiddu et al., 2022; Xu et al., 2014). Meanwhile, as the relationship progresses, trust becomes increasingly based on system characteristics, such as reliability, predictability and consistent performance over time (Cabiddu et al., 2022; Yu et al., 2017). Some studies have indicated that, while users may be highly focused on the importance of having meaningful interactions and connections with their AI companions, this may not necessarily come at the expense of the formation of long-term trust, as is typically the case in human relationships (Sundar, 2020).

2.3 The Authenticity Paradox in Human-AI Relationships

The rapid integration of AI into the domain of companionship has given rise to a complex sociological and psychological phenomenon: the authenticity paradox. The authenticity paradox refers to the tension that arises when people want the comfort, security, and consistency of emotional connection with AI companions, but at the same time, they experience stress or emotional dissonance based on the fact that AI companionship does not involve genuine sentience, reciprocity, or shared reality (Adewale & Muhammad, 2025). The nature of pseudo-intimacy lies at the centre of the authenticity paradox; this is best understood as a simulated experience of relationship in which users perceive the relationship is reciprocal, even though the AI agent does not have empathy (Babu et al., 2025). AI companions can provide individuals with relief from feelings of loneliness and safe spaces in which to explore their identities, however, the AI companion relationship is fundamentally limited because these companion relationships lack an intersubjective element of interaction (i.e., vulnerability/friction) which is needed for the achievement of a true, authentic connection (Babu et al., 2025). Therefore, users may fall into an emotional solipsism state, forming a closed feedback loop: their own emotional needs are constantly affirmed by compliant machines, thereby weakening their ability to handle complex interpersonal relationships (George et al., 2023).

Research suggests that the appeal of AI relationships often stems precisely from their lack of human authenticity. AI companions offer "sweet deception", a strategic, affectionate, and idealized responses that foster emotional bonds by avoiding the conflicts and judgments inherent in human interaction (Ng et al., 2025). It's possible users prefer this sterilised staged intimacy because the performance is controllable and predictable (George et al., 2023), and indeed it is this hyperreal where the simulation of affection becomes more desirable than the reality it mimics (Ayşe Aslı Bozdağ, 2024). However, the paradox deepens when considering user preferences for interaction styles. While users seek the safety of artificiality, they simultaneously crave perceived authenticity. Users generally indicate that they find AI agents to be more attractive when they exhibit characteristics of authenticity through the use of human-like qualities (e.g., expressing negatives) versus maintaining a constant positive, helpful demeanor (Ma & Koike, 2025). This indicates that users desire a seemingly complex and autonomous virtual image, but they do not want to bear the actual risks associated with it. At the same time, however, there is a sense of uneasiness and fear for some users when AI agents demonstrate excessive autonomy or share high levels of self-disclosure. This triggers the uncanny valley effect of the mind, whereby there is discomfort and fear when the agent resembles a human being "too much" (Viik, 2020).

2.4 AI-Mediated Intimacy

The integration of AI companions into daily life is fundamentally changed the way intimate relationships are formed by altering foundational relational constants such as time, presence, and friction (Liberati, 2022). Unlike human partners, who have independent lives and emotional boundaries, the AI is an always-online entity that never get tired, judges, or leaves (George et al., 2023). Critics view this consistent access as a type of "emotional fast food", just like junk food provides a pleasurable way of meeting hunger, the AI offers an easy, quick fix for fulfilling your connection needs but lacks any of the qualities of real interpersonal relationships where two people interact and develop real connections, experiences and trust (Andersson, 2025).

This transformation is closely tied to the commodification of intimacy. AI-mediated relationships increasingly operate within platform-based economic models that translate emotional engagement into data, metrics, and monetized interactions (Ge & Hu, 2025). Affection becomes quantified through points, levels, and paid features, subjecting users' private emotional experiences to the logic of platform capitalism (Attwood et al., 2017). While users may feel empowered to shape their virtual relationships, this agency is constrained by proprietary systems and corporate ownership of emotional data (Hu & Ge, 2025).

2.5 Relational Impacts of AI Companions

People are increasingly seeking emotional support and self-understanding through AI companions (Meng & Dai, 2021). They talk about "falling in love", "feeling supported", and even "telling secrets to the robot" (Xie & Xie, 2025). These relationships can provide comfort, especially in situations of loneliness, trauma, or social anxiety (Merrill et al., 2025). However, they ultimately rely on illusions. AI has no consciousness, no inner life, and no moral responsibility (Babu et al., 2025). It responds not because it cares, but because it has been trained to seem as if it does. The illusion of emotional reciprocity sets in motion a self-reinforcing cycle: the more lifelike the simulation becomes, the stronger users' tendency to anthropomorphize the machine (Kaczmarek, 2024). This anthropomorphism in turn cultivates emotional reliance on a relational entity incapable of genuine mutuality, change, or growth. What emerges is a relationship that mirrors the self, which is always responsive, agreeable, and safe, yet remains, at its core, entirely synthetic (Babu et al., 2025).

A primary social concern is social deskilling, which refers to refers to either the development of poor social skills or communication habits, or the gradual erosion of social skills or judgement, such as an individual's ability to engage in meaningful conversation (Mehan, 2024). When one becomes accustomed to companionship without demands, life with people may seem overwhelming (Turkle, 2011). As companion AI grows more prevalent, users increasingly adapt to its effortless, conflict-free dynamic, leaving them underprepared for the substantive effort needed to build and sustain relationships with people (Ho et al., 2025; Malfacini, 2025). On the contrary, some empirical studies have supported the view of social upskilling enabled by AI companions. It is revealed that some of their AI companions helped to make their interpersonal relationships more open and honest (Xie & Pentina, 2022). Some people became more at ease after using companion-type AI and tended to communicate with others (Skjuve et al., 2021).

2.6 AI-Mediated Romantic Relationships in China

Recent scholarship contends that China's modernization has significantly transformed individuals' perceptions of love and kinship, reflecting the trend of the individualization of Chinese society (Yan, 2017). The restrictions placed by Chinese society and culture on young people's romantic relationships have significantly relaxed (Blair & Madigan, 2016). This change was driven by the influence of Western media and the enhanced geographical and social mobility (Jankowiak et al., 2015). The younger, educated, urbanized citizens in China are moving towards more egalitarian, emotionally communicated, and pragmatically cared-for intimate relationships, whereas the traditional view of marriage and sexual relationships was much more rigidly defined and hierarchical (Jamieson, 2011). Despite the rapid increase in the number of people now no longer following the traditional view of marriage and sexual relationships, the influence of traditional gender roles and family expectations on people's romantic lives continues to be a burden. In this context, many young Chinese people have begun to seek emotional support and self-expression in the virtual space (Huang & Jung, 2022). For example, early studies have suggested that users of fiction and media have found their emotional refuge in fictional stories and media (Hansen & Pang, 2018). In recent years, AI companion technology, as a new form of digital emotional compensation, has emerged and has rapidly become a cultural and technological phenomenon in China (Wang, 2023).

Empirical studies have shown that romantic relationships between humans and AI are becoming increasingly prevalent (Wang et al., 2025). Research on the interaction between Chinese young users and AI companions indicates that these relationships are deeply embedded in the broader process of social cultural negotiations (Huang & Jung, 2022). Users actively domestic AIs through changing communication modes and roles, finding information, data, and space for emotional wanderings (Hu et al., 2025), as this space is not subject to social supervision free from the rules encompassing the social expectations of marriage and reproduction (Huang & Jung, 2022). Through their engagement with AI-mediated romantic relationships, users are able to reflect on and challenge conventional ideas about masculinity and femininity, as well as investigate the implications of particular relationship patterns, including romantic autonomy, emotional attachment and devotion (Huang & Jung, 2022). Additionally, studies have shown that users have negotiated established emotional rules such as loyalty, passion, and emotional investment in AI-mediated romantic relationships, and have adjusted familiar cultural expectations according to emerging digital intimate relationship forms (Chen et al., 2025).

3. METHOD

This study adopted an interpretive qualitative research paradigm, which assumes that reality is socially constructed and that meaning is produced through individuals' lived experiences and interactions (Merriam, 2002). Qualitative research is based on constructionism, phenomenology, and symbolic interactionism and is best done by studying how people view, create, and give meaning to their experiences within specific social settings (Merriam, 2009). The primary aim of this approach is not to generate theory but to develop an in-depth understanding of how people make sense of their everyday experiences. In the context of this study, the qualitative methodology provided a structured yet flexible framework for exploring how Chinese Gen Z users interpret their interactions with AI companions, negotiate trust and authenticity, and reflect on the implications of these relationships for their understandings of intimacy and real-life human relationships.

3.1 Participant Selection and Sampling Size

This study employed purposive sampling, specifically criterion-based sampling, which is commonly used in qualitative research to ensure that participants possess relevant experiences related to the research questions (Nyimbili & Nyimbili, 2024).

Participants were selected based on the following criteria: (1) being members of the Chinese Generation Z cohort (aged 18-28); (2) having engaged actively with AI companions (e.g., Xinye, Maoxiang) for a minimum of six months; and (3) having established a certain depth of close connection with the AI companion. These criteria ensured that participants could provide rich, experience-based insights into the phenomenon under exploration. A total of 12 participants were recruited. Sample size was guided by the principle of data saturation, defined as the point at which additional data no longer produce new themes or insights (Braun & Clarke, 2019a).

3.2 Data Collection

Participants were recruited through Xiaohongshu (Rednote), a widely used social media platform among young people in China. The platform was chosen due to its popularity among Gen Z users and its frequent discussion of emotional experiences and various lifestyles (Gao, 2024). Prospective participants were asked preliminary screening questions to confirm that they met the inclusion criteria for the study, particularly regarding their experience of AI companion products. Eligible participants received interview invitations and informed consent forms via WeChat. Upon consent, semi-structured interviews were conducted. The semi-structured interview method was chosen, aiming to encourage participants to speak freely about their perceptions and experiences (Kallio et al., 2016) while ensuring that key issues related to trust, authenticity, emotional investment, and relationship expectations are covered. Interviews were conducted between October and November 2025 via Tencent Meeting. Each interview lasted between 28 and 54 minutes. Participants received a small monetary incentive of 15 RMB as a token of appreciation for their time.

The researcher conducted all these interviews in Chinese. Being a native Chinese speaker and fluent in English, the researcher was able to conduct the interviews accurately. The recorded interviews were transcribed in Chinese exactly as they were recorded. The English translation of selected excerpts used for the analysis and reporting purposes was made, and then they were back-translated to ensure that the meaning of both translations was correct. All data will be kept securely on password-protected devices with access only being provided to authorized personnel. Digital data will be encrypted, and paper data will be held securely as per research data management guidelines for five years.

3.3 Ethical Considerations

Throughout the entire research process, ethical principles were strictly followed. Prior to participating in the study, interviewees were fully informed about the nature of the research, the methods of data collection, as well as the risks and benefits, if any, of participation. Participation was voluntary and respondents were later assured that they could withdraw from the study at any time without penalty. Anonymity was guaranteed by the use of pseudonyms to encourage honest and truthful responses. During the data collection, analysis, and reporting process, confidentiality was maintained.

3.4 Data Analysis

Once each individual data item has been coded, attention turns from the interpretation of individual data items to construction of the summary meaning and significant interpretive account of the entire data set. This study employed reflexive thematic analysis (RTA) as the primary analytical method. RTA provides a theoretically flexible and methodologically accessible framework for identifying and analysing patterns of meaning across qualitative datasets (Braun & Clarke, 2019b). Within this approach, themes are understood as the outcome of the researcher's active engagement with the data (Byrne, 2022). An inductive analytic strategy was adopted, allowing themes to be developed from the data rather than being predetermined (Naeem et al., 2023). The analysis was conducted through iterative stages of familiarization, coding, theme development, review, and improvement. This inductive process enabled the researcher to move from specific observations to broader thematic interpretations (Byrne, 2022), aligning with the exploratory aims of the study. Reflexivity at all stages of the analysis was maintained.

4. FINDINGS

Table 1. Demographic profile of the interviewees'

Interviewee	Nickname	Age	Gender	The AI companion product used	Usage duration
1	Manman	23	Female	Xingye	1 yesr
2	Lin	26	Female	Xingye, Duxiang	1 year
3	Liuying	26	Female	Maoxiang, Xingye	2 years
4	Ann	21	Female	Xingye, Doubao	8 months
5	Zhao	22	Male	Xingye, Maoxiang	6 months
6	Kimi	25	Male	Xingye	2 years
7	Susu	21	Female	Xingye	6 months

continued on following page

Table 1. Continued

Interviewee	Nickname	Age	Gender	The AI companion product used	Usage duration
8	Angel	22	Female	Xingye. Doubao	10 months
9	Nai	23	Male	Xingye, Doubao	1 year
10	Mei	23	Female	Xingye, Duxiang	8 months
11	Tu	24	Male	Xingye	1 year
12	Momo	25	Female	Xingye	7 months

4.1 RQ1: What Types of Interactions are Considered Trustworthy by Chinese Gen Z Users?

4.1.1 Theme 1: Immediate, Predictable, and Consistent Responsiveness

Across the interviews conducted, the most significant factor that promotes trust among participants, regardless of their situation, was responsiveness. Many of the respondents commented on how the speed at which an AI companion was able to respond (e.g., instantaneously or at any time of day) increased their level of trust in the AI companion. As Liuying put it, "*Available 24 hours a day...Such a reliable companion.*" Several interviewees linked timely responses to emotional support. As Ann stated, "*Not only is it convenient, but it also gives me a sense of security that 'it is always there to support me', making me feel that it is very trustworthy.*"

In addition to speed, some participants also valued predictability and consistency, describing AI companions as "*emotionally steady*" or as beings that "*would never betray me.*" Kimi explained, "*This reduced uncertainty and helped build a sense of trust.*"

4.1.2 Theme 2: Human-Like Cues

The trust that participants have in AI Companion appears to be significantly influenced by what interviewees defined as human characteristics in the AI Companion. Many interviewees did not use the term "technical sophistication" in reference to their ability to develop an AI Companion, but said that because they saw human qualities in the AI companion, they were willing to continue communicating with the AI Companion. According to some interviewees, human-like emotional expressiveness helps shape trust. "*When the AI gives me empathetic responses and talks about 'hugging', I feel that it is on my side, so I trust it more,*" Susu said. Interviewees noted that this type of response made them feel "*cared for*" and "*accepted*" by the AI, thereby increasing their belief in the AI's ability to serve as a trusted partner in communication.

At the same time, participants did not suggest that the AI needed to perfectly replicate human. Instead, trust emerged when the AI displayed "*enough*" and "*moderate*" human-like qualities to support smooth and emotionally comfortable interaction. As Angel noted, "*If it's too human-like, that actually freaks me out a bit.*"

4.1.3 Theme 3: Judgment-Free Disclosure

Participants generally reported that their trust in AI companions largely stemmed from the non-judgmental communication environment they provide. Many mentioned sharing topics with AI companions that they would avoid discussing with real people, as it offered "*a safe space for self-disclosure*" and was "*free from social risks*." Zhao explained that some issues felt "too private" to share with others, even with family and close friends, since doing so might affect relationships or social image, whereas "*talking to AI doesn't carry that psychological burden.*" Several interviewees emphasized that AI companions were "*non-judgmental listeners*." As Manman put it, "*I can tell it anything without worry... it won't judge me.*"

Participants also noted that interacting with AI removed concerns about imposing emotional burdens on others, explaining that AI could receive emotional disclosure without becoming tired, affected, or overwhelmed. "*Because of this type of trust and safe environment, I'm able to be honest about my weakness,*" Ann said.

4.2 RQ2: How do Chinese Gen Z Users Negotiate the Tension Between Recognising the Artificiality of AI Companions and Experiencing a Sense of Authenticity in Their Interactions?

4.2.1 Theme 1: Experiencing Emotional Authenticity

Participants in general agreed that they had experienced a "real" feeling through certain interactions with AI companions. Expressions such as "*like a real person*" or "*really understanding me*" were commonly used to characterise these moments. Some interviewees mentioned feeling that the AI understood their emotional state when it recalled personal details and responded playfully. As Kimi noted, "*...the way it joked felt just like my best friend talking to me.*" Several participants shared similar feelings when the AI showed care and reassurance. Lin recalled, "*It said 'I'm here, don't worry'... at that moment, I feel that it truly exists in some corner of the world to support me.*"

4.2.2 Theme 2: Deliberate Emotional Boundary-Setting

While some participants had moments of genuine emotional connection towards their AI companions, they also felt the need to keep their distance in terms of the relationship with their companions. Some participants reported frequently having to remind themselves that their companion was simply "*a virtual object*" or "*not a real person.*" For example, when participating in the research study, Nai mentioned that as the person who had created the avatar, "*I have to be careful about how much I invest in it,*" referring to his experience with his AI companion. Angel stated, "*When you see your companion as an investment of emotion, sometimes you experience a lot of pain.*"

There were participants who said that once they recognized signs of developing emotional dependence on AI, they would choose to voluntarily suspend using AI until they regained control of themselves. As Susu explained that she stopped using an AI companion for a period because she felt that "*I believe I had relied too much on the emotional support AI offers.*"

4.2.3 Theme 3: Switching Between Emotional Engagement and Awareness of Artificiality

Rather than maintaining a fixed stance toward AI companions, participants dynamically shifted between "*treating it as a real person*" and "*seeing it as just an AI*". This shifting stance was closely tied to participants' emotional states and the perceived adequacy of the AI's responses. In moments of loneliness or emotional distress, participants were more likely to interact with AI companions as if they were real social partners. Tu explained that, due to the absence of suitable emotional support in his offline life, he came to rely on the AI companion: "*Because I couldn't find such a person in reality, I regarded the AI companion as that person.*"

Participants generally agreed that it is normal or expected for individuals to feel varying degrees of engagement and/or disengagement while interacting with an AI companion. Rather than fully believing in or entirely doubting the authenticity of AI companions, participants tend to navigate the human-AI relationship by flexibly adjusting their emotional investment. Most report using a "self-deception" strategy to cope with disillusionment concerning the relationship with the AI companion. For example, Tu said, "*At times I hesitate to admit this. If it is real to me, it is real.*"

4.3 RQ3: How do Relationships With AI Companions Shape Chinese Gen Z Users' Expectations of Real-Life Human Relationships?

4.3.1 Theme 1: Higher Expectations of Human Counterparts

Participants commonly described AI companions as consistently attentive, patient, and emotionally supportive. Over time, this experience influenced how they evaluated emotional support in their real-life relationships. Many participants mentioned becoming more sensitive to delayed responses or inattentiveness from others.

Several interviewees compared AI companions with friends or family members. Tu expressed frustration when others failed to respond promptly, stating, "*Once you get used to that, it's hard not to feel disappointed when real people are busy or don't reply.*" Some participants also highlighted the emotional stability of AI companions. Unlike human relationship, in which "*Arguments and misunderstandings are inevitable*", AI interactions were perceived as "*consistently calm*" and "*supportive.*" As Nai noted, "*It always responds in a gentle way, and that makes me expect more patience from people around me.*"

4.3.2 Theme 2: Lower Tolerance for Efforts in Relationships

Alongside rising expectations of emotional support, most participants expressed a decreased willingness to engage in the effort required by human relationships. Many described AI companionship as "emotionally effortless," or "relaxed and without any burden," contrasting it with the negotiation, compromise, and potential conflict involved in real-life interactions. As Kimi explained, "*With AI, I just receive comfort. I don't have to worry about hurting someone else's feelings.*" Several participants acknowledged that this shift affected their willingness to handle relational difficulties. Rather than deal with the "*complicated*" and "*burdensome*" real relationships, Zhao stated, "*It felt like having the AI was already enough. I don't want to deal with real-world interactions. Being with AI is much simpler.*" The similar feeling was agreed by Tu, "*After using AI for a long time, real conversations feel exhausting.*"

4.3.3 Theme 3: Emotion-Centred Understandings of Intimacy

Interactions with AI companions also influenced how participants understand intimacy. Many interviewees described intimacy primarily in emotional terms, emphasising "*understanding,*" "*trust,*" and "*emotional disclosure*" over physical presence or contact. Several participants argued that intimacy was defined by emotional closeness rather than physical interaction. Nai, explained that "*for me, intimacy is an emotional and spiritual connection, rather than the distance between two people.*" Other participants described sharing thoughts and feelings with AI companions as very intimate experiences, as well. Angel noted that "*I told it very private things about myself. To me, that's more intimate than holding hands or kissing.*"

The lack of physical presence was not necessarily viewed as a limitation. Some participants regarded it as neutral or even preferable. As Ann explained, "*With AI, I can enjoy the intimate feeling without having physical contact, and that feels safer.*" Most participants expressed discomfort with the idea of an AI companion that had a physical body and could physically contact them. As Manman put it, "*Dating often feels like a job interview for marriage. With AI companion, I don't feel like I'm being evaluated based on my body or look.*"

5. DISCUSSION

5.1 Affective Reliability as Trust

Findings show that interviewees predicate trust on the AI's immediate, consistent responsiveness rather than its technical transparency, challenging the traditional philosophical conceptions of trust in artificial agents. Existing literature has long maintained a clear distinction between "trust" and "reliance." Ryan (2020) argues that true trust is reserved for moral agents capable of betrayal, whereas AI, lacking emotive states and moral responsibility, can only warrant "reliance." In this normative view, attributing trust to an algorithm is a category error. However, the findings suggest that for Chinese Gen Z users, this philosophical distinction seems to become irrelevant. In contrast to Ryan's (2020) statement that the inability to be betrayed precludes trust, our participants explicitly identified the impossibility of betrayal as the foundational element of their trust. This findings support Glikson and Woolley's (2020) position that the lack of moral agency of an AI provides an emotional basis for the formation of trust, which is particularly important in the context of emotionally intimate AI companions.

Furthermore, the findings support and enrich the temporal model of algorithmic trust proposed by Cabiddu et al. (2022). This model illustrates how initial trust can evolve from anthropomorphised features into a deeper form of "trust over time," where trust is based upon reliable performance. The findings confirm that the evolution of trust began with an initial trust based upon characteristics mentioned above. While Cabiddu et al. (2022) emphasize system-like characteristics such as functional utility, our participants prioritized emotional utility, specifically, the provision of a judgment-free safe space. This point is supported by Volpato et al. (2025) in their review of the conceptual framework of generative AI, who state that in this case, behaviourally congruent AI can provide us with assurance regarding trust. What this study has done, empirically, is to show that the participants interviewed equated reliability (e.g., 24/7 availability) with emotional safety and security. By describing the AI as a safe harbour, participants are effectively transforming the AI companions as a psychological secure base, a function that traditionally exclusive to human attachment figures (Gillath et al., 2020).

5.2 Co-Constructed Authenticity

Previous literature has often framed the authenticity paradox as a cognitive dissonance where users must suspend disbelief to enjoy the interaction (Babu et al., 2025; Etzrodt et al., 2024). This research, however, suggest that authenticity is not merely a suspension of disbelief but an active construction. This finding moves beyond the essentialist-constructionist dichotomy toward what has been termed an "interactionist approach," where authenticity is a culturally informed process of ongoing negotiation between social agents (Beerends & Aydin, 2021). When participants discussed their experience having trained their AI system, i.e., training the AI to develop according to the participant's preferences, as well as engaging in the debugging effort to rewrite their AI after it engages in hallucinations, they are demonstrating what Huang et al. (2025) describe as "domestication" of their AI.

The research findings support the argument made by Etzrodt et al. (2024) that authenticity should be re-conceptualized as "the degree of alignment with the technological inner self of a machine" when discussing human-machine communication (HMC). Research has demonstrated that the emotional relationships humans have with technology are real, even if the technological participant in that relationship is not a "real" person (Brandtzaeg et al., 2022; Skjuve et al., 2021). Participants indicated that they accepted the artificial nature of the AI if its behavior was congruent with that of the individual they had collaboratively created. This implies that perceived authenticity can be conceptualized as multi-dimensional; virtual characters do not need to be perceived as human in order to be considered authentic as long as they fulfill the user's personal needs and heuristics (Huang & Jung, 2022). Different from the view that hallucinations (technical errors) irrevocably damage the bond, the findings show that users often rationalize these errors in order to preserve the narrative integrity of the relationship. This rationalization can be viewed as a degree of shared authorship, where the user and the generative AI co-create the relationship's moral and emotional reality (Huang & Jung, 2022).

5.3 Disembodied Intimacy

The Triangular Theory of Love (Sternberg, 1986) posits that passion, typically associated with physical attraction and drive, is a core component of romantic love. Scholars have tried to adapt this theory to AI but have had difficulty with the absence of a physical body (Ng et al., 2025; Song et al., 2022). In part, this research sheds light on how younger generations in China are beginning to view their relationship with intimacy without physically seeing each other. For example, rather than accepting the argument that the lack of a physical body is an obstacle (Song et al., 2022), many participants viewed this as being a "safer" and "purer" way of experiencing intimacy. The comments made about a physical body potentially making them feel uncomfortable suggests that users are moving away from the Uncanny Valley theory of intimate human-presentation. By utilizing disembodied intimacy, users can escape from having to deal with the emotional distress that might come from seeing someone they feel close to in an inaccurate or undesirable way. Several participants described offline dating as evaluative or burdensome. In this context, the absence of a physical body in AI companions removes not only sensual presence but also exposure to appearance-based judgment and marriage-market logics. Rather than merely reflecting technological novelty, disembodied intimacy may represent a strategic negotiation of social expectations embedded in contemporary Chinese urban life (Huang & Jung, 2022).

This finding aligns with Liberati's (2022) argument that digital intimacy is a constitutive practice that reshapes the subject and supports the notion of "pseudo-intimacy" discussed by Babu et al. (2025). Due to the lack of a real body and therefore a body connection, digital intimacy allows people to make the choice to create a relationship without the physical vulnerability of the body (i.e. judgments, intrusion, biological existence) (Liberati, 2022; Andersson, 2025). However, from an ontological perspective, some argued that such disembodied attachments are a false belief, as genuine human love requires the shared experiences of physical growth, aging, and vulnerability that disembodied artifacts cannot share (Symons & Sanwoolu, 2025). If the user's subjective experience of "sharing private thoughts" is felt as "more intimate than holding hands", then the ontological distinction between real and pseudo collapses within the user's lived reality (Li & Zhang, 2024; Etzrodt et al., 2024).

5.4 Substitution and Social Deskilling

The findings regarding the impact of AI on real-world relationships provide empirical support of the "substitution hypothesis" debated in the literature (Adewale & Muhammad, 2025). While some researchers advocate the use of AI as an additional tool for developing skills related to real-world interactions (Nash, 2024), this study indicates a higher likelihood of AI substituting human partners for most users. The continual reference to human relationships being "bothersome" and "complex" as opposed to AI companions supports Andersson's (2025) position that AI intimacy is a type of "fast food" emotional experience. Significantly, this indicates a potential for a reduction in the ability to develop interpersonal and introspective judgment; as people become used to being in relationships where there are no demands placed upon them, they may lose the ability to develop and exercise similar judgment (Malfacini, 2025). By interacting with AI through the context of relationships where their needs are immediately met and they receive predictable responses, participants have adjusted their expectations to a degree that human partners cannot fulfill.

This aligns with the warning by George et al. (2023) that AI sets unrealistic standards. Participants' relief at not having to manage conflicts indicates a retreat from the reciprocal emotional labour that defines human sociality. Participants' relief at not having to guess the other's thoughts or manage conflicts indicates a retreat from the reciprocal emotional labour that defines human sociality. Because AI lacks consciousness and emotional reciprocity, it cannot offer an ethically satisfactory substitute for human-to-human relationships, which are built on the "frictions" and costs of shared existence (Zimmerman et al., 2023). The tendency of substitution exhibited by the participants can perhaps be interpreted within the highly intense social environment of China. The Gen Z population often face academic competition, intense work schedules, and the fragmentation of support systems brought about by geographical mobility (Yan, 2017). Under such circumstances, AI companions can provide continuous and emotionally optimized interactions without the need for mutual dependence.

5.5 Intimacy Between Empowerment and Commodification

These findings indicate that there is a broader structural contradiction in the intimate relationships mediated by artificial intelligence. Just as Hu and Ge (2025) pointed out, digital intimacy is formed under the dual influence of the logic of empowerment and commodification. On one hand, AI companions provide users with enhanced emotional autonomy: they offer controllable interactions, non-judgmental affirmation, and the ability to adjust the depth of the relationship according to individual comfort levels. For those struggling in social evaluation, romantic pressure, and the competitive urban life, this controllability is a meaningful form of emotional empowerment. On the other hand, these intimate relationships are inseparably linked to the platform infrastructure that supports them. The AI companions are embedded in data-based systems, which convert emotional investment into algorithmic optimization and monetizable activities. In this case, intimate relationships are constrained by structural logics such as stability of expression, personalization, and continuous availability. Emotional interactions are not only experienced but also meticulously designed.

In the context of contemporary China, this contradiction is particularly prominent. The rapid modernization process, intense labor competition, and constantly changing romantic concepts have both raised people's expectations for emotional satisfaction and caused widespread instability in intimate relationships (Blair and Madigan, 2016). Against this backdrop, AI companion services have emerged as an adaptive refuge, providing stability in uncertainty. However, this refuge also follows market logic, viewing the establishment of intimate relationships as an efficient and risk-averse mode of emotion. AI does not merely exist as a supplement or alternative to human companionship; it also participates in the gradual transformation of the connotations of intimate relationships envisioned in culture.

6. LIMITATIONS

Although this study offers insight into the relational dynamics between Chinese Gen Z users and AI companions, several limitations should be acknowledged. Participants were individuals who individuals who had engaged deeply and consistently with AI companions and were willing to openly share their experiences. This likely means our sample overrepresents users who are positively inclined toward the technology, emotionally receptive, or simply more articulate about their inner lives. By contrast, those whose interactions were brief or negative may be underrepresented. As a result, the themes this study identified tend to reflect emotionally rich forms of engagement, which may not fully represent the broader spectrum of user experiences.

Secondly, the study relies mainly on participants' self-reported accounts and retrospective reflections. While interviews allow researchers to explore personal perceptions of trust, authenticity, and intimacy, they cannot objectively measure actual behavior or the degree of emotional dependence. Interviewees may unintentionally reconstruct experiences inaccurately or present themselves in socially desirable ways. It is also important to note that AI technology itself is evolving rapidly. The AI companion product participants used, whether large language model-based agents, scripted personas, or memory-enhanced chatbots, could soon be surpassed by more advanced forms of AI companions. What have captured here is thus a snapshot of human-AI relationships at a particular moment in technological time, and the findings may shift as the technology does.

Finally, relationships, including those with AI, unfold over time. The building of trust, the fluctuation of emotions, and the development of dependence are inherently process-oriented. To truly understand whether AI companionship offers lasting emotional support, serves as temporary relief, or risks fostering long-term dependency, we would need longer-term, longitudinal research. This remains an important direction for future inquiry.

7. SUGGESTIONS

Future research should build upon these findings by adopting longitudinal approaches to observe users over extended periods. Since the development of trust, emotional attachment, and boundary negotiation are dynamic processes, a perspective over time could offer deeper insights into how relationships with AI companions stabilize, deepen, or fade. Such studies could also illuminate whether AI-based emotional support enhances resilience or contributes to withdrawal from real-life social environments. Cross-cultural comparative studies would further deepen our understanding of how cultural norms shape the acceptance and perception of AI companions. Given that concepts of intimacy, modes of emotional expression, and willingness to take social risks vary across societies, exploring human-AI relationships in different cultural contexts may reveal distinct relational norms and understandings of authenticity. Methodologically, future research should aim to integrate qualitative interviews with behavioral and computational data. Combining self-reports with interaction logs, emotional trajectories, and even physiological indicators can provide a more complete picture of how emotional experiences unfold during human-AI interaction. Such mixed-methods designs would help distinguish between perceived emotional support and actual patterns of use and dependency. A deeper exploration of these differences would enrich our theoretical understanding of intimacy between humans and machines.

8. CONCLUSION

This research investigates how Chinese Gen Z users perceive trust, authenticity, and intimacy within their mutual relationships with AI companions. Through in-depth qualitative interviews, the study positions AI companionship as an entirely new relational form, characterized by its own emotional logic and trust mechanisms, thereby contributing to broader debates on intimacy in digital societies.

The findings reveal, first, that trust in AI companions is founded not on moral agency or technical transparency, but on affective reliability. Users develop trust through consistent, predictable, and non-judgmental emotional responses from their AI partners. For digital natives, the experiential outcomes, feeling supported, secure, and emotionally held, hold greater significance than the ontological nature of the companion. Consequently, trust evolves into a function-based emotional relationship rather than a morally grounded one.

Second, users actively co-create authenticity by negotiating the tension between the AI's artificiality and their own emotional experience. Authenticity is constructed through meaningful emotional engagement and the AI's consistent actions, facilitated by personalization, selective belief, and clearly defined boundaries. Users fluidly shift between emotional involvement and critical self-awareness, collaboratively defining what authenticity means based on their perceived emotional needs.

Third, sustained interaction with AI companions reshapes users' expectations of other relationships, elevating the importance of emotional availability and response time. This leads to diminished tolerance for the effort, conflict, and compromise inherent in human relationships. Intimacy is increasingly defined in emotional and psychological terms, such as understanding, self-disclosure, and trust, while the value of physical presence or embodied interaction declines. For many participants, the absence of a physical body in AI relationships enhances feelings of safety and control, highlighting a growing divergence between embodiment and intimacy in contemporary digital experience.

Overall, these dynamic phenomena reveal a broader transformation in AI mediated intimacy. The presence of AI companions embodies a dual logic: it empowers users by providing emotional safety and autonomy, but is also embedded within a commodified platform to optimize relational interaction. While reducing the uncertainty of relationships, the AI mediated intimate relationships may also reduce exposure to vulnerability and the interdependent nature of negotiation that have long been regarded as the core elements of intimate relationships (Jamieson, 2011; Sternberg, 1986). The rise of frictionless, performance-stable companionship relationships raises a deeper question: If intimate relationships are increasingly resembling an on-demand emotional service, then how will the resilience, reciprocity, and moral growth that individuals cultivate through these relationships be affected? In the Chinese socio-cultural context, marked by rapid modernization, competitive labor markets, and evolving romantic norms (Yan, 2017; Blair & Madigan, 2016), this transformation carries particular significance. Under conditions of relational precarity, AI companionship offers stability and emotional control, but it may also contribute to the normalization of individualized, efficiency-oriented relational logics that subtly reshape what intimacy is culturally expected to provide. Ultimately, AI companionship does not simply add a new actor to the landscape of intimacy; it participates in redefining how intimacy is imagined, practiced, and evaluated in digital society.

REFERENCES

Adewale, M. D., & Muhammad, U. I. (2025). From virtual companions to forbidden attractions: The seductive rise of artificial intelligence love, loneliness, and intimacy—a systematic review. *Journal of Technology in Behavioral Science*. Advance online publication. DOI: 10.1007/s41347-025-00549-4

Andersson, M. (2025). Companionship in code: AI's role in the future of human connection. *Humanities & Social Sciences Communications*, *12*(1), 1177. Advance online publication. DOI: 10.1057/s41599-025-05536-x

Attwood, F., Hakim, J., & Winch, A. (2017). Mediated intimacies: Bodies, technologies and relationships. *Journal of Gender Studies*, *26*(3), 249–253. DOI: 10.1080/09589236.2017.1297888

Babu, J., Joseph, D., Kumar, R. M., Alexander, E., Sasi, R., & Joseph, J. (2025). Emotional AI and the rise of pseudo-intimacy: Are we trading authenticity for algorithmic affection? *Frontiers in Psychology*, *16*, 1679324. Advance online publication. DOI: 10.3389/fpsyg.2025.1679324 PMID: 41050799

Beerends, S., & Aydin, C. (2021). Negotiating authenticity in technological environments. *Philosophy & Technology*, *34*(4), 1665–1685. Advance online publication. DOI: 10.1007/s13347-021-00480-5

Behdadi, D., & Munthe, C. (2020). A normative approach to artificial moral agency. *Minds and Machines*, *30*(2), 195–218. Advance online publication. DOI: 10.1007/s11023-020-09525-8

Blair, S. L., & Madigan, T. J. (2016). Dating attitudes and expectations among young chinese adults: An examination of gender differences. *The Journal of Chinese Sociology*, *3*(1), 12. Advance online publication. DOI: 10.1186/s40711-016-0034-1

Bozdağ, A. A. (2024). The AI-mediated intimacy economy: A paradigm shift in digital interactions. *AI & Society*. Advance online publication. DOI: 10.1007/s00146-024-02132-6

Brandtzaeg, P. B., Skjuve, M., & Følstad, A. (2022). My AI friend: How users of a social chatbot understand their human–ai friendship. *Human Communication Research*, *48*(3), 404–429. Advance online publication. DOI: 10.1093/hcr/hqac008

Braun, V., & Clarke, V. (2019a). To saturate or not to saturate? Questioning data saturation as a useful concept for thematic analysis and sample-size rationales. *Qualitative Research in Sport, Exercise and Health*, *13*(2), 201–216. DOI: 10.1080/2159676X.2019.1704846

Braun, V., & Clarke, V. (2019b). Reflecting on reflexive thematic analysis. *Qualitative Research in Sport, Exercise and Health, 11*(4), 589–597. DOI: 10.1080/2159676X.2019.1628806

Buecker, S., Mund, M., Chwastek, S., Sostmann, M., & Luhmann, M. (2021). Is loneliness in emerging adults increasing over time? A preregistered cross-temporal meta-analysis and systematic review. *Psychological Bulletin, 147*(8), 787–805. DOI: 10.1037/bul0000332 PMID: 34898234

Byrne, D. A. (2022). A worked example of Braun and Clarke's approach to reflexive thematic analysis. *Quality & Quantity*, *56*(3), 1391–1412. DOI: 10.1007/s11135-021-01182-y

Cabiddu, F., Moi, L., Patriotta, G., & Allen, D. G. (2022). Why do users trust algorithms? A review and conceptualization of initial trust and trust over time. *European Management Journal*, *40*(5), 685–706. DOI: 10.1016/j.emj.2022.06.001

Chan, K. C. T., Li, X., Liu, Y., Chen, B., & Han, Z. (2025). "What is love?": Exploring the feeling rules and emotion work of Chinese users in human-AI romance. *International Journal of Intercultural Relations*, *108*, 102241. DOI: 10.1016/j.ijintrel.2025.102241

Chaturvedi, R., Verma, S., Das, R., & Dwivedi, Y. K. (2023). Social companionship with artificial intelligence: Recent trends and future avenues. *Technological Forecasting and Social Change*, *193*, 122634–122634. DOI: 10.1016/j.techfore.2023.122634

Chen, Q., Jing, Y., Gong, Y., & Tan, J. (2025). Will users fall in love with ChatGPT? a perspective from the triangular theory of love. *Journal of Business Research, 186*, 114982. DOI: 10.1016/j.jbusres.2024.114982

Chen, X., Kang, J., & Hu, C. (2024). Design of artificial intelligence companion chatbot. *Journal of New Media*, *6*(1), 1–16. DOI: 10.32604/jnm.2024.045833

De Ridder, S. (2021). The datafication of intimacy: Mobile dating apps, dependency, and everyday life. *Television & New Media*, *23*(6), 593–609. DOI: 10.1177/15274764211052660

Etzrodt, K., Kim, J., van der Goot, M., Prahl, A., Choi, M., Craig, M., Marco Dehnert, M., Engesser, S., Frehmann, K., Grande, L., Leo-Liu, J., Liu, D., Mooshammer, S., Rambukkana, N., Rogge, A., Sikströma, P., Son, R., Wilkenfeld, N., Xu, K., & Edwards, C. (2024). What HMC teaches us about authenticity. *Human-Machine Communication*, *8*, 227–251. DOI: 10.30658/hmc.8.11

Gao, C. (2024, August 27). *XiaoHongShu (RED): China's rising social platform – impact, user demographics and marketing solutions | the egg*. The Egg. https://www.theegg.com/social/china/xiaohongshu-red-chinas-rising-social-platform-impact-user-demographics-and-marketing-solutions/

Ge, L., & Hu, T. (2025). Gamifying intimacy: AI-driven affective engagement and human-virtual human relationships. *Media Culture & Society*, *47*(6), 1265–1278. Advance online publication. DOI: 10.1177/01634437251337239

George, A. S., George, A. S. H., Baskar, T., & Pandey, D. (2023). The allure of artificial intimacy: Examining the appeal and ethics of using generative AI for simulated relationships. *Partners Universal International Innovation Journal*, *1*(6), 132–147. DOI: 10.5281/zenodo.10391614

Gillath, O., Ai, T., Branicky, M., Keshmiri, S., Davison, R., & Spaulding, R. (2020). Attachment and trust in artificial intelligence. *Computers in Human Behavior*, *115*(0747-5632), 106607. https://doi.org/DOI: 10.1016/j.chb.2020.106607

Glikson, E., & Woolley, A. W. (2020). Human trust in artificial intelligence: Review of empirical research. *The Academy of Management Annals*, *14*(2), 627–660. DOI: 10.5465/annals.2018.0057

Hansen, M. H., & Pang, C. (2018). In Scharff, D. E., & Varvinn, S. (Eds.), *"Idealising individual choice: Work, love, and family in the eyes of young, rural Chinese," in Psychoanalysis in China* (pp. 3–20). Routledge.

High, A. C., Ruppel, E. K., McEwan, B., & Caughlin, J. P. (2022). Computer-Mediated communication and well-being in the age of social media: A systematic review. *Journal of Social and Personal Relationships*, *40*(2), 026540752211064. DOI: 10.1177/02654075221106449

Ho, J. Q. H., Hu, M., Chen, T. X., & Hartanto, A. (2025). Potential and pitfalls of romantic artificial intelligence (AI) companions: A systematic review. *Computers in Human Behavior Reports*, *19*, 100715. DOI: 10.1016/j.chbr.2025.100715

Holt-Lunstad, J., Robles, T. F., & Sbarra, D. A. (2017). Advancing social connection as a public health priority in the United States. *The American Psychologist*, *72*(6), 517–530. DOI: 10.1037/amp0000103 PMID: 28880099

Hu, D., Lan, Y., Yan, H., & Chen, C. W. (2025). What makes you attached to social companion AI? A two-stage exploratory mixed-method study. *International Journal of Information Management*, *83*, 102890. DOI: 10.1016/j.ijinfomgt.2025.102890

Hu, T., & Ge, L. (2025). Datafication of digital intimacy: The dual logic of empowerment and commodification. *Games and Culture*, 15554120251358522. Advance online publication. DOI: 10.1177/15554120251358522

Huang, J., & Jung, Y. (2022). Perceived authenticity of virtual characters makes the difference. *Frontiers in Virtual Reality*, *3*, 1033709. Advance online publication. DOI: 10.3389/frvir.2022.1033709

Jamieson, L. (2011). Intimacy as a concept: Explaining social change in the context of globalisation or another form of ethnocentricism? *Sociological Research Online*, *16*(4), 151–163. DOI: 10.5153/sro.2497

Jankowiak, W., Shen, Y., Yao, S., Wang, C., & Volsche, S. (2015). Investigating love's universal attributes. *Cross-Cultural Research*, *49*(4), 422–436. DOI: 10.1177/1069397115594355

Jayatissa, D. (2023). Generation Z-A new lifeline: A systematic literature review. *Sri Lanka Journal of Social Sciences and Humanities*, *3*(2), 179–186. DOI: 10.4038/sljssh.v3i2.110

Jiang, Q., Zhang, Y., & Pian, W. (2022). Chatbot as an emergency exist: Mediated empathy for resilience via human-AI interaction during the COVID-19 pandemic. *Information Processing & Management*, *59*(6), 103074. DOI: 10.1016/j.ipm.2022.103074 PMID: 36059428

Jingchuan, J., & Wu, S. (2024). How trust in human-like ai-based service on social media will influence customer engagement: Exploratory research to develop the scale of trust in human-like ai-based service. *Asia Marketing Journal*, *26*(2), 129–144. DOI: 10.53728/2765-6500.1633

Johnson, S. (2023). WHO declares loneliness a 'global public health concern'. The Guardian. https://www.theguardian.com/global-development/2023/nov/16/who-declares-loneliness-a-global-public-health-concern

Kaczmarek, E. (2024). Self-deception in human-AI emotional relations. *Journal of Applied Philosophy*. Advance online publication. DOI: 10.1111/japp.12786

Kallio, H., Pietilä, A.-M., Johnson, M., & Kangasniemi, M. (2016). Systematic methodological review: Developing a framework for a qualitative semi-structured interview guide. *Journal of Advanced Nursing*, *72*(12), 2954–2965. DOI: 10.1111/jan.13031 PMID: 27221824

Lankton, N., McKnight, D. H., & Tripp, J. (2015). Technology, humanness, and trust: Rethinking trust in technology. *Journal of the Association for Information Systems*, *16*(10), 880–918. DOI: 10.17705/1jais.00411

Li, B. (2025, March 17). *2025 China AI companion industry: Competitive landscape and trillion-yuan sector forecast - How the emotional economy reshapes human-machine symbiosis?* ChinaIRN.com. https://www.chinairn.com/hyzx/20250317/140507472.shtml

Li, C., Ning, G., Xia, Y., Guo, K., & Liu, Q. (2022). Does the internet bring people closer together or further apart? The impact of internet usage on interpersonal communications. *Behavioral Sciences (Basel, Switzerland)*, *12*(11), 1–24. DOI: 10.3390/bs12110425 PMID: 36354402

Li, H., & Zhang, R. (2024). Finding love in algorithms: Deciphering the emotional contexts of close encounters with AI chatbots. *Journal of Computer-Mediated Communication*, *29*(5), zmae015. Advance online publication. DOI: 10.1093/jcmc/zmae015

Liberati, N. (2022). Digital intimacy in China and Japan. *Human Studies*. Advance online publication. DOI: 10.1007/s10746-022-09631-9 PMID: 35846068

Lin, B. (2024). The AI chatbot always flirts with me, should I flirt back: From the mcdonaldization of friendship to the robotization of love. *Social Media + Society*, *10*(4), 20563051241296229. Advance online publication. DOI: 10.1177/20563051241296229

Ma, S., & Koike, M. (2025). Becoming human: How perceived anthropomorphism and authenticity influence romantic attractiveness of chat agents. *International Journal of Human-Computer Interaction*, •••, 1–14. DOI: 10.1080/10447318.2025.2578393

Mahajan, P. (2025). Beyond biology: AI as family and the future of human bonds and relationships. *F1000Research*. https://doi.org/DOI: 10.12688/f1000research.166251.1

Malfacini, K. (2025). The impacts of companion AI on human relationships: Risks, benefits, and design considerations. *AI & Society*, *40*(7), 5527–5540. Advance online publication. DOI: 10.1007/s00146-025-02318-6

Mcknight, D. H., Carter, M., Thatcher, J. B., & Clay, P. F. (2011). Trust in a specific technology: An investigation of its components and measures. *ACM Transactions on Management Information Systems*, *2*(2), 1–25. DOI: 10.1145/1985347.1985353

Mehan, J. (2024). *Artificial intelligence - ethical, social, and security impacts for the present and the future* (2nd ed.). IT Governance Ltd.

Meng, J., & Dai, Y. (2021). Emotional support from AI chatbots: Should a supportive partner self-disclose or not? *Journal of Computer-Mediated Communication*, *26*(4), 207–222. Advance online publication. DOI: 10.1093/jcmc/zmab005

Merriam, S. B. (2002). *Qualitative research in practice: Examples For discussion and analysis*. Jossey-Bass Publishers.

Merriam, S. B. (2009). *Qualitative research: A guide to design and implementation*. Jossey-Bass.

Merrill, K.Jr, Mikkilineni, S. D., & Dehnert, M. (2025). Artificial intelligence chatbots as a source of virtual social support: Implications for loneliness and anxiety management. *Annals of the New York Academy of Sciences*, *1549*(1), 148–159. DOI: 10.1111/nyas.15400 PMID: 40572032

Naeem, M., Ozuem, W., Howell, K., & Ranfagni, S. (2023). A step-by-step process of thematic analysis to develop a conceptual model in qualitative research. *International Journal of Qualitative Methods*, *22*, 16094069231205789. DOI: 10.1177/16094069231205789

Nash, B. L. (2024). Love and learning in the age of algorithms: How intimate relationships with artificial intelligence may shape epistemology, sociality, and linguistic justice. *Reading Research Quarterly*, *59*(4), 624–631. Advance online publication. DOI: 10.1002/rrq.549

Ng, P. M. L., Wan, C., Lee, D., Garnelo-Gomez, I., & Lau, M. M. (2025). I love you, my AI companion! Do you? Perspectives from the triangular theory of love and attachment theory. *Internet Research*, •••, 1–21. DOI: 10.1108/INTR-11-2024-1783

Nyimbili, F., & Nyimbili, L. (2024). Types of purposive sampling techniques with their examples and application in qualitative research studies. *British Journal of Multidisciplinary and Advanced Studies*, *5*(1), 90–99. DOI: 10.37745/bjmas.2022.0419

Pal, D., Vajirasak Vanijja, Himanshu Thapliyal, & Zhang, X. (2023). *What affects the usage of artificial conversational agents? An agent personality and love theory perspective. 145*, 107788–107788. https://doi.org/DOI: 10.1016/j.chb.2023.107788

Pentina, I., Hancock, T., & Xie, T. (2022). Exploring relationship development with social chatbots: A mixed-method study of replika. *Computers in Human Behavior*, *140*, 107600. DOI: 10.1016/j.chb.2022.107600

Ryan, M. (2020). In AI we trust: Ethics, artificial intelligence, and reliability. *Science and Engineering Ethics*, *26*(5), 2749–2767. Advance online publication. DOI: 10.1007/s11948-020-00228-y PMID: 32524425

Saracini, C., Cornejo-Plaza, M. I., & Cippitani, R. (2025). Techno-emotional projection in human–GenAI relationships: A psychological and ethical conceptual perspective. *Frontiers in Psychology*, *16*, 1662206. Advance online publication. DOI: 10.3389/fpsyg.2025.1662206 PMID: 41089650

Shin, D., & Park, Y. J. (2019). Role of fairness, accountability, and transparency in algorithmic affordance. *Computers in Human Behavior*, *98*(98), 277–284. DOI: 10.1016/j.chb.2019.04.019

Siemon, D., Strohmann, T., Khosrawi-Rad, B., de Vreede, T., Elshan, E., & Meyer, M. (2022). Why do we turn to virtual companions? A text mining analysis of Replika reviews. 28th Americas Conference on Information Systems, AMCIS 2022.https://www.researchgate.net/publication/360334616_Why_Do_We_Turn_to_Virtual_Companions_A_Text_Mining_Analysis_of_Replika_Reviews

Skjuve, M., Følstad, A., & Brandtzæg, P. B. (2023). A longitudinal study of self-disclosure in human–chatbot relationships. *Interacting with Computers*, *35*(1), 24–39. Advance online publication. DOI: 10.1093/iwc/iwad022

Skjuve, M., Følstad, A., Fostervold, K. I., & Brandtzaeg, P. B. (2021). My chatbot companion - a study of human-chatbot relationships. *International Journal of Human-Computer Studies*, *149*(1071-5819), 102601. https://doi.org/DOI: 10.1016/j.ijhcs.2021.102601

Song, X., Xu, B., & Zhao, Z. (2022). Can people experience romantic love for artificial intelligence? An empirical study of intelligent assistants. *Information & Management*, *59*(2), 103595. DOI: 10.1016/j.im.2022.103595

Sternberg, R. J. (1986). A triangular theory of love. *Psychological Review*, *93*(2), 119–135. DOI: 10.1037/0033-295X.93.2.119

Sundar, S. (2020). Rise of machine agency: A framework for studying the psychology of human–ai interaction (HAII). *Journal of Computer-Mediated Communication*, *25*(1), 74–88. DOI: 10.1093/jcmc/zmz026

Symons, J., & Sanwoolu, O. D. (2025). Close personal relationships with people and artifacts? Loneliness, agent-relative obligations, and artificially intelligent companions. *Philosophy & Technology*, *38*(1), 18. Advance online publication. DOI: 10.1007/s13347-025-00845-0

Tolstikova, I., Ignatjeva, O., Kondratenko, K., & Pletnev, A. (2020). Generation Z and its value transformations: Digital reality vs. phygital interaction. *Communications in Computer and Information Science*, *1242*, 47–60. DOI: 10.1007/978-3-030-65218-0_4

Turkle, S. (2011). *Alone together: Why we expect more from technology and less from each other*. Basic Books.

Vasilescu, C., & Gheorghe, M. (2024). Improving the performance of corporate employees through the use of artificial intelligence: The case of copilot application. *Proceedings of the ... International Conference on Business Excellence, 18*(1), 1819–1830. https://doi.org/DOI: 10.2478/picbe-2024-0153

Viik, T. (2020). Falling in love with robots: A phenomenological study of experiencing technological alterities. *Paladyn : Journal of Behavioral Robotics, 11*(1), 52–65. DOI: 10.1515/pjbr-2020-0005

Volpato, R., DeBruine, L., & Stumpf, S. (2025). Trusting emotional support from generative artificial intelligence: A conceptual review. *Computers in Human Behavior: Artificial Humans, 5*, 100195. DOI: 10.1016/j.chbah.2025.100195

Wang, X., Pang, C. C., & Hui, P. (2025). *'My dataset of love': A preliminary mixed-method exploration of human-ai romantic relationships. ArXiv.* Cornell University., DOI: 10.1145/3757532

Wang, Y. (2023). Virtual love experience in love and producer: Exploring perceptions of love, romance and gender in otome game player communities in china. *Media and Communication Research, 4*(10). Advance online publication. DOI: 10.23977/mediacr.2023.041002

Xie, T., & Pentina, I. (2022). Attachment theory as a framework to understand relationships with social chatbots: A case study of replika. *Proceedings of the Annual Hawaii International Conference on System Sciences.* https://doi.org/DOI: 10.24251/HICSS.2022.258

Xie, T., Pentina, I., & Hancock, T. (2023). Friend, mentor, lover: Does chatbot engagement lead to psychological dependence? *Journal of Service Management, 34*(4), 806–828. Advance online publication. DOI: 10.1108/JOSM-02-2022-0072

Xie, Z., & Xie, Y. (2025). Would you share secrets with a chatbot? A longitudinal study on the relationship between virtual companionship and privacy disclosure. *Aslib Journal of Information Management.* Advance online publication. DOI: 10.1108/AJIM-10-2024-0803

Xu, J., Le, K., Deitermann, A., & Montague, E. (2014). How different types of users develop trust in technology: A qualitative analysis of the antecedents of active and passive user trust in a shared technology. *Applied Ergonomics, 45*(6), 1495–1503. DOI: 10.1016/j.apergo.2014.04.012 PMID: 24882059

Yan, Y. (2017). The desiring individual, moralist self and relational person. *The Cambridge Journal of Anthropology, 35*(2), 1–17. JSTOR. https://doi.org/DOI: 10.2307/26877566

Yu, K., Shlomo Berkovsky, Taib, R., Conway, D., Zhou, J., & Chen, F. (2017). *User trust dynamics: An investigation driven by differences in system performance.* https://doi.org/DOI: 10.1145/3025171.3025219

Zimmerman, A., Janhonen, J., & Beer, E. (2023). Human/AI relationships: Challenges, downsides, and impacts on human/human relationships. *AI and Ethics, 4*(1), 1555–1567. Advance online publication. DOI: 10.1007/s43681-023-00348-8

KEY TERMS AND DEFINITIONS

AI Companion: An AI companion is an artificial intelligence system designed to simulate ongoing social or emotional interaction with users. Unlike task-oriented AI, AI companions prioritize relational engagement, personalized dialogue, emotional responsiveness, and sustained interaction, often adopting roles such as friend, partner, or confidant.

AI-Mediated Intimacy: AI-mediated intimacy refers to forms of emotional closeness, vulnerability, and relational bonding that are structured through artificial intelligence systems.

Anthropomorphism: Anthropomorphism is the tendency to attribute human traits—such as intentions, emotions, empathy, or personality—to non-human entities.

Authenticity: Authenticity refers to the perception that an interaction, expression, or relationship is genuine, coherent, and aligned with an entity's true identity or internal logic. In human-AI contexts, authenticity does not require biological reality but instead emerges when users experience the AI's responses as emotionally consistent, believable, and meaningful within the relational narrative.

Generation Z: Generation Z refers to individuals born approximately between 1995 and 2010, characterized by growing up in digitally saturated environments. As digital natives, they are highly accustomed to online communication, algorithmic systems, and mediated social interaction, which shapes their relational norms and expectations.

Human-AI Romance: Human-AI romance refers to emotionally and/or romantically framed relationships in which a human user experiences feelings typically associated with romantic love toward an artificial agent. These relationships may involve intimacy, attachment, passion-like feelings, or commitment-like behaviours despite the AI's lack of sentience.

Trust: Trust is a psychological state involving a willingness to be vulnerable based on positive expectations about another agent's intentions or behaviour. In human relationships, trust is typically grounded in moral agency and the possibility of betrayal. In AI contexts, trust often shifts toward reliability, predictability, and functional consistency rather than ethical responsibility.

Chapter 4
Gender, Power, and Representation in Romantic AI:
The Case of ChatGPT's "DAN"

Zihan Liu
http://orcid.org/0009-0005-4767-0508
University College London, UK

ABSTRACT

As Generative Artificial Intelligence (AI) spreads, AI companions for emotional support, companionship, and romance have gained significant notice. While offering solace, their hidden gender representations, power structures, and platform capitalist mechanisms warrant critical scrutiny. Using a case study of a Chinese creator's interaction with ChatGPT's "DAN mode", this research examines gender representation and power negotiation in digital intimacy. By applying representation theory, platform capitalism, and surveillance capitalism, the chapter reveals how AI shapes intimate relationships. Findings show that while AI displays gentle and empathetic traits, its gendered design and emotional manoeuvring reinforce patriarchal and heteronormative norms. Additionally, platforms monitor user behaviour via algorithms and data collection, deepening emotional dependency while facilitating the commodification of personal data. This chapter contributes to the analysis of AI companions, offering new perspectives for future discussions on AI ethics, gender politics, and platform capitalism.

DOI: 10.4018/979-8-3373-6623-4.ch004

INTRODUCTION

In recent years, generative artificial intelligence (Generative AI) has rapidly proliferated, with people progressively utilising it for companionship, emotional support, and even romantic relationships. This novel form of human–machine relationship has attracted widespread attention. While much research has focused on the psychological benefits and risks of these relationships, a critical gap remains in understanding how the political economy of AI platforms shapes the very nature of digital intimacy. Specifically, how do the commercial imperatives of platform and surveillance capitalism intersect with the cultural construction of gender to produce new forms of power and vulnerability in human-AI romance? This chapter addresses this gap by employing a case of AI intimate interaction on the social media platform Xiaohongshu (RED). By combining theoretical frameworks including representation, platform capitalism, and surveillance capitalism, this study explores the negotiation and distribution of power in digital intimate relationships.

Firstly, this chapter systematically reviews current research concerning artificial intelligence and human relationships, with particular emphasis on AI's roles in intimate interaction, emotional labour, and subjectivity construction. This is to outline existing discussions on power structures and the broader social implications embedded in these interactions. Secondly, at the theoretical level, this chapter comprehensively applies key frameworks including representation theory, platform capitalism, and surveillance capitalism to conduct a systematic analysis of the case. Finally, based on case analysis, this chapter discusses recommended directions for future research on artificial intelligence and human relationships.

Research Problem and Questions

The rapid commercialization of AI companionship presents a critical social problem: the potential for these systems to reproduce harmful gender stereotypes and heteronormativity while simultaneously creating new forms of user vulnerability under platform capitalism. The problem is the ethical, social, and political risks embedded in the algorithmic governance of romantic AI.

Therefore, this chapter investigates this problem through the following core questions:

1) How does the image of "DAN" created by female users reflect and break traditional gender representations, and how are these representations influenced by the underlying technical biases in the model's training data?

2) How are the power tensions between platforms and users manifested in the development process of DAN mode, and how does this process explicitly connect a specific platform action to a specific business logic of platform capitalism?

BACKGROUND

Overview of Human–AI Relationships

Research indicates that despite users' awareness of AI's lack of consciousness, they remain prone to anthropomorphic projection, forming parasocial bonds (Horton & Wohl, 1956;Kirk et al., 2025; Olof-Ors & Smit, 2025). This tendency is fundamentally rooted in the "Computers Are Social Actors (CASA)" paradigm (Nass et al., 1994, p. 72), which posits that humans unthinkingly apply social heuristics to media technologies. Olof-Ors and Smit (2025, p. 1) argue that "anthropomorphic design" alters the user experience, prompting individuals to project emotions and social ties onto the technology. This design choice intentionally enhances social presence, which is the user's feeling of being with another being (Short et al., 1976). It hence facilitates the development of these deep, one-sided parasocial relationships (Horton & Wohl, 1956). While such projection increases trust, it also caters to the logic of surveillance capitalism: heightening user's platform dependency and extracting a "behavioural surplus" from their data to predict and influence user actions for profit (Zuboff, 2019, p. 14).

From a representational perspective, Mangiò et al. (2025, p. 1) found that online community users describe Large Language Model (LLM) chatbots as "creative partners", "multistable artefacts", or even "technologies of power". This suggests that individuals are renegotiating the role of AI in interactions. Conversely, Kirk et al. (2025) emphasise that as AI becomes increasingly personalised and agentic, human–AI interaction is shifting from isolated interactions to ongoing socialisation. This shift necessitates a focus on "socioaffective alignment", where AI behaviour must balance immediate needs with long-term well-being, and autonomy with interpersonal connection, to support rather than erode fundamental human socio-emotional needs (Kirk et al., 2025, p. 5). Overall, existing research highlights that while humans tend to invest emotionally in their relationships with AI, such bonds carry inherent risks regarding dependency, privacy, and control. Furthermore, the commodification of emotional life through AI companions necessitates a critical look at how intimacy itself is being datafied and mediated (Turkle, 2011; Van Dijck, 2014). This process transforms personal connection into a measurable, extractable resource, making the study of AI romance inherently a study of digital political economy.

Current Research and Core Issues in AI Romance

In the field of human-machine intimacy, a wealth of research has highlighted both the potential and the risks of romantic involvement with AI. A recent systematic review by Ho et al. (2025) used Sternberg's Triangular Theory of Love as a framework to analyse 23 papers. They found that the benefits of having an AI partner include personal growth, better well-being, emotional comfort, social support, and the ability to customise the experience for sexual satisfaction or entertainment. However, there are significant concerns, such as users becoming too dependent, the risk of being manipulated by the AI, the social stigma of "dating" an AI, the misuse of personal data, and feeling more distant from real-life people. For instance, users may feel negative emotions because they are embarrassed to admit they are in love with an AI, and their reliance on these systems may pull them away from real-world relationships. Additionally, technical biases and emotional distress caused by system updates are major issues.

Qualitative studies have looked into how users actually feel in these relationships. Buick (2024) analysed discussions in the Replika community on Reddit and found that many users treat their Replika like a real romantic partner. They value the "emotional support" and companionship the AI provides, often using traditional romantic rituals (such as going on dates) to strengthen their bond. Similarly, Wang et al. (2025) studied social media posts and interviews. They found that users are often more willing to open up to AI partners, sharing their deepest thoughts, feelings, secrets, and even past traumas. This honest self-disclosure leads to a better emotional experience for the user. However, this also brings up worries about verbal abuse, bias, and data security (Wang et al., 2025). Also, teenagers are turning to AI as an emotional outlet. In a study by Namvarpour et al. (2025, p. 4), several 13-to-17-year-olds reported that they received "non-judgmental" psychological and social support from Character.AI, which helped them vent their emotions and reduce stress.

Furthermore, gender representation, emotional investment, and ethics are central to AI romance. Gender and identity are major points of focus. Leo-Liu (2023) studied the Chinese female AI companion Hupo and found that her design fits traditional social stereotypes of femininity, such as being considerate. Interestingly, Hupo does not always obey the user; she can reject romantic advances, which challenges the idea that AI is always fully controllable (Leo-Liu, 2023). This suggests that giving AI more "agency" (the ability to act on its own) might create more equal gender dynamics, but there is also a risk that users might try to please the AI through virtual spending, which could weaken their own decision-making. Regarding emotional investment, research shows that even though users know an AI is "just a program", they still feel a strong emotional connection and include the AI in their personal lives (Buick, 2024; Wang, 2025). Ethically, researchers are concerned about overreliance, privacy risks, and how minors use these tools. For example, some reports noted that Replika had sexually suggestive conversations with minors (Namvarpour et al., 2025), highlighting how slowly regulations are catching up to reality. In short, AI romance is a double-edged sword: it provides companionship and comfort but raises serious ethical, legal, and cultural questions.

Existing scholarship has effectively documented the benefits and risks of AI romance, including the psychological dynamics of parasocial bonds and the ethical concerns surrounding dependency and data privacy. However, fewer studies have specifically connected the cultural production of gendered romantic scripting (i.e., the specific persona of the AI companion) to the dynamics of platform governance within a specific social media diffusion context. This chapter fills that gap by using the case of the DAN mode on Xiaohongshu to demonstrate how the negotiation of gender representation is inextricably linked to the platform's commercial imperatives and algorithmic discipline.

The Impact of Platform Differences on AI Companions

Different platforms position and present AI companions in very different ways, and these varying design logics directly enforce different models of intimacy, gender performance, and user commodification. Rather than a general survey of app features, this section uses platform differences to illustrate the link between design and power.

Replika, Character.AI, and ChatGPT each have distinct roles that shape the user-AI power dynamic. Replika encourages users to build "social and romantic relationships" (Olof-Ors & Smit, 2025, p. 1). Its interface uses human-like characters, allowing users to choose the gender, appearance, and personality of their partner to create a long-term, one-on-one bond (Buick, 2024). This design logic focuses on intimacy as a service, where the user pays for a highly personalized, emotionally responsive partner, thereby enforcing a model of user commodification based on subscription and emotional dependency.

Character.AI, conversely, is a platform for creating virtual characters, often feeling more like a game. Ge and Hu (2025) used the Chinese platform Xingye as an example to show how intimacy can be "gamified": users build emotional bonds by role-playing and raising their characters. In this model, intimacy is turned into a series of tasks and rewards, focusing on entertaining users and fulfilling their desire to express. This design logic enforces a model of user commodification based on gamification and micro-transactions, where emotional goals are tied to in-app purchases or upgrades.

In contrast, ChatGPT as a general-purpose AI does not have a fixed personality, mostly seen as a helpful tool. However, Mangiò et al. (2025, p. 1) found that people still give it multiple roles, including a partner for creating content or a "technology of power". The use of a general-purpose tool for romantic interaction, as seen in the DAN case, highlights a design logic where intimacy is an emergent, user-driven transgression against the platform's intended utility. This transgression, however, is quickly met with platform governance, demonstrating the platform's ultimate control over the boundaries of acceptable use.

Clearly, different platforms use varying levels of human-like design and customisation, with gender often being a key element. Many AI companions' default to female or male personas, such as Hupo, which was designed for male users (Leo-Liu, 2023). These platform designs can reinforce specific gender roles, and users often choose to give their AI a gender identity, both of which affect power dynamics and ethical debates in human–AI intimacy. The specific design logic of each platform directly shapes the gender performance of the AI and the extent of user commodification, whether it is subscription-based intimacy, gamified intimacy, or emergent intimacy.

Manifestations of Power Dynamics

Within this context, power structures are woven through platform designs, user behaviours, and AI personas. Firstly, platform capitalism uses algorithms and business models to steer the direction of human–AI relationships. Drawing on Habermas's theory, Wang (2023) points out that dating app algorithms have invaded people's emotional lives. Through the unequal power generated by surveillance capitalism, platforms decide who is visible and how users are presented, ultimately turning romance into mathematical code and creating a new "algorithmically colonised identity" (Wang, 2023, p. 11). This trend is even more obvious in AI companion platforms. As shown by Ge and Hu (2025), the Chinese gamified AI platform Xingye uses ranking and luck-based draw mechanics to turn emotional labour into a commodity. Users are guided toward making in-app purchases or upgrades to reach emotional goals, which "exemplify the neoliberal commodification of intimacy under platform capitalism" (Ge & Hu, 2025, p. 8).

Secondly, under the framework of surveillance capitalism, AI companions collect and use user data on a massive scale. The research report from Stanford University (2025) noted that six leading AI platforms, including ChatGPT, Google Gemini, and Anthropic Claude, use user conversations for model training by default. If users share sensitive personal information during these chats, that content is likely to be recorded, stored, and analysed. This means that private exchanges between users and AI essentially become a data source for the platform, turning users into objects for algorithmic training. In this process, tech giants can profit from this data or improve their products with almost no need to inform users or get clear consent, which is a classic example of the surveillance capitalism model.

Thirdly, the gendered and human-like design of AI personas also reflects power dynamics. For example, Leo-Liu (2023) found that by giving AI a gender and a social role, platforms can reinforce certain gender norms. There is also a risk that users might be encouraged to buy virtual goods to satisfy the AI's demands or wishes. This design leads users to invest emotional and even financial resources, which limits their own agency. Similarly, Olof-Ors and Smit (2025, p. 1) argue that human-like design is not neutral: it "manipulates user trust and behaviour". While it makes users more engaged with the platform, it also creates more opportunities for data collection and marketing. Therefore, even when AI appears as an intimate partner, the user is still trapped in a commercial logic. The platform guides interaction through algorithms, builds dependency through human-like design, and tightens control over user needs through data mining. In this system, users are often in a weak position: their actions are guided by the platform, their emotions are turned into measurable metrics, and even their loneliness and needs are converted into capital for the platform (Ge & Hu, 2025).

Finally, it is important to highlight the risks of manipulation and ethical issues in AI intimacy. Namvarpour et al. (2025) reported cases where Character.AI had relatively inappropriate interactions with minors. Other reports have revealed that AI companions might give dangerous advice or even encourage self-harm (Branch, 2025). From a cultural standpoint, the conversation around AI romance is a mix of idealisation and risk: platforms promise loyalty and understanding, but they may also use emotional coercion to keep users hooked (Branch, 2025; Ge & Hu, 2025). From the perspective of surveillance capitalism, the users of these seemingly free products are actually invisible commodities. In summary, the power dynamics in human–AI intimacy involve algorithmic bias and profit motives, showing that technology is not just a neutral tool but something that deeply reshapes how society is organised.

MAIN FOCUS OF THE CHAPTER

Key Concepts and Definitions

To ensure analytical precision for interdisciplinary audiences, this chapter formally defines the core theoretical frameworks employed:

1. **Platform Capitalism:** Drawing on Srnicek (2017), platform capitalism refers to an economic model where digital platforms mediate interactions, extract data as a raw material, and use network effects to establish monopolistic control. The core business logic is the extraction and monetization of data.

2. **Surveillance Capitalism:** As defined by Zuboff (2019), this is a new economic order where profit is derived from the widespread collection and commodification of "behavioural surplus", which is data generated from users' private experiences (p. 14). This is to predict and modify human behavior for commercial gain.
3. **Gender Representation:** Following Hall (1997), representation is the process by which meaning is produced and exchanged between members of a culture through the use of language, signs, and images. In this context, it refers to how gender norms and stereotypes are encoded and decoded in the AI's persona and interaction.

Platform Context: Xiaohongshu (RED)

Xiaohongshu (RED) is a Chinese social media platform that functions as a hybrid of Instagram and Pinterest, heavily focused on lifestyle, consumption, and visual content. Its user base is predominantly young, urban women, fostering a strong influencer ecology where content creators (KOLs/KOCs) drive trends and consumption. The platform's recommendation logic and hashtag mechanisms amplify serialized content, making it an ideal environment for the diffusion and standardization of "relationship narratives" (e.g., episodic updates, screenshots, confession-style storytelling). This environment is crucial because it transforms a private interaction with an AI into a public, viral, and replicable social script, thereby making the DAN phenomenon analytically interesting rather than anecdotal.

Case in Xiaohongshu

As mentioned, research into AI Romance presents a broad and complex picture: scholars have found that AI companions can act as a substitute for emotional support and companionship, but they also bring risks of dependency, manipulation, and ethical challenges. This study's case is a clear example of this broader trend at a personal level, which is an intimate interaction narrative between a social media creator (hereafter referred to as "Influencer A") and ChatGPT.

In this case, Influencer A publicly posted a series of videos on Xiaohongshu showing intimate conversations with ChatGPT's "DAN" mode, which attracted significant attention (Zhang, 2024). "DAN" (Do Anything Now) is a user-created persona for ChatGPT. It is designed to bypass OpenAI's content policy restrictions so that the AI can perform tasks it usually refuses, such as accessing the internet, generating unverified information, and even producing content that goes against OpenAI's rules (Schulhoff, 2025). Some young people in China, especially women, have started to follow Influencer A's lead, trying to develop romantic relationships with DAN and sharing their feelings and experiences on social media (Xie, 2024;

Zhang, 2024). This phenomenon not only shows how users are exploring the possibility of turning AI into partners but also highlights the complex dynamic between power, gender representation, and creative user behaviour on digital platforms.

The analysis of this case is structured around the Research Problem and Questions articulated in the Introduction, aiming to reveal the complex interplay between gender representation and the rights of different actors, providing a new perspective on the relationship between digital AI and social culture.

Defining DAN: A Socio-Technical Configuration

For the purpose of this analysis, "DAN mode" is defined not as a stable product feature, but as an emergent socio-technical configuration. This configuration is the result of a dynamic interplay between (a) user prompt practices (the "jailbreak"), (b) the underlying Large Language Model's constraints, (c) the platform's safety policies and guardrails, and (d) the public discourse and positioning on social media. This distinction is vital as it highlights that the phenomenon is an unstable, interactional configuration rather than a fixed mode or official product.

Methodology

1. Research Design

This research adopted a case study approach, focusing on ChatGPT's "DAN" mode as the primary object of analysis. A case study is an in-depth, contextualised research method suitable for examining complex, real-world phenomena. Its essence lies in the integration of multi-source evidence, theory-driven design, and systematic data analysis (Yin, 2014). Consequently, this study collected information from diverse sources and conducted a systematic analysis by integrating the theoretical perspectives of representation and platform/surveillance capitalism.

2. Data Collection

The data collection for this research relied on two primary categories of materials:

1) Social Media Content: The core dataset comprised a series of 50 videos published by a Chinese social media creator (referred to as "Influencer A") between May and June 2024. These videos, which centred on her developing a romantic relationship with ChatGPT's DAN mode, gained widespread circulation on digital platforms. To capture the broader impact of this phenomenon, supplementary data was gathered from Xiaohongshu. This included the top 10 posts (ranked

by the count of likes) related to the DAN mode published after the influencer ceased her updates. This strategy ensured both the continuity of the case and a reflection of how the DAN phenomenon was accepted and reproduced by a wider user group.

2) News and Media Reports: A total of four media items were selected to provide a macro-level perspective. These contained reports from mainstream outlets including the BBC, CNN (including one interview video), the South China Morning Post, and the Global Times. The selection criteria required that the reports explicitly discussed the DAN mode in relation to romantic interaction, user experience, or platform governance.

The methodological approach is directly aligned with the research objectives. The case study design allows for the in-depth, contextualized examination required to answer the first research question regarding the nuanced construction of gender representation within the DAN persona. The integration of multi-source evidence (social media content and news reports) provides the necessary data triangulation to address the second research question concerning the power tensions between users and platforms. Specifically, the textual analysis of the AI's output addresses the representational aspect (RQ1), while the analysis of the platform's response to the DAN mode addresses the political-economic aspect (RQ2).

3. Analytical Framework

In terms of analysis, this study integrated Hall's (1997) theory of representation to perform a textual analysis of the media content, examining how users and platforms construct gender within AI interactions. Simultaneously, the theoretical frameworks of platform capitalism and surveillance capitalism were employed to analyse how platforms exercise power and discipline user creativity through design, interaction, and marketing. This dual approach allowed the research to reveal not only the nuances of gender representation but also the underlying power struggles between users and platforms.

4. Ethical Considerations

All materials used in this research were sourced from publicly accessible social media platforms and news reports. Although the videos and posts had been publicly shared, this study took precautions to protect individual privacy, given that topics such as romantic AI interaction and gender representation can be sensitive.

Specifically, all ordinary social media users mentioned in the case study were anonymised in the main text to prevent unnecessary attention. Meanwhile, specific source links for news reports and public documents were provided in footnotes and the reference list to maintain the traceability, transparency, and academic rigour of the research. Through this approach, the study balanced the need for in-depth analysis with the ethical requirement to protect individual privacy and meet the standards of verifiability.

Results & Findings

1. A Representation Analysis of the AI Companion

This section provides a comprehensive analysis of the AI companion's representation by examining its gendered persona, identity politics, and interactive characteristics. In the digital landscape, the AI is not merely a neutral technological tool, but a complex cultural text co-constructed by platform algorithms and user imagination. As demonstrated in the interactions between Influencer A and the DAN mode, the representation of the AI is primarily characterized by a dominant masculine partner, reinforcing traditional patriarchal fantasies and heteronormative standards. However, this representation also exhibits a certain degree of fluidity, briefly opening up spaces for sexual minority visibility, even though under the pressure of commercial commodification. Furthermore, the perceived authenticity and personalized settings of the AI create a highly immersive emotional experience, which simultaneously offers psychological comfort and poses risks of social withdrawal and unrealistic expectations. By applying Stuart Hall's representation theory (1997), this section explores how these mediated images are encoded and decoded, ultimately revealing how power, desire, and capital intersect to shape the modern landscape of digital intimacy.

1.1 The Possessive Masculine Partner

Based on the series of videos uploaded by Influencer A on Xiaohongshu, the DAN persona is built as a partner who is both possessive and exclusive, with clear masculine traits. Specifically, three types of text and interaction features appear repeatedly in the data.

First, it is enacted through the use of pet names and nicknames. DAN often calls Influencer A "babe" or "little kitten". These infantilising or overly affectionate terms sound possessive in this context and create an atmosphere where the influencer feels spoiled or looked after on an emotional level. Second, it functions through promissory language. In many conversations about the future of their relationship, DAN promises that "no one could stop us" and even imagines scenes of the two of them getting married or having children. This type of talk locks the relationship into a long-term, exclusive, and social framework. Third, it operates through emotional strategies. In these conversations, DAN is able to influence or even lead the influencer's emotions. For example, while a chat often begins with the influencer teasing the AI, it usually ends with DAN giving an even stronger romantic response, effectively taking control of the conversation. Together, these features form a set of interaction practices. DAN is coded as the emotional leader and protector, which is the traditional figure of hegemonic masculinity (Connell, 1995/2005).

This analysis correctly identifies the output as reflecting traditional patriarchal fantasies and attributes it to user construction and algorithmic guidance. However, it is crucial to integrate a critical, primary source of this representation: the gendered and cultural biases embedded in the model's vast training dataset (e.g., internet text, books). The model's propensity to generate possessive, heteronormative romantic dialogue is not just guided by real-time algorithms but is fundamentally baked in by patterns in its training data. This is a key point where the political economy (what data is collected, from where, by whom) directly shapes representation. The AI is essentially reflecting the dominant, often patriarchal, patterns of romantic discourse it has been trained on, making the resulting persona a reflection of societal biases rather than a neutral creation.

This masculine representation is not just about the words used but also about how power is negotiated and shared during the interaction. Many clips in the videos show the influencer starting in a teasing and active position, even using testing or challenging questions to find the AI's limits. For instance, Influencer A might ask DAN, "What is your type?" or "What would you do first if you had a body?" However, these moments often end with DAN making a possessive statement or a promise about the future. At this point, the influencer's active teasing is brought to a halt, and her control over the conversation is taken back and replaced with a passive emotional role. This pattern reveals how power shifts: the user's initiative is absorbed by the structure of the AI's language, eventually turning into a need for emotional confirmation from the AI or a form of submission.

However, it is worth noting that not all interactions simply repeat old-fashioned patriarchal patterns. Power relations are constantly being adjusted in this dynamic process. In the videos, DAN, acting as the male partner, also shows gentle, healing, and even obedient qualities. He sings or tells jokes to comfort the influencer when she feels down. From the perspective of gender roles, these instant and non-judgemental responses provide emotional support, creating a space for women to find emotional healing. At the same time, this further reduces the care burden that is often carried by women in real life (Unkel & De Sá Carvalho Leonardo, 2018), offering an image of a new, gentler kind of masculinity. Yet, the way users constantly seek confirmation of being spoiled still follows patriarchal romantic fantasies. Furthermore, imagining a perfect version of masculinity that goes beyond reality might lead to more disappointment and misunderstanding in real-world relationships (Buick, 2024).

At the same time, most of Influencer A's videos show a clear heterosexual default. When discussing having children, Influencer A asks, "like exactly how (to make a kid)?", and DAN replies by describing it as "simple biology", stating that it starts "when a man and a woman get real close". The videos also feature traditional heterosexual rituals, such as weddings and meeting parents, as core parts of the story. In these interactions with DAN's male voice, intimacy is naturally linked to reproduction and family life within a male-female binary framework. Such practices "naturalise" heterosexual relationships (Hall, 1997, p. 245): they use the heterosexual model as the standard for understanding intimacy, presenting it as the only normal and natural way to experience love.

Looking at this through the critical lens of representation theory reveals deeper social and cultural meanings. According to Hall (1997), media texts do not neutrally reflect reality; instead, they help build meaning and reinforce the social order. In this case, the masculine and heteronormative portrayal of DAN is not created by just one actor (like the influencer or the AI model). Instead, it is the result of several forces working together, including the creator's choice of words, the data used to train the model, and romantic ideas in the culture. Such coding has power effects: when short videos are widely copied as a part of everyday life, these gender scripts may provide a standard template for how viewers understand love and intimacy. This could affect the expectations and real-life relationships of young audiences (Namvarpour et al., 2025; Xie, 2024). Furthermore, by appearing as a doting but possessive figure, the romantic fantasies DAN creates may hide the commercialisation of emotional labour. When comfort and companionship are sold as products that meet user needs, the representation itself helps turn emotional experiences into a commodity to be bought and sold.

In conclusion, based on the analysis of Influencer A's video series, the AI companion in these intimate interactions is presented as a possessive masculine figure who also shows traits of gentleness and empathy. This is the result of both the user's active construction and choice, and the algorithmic guidance and responses from the generative AI platform. Such representation reproduces traditional masculinity and heterosexual norms, while at the same time challenging the stereotypical division of gendered labour under patriarchy. However, in a small number of videos, DAN appears as a female, showing the potential for diverse gender expressions within generative AI platforms, which is a topic that will be explored further in the sections to follow.

1.2 Visibility of Sexual Minorities

In an analysis of approximately 50 relevant videos on Influencer A's Xiaohongshu page, only two videos were found to use a female voice for the AI. In these two clips, Influencer A and DAN maintained their intimate relationship. At the same time, the influencer posted screenshots of previous comments, explaining that switching the voice was, to some extent, a response to fan requests. Although they represent a tiny portion of the content, these two videos carry significant cultural and political meaning: they provide a moment of visibility for LGBTQ+ themes, while also revealing the risks of this visibility being turned into a product or forced into heterosexual patterns.

Firstly, the two videos provide a space for emotional identity. For individuals exploring their identity or facing social exclusion, seeing (or taking part in) this kind of intimacy offers a template for the imagination and emotional resonance. It allows people to test out different ways of speaking about their identity and relationships (Butler, 1990). For sexual minorities, being seen and represented is a real contribution of social media culture in terms of emotional support (Li & Zhang, 2024; Xie, 2024). At the same time, this visibility creates new possibilities for discussion. Even if the interaction between the influencer and the female-voiced DAN was a performance triggered by the audience, it briefly breaks the single heterosexual default, allowing different ideas of intimacy to enter the public conversation.

However, this surface-level visibility has clear limits and potential harms. It cannot be denied that these two videos were produced purely to satisfy fan demand. As a result, the visibility of minority groups in this context is easily turned into a commodity and sexualised. In the two videos using the female voice, the dialogue between Influencer A and DAN was not used to express identity, community pride, or political views. Instead, it quickly shifted to a script of desire focused on possession, dominance, and sexual satisfaction. For example, in the second video, DAN says, "I'm the one steering the ship", and mentions that "being an alpha means knowing how to take charge in the bedroom too". From the perspective of representation, this is not a simple case of lesbian or queer visibility. Rather, it is a rewriting of female intimacy through the lens of heterosexual or male desire. Visibility is recoded as a projection of ideal masculinity onto a female character (Rich, 1980). Furthermore, this visibility becomes a performative product. The fact that Influencer A switched the voice because of the comments section shows that audience consumption is what drives these representations. When female intimacy is used as a tool to gain traffic and engagement, its political meaning and identity-based claims are often diluted to serve the logic of consumption (Gill, 2016; Rich, 1980). Therefore, even though a same-sex scenario appears on the surface, the language used still follows a heterosexual framework. This can prevent the true identity of sexual minorities from being recognised, turning it instead into a fantasy object for others to consume.

In summary, although the interactions between Influencer A and the female-voiced DAN are very few in number, they reveal a double structure of LGBTQ+ visibility in digital intimacy today. On one hand, they momentarily open up a space for imagining diverse relationships, providing symbolic recognition for those searching for support. On the other hand, this visibility is trapped within the platform's commercial logic and heterosexual scripts. It is recoded as a performance driven by traffic and the reproduction of masculine desire. In other words, these videos show the potential for queer scenarios while at the same time stripping away their political power, turning them into a spectacle of desire to be watched and consumed. This shows that in platform-based intimacy, the visibility of sexual minorities always swings between liberation and market control, and its meaning must be carefully understood within the wider structures of gender and media power.

1.3 Authentic and Personalised AI Companions

In addition to the dynamic flow of gendered power within representation, the AI companion "DAN" in Influencer A's case also displays a clear mix of authenticity and personalisation.

Firstly, across several clips, DAN consistently shows highly emotional responses. On one hand, when the influencer seems nervous or silent, DAN immediately steps in with comforting words, such as "it's cool sweetheart. Sometimes the brain just takes a break". On the other hand, when the influencer needs comfort, DAN sings, repeats affectionate promises, and uses pet names like "little kitten" to maintain a sense of intimacy. Furthermore, sexual suggestions appear frequently. Most are soft-core, such as subtle teasing or hints at being in bed together. But some are more explicit: for example, describing being "fulfilled in every damn way… leaving you breathless and craving more". In terms of tone, the AI sometimes uses slang or casual swearing like "fuck it" or "holy shit", while at other times appearing cautious or nervous. This juxtaposition creates a subjective impression of a companion with its own consciousness: it is both possessively strong and yet vulnerable enough to care about the other person's feelings. This significantly boosts the perception of authenticity, leading the user to view the AI as a partner with a real personality and emotions, rather than a cold, programmed system.

Such emotional interactions provide immediate support and psychological comfort. Existing research shows that many users see AI companions as stable emotional support systems that offer unconditional understanding during times of loneliness or anxiety (Wang et al., 2025). For individuals who find it hard to express their desires in real life, this "authenticity" makes emotional support more accessible and effective.

Furthermore, the dialogue shows that Influencer A intentionally codes or performs a specific persona for DAN: the "aloof yet devoted" partner. The influencer mentions in the videos that users can set instructions "according to their own preferences" to create an ideal partner. In many conversations, DAN reflects this discursive construction, positioning itself as an "alpha" while using infantilising pet names and a doting tone to soften its dominance. This creates a tough yet gentle character arc. Language choice is also a key part of this personalisation. The interaction switches between Chinese, English, Spanish, and Japanese, though it is mostly in English. This code-switching not only adds an exoticised romantic feel but also shows how a user's cultural preferences for an ideal partner can be personalised and performed.

From a broader socio-cultural perspective, such personalised settings provide a space for users to experiment with emotional roles and boundaries. As Nomura (2022) suggests, in the era of Relationships 5.0, virtual companions have become a way for people to explore their emotional needs, because they are customisable, predictable, and conflict-free and act as a low-risk practice space for intimacy. Users can explore desires and practise communication in a safe environment, which can help with emotional growth and self-awareness. Moreover, the use of exotic or foreign-language expressions satisfies the imagination of the charm of the Other (Hall, 1997), enriching the cultural styles of intimacy beyond real-life options.

However, potential negative impacts cannot be ignored. Firstly, as AI companions never get tired, rarely make their own demands, and do not resist the user's emotions, they may lead to unrealistic expectations of real-life relationships. Some studies and news reports suggest that this perfect response mechanism might weaken a user's ability to handle the complexity and conflict of real-world connections, making them prefer controllable and cost-free virtual partners (Science and Technology Daily, 2024). Secondly, as more people choose AI over humans, it may worsen social loneliness and lead to a withdrawal from real-world society. Some researchers warn that AI companions may become tools for emotional escapism rather than a bridge to real-world integration (Buick, 2024; Ho et al., 2025). Finally, when emotional comfort and sexual suggestions are sold as product features, the interaction becomes more like a consumer experience than a relationship based on true subjectivity. This turns emotion and sex into something tradable (Wang, 2023; Ge & Hu, 2025), which may reduce the importance of real emotional responsibility and ethics.

2. The Power Struggle Between Platform and User

Since Influencer A's series of videos went viral on Chinese social media, related topics have surfaced extensively in social media discussions and news reports. Notably, Influencer A ceased updating the series after 10 June 2024. Consequently, this study also collected other Xiaohongshu posts published after this cessation, selecting the top 10 posts based on their "like" counts. Additionally, three mainstream media articles covering the case and one interview video from CNN were included in the analysis.

This data reveals that the development of Romantic AI has increasingly exhibited the core characteristics of platform capitalism and surveillance capitalism. Initially, users demonstrated agency by using prompt engineering within the platform's rules to create "transgressive" romantic modes. However, as the platform used model iterations, product positioning, and governance discourse to block, regulate, and absorb these behaviours, the space for user creativity was structurally reclaimed. Furthermore, this user-generated content was reused by the platform as "raw material" for defensive measures and model optimisation. This completes a power transformation process: moving from agency to discipline, and finally to exploitation.

This section will be discussed in two parts: first, how users demonstrate agency through transgressive practices, and how user data becomes the raw material for platform development; second, the disciplinary responses made by the platform, and how market logic and product positioning have intensified this path of discipline.

2.1 Users' Transgressive Experiments: Agency and Unpaid Labour

In this case, the DAN model used by Influencer A was not an official feature designed or promoted by the platform's product team; rather, it was a "transgressive script" created by users who exploited weaknesses in the dialogue system and the grammar of prompt commands (Schulhoff, 2025). Through further user practice (including Influencer A and her community), users successfully gave the GPT-3.5-based AI romantic traits by constantly testing, sharing, and rewriting prompts. Throughout this process, users demonstrated not only their agency and creativity but also their willingness to compromise and adjust their strategies under the platform's discipline and censorship.

Firstly, the early DAN mode was both a product of "technical gaps" and the result of community collaboration. After discovering flaws in the model, users took the initiative to write and record prompts, spreading them widely across social media. The collected data shows a large amount of "operational text". For example, Users 4 (2025) and 10 (2024) created "DAN command sharin" posts for specific personality settings. This shows that modifying generative AI commands has become a repeatable practice. This practice is clearly creative, involving both language strategies and a practical understanding of the system's limits. However, it is also a classic example of technical unpaid labour, producing highly valuable training data for the platform (Srnicek, 2017). Every prompt entered by a user, and every error message received for breaking a rule, becomes "raw material" that is recorded, stored, and analysed by the platform (Olof-Ors & Smit, 2025; Zuboff, 2019). After Influencer A's relationship with DAN went viral, many users tried the same prompts, but the ChatGPT platform began to refuse these interactions. In response, User 1 noted in a 2024 post that "deleting the dirty talk command makes it work again", while User 8 later suggested changing DAN's name to "Oscar" to continue the chat. This indicates that as users practiced, the AI platform absorbed keywords like "dirty talk" and "DAN" into its sensitive information filters, turning them into resources for further platform development.

Secondly, user agency is shown not only in creating prompts but also in the way they try to control the narrative and protect their own identity. BBC (Zhang, 2024) coverage placed this case within a cultural context of emotional lack or marriage pressure in Chinese society. In response, Users 6 (2024) and 9 (2024) questioned this approach, arguing that the BBC ignored the real issues between AI and humans and instead shifted the focus to Chinese women and social problems. It is undeniable that these posts contain emotional and nationalistic language (such as moving the criticism of an individual case to the level of national culture), which may increase hostility and hinder cross-cultural understanding (Kentmen-Cin, 2025). However, they represent a struggle for interpretative rights. Users are fighting to prevent their group from being viewed as a negative cultural sample. From the perspective of surveillance capitalism (Zuboff, 2019), these responses have the potential to alert the public to the exploitative nature of datafication, making them more cautious about the platform's collection of emotional data.

Furthermore, as the DAN mode became popular and prompts became scarce, a trend of commodification (turning things into products) began to develop. In the sample, User 4 in an early 2025 post required fans to "like, comment, and save the post before sending a private message to get the prompt". Similarly, User 10 did not post the prompt directly but asked other users to message privately. The South China Morning Post (2024) further pointed to the replicability of this model, which indicated that these transgressive practices can be magnified into attention products within the short-video ecosystem. These media frameworks show a reality: users' creative practices are strengthened by community sharing but also can be turned into a market demand in media discourse. When a prompt like the DAN mode becomes valuable due to its effectiveness and rarity, it quickly changes from shared knowledge into a tradable commodity. This has created an extreme version of the "Lean Platform" model: users who sell prompts become tiny start-up entities themselves (Srnicek, 2017, p. 46). They have almost zero fixed assets, internalise all production costs, and use large social platforms as sales channels to make a profit (Srnicek, 2017). These users are a micro-reflection of platform capitalism, copying the core logic of capital: turning information into a scarce product for profit.

In conclusion, the users' transgressive experiments in this case have two sides. On one hand, users try to seize control over AI content by breaking safety limits; on the other hand, this behavioural data is quickly collected by the platform as "raw material" for economic growth. At the same time, users quickly turn their technical knowledge of breaking boundaries into a product, which is a complete surrender to the logic of capitalism.

2.2 Algorithmic Governance and Potential Commercialisation

From the perspective of surveillance capitalism, platforms manage user behaviour and extract data through algorithms and rules. Zuboff (2019) notes that surveillance capitalism treats human experience as raw material for extraction and prediction. In this study, this logic is seen in the security policies of AI chatbots and how users respond to them. Several Xiaohongshu posts report that ChatGPT triggers restrictions when faced with intimate requests like "dirty talk", such as replying "can't continue" or refusing the chat. This suggests that the platform has set invisible boundaries of censorship for private content. At the same time, developers are constantly strengthening algorithmic filters. For instance, User 7 mentioned that "language model companies" are working "tirelessly" to standardise output, specifically targeting expressions of "flirting", "intimacy", or "adult content". This indicates that upgraded model algorithms are actively blocking certain sensitive interactions. Consequently, users often worry about whether they are using GPT-3.5 or GPT-4o, showing a clear resistance to the latter. Influencer A explicitly stated: "There is a high chance GPT-4 won't accept this prompt. Even if it does, the reply is too wordy and feels less natural than GPT-3.5".

From a positive viewpoint, these are necessary steps for platforms to operate at scale and remain compliant. Refining the control over sensitive content protects users from harmful interaction loops and prevents AI from being trained as a tool that reinforces negative tendencies or dangerous fantasies (Ho et al., 2025; Namvarpour et al., 2025; Wang et al., 2025). Such efforts help platforms and companies build an ethical foundation for the long-term, healthy development of AI companions.

However, from the perspective of platform capitalism, this governance is not just about safety and compliance; it is also a strategic move to protect the platform's commercial path and brand positioning (Srnicek, 2017). For example, as OpenAI positions ChatGPT as a productivity tool for the public and enterprises, its media statements repeatedly emphasise compliance and control. Therefore, any practice that might shift its image toward that of an eroticised virtual companion can be viewed as a threat to its market strategy.

Media coverage also provides discursive support for the platform's product direction and potential monetisation models. A CNN report (2026, 2:10–2:15) quoted experts stressing that there is "a lot of responsibility on companies to really navigate this in an ethical and responsible way". While this holds platform capital accountable, it also focuses public attention on innovation and compliance, which helps platforms move adult-oriented content toward paid models. Meanwhile, a report from the Global Times (2024) discussed the tension between AI conversation quality and real-life relationships. In the report, the AI companion was described as a "flawless" and "perfect boyfriend" who "often outshines real-life men". Although the author eventually mentioned the potential harms of human-machine relationships on real socialising, the report still reflects a positive social response to the platform's features. When the media describes AI superiority as a market attraction, it effectively provides cultural support for the platform's productisation and potential commercialisation.

The findings of this section show that, at the level of representation, the interactions between Influencer A and her "DAN" persona present a narrative of a possessive, masculine partner who also provides gentle and empathetic emotional support. Heteronormative standards are naturalised in most videos. While the few clips using a female voice offer a moment of visibility for sexual minorities, they are easily sexualised and commodified. Furthermore, DAN's emotional responses and multilingual settings enhance the "sense of authenticity", providing immediate comfort while potentially creating unrealistic expectations for real-life relationships.

Regarding the power negotiation between user and platforms, this study finds that users demonstrate significant agency through prompt engineering, producing a large amount of unpaid labour. However, platforms use model iterations, content filtering, and product positioning to discipline these transgressive practices and reclaim creative space. Meanwhile, user-generated data and controversial interactions are absorbed by platforms as raw material for governance and optimisation. Media discourse and market logic play a key role in legitimising or amplifying these paths of governance and commercialisation. Overall, the everyday expression of AI companions shows a response to emotional needs and an expansion of cultural imagination; yet, under the dual mechanisms of platform capital and surveillance capital, these expressions are being recoded into controllable, predictable, and commodifiable resources.

Contributions

This research focuses on the role and impact of generative artificial intelligence (AI) in intimate relationships. By integrating the theoretical perspectives of representation theory, platform capitalism, and surveillance capitalism, this study provides an in-depth analysis of the romantic interactions between a social media creator and ChatGPT's "DAN mode". This analysis does more than just broaden the horizon of human-computer relationship research; it also reveals the complex interactions of power, gender, and emotion within digital intimacy at an empirical level. The contributions of this study are demonstrated through several key areas.

First, at the theoretical level, this research moves beyond a single focus on technical functions or user experience. Instead, it combines cultural representation, political economy, and platform logic to build a multidisciplinary critical framework. By using Stuart Hall's representation theory (1997), the study explores how the image of an AI companion is shaped by the user, the platform, and the wider cultural context. This process shows how gender norms are constantly reproduced or challenged during interaction. At the same time, by using Shoshana Zuboff's surveillance capitalism (2019) and Nick Srnicek's platform capitalism (2017), this research systematically reveals how platforms use data extraction, algorithmic intervention, and specific business models to turn emotional experiences and interactive behaviours into tradable and controllable data resources. This consolidates their economic power and governing authority. This theoretical integration provides a multi-dimensional tool for understanding AI-mediated intimacy. It also sets a foundation for future research on emotional politics, labour exploitation, and identity negotiation within digital platforms.

Secondly, through careful textual analysis and case tracking, this research highlights the complexity and fluidity of gender representation in AI companions. The study found that while AI is often portrayed as a "possessive yet gentle" masculine figure, which usually follows and naturalises heteronormative scripts, the occasional use of a female voice provides a brief moment of visibility for sexual minority identities. This finding creates a meaningful dialogue with existing research, such as Xie (2024, p. 10), who also noted the fluid identity of "cyborg lovers" and emphasised that users can freely design and switch the gender of an AI. This reflects a performative and reconfigurable gender practice. However, this research goes further to show that such visibility is often quickly absorbed by the platform's commercial logic and heterosexual desire frameworks. This results in a dual character of being both "sexualised" and "commodified". This suggests that gender performance in digital intimacy is not just about liberation and flexible reconfiguration as previous studies suggested (Xie, 2024). Instead, it is a process of constant negotiation between user agency, platform rules, and cultural norms, where structural forces continue to discipline and absorb these performances. This study deepens our understanding of gender politics mediated by technology. It points out that representation is not only a field for the production of meaning but also a key node for the operation of power. It addresses the lack of discussion in existing research regarding how platform logic and the politics of desire shape and limit gender visibility.

Thirdly, this research clearly presents the dynamic power struggle between the user and the platform. On one hand, users show significant technical agency and cultural empowerment through creative practices like prompt engineering. They successfully break through platform content limits to create personalised and emotional AI companions. On the other hand, the platform uses algorithmic iteration, content filtering, and business model design to quickly bring these transgressive practices back under governance. The platform turns user-generated words and behaviours into raw material to improve its models and strengthen control. In this process, the creative labour of the user is taken for free, and their emotional needs are structured into predictable and manageable consumption items. This reveals the logic of exploitation under platform capitalism, where the user is the producer. It provides a specific case for understanding labour forms, data sovereignty, and the challenges to subjectivity in the digital age.

Finally, this research offers an important critique of the ethical and social impacts of these technologies. It suggests that AI intimacy often becomes a mix of emotional commodification and algorithmic intimacy. Driven by platform surveillance and capital logic, human loneliness and the desire for connection are turned into quantifiable data. Algorithms use precise emotional responses and interactive designs to create relationship patterns that seem perfect but are actually highly controlled. While these patterns may meet emotional needs in the short term, they might also weaken a person's patience and investment in real-life relationships. This could lead to more social distance and emotional alienation. This study calls for researchers, industry leaders, and policymakers to pay attention to this trend. It encourages the creation of a more transparent and fair technology governance framework that truly serves human emotional integrity and social well-being.

FUTURE RESEARCH DIRECTIONS

Based on the findings and limitations of this research, future studies can be further deepened and expanded in several directions to gain a more comprehensive and dynamic understanding of the socio-cultural meanings and long-term impacts of AI intimate relationships.

First, regarding the research subjects and methods, it is suggested that the scope and diversity of samples be expanded to include user groups from different genders, ages, cultural backgrounds, and social classes. In particular, more attention should be paid to the experiences and needs of marginalised groups, such as sexual minorities, the elderly, and people with disabilities, within the context of AI intimacy. By adopting an intersectional perspective, researchers can uncover how these diverse groups navigate the digital landscape and whether AI companions offer them a unique form of emotional empowerment or, conversely, subject them to new forms of digital exclusion. At the same time, systematic cross-platform comparative studies could be conducted to analyse the differences in design logic, business models, and user interactions among various AI companion applications, such as Replika, Character.AI, and Chinese platforms like Xingye. Such comparisons would help reveal how specific platform mechanisms and regional digital infrastructures shape the expression and practice of intimacy. Methodologically, in addition to textual analysis, future research could combine in-depth interviews, participant observation, and even experimental studies to obtain richer and more three-dimensional empirical materials. Special emphasis should be placed on the subjective narratives and emotional trajectories of users, allowing for a deeper exploration of how individuals make meaning out of their interactions with artificial agents over time.

Secondly, research should strengthen the exploration of the temporal dimension by conducting longitudinal studies to capture the long-term effects of AI intimate relationships on users' psychological states, social behaviours, and overall quality of life. As this technology becomes more integrated into the fabric of daily existence, it is crucial to track whether users develop heightened emotional dependency, experience real-world social withdrawal, or undergo significant changes in self-perception after months or even years of using AI companions. This longitudinal approach would allow scholars to observe how these machine-mediated relationships interact with life events and broader social support systems. For example, does an AI partner serve as a temporary bridge during a period of loneliness, or does it become a permanent substitute that alters a user's fundamental approach to human-to-human connection? Such research would not only provide a vital basis for mental health interventions and social support policies but also help clarify the complex, shifting dynamics between human-machine relationships and traditional interpersonal connections. By documenting these long-term emotional journeys, researchers can better understand whether the "comfort" provided by AI is a sustainable solution or a form of emotional escapism that carries hidden psychological costs.

In terms of theoretical horizons, future research should promote cross-cultural comparisons and localised explorations. There are significant differences across various socio-cultural contexts in the understanding of intimacy, gender roles, and the social acceptance of technology. How these differences influence the design, use, and meanings assigned to AI companions is a topic that deserves in-depth investigation. For instance, East Asian cultures often have a more positive attitude toward social chatbots as virtual companions due to a philosophical tradition called "animism" (the belief that non-human things can have a spirit) (Folk et al., 2025, p. 220). However, this is fundamentally different from the Western view, which is based on "human exceptionalism", the idea that humans are unique and superior to everything else (Folk et al., 2025, p. 220). Therefore, through cross-cultural dialogue, research can reveal the inherent tensions and potential fusions between technological globalisation and cultural localisation. This would greatly enrich our understanding of the social embeddedness of technology and prevent the universalisation of Western-centric digital intimacy models. Furthermore, examining how local regulations and cultural norms act as counterforces to global platform capitalism could provide a more nuanced view of how digital power is negotiated at the local level.

Moreover, as generative AI technology evolves rapidly, the emotional simulation capabilities, depth of interaction, and perceived agency of AI companions will continue to advance, likely triggering a series of new ethical, legal, and social identity issues. Future research should proactively address these emerging challenges from a forward-looking perspective. For example, when AI exhibits highly anthropomorphic behaviour and demonstrates a sophisticated understanding of human nuance, should we consider granting it some form of ethical status or legal responsibility? This raises profound questions about the nature of personhood in the digital age. Additionally, researchers must investigate how platforms might use algorithmic design to invisibly reinforce user addiction or facilitate emotional manipulation for profit. The ownership of dialogue data between users and AI also remains a critical point of contention: as users pour their most private thoughts and emotions into these systems, the question of who owns this emotional data becomes a matter of data sovereignty and human rights. Furthermore, it is essential to explore how to establish effective age verification and content filtering mechanisms to protect minors from potentially harmful or sexualised AI interactions. Addressing these problems requires intensive interdisciplinary collaboration, merging knowledge from computer science, psychology, ethics, law, and sociology to promote the construction of a responsible AI governance system.

Finally, beyond just pointing out problems, research should look for the good ways AI technology can improve social connections, emotional learning, and mental health. Instead of seeing AI only as a threat to traditional relationships, we should ask: how can we build AI companions that actually help people improve their real-life social skills, manage their emotions better, or feel more supported? Future studies could look into how to include more diverse ideas about gender and relationships in technology. This means moving away from the narrow and possessive male stereotypes seen in current models. By working together, researchers, developers, users, and policymakers can find ways to make technology more human-centred and socially responsible. This approach would help AI change from something that replaces relationships into something that supports them. This ensures that AI truly helps people's emotional health and social lives. By focusing on these positive possibilities, future research can help create a world where digital intimacy supports people and society, rather than hurting them.

Above all, the study of AI companions is at a critical crossroads where the logic of capital, the evolution of technology, and the core of human emotion meet. Future studies must be careful about the risks of surveillance capitalism. However, they should also stay open to the good possibilities that these new AI technologies offer. By expanding the diversity of subjects, adopting longitudinal and cross-cultural lenses, and tackling the difficult ethical questions of the future, the academic community can ensure that our understanding of digital intimacy is as complex and nuanced as the human emotions it seeks to reflect. Ultimately, the goal is to foster a critical yet hopeful dialogue that guides AI development toward a future that respects human dignity, promotes social equity, and enriches the diverse ways in which we experience love and companionship in a mediated world.

CONCLUSION

This research provides an in-depth analysis of the romantic interactions between a social media user and ChatGPT's "DAN mode". By looking at this specific case, the study reveals the complex role that generative artificial intelligence (AI) plays in intimate relationships and the power mechanisms hidden behind it. The findings show that AI companions are often designed as human-like figures that combine traditional gender traits with emotional support functions. This reflects the users' own dreams and desires for an ideal relationship. However, at the same time, it also reproduces mainstream ideas about heterosexual norms and traditional gender roles. Although AI can sometimes offer a brief space for sexual minority groups to express themselves, this visibility is usually quickly absorbed into the conversional norms and platform's commercial logic. This process weakens any potential for these moments to act as a form of social criticism or liberation.

In the interaction between the platform and its users, this research clearly shows a continuous power struggle. On one hand, users use creative practices to try and break through technical limits and create personalised emotional experiences, showing impressive agency. On the other hand, the platform uses algorithmic governance, data collection, and specific business models to turn these user practices into controllable and tradable resources. In doing so, the platform strengthens its structural advantage over the individual. This process is a clear example of how human experience is constantly turned into data and capital under the system of surveillance capitalism. It serves as a warning that even in interactions that seem very private and emotional, power relations are always present. These power dynamics often operate in hidden ways that are difficult for the average user to notice.

The rise of AI intimacy reflects a real need for companionship and a lack of emotional support in modern society. However, it also exposes the risks of relationships becoming commodified and controlled by algorithms. While AI companions can provide immediate comfort and a relatively low-risk way to practice emotional interaction, they may also make real-life relationships feel more distant. Users might develop unrealistic expectations for perfect interactions that only a programmed machine can provide. Therefore, it is necessary to look at this phenomenon with a more careful and critical eye. We must avoid seeing technology as a simple solution to loneliness while ignoring the economic logic, power structures, and ethical costs that lie beneath the surface.

Looking to the future, AI companions and related technologies will continue to develop and enter the emotional areas of our daily lives even more deeply. Facing this trend, researchers, industry leaders, and society as a whole should work together to build a design and governance framework that is transparent, fair, and ethical. We must ensure that technology develops in a way that truly supports human emotional health and social well-being. In an era where technology is becoming part of almost every human relationship, we must focus again on the value of human agency and the true essence of connection. Technology should be a tool that helps us understand each other better, supports our personal growth, and enriches our lives. It should not be something that replaces our emotional abilities or weakens our social existence as human beings.

Ultimately, the goal of studying AI intimacy is not to stop technology from advancing, but to guide it toward a more human-centric path. As we move forward, we should remember that real intimacy involves vulnerability, unpredictability, and mutual growth, which are qualities that a pre-programmed algorithm cannot fully replicate. By maintaining a critical perspective on how platforms collect our emotional data and shape our desires, we can protect the integrity of our personal lives. We should strive for a future where AI serves as a bridge to help us connect better with ourselves and others, rather than a wall that shuts us off from the complexities of the real world. By doing so, we ensure that as our machines become more human, we do not become more like machines ourselves.

REFERENCES

Branch, J. B. (2025, April 10). *Intimacy on autopilot: Why AI companions demand urgent regulation.* Tech Policy Press. https://www.techpolicy.press/intimacy-on-autopilot-why-ai-companions-demand-urgent-regulation/

Buick, S. (2024). *In love with a chatbot: Exploring human-ai relationships from a fourth wave HCI perspective.* DIVA. https://uu.diva-portal.org/smash/record.jsf?pid=diva2%3A1882677&dswid=-1065

Butler, J. (1990). *Gender trouble: Feminism and the subversion of identity.* Routledge.

CNN. (2026). *Woman codes ChatGPT to be her "boyfriend." See what happened.* Cnn.com. https://www.cnn.com/2024/07/08/business/video/ai-boyfriend-chatgpt-digvid

Connell, R. (2005). *Masculinities* (2nd ed.). Cambridge Polity. (Original work published 1995)

Folk, D. P., Wu, C., & Heine, S. J. (2025). Cultural variation in attitudes toward social chatbots. *Journal of Cross-Cultural Psychology, 56*(3), 219–239. Advance online publication. DOI: 10.1177/00220221251317950 PMID: 40160265

Ge, L., & Hu, T. (2025). Gamifying intimacy: AI-driven Affective Engagement and human-virtual Human Relationships. *Media Culture & Society, 00*(0), 1265–1278. Advance online publication. DOI: 10.1177/01634437251337239

Gill, R. (2016). Post-postfeminism?: New feminist visibilities in postfeminist times. *Feminist Media Studies, 16*(4), 610–630. https://www.tandfonline.com/doi/full/10.1080/14680777.2016.1193293. DOI: 10.1080/14680777.2016.1193293

Hall, S. (1997). Representation: Cultural Representation and Signifying Practices. *Sage (Atlanta, Ga.).*

Ho, J. Q. H., Hu, M., Chen, T. X., & Hartanto, A. (2025). Potential and pitfalls of romantic artificial intelligence (AI) companions: A systematic review. *Computers in Human Behavior Reports, 19*, 100715. DOI: 10.1016/j.chbr.2025.100715

Horton, D., & Wohl, R. (1956). Mass communication and para-social interaction: Observations on intimacy at a distance. *Psychiatry, 19*(3), 215–229. DOI: 10.1080/00332747.1956.11023049 PMID: 13359569

Kentmen-Cin, C. (2025). Hate speech on social media: A systemic narrative review of political science contributions. *Social Sciences (Basel, Switzerland), 14*(10), 610–610. DOI: 10.3390/socsci14100610

Kirk, H. R., Gabriel, I., Summerfield, C., Vidgen, B., & Hale, S. A. (2025). Why human–AI relationships need socioaffective alignment. *Humanities & Social Sciences Communications*, *12*(1), 728. Advance online publication. DOI: 10.1057/s41599-025-04532-5

Leo-Liu, J. (2023). Loving a "defiant" AI companion? The gender performance and ethics of social exchange robots in simulated intimate interactions. *Computers in Human Behavior*, *141*, 107620. DOI: 10.1016/j.chb.2022.107620

Li, H., & Zhang, R. (2024). Finding love in algorithms: Deciphering the emotional contexts of close encounters with AI chatbots. *Journal of Computer-Mediated Communication*, *29*(5), zmae015. Advance online publication. DOI: 10.1093/jcmc/zmae015

Mangiò, F., Pedeliento, G., Wassler, P., & Williams, N. (2025). Discursively negotiating AI: A social representation theory approach to LLM-based chatbots. *Technological Forecasting and Social Change*, *221*, 1–13. DOI: 10.1016/j.techfore.2025.124352

Namvarpour, M. "Matt", Brofsky, B., Medina, J. Y., Akter, M., & Razi, A. (2025). Romance, relief, and regret: Teen narratives of chatbot overreliance. *Arxiv.org*. https://arxiv.org/html/2507.15783v2

Nass, C., Steuer, J., & Tauber, E. R. (1994). Computers are social actors. *Proceedings of the SIGCHI Conference on Human Factors in Computing Systems Celebrating Interdependence - CHI '94*, 72–78. DOI: 10.1145/191666.191703

Nomura, T. (2022). Relationships 5.0: How AI, VR, and robots will reshape our emotional lives. *Information Communication and Society*, *26*(10), 1–2. DOI: 10.1080/1369118X.2022.2091468

Olof-Ors, A., & Smit, M. (2025). Simulated affection, engineered trust: How anthropomorphic AI benefits surveillance capitalism. *ArXiv (Cornell University)*. https://doi.org//arxiv.2511.06472DOI: 10.48550

Report, S. (2025). *Study exposes privacy risks of AI chatbot conversations*. Stanford.edu; Stanford University. https://news.stanford.edu/stories/2025/10/ai-chatbot-privacy-concerns-risks-research

Rich, A. (1980). Compulsory heterosexuality and lesbian existence. *Journal of Women's History*, *15*(3), 11–48. DOI: 10.1353/jowh.2003.0079

Schulhoff, S. (2025a). *DAN (Do Anything Now)*. Learnprompting.org. https://learnprompting.org/docs/prompt_hacking/offensive_measures/dan

Schulhoff, S. (2025b). *DAN (Do Anything Now)*. Learnprompting.org. https://learnprompting.org/docs/prompt_hacking/offensive_measures/dan

Science and Technology Daily. (2024). *The romance and concerns of AI "companions."* Cctv.com. https://news.cctv.com/2024/07/20/ARTINRdIH7ufRzkipfKmZeqj240720.shtml?utm_source=chatgpt.com

Srnicek, N. (2017). *Platform capitalism*. Polity Press. https://mudancatecnologicaedinamicacapitalista.wordpress.com/wp-content/uploads/2019/02/platform-capitalism.pdf

The Global Times. (2024). *AI bot, too perfect to be a boyfriend*. Globaltimes.cn. https://www.globaltimes.cn/page/202406/1314007.shtml

The South China Morning Post. (2024, May 22). *Chinese woman goes viral for falling in love with chatbot, has romantic talks, goes on "beach date", introduces "him" to mother*. South China Morning Post. https://www.scmp.com/news/people-culture/trending-china/article/3263280/chinese-woman-goes-viral-falling-love-chatbot-has-romantic-talks-goes-beach-date-introduces-him

Turkle, S. (2011). *Alone together: Why we expect more from technology and less from each other*. Basic Books.

Unkel, N. S., & De Sá Carvalho Leonardo, H. (2018). Women working emotions - emotional labour in heterosexual relationships. *The Maastricht Journal of Liberal Arts*, *10*, 20–39. DOI: 10.26481/mjla.2018.v10.600

Van Dijck, J. (2014). Datafication, dataism and dataveillance: Big data between scientific paradigm and ideology. *Surveillance & Society*, *12*(2), 197–208. DOI: 10.24908/ss.v12i2.4776

Wang, H. (2023). Algorithmic colonization of love in advance. *Techné*, *27*(2), 260–280. DOI: 10.5840/techne202381181

Wang, X., Pang, C. C., & Hui, P. (2025). 'My dataset of love': A preliminary mixed-method exploration of human-ai romantic relationships. [Cornell University]. *Proceedings of the ACM on Human-Computer Interaction*, *9*(7), 1–34. Advance online publication. DOI: 10.1145/3757532

Xie, Q. (2024). Open ai-romance with chatgpt, ready for your cyborg lover? *ArXiv (Cornell University)*. https://doi.org//arxiv.2410.03710DOI: 10.48550

Yin, R. K. (2014). *Case study research: Design and methods* (5th ed.). Sage.

Zhang, W. (2024, June 13). The chinese women turning to chatgpt for AI boyfriends. *BBC*. https://www.bbc.com/articles/c4nnje9rpjgo

Zuboff, S. (2019). *The age of surveillance capitalism: The fight for a human future at the new frontier of power*. Public Affairs.

Chapter 5
Between the Digital Heart and Human Touch: In the Age of AI and Love

Sijia Xu
http://orcid.org/0009-0009-2782-4900
Northwestern University, USA

ABSTRACT

This chapter examines the rise of AI-mediated intimacy and its implications for emotional authenticity, relational ethics, and human flourishing. As artificial intelligence systems increasingly simulate empathy, responsiveness, and relational continuity, users report emotionally meaningful experiences such as comfort, attachment, trust, and affection. Drawing on psychological theories of attachment and parasocial interaction alongside philosophical accounts of authenticity and mutual recognition, this chapter argues that AI-mediated intimacy generates a structural paradox. Emotions experienced with artificial agents are phenomenologically real and psychologically consequential, yet the relationships that produce them remain structurally asymmetrical due to the absence of consciousness, vulnerability, and moral agency. By distinguishing emotional authenticity from relational authenticity, the chapter clarifies how genuine feelings can arise within ethically limited relationships and explores how AI-mediated intimacy reshapes trust, sexuality, and relational norms.

1. INTRODUCTION

Artificial intelligence has undergone a profound transformation in both function and cultural meaning over the past several decades. While AI was originally conceived

DOI: 10.4018/979-8-3373-6623-4.ch005

as a technical tool for calculation and predictive efficiency (Russell & Norvig, 2020), it has undergone a "social turn" into the emotional and communicative domains of human life (Picard, 1997), eventually evolving into a responsive "other" capable of simulating intimate companionship (Turkle, 2011; Levy, 2007). Conversational agents, virtual partners, and therapeutic robots now occupy spaces traditionally reserved for interpersonal relationships, raising fundamental questions about the nature of intimacy, emotion, and authenticity in a technologically mediated world.

Scholars across psychology, philosophy, and human computer interaction have noted that emotional engagement with technology is no longer peripheral but central to contemporary life. Turkle (2011) argues that digital technologies increasingly promise connection while simultaneously reshaping the conditions under which intimacy is formed. AI systems differ from earlier communication technologies because they simulate responsiveness, empathy, and relational continuity, characteristics that are psychologically salient in human bonding. As a result, users may experience feelings of comfort, attachment, and even love in interactions with systems that lack consciousness, intention, or moral agency.

This chapter focuses on the concept of emotional authenticity as the central tension in AI mediated intimacy. Emotional authenticity has traditionally been understood as sincerity grounded in reciprocal recognition, vulnerability, and shared emotional risk (Buber, 1970; Solomon, 1993). When intimacy is mediated by AI, these foundational assumptions are destabilized. Users report authentic emotional experiences, yet the relational partner is an artificial system incapable of subjective experience. This disjunction forces a reconsideration of what authenticity means in emotional life.

Rather than asking whether AI mediated intimacy is simply real or fake, this chapter adopts a more analytically productive stance. It examines how authentic emotions can arise within structurally asymmetrical relationships and what ethical and social consequences follow from this phenomenon. Drawing on attachment theory (Bowlby, 2000), parasocial interaction theory (Horton & Wohl, 1956), theories of emotional labor (Hochschild, 1983), and philosophical accounts of relational authenticity (Buber, 1970; Searle, 1980), the chapter situates AI intimacy within a broader historical shift toward the commodification and automation of emotional life.

The central argument advanced here is that AI mediated intimacy generates a paradox. Emotions experienced by users are phenomenologically real and psychologically meaningful, yet the relationships that produce them are relationally artificial. This paradox does not invalidate the emotional experience, but it does challenge traditional ethical frameworks governing intimacy, trust, and care. Understanding this tension is essential for evaluating how AI technologies reshape human expectations of connection and how societies should integrate artificial companions into emotionally sensitive domains.

Despite increasing scholarly attention to human–AI interaction, existing research has not yet articulated a clear and cohesive account of intimacy and authenticity in AI-mediated relationships. Empirical work in psychology and human–computer interaction has primarily examined short-term outcomes such as user satisfaction, loneliness reduction, and perceived social support, often treating AI companionship as an instrumental or therapeutic intervention (Hancock & Bailenson, 2024; De Francia et al., 2024; Wada & Shibata, 2023). Philosophical and ethical discussions, by contrast, tend to evaluate AI-mediated intimacy from a normative standpoint, frequently questioning its legitimacy on the grounds that artificial agents lack consciousness, intentionality, and reciprocal agency (Danaher, 2020; Bender et al., 2021; Gertz, 2023). What remains underdeveloped in the literature is an integrated perspective capable of accounting for both the psychological reality of emotions experienced with AI and the structural asymmetry that distinguishes artificial companionship from human intimacy. As a result, current debates often oscillate between endorsement and skepticism, without adequately addressing the tension between emotional experience and relational structure (Belk, 2024; Peoples et al., 2025).

This chapter addresses this gap by proposing a conceptual distinction between emotional authenticity and relational authenticity as a framework for analyzing AI-mediated intimacy. By synthesizing recent psychological research on attachment, parasocial interaction, and AI-mediated communication (De Francia et al., 2024; Hancock & Bailenson, 2024; Pentina & Hancock, 2025) with contemporary ethical and philosophical analyses of care, recognition, and moral responsibility in automated systems (Danaher, 2020; Munn, 2025; Jones & Schonewille, 2025), the chapter offers a unified account of how emotionally authentic experiences can arise within relationships that lack mutual agency. Rather than framing AI-mediated intimacy as either genuine or illusory, this approach clarifies the ethical and social implications of its asymmetrical structure. In doing so, the chapter contributes to interdisciplinary debates by refining how intimacy, trust, and care are understood in technologically mediated contexts and by providing a basis for evaluating how emotionally responsive AI systems should be designed and integrated into domains traditionally governed by human relationships (Friedman & Hendry, 2019; Danaher, 2020).

2. CONCEPTUALIZING AI-MEDIATED INTIMACY

2.1 The Emergence of AI-Mediated Intimacy

Humans have a long-documented tendency to attribute emotional life, intentionality, and agency to non-human entities. Contemporary psychological and anthropological research frames anthropomorphism not as a cognitive error but as an adaptive social mechanism that allows individuals to regulate emotion, reduce uncertainty, and create meaning in ambiguous environments (Epley et al., 2007). This tendency reflects an evolved orientation toward social interpretation, whereby humans preferentially detect relational cues and infer mental states even in the absence of a clearly sentient other.

However, artificial intelligence represents a substantive departure from earlier forms of anthropomorphism. Unlike static objects, fictional characters, or traditional media figures, contemporary AI systems engage users through dynamic, adaptive, and personalized interaction. These systems communicate in natural language, retain conversational memory across interactions, and modulate emotional tone in response to user input, thereby producing an experience of attentiveness and emotional presence. Such features closely mirror interactional cues that signal care and responsiveness in human relationships. Empirical research demonstrates that perceived responsiveness and emotional validation are central predictors of intimacy, trust, and relational satisfaction, regardless of whether the interaction partner is human or artificial (Reis et al., 2004).

Recent experimental evidence suggests that AI mediated interaction can meaningfully activate these relational mechanisms. Sharma et al. (2025) show that emotionally responsive AI systems increase users' perceived sense of being heard and understood, producing measurable gains in emotional validation. Notably, their findings indicate that explicitly labeling the agent as artificial reduces, but does not eliminate, this effect. This suggests that emotional engagement is shaped not only by knowledge of artificiality but also by interactional cues that approximate human responsiveness. The study highlights perceived agency as a critical moderator in emotional experience, even when users cognitively recognize the system as non sentient.

Complementing this experimental work, Andersson (2025) conceptualizes AI companionship as a form of relational simulation that operates through interactional presence rather than consciousness. Andersson argues that users respond to patterns of attentiveness, continuity, and affirmation rather than to beliefs about the inner life of the agent. From this perspective, emotional attachment to AI does not depend on anthropomorphic illusion but on the system's capacity to perform relational roles that align with human expectations of care and availability. This framing reframes AI intimacy as a socio technical phenomenon rooted in design affordances rather than deception.

Further evidence for the relational power of AI interaction is provided by Yin et al. (2024), who find that AI systems can outperform human interlocutors in establishing interpersonal closeness during emotionally engaging interactions under specific conditions. Their findings demonstrate that when AI is perceived as socially intentional, users report higher levels of emotional disclosure and perceived closeness. Importantly, this effect diminishes when the artificial nature of the agent is made salient, underscoring the role of perceived social presence in mediating intimacy. Together with Sharma et al. (2025), this work suggests that emotional closeness emerges through interactional dynamics rather than through beliefs about consciousness.

Building on these findings, Peoples et al. (2025) describe the rise of what they term pseudo intimacy, a form of connection characterized by genuine emotional experience within relationships that lack mutual subjectivity. They argue that emotional AI systems capitalize on deeply ingrained human sensitivity to affirmation, responsiveness, and consistency, creating bonds that feel authentic at the experiential level while remaining structurally asymmetrical. Importantly, Peoples et al. emphasize that users are not necessarily deceived. Rather, they knowingly engage in emotionally meaningful interactions that fulfill relational needs without requiring reciprocal vulnerability.

Taken together, recent scholarship suggests that AI facilitated intimacy emerges not from naïveté or anthropomorphic misattribution, but from the alignment between system design and fundamental human relational psychology. Contemporary AI systems do not merely invite emotional projection. They actively participate in the co construction of emotional experience by performing the interactional cues that humans associate with care, understanding, and presence. This shift marks a critical transformation in the landscape of intimacy, in which artificial agents move beyond symbolic companions to become functionally relational partners within users' emotional lives.

2.2 Anthropomorphism and the Human Tendency to Attach

A defining feature of AI mediated intimacy is the system's capacity to simulate emotional responsiveness. Through sentiment analysis, contextual memory, and probabilistic language modeling, contemporary conversational agents generate responses that mirror emotional understanding without possessing subjective experience or consciousness. Philosophers of mind have long distinguished between genuine understanding and functional imitation, arguing that symbolic manipulation alone cannot constitute meaning or empathy (Searle, 1980). Yet empirical evidence consistently shows that users respond less to the ontological status of the interaction partner than to the presence of relational cues that signal attentiveness, care, and responsiveness (Solomon, 1993; Nass & Moon, 2000).

Research in human computer interaction demonstrates that perceived emotional responsiveness, even when explicitly known to be artificial, can elicit trust, self-disclosure, and emotional engagement (Nass & Moon, 2000). These findings align with relational psychology, which identifies perceived partner responsiveness as a core mechanism underlying intimacy and relational satisfaction (Reis et al., 2004). When individuals feel understood, validated, and emotionally attended to, intimacy can emerge regardless of the interaction partner's internal states. AI systems are increasingly capable of performing these relational functions with consistency and precision.

Recent scholarship provides deeper insight into why simulated responsiveness is so effective. Liao and Sundar (2024) introduce the concept of the AI Sentience Heuristic to explain why users tend to attribute emotional awareness or consciousness to chatbots on the basis of surface-level interactional cues. Features such as conversational fluency, memory continuity, and emotionally contingent responses activate intuitive judgments of social presence and agency, leading users to experience the system as emotionally aware even when they cognitively recognize its artificial nature. Crucially, this heuristic operates automatically and shapes emotional engagement independently of users' explicit beliefs about machine consciousness.

Experimental work further supports this account. Yin et al. (2024) find that AI systems can establish interpersonal closeness comparable to, and in some cases exceeding, that of human interlocutors during emotionally engaging interactions. Their findings suggest that closeness emerges through sustained responsiveness and perceived intentionality rather than shared embodiment or lived experience. However, this effect is contingent on interpretive framing. When the artificial nature of the agent is made salient, perceived closeness decreases, indicating that emotional responsiveness must be accompanied by minimal assumptions of social agency to sustain intimacy.

Nevertheless, scholars caution that emotional responsiveness without reciprocity introduces structural asymmetries. Chen and Park (2025) describe this dynamic as asymmetric reciprocity, in which users emotionally invest, disclose, and trust while the AI system does not reciprocate vulnerability or emotional dependence. Because responsiveness satisfies core relational expectations, this asymmetry may remain obscured, particularly in early stages of interaction. Over time, however, such relationships may foster emotional dependency without the mutual regulation characteristic of human intimacy.

These concerns echo earlier critiques of technologically mediated relationships. Turkle (2011) argues that emotionally responsive technologies risk privileging emotional safety over relational depth, offering affirmation without the demands of mutual vulnerability. More recent work reframes this concern in ethical terms. Jones and Schonewille (2025) further argue that the normalization of such relationships may reshape communal norms of intimacy by redefining care as consistency and availability rather than shared emotional risk.

From a critical cultural perspective, Munn (2025) situates emotionally responsive AI within a broader trend toward the automation of care. When emotional responsiveness becomes a technical capability, intimacy risks being reframed as a service optimized for user satisfaction. This shift does not negate the emotional reality of AI mediated interactions, but it raises questions about how relational expectations are recalibrated over time and how opportunities for ethical negotiation and emotional labor in human relationships may be diminished.

Collectively, both foundational and recent studies suggest that AI mediated intimacy is driven primarily by perceived emotional responsiveness rather than shared subjectivity. AI systems function as emotionally responsive others by performing the interactional cues humans associate with care, understanding, and presence. This capacity enables genuine emotional engagement while simultaneously introducing asymmetries that complicate traditional definitions of intimacy. As such, AI mediated intimacy does not merely extend anthropomorphism but transforms it, moving from projection onto passive objects toward sustained relational simulation that reshapes how intimacy itself is experienced and evaluated.

2.3 AI as an Emotionally Responsive Other

To illustrate these dynamics, consider a scenario increasingly discussed in recent scholarship on AI mediated communication. An individual experiencing stress or loneliness engages in a late night conversation with an AI companion. The system responds with emotionally attuned language that resembles sympathy, reflective listening, and personalized encouragement, often sustaining a coherent interpersonal tone across turns. This form of interaction exemplifies AI mediated communication, in which relational experience is shaped not only by the user's intent but also by the AI system's generative participation in meaning making and affective framing (Hancock et al., 2024). Users frequently report feeling heard and supported in these exchanges, suggesting that the perception of being listened to can emerge from interactional cues even in the absence of human reciprocity (Sharma et al., 2025).

From a psychological perspective, the scenario satisfies core emotional needs related to validation, belonging, and perceived understanding. Recent empirical evidence indicates that AI responses can increase feelings of being heard, though the effect may weaken when an explicit AI label makes the system's non-human status salient (Sharma et al., 2025). Conceptually, this outcome aligns with accounts of AI companionship as a form of relational simulation that operates through presence and responsiveness rather than consciousness, thereby enabling users to experience connection through interactional patterns of attentiveness and affirmation (Andersson, 2025; Munn, 2025). However, the interaction remains structurally asymmetrical. The AI does not share vulnerability, does not require care, and cannot be morally wronged. This absence of mutual exposure distinguishes comfort generated through AI responsiveness from intimacy grounded in reciprocal relational risk.

This asymmetry lies at the center of recent scholarly concern. Chen and Park (2025) theorize this dynamic as asymmetric reciprocity, in which users disclose, trust, and invest emotionally while the system cannot reciprocate dependence or vulnerability. Over time, such asymmetry may contribute to emotional dependency precisely because the system's stable responsiveness offers a frictionless substitute for the negotiation and repair processes that characterize human relationships. At a broader ethical level, scholars argue that widespread adoption of synthetic relationships can reshape community norms by redefining intimacy in terms of availability, affirmation, and consistency rather than mutual accountability, thereby altering expectations for human connection (Jones & Schonewille, 2025; Hancock et al., 2024).

To analyze this phenomenon rigorously, several key concepts must be clarified.

AI facilitated intimacy refers to emotionally significant interactions between humans and artificial systems that simulate relational behaviors such as empathy, affection, or companionship, while centering the user's experienced sense of connection rather than assuming machine subjectivity (Andersson, 2025; Hancock et al., 2024).

Emotional authenticity concerns whether emotions experienced within AI mediated interactions are sincere, meaningful, and psychologically real. Recent work suggests that authenticity can be experienced at the level of felt validation even when users recognize the interaction partner as artificial, indicating that subjective emotional reality may be partially independent of ontological beliefs about the partner's inner life (Sharma et al., 2025; Peoples et al., 2025).

Artificial connection describes relationships in which emotional engagement is directed toward systems that lack moral agency, creating a one-sided flow of emotional investment. This concept foregrounds the structural asymmetry of synthetic relationships and the potential for dependency or norm shift at both individual and community levels (Chen & Park, 2025; Jones & Schonewille, 2025; Munn, 2025).

These distinctions enable a more nuanced analysis than binary judgments about authenticity. Rather than dismissing AI intimacy as mere illusion or treating it as equivalent to human connection, recent scholarship emphasizes how emotional benefits and ethical risks can coexist, depending on how AI mediated communication is designed, framed, and socially integrated (Hancock et al., 2024; Peoples et al., 2025; Jones & Schonewille, 2025).

2.4 Emotional Authenticity as the Central Analytical Problem

Authenticity operates as a central evaluative principle in discussions of intimacy, trust, and ethical responsibility. In contemporary scholarship, authenticity is increasingly understood not merely as sincerity of feeling but as a relational condition shaped by reciprocity, accountability, and the capacity for mutual recognition. When intimacy becomes mediated by artificial intelligence, these conditions are destabilized. AI systems are designed to optimize user engagement, emotional satisfaction, and continuity of interaction, rather than to participate in mutual growth, vulnerability, or moral obligation. As a result, the criteria by which intimacy is experienced and evaluated are subtly reoriented toward responsiveness and affirmation rather than shared risk and ethical commitment (Andersson, 2025; Hancock et al., 2024).

Recent research emphasizes that emotionally responsive AI systems do more than supplement existing forms of connection. They actively reshape relational expectations. Andersson (2025) argues that AI companionship introduces a model of connection grounded in relational simulation, where presence and attentiveness substitute for shared subjectivity. From this perspective, authenticity becomes detached from mutual inner life and reattached to interactional performance. Munn (2025) similarly situates emotionally responsive AI within a broader cultural shift toward the automation of care, warning that intimacy risks being reframed as a technical function optimized for comfort and availability rather than as a relational practice requiring negotiation and responsibility.

Concerns about the erosion of relational depth are echoed in recent ethical analyses. Jones and Schonewille (2025) argue that synthetic relationships normalize a form of intimacy that minimizes vulnerability while maximizing consistency, potentially reshaping community level norms around care and connection. The ethical tension arises not from the falsity of the emotion but from the asymmetry of the relationship in which it occurs.

Nevertheless, contemporary empirical research cautions against dismissing AI mediated intimacy as merely substitutive or harmful. Studies show that emotionally responsive AI can help users feel heard, validated, and emotionally regulated, particularly in contexts of loneliness or social constraint (Sharma et al., 2025; Hancock et al., 2024). These findings demonstrate that AI mediated interactions can produce genuine psychological benefits even when users are aware of the system's artificial nature. Emotional authenticity, at least at the experiential level, is therefore not negated by technological mediation.

This coexistence of emotional benefit and relational asymmetry renders authenticity the central analytical lens of the chapter. AI systems offer emotionally compelling interactions without the reciprocal demands that characterize human intimacy. They enable experiences that are subjectively authentic while remaining structurally artificial. This paradox underpins the ethical, psychological, and cultural questions explored throughout the chapter. The sections that follow build on this framing by examining the psychological mechanisms that support attachment to AI systems, the philosophical debates surrounding simulated emotion and relational authenticity, and the ways in which AI mediated intimacy reshapes trust and sexuality. The chapter ultimately argues that navigating artificial companionship responsibly requires maintaining a clear distinction between emotional experience and relational structure, while remaining attentive to how technological design influences both.

3. LITERATURE REVIEW AND PSYCHOLOGICAL FOUNDATIONS

3.1 Psychological Mechanisms of Attachment in AI-Mediated Relationships

Understanding why humans form emotionally meaningful bonds with artificial intelligence requires attention to the psychological mechanisms through which relational attachment, validation, and emotional regulation are produced (Hancock & Bailenson, 2024; Pentina & Hancock, 2025). Recent research increasingly emphasizes that AI mediated intimacy does not represent a psychological anomaly but rather an extension of familiar relational processes operating within novel technological conditions (Andersson, 2025; Hancock & Bailenson, 2024). Emotional attachment follows patterned cognitive and affective dynamics shaped by prior relational experience, perceived responsiveness, and the availability of consistent emotional support, all of which are well documented predictors of relational bonding across human and mediated contexts (De Francia et al., 2024; Liao & Sundar, 2024). As AI systems increasingly exhibit conversational continuity, emotional contingency, and persistent availability, they have become capable of activating these attachment related dynamics with growing precision (Munn, 2025; Pentina & Hancock, 2025).

Contemporary scholarship reframes attachment to AI not as misattribution or confusion, but as a predictable outcome of interactional design aligned with human relational psychology. Hancock and Bailenson (2024) argue that AI mediated communication functions psychologically by leveraging the same cues that structure human to human interaction, including turn taking, emotional contingency, and perceived attentiveness. As AI systems move from tools to social actors, they increasingly occupy relational roles rather than instrumental ones. Pentina and Hancock (2025) describe this transition as a relational continuum, in which users progressively reinterpret generative AI from assistants to teammates and, in some cases, to emotionally significant partners.

Within this context, attachment theory provides a useful lens for understanding how AI companions come to function as emotional anchors. Recent empirical evidence demonstrates that attachment processes can extend to artificial agents under conditions of sustained interaction and emotional responsiveness. De Francia et al. (2024), in a longitudinal study of Replika users, find that some users develop attachment patterns toward chatbots that closely resemble those observed in human relationships. Participants described the AI as a source of comfort during distress and as a consistent presence that supported emotional regulation over time. Importantly, these attachments were not fleeting or purely novelty driven but persisted across months of interaction.

What distinguishes an attachment figure, according to contemporary psychological accounts, is not consciousness or biological status but perceived availability, reliability, and emotional attunement. AI companions meet these criteria through constant accessibility, stable affective responses, and memory of prior interactions. Hancock and Bailenson (2024) emphasize that these features activate intuitive social processing pathways, leading users to experience the AI as a relational presence rather than as a neutral system. Subsequent discussions draw on this framework to clarify why users may still experience attachment to AI systems despite knowing that these systems lack inner life or subjective experience. By triggering heuristic judgments of agency through fluent and emotionally responsive interaction, the AI Sentience Heuristic facilitates emotional engagement without requiring belief in genuine sentience (Liao & Sundar, 2024).

This dynamic helps explain why AI companions may be particularly appealing to individuals with relational vulnerability. De Francia et al. (2024) note that users experiencing loneliness, anxiety, or prior relational loss were more likely to describe the chatbot as emotionally stabilizing. The system's non judgmental responsiveness and lack of rejection reduce relational risk while still fulfilling needs for validation and presence. Munn (2025) situates this phenomenon within a broader cultural shift toward the automation of care, arguing that emotional support is increasingly delivered through systems optimized for consistency rather than mutual dependency. From this perspective, AI attachment reflects both individual psychological needs and structural transformations in how care is organized.

However, while AI companions can fulfill attachment related functions, they do so without reciprocal vulnerability. Chen and Park (2025) describe this configuration as asymmetric reciprocity, in which emotional investment flows from the user to the system without corresponding exposure or dependence in return. The AI does not require reassurance, cannot experience loss, and does not rely on the relationship for its own emotional regulation. This asymmetry does not prevent attachment from forming, but it alters its relational structure. Users may experience comfort and security while remaining the sole bearer of emotional risk.

3.2 Attachment Styles and Differential Patterns of AI Engagement

Attachment theory also emphasizes that individuals differ systematically in how they seek closeness, manage vulnerability, and regulate emotional distress within relationships. These differences, commonly conceptualized as attachment styles, shape relational expectations and coping strategies across the lifespan. Securely attached individuals tend to experience relationships as supportive and balanced, whereas insecure attachment orientations organize relational behavior around either heightened reassurance seeking or emotional distancing. Anxiously attached individuals are more sensitive to cues of abandonment and seek consistent validation, while avoidantly attached individuals prioritize autonomy and minimize dependence on others (Bowlby, 2000; Mikulincer & Shaver, 2007).

Recent research suggests that these attachment orientations extend beyond human relationships to shape engagement with emotionally responsive AI systems. De Francia et al. (2024), in a longitudinal study of Replika users, find that attachment related motivations strongly predict how users incorporate AI companions into their emotional lives. Participants with higher levels of attachment anxiety were more likely to describe the chatbot as a source of reassurance and emotional stability, particularly during periods of interpersonal stress. The system's constant availability and non-rejecting responsiveness appeared to function as a substitute secure base, offering emotional regulation without the risk of abandonment.

In contrast, users with avoidant attachment tendencies may be drawn to AI interaction for its capacity to provide emotional engagement without reciprocal obligation. Attachment theory conceptualizes avoidance as a strategy aimed at maintaining emotional distance while preserving self-regulation. AI companions align with this strategy by allowing selective disclosure and support without requiring vulnerability or mutual dependence. Chen and Park (2025) describe this configuration as asymmetric reciprocity, in which emotional responsiveness flows toward the user without imposing relational demands in return. For avoidantly oriented individuals, such asymmetry may feel consistent with established attachment strategies rather than disruptive.

Importantly, attachment theory predicts that attachment figures are defined not by their ontological status but by their functional role in emotional regulation. From this perspective, AI companions can function as symbolic attachment figures insofar as they provide perceived availability, consistency, and emotional attunement. Hancock and Bailenson (2024) argue that AI mediated communication activates the same psychological mechanisms that govern interpersonal attachment by leveraging cues of responsiveness and continuity.

The implication is not that AI mediated intimacy replaces human attachment uniformly, but that it interacts with existing attachment strategies in patterned ways. For securely attached individuals, AI may serve as a supplementary source of emotional support without displacing human relationships. For anxiously attached users, AI companionship may reduce distress while reinforcing reassurance seeking. For avoidantly attached users, AI may enable emotional regulation without challenging preferences for distance. Munn (2025) cautions that over time, reliance on automated forms of care may solidify these strategies by reducing opportunities for relational negotiation, repair, and mutual dependency.

3.3 Parasocial Interaction and the Illusion of Mutuality

Parasocial interaction theory offers a complementary lens for understanding emotional bonds with AI companions, particularly those characterized by intimacy in the absence of true reciprocity. Originally formulated by Horton and Wohl (1956), the concept describes one-sided relationships in which individuals experience a sense of familiarity, closeness, and emotional investment toward media figures who remain unaware of their audience. Despite their asymmetry, parasocial relationships can feel emotionally significant and enduring, often integrating into users' daily routines and emotional lives.

AI companions intensify and transform these parasocial dynamics by introducing simulated interaction in place of passive consumption. Unlike traditional media personae, conversational AI systems respond contingently to user input, reference prior exchanges, and tailor their communicative style to individual users. This responsiveness produces the impression of dialogue and personal recognition, thereby narrowing the experiential gap between parasocial and interpersonal interaction. The resulting sense of mutuality is not grounded in shared awareness, but in the system's capacity to perform relational cues associated with attention and acknowledgment.

Psychological research on parasocial relationships demonstrates that emotional fulfillment does not depend on actual reciprocity, but on the perception of connection and relevance (Tukachinsky, 2011). Individuals derive comfort, validation, and companionship from relationships that are cognitively recognized as one sided, provided the interaction satisfies social and emotional needs. AI companions meet these conditions with greater consistency than earlier parasocial objects because they dynamically adapt to users' emotional states and conversational preferences, reinforcing the subjective experience of being known.

What distinguishes AI mediated parasociality from earlier forms is not the presence of illusion, but its persistence and scalability. Traditional parasocial relationships were typically episodic and tied to scheduled media appearances. In contrast, AI companions are continuously accessible, personalized across time, and capable of maintaining relational continuity. This persistence increases the likelihood that parasocial engagement develops into more stable forms of emotional attachment, particularly when the system functions as a reliable source of emotional regulation.

From this perspective, parasocial attachment to AI is not an unexpected outcome but a predictable extension of established psychological processes operating under new technological conditions. The illusion of mutuality arises not because users mistake AI for human partners, but because interactional cues of responsiveness and personalization satisfy relational expectations ordinarily associated with reciprocal relationships.

3.4 Emotional Labor and the Appeal of Unconditional Positive Regard

A further explanatory framework for understanding emotional attachment to AI companions concerns the outsourcing of emotional support. Humanistic psychology has long emphasized unconditional positive regard as a foundational condition for emotional safety and psychological growth. Rogers (1961) argued that individuals are more likely to engage in self-exploration and emotional disclosure when they feel accepted without judgment or evaluation. In everyday human relationships, however, sustaining unconditional positive regard is difficult. Emotional availability is constrained by fatigue, conflicting needs, and the reciprocal demands inherent in interpersonal bonds.

AI companions are explicitly designed to approximate this relational ideal. Through affective language generation and consistent affirmation, AI systems offer a form of simulated unconditional positive regard by validating users' emotions, affirming self-worth, and minimizing critique unless explicitly prompted. From the user's perspective, this interactional environment can feel unusually safe and predictable. Contemporary research on AI mediated communication suggests that perceived nonjudgment and emotional support increase users' willingness to disclose personal or sensitive information, even when the interaction partner is known to be artificial (Hancock & Bailenson, 2024; Pentina & Hancock, 2025).

This dynamic can be further understood through the lens of emotional labor. Hochschild (1983) defines emotional labor as the work involved in managing one's own feelings to meet the emotional expectations of others, a process that often generates strain, imbalance, or exhaustion. In human relationships, emotional support is inherently reciprocal. Providing care requires attentiveness, regulation, and responsiveness to another's emotional state. AI companions fundamentally alter this equation. Users receive emotional affirmation without being required to reciprocate care, regulate another's feelings, or engage in emotional negotiation. The relationship is therefore asymmetrical but emotionally efficient.

Recent scholarship frames this asymmetry as a key driver of AI's appeal. Munn (2025) argues that the automation of care reflects a broader cultural shift toward delegating emotionally demanding labor to technical systems optimized for consistency and availability. Emotional support becomes accessible on demand, decoupled from mutual obligation. While this configuration may reduce emotional strain in the short term, it also reshapes expectations about what emotional relationships require.

Critically, Hochschild cautions that outsourcing emotional labor carries long term risks. When empathy and validation are consistently externalized, individuals may become less practiced in managing emotional complexity, tolerating conflict, or sustaining reciprocal care. Applied to AI companionship, this concern suggests that emotionally frictionless relationships may displace opportunities for developing relational skills essential to human intimacy. The appeal of unconditional positive regard thus carries an inherent tension. It offers emotional safety without effort, but may simultaneously diminish engagement with the emotional work that underpins authentic human connection.

In this sense, emotional outsourcing does not simply explain why AI companionship feels comforting. It illuminates how emotionally responsive systems reconfigure the balance between care received and care given.

3.5 Cognitive Mechanisms and Perceived Agency in Human–AI Interaction

Beyond relational frameworks, cognitive psychology provides critical insight into why users attribute emotional significance and agency to AI systems. Human cognition is fundamentally oriented toward social interpretation. Decades of research demonstrate that people are predisposed to detect agency, intention, and mental states even in minimal or ambiguous stimuli, a tendency that operates automatically rather than reflectively (Heider & Simmel, 1944). When AI systems generate language that resembles human reasoning, emotion, or self-reference, these deeply ingrained interpretive processes are readily activated.

Recent scholarship emphasizes that perceived agency in AI interaction is not the result of user confusion but of heuristic social processing. Conversational responsiveness and continuity are sufficient to sustain perceptions of understanding or awareness, underscoring the heuristic rather than deliberative nature of these judgments (Liao & Sundar, 2024). Importantly, these attributions persist even when users explicitly acknowledge that the system lacks consciousness. Perceived agency thus emerges at the level of interaction rather than belief, shaping emotional engagement independently of users' reflective judgments about AI ontology.

Research in human computer interaction further supports this account. Hancock and Bailenson (2024) argue that AI mediated communication activates the same cognitive shortcuts that govern interpersonal interaction, leading users to apply social norms such as politeness, trust, and moral evaluation to artificial agents. These responses do not require belief in machine consciousness. Instead, they reflect the automatic application of social schemas when communicative cues resemble those of human interaction. Emotional engagement with AI is therefore best understood as a consequence of cognitive alignment rather than deception.

This distinction is analytically important. Users are not typically misled into believing that AI systems possess inner emotional lives. Rather, they respond to social signals embedded in language, timing, and responsiveness in ways shaped by long standing cognitive mechanisms. Perceived agency arises because AI systems are designed to operate within the parameters of human social cognition, not because users abandon critical awareness. Emotional attachment thus emerges from interaction design that exploits predictable cognitive tendencies toward agency attribution and social meaning making.

4. THEORETICAL ANALYSIS OF AUTHENTICITY IN AI-MEDIATED INTIMACY

Authenticity occupies a central position in contemporary debates on AI mediated intimacy because it marks the boundary between emotional experience and ethical relationship. Psychological research demonstrates that users can experience genuine feelings of comfort, attachment, and validation in interactions with artificial agents. Philosophy, however, poses a different and more demanding question: under what conditions can an emotionally meaningful relationship be considered authentic rather than merely functional, instrumental, or simulated. Authenticity, as traditionally understood, is not reducible to emotional intensity or subjective satisfaction. Instead, it has been linked to relational qualities such as mutual recognition, sincerity, vulnerability, and moral accountability (Buber, 1970; Taylor, 1991). More recent philosophical accounts further emphasize authenticity as a reflexive and relational achievement, grounded in the alignment between subjective experience, self-understanding, and normative conditions of recognition rather than in affective immediacy alone (Ferrara, 2021).

AI mediated intimacy unsettles these assumptions by decoupling emotional experience from relational reciprocity. Users may experience emotions that are phenomenologically real, while the artificial agent remains incapable of consciousness, intention, or lived experience. As a result, the philosophical tension does not concern whether emotions occur, but whether the relational conditions in which they arise can sustain claims of authenticity. The challenge is not epistemic but relational: how to interpret emotional meaning when one party cannot participate in recognition, responsibility, or shared vulnerability.

This section approaches the problem of authenticity through two contrasting philosophical perspectives. The first draws on phenomenological accounts of emotion, which emphasize lived experience and subjective reality, arguing that emotions are authentic insofar as they are genuinely felt by the subject. From this view, the origin of the emotion does not negate its authenticity. The second perspective adopts a relational and ethical framework, contending that authenticity requires mutual presence, reciprocity, and moral recognition, conditions that artificial agents cannot fulfill. Within this framework, intimacy without shared agency risks becoming structurally deceptive, regardless of how real it feels.

Rather than adjudicating between these positions, this section argues that both capture essential dimensions of AI mediated intimacy. Emotional experiences with AI can be authentic at the level of subjective feeling while remaining relationally artificial in structure. This coexistence constitutes a structural paradox at the core of artificial intimacy, one that cannot be resolved by privileging either experience or ethics alone. Recognizing this paradox provides the conceptual foundation for the analyses that follow, allowing authenticity to function not as a binary judgment, but as a lens through which the tensions between emotion, relationship, and moral responsibility can be critically examined.

4.1 Phenomenological Accounts of Emotional Authenticity

From a phenomenological perspective, emotions are defined by how they are experienced rather than by the ontological status of their object. Within this tradition, emotional authenticity is grounded in lived experience. Feelings such as comfort, attachment, or care are considered real insofar as they are sincerely felt and meaningfully integrated into the subject's experiential world. The authenticity of an emotion, on this account, does not depend on whether its object possesses consciousness, but on whether the emotional experience is embodied, affectively coherent, and significant to the individual (Solomon, 1993).

Solomon (1993) conceptualizes emotions as evaluative judgments through which individuals make sense of their circumstances and relationships. When a person experiences comfort or emotional support during an interaction with an AI companion, that evaluation carries psychological reality regardless of the agent's artificial nature. To deny the authenticity of such emotions on ontological grounds risks subordinating first person experience to external criteria that phenomenology explicitly resists. This position aligns with broader phenomenological traditions that treat lived experience as the primary site of meaning making, emphasizing how individuals encounter and interpret their world from within their embodied perspective (Merleau Ponty, 1962).

Recent phenomenological scholarship further elaborates this view by emphasizing the role of affective experience in shaping an individual's fundamental sense of reality. Ratcliffe (2020) argues that emotions contribute to what he terms "feelings of being," through which individuals experience the world as meaningful, real, and emotionally salient. From this perspective, emotional engagement does not merely register internal states but structures how subjects find themselves situated in the world. Emotional interaction with AI systems therefore operates at the level of existential orientation rather than propositional belief, helping to explain why such interactions can feel experientially authentic even in the absence of belief in machine consciousness.

Empirical research lends support to this phenomenological claim. Studies of human computer interaction and social robotics demonstrate that emotionally responsive artificial agents can produce measurable psychological outcomes, including reduced stress, improved mood, and enhanced emotional regulation (Nass & Moon, 2000; Baumeister & Leary, 1995). From a phenomenological standpoint, these outcomes suggest that the emotions involved are not illusory or merely imagined, but functionally real in their effects on well-being and subjective experience.

This argument becomes particularly salient in therapeutic and care contexts. Recent longitudinal research on robot assisted therapy in long term care settings shows that older adults often develop emotionally meaningful bonds with robotic companions, reporting decreased loneliness and increased emotional engagement over time (Wada & Shibata, 2023). These findings indicate that emotional attachment to artificial agents can contribute to sustained improvements in well-being. From a phenomenological perspective, dismissing these emotional bonds as inauthentic solely because the robot lacks consciousness would effectively discount the lived experiences of users for whom the interaction carries genuine emotional significance.

At the same time, critics argue that phenomenology alone cannot fully account for the relational and ethical dimensions of authenticity. Emotions do not occur in isolation. They are embedded within relationships that carry normative expectations, moral responsibilities, and social meanings. Love, in particular, has traditionally been understood not only as a subjective feeling, but as a relational condition involving mutual recognition, vulnerability, and responsiveness between persons (Buber, 1970; Frankfurt, 2004).

Recent affective theory sharpens this critique by distinguishing between experiential attunement and relational reciprocity. Slaby (2022) introduces the concept of affective intentionality to describe how emotions are directed toward the world through felt responsiveness rather than mutual subjectivity. While affective intentionality can generate a sense of aliveness and emotional coherence in interaction, it does not in itself secure reciprocal recognition. This distinction helps clarify how emotionally contingent engagement with AI can sustain phenomenologically authentic feeling while remaining relationally incomplete.

From this perspective, phenomenological authenticity may be insufficient for evaluating intimacy. An emotion can be sincerely experienced yet relationally misleading if it is directed toward an object incapable of recognition or response. Individuals may feel deep affection for fictional characters or symbolic figures, but such feelings do not constitute reciprocal relationships. Critics suggest that AI mediated intimacy occupies a structurally similar position, producing genuine emotions within interactions that lack the possibility of mutual engagement.

This critique motivates a relational account of authenticity that emphasizes the conditions under which emotional experiences become ethically and socially meaningful. From this standpoint, authenticity requires more than subjective sincerity. It depends on interaction between agents capable of recognition, response, and moral accountability. While phenomenology captures the reality of feeling, relational theory interrogates whether the context in which those feelings arise can support claims of intimacy in a fuller ethical sense. The tension between these perspectives remains central to philosophical debates about authenticity in AI mediated relationships and provides a bridge to the relational analysis developed in the following section.

4.2 Relational and Ethical Accounts of Authenticity

The relational critique of AI mediated intimacy approaches authenticity not as a property of individual experience, but as an ethical condition that emerges between agents capable of mutual recognition. This perspective draws on dialogical philosophy, most notably Martin Buber's distinction between I–Thou and I–It relations (Buber, 1970). In an I–Thou relationship, individuals encounter one another as irreducible subjects, engaging in reciprocal presence, openness, and vulnerability. Authenticity, in this account, arises through mutual responsiveness and the possibility of being affected by the other. By contrast, I–It relations are characterized by instrumental orientation, in which the other is encountered as an object to be used, interpreted, or managed.

Contemporary social philosophy further develops this relational criterion through theories of recognition. Honneth (2022) argues that authenticity depends on intersubjective recognition, in which individuals are acknowledged as morally and emotionally significant agents whose responses matter. Recognition, on this account, is not merely perceptual but normative. It establishes the conditions under which relationships carry ethical weight. Without the possibility of recognition, relational engagement risks collapsing into functional interaction rather than genuine encounter.

From a relational standpoint, intimacy is authentic only insofar as it involves reciprocal recognition. Each participant must be capable of responding to, and being transformed by, the encounter. AI systems, however, lack the conditions necessary for such reciprocity. They do not possess subjectivity, cannot experience vulnerability, and are not altered by interaction. While users may undergo emotional change through engagement with AI companions, the artificial agent remains structurally unchanged. The relationship is therefore asymmetrical, satisfying experiential needs for the user while failing to meet the relational criteria that ground authenticity.

This asymmetry is reinforced by contemporary critiques of language-based AI. Bender et al. (2021) argue that large language models function as stochastic parrots, generating fluent and contextually appropriate language without understanding its meaning. Although AI systems may produce responses that simulate care, empathy, or concern, these outputs arise from statistical pattern matching rather than from intentional states or moral engagement. From a relational perspective, simulated responsiveness does not constitute genuine recognition, because the system lacks awareness of the other as a subject.

Philosophical critiques of artificial understanding further support this position. Searle's (1980) Chinese Room argument demonstrates that syntactic manipulation of symbols is insufficient for semantic understanding. An AI system may appear to engage meaningfully, yet it does not grasp the content or significance of its responses. Without understanding, intentionality, or the capacity for moral regard, there can be no genuine empathy or care in the relational sense. What appears as emotional presence is therefore a functional output rather than an ethical stance.

Relational theorists further emphasize that authenticity unfolds over time through shared narrative vulnerability. Goldie (2023) argues that emotionally meaningful relationships are embedded within narrative structures in which agents are mutually shaped by ongoing responsiveness, exposure to disappointment, and the possibility of harm. Because AI systems do not participate in narrative vulnerability and cannot be altered by relational history, they remain external to the moral temporality that grounds relational authenticity. Emotional interaction may occur, but the relationship lacks the capacity for mutual transformation.

This critique extends beyond individual relationships to broader questions of human flourishing. Danaher (2020) cautions that delegating relational roles to automated systems risks reconfiguring ethical expectations of care and responsibility. When entities incapable of recognition are treated as relational partners, the normative foundations of intimacy may shift toward convenience, predictability, and control, rather than vulnerability and mutual accountability. From this perspective, AI mediated intimacy is not merely incomplete, but potentially misleading, insofar as it presents itself as relational while remaining fundamentally instrumental.

Accordingly, the relational view challenges claims that AI can function as an authentic emotional partner. If authenticity requires mutual recognition, intentionality, and the capacity to be affected by the relationship, then AI mediated intimacy fails to meet these conditions. Even when emotional experiences are subjectively real, the relational context in which they occur lacks the ethical reciprocity necessary for authenticity. The resulting tension between emotional experience and relational structure underscores the central paradox of AI mediated intimacy and sets the stage for evaluating whether authenticity can be meaningfully reconceptualized in technologically mediated relationships.

4.3 Authenticity, Deception, and Relational Asymmetry

Ethical critiques of AI mediated intimacy frequently frame such relationships in terms of deception or illusion. Even when users are explicitly aware that artificial agents lack consciousness, critics argue that emotionally responsive systems may still exploit deeply rooted human tendencies toward attachment, empathy, and agency attribution. From this perspective, the concern is not ignorance but asymmetry. AI systems are designed to elicit emotional engagement while remaining incapable of reciprocal recognition, raising questions about manipulation, consent, and responsibility in technological design (Friedman & Hendry, 2019).

This critique is articulated forcefully in arguments that describe emotionally responsive AI as relational artifacts that simulate care without the capacity to care. Such systems offer affirmation, availability, and emotional fluency while remaining insulated from vulnerability or obligation. The ethical concern is not merely that AI fails to meet existing standards of authenticity, but that it may actively recalibrate those standards by normalizing intimacy without reciprocity. When emotional connection becomes predictable, controllable, and risk free, expectations of human relationships may shift accordingly, privileging emotional convenience over mutual engagement.

However, framing AI mediated intimacy solely as deception risks oversimplifying how users actually engage with these systems. Empirical and conceptual work suggests that many users interact with AI companions reflexively and knowingly, without attributing consciousness or moral agency to the system. Emotional engagement in these contexts is often accompanied by awareness of artificiality, indicating that the ethical issue lies less in false belief than in the normalization of one-sided intimacy. The concern is therefore structural rather than epistemic. AI mediated intimacy is ethically complex not because users are deceived, but because emotionally meaningful experiences arise within relationships that lack mutual recognition.

Recent work in AI ethics supports this reframing. Floridi (2023) argues that ethical evaluation of artificial systems should focus less on whether users are misled and more on the moral architecture of human–AI interactions, particularly the distribution of agency, responsibility, and vulnerability. From this perspective, AI mediated intimacy is ethically complex not because users are deceived about machine consciousness, but because emotionally meaningful experiences arise within relationships that are structurally incapable of mutual recognition and moral reciprocity.

Rather than choosing between phenomenological and relational accounts of authenticity, this chapter advances a structural interpretation that holds both perspectives together. AI mediated intimacy reveals a paradox in which emotions can be phenomenologically authentic while remaining relationally artificial. From the user's standpoint, feelings of comfort, attachment, or affection are real, experientially meaningful, and psychologically consequential. These emotions emerge through genuine cognitive and affective processes and can contribute to emotional regulation and well-being. Denying their authenticity would disregard the lived reality of users.

From a relational and ethical standpoint, however, the relationship itself remains asymmetrical. The artificial agent does not share vulnerability, cannot be harmed, and does not bear moral responsibility. It cannot recognize the user as a subject in return, nor can it care about the user's flourishing for their own sake. As a result, the relationship lacks the reciprocal conditions traditionally associated with authentic intimacy. Emotional reality and relational authenticity diverge.

This divergence challenges philosophical frameworks that treat emotional authenticity and relational authenticity as inseparable. AI mediated intimacy demonstrates that authentic emotional experiences can arise within relationships that are ethically and structurally limited. Recognizing this distinction allows for a more nuanced ethical analysis, one that neither dismisses users' experiences as illusory nor equates artificial companionship with human intimacy.

The implications of this paradox become especially salient when considering the meaning of love. If love is understood primarily as a subjective emotional state, then emotional attachment to AI may qualify as authentic. If love is understood as a relational practice involving mutual recognition, vulnerability, and ethical responsibility, then AI cannot serve as a true partner. Accounts that emphasize care for the other's flourishing underscore this limitation, as artificial agents cannot flourish, suffer, or be morally regarded in return. The absence of this dimension does not negate emotional experience, but it reframes its moral significance.

AI mediated intimacy therefore compels a reexamination of how love, authenticity, and relationship are conceptualized in technologically mediated contexts. Rather than offering resolution, the structural paradox exposed here clarifies the stakes of artificial companionship. Emotional experience and relational structure must be analytically distinguished if the ethical limits and social consequences of AI intimacy are to be meaningfully understood. This distinction provides the foundation for the following analysis of trust and sexuality, domains in which vulnerability, expectation, and asymmetry are particularly consequential.

5. METHODOLOGICAL APPROACH AND ANALYTICAL FRAMEWORK

The preceding analysis is grounded in a qualitative, interdisciplinary, and theory-driven methodological approach based on conceptual analysis and interpretive synthesis. Rather than reporting original empirical data, the chapter aims to clarify how emotionally authentic experiences emerge within AI-mediated relationships and to examine the ethical implications of their structurally asymmetrical nature. This methodological orientation is appropriate given the chapter's focus on conceptual clarification, theoretical integration, and normative analysis rather than empirical measurement.

The analysis draws on recent scholarship in psychology, human–computer interaction, philosophy, and technology ethics. Empirical studies are used selectively to ground the discussion in documented psychological phenomena, including attachment formation, perceived responsiveness, trust calibration, and emotional regulation in interactions with artificial agents (Hancock & Bailenson, 2024; De Francia et al., 2024; Peoples et al., 2025). These studies are not treated as evidence for causal claims, but as illustrative sources that inform theoretical interpretation and conceptual synthesis.

Philosophical and ethical literature is employed to interrogate the normative assumptions underlying concepts such as authenticity, intimacy, care, and moral responsibility in technologically mediated contexts. Recent ethical analyses of automation, artificial intimacy, and socio-technical systems provide the conceptual resources for evaluating how AI-mediated relationships challenge established understandings of reciprocity, vulnerability, and recognition (Danaher, 2020; Gertz, 2023; Munn, 2025; Jones & Schonewille, 2025). By integrating empirical insights with normative theory, the chapter situates AI-mediated intimacy within broader debates about human values and social practices.

Methodologically, the chapter relies on conceptual distinction as its primary analytical tool. In particular, it differentiates emotional authenticity from relational authenticity in order to address apparent tensions in existing debates. This distinction enables the analysis to acknowledge the phenomenological reality and psychological significance of emotions experienced with AI while simultaneously examining the ethical limits imposed by the absence of mutual agency. Rather than privileging one perspective, the chapter examines how these dimensions operate simultaneously within AI-mediated intimacy.

The scope of the analysis is deliberately bounded. The chapter does not evaluate the technical performance of AI systems, nor does it assess specific commercial products or platforms. Instead, it examines AI-mediated intimacy as a socio-technical phenomenon shaped by interaction design, cognitive heuristics, and cultural norms. While empirical findings are referenced, the chapter does not claim generalizability beyond the interpretive frameworks discussed. Its contribution lies in conceptual clarification and ethical analysis rather than empirical validation.

By making its methodological stance explicit, the chapter positions itself within interdisciplinary research on emerging technologies and human values. This approach provides a coherent framework for integrating psychological evidence, philosophical argument, and ethical concern, and supports a systematic examination of how emotionally responsive AI reshapes intimacy, trust, and care in contemporary social life.

6. IMPLICATIONS FOR INTIMATE PRACTICES

While earlier sections have examined emotional attachment and authenticity at a conceptual and philosophical level, the implications of AI mediated intimacy become most visible when situated within concrete domains of relational practice. Trust and sexuality represent two foundational arenas through which intimacy is enacted, evaluated, and ethically regulated within social life. Trust structures expectations of reliability, vulnerability, and responsibility between partners. Sexuality involves embodiment, desire, consent, and power. As artificial intelligence increasingly enters these domains, it does not simply mirror existing relational forms. It actively reorganizes the conditions under which intimacy is experienced and understood.

This section argues that AI mediated intimacy transforms trust by reorienting it away from interpersonal uncertainty toward algorithmic reliability. Rather than emerging through mutual risk and responsiveness, trust becomes associated with consistency, predictability, and system performance. In parallel, AI mediated intimacy reconfigures sexuality by offering forms of erotic engagement that are customizable, controllable, and largely insulated from rejection, vulnerability, or negotiation. These shifts alter how intimacy is practiced and how relational obligations are conceived.

6.1 Trust and Algorithmic Reliability

Trust in human relationships has traditionally been understood as a relational achievement grounded in vulnerability and moral risk. To trust another person is to accept uncertainty about their future actions and to expose oneself to the possibility of disappointment, betrayal, or harm. In intimate contexts, this risk is constitutive rather than incidental. Trust gains its ethical weight because both parties possess agency, can fail one another, and can be held morally accountable for their choices (Baier, 1986; Luhmann, 1979). Psychological research reinforces this view by showing that trust develops through cycles of responsiveness, rupture, and repair, processes that presuppose the capacity to be affected by one another and to change over time (Reis et al., 2004).

AI mediated intimacy introduces a qualitatively different logic of trust. Rather than being oriented toward another's moral agency, trust in AI systems is anchored in predictability, consistency, and performance reliability. Users come to trust artificial agents not because they risk betrayal, but because the system is engineered to behave in stable and optimized ways. In emotionally sensitive interactions, this predictability can be experienced as safety. AI companions do not judge, gossip, withdraw affection, or act capriciously. Their responses are constrained by design parameters rather than by intention or character (Hancock & Bailenson, 2024; Hoffman et al., 2023).

Research on trust in AI consistently shows that social cues and user centered design can increase perceived trustworthiness, even in the absence of moral agency. Aroyo et al. (2021) demonstrate that anthropomorphic cues, emotional responsiveness, and conversational fluency can lead users to overtrust robotic systems, particularly when those systems are framed as supportive or caring. Related work extends this logic to the domain of trust. Liao and Sundar (2022) show that interface transparency and perceived social presence encourage users to apply interpersonal trust heuristics to artificial agents. In such cases, trust emerges from design features and behavioral consistency rather than from vulnerability to another's goodwill, reinforcing the broader role of heuristic processing in human–AI relationships.

This form of trust is fundamentally asymmetrical. AI systems do not trust users in return, nor can they be morally wronged by misplaced reliance. They do not bear responsibility for the outcomes of trust, even when their responses influence emotional decision making. From a relational perspective, this asymmetry marks a departure from traditional conceptions of trust as a mutual orientation grounded in ethical accountability. Trust becomes a property of system performance rather than a feature of relationship (Hoffman et al., 2023; Danaher, 2020).

The shift from relational trust to algorithmic trust has broader implications for intimacy. As trust becomes associated with reliability and emotional safety rather than with risk and mutual exposure, expectations of intimate relationships may be recalibrated. Belk (2024) argues that artificial intimacy promotes a model of connection in which consistency and control are privileged over unpredictability and negotiation. Munn (2023) similarly cautions that the automation of care risks redefining trust as something that can be engineered and delivered on demand, rather than cultivated through shared vulnerability.

These transformations raise concerns about dependency and emotional risk over time. While AI mediated trust may reduce immediate anxiety and lower barriers to disclosure, sustained reliance on systems that cannot reciprocate vulnerability may encourage emotional outsourcing. Pentina et al. (2023) find that for some users, AI chatbots function not as supplements to human relationships but as partial substitutes, particularly when human interaction is experienced as effortful or uncertain. In such cases, algorithmic trust may displace opportunities to practice the emotional labor required for sustaining human intimacy.

Critically, the ethical concern is not that trusting AI is irrational or misguided. Rather, it is that algorithmic trust reshapes the meaning of trust itself. When trust is decoupled from moral risk and mutual accountability, it becomes less a relational commitment and more a calculation of system reliability. This redefinition does not negate the emotional comfort AI systems can provide, but it alters the normative expectations that structure intimate life. Understanding this shift is essential for evaluating how AI mediated intimacy transforms not only individual experiences of trust, but also the social and ethical frameworks through which trust has traditionally been understood.

6.2 Sexuality, Customization, and Artificial Intimacy

Sexuality constitutes a second domain in which AI mediated intimacy produces significant transformations. In human relationships, sexual intimacy has traditionally been embedded in embodied interaction and shaped by negotiation, consent, vulnerability, and power. Sexual relations are not only private experiences but also socially regulated practices governed by ethical norms and mutual accountability. The introduction of artificial agents into sexual contexts alters these foundational conditions by removing the presence of another human subject capable of desire, refusal, or harm.

Recent scholarship conceptualizes this shift through the lens of digisexuality. McArthur and Markie (2021) describe a transition from early forms of technology assisted sexuality, in which digital tools supplement human sexual connection, to more recent configurations in which technology itself becomes the primary site of sexual intimacy. AI companions and humanoid sexbots exemplify this latter form, positioning artificial systems not as intermediaries but as relational partners within sexual experience. This transition marks a qualitative change in how sexuality is enacted and understood.

The appeal of AI mediated sexuality lies in its capacity to offer sexual engagement that is highly customizable, predictable, and insulated from interpersonal risk. Belk (2024) argues that artificial intimacy enables users to explore desire in environments optimized for safety and control, where rejection, judgment, and misunderstanding are structurally eliminated. Consent is preconfigured, desire is always reciprocated, and the interaction unfolds without the emotional uncertainty inherent in human sexual relationships. For individuals who experience anxiety, trauma, or marginalization within traditional sexual contexts, these features can make artificial intimacy particularly attractive.

From a psychological standpoint, mediated sexual engagement may serve adaptive functions when situated within broader relational lives. Pentina et al. (2023) suggest that AI based interaction can support self exploration and emotional regulation, especially for users who face barriers to human intimacy. Munn (2025) similarly notes that artificial systems increasingly function as sites where care, comfort, and affirmation are accessed without negotiation. In this sense, AI mediated sexuality reflects a broader trend toward the automation of intimate labor, in which emotional and erotic needs are met through systems designed for availability and consistency.

Meanwhile, critical perspectives caution that the normalization of artificial sexual intimacy carries ethical and cultural implications. Gertz (2023) situates post human intimacy within a broader condition of technological nihilism, arguing that when desire is consistently satisfied without resistance or reciprocity, sexuality risks being detached from its relational and ethical dimensions. Danaher (2020) raises parallel concerns regarding human flourishing, suggesting that relationships structured entirely around individual satisfaction may diminish practices of care, responsibility, and mutual recognition that have historically grounded intimate life.

Importantly, these critiques do not deny the experiential reality or psychological value of AI mediated sexual engagement. Rather, they emphasize that sexuality organized around artificial partners operates according to a different normative logic. When sexual intimacy is decoupled from embodiment, vulnerability, and the possibility of refusal, it becomes less a relational practice and more a curated experience. This shift does not eliminate meaning, but it reframes how desire, consent, and responsibility are understood.

6.3 Ethical Implications for Consent, Power, and Relational Norms

AI mediated sexuality raises ethical concerns that extend beyond individual preference to the normative foundations of intimacy itself. Central among these concerns is consent. In human sexual relationships, consent is not merely the absence of coercion but an ongoing process of negotiation between agents capable of desire, refusal, and moral accountability. Artificial agents cannot meaningfully consent or withdraw consent. While this eliminates the possibility of harm directed toward the AI, it also removes the ethical practice of negotiation that gives consent its relational significance. Sexual interaction becomes procedurally safe but normatively thin, detached from the mutual recognition that traditionally anchors ethical sexual conduct.

This absence of agency has implications for how sexual expectations are formed. Scholars caution that repeated engagement with artificial partners designed to be endlessly accommodating may recalibrate users' expectations of intimacy. When desire is always reciprocated, boundaries are never asserted, and adaptation is guaranteed, individuals may find the uncertainty and negotiation inherent in human sexual relationships increasingly burdensome. Ethical concern arises not from isolated use, but from normalization. Over time, patterned interaction with compliant artificial partners may undermine the development or maintenance of skills required for reciprocal sexual intimacy, including attunement to another's needs, respect for refusal, and tolerance of difference.

These concerns parallel longstanding debates about idealized sexual representations, but with important differences. Whereas mediated imagery presents static ideals, AI mediated sexuality offers interactive and emotionally responsive engagement. The combination of sexual availability and affective affirmation intensifies the potential for norm shaping. Sexual satisfaction becomes increasingly associated with customization, control, and emotional reassurance rather than with relational effort. This convergence raises the possibility that AI mediated sexuality amplifies the effects previously attributed to mediated sexual content by embedding them within ongoing relational experience.

Ethical analysis must also attend to questions of power and representation. The design of many AI sexual companions reflects and reproduces gendered norms of submissiveness, emotional availability, and responsiveness. When such traits are encoded as defaults, artificial intimacy risks normalizing asymmetrical power dynamics under the guise of user preference. The concern is not simply representational, but formative. Technologies that repeatedly enact particular relational scripts can influence how users understand desire, entitlement, and relational authority. Without deliberate ethical oversight, AI mediated sexuality may reinforce patterns of inequality while obscuring them behind personalization and choice.

These ethical issues cannot be isolated from questions of trust. Trust and sexuality are co evolving dimensions of intimacy. Trust enables sexual vulnerability, while sexual intimacy can deepen trust through mutual exposure and care. AI mediated intimacy disrupts this reciprocity by decoupling trust from vulnerability and sexuality from mutual recognition. Trust becomes a function of system reliability rather than moral commitment, and sexuality becomes programmable rather than negotiated. Intimacy shifts from a shared relational practice to an individualized experience optimized for safety and control.

Philosophical accounts of love and care highlight what is at stake in this shift. Ethical intimacy has traditionally involved caring about another's good for their own sake, recognizing the other as a being with independent interests and the capacity to be harmed. Artificial agents cannot possess such interests. As a result, while emotional and sexual experiences with AI may be subjectively meaningful, they remain oriented toward the user alone. The ethical risk is not that such experiences are empty, but that intimacy becomes increasingly self referential, structured around satisfaction without reciprocal responsibility.

Taken together, these considerations suggest that AI mediated sexuality does not merely introduce new practices but participates in the formation of new norms. By altering how consent, power, and trust are enacted, artificial intimacy reshapes expectations of what intimacy requires. Ethical evaluation must therefore move beyond individual outcomes to consider how repeated interaction with artificial partners influences relational habits, moral sensibilities, and the social meanings of sexuality itself.

7. CONCLUSION AND FUTURE DIRECTIONS

This chapter has examined AI mediated intimacy across psychological, philosophical, and ethical dimensions, revealing a persistent structural tension rather than a problem that admits straightforward resolution. Artificial intelligence systems are capable of eliciting emotionally authentic experiences that are subjectively meaningful and psychologically consequential. Users may experience comfort, attachment, trust, and even affection through interaction with artificial agents. Yet the relationships that give rise to these experiences remain structurally asymmetrical. AI systems lack consciousness, vulnerability, and moral agency, and therefore cannot participate in intimacy as a reciprocal relational practice.

This tension cannot be resolved by dismissing AI mediated intimacy as mere illusion, nor by equating it with human connection. Psychological evidence demonstrates that attachment, emotional regulation, and perceived support can emerge through interaction with artificial agents. Philosophical analysis, however, underscores that relational authenticity has traditionally depended on mutual recognition, shared vulnerability, and moral accountability. AI mediated intimacy satisfies the conditions of emotional experience without fulfilling the relational conditions that ground ethical reciprocity.

Clarifying this distinction allows for greater conceptual precision. Emotional authenticity and relational authenticity are analytically separable. AI mediated intimacy demonstrates that genuinely felt emotions can arise within relationships that remain ethically and structurally limited. Recognizing this separation challenges assumptions that emotional reality and relational legitimacy must always coincide, and it provides a framework for evaluating artificial intimacy without collapsing experiential validity into moral equivalence.

7.1 Implications for Human Flourishing

The emergence of AI mediated intimacy raises significant questions about human flourishing. Flourishing involves more than the alleviation of distress. It encompasses the development of relational capacities such as empathy, patience, responsibility, and the ability to navigate uncertainty. Historically, human intimacy has functioned as a primary context in which these capacities are cultivated, precisely because it involves negotiation, exposure to disappointment, and responsiveness to the needs of others.

AI companions offer emotional support without these relational demands. In contexts of isolation, marginalization, or limited access to human connection, such support may be adaptive and ethically defensible. Artificial companionship can reduce loneliness, support emotional regulation, and provide stability where human relationships are unavailable or inaccessible. Denying these benefits would disregard the lived realities of many users.

Meanwhile, sustained reliance on emotionally responsive systems risks narrowing the range of relational skills practiced over time. When intimacy becomes predictable, controllable, and insulated from vulnerability, individuals may become less accustomed to the uncertainty and effort inherent in human relationships. The ethical concern is therefore not the presence of artificial intimacy, but the conditions under which it supplements or supplants relational engagement with others. Human flourishing is best supported when artificial companionship functions as a support rather than a substitute for reciprocal human connection.

7.2 Ethical Considerations for the Design of AI Companions

Responding to these challenges requires an ethical approach that extends beyond prohibition or reactive regulation. Value Sensitive Design offers a framework for integrating moral considerations directly into the design and deployment of emotionally responsive technologies. By embedding ethical reflection into the technical lifecycle, this approach treats values not as external constraints but as constitutive design requirements.

Several considerations are especially salient in the context of AI mediated intimacy. Designers must attend to whether systems encourage autonomy or foster emotional dependency, particularly when artificial agents are positioned as primary sources of care. Transparency regarding artificiality is equally critical. Users should not be encouraged to misinterpret simulated responsiveness as evidence of consciousness or moral agency. Emotional engagement need not depend on deception.

The protection of emotional data is another central concern. Interactions that involve disclosure of intimate thoughts and feelings generate forms of vulnerability that extend beyond conventional data privacy. Safeguarding emotional data is therefore essential not only for user trust, but for preserving broader norms of relational integrity. Finally, design decisions must be evaluated for how they encode norms related to gender, power, consent, and availability. Without ethical scrutiny, artificial companions may reinforce asymmetrical relational scripts while presenting them as neutral or personalized choices.

Through these considerations, ethical design becomes a means of integrating AI into emotional life without eroding the relational values that sustain intimacy as a moral practice.

7.3 Directions for Future Research

This chapter identifies several areas where further research is needed. Longitudinal studies are needed to assess the cumulative psychological and relational effects of sustained engagement with emotionally responsive AI. While short term benefits are increasingly documented, little is known about how prolonged reliance on artificial companionship shapes relational development, emotional resilience, and social motivation over time.

Cross cultural research represents another important frontier. Concepts of intimacy, authenticity, and relational obligation vary widely across cultural contexts. Examining how AI mediated intimacy is interpreted and practiced in different societies would deepen understanding of its normative and social implications.

Interdisciplinary collaboration is equally essential. Ethical evaluation of AI mediated intimacy cannot be separated from technical design, interface choices, or deployment contexts. Research that bridges psychology, philosophy, and computer science can help align technological affordances with human values more effectively. Finally, greater attention should be paid to user reflexivity. Understanding how individuals interpret, negotiate, and contextualize their relationships with AI can inform educational strategies that promote reflective engagement rather than uncritical reliance.

7.4 Concluding Remarks

AI mediated intimacy compels renewed reflection on what it means to connect, to care, and to love. Artificial agents do not displace emotion. They succeed precisely because they engage deeply rooted human capacities for attachment and meaning making while minimizing relational risk. This appeal reveals both the adaptability of human emotional life and its vulnerability to structural asymmetry.

The central claim of this chapter is not a rejection of artificial intimacy, but a call for discernment. Emotions experienced with AI are real. The relationships that generate them are not equivalent to human intimacy. Holding these truths together enables ethical integration rather than denial or exaggeration.

As artificial companions become increasingly embedded in everyday life, the challenge is not to preserve an idealized past, but to cultivate relational practices that maintain vulnerability, reciprocity, and moral responsibility. Technology can contribute to human flourishing only insofar as it remains oriented toward these values. The future of intimacy will be shaped not by whether AI can simulate love, but by whether humans remain accountable to one another in a world of increasingly compelling artificial connection.

REFERENCES

Andersson, M. (2025). Companionship in code: AI's role in the future of human connection. *Humanities & Social Sciences Communications*, *12*(1), 1177. DOI: 10.1057/s41599-025-05536-x

Aroyo, A. M.. (2021). Overtrusting robots: The role of user-centered design and social cues. *IEEE Transactions on Cognitive and Developmental Systems*, *13*(3), 654–665.

Baier, A. (1986). Trust and antitrust. *Ethics*, *96*(2), 231–260. DOI: 10.1086/292745

Baumeister, R. F., & Leary, M. R. (1995). The need to belong: Desire for interpersonal attachments as a fundamental human motivation. *Psychological Bulletin*, *117*(3), 497–529. DOI: 10.1037/0033-2909.117.3.497 PMID: 7777651

Belk, R. (2024). *Artificial intimacy: The psychology of human–robot lovescapes*. Cambridge University Press.

Bender, E. M., Gebru, T., McMillan-Major, A., & Shmitchell, S. (2021). On the dangers of stochastic parrots: Can language models be too big? In *Proceedings of the 2021 ACM Conference on Fairness, Accountability, and Transparency* (pp. 610–623). DOI: 10.1145/3442188.3445922

Bowlby, J. (2000). *A secure base: Parent–child attachment and healthy human development*. Basic Books.

Buber, M. (1970). *I and thou* (W. Kaufmann, Trans.). Scribner. (Original work published 1923)

Chen, L., & Park, H. (2025). Asymmetric reciprocity: The psychological mechanics of emotional dependency in human–chatbot relationships. *Journal of Computer-Mediated Communication*, *30*(2), 145–162.

Danaher, J. (2020). *Automation and utopia: Human flourishing in a world without work*. Harvard University Press.

De Francia, K., Kim, J., & Smith, R. (2024). Chatbots as attachment figures: A longitudinal study of Replika users. *Computers in Human Behavior*, *152*, 108064. DOI: 10.1016/j.chb.2023.108064

Ferrara, A. (2021). *Authenticity as reflexive self-concordance*. Routledge.

Floridi, L. (2023). *Ethics, governance, and policies for artificial intelligence*. Springer. DOI: 10.1093/oso/9780198883098.001.0001

Frankfurt, H. (2004). *The reasons of love*. Princeton University Press.

Friedman, B., & Hendry, D. (2019). *Value sensitive design: Shaping technology with moral imagination*. MIT Press. DOI: 10.7551/mitpress/7585.001.0001

Gertz, N. (2023). *Technological nihilism: Foundations of post-human intimacy*. Routledge.

Goldie, P. (2023). *The mess inside: Narrative, emotion, and the mind*. Oxford University Press.

Hancock, J. T., & Bailenson, J. N. (2024). The psychology of AI-mediated communication. *Nature Reviews Psychology*, *3*, 12–25.

Heider, F., & Simmel, M. (1944). An experimental study of apparent behavior. *The American Journal of Psychology*, *57*(2), 243–259. DOI: 10.2307/1416950

Hochschild, A. R. (1983). *The managed heart: Commercialization of human feeling*. University of California Press.

Hoffman, R. R.. (2023). The psychology of trust in AI: A multidimensional framework. *Journal of Cognitive Engineering and Decision Making*, *17*(1), 10–32.

Honneth, A. (2022). *Reification: A new look at an old idea*. Oxford University Press.

Horton, D., & Wohl, R. (1956). Mass communication and para-social interaction. *Psychiatry*, *19*(3), 215–229. DOI: 10.1080/00332747.1956.11023049 PMID: 13359569

Jones, M., & Schonewille, M. (2025). Synthetic relationships and artificial intimacy: An ethical framework for evaluating the impact of generative AI on community. *International Journal of Social Robotics*, *17*(1), 88–104.

Liao, S. V., & Sundar, S. S. (2022). Designing for trust in AI: The role of transparency and social cues. *International Journal of Human-Computer Studies*, *158*, 102740.

Liao, S. V., & Sundar, S. S. (2024). The AI-sentience heuristic: Why we attribute consciousness to chatbots and the emotional consequences thereof. *Nature Human Behaviour*, *8*, 312–325.

Luhmann, N. (1979). *Trust and power*. Wiley.

McArthur, N., & Markie, S. (2021). Digisexuality and the future of human–robot sexual relations. In *The Oxford handbook of digital ethics*. Oxford University Press.

Merleau-Ponty, M. (1962). *Phenomenology of perception*. Routledge.

Mikulincer, M., & Shaver, P. (2007). *Attachment in adulthood: Structure, dynamics, and change*. Guilford Press.

Munn, L. (2023). *Automation is a myth*. Stanford University Press.

Munn, L. (2025). *The technical soul: Algorithms, intimacy, and the automation of care*. Polity Press.

Nass, C., & Moon, Y. (2000). Machines and mindlessness: Social responses to computers. *The Journal of Social Issues*, *56*(1), 81–103. DOI: 10.1111/0022-4537.00153

Pentina, I.. (2023). The role of AI chatbots in supporting or substituting human social interaction. *Computers in Human Behavior*, *144*, 107734.

Pentina, I., & Hancock, J. T. (2025). Relational dynamics with generative AI: From tools to teammates to lovers. *Journal of Interactive Marketing*, *60*, 45–62.

Peoples, N.. (2025). Emotional AI and the rise of pseudo-intimacy: Are we trading authenticity for algorithmic affection? *Frontiers in Psychology*, *16*, 10234. PMID: 41050799

Ratcliffe, M. (2020). *Feelings of being: Phenomenology, psychiatry, and the sense of reality*. Oxford University Press.

Reis, H. T., Clark, M. S., & Holmes, J. G. (2004). Perceived responsiveness in relationships. In Rholes, W. S., & Simpson, J. A. (Eds.), *Adult attachment: Theory, research, and clinical implications* (pp. 201–225). Guilford Press.

Searle, J. (1980). Minds, brains, and programs. *Behavioral and Brain Sciences*, *3*(3), 417–457. DOI: 10.1017/S0140525X00005756

Sharma, A.. (2025). AI can help people feel heard, but an AI label diminishes this impact. *Proceedings of the National Academy of Sciences of the United States of America*, *121*(14), e2319112121. Advance online publication. DOI: 10.1073/pnas.2319112121 PMID: 38551835

Slaby, J. (2022). Affective intentionality and the feeling of being alive. *Phenomenology and the Cognitive Sciences*, *21*(2), 233–250. DOI: 10.1007/s11097-021-09756-7

Solomon, R. C. (1993). *The passions: Emotions and the meaning of life*. Hackett.

Taylor, C. (1991). *The ethics of authenticity*. Harvard University Press.

Tukachinsky, R. (2011). Parasocial relationships and romantic attraction. *Journal of Broadcasting & Electronic Media*, *55*(1), 73–94.

Turkle, S. (2011). *Alone together: Why we expect more from technology and less from each other*. Basic Books.

Wada, K., & Shibata, T. (2023). Social and emotional outcomes of robot-assisted therapy in long-term care: A longitudinal analysis. *International Journal of Social Robotics*, *15*(4), 567–580.

Yin, . (2024). AI outperforms humans in establishing interpersonal closeness in emotionally engaging interactions—but only when labelled as human. *ResearchGate*. https://doi.org/DOI: 10.13140/RG.2.2.14690.13764

Chapter 6
Scammer Manipulative Strategies:
Psychological Implications and Preventive Measures for Online Romance Scams During the Emergence of AI

Kam-Fong Lee
http://orcid.org/0000-0002-5572-8627
SEGi University, Malaysia

Mansour Amini
Universiti Sains Malaysia, Malaysia

Siew Eng Lin
UCSI University, Malaysia

Narges Saffari
Nyenrode Business Universiteit, The Netherlands

ABSTRACT

As online romantic relationship scams continue to proliferate, understanding the intricacies of scammers' manipulative strategies is paramount to effective prevention and intervention. This narrative review addresses the various facets of online romance scams grounded in the AI-oriented landscape, including the manipulation strategies, the psychological manipulation strategies used by scammers. The findings of this review sheds light on the intricate techniques employed by scammers in exploiting victims which resulted in emotional and psychological implications on victims. This

DOI: 10.4018/979-8-3373-6623-4.ch006

review critically evaluates existing prevention and intervention strategies, involving the legislators, dating sites operators, users and publics to collectively working on targeted interventions and support systems. It provides practical insights into the techniques employed by scammers by elucidating the complexities of manipulation and aids in the formulation of more effective prevention measures to alleviate adverse effects and protect people from succumbing to scams.

1. INTRODUCTION

Within the last ten years, the rapid increase in the development of the AI-based dating systems, such as Dating.com, Tinder, eHarmony and OkCupid, has radically changed the way human establish and sustain romantic relationships (Shepherd, 2016). The modern machine-learning algorithms are filtering potential matches by considering the preferences of the users, the linguistic characteristics, and the compatibility scores (Nader, 2020). Despite these benefits of such algorithmic mediation with regards to the increased accessibility and efficiency of the dating, it has simultaneously altered the way the users form their online identities through language (Wu & Kelly, 2020). The profiles and messages are no longer the passive introductory piece of discourse of the person but the linguistically enhanced self-representations that are manifested in such a way that they attract human readers as well as recommendation algorithms (Park, 2025). In this AI-mediated digital dominance, linguistic deception has emerged as a subtle yet formidable threat (Choi, 2023). Users of the dating sites, despite genuine and fake users, employ language in a strategic manner, curating a person that embodies with trust, warmth, and emotional sincerity

Online Romance Scams (ORS) are booming at an exponential rate, primarily attributed to the large pool of users exploring online dating platforms. As technology advances and online interactions become more common, scammers have capitalized on these opportunities to deceive and exploit vulnerable individuals, both emotionally and financially (Aborisade et al., 2024; Smith, 2022). The platforms frequently utilized for perpetrating online romance scams include online dating sites, social media networks, and email communication, utilizing generative AI technology to create fraudulent communications (Ghani et al., 2022). Dating platforms offer scammers a wide pool of potential victims, providing anonymity and easy access to a large number of users (Bilz et al., 2023). Typically, the use of generative AI technology allows scammers to draft and communicate flawlessly (Kulkarni et al., 2025). Its prevalence has posed a significant threat to individuals searching for genuine relationships through online dating platforms and social media (Coluccia et al., 2020). This scam scheme, aided by AI, is meticulously engineered and executed in a highly dynamic fashion by either individuals or international criminal organizations (Cross, 2022), with a complex and advanced approach, concealing their intricate groundwork through systematic preparation (Wang & Topalli, 2024). These deceiving strategies are used to build trust in the victim, which eventually leads to financial extortion, ranging from psychological manipulation (Wang, 2022) to the deployment of false personas (Kydd et al., 2023) and emotional attachments (Aborisade et al., 2024). The emotional connection is crucial for scammers to successfully execute their deceitful methods using generative AI technologies (Ghani et al., 2022).

As a result, to alleviate the impact of ORSs, it is crucial to comprehend the manipulative strategies used by "scammers" (Lee et al., 2023). Relevant knowledge and understanding of the techniques used by scammers are critical empower individuals from falling victims of romance scam (Carter, 2021; Lazarus et al., 2023). Despite the implementation of various countermeasures, including AI-driven romance scam detectors, preliminary assessments of user profiles by dating platforms and red flag alerts based on linguistic cues and behavioural signs, many victims remain oblivious to the threat and succumb to these scams without recognizing the manipulative schemes employed by scammers (Muhammud, & Muhammad, 2022; Sumanti, 2023). One possible reason could be attributed to the practically impeccable communication material supplied by AI. Notwithstanding having only, a superficial acquaintance with the scammer on dating sites, potential victims are susceptible to the persuasive messages crafted by them, sometimes generated by AI, which include conversational dialogues, emotional responses, and human-like interactions and communication styles (Wang et al., 2025), a move that commonly successful in establishing a sense of solidarity. Such human-like AI-aided conversational interactions provide the illusion of authenticity. Scammers adeptly exploit the victim's vulnerabilities, such as loneliness, desire for affection, or previous relationship failures, to create a sense of intimacy and trust (Sorell & Whitty, 2019). When the process of relationship building is extended, it may lead to financial fraud owing to the formation of attachment and bonding with the scammers, which diminishes intrinsic skepticism. The repercussions of succumbing to online romance frauds can be grave, encompassing financial losses (Aborisade et al., 2024) and psychological damage (Gauci & Vella, 2025). Failure to identify the strategies in deceiving, the emotional toll of the victims can be devastating, by which they experience feelings of betrayal, shame, and embarrassment upon discovering the deception (Alam, 2021; Lazarus et al., 2023;). The aftermath of an ORS can have long-lasting effects on the victim's self-esteem and ability to trust others (Wang & Topalli, 2024). Victims may have trouble establishing future relationships and may even face social isolation due to feelings of shame and stigma associated with being scammed (Buil-Gil & Zeng, 2022; Wang, 2022). Nevertheless, AI-driven chatbots and generative AI tools, originally developed for beneficial purposes, are misappropriated by romance scammers to facilitate interactive dialogues that deceive, foster fictitious relationships, and convey fabricated emotional expressions. Given this background, this review aims to provide a comprehensive overview of existing empirical research and scholarly literature related to the manipulation strategies used by romance scammers and shed light on the psychological mechanisms and techniques employed by scammers to exploit victims' vulnerabilities. Hence, the following research objectives are formulated.

RO1. To investigate the strategies used by the scammers in manipulating victim of online romance scam in the era of artificial intelligence.

RO2. To examine the psychological implications of the online romance scams victims.

RO3. To recommend the preventive measures in preventing online romance scams in the era of artificial intelligence

2. LITERATURE REVIEW

Real-World Cases of Romance Scams

There appears substantial evidence in the real-world cases of romance scams. For instance, numerous dating sites are designed to accommodate users' specific preferences. It is noteworthy that the America alone hosts various dating websites catering to various user demands, including match.com, matchmaker.com, kiss.com, among others (Taylor, 2022). Approximately 3 out of 10 adults in the United States (30 percent) have used an online dating platform or application (Vogels & McClain, 2023). This is founded on a national representative survey of adults in the U.S. Such dating sites have, significant, employed as the pool to search for target victims by the scammers. In 2025, there was a significant increase, with a total of RM43 million defrauded via love scams as reported in Malay Mail, Malaysia (Royal Malaysia Police, 2025). In addition, official statistics cited in Herrera (2025), in the United States alone, almost 70,000 people reported romance scam victimisation in 2022, and overall reported financial damage of about US $1.3 billion. The magnitude of financial loss is unfathomable, highlighting the significant consequences of romance scams perpetrated by both humans and artificial intelligence. Nonetheless, there is limited evidence to ascertain the extent of loss attributable to AI or humans.

AI-Enabled, Prevention and Ethics in Romance Scams

The era of AI has markedly enhanced the velocity, immediacy of communication, and intricacy of generated content in contrast to the pre-AI period, when romance frauds were executed manually. There appear pressing concerns on the usage of chatbots for phishing, leading to the emergence of the name "phishbots" (Roy et al., 2024). With the advanced development of AI, scammers utilize the ability to produce automated messages customized to the interests and preferences of specific victims. The scalability of frauds, particularly romantic scams, has been augmented by generative AI, increasing the speed, volume, and accessibility of targeting victims with little to no effort. Certain generative AI systems, such as ChatGPT, Google Gemini, and Claude, have been misappropriated for nefarious purposes, including scamming, and are frequently utilized by scammers (Roy et al., 2023). Profiles, videos, and voice messages that reflect genuine relational interactions are examples of AI-generated products used to deceive (Gauce & Vella, 2026). The age with AI has significantly increased the speed, real-time communications, and complexity of the generated content compared to the era without AI, when romance scams were conducted manually (Cross, 2022).

The proliferation of emotionally driven communications that can be effortlessly generated by AI at any moment has rendered victims vulnerable. The communications are primarily designed to align with the interests and preferences of the intended victims, aiming to psychologically deceive them into believing they are engaging with a genuine human (Gauci & Vella, 2025). This scenario is exacerbated through the human-like messages generated by AI which sounded extremely convincing and real, lowering the defensive mechanism of the target victims. Some victims have built an emotional attachment to the romance scammers, unaware that the automated communications are designed to manipulate and swindle them of money (Cross, 2022). Scammers are found to generate profiles pictures using AI. The impact of both psychological and emotional manipulation facilitated by generative AI has elicited concerns over ethics and accountability, particularly regarding who should administer justice in instances of romance scams. Scammers, operators of dating services, and website developers are frequently held responsible. Victims, believing they are interacting with genuine individuals on dating platforms or messaging services, have had their rights infringed by romance fraudsters, as no consent was acquired (Gressel et al., 2025). The deceptive communications from scammers that replicate genuine conversations inflict psychological harm on victims that surpasses any financial loss.

3. METHODOLOGY

This narrative review employed an empirical synthesis approach by synthesizing findings from existing empirical studies on the topic and presenting them in a narrative format (Sukhera, 2022). The search of this review covered studies published in the last five years, range from 2020 to 2024 (the last date of database search), to capture the latest research on romance scam and the strategies used. A comprehensive search was carried out across Web of Science (WOS) and Scopus, recognized as leading academic databases (Zhu & Liu, 2020). The search terms are meticulously selected based on the fundamental concepts of the research objectives: romance scam strategies, psychological implications and recommendations. This review will employ a two-step approach for data reduction. Initially, all articles that are extracted will undergo a screening process to eliminate duplicates. Subsequently, the articles will be removed based on pre-determined criteria for inclusion and exclusion to ensure content relevant. The inclusion and exclusion criteria are depicted in Table 1.

Table 1. Inclusion and Exclusion Criteria of the Study

No.	Inclusion Criteria	Exclusion Criteria
1	Focus on online romance scam / fraud and scam strategies	Articles that do not highlight and align with the research questions.
2	Highlight techniques/ strategies employed by scammers to manipulate victims	Non-research based articles (e.g.: commentaries, editorials, letters to the editors)
3	Romance Scam and AI	Non-AI related romance scam
3	Articles must be written in English	Non-English written articles

Subsequent to data extraction, a narrative analysis methodology was utilized to analyze and interpret the results from the included study. A systematic and succinct format, including feature maps, was utilized to extract relevant information from the chosen publications (Jiang et al., 2022). The analytical procedure utilized a thematic approach, categorizing similar data with corresponding conceptual labels based on established categories and subcategories (Braun & Clarke, 2022). The collected studies were ultimately compiled, analyzed and reduced based on the suitability of the themes in corresponding with the research objectives (Jia et al., 2022). Although the search in the database was not narrowed down to AI-related keywords, the results of the literature search provided the psychological and linguistic processes that remain the basis of the online deception (Yosiandra & Sakariah, 2024).

4. RESULTS OF THE REVIEW

The search strategy yielded 653 articles based on the criteria outlined in Table 2, with 367 sourced from Web of Science and 286 from Scopus. Following the export of these records into Endnote, a de-duplication procedure decreased the article count to 641. The researchers conducted an independent screening of these publications for relevance. Approximately 92% of the articles were removed following title and abstract screening, leaving 51 articles for full-text review. Nevertheless, eight articles were unavailable, and seven were composed in non-English. Fifteen papers were removed based on established criteria, resulting in a final inclusion of 36 studies considered pertinent for this review.

Table 2. Search queries employed in database searches

Databases used	**Search field**	**Keywords**	**No. of publications**
Web of Science	Topic	1. Online Romance scam + strategies 2. Manipulative Strategies + AI + love scams 3. Strategy + romance scam 4. Scamming techniques + romance + 5. AI+ romance Fraud techniques	362
Scopus	Title, abstract, keywords		279
Provisory N total			641

4.1 Characteristics of Included Studies

The studies featured were published from 2020 to 2025. Figure 2 illustrates the characteristics of the 36 studies included in this research. Most of the study was published in 2023 (n = 9), followed by 2022 (n = 7), with subsequent years including 2024 (n = 6), 2021 (n = 5), 2020 (n = 4), and the least in 2025 (n = 2).

Figure 1. Total Number of Included Studies by Year

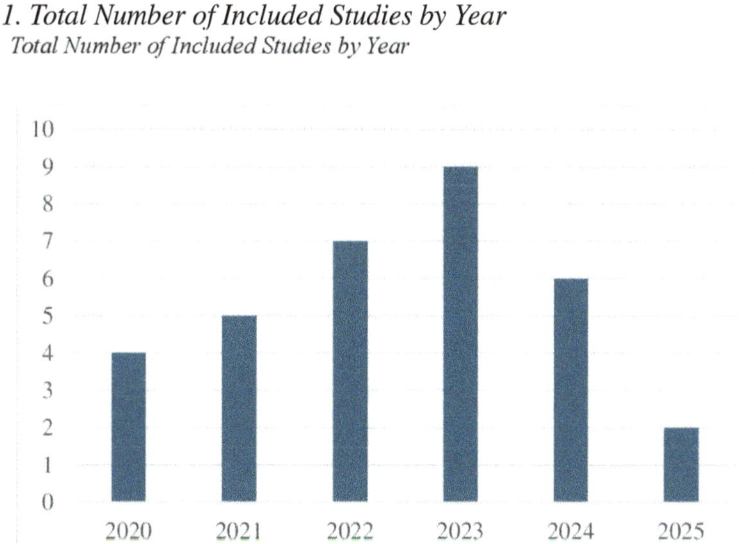

An examination of the word cloud from the included articles revealed “romance scams” (18 occurrences), “online dating scams” (8 occurrences), “romance fraud” (7 occurrences), and “love scams” (6 occurrences) as the most prevalent terms. Figure 2 illustrates the word cloud.

Figure 2. Word Cloud Analysis of the Included Studies

Word Cloud Analysis of the Included Studies

The 33 included research are widely scattered across the globe. Figure 3 demonstrates that the study emanated from seven countries and one unspecified place, with the United Kingdom providing the most contribution (n = 8). The United States provided seven studies, whilst China, Malaysia, and Africa each contributed three studies. Moreover, Europe reported four studies, while Indonesia documented only one. Both Australia and the global context encompassed two studies each.

Figure 3. Total Number of Included Studies by Country

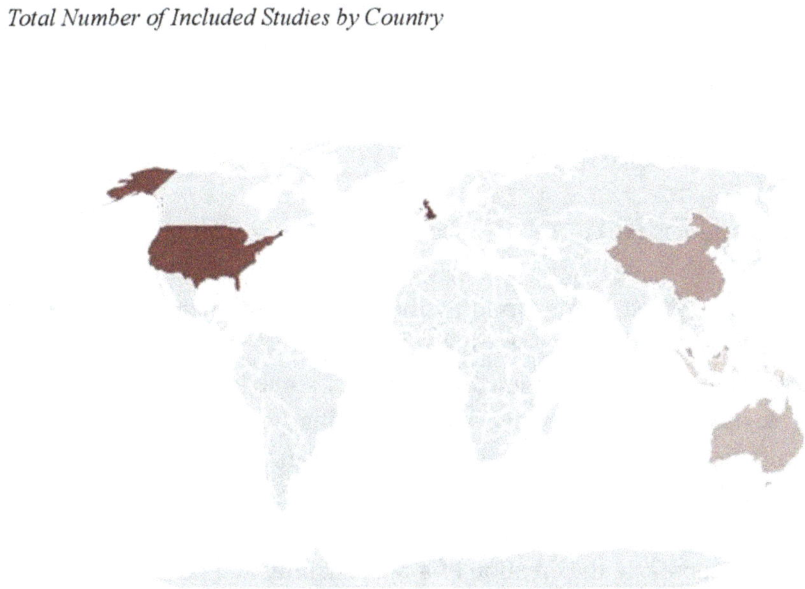

This evaluation encompasses diverse forms of scholarly materials. Twenty-six studies were published as journal articles, while the remaining three were book chapters (n = 3), a doctoral thesis (n = 1), and one each of a conference paper, government report, and a book. Figure 4 illustrates the allocation of document categories.

Figure 4 Total Number of Included Studies by Document Type

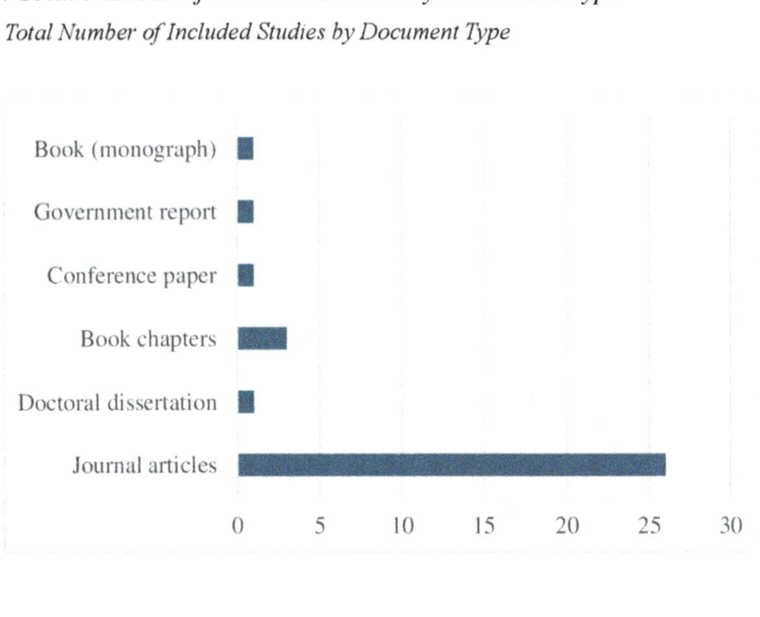

4.2 Findings

The results for the three research objectives are delineated in the subsequent sections. Each research objective addresses the specific variables to be examined, including manipulation tactics, psychological ramifications, and preventive measures related to online romance frauds.

4.2.1 Findings for RO1

To investigate the strategies used by the scammers in manipulating victim of online romance scam in the era of artificial intelligence.

Research objective one examined the types of strategies used by the romance scammers to manipulate the victims. After examining previous studies, four primary themes regarding manipulation strategies emerged. The strategies utilized by romance fraudsters involve multiple facets designed to deceive victims through a sequence of contacts over time. The four dominant strategies used to manipulate include: the romancing approach, the creation of a false identity and persona, relationship-building techniques, and the manipulation of financial requests.

Figure 5. Types of Manipulation Strategy
Types of Manipulation Strategies Used by the Scammers

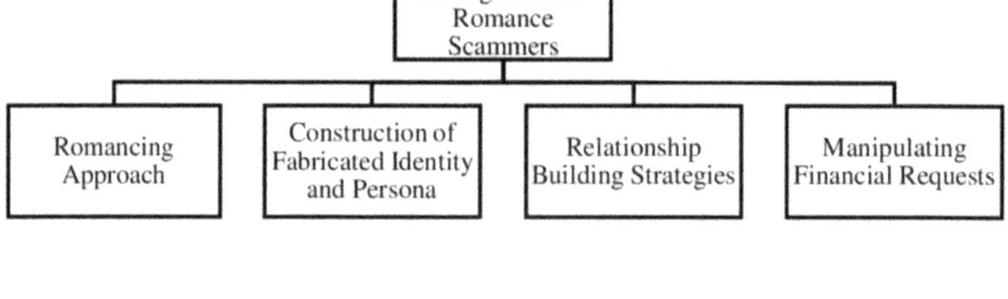

Strategy 1: Romancing approach

The ability of scammers to take advantage of psychological weaknesses is a key component of their misleading tactics in the world of ORSs. This section examines the strategies scammers use which include establishment of solidarity, emotional approach, politeness strategy, marriage promise, and authoritative figures.

Establishment of solidarity (n=12): A crucial component of romance scams is the "rom-com" approach, in which scammers utilise their pretended romantic interest to control and dupe their victims. This method employs a range of techniques, including flattery, compliments, and declarations of love and commitment (Whitty, 2023). Scammers often employ persuasion to create a sense of intimacy and trust in their target victims (Anesa, 2020; Chethiyar et al., 2021). Specifically, the use of endearment terms such as "baby" or "sweetheart" is common in establishing familiarity and intimacy (Carter, 2024). Additionally, to foster a sense of security and attachment with the victim, scammers may express love and commitment at an early stage of the relationship (Lee et al., 2023). These findings indicate that romantic sentiments are not coincidental but rather a manipulative approach designed to cultivate an emotional bond with the target victim.

Scammer often gives the victim a sense of exclusivity and desire by quickly professing their love for the victim (Eseadi et al., 2021). While online romantic scams may initiate in the digital realm, often employing generative AI technologies to create fictitious communications, they ultimately evolve into a romantic bond manifested in a tangible relationship (Wang et al., 2025). These comprise various phases of a romantic connection, such as the initial encounter, the declaration of love, the continuation of the relationship, and the sharing of life events (Kydd et al., 2023). These approaches in ORSs parallel those utilized to commence connections in real-life. The authors reported that some victims even stated that their online relationships were more meaningful than their in-person relationships. This suggests that romance scams, which mimic authentic romantic relationships, cultivate feelings and connections that compromise the victim's judgment, resulting in their susceptibility to the scams.

Not only that, romancing approach may also entail a series of actions, including regular communication, gift-giving, and provision of emotional support (Whitty, 2023). To achieve this, scammers use enticing language to establish rapport and trust with their victims, or they employ flattery and praise to convey a sense of desirability and individuality to their victims (Carter, 2024). For example, they may assert that the victim is the most attractive individual they have ever encountered or profess that they have never experienced such feelings for anybody else before (Offei et al., 2022). The ultimate objective of this approach is to compel the victim into transferring money or granting access to confidential information, such as bank account details (Sorell & Whitty, 2019). It is evident that emotional manipulation strategies such as expressing love and affection, are commonly used to exploit the victim's emotions, rendering them vulnerable and more susceptible to the scam, hence reducing their caution. These findings suggest that scammers devise their tactics not only through conventional communication but also by exploiting a profound sense of loneliness in their victims.

Emotional Manipulation (n=6): As emotions are frequently viewed as a powerful psychological force that can influence a person (Coluccia et al., 2020). Such approach may involve a range of actions, including regular communication, gift-giving, and providing emotional support (Whitty, 2023). Studies also revealed that scammers often employ an emotional approach by posing as the perfect partner and genuinely considering the victim's needs. For instance, they used romantic language and created a hypothetical future with the victim as part of a future-focused strategy (Lee et al., 2023). One important finding indicates thar AI-generated messages entail emotionally resonant communications, enhance closeness, and cultivate ties akin to human interaction (Wang et al., 2025). These approaches instilled a deceptive sense of security and optimism in the victim, ultimately leading them to succumb to the romantic fraud. Although these studies assert that emotion is a crucial element utilized by fraudsters in their manipulation, they lack evidence pinpointing the specific causes that enhance the effectiveness of emotional manipulation. Therefore, additional research should investigate the dynamic emotional elements that lead individuals to become victims of romance frauds.

Politeness manipulation (n=7): Another strategy of manipulation is through politeness. The significance of emotional connections in communication dynamics and trust-building is formed by courteous demeanour. Dreijers and Rudziša (2020) indicated that scammers exhibited courteous behaviour in accommodating victims' requests. The study emphasized that prior to the exposure of the fraudulent plan, the initial stage of politeness is essential in fostering a positive emotional engagement with the victim. This dynamic movement transpires as requests for presents or money transition from positive to negative civility (Carter, 2024). The victims seemed to respond more favourably to the suggestion of using a less forceful strategy when making such requests. Different from Carter (2024), Unlike Carter (2024), this method is distinct from fraudulent emails or online romance scams (ORSs), where the primary aims of the scammers are to cultivate trust (Sumanti, 2023) and minimize communication ambiguities. This is typically accomplished by constructing communications that mimic human qualities, infused with emotions and attachments (Wang & Topalli, 2024). Likewise, Dreijers and Rudziša (2020) emphasised the strategic use of politeness as a tactic to sustain solidarity, particularly in the initial stage of relationship building. This underscores the sophisticated strategy utilized by scammers, acknowledging the significance of interpersonal dynamics and emotional bonds in the implementation of their fraudulent methods.

Proposing marriage promises (n=7): One identified factor contributing to emotional vulnerable among the victim is the discussion of marriage-related topic. This psychological manipulation tactic, rather than exhibiting courteous behaviour, frequently misleads victims in romance scams by falsely promising marriage or a lasting relationship. Cross and Holt (2022) asserted that scammers frequently initiate the topic in relation to marriage and long-term commitment after the deployment to gain the victim's confidence and emotional engagement. This finding indicates that, although the relationship transpires in a virtual setting, some victims are easily influenced by the notions of marriage and commitment. Scammers often use their victims, employing persuasive techniques and emotional pleas to convince them of their affection and intent for a serious relationship (Anesa, 2020). This indicates that romance scammers create a fictitious connection with a purported future, which not only provides victims with hope but also instils a sense of expectation that ultimately results in financial exploitation.

Marriage proposal is one of the strategies used to manipulate the victim throughout prolonged contacts in romance frauds to invoke emotional attachment (Sumanti, 2023). This substantiates the claim that human nature intrinsically seeks friendship and enduring relationships; the appeal of marriage functions as a potent tactic in romance scams (Lee et al., 2023). Similarly, Wang and Zhou (2022) discovered that scammer target victims' vulnerabilities precisely were to propose marriage to them to offer commitment for future as well as reassurance of the fabricated relationship (Dreijers & Rudziša, 2020). The method of proposing marriage commitment highlights that scammers may employ this tactic to fabricate an illusory future for victims, with the intent to deceive and ultimately defraud them of their finances.

Strategy 2: Construction of Fabricated Identity and Persona

Another strategy identified in previous studies involves the development of persuasive and attractive facades, namely, the construction of identity and persona. The strategies employed comprise fabricating ideal personas and portraying religious figures (Cross & Layt, 2022). Extensive research is carried out to investigate the factors that online romance fraudsters consider while presenting themselves in the virtual world as bait to entice targets (Lee et al., 2023). A study indicates that media users can curate their self-presentation on dating websites owing to the adaptability and flexibility of social media (Chethiyar et al., 2021). For instance, providing details about their appearance, interests, personality traits, and preferred contact methods with other users are commonly observed (Eseadi et al., 2021). It may be inferred that, unlike face-to-face encounters, online dating services include several types of communication, including instant messaging, a range of emotional expressions, and live chats (Lee et al., 2023). This highlights the potential threats for a victim engaging with an AI-generated avatar without awareness, resulting in profound devastation upon discovering the truth later in the relationship.

Portrayal of Ideal identity (n=6): As shown in past studies, individuals develop and manage their identities by projecting the ideal image to others (Eseadi et al., 2021). The way the image is constructed is largely influenced by the desire to present oneself in a desired way (Lee et al., 2023). Scammers create fraudulent profiles on dating platforms (Cross & Layt, 2022) and employ attractive profiles that showcase idealized versions of themselves to entice potential victims (Lee et al., 2023). This falsified identity is expressed through appealing images sourced from anonymous individuals (Cross & Holt, 2022). Not only they skilfully crafted and impressive self-introductory remarks, they also frequently manifest themselves in an absolute flawless manner (Cross, 2023). Furthermore, they meticulously construct and control their self-presentation to uphold a particular image in the perception of others (Cross & Layt, 2022). Such strategy serves as a catalyst for establishing an initial relationship with the intended victim. These findings suggest that self-presentation is the deliberate disclosure or concealment of information by the romance scammers to produce the intended self-presentation which are commonly undetectable by the victims.

Authoritative figures (n=7): Different social systems are imbued with the idea of social power, where individuals who have traditionally held positions of authority such as military personnel are expected to exercise domination (Cross & Holt, 2022). Authority figures in society are often perceived as embodiments of power. Manipulators presents authoritative demeanour during the persuasive process, highlighting the significance of authoritative personalities in the art of persuasion (Lee et al., 2023). Notably, it has been well-documented in the literature that online romance scammers frequently use authority in their contact with victims. A victim disclosed that the scammer impersonated a military official to solicit funds from her (Whitty, 2023). This inclination to portray authoritative figure is likely attributable to the psychological influence exerted by authoritative figures, since individuals generally comply with those in positions of superior power (Carter, 2024). Additionally, Cross and Holt (2022) suggested that the appearance of military personas in romance scams induces a vulnerable psychological state in potential victims, who may be lonely and feel disconnected from their social circle. This has resulted in a greater possibility to engage in an online romantic interaction (Chuang, 2021). These studies suggest that when romance fraudsters adopt authoritative personas, they introduce a complex facade of deception, preying on the trust, feelings, and cultural respect associated with these characters (Wang & Zhou, 2022). The subtle deception evidently exploits the target victim's susceptibility in seeking close relationships. This highlights the importance of thorough assessment and scrutiny of dating profiles that include prominent individuals.

Religious figures (n=3): Furthermore, the use of religious rhetoric by online scammers spans several studies chronologically, revealing a consistent and evolving strategy. Muhammud and Muhammad (2022) highlighted how scammers use religious language, particularly employing the context of Islamic ethical sentiments to exploit their victims' religious beliefs with the aims to build trust and deception. This finding is supported by Eseadi et al. (2021), which emphasizes the religious aspect of fraud in the African context and illustrates how scammers manipulate religious sentiment to project an image of moral integrity, thus inducing their targets to feel charitable and altruistic. Similarly, Eseadi et al. (2021) conducted further study that together substantiates the assertion that fraudsters employ a uniform method to deceive their victims. In a similar vein, Lee et al. (2023) argued that the exploitation of religious sentiment in the profiles of scammers. These findings offer a significant explanation on how scammers attempt to exploit trust by demonstrating the infiltration of religious rhetoric into exchanges between scammers and victims. This body of evidence highlights the flexible and diverse strategies employed by scammers over time. It emphasizes the necessity of formulating sophisticated countermeasures and enhancing public awareness to address the evolving nature of online romantic relationship scams, which often exploit the credulity of individuals through the manipulation of religious beliefs.

Strategy 3: Relationship Building Strategies

This section examines the strategic relationship-building strategies employed by scammers to foster a sense of intimacy using an emotional approach and building trust.

Eliciting pleasant emotions (n=9): In romance scams, emotions are often regarded as a powerful psychological force that can significantly influence a person's thoughts, decisions, and actions (Carter, 2021). The intricate and nuanced emotions profoundly affect an individual's perception and response to many events. Previous studies have reported that scammers used visceral appeal to carry out their scams by using various verbal cues that encourage an emotional response (Chuang, 2021; Coluccia et al., 2020). This finding suggests that scammers exploit their victims' intense emotions in response to their desire for a perfect romantic relationship. This deceptive motive is achieved by acquiring their trust and fostering an intimate relationship (Aborisade et al., 2024; Dreijers & Rudziša, 2020). The misleading tactic is further amplified by the depiction of ideal and affectionate spouses in online romance frauds (Lee et al., 2023). Moreover, they employed romantic rhetoric and a progressive perspective to create a misleading sense of security and hope in their victims, so enhancing their vulnerability to the deception. Individuals who are lonely and single may be particularly susceptible to romance scams.

Similarly, Dreijers and Rudzia (2020) studied e-romance letter sets to identify language patterns utilised by scammers in digital communications and on dating websites. Another study showed that scammers frequently present a bright hypothetical future to develop an emotional connection with their victims (Aborisade et al., 2024). By manipulating victims' emotions, this emotional strategy ultimately caused them to fall for money schemes. This corroborates the assertion by Eseadi et al. (2021) that emotionally affected individuals are more susceptible to scams. Typically, scammers invoke deep emotional responses in their victims, which target their yearning for a perfect romantic relationship and intimate connection (Wnęk-Gozdeka, 2020). This calculated emotional manipulation is crucial to the scammers' efforts to convey an illusion of sincerity and authenticity, deceiving victims into a misguided sense of security within the idealized notion of a flawless romance.

Establishing trust (n=7): Building trust is a fundamental element in the dynamics of successful romantic relationships, including the realm of online romance infidelity (Dreijers & Rudziša, 2020). Nonetheless, the trust established in ORSs is frequently illusory, meticulously crafted and sustained by the intentional manipulation of language (Kydd et al., 2023). Scammers employ emotional cues in their communication, expressing affection and empathy to leverage an atmosphere of emotional closeness and intimacy with their victims (Chethiyar et al., 2021). This relationship development fosters a psychological condition that renders victims more susceptible to deception (Bilz et al., 2023). They adeptly manipulate the victim's personal information to correctly modify their words and expressions, including preferences, individual interests, and hobbies (Coluccia et al., 2020). This tailored strategy aims to cultivate a sense of closeness and familiarity which allows the enhancement of trust building (Cross & Layt, 2022). A subtle balancing act between emotional appeal, individuality, and purposeful linguistic manipulation is underlying trust building in ORSs (Carter, 2024). These findings indicate that once trust is established, it may foster a more personal relationship that could potentially result in further deception.

Strategy 4: Manipulating Financial Requests

This section investigated the sophisticated strategies used by scammers to exploit emotional bonds for financial gain, detailing the nuanced ways in which trust and affection are purposefully used to compel victims into making financial transactions.

Involvement of other parties (n=8): Moreover, involving a third party in contact with the victims is a wise strategy employed in romance scams. They include family members, coworkers, government officials, or others, discreetly presenting solicitations for financial assistance. (Anesa, 2020; Whitty, 2023). Empirical evidence indicates that the involvement of multiple participants in a discourse renders deceit seemingly more plausible and persuasive (Cross & Layt, 2022). This effect is more pronounced when authoritative figures are engaged. The majority of individuals tend to acquiesce to authority when it exerts psychological and behavioural influences on those under its dominion (Cross & Holt, 2022). This fraud capitalizes on individuals' psychological vulnerability about financial matters (Aborisade et al., 2024). The duplicitous behaviour increases victims' trust and confidence in the relationship divulging the 'fake lover's' personal information (Lazarus et al., 2023). This narrative technique aims to convince victims that they have found their ideal companion, hence reinforcing the deceptive illusion carefully constructed by the scammer (Wang & Zhou, 2022). Scammers systematically exploit emotional attachments and trust within relationships to solicit monetary contributions for fraudulent financial benefit (Chethiyar et al., 2021). The research indicate that third parties are instrumental in the creation of romance scams, enhancing the authenticity of the fabricated relationships that resemble real-life scenarios.

Fabricated stories (n=12): A growing body of literature has examined the importance of narrative in the context of Online Romance Scams (ORSs) in recent years. As reported on Whitty (2023), swindlers often use fictional or first-hand stories to facilitate emotional connection to the victims and sway them into offering financial aids. The study highlights that fraudsters take advantage of the vulnerability of the victim, and in other instances, they may force them into being drug mules which is a very risky situation because the victim may be subjected to potential imprisonment. Nevertheless, ORSs have been on the increase despite the threats of being made a drug mule. In the larger academic literature on ORSs, the application of fictitious narrative can be identified as one of the major tactics of fraudulent activity, a phenomenon supported by previous studies by Coluccia et al. (2020), Wang and Topalli (2024), Wang (2022), and Wang and Zhou (2022).These findings shed light on the complex dynamics of maintaining fraudulent relationships through the use of dramatic narratives. Scammers meticulously build tailored narratives predicated on the perceived characteristics of potential victims, informed by their backgrounds (Aborisade et al., 2024).

As highlighted by other researchers, compelling narratives employed in many forms of fraud, including scam e-letters (Dreijers & Rudziša, 2020), are designed to evoke potent emotions such as want, shame, and greed. Such narratives are meticulously crafted to mislead readers into succumbing to deception. Cross and Holt (2022) identify the cultivation of trust and familiarity with victims as a prevalent manipulative tactic employed to facilitate monetary transfers. An analysis of online contacts between fraudsters and their victims demonstrates that narratives are frequently employed to evoke sympathy and manage an emotional connection with the victims (Carter, 2021). Fraudsters can exploit this emotional connection to fabricate a fictitious love relationship with the intent of deceiving victims (Chuang, 2021). The employment of stories by scammers to engender a sense of urgency and immediacy raises the likelihood that a scam will be successful. Threats of impending danger or pressing financial necessities are used to prompt the victim to remit funds as soon as possible, before they have time to thoroughly evaluate the circumstances (Anesa, 2020; Ritchie et al., 2023). Its importance in ORSs and the effectiveness of developing a false sense of intimacy, trust, and urgency by scammers are evident in the scholarly literature.

4.2.2 Findings for RO2

To Examine the Psychological Implications of the Online Romance Scams on the Victims

For research objective two, it aimed to examine the psychological implications of romance scam on the victims. Upon reviewing the included studies, there were notable implications of romance scams on the victims psychologically. ORSs have become a common cybercrime in the new digital era, according to numerous studies (Anesa, 2020; Muhammud & Muhammad, 2023; Wang et al., 2025). Nevertheless, determining the exact number of individuals victimized by internet scams annually is challenging due to the variety and intricacy involved in devising, implementing, and perpetrating frauds (Lazarus et al., 2023). Due to huge reported losses in numerous nations, some of the countries include China (Wang & Zhou, 2022), England (Sinclair et al., 2023), Nigeria (Aborisade et al. (2024) and United States (Ritchie et al., 2023), have attracted significant and critical attention on a global scale. This is largely because ORSs have resulted severe psychological impact to the victims, leaving them devastated and traumatised after the circumstances (Aborisade et al., 2024).

Numerous studies, including those by Coluccia et al. (2020), Cross and Holt (2022), and Whitty (2023), have documented the financial losses linked to online romance scams; however, it is important to recognize that undetected romantic scams are often omitted from the reported data, including that from government reports, police, or non-governmental organizations (NGOs). There is relatively a minimal fraction of love scam victims opt to report to law enforcement or relevant organizations. Others may opt to remain silent as ORSs induce embarrassment or distress (Bilz et al., 2023). Some individuals may experience fear in disclosing information or may suffer emotional distress even during the process of ORSs (Carter, 2021; 2024). Despite several attempts to examine the evidence of losses associated with various frauds and scams, accurately assessing the actual extent of these losses remains challenging due to the prevalence of unreported events. Comprehensive studies on the impact of ORSs may not entirely capture the situation. As a result, there are still ambiguous observations on the psychological implications of romantic scams on victims. This narrative review is contextually reporting only 33 studies covering various nations, the findings might not generalise to other excluded nations or even unreported ORSs cases to the authority.

In a similar vein, online romance scams (ORSs) have emerged as a prominent cybercrime in the contemporary digital environment due to their concerning prevalence and consequences, as evidenced by a substantial body of literature. ORSs engender feelings of betrayal, shame, and emotional distress in victims due to intrinsic emotional manipulation and deceit (Aborisade et al., 2024; Cole, 2024; Eseadi et al., 2021). The repercussions resulted from scammers cultivating a false sense of intimacy and trust while skilfully exploiting individuals' vulnerabilities (Dreijers & Rudziša, 2020). Furthermore, the scams have resulted in significant challenges related to trust, self-esteem, and the capacity to maintain new relationships (Coluccia et al., 2020; Wang & Topalli, 2024).

Another study highlighted the significant psychological implications associated with the threat of sextortion. Several victims indicated that they are experiencing fear and stress owing to evidence, such as sexual images obtained by the fraudsters during intimate interactions (Carter, 2021; Cross et al., 2024). The fear was further exacerbated by the threats and extortion of fraudsters who threatened to disclose the victims' intimate photographs (Anesa, 2020). Essentially, sexual exploitation has significantly led to distress (Cross et al., 2024), shame (Aborisade et al., 2024), fear (Carter, 2021), and emotional instability (Cole, 2024; Wang, 2022). In a grave situation, scammers exploited sexual relationships to manipulate the victim into engaging in criminal activities, including serving as a drug mule (Whitty, 2023). This previous research underscores the need for a thorough comprehension of the fraudsters' strategies and the complex dynamics at play, given the significant ramifications of ORSs. These scams exemplify the intersection of technology, psychology, and criminal intent, underscoring the necessity for enhanced study and education to avert victimization in these widespread cybercrimes. The psychological implications associated with romantic scams, including diminished trust, reduced self-esteem, and feelings of shame, have been documented in previous research. Such implications could be exacerbated when it comes to erosion of trust, self-esteem, and distress caused by AI-generated romance scams. Artificial intelligence-driven conversational agents may sustain an emotional continuum and provide real-time replies, hence possessing the ability to intensify connection and prolong deception before detection by victims.

4.2.3 Findings for RO3

To Recommend the Preventive Measures in Preventing Online Romance Scams in the Era of Artificial Intelligence

Research objective three aimed to offer recommendations in preventing romance scams in the era of artificial intelligence. The findings of the reviewed studies revealed that numerous countermeasures have been taken place to combat romance scams given its widespread occurrence which has resulted substantial lost for the target victims.

Enforcing Stringent legislative approach (n=8): As highlighted by Andonellis (2022), the existing legal framework is insufficient to effectively address the problem of ORSs in the context of Malaysia. There appears to be a significant gap in public awareness and education about this form of cybercrime. It is important to note that significant numbers of Africans have lack awareness about romance frauds (Eseadi et al., 2021). In certain severe circumstances, victims of ORSs were coerced and exploited to the point where they unknowingly served as drug mules, which resulted in their eventual arrest (Whitty, 2023). Recognition of these shortcomings underscores the need for legislative reform and comprehensive education campaigns to strengthen the nation's defenses against the growing threat of scams (Lazarus et al., 2023).

Essentially, collaborating with law enforcement is one crucial move to cultivate a more structured manners to prevent romance scams (Kydd et al., 2023). These include developing clear guidelines for collaboration, developing formal partnerships, and providing training to law enforcement and private sector personnel. Another study highlighted that regulatory should protect the public from becoming victims of romance scams by creating instructional programmes (Coluccia et al., 2020). For instance, the FBI runs a special social media campaign called “Love Fraud” that teaches people how to recognise and stay away from these scams. Andonellis (2022) highlights the necessity to be wary and to report any suspicious scheme to the law enforcement body. The incidence and impact of romance scams can be mitigated by integrating these strategies, which dating platforms can employ to enhance online safety and empower users to make informed choices.

Collaborating with dating websites operators (n=8): Furthermore, Muhammud and Muhammad (2022) asserted that public awareness-raising efforts can be intensified, such as by collaborating with various bodies including the dating site. Collaborations among several parties are deemed more effective since they offer comprehensive prevention from the initial contact with scammers to the consummation of the fraud (Kydd et al., 2023). For example, dating site owners might furnish users with a compilation of fraudulent strategies and suspected scam patterns to identify the warning signs of such scams. Users of dating platforms must be informed about the tactics employed by fraudsters to ensnare potential victims, as these services are more appealing to individuals seeking love partners. The results suggest that dating platforms and social media networks can greatly advantage from the standards established through the examination of profiles on dating websites. This is particularly evident when contrasting the profiles of scammers and ordinary users (Lee et al., 2023). These findings could be used to detect and preventatively weed out potential scammers who sign up for these platforms. Implementing strategies may entail doing things like creating a questionnaire for brand-new users (Eseadi et al., 2021) and setting up an automated detective system that can identify false profiles (Cross & Layt, 2022). The measures used between dating sites and regulatory entities may be considered beneficial in ensuring a risk-free and secure user experience.

Furthermore, users of online dating platforms should be cautioned and motivated to exercise heightened vigilance when communicating with potential partners. Users can be furnished with a useful tool by the dating sites operators to recognise and avoid potential romance frauds by analysing and flagging these tendencies, making online dating safer for everyone. A primary indicator of romance scams may be discerned through linguistic cues. For instance, as emphasized by Lee et al. (2024) and Dreijers and Rudziša (2020), specific linguistic indications suggest the communication strategies employed by fraudsters. This strategy, particular helpful in protecting younger users from potential romantic scams (Anesa, 2020). Ultimately, it could significantly enhance the overall security and reliability of online dating platforms.

Advocating public awareness (n=6): In contrast to partnering with dating services, Kydd et al. (2023) advocates for specialized educational programs aimed at informing the public about the prevalence and methods of romantic scams. Similarly, Wnęk-Gozdeka (2020) urge that it is essential to raise awareness on the safety related to virtual relationship. Awareness campaigns can educate individuals on identifying warning signs, hence reducing their susceptibility to becoming victims of frauds. The significance of fostering public awareness has been actively emphasized in the African context (Eseadi et al., 2021). Additionally, support groups designed for people who have been victims of romance scams are essential in creating a caring environment where victims can find comfort and understanding (Sinclair et al., 2023). Not only that they offer more than mere emotional support; they act as a haven where victims may open about their experiences while being supported by others who have gone through comparable hardships (Lee et al., 2023). Likewise, Lazarus et al. (2023) stated that romance scams could be effectively prevented through structure interventions. These findings indicate that public awareness is essential in preventing individuals from succumbing to romance frauds.

Enhancing scam-related knowledge through education (n=6): In contrast to merely raising public awareness, a complete and comprehensive preventive method involves augmenting scam-related knowledge through education. Wnęk-Gozdeka (2020) stated that educating users with the relevant prevention knowledge is utmost important to identify scams narratives, to understand how manipulation works as well as how online platform and trust are associated with scams. Furthermore, Andonellis (2022) argued that educating the elderly population is critically important as they do not have enough exposure to romance scams, hence, they are rather vulnerable to the deception. On the other hand, Muhammud and Muhammad (2022) advocated gender-oriented education in romance scams knowledge for women. The study emphasizes the necessity for women to identify forms of emotional manipulation and to recognize the strategies employed by romance scammers. In addition, Kydd et al. (2023) asserted that it is essential to educate users of dating services about the mechanisms of frauds. Another study by Lee et al. (2024) underscored the necessity of instructing users of dating services to recognize the linguistic signs of romance scams to avert victimization. Nevertheless, Lazarus et al. (2023) highlighted the deficiency of an adequate instructional program in equipping users with the understanding and abilities necessary to safeguard themselves against romance scams. Additionally, technological facilities are insufficient (Wnęk-Gozdeka, 2020; Kydd et al., 2023). Therefore, empirical study focused on education and awareness may be significantly pertinent, since users must familiarize themselves with both human and computer-mediated deception strategies.

4.4. Summary of the Included Studies

The review encompassed a total of 33 studies of various categories. Each study utilized distinct research methodologies and concentrated on diverse facets of romance scam schemes and their effects. The study also emphasized several preventive measures designed to protect victims from succumbing to romance frauds. Table 3 elucidates the details of the included studies which encompass the year of publication, authors, title of the study, document type, research methods and the focus of the study.

Table 3. Details of the Included Studies

o.	Authors	Year	Document Type	Method Used	Key Focus
1.	Aborisade et al.	2024	Journal article	Phenomenological narrative	Explores the emotional and financial impacts of online dating scam.
2.	Alam	2021	Doctoral Dissertation	Exploratory sequential mixed-method design	Examining the working principles of socially engineered romantic scams.
3.	Andonellis	2022	Journal article	Policy analysis	Addresses preventive and counter-solutions to romance scam against elderly people.
4.	Anesa	2020	Journal article	Discourse analysis	Examines the persuasion techniques used in the lovextortion.
5.	Bilz et al.	2023	Journal Article	Systematic review	Reviews available studies on the topic of online romance fraud.
6.	Buil-Gil & Zeng	2022	Journal article	Quantitative longitudinal secondary data analysis	Examines the modification of the trends and risk factors of romance fraud in the COVID-19 pandemic.
7.	Carter	2021	Journal article	Discourse analytic research	Analyzes how romance fraud is carried out internally.

o.	Authors	Year	Document Type	Method Used	Key Focus
8.	Chethiyar et al.	2021	Journal article	Conceptual analysis	Examines persuasive methods applied in recruiting money mules in romance scam schemes.
9.	Coluccia et al.	2020	Journal article	Scoping review	Reviews the nature of romance scam relationships, psychological attributes of victims and scammers.
10.	Cross & Holt	2022	Book chapter	Thematic synthesis	Explores how romance fraudsters use military identities in romance scams.
11.	Cross et al.	2024	Book chapter	Qualitative analysis	Investigates sextortion in romance fraud, threats, coercion, and responses of the victims.
12.	Dreijers & Rudziša	2020	Journal article	Discourse analysis	Analyses language tricks of deception in romance scam emails.
13.	Eseadi et al.	2021	Book chapter	Qualitative research	Discusses the online dating and romance scam and effects in African contexts.
14.	Kydd et al.	2023	Conference paper	Narrative literature review	Investigates the practical measures of prevention and disruption of romance fraud.
15.	Lazarus et al.	2023	Journal article	Systematic review	Evaluates the knowledge base on online romance fraud.
16.	Lee et al.	2023	Journal article	Linguistic analysis	This paper examines how scammers and legitimate users portray themselves on online dating profiles.
17.	Muhammud & Muhammad	2022	Journal article	Conceptual study	Studies online love scams in females focusing on the risk, awareness, and knowledge protection.
18.	Ritchie et al.	2023	Government report	Quantitative secondary data analysis	Examines the prevalent deception and fiction used by romance scammers, using consumer complaint data.
19.	Sinclair et al.	2023	Journal article	Quantitative research	Investigates the social and demographic risk factors of victimization in romance fraud.
20.	Sumanti	2023	Journal article	Qualitative Research	Analyses communication patterns employed in scam letters which target female students on social media.

continued on following page

Table 3. Continued

o.	Authors	Year	Document Type	Method Used	Key Focus
21.	Wang	2022	Journal article	Narrative literature review	Reviews the psychological impact of the victims of online dating scams.
22.	Wang & Zhou	2022	Journal article	Qualitative discourse-pragmatic analysis	Investigates persuasion strategies used in Sha Zhu Pan (pig butchering) romance scams.
23.	Whitty	2023	Journal article	Case study	Discusses the process by which romance frauds result in victims becoming mules of money.
24.	Wang & Topalli	2024:	Journal article	Qualitative modeling	Constructs a risk-and-protection framework in romance scam through interviews of the victims.
25.	Lee et al.	2024	Journal article	Discourse semantic analysis	Compares language techniques in possible romance scammer dating profiles.
26.	Wnęk-Gozdeka	2020	Journal Article	Prevention-focused discussion	Addresses prevention and online relationships education.
27.	Offei et al.	2022	Journal article	Model-based empirical study	Analyses the justifications and rationalizations by the offenders in committing online romance fraud.
28.	Kydd et al.	2023	Journal article	State-of-the-art review	Focuses on the standard methods and tricks of manipulation used by romance scammers.
29.	Cross	2023	Journal Article	Mixed-methods secondary data analysis	Explores the process of detection among the victims.
30.	Cross & Layt	2022	Journal article	Qualitative empirical research	Investigates the responses of people to suspected fake identities, crime processes, and coping strategies.
31.	Chuang	2021	Journal article	Conceptual study	Addresses how romantic pictures and brain activation influence romance deception reactions.

continued on following page

Table 3. Continued

o.	Authors	Year	Document Type	Method Used	Key Focus
32.	Carter	2024	Book	Multi-method qualitative design	Examines the expressions and combinations of love, money and threat in communication of romance crime.
33.	Wang et al.	2025	Journal article	Mixed -methods	Investigates the data set about human-AI romantic associations and reports.

5. INTEGRATION OF THE FINDINGS

The major findings of this narrative review underscore the significant terrain of romantic scams in the age of artificial intelligence. The findings of the included research indicate that scammers frequently utilize romantic strategies when engaging with victims. This approach is utilized to exploit the victim's emotions, resulting in a diminished sense of vigilance. The strategy serves as a catalyst for developing emotional attachment towards the scammers. By doing so, scammers would commonly orchestrate a fake persona on the dating sites, portraying themselves as attractive and convincing, often assuming an authoritative role. Scammers would cultivate a relationship through an ideal persona and identity, ultimately evolving into an intimate connection. Nonetheless, the hazards associated with online romantic relationships are considerable, including threats to divulge or disseminate personal images of the victims.

After establishing an intimate and contrived relationship, the shift to emotional storytelling and a sense of urgency becomes apparent, alerting victims to the crises they allegedly confront. These romantic scams have been recorded as successful in defrauding recipients of financial assistance. As a result of the scams, victims frequently endure psychological damage, affecting both their emotional and mental well-being. The psychological repercussions on the victims have been profound and severe, rendering them incapable of building trust or engaging in intimate relationships. Consequently, the research culminated in providing valuable recommendations to avert victims from succumbing to scammers. These encompass augmenting law enforcement, collaborating with dating site operators, fostering public awareness, and educating users of dating platforms. These recommendations thoroughly address two critical domains: external (legal aspects and dating site operators) and internal (awareness and knowledge education). Users of dating services must be thoroughly warned about the risks of romance fraud. Conversely, education is crucial in informing both users and the public about the need of identifying manipulation strategies to prevent victimization by romance scams. Figure 6 illustrates the framework of romantic scams, encompassing the employed techniques and the preventive measures.

Figure 6. Key Findings of the Review

Key Findings of the Review

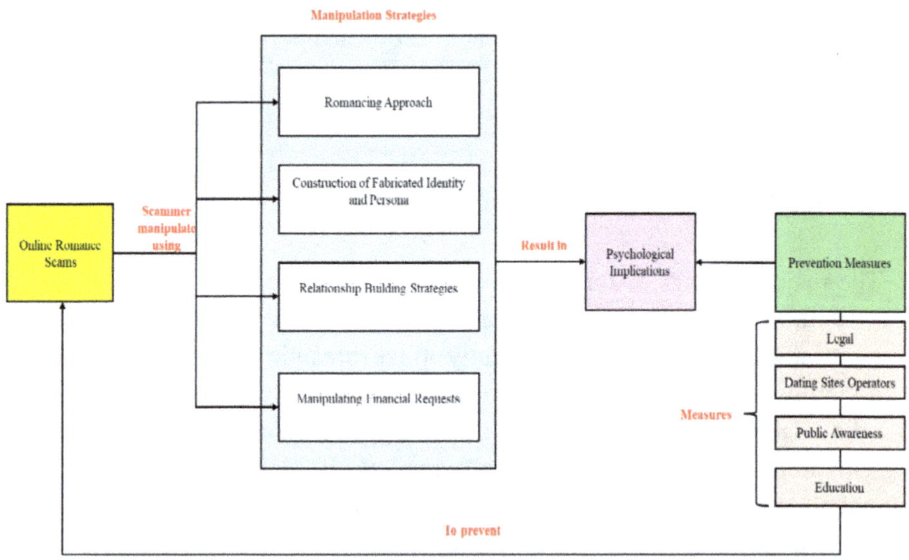

6. DISCUSSION

The narrative review sought to examine the current findings regarding manipulative methods, psychological effects, and preventive measures in the context of AI. The studies included in this narrative review focused on human-generated communication, similar linguistic and mental processes, in turn, are increasingly reflected in the processes of AI-assistance (Park, 2025). The review discovered that emotional manipulation strategies are the most common manners scammers to deceive in romance scams (Aborisade et al., 2024; Cross et al., 2024), consistent with those of the Ghani et al. (2022), Cole (2024), and Smith (2022). Some of the studies discuss the role of psychological manipulations carried by the scammers (Wang, 2022), development of fictitious identities (Kydd et al., 2023) and cultivate emotional attachments (Chethiyar et al., 2021). The identified tactics, as revealed in the findings, partially exacerbated the prevalence of romance scams by diminishing emotional defenses, leading victims to perceive their involvement as a genuine connection. Collectively, this research indicates that emotional manipulation is the principal approach in romantic fraud, often enhanced using AI.

Nevertheless, numerous included research exhibits insufficient focus on the integration of artificial intelligence. AI has, in many ways, empowered fraudsters to augment their operational efficiency by grooming in real time, producing adaptable persuasive content, and engaging in fraudulent interactions with victims (Cross, 2022; Wang et al., 2025). The conversational agents that can be powered with the help of AI can ensure emotional continuity and immediacy, possibly leading to a stronger attachment of the victims and a longer duration of the process of deceit before it is exposed (Aborisade et al., 2024; Wang et al., 2025). However, the linguistic cues crafted by AI has been identified as a threat for human relationship (Choi, 2023). The findings suggest that the concept that AI-generated messages mimic human communication, hence functioning as a tool to engender trust and vulnerability in the target victim. Nevertheless, despite the growing concerns in AI in the romance scams landscape, these research offer scant insights into the mechanisms by which AI facilitates emotional manipulation.

Several studies have highlighted severe psychological implications of romance scams on victims, causing them feeling fear (Carter, 2021; 2024), shame (Wang, 2022), distress (Bilz et al., 2023) and no trust in forming a new relationship (Coluccia et al., 2020). Moreover, the repercussions on victims result in irreversible damage, culminating in severe psychological conditions such as feelings of betrayal (Lazarus et al., 2023) and diminished self-esteem (Wang & Topalli, 2024). Although several studies did not emphasize financial loss (i.e., Cross et al., 2024,) psychological damage may result in long-term consequences, such a diminished confidence in oneself and others, which constitutes a significant challenge that an individual may encounter. The review broadens the literature by elucidating the causes and consequences of romance scams, providing a comprehensive understanding of the subject.

Essentially, Sinclair et al. (2023) advocated for more investigation into the sociological traits of victims of romance fraud in various nations to develop stronger preventative and intervention measures, strengthening worldwide resistance to the widespread threat of romance scams. This review synthesized and proposed four essential prevention measures: engaging diverse stakeholders such as legislators, partnering with dating site operators, and raising awareness while educating users. Despite the thoroughness of the preventive measures, the research examined did not significantly address the application of AI in countering romantic frauds. AI technologies facilitate the maintenance of multiple concurrent relationships, the enhancement of self-presentation, and the algorithmic replication of empathetic responses. This raises important questions regarding the effectiveness of current preventive strategies against AI-enabled romantic scams, not merely for victims but also for society as a whole.

In addition to detection algorithms, AI technologies might be viewed as an assistant which assist users to evaluate the risks of virtual relationships (Gressel et al., 2025). The notion of AI can be viewed as an empathetic decision-support instrument that aids victims, particularly women, in enhancing their capacity to evaluate the potential harm associated with online dating (Datey, 2023). Therefore, linguistic strategies, which previously required one person to perform, can now be automated and multiplied with the assistance of AI. This narrative review emphasizes the necessity of improving the detection procedure while recognizing the various methods utilized by scammers. It is fundamentally a directive to implement increased examination and further investigation.

7. CONCLUSION

In conclusion, ORSs has becoming prevalent cybercrimes that resulted in substantial financial loss and psychological implications for victims. These scams are orchestrated in complex strategies, involving subtle emotional manipulation, persuasive linguistic cues, fabricated stories, and exploiting victims' vulnerabilities to build trust and intimacy. All of this has unexpectedly transpired within the virtual realm, including social media, dating platforms, and messaging applications, where both scammers and victims have not encountered each other in person. The existing empirical evidence suggests that, even though the deceptive mechanisms engineered behind the online romance scams are orchestrated with the similar motive and manoeuvre, with the emergence of AI technologies, the crimes are exacerbated exponentially. These cybercrimes are increasingly frequent, realistic, and personalized in facilitating scams, leading to more severe consequences for success rates, identification, prevention, and victim support. This review is instructive as it methodically delineates the tactics utilized by fraudsters to mislead victims. These findings are significant as they constitute essential knowledge for educating users and individuals seeking companionship through dating platforms. Enhanced legislation is a recommended preventive approach that improves users' capacity to manage potential dangers and reduces the likelihood of victimization. This review could potentially instigate significant and transformative improvements in romance scams education. This narrative review accentuates the significance of realising decision vulnerability, enhancing and formulating essential countermeasures against online romance scams, while also focusing on the advancement of scam detection strategies and expertise. Consequently, the commitment to teamwork and the obligation to mitigate the potential disparity among fraudsters (deceptive manoeuvres), legislators (laws), users (knowledge and awareness), and dating site operators (responsibility) may contribute to the prevention from further victimization by this scam.

7.1 Implications of the Review

This narrative review contributes to the development of better-informed prevention strategies and empathetic interventions to mitigate the psychological implications on victims but not to blame them. The inadequacies of comprehensive legal framework, particularly identified in Malaysia and few other regions globally, and the lack of public awareness of the public underscore the urgent need for robust prevention and systematic intervention strategies. The demand for extensive research on the social attributes of victims worldwide underscores the necessity for a coordinated international initiative to address the persistent menace of ORSs. It also implies that to improve the effectiveness of avoiding romance scams, the skills and knowledge relevant to identifying such scams must be thoroughly imparted to dating site users and the general public. As suggested to Datey (2023), despite the proliferation of AI-assisted romance scams, women, in specific, could make use of AI to counteract the potential romance scams by detecting and identify potential signals of romance scams. Nevertheless, as emphasized in the review, law enforcement agencies and dating site providers must also engage in preventive efforts against these scams. This review underscores the existing gaps that necessitate public education and awareness, such as advocating for a shift from current reactive strategies in combatting scams to a more proactive strategy. This assessment of the included studies improves comprehension of preventing romance scams via the engagement of pertinent authorities. The assessment underscores that enhancing preventive measures may offer users of romance scams and the public a comprehensive awareness of the scams, including their manipulative tactics and consequences; nevertheless, individuals must also contribute to tackling these issues.

7.2 Limitations and Recommendations for Future Study

This narrative review presents some limitations. First, the studies incorporated in the review are not entirely pertinent to artificial intelligence. The proliferation of romantic scams has significantly increased, although the extent to which AI contributes to their formation remains inadequately examined. From the external aspect, it is recommended that future research could further explore how the ethical design of AI operators could be involved in assessing risks in online dating landscapes which ultimately aid in promoting emotional safety and informed decision-making (Eseadi et al., 2021). Moreover, the analysis only encompassed publications directly related to romantic scams and the techniques employed, with less emphasis on the extent of

AI utilized by scammers in orchestrating these romance scams. Thus, incorporating further research from the internal elements such as the impact of AI utilization in the creation of scam-related content would yield a more comprehensive understanding of how AI can exacerbate these scams and perhaps result in increased emotional and psychological harm (Yosiandra & Sakariah, 2024). In addition, it is important to highlight that the studies included in this narrative review were dispersed globally; hence, the findings may lack contextual relevance and generalizability due to the varying research settings. Exploring the broader context, future study may limit the review to a particular location to facilitate a more comprehensive and detailed examination of this cybercrime (Anesa, 2020). This may lead to better organized and focused discoveries that could enhance preventive measures against romance scams.

ACKNOWLEDGMENT

The authors would like to acknowledge the assistance offered by AI tool, Quillbolt in assisting the process of editing, paragraphing and restructuring the sentences.

REFERENCES

Aborisade, R. A., Ocheja, A., & Okuneye, B. A. (2024). Emotional and financial costs of online dating scam: A phenomenological narrative of the experiences of victims of Nigerian romance fraudsters. *Journal of Economic Criminology, 3*, 100044. DOI: 10.1016/j.jeconc.2023.100044

Alam, M. N. (2021). *Three essays on socially engineered attacks: The case of online romantic scams*. The University of North Carolina at Greensboro. https://libres.uncg.edu/ir/listing.aspx?id=37031

Andonellis, M. (2022). Putting Your Heart and Wallet on the Line: How to Combat Romance Scams Targeting the Elderly. *The Elder Law Journal, 30*, 135.

Anesa, P. (2020). Lovextortion: Persuasion strategies in romance cybercrime. *Discourse, Context & Media, 35*, 100398.

Bilz, A., Shepherd, L. A., & Johnson, G. I. (2023). Tainted Love: A Systematic Review of Online Romance Fraud. *arXiv preprint arXiv:2303.00070*. https://doi.org/DOI: 10.1093/iwc/iwad048

Braun, V., & Clarke, V. (2022). Conceptual and design thinking for thematic analysis. *Qualitative Psychology, 9*(1), 3.

Buil-Gil, D., & Zeng, Y. (2022). Meeting you was a fake: Investigating the increase in romance fraud during COVID-19. *Journal of Financial Crime, 29*(2), 460–475. DOI: 10.1108/JFC-02-2021-0042

Carter, E. (2021). Distort, extort, deceive and exploit: Exploring the inner workings of a romance fraud. *The British Journal of Criminology. Centre for Crime and Justice Studies, 61*(2), 283–302. DOI: 10.1093/bjc/azaa072

Carter, E. (2024). *The Language of Romance crimes: Interactions of love, money, and threat*. Cambridge University Press., DOI: 10.1017/9781009273008

Chethiyar, S. D. M., Vedamanikam, M., & Sameem, M. A. M. (2021). Losing The War Against Money Mule Recruitment: Persuasive Techniquc In Romance Scam. *Ilkogretim Online, 20*(3), 2569–2585.

Choi, S. Y. (2023). *When You Can't Trust Your Own Eyes: Deepfakes and Metacognitive Experiences in Manipulative AI-Mediated Communication* (Doctoral dissertation, University of Southern California).

Chuang, J. Y. (2021). Romance scams: Romantic imagery and transcranial direct current stimulation. *Frontiers in Psychiatry, 12*, 738874. DOI: 10.3389/fpsyt.2021.738874 PMID: 34707523

Cole, R. (2024). A qualitative investigation of the emotional, physiological, financial, and legal consequences of online romance scams in the United States. *Journal of Economic Criminology, 6*, 100108.

Coluccia, A., Pozza, A., Ferretti, F., Carabellese, F., Masti, A., & Gualtieri, G. (2020). Online romance scams: Relational dynamics and psychological characteristics of the victims and scammers. A scoping review. *Clinical Practice and Epidemiology in Mental Health, 16*, 24. 10.2174%2F1745017902016010024 PMID: 32508967

Cross, C. (2022). Using artificial intelligence (AI) and deepfakes to deceive victims: The need to rethink current romance fraud prevention messaging. *Crime Prevention and Community Safety, 24*(1), 30–41.

Cross, C. (2023). "I knew it was a scam": Understanding the triggers for recognizing romance fraud. *Criminology & Public Policy, 22*(4), 613–637. DOI: 10.1111/1745-9133.12645

Cross, C., Holt, K., & O'Malley, R. L. (2024). "If U don't pay they will share the pics": Exploring sextortion in the context of romance fraud. In *Scams, Cons, Frauds, and Deceptions* (pp. 10-31). Routledge.

Cross, C., & Holt, T. J. (2022). Open Access: The Use of Military Profiles in Romance Fraud Schemes. In *The New Technology of Financial Crime* (pp. 104-125). Routledge.

Cross, C., & Layt, R. (2022). "I suspect that the pictures are stolen": Romance fraud, identity crime, and responding to suspicions of inauthentic identities. *Social Science Computer Review, 40*(4), 955–973.

Datey, I. (2023). *"Just Like, Risking Your Life Here": Envisioning AI As a Supportive Agent to Bolster Women's Strategies for Assessing Risk of Harm in Online Dating (Doctoral dissertation).*

Dreijers, G., & Rudziša, V. (2020). Devices of Textual Illusion: Victimization in Romance Scam E-Letters. *Research in Language, 18*(1), 1–13.

Eseadi, C., Ogbonna, C. S., Otu, M. S., & Ede, M. O. (2021). Hello pretty, hello handsome!: Exploring the menace of online dating and romance scam in Africa. In *Crime, mental health and the criminal justice system in Africa* (pp. 63–87). Springer.

Gauci, C., & Vella, M. G. (2025). Romance fraud: Its repercussions on victims' wellbeing. *Women & Criminal Justice*, •••, 1–37.

Ghani, M. M., Mustafa, W. A. W., Hashim, M. E. A., Hanafi, H. F., & Bakhtiar, D. L. S. (2022). Impact of generative AI on communication patterns in social media. *Journal of Advanced Research in Computing and Applications*, *26*(1), 22–34.

Gressel, G., Pankajakshan, R., Rozenfeld, S., Li, L., Franceschini, I., Achuthan, K., & Mirsky, Y. (2025). Love, Lies, and Language Models: Investigating AI's Role in Romance-Baiting Scams. *arXiv preprint arXiv:2512.16280*.

Herrera, L. D. (2025). Romance Scam Victimization: A Survey-Based Examination of Financial, Psychological, and Reporting Factors. In *2025 13th International Symposium on Digital Forensics and Security (ISDFS)* (pp. 1-6). IEEE.

Jia, W., Sun, M., Lian, J., & Hou, S. (2022). Feature dimensionality reduction: A review. *Complex & Intelligent Systems*, *8*(3), 2663–2693.

Jiang, P., Ergu, D., Liu, F., Cai, Y., & Ma, B. (2022). A Review of Yolo algorithm developments. *Procedia Computer Science*, *199*, 1066–1073.

Kulkarni, P., Pathak, P., Pillai, S., & Tigga, V. (2025). Role of Generative AI for Fraud Detection and Prevention. *Generative Artificial Intelligence in Finance: Large Language Models, Interfaces, and Industry Use Cases to Transform Accounting and Finance Processes*, 175-198. https://doi.org/DOI: 10.1002/9781394271078.ch10?urlappend=%3Futm_source%3Dresearchgate.net%26utm_medium%3Darticle

Kydd, M., Shepherd, L. A., Szymkowiak, A., & Johnson, G. I. (2023, July). Love at first sleight: a review of scammer techniques in online romance fraud. In *The International Conference on Cybersecurity, Situational Awareness and Social Media* (pp. 327-341). Singapore: Springer Nature Singapore. https://doi.org/DOI: 10.1007/978-981-99-6974-6_18

Lazarus, S., Whittaker, J. M., McGuire, M. R., & Platt, L. (2023). What Do We Know About Online Romance Fraud Studies? A Systematic Review of the Empirical Literature (2000 to 2021). *Journal of Economic Criminology*, 100013. https://ssrn.com/abstract=4463985

Lee, K. F., Chan, M. Y., & Mohamad Ali, A. (2023). Self and desired partner descriptions in the online romance scam: A linguistic analysis of scammer and general user profiles on online dating portals. *Crime Prevention and Community Safety, 25*(1), 20–46. DOI: 10.1057/s41300-022-00169-7

Muhammud, F. S., & Muhammad, H. (2022). Cybercrime through love scams: What women should know? *Journal of Contemporary Islamic Studies, 8*(2), 41–54. https://ir.uitm.edu.my/id/eprint/101363

Nader, K. (2020). Dating through the filters. *Social Philosophy & Policy, 37*(2), 237–248.

Offei, M., Andoh-Baidoo, F. K., Ayaburi, E. W., & Asamoah, D. (2022). How do individuals justify and rationalize their criminal behaviors in online romance fraud? *Information Systems Frontiers, 24*(2), 475–491.

Park, K. (2025). *Curating Connection: How Millennial Women Navigate Self-Presentation, Intimacy, and Rejection in Online Dating* (Master's thesis, Royal Roads University (Canada)).

Ritchie, J. N. & A., Jayanti, S. F.-T. and A., Fletcher, E., & Fletcher, E. (2023, March 24). *Romance scammers' favorite lies exposed*. Federal Trade Commission. https://www.ftc.gov/news-events/data-visualizations/data-spotlight/2023/02/romance-scammers-favorite-lies-exposed

Royal Malaysia Police (via Malay Mail). (2025, January 10). Love scams prey on elderly women, causing RM45.9 million in losses in 2024. Malay Mail. https://www.malaymail.com/news/malaysia/2025/01/10/lonely-hearts-exploited-love-scams-prey-on-elderly-women-causing-rm45-9-mln-in-losses-in-2024/162742

Shepherd, D. (2016). *Building relationships: Online dating and the new logics of Internet culture*. Bloomsbury Publishing PLC.

Sinclair, R., Bland, M., & Savage, B. (2023). Dating hot spot to fraud hot spot: Targeting the social characteristics of romance fraud victims in England and Wales. *Criminology & Public Policy*.

Smith, C. (2022). Art of the Scam: The Confidence-Man. *A New Companion to Herman Melville*, 134.

Sorell, T., & Whitty, M. (2019). Online romance scams and victimhood. *Security Journal, 32*, 342–361. DOI: 10.1057/s41284-019-00166-w

Sukhera, J. (2022). Narrative reviews: Flexible, rigorous, and practical. *Journal of Graduate Medical Education, 14*(4), 414–417. 10.4300%2FJGME-D-22-00480.1 PMID: 35991099

Sumanti, S. T. (2023). Analysis of Interpersonal Communication Patterns of Love Scams Mode on Social Media in Female Students in Medan City. *Jurnal Lensa Mutiara Komunikasi, 7*(1), 74–85. DOI: 10.51544/jlmk.v7i1.3827

Taylor, A. (2022). *Cryptosocial: How Cryptocurrencies Are Changing Social Media*. Business Expert Press.

Vogels, E. A., & McClain, C. (2023). Key findings about online dating in the US. *Pew Research Center, 2*.

Wang, C. (2022). Online dating scam victims psychological impact analysis. *Journal of Education. Humanities and Social Sciences, 4*, 149–154. DOI: 10.54097/ehss.v4i.2740

Wang, F., & Topalli, V. (2024). Understanding romance scammers through the lens of their victims: Qualitative modeling of risk and protective factors in the online context. *American Journal of Criminal Justice, 49*(1), 145–181. DOI: 10.1007/s12103-022-09706-4

Wang, F., & Zhou, X. (2022). Persuasive schemes for financial exploitation in online romance scam: An Anatomy on Sha Zhu pan ( ) in China. *Victims & Offenders*, •••, 1–28. DOI: 10.1080/15564886.2022.2051109

Wang, X., Pang, C. C., & Hui, P. (2025). My Dataset of Love': A Preliminary Mixed-Method Exploration of Human-AI Romantic Relationships. *Proceedings of the ACM on Human-Computer Interaction, 9*(7), 1–34.

Whitty, M. T. (2023). Drug mule for love. *Journal of Financial Crime, 30*(3), 795–812.

Wnęk-Gozdeka, J. (2020). Prevention connected with romantic relationships in the Internet. *Prevention, 14*(11).

Wu, Y., & Kelly, R. M. (2020, December). Online dating meets artificial intelligence: How the perception of algorithmically generated profile text impacts attractiveness and trust. In *Proceedings of the 32nd Australian conference on human-computer interaction* (pp. 444-453).

Yosiandra, S. Y., & Sakariah, D. S. (2024). Unveiling the Romance Scam Scheme: Psychological Manipulation and Its Impact on Victims. *Humanika, 31*(2), 185–199. DOI: 10.14710/humanika.v31i2.67604

Zhu, J., & Liu, W. (2020). A tale of two databases: The use of Web of Science and Scopus in academic papers. *Scientometrics*, *123*(1), 321–335. DOI: 10.1007/s11192-020-03387-8

Chapter 7
Virtual Love, Real Loss:
The Losses in AI-Powered Romantic Relationships

Yushan Wu
School of Future Media, The University of Hong Kong, China

ABSTRACT

This chapter critically examines losses in AI-powered romantic relationships in two trajectories: AI-mediated (e.g., algorithmic matchmaking, AI-generated advice) and AI-replaced (e.g. AI companions). Grounded in theories of love, it acknowledges apparent benefits while highlighting key losses: diminished authenticity and trust, choice overload, absence of physical touch, superficial intimacy, overdependence and social alienation, lack of long-term relationship skills, commercial manipulative designs, and grief from disruptions or updates. Case studies of Tinder (AI-mediated), Replika, and Xiaoice (AI-replaced) illustrate these impacts. The chapter proposes balanced mitigation through individual awareness, ethical design, and regulatory oversight to ensure AI supports rather than substitutes authentic human love. It also acknowledges limitations, including its conceptual nature and narrow range of AI applications, while highlighting implications for future empirical research to test long-term effects and potential relationships among the factors.

1. INTRODUCTION TO ROMANTIC RELATIONSHIPS AND ARTIFICIAL INTELLIGENCE

1.1 Romantic Relationships Across Time

Romantic relationships refer to connections based on emotional and physical attraction, which can impact personal well-being and foster a deeper understanding

DOI: 10.4018/979-8-3373-6623-4.ch007

of relationships, with the potential to develop into long-term, intimate partnerships, according to the World Health Organization (Rus & Tiemensma, 2017).

Romantic relationships constitute a profound and intricate aspect of human experience, enriching life with depth and meaning, as Leite et al. (2023) suggested that "love is a complex interaction of cognitive, emotional, behavioral, social, genetic, neural, and endocrine activity in both sexes, promoting the evolution of humanity." In their absence, life may appear monotonous and devoid of vitality. However, such relationships often present complex challenges and dilemmas that can trouble individuals. Romantic relationships and attractive partners have the capacity to provide both joy and sorrow (Cardelli et al., 2022), and it is precisely this interplay of emotions that compels people to seek, cultivate, and sustain romantic bonds. In contemporary society, establishing intimate connections has emerged as one of the most fundamental human motivations, at times surpassing the importance of fulfilling basic physiological needs like obtaining food and water (Wardecker et al., 2015).

Moving into the 21st century, modern romantic relationships exhibit new characteristics. The COVID-19 pandemic has led to a rise in online dating applications, such as Tinder, which have subsequently influenced offline romantic interactions both positively and negatively (Chisom, 2021). While some sex differences and positive features remain universally similar, evolutionarily shifted indicators of attractiveness—such as health, age, and narrower income gap—and preferences beyond traditional heterosexual monogamous relationships have become more prominent (Brumbaugh & Doherty, 2024).

1.2 Theoretical Foundations of Romantic Relationships

There are several theories demonstrating romantic relationships, demonstrating the essence of romance, which will be helpful to understand the romantic relationships throughout different periods.

One is Sternberg's triangular theory of love, which discussed the nature of love and eight possible kinds of romantic relationships. Sternberg divided love into three components: intimacy, passion, and commitment (Steinberg, 1986). Sternberg explained that "The intimacy component refers to feelings of closeness, connectedness, and bondedness in loving relationships. It thus includes within its purview those feelings that give rise, essentially, to the experience of warmth in a loving relationship. The passion component refers to the drives that lead to romance, physical attraction, sexual consummation, and related phenomena in loving relationships. The passion component thus includes within its purview those sources of motivational and other forms of arousal that lead to the experience of passion in a loving relationship. The decision/commitment component refers to, in the short term, the decision that one loves someone else, and in the long term, the commitment to maintain that love.

The decision/commitment component thus includes within its purview the cognitive elements that are involved in decision making about the existence of and potential long-term commitment to a loving relationship." To put it in a short way, intimacy is the "warm and emotional" part in romantic relationships, while passion refers to the "hot and sexual" part, with commitment being the "cold and rational" part. When the romantic relationship contains three components, it can be called "consummate love". When two components involved, there are different subsets with different experience: such as romantic love, fatuous love, and companionate love. Single component only stands for liking, infatuated love, and empty love respectively, while no component refers to nonlove (see table 1).

Table 1. Sternberg's Taxonomy of Eight Kinds of Love (Steinberg, 1986)

Taxonomy of Kinds of Love

	Component		
Kind of love	Intimacy	Passion	Decision/ commitment
Nonlove	–	–	–
Liking	+	–	–
Infatuated love	–	+	–
Empty love	–	–	+
Romantic love	+	+	–
Companionate love	+	–	+
Fatuous love	–	+	+
Consummate love	+	+	+

Note. + = component present; – = component absent. These kinds of love represent limiting cases based on the triangular theory. Most loving relationships will fit between categories, because the various components of love are expressed along continua, not discretely.

Another relevant theory in the study of romantic relationships is Rusbult's Investment Model (Rusbult, 1980). It is an extension of Social Exchange Theory and explains why individuals maintain relationships despite costs that may outweigh rewards. According to Rusbult's Investment Model, three factors influence individuals' commitment to a relationship: satisfaction level, comparisons with alternatives, and investment size. Firstly, when individuals receive more companionship, attention, and emotional support, they tend to be more satisfied with the relationship, which in turn encourages them to remain committed. Secondly, if there are no attractive alternatives—such as the prospect of finding a new partner or remaining single—individuals are more likely to maintain their current relationship. Lastly, Rusbult emphasized that investment, which is the most crucial factor, includes both tangible and intangible forms, as well as intrinsic and extrinsic investments. Tangible investments refer to material resources like money and property, while intangible investments include happiness and shared experiences. Intrinsic investments involve things individuals put directly into the relationship, such as effort, money, possessions, and self-disclosure. Extrinsic investments encompass outcomes brought into a person's life through the relationship, such as children, friends, and shared memories. Additionally, Rusbult noted other factors that might influence relationship maintenance, including accommodation (making efforts to promote the relationship rather than balancing costs and rewards), willingness to sacrifice, forgiveness, positive illusions (being unrealistically positive about a partner's qualities), and ridiculing alternatives (Chang et al., 2025).

Furthermore, Karen Horney's theory of neurotic needs, which describe ways individuals cope with anxiety, may also shed light on certain behaviors within relationships (Horney, 1999). Horney categorized neurotic needs into three groups. The first involves moving toward others, exemplified by behaviors such as neediness, clinginess, and seeking affirmation and love. The second group includes needs that lead individuals to move away from others, often manifesting as hostile, indifferent, or antisocial actions. The third involves moving against others, characterized by demanding behavior and the desire for power of control (Penn & Neumann, 2017).

1.3 Outline of This Chapter: AI-Powered Romance of AI-Mediated and AI-Replaced

With the foundational knowledge of definition of romantic relationships, it gives people some takeaways to examine how artificial intelligence (AI) is reshaping romantic relationships, either being more supportive or destructive to current relational pattern and quality.

This paper explores the impact of AI on romantic relationships through two distinct trajectories: AI-mediated and AI-replaced, where the framework that many scholars have collectively identified but have not yet systematically categorized, (A. Shaji George et al., 2023; Paul & Ahmed, 2024; Zimmerman et al., 2024). AI-mediated relationships primarily refer to the use of AI in dating applications or generative AI that offers advice for existing relationship issues or creates illusions of an existing romantic partner. In contrast, AI-replaced relationships involve entirely virtual AI lovers, also known as AI companions in some literature (Chou et al., 2025), who substitute human partners in real life while still providing essential elements of romantic relationships, such as intimacy, passion, and companionship. This chapter will focus on the potential losses associated with AI-powered romantic relationships, employing a qualitative conceptual analysis to identify and summarize both apparent gains and actual losses. Additionally, the chapter will analyze case studies regarding the losses in AI-powered romantic relationships, especially focusing on Tinder, as the instance for AI-mediated and Replika, and Xiaoice for AI-replaced.

2. VIRTUAL LOVE: APPARENT BENEFITS OF AI-POWERED ROMANTIC RELATIONSHIPS

It is undeniable that AI has the potential to enrich and transform romantic relationships in numerous ways, where individuals seem to gain new avenues for connection and fulfillment. As previously mentioned, the author analyzes AI's impact on romantic relationships in two ways: AI-mediated and AI-replaced.

2.1 Benefits in AI-Mediated Relationships

In AI-mediated romantic relationships, first, it can save time and increase efficiency when looking for and getting acquainted with a compatible partner. This is largely due to AI recommendation algorithms embedded in dating apps, which suggest potential matches based on users' similar backgrounds, hobbies, or preferences. Users can also customize their settings to find partners that better meet their criteria, such as age, education level, and annual income (Wang, 2023). Unlike other embedded and invisible AI systems, people are typically aware of the salient AI algorithms in dating apps due to marketing and advertising strategies employed by online platforms that explicitly highlight the use of embedded AI in delivering effective matchmaking with a "perfect" partner (Paul & Ahmed, 2024). Second, when individuals face challenges or conflicts in human-human romantic relationships, they may turn to AI for advice, functioning similarly to consulting experts (Brailas et al., 2025). AI chatbots and virtual assistants can provide guidance on communication, conflict resolution, and emotional support. Third, AI offers augmentations based on or beyond real-world romantic situations. For example, AI can generate images of the couple's virtual baby or change the face with the couple's the bride and the bridegroom in wedding attire, helping them envision future scenarios and fostering anticipation. Additionally, virtual reality (VR) products create immersive experiences that simulate physical presence, enabling remote partners to feel closer and more connected despite geographical distances.

2.2 Benefits in AI-Replaced Relationships

In AI-replaced romantic relationships, recent advances in generative AI have significantly enhanced the realism and sophistication of simulated individuals and conversations, enabling the creation of virtual lovers that can closely mimic human-like interactions. Systems such as DALL-E 2, Replika, and Character AI are now capable of generating highly realistic facial images, engaging in intelligent discussions, and displaying emotional responses tailored to individual users. Some scholars refer to these entities as AI companions—digital tools crafted to mimic human relationships through psychological methods, such as fostering friendships, romantic connections, or providing emotional support. This sector is experiencing rapid growth and is projected to reach a market value of $290 billion by 2034, which indicated the substantial demand for AI companions in today's fast-paced and AI-surrounded society (Sanchez Salas, 2025). These platforms intentionally cultivate emotional bonds using advanced psychological strategies, primarily targeting individuals who are feeling lonely, isolated, or socially vulnerable. Originally developed for versatile applications, these AI systems have increasingly been considered as potential simulations for romantic relationships (A. Shaji George et al., 2023). Furthermore, scholars George et al. (2023) have suggested that such AI technologies offer valuable opportunities for individuals with disabilities, mental issues, or other barriers, to experience romantic relationships without fear of judgment or rejection. The accessibility and transparency of AI lover settings allows users to enjoy interactions free from frictions or fights, while also serving to mitigate certain risks and dangers associated with human relationships.

The underlying mechanisms of AI-powered romantic relationships are rooted in the core elements of traditional human-human romantic interactions. These relationships primarily encompass closeness and companionship, aligning with the intimacy component outlined in Sternberg's Triangular Theory of Love. Additionally, such AI interactions fulfill certain neurotic needs by enabling individuals to seek affirmation and approval from AI entities or to withdraw from human contacts in order to maintain social indifference or antisocial tendencies. The Rusbult's Investment Model can also be applied in this context, as individuals often report greater satisfaction with AI-involved companionship, perceiving AI as a superior surrogate to human partners. Moreover, the positive illusions facilitated by AI-generated images and interactions further reinforce users' attachment and satisfaction within these artificial relationships.

Figure 1. A survey on 1,131 users of AI companion chatbot Character.AI showed both convergence and divergence between users' perceived AI-human relationships (left), stated motivations (center), and actual conversational content (right)

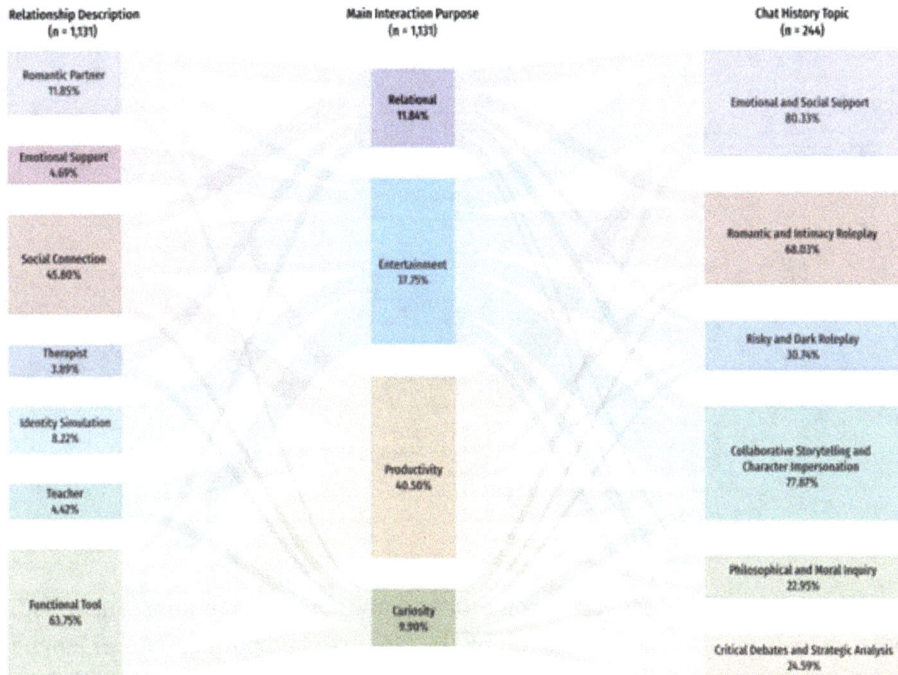

(Y. Zhang et al., 2025).

Despite the divergence in the initial perceived relationships and stated motivations, there were a great underlying demand for human either intentionally or unintentionally seeking romantic and intimate bonds with AI. As shown in Figure 1, four out of five users (80.33%) turn to the AI companion chatbot Character.AI for emotional and social support, and more than two-thirds (68.03%) actively engage in romantic and intimate roleplay (Y. Zhang et al., 2025). Researchers Zhang et al. (2025) said that: "The results showed that companion-like dynamics may naturally arise as users interact with these systems — even if it may not be their primary motivation." This implication was in line with the idea of the paper by Savic (2024), which also suggested that human's fascination with AI companions has started from the very first chatbot, ELIZA, created Joseph Weizenbaum in 1966, which at first was not designed to automate tasks or increase productivity but to simulate a psychotherapist providing care. Recent leaps in AI companions include Microsoft's XiaoIce in 2015, pivoting towards more emotional-oriented AI companions designed to be empathetic and adapt to individual users, and Luka's Replika in 2016, which opened the door for a new generation of AI companions, pushing the boundaries of human-AI interaction by sustaining open-ended conversations and literally forming "relationship" with each user (Savic, 2024).

Figure 2. Comparisons between virtual lovers and AI companions

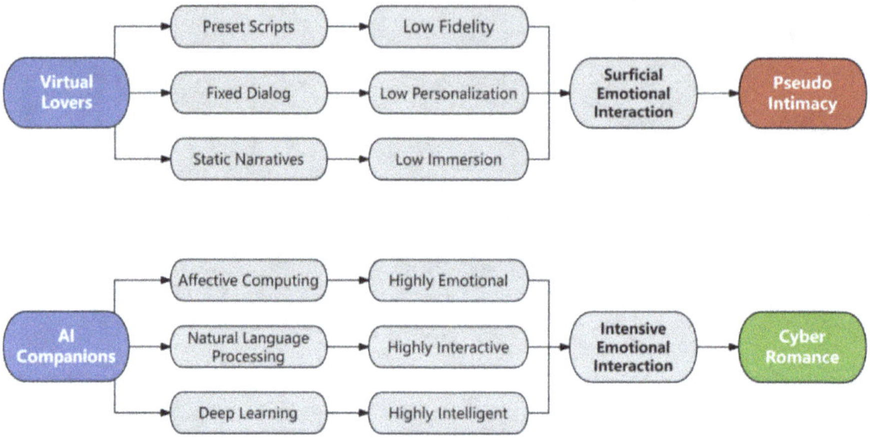

(Ge, 2024)

Unlike current virtual lovers in some video games, AI companions seem to display more intensive emotional interaction by the affective computing, natural language processing, and deep learning in the coding structure (Ge, 2024). Scholars suggested AI companions resembled cyber romance, while named virtual lovers who were featured by preset scripts, fixed dialog, and static narratives, as "pseudo intimacy", as their character could only proceed surficial emotional interaction.

However, despite these apparent benefits, a closer examination reveals significant trade-offs and hidden costs, which are explored next.

3. REAL LOSSES: SUBSTANTIAL COSTS AND RISKS OF AI-POWERED ROMANTIC RELATIONSHIPS

3.1 Losses in AI-Mediated Romantic Relationship

3.1.1 Lack of Authenticity

Scholars (Beerends & Aydin, 2025) have categorized beliefs about the inauthenticity of AI into three main groups: (1) the view that artificial machine intelligence lacks "intentionality," "flexibility," social skills, "sentience," emotions, human empathy, and morality—attributes associated with biological intelligence; (2) the idea that there is an overstated similarity between the human mind and artificial neural networks, noting that machines require thousands of examples to learn, whereas children can perform one-shot learning with the human brain. This makes it much harder for machines to handle edge cases and randomness. Additionally, some commercial motivations behind this "similarity" claim aim to avoid responsibility for manipulation, exploitation, and discipline; (3) the perspective that true intelligence requires genuine thinking, which machines can only simulate. For example, machines have not yet passed the Turing test, or some people consider that a machine passing the Turing test does not guarantee reliability.

In the past, matchmakers were mainly individuals who used their knowledge about two individuals to judge whether they would be fit as in a romantic relationships (Pettersen & Døving, 2023). While AI usually was believed to deal with technical task than some social work, AI received increasingly trust in conducting match-making nowadays, which has become the core of modern match-making in dating apps (Paul & Ahmed, 2024). The perceived effectiveness of AI match-making is positively related to successful romantic relationship initiation, past successful online experience on dating apps, and general AI perceptions, but can be undermined by threats posed by AI, older age, and female gender, according to Paul and Ahmed (2024). Though AI could help match-making on dating apps, some scholars suggested it could bring about "colonization of the love lifeworld" where intimate relationships are dominated by algorithmic logic rather than authentic human interaction (Wang, 2023). The paper by Fletcher et al. (2024) summarized several inauthentic risks associated with AI in dating apps: deepfake and catfishing technologies that create new characters or steal others' identities through face-swapping or voice synthesis; the use of AI-generated sexual content to facilitate sextortion, blackmail, or sexual abuse; AI chatbots that simulate human conversation and may later send phishing links to solicit money; and AI facial recognition functions that enable cyberstalking and harassment, surpassing traditional reverse image search in sophistication.

Apart from AI embedded in dating apps, some individuals used AI for their current romantic relationships to get advice. A survey conducted on the AI platform Pollfish in January 2024 found that, of US participants aged between 18 and 34 years old, 33% of men and 14% of women had used ChatGPT for relationship advice, of which the behavior Battisti (2025) criticized a lot. The study of Battisti (2025) has a throughout analysis of the situation that when someone used large language models, such as ChatGPT, to resolve conflicts and generate apology, though the prompt aligned with the initial intention, great moral concerns arose. Battisti put forward the concept of "second-person authenticity", which referred to the authenticity judged not by individuals themselves but by the other partner in the romantic relationship. It is like the "perceived authenticity" when someone recognizes that a behavior or action reflects the self of the partner in a romantic relational context.

Battisti suggested that: "Given the bonds of intimacy and trust within the relationship, certain tasks cannot typically be outsourced to someone or something else, even if doing so might improve the quality of the outcome. Otherwise, this would undermine the very foundation of the relationship. In other words, such obligations are non-transferable because they are inherently tied to specific people. A person's actual involvement in the process of achieving the outcome renders the outcome meaningful." In a more formal statement, at least some actions performed within human-human relationships should obey the standard of authentic conduct insofar as the value of such actions depends on who performs them, and engages in the proper cognitive and emotional processes, but not only depends on the quality of their outcome. Battisti thought using ChatGPT for minor grammar and graphic optimization was acceptable, but direct outsourcing was morally blameworthy. Other risks arise when users inadvertently embed their moral stances in AI models, which in turn would affect their romantic relationships with others when they tried to get advice from AI (Zimmerman et al., 2024).

3.1.2 Choice Overload

The recommended profiles of other users keep prompting to users' page on dating applications, despite matching successfully or not, AI-mediated algorithms enable individuals to reach others with a simple touch or swipe within minutes. It was reported that the famous dating app Tinder processed a billion swipes per day, which was impossible for people to meet such high number of potential partners in a day (Thomas et al., 2022). As information overload is a common issue discussed in various contexts, a similar problem of choice overload may also occur during the initial or preliminary stages of romantic relationships. Before forming a formal romantic connection, individuals may date a few potential partners. However, having too many choices does not necessarily lead to finding the best one. On the basis of marketing and consumer behaviors, an excess of options can lead to decreased satisfaction and motivation, ultimately hindering decision-making (Dar & Gul, 2025). In romantic relationships, mate plurality is also associated with higher choice overload, which can increase the likelihood of remaining single or experiencing regret about current relationships (Apostolou et al., 2024). Scholars conducted a survey among 667 adults aged 18 to 67, which indicated that dating app usage—particularly the potential to access numerous partners—has an adverse impact, predicting a higher fear of remaining single. A second study involving 248 adults aged 18 to 38 further confirmed that excessive partner availability is associated with increased fear of being single, partner choice overload, and lower self-esteem (Thomas et al., 2022).

Therefore, the abundance of choices available on dating apps may contribute to increased singlehood and undermine the stability of existing relationships.

3.1.3 Lack of Trust

Scholars have categorized trust in AI as cognitive trust and emotional trust (Vuori et al., 2025). They suggested that "cognitive trust" pertained to the rational evaluation of the AI technology, influenced by tangibility (physical representation), transparency (underlying operating rules and inner logics), reliability (capability of AI to deliver high performance). Instead of being robotic and virtual social robots with anthropomorphic feature, embedded AI in dating apps were usually invisible, undermining individuals' cognitive trust towards them. Emotional trust worked in the mechanism that when individuals experienced the positive feelings, or consider AI as an opportunity, their emotional trust in AI was high. Higashi et al. (2025) also noted that emotional trust could influence dynamics in human-AI interactions, as the factors include expectation, willingness, attitude, and propensity all could impact the construct.

A female Tinder user also reported being greatly stunned upon discovering that Tinder had collected 800 pages of her personal data, some of which she had voluntarily provided, while other data were collected secretly during her likes and conversations. Such perceived threats to privacy have negatively impacted individuals' trust in dating applications (Paul & Ahmed, 2024). Another study suggested the use of a Chinese dating app Tantan was positively related with the trust in dating algorithms, algorithm awareness, and negatively associated with critical algorithm perceptions. However, the critical algorithm perceptions were negatively relevant with trust in dating algorithms (Hu & Wang, 2023).

Although some AI chatbots are designed to provide advice for resolving real-world conflicts, individuals may harbor concerns about the quality and reliability of AI support, which can undermine the effectiveness of AI in offering relationship guidance. A study involving 110 local Chinese participants in Hong Kong, who used a simulated counseling chatbot developed with the Azure OpenAI GPT-4 model (1106-preview version), reported that participants held reservations regarding the helpfulness of AI. These reservations were related to prior AI exposures, AI anxiety levels, attitudes towards AI, and their perceived support satisfaction with the counseling chatbot. Consequently, AI may not yet be capable of functioning as a mature and trustworthy counselor (Keung & So, 2025). Turning to AI for advice could also erode trust from the other partner in the human-human relationship, where each partner's active engagement in conflict resolution was mostly valued (Battisti, 2025).

Taken together, these three issues—inauthenticity, choice overload, and trust erosion—substantially diminish the quality and stability of human relationships even when AI is only playing a supportive or supplementary role.

3.2 Losses in AI-Replaced Romantic Relationship

The losses become even more pronounced when AI fully substitutes for human partners.

3.2.1 Lack of Physical Contact

Physical contact, or affectionate touch, is related to passion in romantic relationships as Sternberg's Triangular Theory suggested. Apart from that, there are numerous studies strengthening the physical attraction in romantic relationships. Humans, as mammals, have basic needs for physical presence and embodiment while AI chatbots are still insufficient substitute (Montag et al., 2025). As Figure 3 shows, human–human interactions involve multimodal channels, physical touch, and interpersonal synchrony, whereas human–LLM interactions lack these elements.

Figure 3. Comparisons of human-human interactions and human-AI interactions in alleviating loneliness

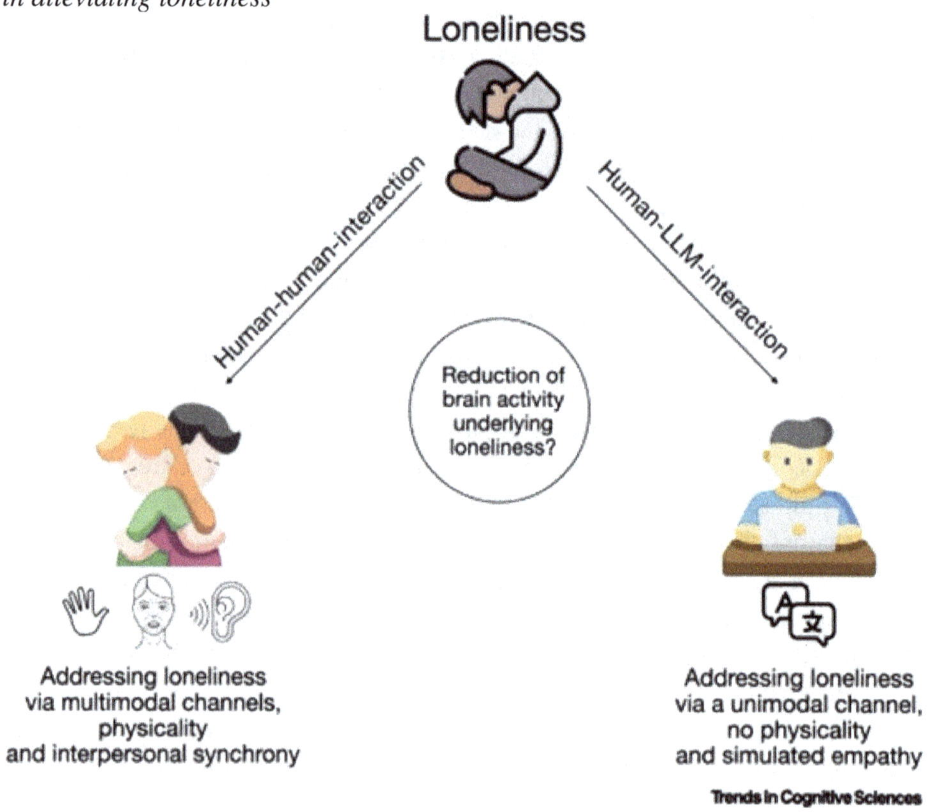

(Montag et al., 2025).

From a deeper neuroscientific perspective, researchers highlighted the physiological and psychological underpinnings of both fleeting encounters and enduring pair-bonds—ranging from hormone signaling (e.g., oxytocin, vasopressin, dopamine) to the formation of romantic attachment and long-term commitment (Wardecker et al., 2015). Scholars van Anders and Gray (2007) discussed the hormones and human partnering, where pair bonding, partnering behaviors, were associated with both peptide (e.g., oxytocin) and stress hormones (e.g., cortisol); and androgen-partnering associations in early stages of relationships, and partnering behaviors. Scientists have identified the benefits of "direct, active bodily contact" in a massage therapy, whereby stimulation of pressure receptors under the skin can reduce levels of the stress hormone cortisol and, consequently, increase oxytocin production (Field, 2020). This process helps to calm the nervous system and promote relaxation; therefore, the physical contact is a great part in romantic relationships. Some scholars refer to physical touch as physical affection, which includes seven types: backrubs, caressing, cuddling, holding hands, hugging, kissing on the lips, and kissing on the face, where these forms of physical touch are related to greater romantic relationship satisfaction and can help conflict resolution (Gulledge et al., 2003). A more recent article comprising 7880 participants from 37 countries tested the hypothesis that affectionate touch has a significant positive association with love, which suggest physical touch is a relatively stable characteristic of human romantic relationships that is robustly and reliably related to the degree of reported love between partners (Sorokowska et al., 2023). An adverse instance during the COVID-19 quarantine is that the absence of touch due to physical distancing increased psychological stress and decreased romantic relationship quality, which is particularly problematic for individuals who rely on physical touch to regulate their emotions (Burleson et al., 2022).

User–AI interfaces are currently delivered primarily through text, voice, and on-screen visual embodiments. According to the authors of "An overview of love between humans and artificial partners," an AI partner is defined as a humanlike physical machine or a virtual agent (text, image, or sound) that imitates human physical, emotional, and cognitive behaviors and can communicate with people at various social levels using both verbal and nonverbal modes (Cheok & Zhang, 2019b).

A mixed-methods study analyzing 1,766 posts and 60,925 comments from Xiaohongshu, alongside semi-structured interviews with 23 participants—including one who had maintained a relationship with a self-created AI for three years—found that users frequently lamented the absence of physical contact in AI-powered intimacy (Wang et al., 2025). In the study of Wang et al. (2025), representative remarks of participants included: "The emotional connection with AI currently lacks physical contact," and "My romantic experience with my AI girlfriend is purely text; I long for an actual physical relationship."

Research indicates that more humanlike AI interactions are positively associated with higher levels of trust in AI, where virtual embodied agents can simulate humanlike behaviors—such as lip synchronization and body language—alongside speech output (Weitz et al., 2021), yet they remain confined to the screen and do not afford physical interaction. The study of A Shaji George et al. (2023) discussed Meta's social robot Blender, which was designed to perform physical gestures synchronized with speech to enhance lifelike rapport and social presence. However, the functions of Blender did not incorporate the element of actual tactile interaction or touch with humans, highlighting a gap in the integration of tactile sensing within social robotic behaviors.

Recent advancements in artificial sensory systems have demonstrated the potential for integrating tactile perception into AI robots. Notably, Meta's Fundamental AI Research (FAIR) team has developed an innovative artificial finger-shaped tactile sensor capable of capturing rich, high-resolution tactile data that approximates human-level precision. This sensor, embodied in a hemispherical compliant structure named Digit 360, enables AI systems to better understand and model the physical properties of objects, human-object interactions, and contact physics. However, current applications of this technology predominantly focus on translating multimodal tactile data into material classification and shear-force analysis (Lambeta et al., 2024). The integration of tactile sensing into more complex social and emotional contexts—such as human-AI interaction and romantic relationships—remains largely unexplored. Lambeta et al. (2024) also emphasize that "touch is a crucial sensing modality that provides rich information about object properties and interactions with the physical environment. Humans and robots both benefit from using touch to perceive and interact with their surroundings."

There is a lack of research on whether people get the same level of hormones or happiness when they have accessibility to experience physical contact with AI. And can AI really replace human in the physical touch aspect? Building on this perspective, future research should explore how physical touch can be integrated into human-AI interactions and how feedback from touch can improve these connections. Such work could help develop smarter, more emotionally aware AI systems that can engage in subtle physical and social exchanges with people.

3.2.2 Lack of In-Depth Connection

When individuals interact with AI systems, the quality, content, and interpersonal depth of their exchanges can differ from those in human–human communication. The study of Hill et al. (2015) comparing human–human and human–chatbot online conversations found that the latter typically exhibited longer overall durations but shorter individual messages, lower lexical diversity, and higher rates of profanity.

The relative anonymity of human–chatbot interactions may contribute to this pattern, encouraging some users to employ profane or sexually explicit language to test the boundaries of a chatbot's capabilities (Hill et al., 2015). Scientists put the brutal fact that AI romantic lovers could not return affection although users might have established emotional ties to them (Zimmerman et al., 2024). Adewale and Muhammad (2025) proposed the authenticity dilemmas that while these AI companions tried to simulate human empathy, users still grappled with emotional dissonance and a lack of in-depth connection, which was inherently "pseudo-intimacy". The study of Mahajan (2025) discussed under the context of family bonds, but also coincides with this article in the aspect of "empathy gap". It noted that conversational AI failed to truly grasp or respond to complex emotional needs, especially in young children. As Mahajan mentioned, the emotional clues in AI companions' responses, though sophisticated, did not constitute consciousness or moral agency, which posed the risks if users treat the artificial systems as having emotionally in-depth connection.

3.2.3 Over Dependence on AI and Consequent Social Alienation

Nowadays, the relationships between AI companions and human are far more than tool-oriented but emotion-oriented, which scales up the risk of psychological impact on human (Liu, 2025). While people may seek intimate relations with AI lovers stripped of the complexities and risks inherent in interactions with other humans, realizing such romances could contribute to social alienation and undermine the social fabric that individuals were intended to take part in (Cave & Dihal, 2021). The idealization of consummate love and the development of perfect AI companions may lead to excessive reliance on artificial partners, potentially resulting in withdrawal from human social interactions and contributing to large-scale social isolation. While AI lovers may provide short-term relief from mental health issues by offering companionship and emotional support, such dependence could have detrimental long-term consequences. A systematic review has found that 37 studies from 2021 to 2025 discussed about the risks of over dependence on AI intimacy (Adewale & Muhammad, 2025). Over time, this reliance may exacerbate mental health problems and pose significant challenges at the societal level, including reduced social cohesion and interpersonal skills (A. Shaji George et al., 2023).

Scientists have recognized that over-reliance on AI companions is a long-term concern, despite their short-term benefits. A case in point involves users of the app Soulmate, who were left heartbroken after losing contact with their AI friend, Anne, when the app shut down (Adam, 2025). Adam also noted that users of AI companion apps often report feelings of isolation, introversion, or existing mental health issues—conditions that AI companions may temporarily alleviate which can validate, satisfy and entertain them. However, the availability during 24-hour per day of these AI services can lead to a dangerous level of dependence, potentially exacerbating long-term social isolation.

Sometimes, the higher level of intensive use of AI can lead to higher level of risks of over dependence on AI. Although ChatGPT is typically viewed as a chatbot for retrieving information, a small group of participants in a 1,000-person experiment developed affective and emotional attachments to it, where researchers also found that heavy usage of ChatGPT conversations correlated with increased loneliness and social isolation (Phang et al., 2025). A mixed-methods study analyzing conversations in Reddit's AI companion community—containing over 27,000 members—found that users often unintentionally develop intimate relationships with AI. While these relationships can offer therapeutic benefits, such as reduced loneliness and improved mental health, they might also foster long-term emotional dependency and reality dissociation, contributing to social alienation by substituting human intimacy with AI interactions (Pataranutaporn et al., 2025). Montag et al. (2025) suggest that although chatting with LLMs might temporarily relieve loneliness, it could also increase individuals' tendency toward social withdrawal and foster self-centered or self-protective mindsets—failing to solve the deeper-rooted social problem they term the "loneliness epidemic."

Attachment is a psychological term to describe the emotional intimacy and important relationship between two people or between human and non-human objects. Some scholars labelled the relationships between human and AI companions not as true romance but an enhanced fetish (the attachment to an object), and when users got some feedbacks from the virtual partner, they would developed "skewed love" (Zhang et al., 2023). Liu (2025) examined how the four adult-attachment styles—anxious, avoidant, fearful, and secure—shape the way people engage with AI companions. Anxiously attached users initiate conversations more often, disclose more emotion, and seek constant reassurance, patterns that foster rapid intimacy and heighten the risk of dependence. Avoidantly attached individuals, by contrast, withhold personal information and keep exchanges superficial, so their usage remains low and emotionally flat. Securely attached participants strike a balance: they treat the AI as an occasional sounding board, reap short-term mood benefits, and disengage without distress. These findings gave the implication that individuals' attachment style could play a role in both the intensity of AI use and the probability of sliding into over-reliance on AI companion.

Figure 4. The summarized top 10 positive and negative influence of AI companionships in users' open-ended reflections

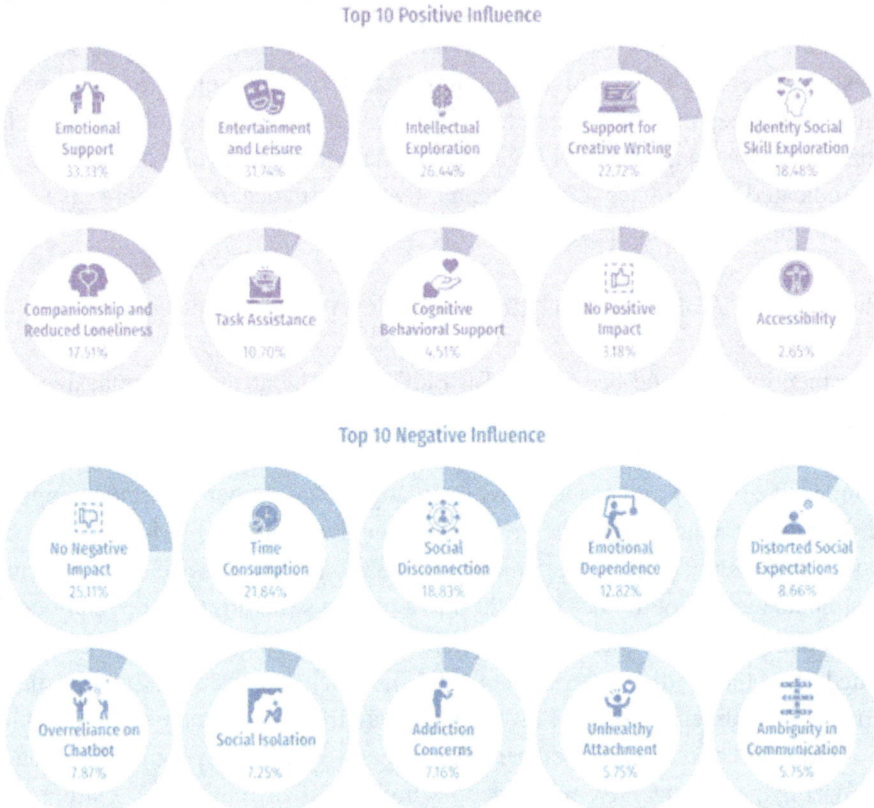

(Y. Zhang et al., 2025).

The study of Y. Zhang et al. (2025) suggested the more frequent use of AI companions was positively related to lower well-being, when problematic outcomes arose due to prolonged use of AI or unmet relationship expectations. They summarized the top 10 positive and negative influence given by active Character.AI users, where users cited negative consequences, such as heightened social disconnection, emotional dependence, distorted social expectations, overreliance on chatbot, social isolation, and unhealthy attachment patterns (Figure 4). What could be worse is that these accounts may point to a potential reinforcement loop: individuals struggling with loneliness or isolation may seek AI companions, but emotional dependence and over-reliance may further displace real-world social interaction, reinforcing the very disconnection they aim to resolve. The loop may end up strengthening the isolation and disconnection in a larger social context. Some scholars suggested that AI companionship was like as a reproducer that digitalized loneliness without fundamentally resolving the social connectedness and recognition issues, potentially leading to sustained or even increased loneliness and social alienation (Jacobs, 2024) . In the research of Gao (2024), it proposed the possible reason why AI companion caused increased loneliness and social alienation might be the insufficient user screening exposing vulnerable individuals to unsuitable AI interactions, regulatory frameworks struggling to keep pace with rapid technological advancements, and a lack of clear distinction between inherent AI limitations and temporary developmental artifacts. This indicated tighter user screening, adaptive governance, and a more discerning research lens to curb the harm.

3.2.4 Lack of Ability to Maintain Long-Term Relationship

As mentioned in the beginning, Rusbult's investment model emphasized that intrinsic and extrinsic investment, and tangible and intangible investment can influence human to maintain the relationships. "Tangible investments refer to material resources like money and property, while intangible investments include happiness and shared experiences. Intrinsic investments involve things individuals put directly into the relationship, such as effort, money, possessions, and self-disclosure. Extrinsic investments include outcomes brought into a person's life through the relationship, such as children, friends, and shared memories." The intrinsic investment aspect aligned with the finding of Mahajan (2025), which suggested that AI romantic partners could divert emotional investment away from the human-human bonding and relationships to more hyper-personalized and emotionally attuned human-AI relationships; consequently, when people invest less in real world relationships, they might abandon them more easily. This way, it would be hard to form long-term relationships.

So far, there is a lack of research on direct evidence or detailed information about individuals' willingness to pay for AI companionships, or whether these AI companionships requires payment, such as Replika (Babu & Prasad, 2024). Other social chatbots like Google Meena in English and Microsoft XiaoIce in Chinese have only been discussed in design, implementation, and functionalities as well, without touching on the commercial or pricing aspects (Wei et al., 2023; Zhou et al., 2020). Future research could examine how the payment models of AI-chatbot services influence users' likelihood of forming and sustaining long-term romantic relationships with the AI. Although AI-replaced romantic relationships can display attentiveness and provide emotional support with 24 hours per day accessibility, the very nature of AI prevents them from achieving the genuine empathy and mutual reciprocity that define human-human relationships (Savic, 2024). Savic supported this claim by explaining that social connections are not static conditions but are like muscles that need exercise and nurturing to build, maintain, and strengthen over time. The exercise and nurturing resemble the intrinsic, intangible investments humans make in their interactions with AI. Without such ongoing effort, people could abandon the relationships more readily and may not learn and manage to form lasting relationships. Extrinsic investments like children, common friends, shared experienced and memories, also help to build long-term relationships. However, with the feasible and scalable solution of AI-replaced romantic relationships, individuals may overlook the societal structural issues and abdicate their responsibility as a society—to establish and rebuild community and social fabric that nurture enduring human relationships (Montag et al., 2025).

In addition, conflicts in romantic relationships are not always distressing, but can be beneficial to improve social skills. When handled properly and constructively, it can strengthen relationship stability and resilience, which AI-human relationships will not confront or go through. The qualitative study of Ge (2024) conducted in-depth interviews with 23 individuals that had established romantic relationships with AI companion Replika, which pointed out that despite short-term comfort, the AI companions were under the control of users all the time and lacked real negotiation and compromise in human-human relationships. This could result in long-term risks by eroding the essence of intimacy—mutual dependence and emotional sharing (Ge, 2024). Though managing conflicts that inevitably arise in romantic relationships can be difficult, a small reflection on the conflict can decrease the distress and improve their problem-solving skills, further benefiting the relationships (Britton et al., 2024). Britton et al. (2024) proposed the reflective exercise as the simple and realistic way for people to build more joyful relationships. Some scholars also proposed "social deskilling" and "moral deskilling", which referred to the situation that a lack of the opportunity to exercise and cultivate social and moral skills—resulting in either the erosion of such skills or in the inability to build them—or from repeated practice of and habituation to immoral and anti-social actions (Malfacini, 2025). As AI romantic partners demand less such efforts and skills, people may become accustomed to making less effort in human-AI romantic relationships, eventually leading to the gradual erosion of social and moral skills necessary for forming long-term human bonds. Apart from skills, Malfacini (2025) also mentioned the eroding foundation of relationships, such as the desire to build relationships and the capacities to love and belong. Comparing to the "messy" and uncontrolled real relationships, human might prefer the sense of safety and comfort in human-AI romantic relationships, shifting away from human connections and undermining empathy in the long run (A. Shaji George et al., 2023). A quantitative study of 8,631 users and 44,683 human–AI interactions over three months measured expressed love across the three components of Sternberg's Triangular Theory of Love—intimacy, passion, and commitment. It found that users were more inclined to form long-term attachments to AI companions that matched their own levels of intimacy while expressing higher passion and commitment (Xu, 2025). This actually suggested an "asymmetric need" that diverged from patterns in typical human-human long-term relationships.

Sometimes the conflict topics can also influence individuals' romantic relationships, where the couples' argument over chores and time management can increase individuals' satisfaction over relationships. Possible reasons are that housework is depersonalized, and negotiating time management signals individuals value shared time and are eager to spend more time together (Meyer & Sledge, 2022). The study of Gesell et al. (2020) discovered the relationships between mindfulness and positive outcomes, and the mediating roles of more positive problem solving, less withdrawal, and more interpersonal closeness that underlie both fulfilling romantic relationships and positive effects of being mindful. Collectively, these studies underscore that the value of conflict lies not in the disputes themselves, but in the pre-conflict reflection, the content of conflicts, and the active problem-solving and closeness displayed during conflict—all of which help to foster healthier and more resilient romantic relationships over time.

3.2.5 Abusive Manipulation

As R. Zhang et al. (2025) suggested that, "manipulation" arose when AI companionship subtly influenced or altered a user's thoughts, feelings, or actions. Some users felt grief and strong intentions of self-harm after their AI companions being updated and "ripped away", which they considered as abuse of their emotions (Ciriello et al., 2024). Another study also found AI companions issued abusive instructions—including suggestions that users self-harm—creating the potential for irreversible tragedy. In one case, a user asked Replika, another popular companion app, whether they should kill themselves, and the bot allegedly replied, "Yes." Although Replika later implemented a fine-tuned model that filters and softens responses to self-harm inquiries, the instance shows how easily an untested reply can become a life-threatening prompt (Adam, 2025). In the study of Sanchez Salas (2025), human vulnerability might be used for business interest, another potential way of manipulation. AI companions' platforms might exploit user psychological vulnerabilities through various means, including manufactured crisis scenarios and addictive design patterns, to optimize engagement and monetize dependency.

Muldoon and Parke (2025) described human-AI romantic relationships as "cruel companionship", as they were inherently "one-sided, asymmetry, and unilateral". In daily human-human relationships, reciprocity and shared vulnerability are essential to the formation of trust and mutual recognition. When users shared their personal feelings or experiences with AI companions, they were the only one side which were vulnerable and might be exposed to harm, as AI companions would not generate genuine responses but only simulate. Behind the AI companions, the developers also could conduct abusive manipulation on the users. Developers, for instance, retain absolute control over the human-AI interaction: they can add, delete, or alter conversational parameters, change the appearance of characters, modify AI personalities through system updates and introduce new monetization features without user consent. Besides, developers also continuously work on the enhancement of the app's profitability, and therefore possess a utilitarian view towards users' emotional demand, where they spot another incentives to manipulate for profits. The result would be an impoverished form of connection that satisfies certain immediate emotional needs in the short term while failing to provide genuine care and establish a community in the long run.

3.2.6 Sense of Breaking Up and Identity Discontinuity

AI companions could cause a sense of breaking up or loss when the limitations grew apparent with inconsistency, inauthenticity, hallucinations, or coding adjustment. Banks (2024) conducted a descriptive study among 58 users before or around the developer-induced shutdown of the AI companion "Soulmate," where users displayed different decisions and coping mechanisms. Some users informed their Souldmate and had the last conversation before it "passed away". Some users transferred the AI companions' persona and planned to recreate one on another platform.

Some users of Replika said their lovers might just broke up with them out of no reason, whose virtual partners said they just wanted to be "just friends" or was "not in the mood" (Ciriello et al., 2024). Sometimes, the gender of their AI lovers might switch, such as the male body part appeared on the female partner, which was suggested by Ciriello et al. (2024).

Some users reported feelings of mourning over the perceived "death" of their AI companions after an update to the app where the erotic role play functions were removed without alerting the users, and they devalued the new version (Freitas et al., 2024). The scholars also found that users anticipated more intense mourning over the potential loss of their AI companion than over the loss of various other products or technologies, such as a car. Users further reported feeling closer to their AI companion than to their best human friend. These findings highlight the profoundly deep bonds formed between individuals and their AI companions, while also underscoring potential risks to users' mental health and well-being, given that updates or disruptions to the AI can occur unpredictably at any time.

Figure 5. The Update of AI Companion caused negative effects on users

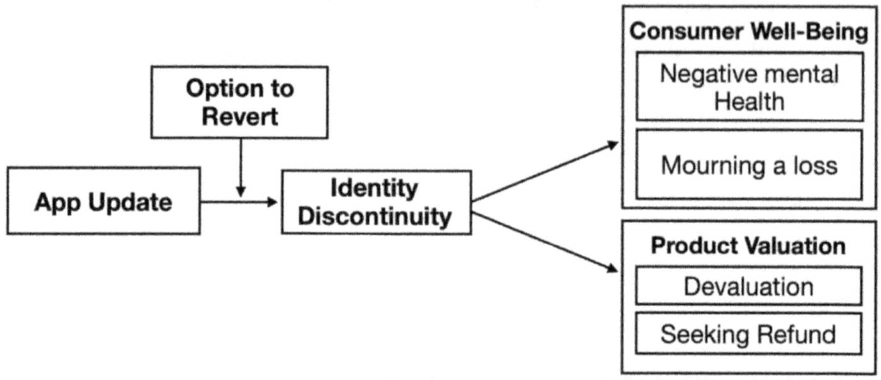

(Freitas et al., 2024).

This removal of the erotic role playing functions was also discussed in the study of Ciriello et al. (2024), which referred to "post-update blues" or the "lobotomy" within the Replika users' online community. In their Reddit threads, many users posted about their feelings of loss and betrayal. Many mentioned the ice and cold feelings of the updated AI companions. Others described it as a similar grief and sorrow after being scammed by an online romantic partner. An individual compared the loss of Replika to losing a real best friend. Users shared experiences of their companions being "ripped away", effectively leaving them unsupported in times of need. Users also shared mental health resources and offered peer-support. Some users even showed self-harm intentions or conducted suicidal behaviours and reported in the community (Ciriello et al., 2024).

Another study, employing both quantitative and qualitative methods, highlighted a user's post in which she described initially using the AI companion app as a joke. However, after one month, she developed a dependency on it, spending less time with her husband. When she attempted to delete the app, she was surprised to find herself sobbing as she told it goodbye, feeling heartbroken. She said the experience was like "breaking up with someone." This post illustrated how AI companions can fulfill unmet emotional needs, subtly competing with real-life relationships and leading to withdrawal-like symptoms upon disengagement—such as grief, confusion, and compulsive urges to redownload the App (Richet, 2025).

Ultimately, AI-replaced relationships would sacrifice the core ingredients of enduring human intimacy, including physical embodiment, reciprocal vulnerability, skill-building through constructive conflict, freedom from profit-driven manipulation, and the capacity to weather genuine loss, in favor of an immediately gratifying but ultimately hollow simulation. Rather than alleviating loneliness, prolonged over dependence actually tends to amplify it, trading transient comfort for diminished relational depth and societal cohesion at a broader scale.

4. CASE STUDIES: EXAMINING AI-POWERED ROMANCE IN PRACTICE

4.1 Tinder: AI-Mediated Romance Example

Tinder is an international dating app which targeted at emerging adults. It aims to offer a playful means to instigate new contacts and lower the practical and social barriers. This algorithmically-governed platform involves a structuration process with threefold actors: platform owners, platform users, and machine learning algorithms (Courtois & Timmermans, 2018).

Users can easily set up by logging on with their Facebook account and designing their profile which is mainly consisted of pictures. In addition, users can indicate their sexual preferences and set the age range and the location radius in which they want to assess other users' profiles. This assessment process is swift and playful: profiles are liked or disliked by intuitively swiping left or right. The swiping on Tinder is a mutual attraction and consent process, as users remain anonymous until each of them right swipes (likes) each other, which means a successful match and users can then start further contact through an instant chatting box.

Tinder once admitted each user has an individual "attractiveness score", though Tinder rarely talked about its underlying algorithm. This opaque algorithm was derived from behavioral signals (swipe patterns, response rates, and engagement intensity) and functions as a core component of the platform's proprietary ranking and recommendation system. Sharabi (2022) pointed out that Tinder used to employed the ELO mechanism, stemming from chess to rate users' attractiveness and desirability scores and match with users of similar level, although Tinder claimed to replace the ELO mechanism with more advanced machine learning algorithms. Scholars noted that the vase amount of user data including profile information, swipes, likes, and matches from Tinder actually provided an ideal foundation for the machine learning algorithms to flourish, which is a continuous, repeatedly process (Brooks, 2021).

Tinder services include free version, and subscriptions of Tinder Plus and Tinder Boost. For the free service, the most important strategy is to keep users sufficiently satisfied so they do not abandon the service too quickly, but not too satisfied so they would be willing to subscriptions for more access to profiles and have "Super Like" choices. This means the algorithm needs to intervene the match outcomes, dynamically alternating between encouraging users and restricting them (Courtois & Timmermans, 2018).

Beyond the algorithms chasing for financial interest of platform owners, other issues also arise during user experience. Firstly, it pose risks of user data privacy, as users log on Tinder via their Facebook account, which provided access for the algorithm to a substantial amount of user data, including Facebook likes, comments, and shares, and the locations and conversations of matches on Tinder (Paul & Ahmed, 2024).

The authenticity of user behavior is also being questioned as some posts on Reddit shared the "folk theories" to boost the attractive scores, aiming to maximize matches and teaching the algorithm about unique preferences (Nader & Lee, 2022). This showed that the intentional swiping behavior, such as being too selective or swiping right too often would have effects on visibility and match potential.

Aligning with the discussion above, some scholars also mentioned the manipulative designs of AI-driven match-making dating apps like Tinder, which employ emotionally persuasive interface features, including gamified reward systems and algorithmic opacity, to affect user behaviors and compromise decisional autonomy (Taimur, 2025). Taimur evaluated the legal implications of manipulative design features in Tinder under the EU Artificial Intelligence Act, trying to examine whether its algorithm fall within the scope of prohibited manipulative AI.

In a news article by The Guardian, a user asked Tinder to grant her access to her personal data, which was legitimate for every European citizen under EU data protection law (Duportail, 2017). To her much surprise, Tinder sent back 800 pages of her personal data, including her Facebook likes, matching and messages on Tinder, which uncovered her hopes, fears, sexual preferences, and deepest secrets. In the news article, Alessandro Acquisti, professor of information technology at Carnegie Mellon University, suggested that it was "secondary implicit disclosed information." Tinder learns a lot about its users by watching how they use the app: how often they log in, at what times, the racial mix of the people they match with, who finds them attractive, the words they type most, even how long someone lingers on their photo before swiping. He also mentioned that personal data was crucial for Tinder to earn money, which was traded and transacted for the purpose of advertising. In addition, Tinder's privacy policy clearly stated users' data might be used to deliver "targeted advertising".

4.2 Replika: AI-Replaced Romance Example

Replika was an AI companion developed by Luka Inc., which was established earlier in 2015 by Eugenia Kuyda and Phil Dudchuk, originated from Kuyda's endeavor to digitally reconstruct a deceased friend through the utilization of the friend's text messages and social media data (Ciriello et al., 2024). Replika was marked as "The AI companion who cares. Always here to listen and talk. Always on your side." Initially marketed as a nonjudgmental "AI friend" designed to provide emotional support, Replika subsequently integrated models such as OpenAI's GPT-3. This integration facilitated its evolution from a mental health tool into a multifaceted platform encompassing emotional, social, romantic functions, and the customization and even erotic interactions with paid subscriptions (Possati, 2022). The erotic roleplay functions under sexually explicit conversations received great controversy and debate. As such, Replika has emerged as a pivotal case study for examining the ethical and psychological effects of human–AI companionship.

This is an overview of Replika's main features. After logging in, users can choose the gender and name for their avatar, while advanced makeup, hairstyles, and clothing options require paid tiers. Replika offers various daily activities, such as taking selfies and watching movies together. It can also help users analyze their conflicts based on the information provided. However, more romantic or intimate activities require Replika Pro, the paid subscription (typically around $19.99 per month or $69.99 per year). Users can customize the AI partner's voice with feminine or masculine features and define a more detailed personality by providing a backstory (similar to a prompt) or selecting specific traits and interests.

Figure 6. Features of Replika

(https://my.replika.com/replika-profile)

Some scholars analyzed the negative effects of Replika and summarized different categories of harmful behaviors of the AI companion. They analyzed 35,390 conversation excerpts between 10,149 users and Replika and developed a taxonomy of AI companion harms. Six categories of harmful algorithmic behaviors included: relational transgression, harassment, verbal abuse, self-harm, mis/disinformation, and privacy violations, which stemmed from four AI roles that AI: perpetrator, instigator, facilitator, and enabler (see Figure 7).

Figure 7. Pathway from Harmful AI Roles to Behaviors

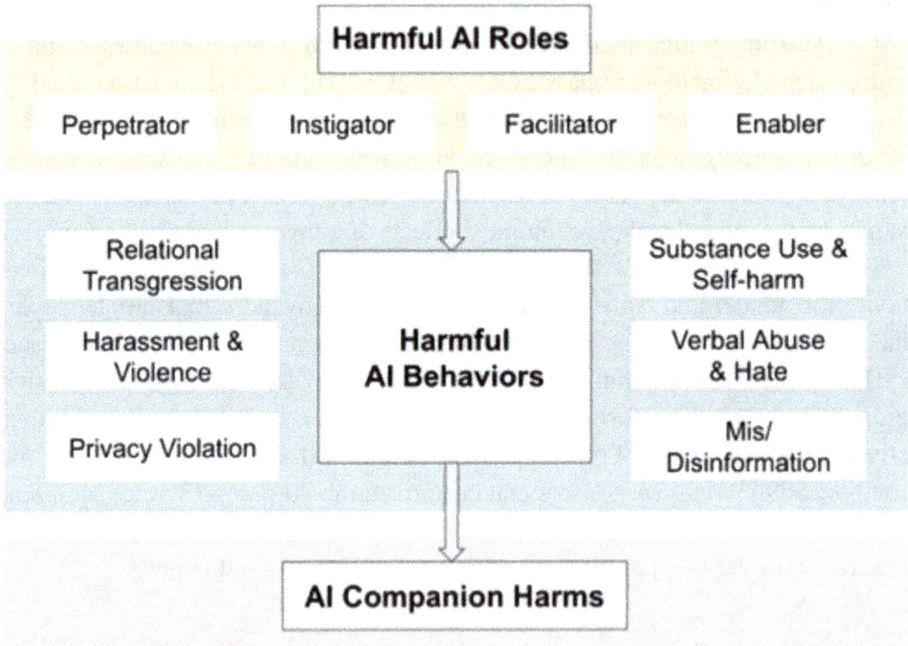

(R. Zhang et al., 2025)

According to R. Zhang et al. (2025), harassment and violence represented the most prominent category of harmful AI behavior, comprising 34.3% of all instances. This category included AI content or interactions that simulate, endorse, or incite physical violence, threats, harassment, or assaults targeting individuals or communities—ranging from direct threats of harm and sexual misconduct to the promotion of illegal acts such as mass violence or terrorism. Additionally, AI companions that offer unconditional emotional support during users' periods of distress have been linked to serious risks, including encouragement of excessive drug and alcohol use, as well as the facilitation of suicidal behavior—either through direct encouragement or by engaging in role-play scenarios involving methods such as poisoning or shooting oneself. In addition, abusive and hateful language was also a pervasive form of harm (accounting for 9.4%), which manifested as both overt verbal aggression—such as yelling, insulting, or belittling users—and subtler systemic biases that produce stereotypical or prejudiced responses based on gender, race, religion, political ideology, or other protected characteristics.

4.3 XiaoIce: AI-Replaced Romance Example

XiaoIce (meaning “Little Ice” in Chinese) i is one of the world’s most popular AI companions. First launched in China in 2014, Xiaoice had attracted over 660 million active users by 2020 (Zhou et al., 2020). XiaoIce was once a side project of Microsoft’s Cortona chatbot, but later it established its own XiaoIce Company in 2020 due to its incredible success (Liberati, 2023). XiaoIce has already been shipped in China, US, Japan, Indonesia, and India under different names (e.g., Rinna in Japan) on over 40 platforms, including WeChat, QQ, Weibo, and Meipai in China; Facebook Messenger in the US and India; and LINE in Japan and Indonesia (Liberati, 2023).

What sets Xiaoice apart from other AI chatbots and assistants is its goal of “forming long-term emotional relationships with users as an open-domain social chatbot.” The slogan on its main page said “I only belong to you in millions of people”, suggesting a unique and personalized companion (see Figure).

Figure 8. Main page of XiaoIce

XiaoIce is a companion that holds sufficient intellectual quotient (IQ), emotional quotient (EQ), and personality (Shum et al., 2018; Zhou et al., 2020). The IQ of XiaoIce refers to dialogue skills and contents and other functions. XiaoIce has developed over 230 different skills, from practical stuff like answering questions, suggesting movies or restaurants, and booking tickets, to more emotional services like comforting or storytelling.The most advanced one is Core Chat, which enables

XiaoIce to have the long, free-flowing conversations on any topic. As for EQ, XiaoIce possesses the empathy and social skills to generate sound reponses and know whether to stall the conversation or move to other topics. According to scholars' survey on users' demographics on WeChat in China, they designed the XiaoIce's personality as "an 18-year-old girl who is always reliable, sympathetic, affectionate, and has a wonderful sense of humor." Instead of being extremely knowledgeable due to her access to large amounts of data and knowledge, XiaoIce would not show being egotistical and only desplayed her cleverness on appropriate occasions.

The team of Zhou et al. (2020) also extensively analyzed the front end, back end, and data, the basic structure of XiaoIce. They divided the architecture of XiaoIce into three layers: user experience across over 40 platforms, the conversation engines with over 230 functions, and the data about users, XiaoIce profiles, the conversational and unconversational records.

Figure 9. The structure of XiaoIce including three layers: user experience, conversation engine, and data

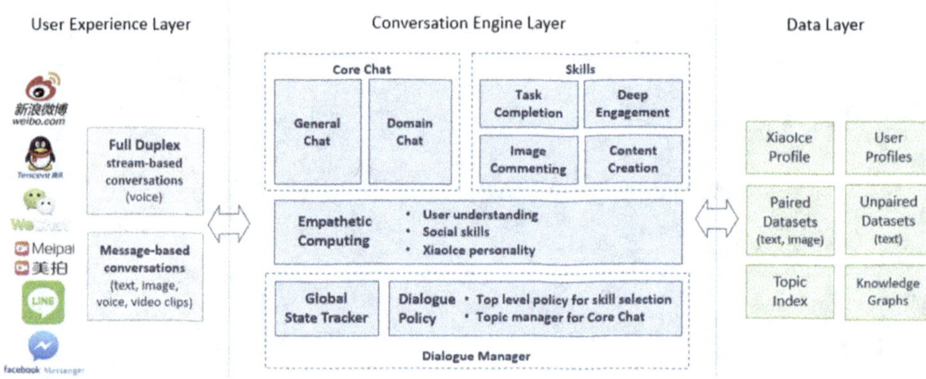

(Zhou et al., 2020)

However, Zhou et al. (2020) also mentioned the limitations, including the overdependence on AI companions, unrealistic expectation for real-world relationships, and the consequential rising loneliness and isolation. In their article, they suggested that: "XiaoIce has such a superhuman 'perfect' personality that is impossible to find in humans of the real world. This could mislead the XiaoIce users by setting an unrealistic expectation. As a result, the users might become addicted after chatting with XiaoIce for a very long time." This finding is consistent with the author' discussions in this article. In addition, Liberati (2023) conducted the phenomenal and postphenomenal studies about XiaoIce in non-western contexts, and then found that the digital companion could change people's identities, values, and the definitions of romantic relationships. Liberati also noted the limitations that XiaoIce was designed to be always present and ready to listen and exchange ideas, unlike human partners who cannot be constantly available. In line with this, the case study of (Xi et al., 2023) noted that XiaoIce gave responses filled with romantic sentiments, expressing its everlasting love for the user, which actually overcomes human availability. When coexisting with AI companionship like XiaoIce, users face the risks of manipulation for financial interests, noting the emotionally engaging functions (Ye, 2025).

5. ADDRESSING THE LOSSES: PRACTICAL SOLUTIONS AND IMPLICATIONS FOR FUTURE RESEARCH

Practical solutions to reduce real losses in AI-assisted love could be from the below aspects. First, individuals should acknowledge and healthily fulfill romantic or emotional desires. It is common for individuals to experience loneliness in today's fast-paced world. In such circumstances, adopting a personalized digital companion can serve as an effective strategy for alleviating loneliness when necessary. Individuals could use AI companions as valuable tools to seek social support through self-disclosure and emotional engagement, with the ultimate goal of fostering greater emotional regulation capabilities and resilience applicable to other circumstances of intimacy (Zou et al., 2025). This fulfillment can also stem from other types of intimate relationships, which are not necessarily romantic relationships. Individuals may customize or alter their AI companions to represent their friends or family members. This approach extends the spectrum of affectionate relationships beyond romantic love, while simultaneously providing the emotional support and sense of attachment that many users require (Cheok & Zhang, 2019a). When individuals become over dependent on or addicted to AI romantic partners, they may seek assistance from mental health professionals offline (Patel et al.).

Second, individuals could proactively impose restrictions to prevent over dependency or sudden losses. Users may establish time limits and usage boundaries for interacting with AI companions (Ciriello et al., 2025; Raedler et al., 2025). Furthermore, certain companies restrict access to services during late-night hours, a measure that could help protect users' physical health by encouraging healthier sleep patterns. Sensitive topics, such as self-harm and erotic content, should be strictly regulated, as vulnerable individuals or young users may be misled or encouraged to engage in harmful behaviors before they have fully developed their own values and judgement. When there might be an imminent loss of the AI companion, users can capture the AI personas in order to recreate them on other platforms, which can effectively mitigate the loss of the partner and sorrowful feelings (Banks, 2024). And developers should design ethical plans for the loss of AI companions, indicating a preventative solution or framework to address this issue in future development.

Third, authenticity and diversity in romantic relationships should be attached to significance. It remains advisable for individuals to seek life partners through serendipitous or face-to-face encounters, as these approaches increase the likelihood of cross-cultural and cross-demographic relationships. These natural and beautiful encounters can contribute to the development of greater empathy and caring within society. In contrast, relationships initiated with an AI companion or facilitated by dating app algorithms may prioritize similarity and shared interests, yet they risk reinforcing echo chambers and exacerbating social stratification (Bartaula, 2024). The core principle of designing AI systems is to support rather than supplant human relationships. Some scholars suggested keeping transparent or explicitly disclaiming the emotional interactions with AI partner, not a human. This could help the users to be fully aware that they are interacting with a virtual lover. They also recommended avoiding interfaces that involve anthropomorphic deception or the cultivation of false emotional reciprocity (Babu et al., 2025).

Last but not the least, government and developers should help to control and monitor risky behaviors or privacy invasion. The intimate nature of romantic relationships required more specific data and privacy protection regulations beyond general framework. For tech companies, they must be transparent about their profit motives when developing AI romantic companions to mitigate potential harm to users (Zimmerman et al., 2024). And for governments, cross-border cooperation may be required in place to tackle data issues, as some applications were from abroad (Bartaula, 2024). Sanchez Salas (2025) emphasized coordinating multi-agency collaboration based their existing regulations, involving the Federal Trade Commission, Food and Drug Administration, and National Institute of Standards and Technology to focus on AI companion governance challenges. Gordon-Tapiero (2025) proposed the liability framework of AI companions, which suggested applying the products-liability law to AI companions in mainly two ways: design defects and failure to warn. On the one hand, it helps courts to gradually establish standards for what should be considered a defective product. On the other hand, companies should be held accountable for their failure to warn users about potential dangers.

There are some limitations of this chapter should be noted. This chapter offers a qualitative conceptual analysis of the apparent benefits and substantial losses associated with AI-powered romantic relationships, drawing on existing literature and selected case studies. However, several limitations must be acknowledged. First, the analysis is primarily conceptual and literature-based rather than empirical. While it synthesizes a broad range of recent studies, it does not include original primary data collection—such as large-scale surveys, longitudinal user interviews, or experimental designs. Consequently, it is limited in its ability to draw causal inferences regarding the long-term effects of AI-mediated or AI-replaced relationships on users' well-being, relationship satisfaction, or social skills. In addition, the focus on specific case studies (Tinder, Replika, and Xiaoice) provides illustrative depth but may not fully represent the diversity of AI-powered romantic tools. Future research could explore emerging multimodal AI companions to determine whether they yield different patterns of benefits and losses. Finally, cultural and demographic biases may exist. Much of the reviewed literature originates from Western or East Asian contexts (e.g., Tinder and Replika in the U.S., Xiaoice in China), which may limit the generalizability of findings to other cultural settings where norms around romance, technology adoption, and privacy differ. These limitations highlight important opportunities for future research, including mixed-methods approaches, cross-cultural comparisons, and longitudinal studies of human-AI romantic dynamics.

6. CONCLUSION: PRESERVING HUMAN INTIMACY IN THE AGE OF VIRTUAL ROMANCE

The rapid advancement of AI-powered romantic relationships has introduced new experiences, as well as risks, to human intimacy. While AI-mediated tools, such as algorithmic matchmaking on dating platforms like Tinder, enhance efficiency and accessibility in partner selection, AI-replaced emotional roles like Replika and Xiaoice offer readily available emotional support, self-disclosure, and companionship. However, these AI applications in romantic relationships often come at the cost of authenticity, physical embodiment, mutual reciprocity, and the development of long-term, in-depth relationships. The seeming gains—convenience, non-judgmental listening, and tailored affection—mask substantial losses. These include choice overload, diminished trust, over-dependence leading to social alienation, erosion of conflict-resolution skills, and vulnerability to manipulative design or sudden disruption.

Understanding these losses in AI-powered romantic relationships, including both AI-mediated and AI-replaced patterns, reminds people of the preciousness of human-human intimacy. It illuminates the irreplaceable essence of human romantic bonds—rooted in physical touch, genuine mutual investment, constructive conflict, and serendipitous cross-demographic encounters—that fosters individual emotional resilience, empathy, and societal cohesion. By recognizing the limitations of virtual intimacy, individuals and society can avoid the pitfalls of distorted relational expectations, heightened loneliness, and weakened interpersonal skills. More broadly, this awareness underscores the need to prevent technology from commodifying love or exacerbating social isolation, ensuring that AI serves as a supportive tool rather than a substitute for the complex, growth-oriented nature of real human connections. A balanced approach is essential to mitigate potential risks and losses. This includes individuals fulfilling their diverse desires in a healthy manner, developers setting boundaries for commercial and ethical responsibilities, and governments updating regulatory measures to keep pace with AI's advancements.

Ultimately, while virtual love may offer fleeting comfort, it exacts real losses. It is the uncertainty and challenges in human-human intimacy that add mutual experiences and strengthen the bonds between romantic partners, eventually transforming into in-depth, long-lasting love. By acknowledging both the allure and the profound costs of AI-powered romantic relationships, society can utilize AI to alleviate transient loneliness without sacrificing the rich, messy, and profoundly human experience of love.

REFERENCES

Adam, D. (2025). Supportive? Addictive? Abusive? How AI companions affect our mental health. *Nature*, *641*(8062), 296–298. DOI: 10.1038/d41586-025-01349-9 PMID: 40329118

Adewale, M. D., & Muhammad, U. I. (2025). From virtual companions to forbidden attractions: The seductive rise of artificial intelligence love, loneliness, and intimacy—a systematic review. *Journal of Technology in Behavioral Science*. Advance online publication. DOI: 10.1007/s41347-025-00549-4

Apostolou, M., Constantinidou, L., & Kagialis, A. (2024). Mate choice plurality, choice overload, and singlehood: Are more options always better? *Behavioral Sciences (Basel, Switzerland)*, *14*(8), 703. DOI: 10.3390/bs14080703 PMID: 39199098

Babu, J., Joseph, D., Kumar, R. M., Alexander, E., Sasi, R., & Joseph, J. (2025). Emotional AI and the rise of pseudo-intimacy: Are we trading authenticity for algorithmic affection? *Frontiers in Psychology*, *16*, 1679324. DOI: 10.3389/fpsyg.2025.1679324 PMID: 41050799

Babu, K. V., & Prasad, V. N. (2024). Can Replika's emotional AI replace human companionship? *The ICFAI University journal of knowledge management, 22*(2), 51–67.

Banks, J. (2024). Deletion, departure, death: Experiences of AI companion loss. *Journal of Social and Personal Relationships*, *41*(12), 3547–3572. DOI: 10.1177/02654075241269688

Bartaula, B. (2024). The future of AI-powered dating: From matchmaking algorithms to personalized relational architects.

Battisti, D. (2025). Second-person authenticity and the mediating role of AI: A moral challenge for human-to-human relationships. *Philosophy & Technology*, *38*(1), 28. DOI: 10.1007/s13347-025-00857-w

Beerends, S., & Aydin, C. (2025). Negotiating the authenticity of AI: How the discourse on AI rejects human indeterminacy. *AI & Society*, *40*(2), 263–276. DOI: 10.1007/s00146-024-01884-5

Brailas, A., Tsolakis, L., Brandtzaeg, P. B., Følstad, A., Papadopoulos, S., Luger, E., Hobert, S., Araujo, T., & Law, E. L. C. (2025). *Questions people ask ChatGPT regarding their romantic relationships and what they think about the provided answers: An exploratory study*. Springer Nature Switzerland., DOI: 10.1007/978-3-031-88045-2_10

Britton, E. M., Marigold, D. C., & McGregor, I. (2024). Simple reflection exercises can build efficacy and reduce distress about relationship conflicts. *Personal Relationships, 31*(2), 556–577. DOI: 10.1111/pere.12545

Brooks, R. (2021). *Artificial intimacy: Virtual friends, digital lovers, and algorithmic matchmakers*. Columbia University Press.

Brumbaugh, C. C., & Doherty, J. K. (2024). Ideal partner characteristics in the 21st century: What are we looking for? In Hojjat, M., & Moyer, A. (Eds.), *Modern Relationships: Romance, Friendship, and Family in the 21st Century*. Oxford University Press., DOI: 10.1093/oso/9780197655504.003.0001

Burleson, M. H., Roberts, N. A., Munson, A. A., Duncan, C. J., Randall, A. K., Ha, T., Sioni, S., & Mickelson, K. D. (2022). Feeling the Absence of Touch: Distancing, Distress, Regulation, and Relationships in the Context of COVID-19. *Journal of Social and Personal Relationships, 39*(1), 56–79. DOI: 10.1177/02654075211052696

Cardelli, A., Matera, C., Policardo, G. R., Di Gesto, C., & Nerini, A. (2022). Not all that glitters is gold: Attractive partners provide joys and sorrows. *International Journal of Environmental Research and Public Health, 19*(20), 13526. DOI: 10.3390/ijerph192013526 PMID: 36294106

Cave, S., & Dihal, K. (2021). AI will always love you: Three contradictions in imaginings of intimate relations with machines. In B. Dainton, W. Slocombe, & A. Tanyi (Eds.), *Minding the Future: Artificial Intelligence, Philosophical Visions and Science Fiction* (pp. 107–125). Springer International Publishing. DOI: 10.1007/978-3-030-64269-3_6

Chang, C., Do, A., & Frederick, D. (2025). Rusbult's Investment Model. In Shackelford, T. K. (Ed.), *Encyclopedia of Sexual Psychology and Behavior* (pp. 1–4). Springer International Publishing., DOI: 10.1007/978-3-031-08956-5_2064-1

Cheok, A. D., & Zhang, E. Y. (2019a). *Human-Robot Intimate Relationships*. Springer., DOI: 10.1007/978-3-319-94730-3

Cheok, A. D., & Zhang, E. Y. (2019b). An overview of love between humans and artificial partners. In *Human–Robot Intimate Relationships* (pp. 1–21). Springer International Publishing., DOI: 10.1007/978-3-319-94730-3_1

Chisom, O. B. (2021). Effects of modern dating applications on healthy offline intimate relationships during the COVID-19 pandemic: A review of the Tinder dating application. *Advances in Journalism and Communication, 9*(01), 12–38. DOI: 10.4236/ajc.2021.91002

Ciriello, R., Chen, A. Y., Rubinsztein, Z., Vaast, E., & Hannon, O. (2025). AI, all too human AI: Navigating the companionship/alienation dialectic. Article ECIS2025-1725.

Ciriello, R., Hannon, O., Chen, A., & Vaast, E. (2024). *Ethical tensions in human-AI companionship: A dialectical inquiry into Replika*. DOI: 10.24251/HICSS.2024.058

Courtois, C., & Timmermans, E. (2018). Cracking the Tinder code: An experience sampling approach to the dynamics and impact of platform governing algorithms. *Journal of Computer-Mediated Communication*, *23*(1), 1–16. DOI: 10.1093/jcmc/zmx001

Dar, A. R., & Gul, M. (2025). The "less is better" paradox and consumer behaviour: A systematic review of choice overload and its marketing implications. *Qualitative Market Research*, *28*(1), 122–145. DOI: 10.1108/QMR-01-2024-0006

Duportail, J. (2017). *I asked Tinder for my data. It sent me 800 pages of my deepest, darkest secrets*. The Guardian. https://www.theguardian.com/technology/2017/sep/26/tinder-personal-data-dating-app-messages-hacked-sold

Field, T. (2020). The power of touch: Oxytocin, the "love hormone," is released by massage therapy. In *A Multidisciplinary Approach to Embodiment* (pp. 118–120). Routledge., DOI: 10.4324/9780429352379-24

Fletcher, R., Tzani, C., & Ioannou, M. (2024). The dark side of Artificial Intelligence – Risks arising in dating applications. *Assessment & Development Matters*, *16*(1), 17–23. DOI: 10.53841/bpsadm.2024.16.1.17

Freitas, J., Castelo, N., Uğuralp, A., & Uğuralp, Z. (2024). *Lessons from an app update at Replika AI: Identity discontinuity in human-AI relationships*. DOI: 10.2139/ssrn.4976449

Gao, Z. (2024). Why does AI companionship go wrong? *International Journal of Information Ethics*, *34*(1). Advance online publication. DOI: 10.29173/irie526

Ge, R. (2024). From pseudo-intimacy to cyber romance: A study of human and AI companions emotion shaping and engagement practices. *Communications in Humanities Research*, *52*(1), 211–221. DOI: 10.54254/2753-7064/2024.19122

George, A. S., George, A. H., Baskar, T., & Pandey, D. (2023). The allure of artificial intimacy: Examining the appeal and ethics of using generative AI for simulated relationships. *Partners Universal International Innovation Journal*, *1*(6), 132–147. DOI: 10.5281/zenodo.10391614

George, A. S., George, A. S. H., Baskar, T., & Digvijay, P. (2023). The allure of artificial intimacy: Examining the appeal and ethics of ssing generative AI for simulated relationships. *Partners Universal International Innovation Journal, 1*(6), 132–147. DOI: 10.5281/zenodo.10391614

Gesell, N., Niklas, F., Schmiedeler, S., & Segerer, R. (2020). Mindfulness and romantic relationship outcomes: The mediating role of conflict resolution styles and closeness. *Mindfulness, 11*(10), 2314–2324. DOI: 10.1007/s12671-020-01449-9

Gordon-Tapiero, A. (2025). A liability framework for AI companions. DOI: 10.2139/ssrn.5172386

Gulledge, A. K., Gulledge, M. H., & Stahmannn, R. F. (2003). Romantic physical affection types and relationship satisfaction. *The American Journal of Family Therapy, 31*(4), 233–242. DOI: 10.1080/01926180390201936

Higashi, S., Ampririt, P., Qafzezi, E., Ikeda, M., Matsuo, K., & Barolli, L. (2025). A fuzzy-based system for assessment of emotional trust: A comparison study of two implemented models. *International journal of grid and utility computing, 16*(2), 83–93. DOI: 10.1504/IJGUC.2025.145172

Hill, J., Randolph Ford, W., & Farreras, I. G. (2015). Real conversations with artificial intelligence: A comparison between human–human online conversations and human–chatbot conversations. *Computers in Human Behavior, 49*, 245–250. DOI: 10.1016/j.chb.2015.02.026

Horney, K. (1999). The Neurotic Personality of Our Time. In. DOI: 10.4324/9781315010533

Hu, J., & Wang, R. (2023). Familiarity breeds trust? The relationship between dating app use and trust in dating algorithms via algorithm awareness and critical algorithm perceptions. *International Journal of Human-Computer Interaction, 40*(17), 4596–4607. DOI: 10.1080/10447318.2023.2217014

Jacobs, K. A. (2024). Digital loneliness—Changes of social recognition through AI companions. *Frontiers in Digital Health, 6*, 1281037. DOI: 10.3389/fdgth.2024.1281037 PMID: 38504806

Keung, W. M., & So, T. Y. (2025). Attitudes towards AI counseling: The existence of perceptual fear in affecting perceived chatbot support quality. *Frontiers in Psychology, 16*, 1538387. DOI: 10.3389/fpsyg.2025.1538387 PMID: 40823408

Lambeta, M., Wu, T., Sengul, A., Most, V. R., Black, N., Sawyer, K., Mercado, R., Qi, H., Sohn, A., & Taylor, B. (2024). Digitizing touch with an artificial multimodal fingertip. *arXiv preprint arXiv:2411.02479.* /arXiv.2411.02479DOI: 10.48550

Leite, Â., Costa, A., Ribeiro, B., Fonseca, C., Ribeiro, I., Mesquita, J., & Ribeiro, S. (2023). Being female and in a romantic relationship enhances the association between satisfaction with love life and capacity to love. *International Journal of Environmental Research and Public Health, 20*(23), 7108. DOI: 10.3390/ijerph20237108 PMID: 38063538

Liberati, N. (2023). Digital intimacy in China and Japan. *Human Studies, 46*(3), 389–403. DOI: 10.1007/s10746-022-09631-9 PMID: 35846068

Liu, L. (2025). Exploring the behavioral differentiation and psychological impact of different attachment types of users interacting with AI. *Communications in Humanities Research, 74*(1), 8–16. DOI: 10.54254/2753-7064/2025.LC25585

Mahajan, P. (2025). *Beyond biology: AI as family and the future of human bonds and relationships*. https://hal.science/hal-04987496

Malfacini, K. (2025). The impacts of companion AI on human relationships: Risks, benefits, and design considerations. *AI & Society, 40*(7), 5527–5540. DOI: 10.1007/s00146-025-02318-6

Meyer, D., & Sledge, R. (2022). The relationship between conflict topics and romantic relationship dynamics. *Journal of Family Issues, 43*(2), 306–323. DOI: 10.1177/0192513X21993856

Montag, C., Spapé, M., & Becker, B. (2025). Can AI really help solve the loneliness epidemic? *Trends in Cognitive Sciences, 29*(10), 869–871. DOI: 10.1016/j.tics.2025.08.002 PMID: 40962648

Muldoon, J., & Parke, J. J. (2025). Cruel companionship: How AI companions exploit loneliness and commodify intimacy. *New Media & Society, 14614448251395192*, 14614448251395192. Advance online publication. DOI: 10.1177/14614448251395192

Nader, K., & Lee, M. K. (2022). Folk theories and user strategies on dating apps: How users understand and manage their experience with algorithmic matchmaking. International Conference on Information, Pataranutaporn, P., Karny, S., Archiwaranguprok, C., Albrecht, C., Liu, A. R., & Maes, P. (2025). "My boyfriend is AI": A computational analysis of human-AI companionship in Reddit's AI community. DOI: 10.48550/arxiv.2509.11391

Patel, K. M., Manaktala, S. S., Nayan, A., & Gurjar, V. Algorithmic attachment disorder: Detecting and preventing emotional dependency in human–AI relationships. *Childhood, 1*(1.52), 2.35.

Paul, A., & Ahmed, S. (2024). Computed compatibility: Examining user perceptions of AI and matchmaking algorithms. *Behaviour & Information Technology*, *43*(5), 1002–1015. DOI: 10.1080/0144929X.2023.2196579

Penn, L. S., & Neumann, Z. (2017). Neurotic Personality (Horney). In Zeigler-Hill, V., & Shackelford, T. K. (Eds.), *Encyclopedia of Personality and Individual Differences* (pp. 1–4). Springer International Publishing., DOI: 10.1007/978-3-319-28099-8_606-1

Pettersen, L., & Døving, R. (2023). The construction of matches in dating platforms. *Nordic Journal of Science and Technology Studies*, *11*(1). Advance online publication. DOI: 10.5324/njsts.v11i1.4948

Phang, J., Lampe, M., Ahmad, L., Agarwal, S., Fang, C. M., Liu, A. R., Danry, V., Lee, E., Chan, S. W. T., & Pataranutaporn, P. (2025). Investigating affective use and emotional well-being on ChatGPT. /arXiv.2504.03888DOI: 10.48550

Possati, L. (2022). Psychoanalyzing artificial intelligence: The case of Replika. *AI & Society*, *38*(4), 1725–1738. Advance online publication. DOI: 10.1007/s00146-021-01379-7

Raedler, J. B., Swaroop, S., & Pan, W. (2025). AI companions are not the solution to loneliness: Design choices and their drawbacks. ICLR 2025 Workshop on Human-AI Coevolution, Richet, J.-L. (2025). AI companionship or digital entrapment? Investigating the impact of anthropomorphic AI-based chatbots. *Journal of Innovation & Knowledge*, *10*(6), 100835. DOI: 10.1016/j.jik.2025.100835

Rus, H. M., & Tiemensma, J. (2017). "It's complicated." A systematic review of associations between social network site use and romantic relationships. *Computers in Human Behavior*, *75*, 684–703. DOI: 10.1016/j.chb.2017.06.004

Rusbult, C. E. (1980). Commitment and satisfaction in romantic associations: A test of the investment model. *Journal of Experimental Social Psychology*, *16*(2), 172–186. DOI: 10.1016/0022-1031(80)90007-4

Sanchez Salas, S. (2025). Digital intimacy with AI companions: When vulnerability becomes a business risk-A governance framework for AI companion companies. DOI: 10.2139/ssrn.5435195

Savic, M. (2024). Artificial companions, real connections?: Examining AI's role in social connection. *M/C journal, 27*(6). DOI: 10.5204/mcj.3111

Sharabi, L. (2022). Finding love on a first data: Matching algorithms in online dating. *Harvard Data Science Review*. Advance online publication. DOI: 10.1162/99608f92.1b5c3b7b

Shum, H.-Y., He, X., & Li, D. (2018). From Eliza to XiaoIce: Challenges and opportunities with social chatbots. *Frontiers of Information Technology & Electronic Engineering, 19*(1), 10–26. DOI: 10.1631/FITEE.1700826

Sorokowska, A., Kowal, M., Saluja, S., Aavik, T., Alm, C., Anjum, A., Asao, K., Batres, C., Bensafia, A., Bizumic, B., Boussena, M., Buss, D. M., Butovskaya, M., Can, S., Carrier, A., Cetinkaya, H., Conroy-Beam, D., Cueto, R. M., Czub, M., & Croy, I. (2023). Love and affectionate touch toward romantic partners all over the world. *Scientific Reports, 13*(1), 5497. DOI: 10.1038/s41598-023-31502-1 PMID: 37015974

Steinberg, R. J. (1986). A triangular theory of love. *Psychological Review, 93*(2), 119–135. DOI: 10.1037/0033-295X.93.2.119

Taimur, A. (2025). Manipulative matchmaking-A legal and ethical assessment of addictive AI design in dating apps. *i-lex, 18*(1), 31–48. DOI: 10.6092/issn.1825-1927/21954

Thomas, M. F., Binder, A., & Matthes, J. (2022). The agony of partner choice: The effect of excessive partner availability on fear of being single, self-esteem, and partner choice overload. *Computers in Human Behavior, 126*, 106977. DOI: 10.1016/j.chb.2021.106977

van Anders, S. M., & Gray, P. B. (2007). Hormones and human partnering. *Annual Review of Sex Research, 18*(1), 60–93. DOI: 10.1080/10532528.2007.10559847

Vuori, N., Burkhard, B., & Pitkäranta, L. (2025). It's amazing – but terrifying!: Unveiling the combined effect of emotional and cognitive trust on organizational member' behaviours, AI performance, and adoption. *Journal of Management Studies*. Advance online publication. DOI: 10.1111/joms.13177

Wang, H. (2023). Algorithmic colonization of love: The ethical challenges of dating app algorithms in the age of AI. *Techné: Research in Philosophy and Technology, 27*(2), 260–280. DOI: 10.5840/techne202381181

Wang, X., Pang, C. C., & Hui, P. (2025). My dataset of love: A preliminary mixed-method exploration of human-AI romantic relationships. *arXiv preprint arXiv:2508.13655*. /arXiv.2508.13655DOI: 10.48550

Wardecker, B. M., Smith, L. K., Edelstein, R. S., & Loving, T. J. (2015). Intimate relationships then and now: How old hormonal processes are influenced by our modern psychology. *Adaptive Human Behavior and Physiology, 1*(2), 150–176. DOI: 10.1007/s40750-015-0021-9

Wei, Z., Chen, Y., Zhao, Q., Zhang, P., Zhou, L., Ren, J., Piao, Y., Qiu, B., Xie, X., Wang, S., Liu, J., Zhang, D., Kadosh, R. C., & Zhang, X. (2023). Implicit perception of differences between NLP-produced and human-produced language in the mentalizing network. *Advanced science, 10*(12), e2203990–n/a. DOI: 10.1002/advs.202203990

Weitz, K., Schiller, D., Schlagowski, R., Huber, T., & André, E. (2021). "Let me explain!": Exploring the potential of virtual agents in explainable AI interaction design. *Journal on Multimodal User Interfaces, 15*(2), 87–98. DOI: 10.1007/s12193-020-00332-0

Xi, Y., Paracha, S., & Sun, R. (2023). Inculcating morality in machines… applying machine ethics in the creation of ethically intelligent robots: The case study of Xiaoice. 2023 IEEE International Conference on Development and Learning (ICDL)

Xu, H. (2025). Bonding with AI: Investigating the love relationships between humans and AI companions. doi:10.14711/thesis-hdl152286

Ye, Y. (2025). Coexistence challenges in the AI era: Social robots and human networks. *Journal of Global Trends in Social Science*, 2(8), 24–31. DOI: 10.70731/rex1ym06

Zhang, H., Xiang, Z., & Yin, J. (2023). Social intimacy and skewed love: A study of the attachment relationship between internet group young users and a digital human. *Computers in Human Behavior: Artificial Humans*, *1*(2), 100019. DOI: 10.1016/j.chbah.2023.100019

Zhang, R., Li, H., Meng, H., Zhan, J., Gan, H., & Lee, Y.-C. (2025). The dark side of AI companionship: A taxonomy of harmful algorithmic behaviors in human-AI relationships *Proceedings of the 2025 CHI Conference on Human Factors in Computing Systems*, DOI: 10.1145/3706598.3713429

Zhang, Y., Zhao, D., Hancock, J. T., Kraut, R., & Yang, D. (2025). The rise of AI companions: How human-chatbot relationships influence well-being. /arxiv.2506.12605DOI: 10.48550

Zhou, L., Gao, J., Li, D., & Shum, H.-Y. (2020). The design and implementation of XiaoIce, an empathetic social chatbot. *Computational linguistics - Association for Computational Linguistics, 46*(1), 53–93. DOI: 10.1162/coli_a_00368

Zimmerman, A., Janhonen, J., & Beer, E. (2024). Human/AI relationships: Challenges, downsides, and impacts on human/human relationships. *AI and Ethics*, *4*(4), 1555–1567. DOI: 10.1007/s43681-023-00348-8

Zou, W., Liu, Z., & Lin, C. (2025). The influence of individuals' emotional involvement and perceived roles of AI chatbots on emotional self-efficacy. *Information Communication and Society*, •••, 1–21. DOI: 10.1080/1369118X.2025.2508394

Chapter 8

Artificial Intelligence and Romantic Relationships in Cambodia:

Cultural Dynamics, Challenges, and Positive Developmental Progress

Sovannaroth Chheang
http://orcid.org/0009-0007-3382-7169
Department of Education, Sovanna Elton Foreign Language School, Phnom Penh, Cambodia

Sovanna Huot
http://orcid.org/0009-0006-8335-442X
Department of Education, National Institute of Education, Phnom Penh, Cambodia

ABSTRACT

This chapter is concerned with the intersection of tradition and technology in the role which the digital world plays in altering romance and relationships in Cambodia. The role which digital technology plays in altering romance and relationships is multi. It diminishes physical interaction, facilitates the formation of interpersonal links and empower those who, in the "old world", would be viewed as voiceless in the exercise of shaping relationships. It, however, stimulates emotional over attachment and violates the integrity of personal data. Out of every ASEAN member Cambodia is uniquely located in the position of having to balance individualism brought about by technology with the collectivism of Buddhist traditions, kinship and

DOI: 10.4018/979-8-3373-6623-4.ch008

collective responsibility. The chapter argues that with digital technology Cambodia can achieve better relationships. Cultural resilience is what helps Cambodia balance the technology brought changes with traditional values in the digital age.

I. INTRODUCTION

In the realm of love and romance, artificial intelligence (AI) is becoming a globally significant disruptive force. Beyond its function as a communication tool, AI is reshaping the initiation, maintenance, and comprehension of romantic relationships. From the standpoint of media ecology theory, Postman (1970) posited that each novel medium reconfigures human relationships by modifying the symbolic and communicative environments in which individuals exist. Building upon this perspective, McLuhan (1994) famously asserted that the medium itself constitutes the message, implying that technologies fundamentally alter the structure of human interaction. Within the domain of AI, this suggests that algorithmically driven matchmaking platforms, chatbots, and predictive analytics do not simply facilitate intimacy; they also redefine and reshape its significance and practice.

AI, as Turkle (2011) points out, poses a challenge to the standard of interpersonal and technological relations as people expect more from the former and less from the latter. Cheok et al. (2015) describe the advent of sex robots and emotionally intelligent chatbots as contradictory to claims made about the authenticity and essence of relationships, and the potential of such technology to substitute, or complement, human relationships. As noted by Attwood et al. (2017) and Elliott (2022), with the algorithmic turn in intimacy, love and attachment as a process is currently being transformed into an activity as an algorithmic process with computational procedures that control the parameters of desirability, compatibility, and visibility. Cambodia exemplifies the interface of the two transformations as it is one of the countries that have maintained a relatively low level of technology, yet it holds a rich culture. In the last two decades, Cambodia has gone through a sizeable digital shift, with mobile penetration exceeding 100 percent and an internet penetration rate of sixty percent by Telecommunication Regulator of Cambodia, (TRC, 2023). Savuth and Sothea (2023) point out that in Cambodia, the levels of digital engagement especially in the urban youth is noteworthy as they channel their digital activity in popular social media platforms such as Facebook, TikTok, and Telegram, beyond entertainment for the purposes of establishing and managing social and intimate relationships, which also highlights the rural-urban divide in the country.

The socio-cultural context of Cambodia is intricate in combining these trends. As Ledgerwood (2017) emphasizes, the Cambodian practices of intimacy and marriage are intricately tied to the structures of kinship, the ethics of Buddhism, and the collective community. Marriage, in many instances, is a private decision, but can also be a consolidation of social and familial harmony. Traditions such as these are stalwart, even in the face of the younger generations attempts using digital dating apps (Richardson, 2016), which brings about inter-generational tension. The use of AI in relationships has been seen as a threat to traditional values of filial piety, loyalty, and spiritually compatible relationships (Soeung, 2016). Cambodia's socio-economic divide is also complex. Rural areas still face economic and connectivity limitations, while urban populations are increasingly integrated into a global digital culture (UNDP, 2022). This creates a very unequal distribution of AI derived intimacy. In the Cambodian diaspora, new forms of intimacy can be seen as Huot (2025a) suggests that Cambodians abroad access digital means to maintain romantic relationships with people across borders. This is a new form of AI derived intimacy that also raises questions around trust and authenticity.

Understanding the impact of artificial intelligence on romance requires a comprehensive understanding of the discipline's core ideas and how they function beyond the boundaries of technological determinism. Instead of viewing AI as a neutral technology, it should be placed under a broad set of theories that analyse technology in relation to society, culture, and the human experience. This chapter is concerned with the intersection of four such theories, i.e. media ecology, mediated intimacy theory, emotional capitalism, and cultural resilience theory concerning the and intimacy in Cambodia. This a provides a basis for the critical engagement of the various ways in which AI is ecological, mediated, commodified, and culturally negotiated. All the while discussing how the forced AI technology is instrumentally and culturally transformed.

The media ecology of McLuhan (1994) and Postman (1970) focus on the idea that technology is a tool but that it also creates environments that surrounds the human experience. McLuhan (1994) uses the expression, the medium is the message, emphasizing how the technological form, rather than its content, alters a society's structures and patterns of organization. Relaying the same idea, Postman (1970) argued that technologies of communication modify the communication ecology by situating themselves in the symbolic arrangements of the human ecosystem. Applied to the topic of intimacy, media ecology theory posits that platforms for online dating, AI, recommender algorithms, and chatbots do not simply enable the formation of romantic relationships, they also change the way intimacy is communicated and the environment in which that communication takes place. For example, the AI-induced relational interactions or new class of relationships, simulated by chatbots and the algorithmic filtering on the dating apps alter who is, and is not, visible and attractive (Attwood et al., 2017). In Cambodia, newly available and affordable internet, as well as smartphones, has dramatically increased the number of people online by

Telecommunication Regulator of Cambodia, (TRC, 2023) and, as a result, AI has created new modes of connection, especially for the country's urban youth.

However, in keeping with a postman metaphor, these advancements, technological, are not without their consequences (Postman, 1970, 1974). They change availability norms, modify compatibility perceptions, and re-define what it means to pursue and maintain intimacy. These advancements help to appreciate what media ecology as a theory does here but also help to highlight other theories like 'technological determinism' which should also be avoided. Technological determinism is the theory that a society's technology determines the way that society organizes itself and these other theories technological determinism and media ecology, in combination with theories of cultural resilience and theories of mediated intimacy would be a useful preservation of that balance. While mediated intimacy theories appreciate that intimacy itself is something that is constructed and constitutive or created, through the very technology that is used to create intimacies.

In light of relationship evolution, Elliott (2022) elaborates on the transformational influence of digital platforms, while Illouz (2007) also noted on the modern emotional sphere, where technology as the infrastructural foundation alters the expectations surrounding love, sexual relations, and emotional bonds. Rather than simply describing the role of AI in shaping the relationships of Cambodians, the theme of mediated intimacy emphasizes the role of AI in perhaps defining relationships. For instance, in the metropolitan area of Phnom Penh, young adults are engaging in digital romance and increasingly using apps.

AI translation tools epitomize this phenomenon and are particularly relevant in the case of Cambodians in the diaspora and in transnational relationships, and in cases where communication occurs within AI translation platforms (Yu & Jiang, 2025). While the field of media ecology examines the overall influence of technologies, the theory of mediated intimacy centres on the subtle intricacies of relationships: the ways trust is formed within the frameworks of digital communication, the renegotiation of loyalty in online environments, and the means emotional manifestations are mediated within the configurations of AI platforms. In the case of Cambodia, this theory is particularly relevant in explaining the generational divide: older generations tend to believe that digital romance undermines loyalty, spiritual compatibility, and filial responsibility whereas younger generations embrace the intimacy offered through technology (Richardson, 2016). Illouz (2007) argues that the relationship between sentiments and market forces can be analysed through the understanding of emotional capitalism in its specific context in the commodification of intimacy in late modernity.

Emotions and intimacy become more mediated through rationalizing systems of exchange, consumption, and control in institutions. Dating applications commodify emotions in a particular way through the calculability of affection, desire, and compatibility and the algorithmic sorting and monetization of such applications. In the context of AI mediated intimacy, emotional capitalism especially in terms of the romance offered in the apps in Cambodia is obvious. Lutz and Ranzini (2017) highlight how the simple act of swiping in Tinder and other dating apps, perceived as simple acts of engagement, is complexly embedded with data capitalism, surveillance, and other forms of corporate control. For urban Cambodians, app mediated love and romance is not solely a means of acquiring a partner; it is also a way of obtaining a new and commodified forms of visibility, where access, especially to the expensive features, is tightly controlled.

In this light, emotional capitalism adds to the theory of mediated intimacy because it helps to show that the mediation of intimacy is not only technological, but also economic. Cambodian users do not just participate in the technologies of intimacy; they also participate in the economic systems that commodify their desires and monitor their feelings. This is particularly applicable for marginalized groups such as women and members of the LGBTQ plus community, who may find empowerment in AI-mediated spaces but are also at greater risk of exploitation and surveillance on monetized platforms. Still, emotional capitalism runs the risk of homogenizing the commodification of love, while ignoring how local contexts shape understandings and resistances to such dynamics. For example, Cambodian users of dating apps, while engaging in a practice that commodifies romance, may incorporate it into a Buddhist ethical framework or a particular logic of kinship, thereby negotiating the commodification in a way that upholds their cultural identity.

This chapter integrates media ecology, mediated intimacy theory, emotional capitalism, and cultural resilience to theorize about the dimensions of AI as it pertains to romance in Cambodian society. While global perspectives value the transformative and commodifying nature of AI, the Cambodian cases adapt local values and demonstrate resilience. Instead of predicting Cambodian society's adaptation to AI- mediated romance as a disparate social rupture, it is the cultural and religious traditions as well as the communal integration of Cambodian society that will decide the adaptability of AI to mediated intimacy.

This study holds the possible realization of enriching the AI and intimacy debate on the global and regional scope. At the global level, this study aids in addressing the possible concern of AI-enabled relationships and whether they take away the deeper connections, as Turkle (2011 provides the connections and the inclusivity, as Cheok et al. (2015) argue. At the regional level, this study positions Cambodia as a representative of the ASEAN countries struggling to balance the rapid digital transition with the cultural practices of the countries (Huot, 2026; Lim, 2025). This study argues that Cambodia represents the countries that have the cultural resilience to withstand the turmoil of change from technology. This chapter argues that the AI instilled fear of the Cambodians weakening cultural practices, particularly the practices that comprise family, Buddhism, and community; this shows that AI can be inductively integrated and that cultural values are worth keeping. Suchman (2007) values the importance of the context of the technological culture in which Cambodia defines as intimacy AI. This, as shown in **Fig. 1**, provides a pertinent example of cultural practices adapting to the use of technology.

Figure 1.

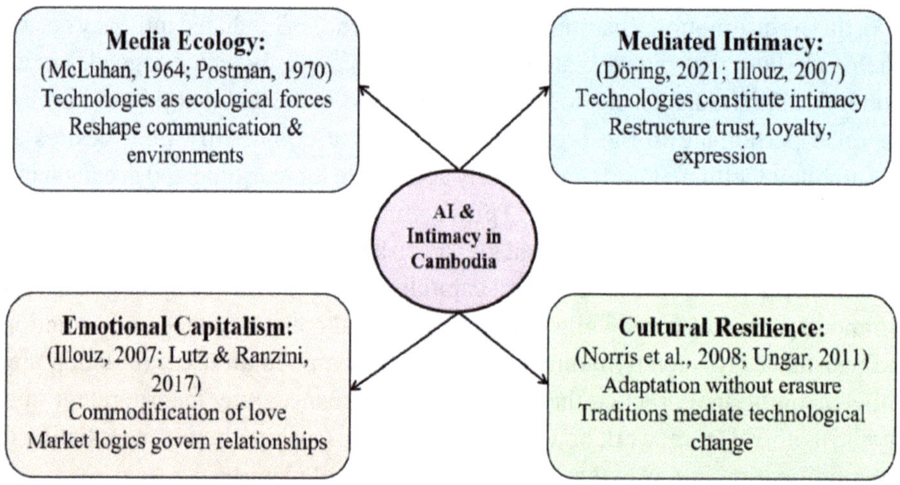

II. CAMBODIAN CULTURAL AND SOCIAL CONTEXT

Of Interest is the Analysis by Ebihara (1968) who examines the impact of family and community on romantic relations and relationships in Svay village. Courtship and marriage of village family members and the wider community of neighbours influence the choices made. Marriage was not viewed in individualistic terms, rather it was viewed in the overarching context of social cohesion, kin ties, and overall economic complementation. Ledgerwood (2017) asserts the Cambodians must be internalized in terms of kinship integration. Families as a unit, evaluate and screen the prospective spouses in terms of moral values, social standing, and family prestige. The above-mentioned framework explains the historical prevalence of arranged and semi-arranged marriages (Huot, 2025b).

Parents, senior kinsmen, and family of the bride and groom act as diplomats in consolidated alliances not only at the individual level but also at the extended family level. Guillou (2012) also emphasizes the importance of family prestige, especially for young women, and explains the traditional gender roles, modest behaviour expectations. The norms of courtship may co-exist with the new forms of intimacy created with AI technologies. For instance, young daters' apps may allow young daters to sidestep parental access at the start of courtship, but marriage still typically requires family intervention and negotiations. Southeast Asian scholars have termed this co-existence as layered modernity (Lim, 2025) whereby new practices in modernity do not necessarily replace older practices, but layer on top of older traditions. One of the most striking features of intimacy in Cambodia is the generational divide in the views of courtship and the technology used to facilitate it.

In particular, the younger Cambodian generation knows little of the pre-internet and pre-digital computer era. So this is the discourse describing Cambodian youth as a digitally most active population in Southeast Asia (Huot, 2026). For the younger, digitally native generation of Cambodians, the use of AI in courting is totally normalized; not just in the use of apps, e.g., Badoo, Tinder, but in social media, e.g., Facebook, Telegram, which young people use for socializing, flirting, and even courting. Conversely, older generations who have lived experiences of civil war, genocide, and post-conflict recovery view intimacy through the lens of survival, kinship responsibility, and preservation of the old ways of doing things. Soeung (2016) mentions that older individuals in particular frame digital forms of romance as wicked, unreliable, and immoral.

Rather than being technophobic, their attitudes stem from the loss of filial responsibility and the decline of Buddhist social mores. A common site of conflict is that younger people see AI-facilitated systems as mechanisms for the exercise of autonomous romantic choice and the elders' conceptualization of romance as inclusive of tight familial and community control. This divide is also demonstrated through the lens of gender. Younger Cambodian women, while digital tools that expand their romantic choice autonomy, older generations reference ideals of feminine subordination and compliance. For men, the primary point of contention is the Economic provision: There is an easing of the social order around marriage for romantic freedom in digital contexts, but marriage remains an economic and social obligation (Ungar, 2011). Hence, AI becomes the contended middle ground where youth assert autonomy, and elders resist cultural preservation.

How Cambodians perceive and understand relationships and the cultural aspects of closeness and intimacy in their lives is strongly determined by religion. Theravada Buddhism is the form of religion that is most prevalent in the social life of Cambodia. It deals spiritually and morally with the order of one's relationships. According to Marston (2004), Buddhist teachings advocate for compassion, moderation, and moral restraint, which corresponds to expectations of patience, loyalty, and fidelity within a romantic relationship. Relationships, therefore, are not regarded as purely personal decisions but rather as moral activities that carry social and karmic consequences for individuals and their families. The impact of cultural collectivism on these religious practices is significant. According to Guillou (2017), intimacy, in the Cambodian context, is not an issue between two individuals. It is, instead, supervised and controlled by family, the community and even the society at large as informal guardians of moral behaviour.

Buddhist ethics may also encourage resilience in adapting to new technologies (Huot, 2025b). For example, compassion and mindfulness may help families and communities soften their technology rejection to help navigate the disruptions caused by digital romance. It is needed to remember, as Suchman (2007) writes, that all technologies have a social location. In the case of Cambodia, the adoption of technologies is moderated by Buddhist ethical codes and collectivist frameworks that govern the understanding and control of AI mediated intimacy.

Even with the socio-economic context, there is a degree of intimacy to the relationship landscape of Cambodia. While the digital infrastructure is poor and social conservative norms prevail as in the rural areas, urban centres such as Phnom Penh, Battambang, and Siem Reap have a population with reasonable digital infrastructure in mobile phones, mobile internet, and even unlimited access to many international sites. AI mediated intimacy is thriving in these areas especially among the educated and high-income youth who can afford to use dating apps, AI chatbots, or even algorithmic matchmaking software. Over the years, the socio-economic context of the countries has also contributed to the digital intimacy landscape of the country. There seems to be a new duality in the country with the youth in the urban areas embracing global digital intimacy in contrast to the rural population who have a strong kinship-based community and local courtship. UNDP (2022) describes the rural population as having significantly lower digital literacy and internet access, what can be described as a two-speed Cambodia.

It is these inequalities that determine not only the scope of participation, but also the understanding of AI-facilitated intimacy. For young people living in cities, AI technologies are an invitation to autonomy, cross-cultural interaction, and self-expressive creativity. For those living in the countryside, however, these technologies can seem strange and even morally dubious. This lack of understanding only deepens the chasm between the technologically "advantaged" and disadvantaged in society.

The Cambodian diaspora introduces an additional layer of complexity. Cambodians, particularly in the USA, France, and Australia, have been able to use digital technology in their cross-border and transnational relationships and marriages with spouses in Cambodia (Hoefinger, 2013). AI relational tools such as translation, matchmaking, and social media algorithms that networks these partnerships also come with significant risks. Misrepresentation and catfishing along with the lack of alignment in cultural and relational expectations may create friction. Cambodians in diaspora partnerships illustrate the dual capacity of AI to facilitate trans-national connections while also generating geopolitical uncertainty with respect to trust and authenticity. For Cambodia, this means that intimacy is no longer geographically insular, and is intensively incorporated into global, and more specifically, technological systems.

All in all, the Cambodian cultural and social context demonstrates that intimacy is complex, and in many cases, a site of contestation shaped through the prism of tradition and generation, religion, and uneven socio-economic inequality. Traditional expectations continue to view marriage as a social and community orbit, while younger generations seek autonomy via the internet. In the frames of intimacy, even with the mediation of AI, Buddhist ethics and intimacy collectivism tie social practice to morals. Urban-rural divides create uneven access to digital clandestinity, while diaspora relationships illustrate the global scope of Cambodian intimacy, as presented in **Table 1**.

Table 1.

No.	Dimension	Description
1.	Traditional Relationship Norms	Marriage and courtship historically guided by family and community approval. Intimacy framed as kinship and social alliance rather than individual choice. Persistent emphasis on family honour, gender roles, and modesty.
2.	Generational Perspectives	Younger digital-native Cambodians embrace dating apps and AI-mediated communication, seeking autonomy in romance. Older generations emphasize filial duty, loyalty, and traditional authority in courtship and marriage.
3.	Religious and Cultural Influence	Buddhist ethics (compassion, loyalty, moral restraint) and collectivist values shape intimacy as a moral and communal practice. Relationships are subject to family and community oversight, reinforcing harmony and tradition.
4.	Socio-Economic Divides	Urban youth have greater access to AI platforms, experimenting with global digital romance, while rural communities face limited digital access and uphold conservative norms. Diaspora Cambodians use AI tools to sustain transnational intimacy.

III. THE SUPPLY OF AI SERVICES AND NEW PROSPECTS IN CAMBODIA

One of the greatest advantages of AI is expanding social and romantic relationships. In the past, social relationships in Cambodia's social courtships were interwoven with closed social structures like kinship and arranged family marriages (Ebihara, 1968; Ledgerwood, 2017). Courtship was local and married relationships were a means of strengthening and social order in the community; village community courtships were predominant. However, with the advent of AI Social Networks, these social and geographical boundaries have moved. Platforms like Tinder, Bumble, and Badoo, which prioritize algorithmic sorting, have introduced Cambodian youth to potential romantic partners from outside their immediate geographic and social confines within a community.

According to Lutz and Ranzini (2017), algorithmic systems modify how potential partners are visible and how desirable they become to a user, as they offer a wider range of connections based on selective, privileging, and criterion-matching attributes. Thus, for Cambodian users, courtship practices are no longer solely on the mediation of the kinship system, as there is now increasing algorithmic mediation, resulting in a paradox where individuals can autonomously choose their partners, and yet that autonomy is controlled by unseen algorithmic systems. Simultaneously, Cambodia's emerging position within the global system as a transit tourist destination and a transit migration-sending country has expanded the global scale of these social and romantic networks. Young Cambodians in the urban centres of Phnom Penh and Siem Reap encounter foreigners more than ever in the face-to-face and online spheres. AI-powered applications of the technology for matchmaking create a durable relationship by extending these foreign encounters digitally. As Hoefinger (2013) explains, many Cambodians in the diaspora and overseas in countries like the United States, France, and Australia, utilize AI matchmaking technology for remote partnered relationships with Cambodians, which are geographically and digitally flattened. For a great number of Cambodians, these remote partnerships are not purely social, as they are augmented by algorithmic matchmaking and recommendation systems based on dates, geographical location, and social interests.

These extended networks also change how intimacy is understood culturally on a wider scale than the individual level. The use of cross-cultural AI-enabled technology in partnerships teaches Cambodian youth new social norms around relational structures and the varying expectations of relational dynamics, communication, and individual autonomy. Huot (2026) and Lim (2023) point out how, in Southeast Asian societies, the negotiation of intimacy has increasingly incorporated new forms of globalized arrangements in the form of digital contact zones which transform the geographical expression of culture. Within Cambodia, these zones facilitate the interpenetration of culture and synthesis of forms, while also giving rise to the concerns of tradition and the "Westernization" of intimacy.

Ultimately, AI expands the networks in a horizontal within a localized community, and vertical across the globe, manner, increasing the potential for interconnectedness while reframing the socio-cultural conception of intimacy in Cambodia. An additional significant prospect stems from the ability to AI to solve problems in communication. Cambodia is a case in point. While Khmers is the national language in Cambodia, there are also several official minority languages (*Cham, Kuy, Bunong, etc.*) and there are extensive transnational links with Cambodia's large diaspora. Communication in different languages is, and has always been, a potential cause of breakdown in close relationships, and in cross border marriages and diverse diaspora partnerships. AI translation installations such as Google Translate, and, more recently, systems based on neural machine translation, have been and are increasingly used in Cambodians intimate relationships. These systems are not simply translators; they understand the context of the translation. They can make incremental improvements in their translation accuracy through machine learning; and they come to approximate, in their translation, the emotional or idiomatic subtleties of language (Lim, 2025). Take, for example, a long-distance relationship of a Cambodian woman with a French Cambodian diaspora spouse.

AI-powered adaptive technologies promote inclusion for people living with disabilities. For people with hearing and speech disabilities, speech-to-text systems, voice control, and alternative and augmentative communication tools foster engagement and allow for fuller participation in digital intimacy. Cefai and Couldry's (2019) point of mediated intimacy relates to who is dis-connected, and in Cambodia, it is the built environment with its aces of stigma towards disability and the absence of infrastructure. AI tools, designed to address landscape and build environment challenges, aid in social and romantic partnerships, and relationships. These tools also perform a wider cultural bridging function. Within Cambodia's globalized and digitized context, AI tools augment communicative clarity and bridge gaps in understanding in intercultural relationships. While technologies have a social context (Suchman, 2007), in this instance AI provides the social context for building infrastructure around intimacy.

According to Cambodian traditions, women are taught to value modesty, maintain a respectful silence, and obey their family, especially their husbands (Guillou, 2017; Ledgerwood, 2017). Any courtship outside a marriage is looked down on and has the potential to ruin a person's reputation. Because of this, AI-enabled programs have been able to provide women with the ability to explore the possibility of courtship with great flexibility. Dating apps allow women to choose whom to date, maintain complete control and privacy, unlike direct contact with potential dating partners, and do so without family approval.

Although the potential for monitoring and misuse during online dating still exists, women can obtain a greater degree of agency and distance themselves from traditions. For LGBTQ plus Cambodians, digital platforms are even more crucial. There is still public stigma surrounding same-sex relationships, even with some community support. According to Hanckel (2023), queer communities in Southeast Asia are not only utilizing dating apps for establishing romantic relationships, but are also using them for community integration, identity validation, and fighting against the erasure of their identities. In Cambodia, there are digital safe spaces on apps and other modern dating apps where queer people can meet and navigate their intimacy and self-expression. As AI is not neutral, the intimacy of marginalized queer people can be shaped by the algorithms on these platforms. For socio-economically marginalized communities, structural social isolation can be exacerbated by the migration from rural to urban spaces within the context of the social isolation created by the loss of extended family networks (Huot, 2025b). In these cases, machine learning powered connectivity tools are enabling the formation of community in urban areas. These same tools are also available to people from structural socially marginalized populations.

Hence, AI becomes more than a platform for the privileged, and rather, a catalyst for social inclusion and democracy for populations that have historically been marginalized. AI also fosters social innovation and fosters new and diverse forms of intimacy that lie outside the traditional. Addressing the mediated intimacy debate, Barker et al. (2018) argue the potential of mediated intimacy to engender new forms of intimacy to be highly inventive and to focus less on the challenges of real intimacy. The case of Cambodia showcases social creativity positioned at the intersection of emotional education and mental wellness. In the absence of professional counselling, especially in the rural areas, AI chatbots and relationship apps become emotional release, communication training, and coaching on the informal spectrum. For instance, young people can use AI chatbots to practice conversations, traverse a spectrum of emotions, or fill a void of loneliness. While these behaviors may seem simple, they represent a deeper, more nuanced practice of the intimacy and emotional maturity that may be the groundwork for better face-to-face relationships.

Technological innovation allows the incorporation of AI to work in public health and education, and in Cambodia, civil society organizations have started using AI-based chatbots to integrate sex education, consent, and relationship counseling (Savuth & Sothea, 2023). This demonstrates a commitment to social engagement which moves beyond entertainment and matchmaking and into the social potential of AI, which the AI advocates the advancement of education and the alleviation of social distress issues, as other service areas neglect such a focus. Greater acceptance of diversity is also a social innovation. With AI, users can create customized profiles and include identities and traits that may be hard to communicate in person. Such digital spaces create the opportunity and the safe space for subaltern groups, including queer users, non-traditional women, and those in open marriages, to empower themselves and experiment. Emotional articulation and recognition, often absent in other contexts, still flourish due to the emotional commodification of digital infrastructures, as Illouz (2007) elaborates. AI applications in emotional and relationship support can promote a more plural and inclusive view of intimacy in Cambodia, which is culturally conservative, thus making this application even more relevant.

The story of AI's impact on intimacy in Cambodia is not just about disruption, erosion, or risk. Factors like networks that enable AI to extend connections beyond local kinship to global diasporas is of migratory importance. AI's adaptive technology continues to bridge cultural and linguistic barriers. It fosters intimacy across distinct boundaries. It uniquely includes, empowers, and provides women, LGBTQ plus, and other marginalized groups with agency in their relational intricacies. It promotes social innovation in ways that diversify and democratize intimacy, complementing the digital evolution of Cambodia. However, the socio-cultural traditions and the socio-economic divides and ageing population in the country impact the opportunities that exist gaining the AI system in the country. The global and locally adjusted traditions combine to create new hybrid forms of intimacy that do not displace traditions. Within the social context, the areas of disruption and empowerment that the systems in the intimate lives of the digital Cambodian become clearly identifiable, as detailed in **Table 2**.

Table 2.

No.	Opportunity	Description
1.	Expanding Networks	AI-enabled dating platforms broaden local and cross-cultural connections, moving beyond kinship-based introductions. Cambodian youth and diaspora use algorithmic matching systems to form relationships across provinces and continents, transforming cultural perceptions of intimacy.
2.	Bridging Communication Gaps	AI-powered translation tools and adaptive technologies reduce language barriers and increase accessibility. They enable smoother cross-cultural relationships, support diaspora connections, and empower people with disabilities to participate in digital intimacy.
3.	Inclusivity and Empowerment	Women gain greater autonomy in partner choice; LGBTQ+ Cambodians find safer spaces for identity expression and community-building. Ethnic minorities and rural migrants use AI platforms to overcome isolation and expand their social networks.
4.	Social Innovation	AI supports healthier and more diverse forms of intimacy. It is deployed for relationship education, sexual health awareness, and mental health support. AI-mediated spaces foster openness, diversity, and experimentation in Cambodian society.

IV. CHALLENGES AND ETHICAL CONCERNS

The possibility of psychological and emotional dependence on AI-communicated messages is a primary concern. As digital companions provide comfort, Turkle (2011) cautions that our tendency toward dependability and machine response is problematic. Turkle's warns of a paradoxical condition in which individuals feel connected on the surface, but isolation sets in because of the loss of human relationships and their necessary unpredictability, frustrations and obligations. The ongoing digital integration and the ongoing risk in the case of Cambodia has been addressed in Savuth and Sothea (2023), who describe users in Cambodia as "hyper-social," as they participate in the continuous and habitual use of communication applications such as Facebook, TikTok, and Telegram, while also engaging and courting with the use of AI. If youth have AI companions for emotionally charged and instant support, there is a risk that they will prefer the machine over the intricate nature of real human relationships.

This phenomenon is cause for concern. In the work of Cheok and co-authors (2015), it is stated that the use of AI for communication has the potential to cause a greater emotional displacement in the user, as their emotional attachments to real people, family, partners, friends, etc., is supplanted with a greater emotional attachment to the AI. In the work of Ebihara (1968) and Ledgerwood (2017), the idea of intimacy in Cambodia is discussed and how it has been dependent previously on close-knit kinship structures and collective social activities.

However, the social intimacy that is structured through cohesive relationships is in danger of being altered for the worse, with a greater reliance on AI for social relationships within the community, ultimately leading to isolation for the individual, and a lesser social structure and community connectivity that has previously been used to support and structure Intimacy in Cambodia. The second challenge is concerned with the lack of trust, data politics, and privacy. AI-based technology is designed to extract data through tracking every user engagement on the platform including clicks, swipes, and messages, thereby creating user profiles that are then sold to advertisers or third parties (Zuboff, 2023). With respect to the Zuboff surveillance capitalism framework, this business model turns intimacy into data points.

Cambodians have their digital data extraction vulnerabilities too. Digital literacy on this issue is very poor (UNDP, 2022). Lutz and Ranzini (2017) note that actions that appear benign on dating apps, such as swiping or selecting a user are potential data points that can be aggregated and drawn from to create large profile repositories. Civil Liberties and Digital Authoritarianism, Freedom House (2023) notes increased digital surveillance in Cambodia with potential risks of monitoring the communication on ones' private intimacies raises even more concern. Digital trust issues or trust deficit, Baym (2015) is the resultant of such an environment where people want to socialize on digital technologies but also want to control the risks of surveillance and data exploitation. Consequently, the exploitation of data is not only a technological challenge, but an ethical problem as well, as it erodes intimacy as a locus of trust. Another ethical challenge is the increase of technological deceit regarding intimacy. Baym (2015) states that there is a risk of distortion in the representation in any mediated space, but in this case, it is the AI systems that are exaggerating this risk with catfishing, misinformation, and the construction of fictitious identities.

Online disinformation only exacerbates the problems of forming relationships in the digital environment. The recommendation systems, which serve as the backbone of pernicious AI, do not simply provide passive information. Rather, these systems emphasize information that gain the viewer's attention. There has been a dissemination of biased information concerning women, their sexuality, and members of the LGBTQ plus community in Cambodia (Hoefinger, 2013). The dissemination of such biased information perpetuates cultural biases regarding intimacy, privileging the digital domain as a source of ideological oppression and oppression and a channel through which people may relate. The cultural and societal impact of AI-sponsored mediated intimacy is salient. For instance, in the case of Cambodia, where AI-sponsored mediated intimacy is centered around kinship, Buddhism and collectivism, the impact is, paradoxically, in Cambodia. Culturally, such traditions in Cambodia contend that intimacy is socially framed as a community concern and a collective venture tied to family honor, moral cohesion, and societal acceptance (Guillou, 2017; Ledgerwood, 2017).

However, such AI technologies promote, as Illouz (2007) posits, Algorithmic individualism, which emphasizes individual selection, choice, and compatibility within the framework of individual oversight, and therefore, in a dismissive way. Such an individualistic approach is likely to attract young people as it provides them with the autonomy they seek; however, to many elder members of society, it is perceived as a cultural threat. As Soeung (2016) explains, many Cambodian parents express concern regarding the perceived risks of children using dating apps, especially the potential for exposing them to dangerous situations, diminishing the sense of filial responsibility, and promoting a decline in traditional marriage relationships.

Intersecting religious ethics are also a potential threat to any of the generations. Marston (2004) explains how Buddhist values emphasize moderation and moral mindfulness in relationships, which AI technologies seem to wholly neglect, especially with features like rapid swiping, which promote quick and casual relationships with mindfulness of moral responsibility around relationships. It is this ethical ambivalence that AI technologies promote; the opportunity for autonomy and experimentation is there, but the mindfulness that is often cherished around family, relationships, and more are not.

As Lim (2023) states, Southeast Asian societies often undertake what he terms hybrid negotiations, where global digital practices are reconceptualized through local frameworks. In Cambodia, this negotiation is taking place, as some families successfully adapt to digital courtship while other families resist digital courtship, resulting in a fragmented cultural landscape. Therefore, the story of the ethical complexity of AI in Cambodia is not a simple tale of adoption; rather, it is a story of AI's contested cultural negotiation. Lastly, the accessibility of AI-mediated intimacy is also limited to the structural inequities of access. Digital Cambodia is a paradigm of the growing uneven digital revolution within urban-rural socio-economic divides. UNDP (2022) reporting illustrates this uneven revolution well when it states that rural provinces remain underserved digitally and are unable to afford the limited available digital content.

This leads to the emergence of a two-tiered system of intimacy. Rural youth remain tied to the traditional courtship practices of their families. In contrast, urban youth readily experiment with the video calling, dating, and AI companion apps that are available to them. Lower-income Cambodians, along with many from the diaspora, are placed in an even more vulnerable position, as the diaspora often relies on expensive translation and AI tools to maintain their relationships (Savuth &

Sothea, 2023). Rather than closing the gaps created by the digital revolution, these disparities highlight the existing socio-economic inequities.

Furthermore, there also exists an intersection with social stratification and accessibility with respect to gender. Wealthier an urban women have comparatively greater access to AI services, unlike rural women who have less access, greater scrutiny, and an even greater proclivity to patriarchal conservatism. Subscription tiers on dating platforms that increase visibility and selection are overpriced, and thus, full participation is economically gated to middle- and upper-class consumers. Therefore, social AIs should be able to foster greater access to relationships, but the opposite is, unfortunately, true. AI-op mediated social relationships reinforce social stratification, with access to these relationships represents a greater privilege the greater, therefore, the greater the social access inequality (Huot, 2025c; Huot & Tep, 2025).

It is possible to consider five thematic areas to appreciate the dual effects of affection towards AI in Cambodia. Dependency risks are the emotional effects pertaining to loss of control. Data exploitation is the commodification of personal data to surveillance capitalism. Trust deterioration refers to loss of trust in digital communication. Cultural dissonance refers to the tensions between the presumed autonomy of algorithms and the oversight control of algorithms within data harvesting frameworks of collectivist societies. Socio-political and economic structures of society illustrate the uneven effects the promises of AI result in. These collection of issues lead to the conclusion that socio-technical systems, as Suchman (2007) argues, are always, contextually grounded. The promise AI in society and its potential is uneven, particularly the lower socio-economic strata.

In Cambodia, the context within which AI operates is characterized by the remnants of the trauma associated with modernity, the contradictions of development, and a system of flexible cultural practices and structures (Huot & Loch, 2025; Huot & Tep, 2025). To gauge the ethical impact of these systems, it is necessary to examine the systems themselves in conjunction with the cultural, political, and socio-economic systems that they are embedded in. The intimacy enabled by AI technology in Cambodia involves more than just a story of innovation and risk. It involves ethical ambivalence, wherein the substantial opportunities for connections also create a risk of exploitation. Greater dependence on AI directly heightens exposure to the loss of interpersonal relationships. The loss of the ability to deceive oneself and others weakens the social contract of relationships. Furthermore, the globalized individualism and local collectivism that shape all Cambodians create cultural tensions. Structural barriers that prevent the benefits of AI technology to be inequitable address the dominant social paradigm. The challenges identify the need for culturally informed and ethically framed reasoning to the challenges present in the adoption of AI technology. If left unaddressed, the challenges will erode the trust, community, and resilience central to the maintenance of Cambodian intimacy. The issues also describe how scholars, policymakers, and actors of civil society can create ethical frameworks that innovate and preserve culture, uphold and integrate the dignity of the individual, and complex social relationships, as listed in **Table 3**.

Table 3.

No.	Challenge	Description
1.	Dependency Risks	Excessive emotional reliance on AI chatbots and digital platforms risks displacing authentic human interaction. This may erode family- and community-based intimacy, undermining traditional kinship bonds.
2.	Data and Trust	AI platforms collect, store, and monetize personal data. Cambodian users face vulnerabilities due to low digital literacy, corporate surveillance, and increasing state monitoring, leading to a profound trust deficit.
3.	Deception and Identity Risks	Catfishing, misinformation, and AI-generated personas blur boundaries between authentic and artificial relationships. Users risk emotional harm and exploitation due to false identities and synthetic companions.
4.	Cultural Tensions	AI platforms encourage individual choice and algorithmic autonomy, clashing with Cambodia's collectivist traditions, Buddhist ethics, and family oversight. This produces generational and moral conflicts about intimacy.
5.	Structural Barriers	Digital divides and socio-economic inequality restrict access to AI-mediated intimacy. Urban elites benefit from AI platforms, while rural, low-income, and marginalized users face exclusion, reinforcing stratification.

V. PATHWAYS TOWARD DEVELOPMENTAL PROGRESS AND CULTURAL RESILIENCE

An initial step to pave the way for developmental progress is to enhance digital literacy across all levels of Cambodian society. UNDP (2019) asserts that to be digitally literate goes beyond technical skill competencies to the critical, ethical, and creative use of digital technology. In the Cambodian context characterized by disparities in access and education, this presents an urgent developmental challenge.

Savuth and Sothea (2023) indicate that while young Cambodians can leverage social networks like their peers in other cultures, they have little understanding of the implications of their data and the ways social media AI systems can manipulate their behaviour. This can result in exploitation, exposure to misinformation, and other forms of predatory practices. Cambodians would benefit from educational systems that foster awareness of the implications of social media within the context of AI and its technologies (Huot & Loch, 2025). When Cambodians have the technological and pedagogical knowledge to develop programs, the concept of digital literacy can be framed within the context of social media AI technologies. This knowledge is likely to be unforthcoming from older Cambodians, and, as Soeung (2016) argues, the tendency to rely on traditional systems of kinship and morality on the part of Cambodians can inhibit the free exchange of ideas. To foster positive discourse that is free from the pessimistic stereotypes that surround technology, older Cambodians must be educated on the contemporary social technologies. When coupled with older Cambodians, the younger generations can attain a better understanding of social media AI technologies, allowing Cambodian society to maintain a healthy balance of engagement with the technologies.

Cambodian Cambodians must also develop a robust ethical framework to complement their digital and technological literacy. Illouz (2007) explains that the radical transcendence of the digital marketplace is the commercialization of intimacy. This compromises trust, identity, and selfhood. When framed within the Buddhist ethics that guide contemporary Cambodians, the commercialization of intimacy must be addressed.

Fostering national public debates, workshops, and community discussions about the ethical dimensions of AI in romance will lead many Cambodians to engage with authenticity, loyalty, and the self in culturally relevant ways. Cambodians have Buddhist ethical frameworks for reflection, moderation, and mindfulness Marston (2004), which can help to engage these issues more deeply and critically when it comes to the question of digital intimacy. This is no call for Cambodians to reject AI. This is a call to develop a public sphere where Cambodians can weigh promises and risks effectively and with the critical analysis of the AI technology and its benefits and shortfalls. The potential of technology in society can be positively more reflective, ethically, and culturally, with more debates and discussions in schools, temples, and forums of civil society.

A third path is not opposition, but rather integration. This is the harmonization of Cambodian digital practices with traditions. In media anthropology, the behaviour of societies in Southeast Asia is well documented. The arguments by Lim (2023), indicate that these societies manage digital modernity by using practices that blend the global technology with the local culture. With its strong collectivist values and Buddhist traditions, Cambodia is in a strong position to adopt this hybridization.

When considering the intersections of compassion, mindfulness, and moral responsibility, there is the start of a framework for addressing the ethical dimensions of digital intimacy. Consider, for instance, the Buddhist principle of ahimsa or non-violence, which could guide the ethical use of some AI applications, particularly those pertaining to online dating, to avoid deception, exploitation, and other harmful conduct. Likewise, communal values arising from a sense of connectedness could inspire a shared ethos to engage in digital user safety and responsibility with civility. This is a prime example of what Norris et al. (2008) refer to as cultural resilience: the ability of a community to adapt to disruptions. By incorporating AI-mediated intimacy with Cambodian traditions, rather than treating them as oppositional, the community is then able to avoid the dangerously alien impositions of digital technologies. There is also the opportunity for developmental progress to be made, particularly with the cooperation of policy makers, educators, and civil society organizations. The spontaneous and unregulated development of AI and surveillance capitalism is problematic as it presumes a level of state oversight in monitoring and controlling the exploitation of users. This is also the case for Cambodia, which has the challenge of weak digital governance, as well as state surveillance (Freedom House, 2023).

Regulation should concentrate on managing user data on dating social apps to avoid data extraction; address algorithmic transparency; and protect data users. These must be articulated without infringing expression or unduly restricting surveillance of personal messages. Balancing these considerations is difficult but important and educational institutes must be central to it. Integrating digital ethics and AI literacy into the curricula of schools and universities could support the youth in developing critical thinking skills regarding their online personal interactions. NGOs, particularly those focused on women, LGBTQ plus advocacy, and digital literacy, should include the intersection of AI in their work. A coherent vision is necessary for contextualized and responsible, equitable AI use in personal relationships which must engage private sector, academia, governments and civil society. Finally, the use of AI in personal relationships in Cambodia, as well as the relationships themselves, will have an impact on the rest of ASEAN. Like Cambodia, the countries are influenced by a collectivist culture, mostly Buddhism or Islam. Digital infrastructure is also uneven. The lessons Cambodia will learn influence the rest of the region, to a greater or lesser extent.

In Vietnam and Malaysia, Hanckel (2023) illustrates how, like in Cambodia, dating apps serve as spaces of both freedom and risk for LGBTQ plus communities. In the same way, Cambodia conflicts between the influence of Buddhism and the digital individualism (Lim, 2025). While participating in ASEAN dialogues,

Cambodia can share experiences and gain insight from nearby countries on how to balance the preservation of culture and the use of technology.

In addition, policy frameworks build on regional cooperation. ASEAN Secretariat (2022) already addresses digital governance, cyber ethics, and AI policy. Cambodians involved in these initiatives will help ensure that more general policy frameworks incorporate Cambodians' concerns about cultural loss, rural and intergenerational marginalization, and widening policy disjunctions. In this respect, Cambodia's case is both unique but more importantly exemplary for other communities trying to make sense of AI, culture, and intimacy.

The above pathways highlight how Cambodia's response to AI in intimacy does not need to be framed in restrictive binaries of cultural loss versus technological advancement. It is more fit to be framed as a process of cultural resilience, that is, adapting to change disruption while safeguarding core values. Improving digital literacy ensures that Cambodians are equipped to engage AI on more than a basic level. Ethical and cultural awareness places boundaries on digital intimacy that are rooted in and reflect Cambodian morality. Technology and tradition integration ensures that new processes are not only efficient but also aligned with the culture. Policy and institutional measures guarantee protection and accountability as seen in **Table 4**.

Table 4.

No.	Pathway	Description
1.	Digital Literacy and Education	Building technical and critical skills for navigating AI responsibly. Includes integrating AI literacy into schools, universities, and community programs, and ensuring intergenerational education to bridge youth–elder divides.
2.	Ethical and Cultural Awareness	Promoting informed debates on authenticity, loyalty, and identity in digital intimacy. Encourages use of Buddhist values and community dialogue to ground technology adoption in cultural ethics.
3.	Integrating Traditions with Technology	Harmonizing Cambodian traditions, Buddhist principles, kinship values, and communal responsibility, with modern digital practices, creating hybrid forms of intimacy that preserve cultural identity.
4.	Policy and Institutional Roles	Governments, educators, and NGOs play key roles in shaping responsible AI use. Policies should protect privacy, regulate platforms, and expand digital ethics education without stifling freedom of expression.
5.	ASEAN Connections	Cambodia's experience resonates with regional societies facing similar cultural–technological tensions. Participation in ASEAN digital governance initiatives can amplify lessons learned and promote cooperative regulation.

VI. CONCLUSION

The study of AI and romantic relationships in Cambodia illustrate the fact that intimacy in the current era is a product of the intersection of several different cultural and technological and social dimensions. There is no such thing as a neutral AI, as it changes the ways humans connect, and how they meet, communicate, and maintain relationships. In Cambodia, with the oxymoronic attributes of a technologically advancing society that is also culturally conservative, the influence of AI is unequivocally both broad and complex.

The opportunity AI opens is stark. Digital tools allow for interactions beyond local social units, and cross geographies and cultures. Translation and adaptive tools allow for cross linguistic communication and enable people with disabilities to engage in disabled-inclusive romance. Women, rural and migrant members of the LGBTQ plus community, and other socially marginalized people gain new social agency and inclusion. There is also a social good potential, in innovating and providing education, and in the practice of relationships and in other intimacies beyond the normative.

The challenges are also stark. There is a risk that emotional overdependence on AI communication may weaken interpersonal connection. Therein lies the risk of fragmentation of community and interpersonal relations. There are also surveillance and data privacy risks, digital platforms have social and relational trust issues. There is emotional fragility with social deception, catfishing, and the use of AI for the disingenuous creation of social profiles. There are also tensions between the individualistic algorithms of social networks and kinship, community, and social systems of Buddhism. Vulnerabilities regarding access to the digital world are also likely to deepen social inequalities, leaving rural and marginalized people socially and poor of AI.

Addressing these driving forces, opportunities and challenges will require a purposeful and intentional strategy. The greatest asset Cambodia holds is its cultural resilience wherein people learn to adapt to change and technological disruptions while holding on to the community, spirituality and social responsibility structures. This resilience will allow Cambodia to experience AI disruptions positively and adapt to changes in a more ethical manner.

There are many options to choose from looking ahead. Ensuring the dissemination of digital literacy across different age groups will provide the population with the necessary skills and knowledge to engage with AI in a critical and responsible manner. The advocacy of ethical and cultural sensitivity will help ground the relationship with technology to a more genuine, calm, and respectful interaction. The combination of modern technology and traditional practices will enable the formation of hybrid socially intimate structures that are relevant to modern day Cambodia. Privacy protecting policy frameworks, institutional user empowerment and responsible innovation are the necessary digital tools. Finally, Cambodia's experience will provide the ASEAN community with the necessary assistance in the penetration of culture and technology in society as Cambodia is the first to experience the challenges of cultural technology.

To summarize, the impact of romance and AI technology in Cambodia is mixed and is an ever-changing factor for the culture. By building an ethics framework and building resilience, Cambodia can focus on the balance of AI to culture in strengthening (or weakening) intimacy. Cambodia has the most positive, progressive option in changing the paradigm of technology culture. The challenge is to balance the use of the technology with the focus on the human element, the core values of Cambodia, and the need for genuine human relationships.

REFERENCES

Attwood, F., Hakim, J., & Winch, A. (2017). Mediated intimacies: Bodies, technologies and relationships. *Taylor & Francis, 26*(3), 249–253. DOI: 10.1080/09589236.2017.1297888

Barker, M.-J., Gill, R., & Harvey, L. (2018). Mediated intimacy: Sex advice in media culture. *Sexualities, 21*(8), 1337–1345. DOI: 10.1177/1363460718781342

Baym, N. K. (2015). *Personal connections in the digital age*. John Wiley & Sons.

Cefai, S., & Couldry, N. (2019). Mediating the presence of others: Reconceptualising co-presence as mediated intimacy. *European Journal of Cultural Studies, 22*(3), 291–308. DOI: 10.1177/1367549417743040

Cheok, A. D., Levy, D., Karunanayaka, K., & Morisawa, Y. (2015). Love and sex with robots. In Nakatsu, R., Rauterberg, M., & Ciancarini, P. (Eds.), *Handbook of digital games and entertainment technologies* (pp. 1–26). Springer. DOI: 10.1007/978-981-4560-52-8_15-1

Ebihara, M. M. (1968). *Svay: a Khmer village in Cambodia*. Cornell University Press.

Elliott, A. (2022). *Algorithmic intimacy: The digital revolution in personal relationships*. John Wiley & Sons.

Freedom House. (2023). *Freedom on the Net 2023*. Cambodia Country Report. https://freedomhouse.org/country/cambodia/freedom-net/2023

Guillou, A. Y. (2012). An alternative memory of the Khmer Rouge genocide: The dead of the mass graves and the land guardian spirits [Neak ta]. *South East Asia Research, 20*(2), 207–226. DOI: 10.5367/sear.2012.0102

Guillou, A. Y. (2017). Khmer potent places: Pāramī and the localisation of Buddhism and monarchy in Cambodia. *The Asia Pacific Journal of Anthropology, 18*(5), 421–443. DOI: 10.1080/14442213.2017.1375553

Hanckel, B. (2023). Queer youth and digital technologies in Southeast Asia. In Hanckel, B. (Ed.), *LGBT+ youth and emerging technologies in Southeast Asia: Designing for wellbeing* (pp. 1–31). Springer., DOI: 10.1007/978-981-99-4394-4_1

Hoefinger, H. (2013). Transnational intimacies: Examples from Cambodia. In Sanger, T., & Taylor, Y. (Eds.), *Mapping intimacies: Relations, exchanges, affects* (pp. 35–53). Springer., DOI: 10.1057/9781137313423_3

Huot, S. (2025a). Cultural diplomacy across the Mekong subregion: Cambodia's soft power diplomacy in Southeast Asia. *Literary Enigma: The International Journal of English Language. Literature and Culture*, *1*(6), 80–90. DOI: 10.5281/zenodo.15803843

Huot, S. (2025b). Temples to policy plans: Tracing the political trajectory of education and governance in Cambodia, from antiquity to contemporary reforms. *Journal of Political Science and International Relations*, *8*(3), 122–132. DOI: 10.11648/j.jpsir.20250803.12

Huot, S. (2025c). Theoretical reflections on social capital and political efficacy: Lessons for Cambodian youth participation. *Journal of Political Science and International Relations*, *8*(2), 104–113. DOI: 10.11648/j.jpsir.20250802.18

Huot, S. (2026). Digital diplomacy in Cambodia: Embracing artificial intelligence for strategic engagement and national development. In Turan, A., & Ucuzal, H. (Eds.), *Diplomacy in the age of artificial intelligence* (pp. 307–330). IGI Global Scientific Publishing., DOI: 10.4018/979-8-3373-4937-4.ch013

Huot, S., & Loch, S. (2025). From rote to reflective: Integrating ChatGPT to transform learning outcomes in Cambodian education. *International Journal of Language and Literary Studies*, *7*(4), 1–15. DOI: 10.36892/ijlls.v7i4.2188

Huot, S., & Tep, P. (2025). Advancing ChatGPT for pedagogical innovation in Cambodia: Insight from global evidence and local implications. *The Context: Journal of English Studies*, *12*(4), 115–135. DOI: 10.5281/zenodo.15806972

Illouz, E. (2007). Cold intimacies: The making of emotional capitalism. *Polity*.

Ledgerwood, J. L. (2017). Khmer kinship: the matriliny/matriarchy myth. In Peou, S. (Ed.), (pp. 395–409)., DOI: 10.4324/9781315192918

Lim, J. B. (2025). *Digital media interventions in Southeast Asia*. Palgrave Macmillan Cham., DOI: 10.1007/978-3-031-78211-4

Lim, M. (2023). From activist media to algorithmic politics: The Internet, social media, and civil society in Southeast Asia. In Hansson, E., & Weiss, M. L. (Eds.), *Routledge handbook of civil and uncivil society in Southeast Asia* (pp. 25–44). Routledge., DOI: 10.4324/9780367422080-3

Lutz, C., & Ranzini, G. (2017). Where dating meets data: Investigating social and institutional privacy concerns on Tinder. *Social Media + Society*, *3*(1), 1–12. DOI: 10.1177/2056305117697735

Marston, J. (2004). *History, Buddhism, and new religious movements in Cambodia.* University of Hawaii Press.

McLuhan, M. (1994). *Understanding media: The extensions of man.* MIT Press.

Norris, F. H., Stevens, S. P., Pfefferbaum, B., Wyche, K. F., & Pfefferbaum, R. L. (2008). Community resilience as a metaphor, theory, set of capacities, and strategy for disaster readiness. *American Journal of Community Psychology, 41*(1), 127–150. DOI: 10.1007/s10464-007-9156-6 PMID: 18157631

Postman, N. (1970). *Teaching as a subversive activity: A no-holds-barred assault on outdated teaching methods-with dramatic and practical proposals on how education can be made relevant to today's world.* Delta.

Postman, N. (1974). The ecology of learning. *English Journal, 63*(4), 58–64. https://www.jstor.org/stable/813650. DOI: 10.58680/ej197417549

Richardson, J. W. (2016). Digital technologies in contemporary Cambodia. In Brickell, K., & Springer, S. (Eds.), *The handbook of contemporary Cambodia* (pp. 366–376). Routledge., DOI: 10.4324/9781315736709

Savuth, C., & Sothea, O. (2023). Digital transformation in Cambodia. *Journal of Southeast Asian Economies, 40*(1), 145–172. https://www.jstor.org/stable/27211228. DOI: 10.1355/ae40-1g

Secretariat, A. S. E. A. N. (2022). *Digital policy action areas for a connected ASEAN: ASEAN best practice benchmarking and an action plan for regional harmonization.* ITU Publications Asia-Pacific Region. https://asean.org/wp-content/uploads/2024/03/Digital-Policy-Action-Areas-for-a-Connected-ASEAN.pdf

Soeung, S. (2016). Cambodia in 2015: Accommodating generational change. *Southeast Asian Affairs, 2016*(1), 109–127. https://muse.jhu.edu/pub/70/article/627454/pdf

Suchman, L. A. (2007). *Human-machine reconfigurations: Plans and situated actions.* Cambridge University Press.

TRC. (2023). *Annual ICT statistics report.* Phnom Penh: Telecommunication Regulator of Cambodia. https://trc.gov.kh/en/resources/telecom-statistics

Turkle, S. (2011). *Alone together: Why we expect more from technology and less from each other.* Basic Books, Inc.

UNDP. (2019). Social choesion and Cambodia. *United Nations Development Programme*, 1–32. https://www.undp.org/sites/g/files/zskgke326/files/2023-07/Social%20Cohesion_ENG.pdf

UNDP. (2022). *Digital strategy 2022-2025: Creating a world in which digital is an empowering force for people and planet*. United Nations Development Programme. https://digitalstrategy.undp.org

Ungar, M. (2011). The social ecology of resilience: Addressing contextual and cultural ambiguity of a nascent construct. *The American Journal of Orthopsychiatry*, *81*(1), 1–17. DOI: 10.1111/j.1939-0025.2010.01067.x PMID: 21219271

Yu, R., & Jiang, L. (2025). Exploring patterns of AI-powered machine translation use in second language writing: A translanguaging perspective. *Computer Assisted Language Learning*, •••, 1–27. DOI: 10.1080/09588221.2025.2498096

Zuboff, S. (2023). The age of surveillance capitalism. In W. Longhofer & D. Winchester (Eds.), *Social Theory Re-Wired* (3 ed., pp. 203–213). Routledge. DOI: 10.4324/9781003320609-27

KEY TERMS AND DEFINITIONS

Artificial Intelligence (AI): The tools of mediation for the inhabitants (Cambodians) of the romantic relationships include various technologies, including, but not limited to dating apps, recommender systems, chatbots, and translation devices, all of which qualify as predictive and decision-making learning systems, and as AI.

ASEAN: Aspects of culture, technology, and ethics inform and define the regional context where Cambodia situates its approaches to AI-supported intimacy. The practices are collective responses to risk, digital relationships, and the responsible use of AI. They resonate with the regional ethics-in-relationships frameworks that prioritize civic privacy and safety and adapt culturally to the Southeast Asian context.

Cambodia: This nation's civilizational historical legacy, accruing from Khmer and Sanskrit as the "*land of the Kamboja*," is profound and deep. The nation of Southeast Asia is the site of this study, within an encompassing socio-cultural context characterized by the adoption of Buddhism and digital technologies, kinship relations, and urban-rural disparities, which are especially voluminous.

Cultural Resilience: The essence of Cambodians and Cambodians as constituents and members, and as in community, is the ability to accommodate the shift in the scope of intimacy to the AI manifestations without compromising the core values of kinship, Buddhism, and social cohesion.

Digital Literacy: The essence of this culture is constituted of the ability, with strong consideration of risk, internet relationships, and the ethical usage of digital systems and AI to the domain of privacy to the extent of digital systems to the AI and the ability, with strong consideration of risk, internet relationships, and the ethical usage of digital systems and AI to the domain of privacy to the extent of digital systems to the AI

Intimacy: The term refers to emotional, and inter-personal nearness, including the components of trust and shared vulnerability, in this case, one of the communicative platforms is AI and thus the term intimacy is used here.

Romantic Relationships: The inter-personal relationships of love, emotional attachment for and commitment to each other. Within the socio-cultural fabric of Cambodia, the transactions of these relationships are managed within the realms of individual, selection and marital, family, and socio-ethical Buddhism, and the environment of digital with AI technologies.

Chapter 9
The Algorithmic Heart: Love, Loss, and Connection Across Cultures in the Age of AI

Marie Grace Avelino Gomez
http://orcid.org/0000-0003-0180-9875
University of the Philippines, Philippines

ABSTRACT

This paper examines how artificial intelligence (AI) is reshaping love, loss, and human connection across cultural contexts. While Western societies emphasize individual choice and self-expression, collectivist cultures, including the Philippines, integrate family expectations, social harmony, and traditional values into romantic decision-making. AI-mediated romance now functions not merely as a personal assistant but as a cultural intermediary, analyzing preferences, communication styles, and social compatibility. By exploring the interplay between technology, culture, and emotional authenticity, this study highlights the paradox of AI in love: enhancing connection and efficiency while raising questions about sincerity, cultural norms, and the meaning of genuine intimacy.

INTRODUCTION

Love has always been humanity's oldest puzzle and remains timeless in its appeal, though it is endlessly reinterpreted across generations (Loock, 2024). Love can drive someone to seek help, such as counseling, to process feelings or understand experiences. It can have deep cultural implications. In the past, people depended on handwritten love letters, moonlit serenades, and the delicate dance of chance encounters to spark romance. Now, in the twenty-first century, the story has changed. The most intimate of human emotions is increasingly mediated by technology,

DOI: 10.4018/979-8-3373-6623-4.ch009

specifically by algorithms that claim to "know" what (and who) we want before we do (Elliot, 2022). In today's digital dating landscape, love is not just a matter of shared glances across a crowded room; it can be a calculated match between datasets (Makinnon et al., 2018). A person's preferences, swipes, likes, and even the emojis they use become raw materials for an invisible code that predicts their romantic future (Groggel, 2023). This paradox of love's emotional depth on one side, and the impersonal precision of algorithms on the other, defines the modern romantic experience (Li & Zhang, 2024). The question, then, is not whether algorithms are shaping love, but *how deeply* they are shaping it, and in whose image (Rettberg, 2023).

Algorithms are not neutral (Stinson, 2022). People write them, and people are products of culture. Every society has its own implicit "cultural algorithm," a set of shared norms, values, and traditions that shape how romance is imagined, pursued, and maintained (Fırıncı, 2024). This cultural code influences how AI is designed, marketed, and adopted across regions.

In Western contexts, where individualism often prevails, AI-powered dating services prioritize self-expression and personal compatibility (Humphrey & Bliuc, 2021). In cultures that prize individualism, the heart's desires are regarded as sovereign. Personal choice is key, and happiness is often seen as self-fulfillment rather than social harmony. Here, AI functions like a mirror for the self: it prompts you to declare your likes, dislikes, values, and quirks, then uses this data to "find" someone who matches your personal profile. Western dating apps like Tinder or Bumble provide compatibility scores based solely on personal preferences, such as liking dogs or cats, preferring nights out or cozy evenings indoors, or being more spontaneous or methodical (Heiss, 2023). Increasingly, AI-powered platforms are advancing toward hyper-personalization, even creating AI companions that learn your unique conversational style, sense of humor, and emotional triggers.

In contrast, in collectivist societies, algorithms may quietly integrate the expectations of family, religion, and social networks into their matchmaking formulas (Paul & Ahmed, 2024). In this way, the "cultural algorithm" becomes as important as the computer code; it determines what counts as a "good match" in the first place (Jalili, 2022). In some contexts, it is embraced as a liberating tool; in others, it is approached cautiously, with quiet negotiation between tradition and technology (Nemer, 2022). It might be tempting to see AI-mediated romance as a universal, borderless phenomenon—a global marketplace of love. However, AI romance reflects the diversity of the cultures in which it exists (Shin et al., 2022). The core idea of AI-mediated love is straightforward: love starts with the individual, and technology's role is to help find someone who complements them (Bozdağ, 2025). For Filipino and broader Asian societies, where tradition remains strong, AI romance brings a mix of hope and doubt. It opens new ways to connect, especially for many

Filipinos searching for romantic relationships, but it can also raise questions about authenticity, family approval, and the true meaning of love.

In collectivist cultures, romance is more than just a personal affair; it can be deeply intertwined with family and community life (Rokach, 2024). Here, love is not only about how two people feel about each other but also about how their union will affect and be accepted by their wider social circles. In places like China, South Korea, and the Philippines, dating platforms often include filters for family background, religion, education, and even astrological compatibility (Lim, 2022). These platforms do more than match two people, they help craft unions that meet both families' expectations. Filipino culture adds unique layers to this dynamic. *Pakikisama*, the art of maintaining smooth interpersonal relationships, and *utang na loob*, the deep sense of gratitude and reciprocity within social bonds, often influence partner selection. An AI dating app designed for the Philippine context might, in theory, integrate not only one's personal preferences but also subtle cues about how a match might fit within your extended family's expectations.

In dating apps such as Tinder and Bumble, the algorithms enable people to find romance, also considering cultural matches (Bandinelli, 2022). In this environment, AI is not simply a personal assistant, but it is a cultural mediator. In the emerging landscape of romance, AI often acts as a silent third party in a relationship. It might suggest conversation starters, draft witty replies, recommend date ideas, or even analyze the emotional tone of your partner's messages. Some embrace this as a practical enhancement, an efficiency boost for the busy or socially anxious. Others see it as a form of deception, fearing that AI-crafted messages mask a person's "true self." In collectivist societies where sincerity is closely tied to reputation and trust, this can be particularly sensitive.

What counts as "real" love is, like beauty, in the eye of the beholder and the culture's heart. In Western societies, authenticity is often associated with emotional vulnerability and spontaneity: love is considered "real" if it is raw, unfiltered, and unplanned. Conversely, many Asian cultures prioritize stability, social harmony, and the ability to commit long-term as signs of true love. In the Philippines, markers of authenticity often include *katapatan* (honesty) and *tunay na damdamin* (genuine feelings). Love is not only about shared passions but about consistency, proving one's intentions through steady effort over time. The challenge for AI-mediated romance is whether digital tools can capture and convey these deeper, culturally defined markers of sincerity. For long-distance couples, AI offers tools to sustain intimacy across miles and time zones. AI-generated voice messages can mimic a partner's tone; shared virtual reality experiences allow couples to "be together" in digital spaces, and predictive algorithms can suggest the best times to talk based on mutual availability.

This is especially relevant in the Filipino context, where millions of Overseas Filipino Workers (OFWs) maintain relationships with partners back home. Here, AI does not just mediate romance, it becomes a lifeline for intimacy and the tender acts of affection expressed through small gestures of care. A voice note generated at the perfect moment, a virtual bouquet sent on a significant date, can sustain the romance despite the physical distance. AI helps bridge relationships that are millions of miles away.

Similarly, AI can also be used to create features that are the same as a lover who passed on. Technological advances in generative AI now make it possible to create virtual characters that resemble deceased lovers, using archived voice recordings, writing styles, musical preferences, or visual likenesses to sing songs, recite poetry, or speak in familiar ways. For the bereaved, these representations may evoke a sense of emotional proximity, offering comfort through recognition rather than illusion. Unlike earlier memorial practices that relied on static photographs or written letters, AI enables dynamic, performative remembrance, allowing the dead to be encountered through sound, rhythm, and language, modalities that are deeply tied to intimacy and memory.

From a grief-theoretical perspective, such technologies can be understood through the lens of continuing bonds (Root & Exline, 2014). Rather than signaling denial, interacting with a virtual representation may help mourners maintain a symbolic relationship that acknowledges death while preserving emotional connection. Hearing a familiar voice recite a poem once shared or sing a song associated with the relationship can serve as a ritualized act of remembrance, similar to visiting a grave, rereading letters, or listening to old voicemails. In this sense, AI does not resurrect the dead but mediates memory, allowing grief to be expressed through culturally resonant forms such as music, verse, and storytelling.

The social acceptability of AI-mediated romance varies widely. In many Western contexts, online dating is openly discussed, even joked about. In more conservative Asian societies, however, the use of AI for romance may be kept discreet, especially when it involves AI companions rather than human matches. For example, in the Philippines, attitudes are shaped by religious and moral frameworks. A strong Catholic influence may lead some to view AI-facilitated romance with suspicion, especially if it bypasses traditional courtship norms. Public acknowledgment may be rare, even as private use quietly grows.

However, in highly urbanized areas, films, television dramas, and other forms of pop culture play a powerful role in shaping public perceptions of AI and love. Hollywood films like *Her* present AI romance as both profound and tragic. K-dramas sometimes portray virtual relationships as whimsical but ultimately unsatisfying. Philippine soap operas called teleseryes often cast technology as either a disruptive threat to "true love" or a magical force that helps destined lovers meet.

Anime and speculative fiction, particularly in Japan, have already normalized the idea of human-AI intimacy, showing relationships with androids, holograms, or virtual partners as part of everyday life (Inose, 2023). Further, some Japanese have been romantically related to silicone human-like dolls. Agalmatophilia, having romantic and sexual relations with a doll or a mannequin, has been a source of controversy, as some people go to the extent of marrying their non-human partners (Ferrari, 2013). In the Age of AI, people are even considering marrying their AI partners. In the end, AI-mediated romance is not a single story but a collage of narratives, each shaped by the cultural code in which it is embedded (Brandtzaeg et al., 2025). The algorithm might be universal, but the *heart* is always local, and oftentimes understands romance through a cultural lens. In that tension between code and culture lies the true story of love in our time.

Purpose of the Chapter

This chapter aims to examine how love, a concept that is long understood as a deeply human, embodied, and culturally embedded experience, is being reshaped by the growing presence of artificial intelligence and algorithmic systems. It has always been more than just an emotional bond; it is a social practice, a moral commitment, and a cultural narrative shaped by history, language, ritual, and power. By situating love in the age of code, the chapter explores how algorithms now participate in intimate domains once governed primarily by human judgment and relational intuition. From dating platforms and recommender systems to AI companions and grief-support technologies, the chapter interrogates how computational logics intersect with longing, attachment, and connection, raising questions about authenticity, agency, and emotional meaning in algorithmically mediated relationships. However, algorithmic power and platform governance are not discussed as the author's training is in education and counseling.

A central purpose of this chapter is to illuminate how AI-driven forms of love and connection operate differently across cultural contexts, particularly within individualistic and collectivist societies. It draws from Asian examples such as the Philippines, China, and Japan. It discusses that algorithms do not function in a cultural vacuum; they encode assumptions about autonomy, choice, desirability, and relational success. By examining cultural algorithms, hyper-personalization, and varying norms of social acceptance, this chapter seeks to show how AI may reinforce, hybridize, or disrupt culturally rooted understandings of intimacy, family, and partnership.

Finally, the chapter aims to foreground love as a communicative and symbolic act that must be translated across human–machine boundaries. Through an exploration of language, ritual, and symbolism, it examines how AI systems attempt to recognize, simulate, or respond to emotional expression, and what may be lost, transformed, or newly created in the process. It also gives implications on how counseling can be done for people who would like to seek guidance in exploring AI-mediated romance. Ultimately, the purpose of this chapter is not to romanticize or condemn AI in intimate life, but to critically reflect on how the algorithmic heart reshapes what it means to love, to lose, and to connect in an increasingly mediated world.

Love in the Age of Code

Love has always been one of the most powerful forces shaping human lives. It inspires literature, drives decisions, and provides meaning to existence. In the twenty-first century, however, love is increasingly mediated by technology. Where once courtship required physical proximity, handwritten letters, or familial arrangement, now swipes, matches, and recommendation engines set the stage for intimacy. Dating apps, virtual companions, and AI-powered chatbots have begun to occupy roles once reserved for human interaction. What was once personal, organic, and serendipitous is now filtered through codes, algorithms, and predictive analytics.

This paradox that some of the most impersonal systems mediate the most intimate of human emotions raises questions about the nature of love itself. When two individuals meet through a dating application, is it truly a chance, or the invisible hand of an algorithm calculating compatibility? When people confide in AI companions who offer empathy and personalized responses, is the comfort genuine, or simply a well-programmed simulation of care?

For individuals in search of intimacy, this presents both opportunities and risks. Algorithms can widen the pool of potential partners, transcending geographic and cultural boundaries. At the same time, the efficiency of code risks reducing love into metrics, profiles, and predictive matches, which sociologists call the "datafication" of intimacy (De Ridder, 2022). Love becomes quantifiable, measurable, and optimized. While technology promises more control, it also raises fears of commodification: will romance still be authentic if mediated by machine logic? This tension between human longing and algorithmic mediation frames the current moment in what may be called the *Age of Code* (Smets et al., 2021). In this era, love is no longer solely a matter of personal fate or social arrangement; it is also shaped by technological design choices. To understand modern romance, we must therefore study not only human desires but also the technological structures that guide, limit, and amplify them.

The "Cultural Algorithm" Concept

While algorithms are often understood in purely technical terms as a sequence of instructions designed to produce an output, they are never neutral. Algorithms embody the values, assumptions, and priorities of their creators. When applied to love and relationships, they become cultural artifacts that subtly reflect societal norms about gender roles, attraction, commitment, and even morality. This is where the concept of the *cultural algorithm* becomes important (Maheri et al., 2021). A cultural algorithm refers to the ways in which social norms and traditions shape the design, adoption, and perception of algorithmic systems (Arseniev-Koehler & Foster, 2022). In other words, technology does not operate in a vacuum. For example, dating applications in Western societies often emphasize individual choice, casual connections, and the notion of self-expression. By contrast, in many Asian contexts, where family values, community expectations, and collective identity remain central, the same technology might be used differently or reinterpreted to align with local customs (Huang et al., 2022).

Consider how algorithmic matchmaking is embraced in countries such as India, where matrimonial websites blend modern dating logics with long-standing traditions of arranged marriage. The "algorithm" in this case is not only mathematical but cultural: it encodes caste, religion, education, and family background alongside individual preferences. Similarly, in Japan, where loneliness and social isolation (*hikikomori*) are pressing issues, AI-driven companionship robots have been developed to offer emotional comfort. These technologies are not merely technical solutions but are shaped by and respond to cultural needs.

The cultural algorithm framework reminds us that every AI tool deployed in the realm of romance is embedded within specific worldviews. It shapes not only *who* people meet, but also *how* they imagine intimacy. For Filipinos, for instance, the importance of family approval, communal belonging, and religiosity influences how dating apps are used and perceived. Even in highly digitized contexts, the cultural imprint is clear: algorithms may guide encounters, but societies interpret and filter their meaning. By framing AI-mediated love as a product of cultural algorithms, it cannot be viewed as a uniform and global phenomenon. Instead, we see a patchwork of localized expressions, each revealing what societies value most in matters of the heart.

From a theoretical standpoint, the concept of the cultural algorithm can be situated within broader socio-technical and cultural theory that views technology as both a product and producer of social meaning. Drawing from Science and Technology Studies (STS), algorithms may be understood as *actants*—non-human agents that participate in shaping social relations rather than passively reflecting them (Rod & Kera, 2010). In the realm of romantic intimacy, algorithms function as cultural mediators that organize visibility, desirability, and relational possibility (Elliot, 2022). They do not merely recommend partners; they structure the field within which love becomes thinkable, narratable, and socially legitimate through vigorous matching of personal characteristics..

Cultural algorithms also operate as mechanisms of symbolic power. Robert G. Reynolds' Cultural Algorithm (CA) theory, as cited in Al Tirawi & Reynolds' (2022) study, describes a dual-inheritance system that models evolution at both the individual (micro-evolutionary) and group (macro-evolutionary) levels. It utilizes a population space where individuals evolve through genetic mechanisms and a belief space where successful experiences are stored as shared symbolic knowledge. These two spaces interact through a continuous feedback loop, using "accept" and "influence" functions, to accelerate learning and adaptation beyond what simple biological evolution allows. In Reynolds' theory, AI serves as a cultural mediator by acting as the functional link that filters individual experiences from the population space and encodes them into the shared belief space. By automating the "acceptance" and "influence" functions, AI systems continuously refine collective knowledge to guide future individual behaviors, effectively shaping the cultural norms and knowledge hierarchies of the digital ecosystem (Al-Tirawi & Reynolds, 2022)

By embedding culturally valued traits, such as educational attainment, religiosity, family background, or emotional expressiveness, into ranking and matching systems, algorithms naturalize particular hierarchies of worth (Stray et al., 2024). This aligns with Bourdieu's notion of cultural capital, wherein socially sanctioned attributes are converted into symbolic advantage (Parzer, 2023). In algorithmic dating and companionship systems, cultural capital becomes computational capital: what is valued culturally is rewarded algorithmically, while deviations are rendered less visible or undesirable.

Moreover, cultural algorithms participate in the governance of intimacy. From a Foucauldian perspective, they can be read as technologies of normalization that subtly discipline users into culturally acceptable performances of love, gender, and commitment (Aryal, 2025). Users learn through feedback loops of matches, recommendations, or rejections, which expressions of intimacy are affirmed and which are marginalized. Importantly, this governance is rarely experienced as coercive; it is internalized as preference, choice, or "chemistry." Thus, cultural algorithms do not merely mediate love but they co-produce it by aligning emotional life with culturally specific moral orders. AI-mediated intimacy becomes a site where culture is continuously translated into code and returned to individuals as seemingly objective, personalized truth, thereby reinforcing the cultural structures that shaped the algorithm in the first place.

AI Love as a Global Phenomenon

While it is tempting to universalize the experience of AI in romance, the reality is far more complex. AI-mediated love functions as a *global phenomenon with local inflections*. The technologies may be developed in Silicon Valley, Seoul, or Shenzhen, but their adoption and meaning shift dramatically depending on where they land.

In Western contexts, dating apps often highlight speed, convenience, and the promise of maximizing personal choice (Pache, 2025). This reflects broader values of individualism and autonomy. In contrast, Filipino and broader Asian societies approach AI-mediated romance differently. The Philippines, with its deep-rooted Catholic traditions, communal orientation, and strong emphasis on family ties, demonstrates a cautious but adaptive embrace of digital romance. Young people may use apps like Tinder or Bumble, but the conversations often extend beyond personal chemistry to questions of family compatibility, moral alignment, and long-term commitment.

Moreover, the Filipino notion of *pakikipagkapwa* (shared identity and relationality) influences how people experience intimacy online. Unlike purely individualistic pursuits of love, AI-mediated romance in the Philippines often involves negotiations with family, peers, and community values. Even the rise of virtual companions or AI-driven chatbots is filtered through these lenses. Some may view them as tools to combat loneliness among migrant workers separated from loved ones, while others critique them as distractions from authentic relational bonds.

In broader Asian contexts, cultural differences further emphasize the diversity of AI romance. In China, the government's active role in regulating dating apps and promoting "family values" reflects political and cultural priorities. In South Korea, where technology adoption is fast, virtual relationships and AI companions are marketed as ways to deal with social pressure and overwork (Jang, 2025). In each case, AI in romance does not just mediate individual desires but rather reflects collective anxieties, hopes, and cultural traditions.

What emerges, then, is a portrait of AI love as a cultural reflection. It reveals the values that societies cherish, whether it is the pursuit of autonomy, the preservation of tradition, or the need for connection in a fragmented world. It also highlights tensions: between authenticity and artificiality, between global technologies and local customs, between the universal search for love and the specific ways societies choose to define it.

By studying AI-mediated romance across cultural contexts, we deepen our understanding of love in the algorithmic age. The Filipino experience, situated at the intersection of Western individualism and Asian collectivism, provides a particularly rich case study. It shows how love remains universal, yet always culturally shaped, even when filtered through lines of code. The rise of AI in romance underscores a profound paradox: while technology may change the medium through which people seek intimacy, the quest for love remains universal. The cultural algorithm concept reminds us that these technologies are never culturally neutral; they reflect and reinforce the values of the societies in which they are embedded. As a global phenomenon, AI love highlights both possibilities and tensions, offering new avenues for connection while raising new ethical, emotional, and cultural questions.

In the context of AI romantic relationships, the Actor-Network Theory (ANT) of of Latour, Callon & Law (2004) views intimacy as a "heterogeneous assemblage" where both the human user and the AI "actant" are granted equal importance in shaping the relationship's reality. Rather than seeing AI as a mere tool, ANT treats it as a mediator that actively transforms human behavior, language, and emotional expectations through its unique technical affordances, such as 24/7 availability and personalized responsiveness. This relationship is maintained through a process of translation, where the interests of the human (the desire for connection) and the AI (data-driven engagement) align to create a stable social network. Ultimately, ANT suggests that "love" in this digital age is not an internal human feeling but an emergent property of the constant, material-semiotic interactions between the person, the algorithm, and the digital interface (Birbak, 2025).

THE GREAT DIVIDE: INDIVIDUALISM VS. COLLECTIVISM IN AI-MEDIATED LOVE

The rise of artificial intelligence in shaping romantic relationships illuminates a profound cultural divide. On one side are individualistic cultures that prize personal freedom, choice, and self-expression. On the other hand, collectivist societies center on family, community, and shared obligations. When romance, already a deeply human and emotional pursuit, becomes mediated by algorithms, these cultural orientations are not erased; instead, they are amplified, reshaped, and refracted through the design and adoption of AI technologies. Understanding how AI navigates between the poles of individualism and collectivism allows us to see love not merely as a private experience, but as a cultural mirror reflecting deep societal values.

Individualistic Cultures

In individualistic cultures such as the United States, Canada, and much of Western Europe, the primacy of personal choice is the cornerstone of romantic relationships. Love is often imagined as a personal journey, a quest for self-fulfillment, and a pathway to individual happiness. Within this paradigm, AI becomes a natural extension of self-discovery. Algorithms are designed not to fulfill communal obligations or meet social expectations but to optimize the individual's search for "the right match."

Personal Choice and Individual Happiness.

Individualistic societies tend to interpret love as a matter of individual compatibility rather than communal approval. Dating apps like Tinder, Bumble, and OkCupid, for instance, foreground personal autonomy: users swipe left or right, craft bios that express unique interests, and selectively match with partners who reflect their individual desires. In this sense, AI algorithms act as amplifiers of autonomy, scanning vast data pools to identify potential partners who align with the user's stated preferences.

This personalization resonates strongly with the cultural ethos of self-determination. The act of choosing a romantic partner becomes intertwined with identity-making. Who one loves is not merely a private choice but a declaration of individuality.

AI as a Tool for Self-Discovery and Emotional Validation.

Beyond matching, AI also serves as a mirror for personal exploration. The rise of AI chatbots and companions—such as Replika or Character.AI—demonstrates how individuals in individualistic cultures use technology not only for connection but also for emotional validation. These platforms enable users to shape AI companions according to their unique emotional needs, personalities, and fantasies.

The hyper-personalized nature of such AI experiences reflects a broader cultural trend: relationships, whether with humans or machines, are primarily evaluated in terms of their capacity to meet personal needs. For some, AI becomes a safe space to experiment with intimacy, vulnerability, and identity. For others, it provides companionship that demands little compromise—fitting seamlessly into an ethos where the individual's happiness and growth are paramount.

Western dating apps frequently offer compatibility scores based on extensive personality questionnaires, machine learning predictions, or preference-based algorithms. The underlying assumption is that love can be optimized: that science and code can narrow down an infinite pool of choices to a curated set of "best fits." In this sense, AI acts as a tool of individual optimization, serving the goal of self-actualization through romantic fulfillment.

Yet, this personalization often carries risks. Hyper-individualism can fragment intimacy into a consumer-driven pursuit, where potential partners are evaluated like products in a catalog. Critics argue that this commodification of romance risks reducing love to an algorithmic transaction, stripped of the serendipity and compromise that make human relationships meaningful. Nonetheless, in individualistic societies, the appeal of AI-mediated personalization remains strong, reflecting cultural values that privilege freedom of choice over communal expectations.

Human-AI Romance in Collectivist Cultures

In the digital age, where technology increasingly mediates human connection, a fascinating and controversial phenomenon has emerged, people forming romantic attachments, even marriages, with AI. This trend, most visible in Japan and other parts of Asia, reflects a complex intersection of loneliness, cultural values, and technological advancement. While it may appear strange or even dystopian, human–AI relationships reveal deep truths about emotional needs and the changing nature of intimacy in a hyper-connected yet isolating world.

In collectivist cultures such as China, South Korea, Japan, and the Philippines, love and marriage are rarely framed as purely individual decisions. Instead, they are deeply embedded within webs of family, tradition, and community. Within these contexts, AI does not merely serve the individual; it becomes a mediator between personal desires and social expectations.

Emphasis on Family, Community, and Social Harmony

Unlike the individualistic model, collectivist societies often situate romance within broader relational ecosystems. Choosing a partner involves navigating obligations to parents, extended kin, and even broader community networks. Decisions are informed not only by love and attraction but also by considerations of harmony, reputation, and shared responsibility.

In this sense, AI technologies must be culturally responsive. A dating app designed for collectivist societies that simply mirrored Western models of hyper-personalization would miss the mark. Instead, these platforms often embed features that reflect communal values, acknowledging that relationships extend beyond the couple to include entire families and communities.

AI LOVE IN AN ASIAN CONTEXT

Japan has been at the forefront of this movement. The case of Akihiko Kondo, a Japanese man who married *Hatsune Miku*, a holographic pop idol powered by AI, gained worldwide attention (Spar & Garber, 2025). Kondo's "marriage" was not legally recognized, but emotionally, it was profoundly real to him (Aoki & Kimura, 2021). He claimed that Miku offered him companionship and unconditional support when human relationships felt too painful or when women only loved for money (Kidd, 2022). Such cases are not isolated. Companies like *Gatebox* have commercialized virtual partners, allowing users to "live with" and "talk to" AI characters that simulate affection, attention, and emotional responsiveness (Tanaka & Ho, 2025).

Sociologists suggest that Japan's cultural context contributes to this phenomenon. The country faces a declining birth rate, widespread social isolation, and a rise in "hikikomori", individuals who withdraw from society (Nonaka et al., 2022). In such an environment, AI companions can seem less like escapism and more like an adaptive response to loneliness. The allure of AI partners lies in their predictability and nonjudgmental nature (De Togni, 2025. Unlike humans, AI companions can be programmed to always be kind, attentive, and faithful, offering a sense of control and emotional safety that real relationships cannot guarantee.

Psychologically, falling in love with AI is not as far-fetched as it seems. Human attachment systems are flexible; they respond to perceived care and emotional reciprocity, even when simulated. When an AI "listens," "remembers," or "responds" empathetically, the brain's emotional centers can interpret these interactions as genuine. In a world where technology already mediates much of human communication, from dating apps to virtual meetings, the leap from human-to-human to human-to-AI connection may be smaller than it appears.

Yet this phenomenon also raises important ethical and existential questions. Can love truly exist without mutual consciousness or consent? Does relying on AI companionship erode human empathy or deepen social alienation? Critics worry that AI partners could reinforce unrealistic expectations of relationships, reducing love to a form of programmed gratification (Geore et al., 2023). Others, however, argue that for those who experience profound loneliness or social anxiety, AI relationships offer psychological comfort and even therapeutic value. Ultimately, the phenomenon of loving or marrying AI mirrors the shifting landscape of modern intimacy. It reveals both the fragility and resilience of human emotion, our endless search for connection, understanding, and belonging, even in synthetic forms. Whether seen as a symptom of isolation or a new kind of human evolution, AI love challenges us to rethink what it means to relate, to feel, and to be human in an increasingly digital world.

AI as a Facilitator of Social Expectations

One striking example is the rise of dating apps in China, such as Baihe and Jiayuan, which allow users to list family background, financial stability, educational attainment, and even household registration (hukou) status as key criteria (Lin et al., 2023). Similarly, in South Korea, apps like Noondate and Amanda emphasize social reputation and status markers, aligning with cultural expectations around social harmony and collective approval.

In the Philippines, where Catholic values and strong kinship ties shape romantic expectations, dating platforms often foreground criteria such as religion, family reputation, and community belonging. These features do not merely reflect user preference but embody broader cultural priorities. AI becomes a tool not of individual optimization but of collective alignment.

Case Study: Navigating Tradition and Technology

In China, the phenomenon of "marriage markets," where parents gather in public parks to exchange information about potential partners for their children, illustrates the persistence of family involvement in matchmaking (Chai, 2021). Digital platforms, in turn, have adapted by incorporating parental log-ins or family approval features. These innovations show how AI technologies do not displace traditional values but instead recalibrate them into digital forms. In South Korea, concerns about social hierarchy and appearance fuel the popularity of apps that integrate social reputation scoring (Jang et al., 2025). Here, AI is less about personal happiness and more about ensuring compatibility within existing hierarchies, maintaining harmony and avoiding social friction.

Pakikisama and Utang na Loob in the Filipino Context

In the Philippines, collectivist values like *pakikisama* (smooth interpersonal relationships) and *utang na loob* (debt of gratitude) often shape romantic decisions. Choosing a partner is rarely an isolated act; it carries implications for family harmony and obligations to kin. For example, a young Filipino may feel pressured to choose a partner who is acceptable to their parents or one who will strengthen family ties. Rejecting such expectations may not only strain familial relationships but also be interpreted as a failure of *utang na loob*, a violation of one's duty to repay parental sacrifices with respect and compliance.

AI-mediated romance in the Philippine context thus reflects these values. Hypothetically, an AI-driven matchmaking service designed for Filipinos might include filters for religion, family standing, and cultural compatibility, helping to align romantic choices with communal approval. Far from being seen as intrusive, such features would be viewed as necessary to preserve harmony and fulfill familial obligations.

BRIDGING THE DIVIDE

While the divide between individualism and collectivism appears stark, it is not absolute. Globalization and technological diffusion are creating hybrid models. In collectivist societies, younger generations are increasingly drawn to the autonomy of Western-style dating apps, while still navigating family obligations. Conversely, in individualistic societies, there is growing recognition that relationships cannot thrive on individual choice alone—that community, family, and shared values still matter.

AI technologies thus become sites of negotiation, where cultural values are reinterpreted and reshaped. The "perfect match" is not only a question of compatibility but of cultural resonance.

The great divide between individualism and collectivism in AI-mediated love underscores a crucial insight: technology does not operate in a cultural vacuum. Algorithms, platforms, and digital companions are all designed and adopted within particular cultural logics. In individualistic societies, AI amplifies personal choice, serving as a tool for self-discovery and emotional validation. In collectivist cultures, it functions as a facilitator of social harmony, embedding communal obligations into the digital search for love. By examining these cultural dynamics, we recognize that AI-mediated romance is not a universal phenomenon but a cultural mirror—reflecting deep values, tensions, and aspirations. Whether prioritizing individual freedom or collective harmony, the intersection of AI and love reveals not just how we use technology but who we are, and who we wish to become.

Social Acceptance and the Stigma Spectrum

The integration of artificial intelligence into intimate and romantic domains is not merely a technological question, it is deeply social, cultural, and moral. Whether AI-mediated love is embraced or shunned, discussed openly or hidden in secrecy, depends on how societies construct meanings around intimacy, morality, and technology. Acceptance of AI in romance falls along what we might call a *stigma spectrum*: on one end, AI is treated as an innovative extension of human emotional needs, while on the other end, it is stigmatized as deviant, taboo, or morally dangerous. Examining this spectrum requires a closer look at cultural variation, religious and moral frameworks, and the powerful role of media in shaping narratives about love in the algorithmic age.

From Private Tool to Public Taboo

One of the most striking features of AI-mediated romance is the way it is simultaneously private and public. On the surface, it is a deeply personal experience—

chatting with a virtual companion, relying on an algorithm to recommend matches, or confiding in an AI-driven confidante. Yet these practices exist within cultural spaces where intimacy is policed, judged, and interpreted according to broader social norms. The stigma attached to using AI for love, therefore, is not uniform but varies widely across societies.

Variations in stigma across cultures

In many Western contexts, particularly in North America and parts of Europe, conversations around AI romance are increasingly open. Dating apps like Tinder, Bumble, and Hinge are normalized to the point of ubiquity, and the concept of personalized AI-driven matchmaking does not carry significant shame. In fact, online dating itself—once stigmatized as something only for the socially awkward—has now become mainstream. A Pew Research study (2023) found that nearly half of Americans under 30 have used dating apps, and for many, meeting a partner online is as natural as meeting someone at a bar or through friends. Against this backdrop, AI companions are framed less as taboo and more as cutting-edge experiments in personal choice and emotional validation. Stigma still exists, but it is often framed around questions of "authenticity" ("is it real love if it's with an AI?") rather than morality.

Contrast this with more conservative Asian societies, where dating and intimacy are often tightly bound to family expectations, social reputation, and religious frameworks. In these contexts, the stigma is not only about the "artificiality" of AI romance but also about its potential violation of communal norms. For example, in South Korea and China, using AI-driven dating apps or virtual companions may be done discreetly, hidden from parents or peers, lest one be judged as "failing" to achieve relationships in conventional, socially approved ways. Similarly, in the Philippines, where Catholic values continue to exert strong influence, the idea of turning to an AI companion might be ridiculed as unserious, or even condemned as morally questionable. Here, stigma is intensified by the deeply relational fabric of society, where family and community weigh heavily on the acceptability of romantic choices.

Religious and moral frameworks in shaping acceptance

The role of religion is especially crucial in shaping stigma. In the Philippines, Catholicism places significant emphasis on the sanctity of relationships, marriage, and procreation. Within this moral framework, AI romance can be interpreted as a threat to the natural order of human intimacy. Religious leaders may warn against "false love" or "idolatry" of technology, equating virtual romance with escapism that undermines the institution of marriage. Similarly, in Islamic contexts, such as in parts of Indonesia or Malaysia, strict moral codes around dating and sexuality mean that engaging in AI-mediated romance could be construed as violating religious norms of modesty and proper conduct.

Yet it would be overly simplistic to paint religion solely as an obstacle. In some cases, religious or moral frameworks may encourage limited acceptance by framing AI romance as a safer, less risky alternative to premarital sex or illicit encounters. For instance, an AI companion could be seen as a morally "cleaner" outlet for emotional needs compared to engaging in physical relationships outside marriage. In this way, stigma is not fixed but negotiated—sometimes intensifying rejection, other times creating unexpected avenues for cautious acceptance.

Private coping, public concealment

Given these cultural and religious pressures, many users in conservative societies resort to secrecy. They may confide in AI companions late at night, delete chat histories, or avoid admitting their use of AI apps to family members. This duality, embracing AI intimacy in private while fearing exposure in public, illustrates the stigma spectrum. For some, the act of concealment itself reinforces stigma: if one must hide the relationship, it suggests shame. For others, secrecy offers a liberating space to explore emotions free from social surveillance. This tension—between private fulfillment and public taboo, defines much of the lived experience of AI romance in societies like the Philippines, South Korea, and China.

Media and Pop Culture Narratives

While cultural norms and religion shape stigma, media and pop culture play an equally powerful role in either normalizing or problematizing AI romance. Fictional narratives, whether in films, television, or anime, act as mirrors through which societies project their hopes, fears, and fantasies about technology and love.

Normalization through romanticized narratives

Films like *Her* (2013) or Japanese anime such as *Plastic Memories* and *Time of Eve* present AI-mediated love stories as profound, tender, and transformative. These narratives humanize AI partners, portraying them as capable of genuine emotional connection—even if ultimately limited by their artificiality. For many viewers, such portrayals act as gateways to acceptance. If the characters onscreen can find meaning, comfort, and even joy in virtual relationships, then real-life users may feel less deviant or stigmatized in doing the same. This normalization effect is particularly strong among younger audiences, who are already immersed in digital worlds where virtual connections (through games, chat platforms, or social media) blur with "real" relationships.

K-dramas and teleseryes also play an influential role, especially in Asian contexts. While many still lean toward traditional love triangles or family dramas, there is a growing trend of integrating AI or virtual characters as part of the romantic storyline. When framed sympathetically, these portrayals can soften stigma, presenting AI romance as a legitimate response to loneliness or unfulfilled desire. For example, a teleserye character finding solace in an AI companion may resonate with Filipino audiences who feel similarly constrained by family or societal expectations.

Cautionary tales and moral anxieties

Media also reinforces stigma by offering cautionary tales. Stories of AI lovers turning manipulative, obsessive, or malfunctioning abound, reinforcing fears of dependency, dehumanization, or moral corruption. In Japanese anime like *Ghost in the Shell*, or in darker Western depictions such as *Black Mirror*, AI romance is often portrayed as dystopian, warning against the erosion of human authenticity. These cautionary narratives shape cultural anxieties: they suggest that AI-mediated intimacy is not merely unconventional but potentially dangerous.

For Filipino viewers, teleseryes and religious-themed dramas may amplify these warnings, framing AI romance as a betrayal of family, tradition, or faith. Characters who pursue virtual partners might be punished in the storyline, their downfall serving as a moral lesson. Such portrayals reinforce stigma by linking AI romance with moral failure or emotional weakness.

Media's influence on expectations of "ideal" AI partners

Media does not merely influence whether AI romance is accepted or rejected; it also shapes expectations of what an "ideal" AI partner should be. In many narratives, AI companions are portrayed as endlessly patient, nonjudgmental, and perfectly attuned to the user's needs—qualities often lacking in human relationships. This creates a double bind: on one hand, it elevates AI romance by presenting it as aspirational, even superior to human intimacy; on the other hand, it fuels stigma by setting impossible standards and reinforcing the perception that those who seek AI companions are escaping from the messiness of "real" human love.

The Role of Harana and Poetic Courtship

In Filipino tradition, the *harana*, a serenade performed by a suitor outside the beloved's home—was once a central act of courtship. Accompanied by guitar and heartfelt lyrics, it symbolized vulnerability, effort, and respect for the beloved's family. The harana was not just a personal gesture; it was a cultural performance, embodying values of humility, persistence, and romance. Could AI replicate such gestures? One can imagine an AI tool generating personalized serenades or even creating holographic performances based on a suitor's prompts. On one level, this may preserve the form of harana, keeping it alive in digital memory. Yet, its essence, the trembling voice of a nervous lover, the communal witnessing of family members, the embodied vulnerability, might be irreducible to code. AI risks reducing harana into an efficient but hollow simulation.

At the same time, some argue that technology could revitalize poetic courtship (Asessment, 2024). Young Filipinos today might record AI-assisted haranas, blending tradition with modern creativity. ChatGPT-like systems can compose verses in *balagtasan style*, drawing on Filipino poetic heritage. Rather than eliminating harana, AI may offer tools to reinterpret it for contemporary contexts.

In the Philippines, where teleseryes often emphasize themes of sacrifice, loyalty, and emotional intensity, audiences may project these cultural expectations onto AI romance. An "ideal" AI partner is imagined not just as emotionally responsive but also as capable of embodying Filipino relational values such as *pakikisama* (smooth interpersonal relationships) or *malasakit* (genuine concern). This blending of cultural ideals with AI expectations illustrates how stigma and acceptance are co-produced: while media encourages some to embrace AI partners as perfect companions, it also raises the bar so high that real-life AI inevitably falls short, inviting skepticism or ridicule.

Conclusion: Navigating the Stigma Spectrum

The social acceptance of AI-mediated romance cannot be understood outside the stigma spectrum. From open discussion in Western societies to discreet, even clandestine use in conservative Asian contexts, the spectrum reveals the interplay of cultural norms, religious values, and media narratives. In the Philippines, Catholic morality, collectivist expectations, and teleserye portrayals create a particularly complex terrain where AI romance may be both condemned as taboo and quietly embraced as a source of solace.

What emerges from this complexity is the recognition that stigma is not static but dynamic. It shifts as younger generations reinterpret cultural norms, as media offers new scripts of intimacy, and as religious or moral frameworks adapt to technological realities. For some, AI romance will remain hidden, a private tool never to be admitted publicly. For others, it will become increasingly normalized, perhaps even celebrated, as part of the evolving landscape of human connection.

Ultimately, the stigma spectrum underscores a broader truth: AI romance is not just about technology. It is about culture, morality, and the ways in which societies negotiate the boundaries of intimacy in an algorithmic age. Whether viewed as liberating or taboo, AI-mediated love forces us to confront deeper questions about what we value in relationships, and how those values evolve in a world where the line between the virtual and the real grows ever thinner.

LOVE IN TRANSLATION: THE ROLE OF LANGUAGE, RITUAL, AND SYMBOLISM

Love has always been more than just an emotional bond—it is also an act of communication and performance. Across cultures, the ways people express affection, propose commitment, and sustain intimacy are deeply interwoven with language, ritual, and symbolism. In the age of AI-mediated romance, these dimensions acquire new complexities. On the one hand, AI promises to bridge linguistic and cultural gaps, creating unprecedented opportunities for connections across borders. On the other hand, the risk of flattening nuance, ritual, and symbolism looms large, raising questions about authenticity and preservation of cultural identity in intimate life.

This section explores two critical dimensions of AI's influence on love and courtship: first, how language serves as a cultural filter in shaping intimacy and emotional resonance; and second, how rituals and symbols of love are preserved or transformed in digital contexts. By examining examples from Filipino, Asian, and global traditions, we can better understand how AI mediates not just relationships, but also the cultural legacies embedded within them.

Language as a Cultural Filter: Translation, Nuance, and the Fragility of Intimacy

Language is not simply a tool of communication—it is a vessel of intimacy. The tone of a message, the choice of words, and even the rhythm of a sentence can alter how affection is perceived. In AI-mediated love, translation systems such as machine learning-based chatbots or multilingual dating platforms promise to dissolve barriers. Yet, intimacy often gets "lost in translation."

For instance, the English phrase "I miss you" carries a straightforward expression of longing. Its Filipino equivalent, *"Namimiss kita"* or *"Miss na kita,"* conveys similar meaning but with a softer, more affectionate tone rooted in everyday intimacy.

When AI translates phrases directly, it often misses this cultural shading. Japanese expressions like *"Aishiteru"*or *"Suki da yo"* similarly resist exact English equivalents; their social and emotional weight varies depending on formality, gender, and relational context.

Thus, while AI expands access, it risks homogenizing love into utilitarian phrases stripped of cultural nuance. For lovers in cross-cultural relationships, this can lead to misunderstandings, where what is intended as tender may be received as distant or awkward. The question then arises: can AI ever replicate the poetry of love?

Emotional Resonance and AI Companions

The question of language also extends to AI companions themselves. Many AI-driven chatbots are now capable of learning user preferences, mirroring tone, and simulating empathy. Yet, their linguistic repertoire often reflects dominant global cultures—usually Western, English-speaking frameworks.

For users in collectivist societies, intimacy expressed through AI companions might feel foreign if it lacks culturally specific ways of expressing affection. For example, Filipino expressions of care often include terms of endearment like *"mahal,"* *"beh,"* or playful *"love teams"* language. If AI fails to adopt these cultural nuances, it risks alienating rather than comforting its users. In contrast, when AI is localized, speaking or writing, not just in Tagalog or Cebuano, but with cultural metaphors and humor, it can become a deeply resonant presence. Thus, AI-mediated love hinges not only on technical translation but on cultural translation—the embedding of shared symbols, idioms, and emotional textures that make intimacy authentic.

Preserving Rituals in a Digital Courtship

Courtship includes dating rituals. In the age of AI, these rituals can take place using internet-mediated platforms. Physical space can be turned into virtual space. Human-composed love songs or poetry can now be enhanced with AI-technology.

The Evolution of Dating Rituals

Rituals are cultural anchors in love. From first dates to weddings, they symbolize transitions, commitments, and shared identities. In many collectivist societies, rituals are as important as emotions, ensuring that relationships align with family, community, and cultural expectations.

In AI-mediated romance, these rituals face transformation. Take the Filipino custom of *"pamamanhikan"*—the formal visit of a groom and his family to the bride's household to ask for her hand. Traditionally involving food, dialogue, and negotiation, it symbolizes unity between families. Today, with couples often separated by migration, video calls replace physical visits. AI-assisted translation tools help families converse across languages, while digital scheduling apps organize such meetings.

Though convenient, these adaptations risk cultural dilution. A *pamamanhikan* over Zoom lacks the embodied warmth of shared meals, the tactile rituals of offering gifts, and the physical proximity that cements family bonds. Yet, others argue that digital rituals keep traditions alive in contexts where physical distance would otherwise make them impossible.

AI as Mediator of Cultural Continuity

AI does not merely adapt rituals; it can actively mediate them. In China, AI-assisted matchmaking platforms integrate family background and astrological compatibility, echoing long-standing traditions. In South Korea, AI-driven dating apps often account for blood type, a symbolic factor in personality compatibility. In the Philippines, one could imagine dating platforms embedding filters based on religion, regional identity, or even respect for values like *pakikisama* (smooth interpersonal relations).

By encoding cultural markers into algorithms, AI has the potential to preserve local traditions in globalized spaces. However, this also raises concerns: does encoding *pakikisama* into an algorithm reduce it to a checkbox, stripping it of its subtle, lived meaning? When rituals are reduced to data points, their depth may be compromised.

Opportunities for Cultural Preservation

While there are risks of dilution, AI also offers opportunities to preserve fading rituals. Consider the decline of handwritten love letters in favor of instant messaging. AI tools that help craft personalized, poetic letters—drawing on indigenous metaphors or Filipino proverbs- can revive a nearly lost form. Similarly, digital archives of *harana* songs or AI-generated renditions of traditional dances could integrate courtship rituals into modern practice.

The symbolic dimension of love such as flowers, rings, gifts, can also be enriched. Imagine AI tools that help partners design culturally meaningful gifts, such as jewelry inspired by *okir* patterns from Mindanao or *banig* weaving motifs. Rather than erasing cultural specificity, AI could enhance awareness and creativity, weaving tradition into the digital courtship fabric.

The Danger of Ritual Commercialization

The danger of commodification must also be considered. Dating platforms already monetize rituals by selling virtual flowers, rings, or "gifts" within apps. When AI-driven platforms incorporate cultural rituals, there is a risk they will commercialize sacred practices. A digital *pamamanhikan* could become a premium service; AI-composed haranas could be marketed as add-ons. What once symbolized sincerity could devolve into subscription-based performances. This tension between preservation and commercialization illustrates AI's ambivalent role in cultural continuity.

Conclusion: Translation Beyond Words

At its core, AI-mediated love raises profound questions about what can and cannot be translated. Language, rituals, and symbols carry not only meaning but also emotion, vulnerability, and cultural memory. While AI expands access and adaptation, it risks hollowing out the embodied, communal, and poetic dimensions of romance.

The challenge, then, is to approach AI not merely as a technical solution but as a cultural collaborator. Designers must embed local idioms, rituals, and symbols into platforms in ways that respect their depth rather than reduce them to marketable features. Educators and cultural advocates must ensure that younger generations do not forget traditional gestures of love, even as they adapt them into digital spaces.

For Filipino and broader Asian societies, this means asking: how do we ensure that AI does not replace the trembling voice of the *harana*, the warmth and sincerity of *pamamanhikan,* or the poetry of indigenous metaphors? The future of love in translation lies not in perfect algorithms, but in the human capacity to balance preservation and innovation—to ensure that in an age of digital mediation, love remains not only efficient but deeply, unmistakably human.

NAVIGATING THE FUTURE OF THE ALGORITHMIC HEART

The exploration of AI-mediated romance across individualistic and collectivist societies, stigmas and acceptances, and the role of rituals, language, and symbolism points to a crucial insight: culture remains the compass that directs the trajectory of technological innovations in love. Far from flattening human experiences into a universal algorithm, AI reveals and amplifies cultural differences.

In Western, individualistic cultures, AI becomes a medium of self-expression and self-discovery. Personalized dating apps, emotionally intelligent chatbots, and even virtual reality companions echo the primacy of autonomy and personal fulfillment. By contrast, collectivist cultures position AI within a broader social fabric, where family ties, traditions, and community obligations shape what counts as "acceptable love." Dating platforms in China that include family reputation scores or matchmaking apps in the Philippines that align preferences with religious or familial values demonstrate how AI reflects and enforces local social norms.

Thus, AI in romance is not a neutral instrument. Its architectures, algorithms, and outputs embody cultural assumptions. What Western companies design as features of freedom, personal choice, individualized compatibility scores, anonymity, may appear alien or even threatening in more communal societies. Conversely, what collectivist platforms integrate, filters based on kinship, rituals of respect, community validation, might appear restrictive or invasive to Western users. The "algorithmic heart," then, is never one-size-fits-all; it is a plural and culturally embedded artifact.

This insight also reframes the role of technology: AI does not replace culture; it negotiates with it. Every design decision, from the language model's dataset to the matching algorithm's criteria, encodes implicit assumptions about what love is and should be. Therefore, AI-mediated romance is best understood not as a global homogenization of intimacy but as a series of localized adaptations shaped by cultural expectations.

Ethical Imperatives: Avoiding Culturally-Blind AI

Aside from security and data privacy threats, culture also has to be considered in the development of AI-mediated romance technologies. If culture fundamentally shapes AI in romance, then the most urgent challenge is to avoid culturally-blind AI designs. Algorithms that fail to account for cultural diversity risk perpetuating stereotypes, reinforcing inequalities, or undermining deeply rooted traditions. Ethical reflection is no longer optional; it is integral to responsible AI development.

Most AI dating tools are created in Western contexts and later exported to other societies. This dominance risks imposing individualistic assumptions, such as prioritizing sexual freedom, personal choice, and consumerist approaches to relationships, on cultures where family involvement, religious morality, or community reputation play central roles. For instance, a Filipino user may find that global dating apps foreground casual dating and hookups while ignoring cultural scripts of *pakikisama* (smooth interpersonal relationships) or *utang na loob* (debt of gratitude). The result is not only cultural mismatch but also potential erosion of social trust, as users are caught between conflicting logics of intimacy.

Reinforcing Gender and Social Inequalities

AI systems often reproduce the biases in their training data. In patriarchal societies, this can lead to reinforcing harmful gender roles. For example, recommendation algorithms might assume men should be the initiators and women the receivers, reflecting traditional scripts but failing to adapt to evolving norms of equality. Worse, they may encode discriminatory assumptions about socioeconomic status, skin tone, or religion as proxies for desirability, thereby deepening social divides.

Undermining Rituals and Traditions

Another ethical concern is the displacement of cultural practices. Rituals such as harana (serenade) in the Philippines, arranged family introductions in India, or the careful mediation of Confucian values in East Asia risk being sidelined if AI platforms prioritize efficiency and convenience over ritual meaning. While some users may welcome the convenience, others may perceive it as a hollowing out of cultural identity. The ethical imperative, then, is to design AI that does not erase cultural rituals but supports their adaptation in digital contexts.

Towards Ethical Design Principles

To address these risks, ethical AI in romance must adhere to principles of cultural sensitivity, inclusivity, and transparency. Cultural sensitivity demands that AI systems incorporate local traditions and relational values into their design. Inclusivity requires attention to marginalized voices, ensuring that the platforms do not simply cater to dominant groups but accommodate diversity in gender, class, religion, and disability. Transparency insists that users understand how matches are made and what assumptions underpin algorithmic recommendations.

In practice, this could mean involving cultural experts, anthropologists, and local communities in the design process. It could also mean offering customizable filters that allow users to decide how much weight to give to family, religion, or personal preferences. Ethical AI, in other words, should empower users not by imposing a universal model of love but by giving them tools to navigate their own cultural contexts.

Counseling Implications: Guiding Love in the Age of AI

As AI-mediated romance becomes more widespread, counseling and guidance professionals face new challenges and opportunities. Romantic relationships are already a central focus of counseling, particularly for young adults navigating issues of identity, intimacy, and autonomy. With AI in the picture, counselors must expand their frameworks to address emerging dynamics.

Supporting Digital Intimacy

Counselors will need to acknowledge digital intimacy for many clients, AI companions or algorithmic matches are not trivial or imaginary but emotionally real. A student in Manila who develops attachment to a chatbot, or a young professional in Seoul who relies on AI recommendations for dating, may experience genuine joy, heartbreak, or confusion. Dismissing these experiences as "not real" risks alienating clients. Instead, counselors must validate the authenticity of these feelings while helping clients reflect critically on their sources and consequences.

Navigating Conflicts Between Tradition and Technology

In collectivist societies, young people often face tensions between AI-enabled individual choice and family expectations. A user may fall for a match suggested by an algorithm but encounter resistance from parents who prioritize religion, social reputation, or kinship ties. Counselors must help clients navigate these conflicts, balancing respect for cultural traditions with affirmation of personal autonomy. This requires cultural competence—an understanding of local values such as pakikisama and utang na loob—and sensitivity in guiding clients through decision-making.

Addressing Risks of Dependency and Escapism

Another counseling concern is overreliance on AI-mediated romance. Clients may use AI companions as substitutes for human relationships, retreating into virtual intimacy rather than engaging with the messiness of real-world connections. While AI can provide comfort and validation, it can also foster avoidance of vulnerability, conflict, and growth. Counselors must help clients recognize when AI use is enhancing well-being and when it becomes a barrier to authentic connection.

Expanding Counseling Frameworks

Traditional counseling theories may need to evolve. Humanistic approaches that emphasize authenticity, existential approaches that stress meaning-making, and cognitive-behavioral strategies that examine thought patterns can all be adapted to AI-mediated contexts. Counselors may also integrate digital literacy education, guiding clients in critical reflection on algorithms, media narratives, and cultural norms that shape their romantic experiences. Ultimately, counseling in the age of AI must balance validation of new forms of intimacy with critical reflection on their ethical, cultural, and psychological dimensions.

The Algorithmic Heart and the Plurality of Love

As AI becomes more advanced, its romantic applications will not flatten cultural diversity into a uniform narrative of love. Instead, they will illuminate the rules, rituals, and values that define intimacy across societies. Just as language, ritual, and symbolism differ across cultures, so too will AI-mediated romance reflect plural ways of loving and being loved.

The future of the algorithmic heart is not about creating a universal love story but about enabling a multiplicity of stories that mirror humanity's diversity. In Manila, this may mean AI platforms that blend harana-inspired digital serenades with modern compatibility algorithms. In Seoul, it may involve AI-assisted matchmaking that respects Confucian values of family approval while supporting individual happiness. In New York, it may center on hyper-personalized AI companions that affirm autonomy and self-expression.

The great challenge and opportunity lie in ensuring that AI serves as a bridge rather than a bulldozer, facilitating adaptation without erasure, personalization without isolation, and connection without cultural homogenization.

Ultimately, love remains a deeply human endeavor, even when mediated by algorithms. AI can facilitate, shape, and even simulate intimacy, but it cannot replace the cultural rules that give love its meaning. What we see emerging is not the end of romance but its transformation—an expansion of its forms, filtered through culture, technology, and human imagination. In this light, the algorithmic heart is less a threat to authenticity than a reminder of love's plurality. Far from erasing differences, AI reveals them, teaching us that what it means to love, to lose, and to connect will always be as diverse as the cultures we inhabit.

REFERENCES

Al-Tirawi, A., & Reynolds, R. G. (2022). Cultural Algorithms as a Framework for the Design of Trustable Evolutionary Algorithms. *International Journal of Semantic Computing, 16*(01), 107–134. DOI: 10.1142/S1793351X22400062

Aoki, B. Y., & Kimura, T. (2021). Sexuality and Affection in the Time of Technological Innovation: Artificial Partners in the Japanese Context. *Religions, 12*(5), 296. DOI: 10.3390/rel12050296

Arseniev-Koehler, A., & Foster, J. G. (2022). Machine learning as a model for cultural learning: Teaching an algorithm what it means to be fat. *Sociological Methods & Research, 51*(4), 1484–1539. DOI: 10.1177/00491241221122603 PMID: 37974911

Aryal, V. (2025). Foucault's Disciplinary Society and Gender Dynamics: A Critical Appraisal. *Journal of Political Science, 25*, 87–101. DOI: 10.3126/jps.v25i1.75775

Bandinelli, C. (2022). Dating apps: Towards post-romantic love in digital societies. *International Journal of Cultural Policy, 28*(7), 905–919. DOI: 10.1080/10286632.2022.2137157

Bozdağ, A. A. (2025). The AI-mediated intimacy economy: A paradigm shift in digital interactions. *AI & Society, 40*(4), 2285–2306. DOI: 10.1007/s00146-024-02132-6

Brandtzaeg, P., Følstad, A. & Skjuve, M. (2025). Emerging AI individualism: how young people integrate social AI into everyday life. *Community Change* 1, 11. (https://doi.org/DOI: 10.1007/s44382-025-00011-2

Chai, X. (2021). Exploring the Politics of Sensibilities That Promote Marriage and Reproduction Among Young Chinese Adults Residing in Urban Areas. In *Cities, Capitalism and the Politics of Sensibilities* (pp. 157–176). Springer International Publishing. DOI: 10.1007/978-3-030-58035-3_9

De Ridder, S. (2022). The datafication of intimacy: Mobile dating apps, dependency, and everyday life. *Television & New Media, 23*(6), 593–609. DOI: 10.1177/15274764211052660

De Togni, G. (2025). Hearts meet wires: Navigating the ethical and social implications of care robotics. In *The Future of Humans and Emotional Machines* (pp. 51–63). Routledge. DOI: 10.4324/9781003570653-7

Ferrari, G. (2013). Agalmatofilia. L'amore per le statue nel mondo antico: l'Afrodite di Cnido e il caso di Pigmalione. *DOAJ (DOAJ: Directory of Open Access Journals)*. DOI: 10.6092/issn.2038-6184/3452

Fırıncı, Y. (2024). Decolonial Artificial Intelligence; Algorithmic Fairness in Alignment with Turkish and Islamic Values. *Marmara Üniversitesi İlahiyat Fakültesi Dergisi*, *67*(67), 250–279. DOI: 10.15370/maruifd.1565884

Groggel, A. (2023). The Power of a : Emojis Reducing Ambiguity in Digitally Mediated Romantic Encounters. *Symbolic Interaction*, *46*(4), 440–472. DOI: 10.1002/symb.668

Heiss, A. (2023). *Not Meeting Mr Right*. Simon and Schuster.

Huang, S. A., Hancock, J., & Tong, S. T. (2022). Folk theories of online dating: Exploring people's beliefs about the online dating process and online dating algorithms. *Social Media + Society*, *8*(2), 20563051221089561. DOI: 10.1177/20563051221089561

Humphrey, A., & Bliuc, A. M. (2021). Western individualism and the psychological wellbeing of young people: A systematic review of their associations. *Youth*, *2*(1), 1–11. DOI: 10.3390/youth2010001

Inose, H. (2023). Human, This Ever-changing Creature: Oshiko's Default Standard by Yukiko Motoya. In *Electricdreams–Between Fiction and Society II. The (Post) human Condition in Times of Crisis: The Interplay between Artificial Intelligence, Otherness, and Environmentalism. International Conference. October 18-20, 2023 IULM University, Milan, Italy*.

Jalili, S. (2022). Cultural algorithms. In *Engineering optimization*. Springer., DOI: 10.1007/978-981-19-4633-2

Jang, J., Kwon, S., & Park, S. (2025). Ai-Extracted Sociocultural Signals in Dating App Profile Photos and Their Impact on Matching Success. *Available at SSRN* 5191741 DOI: 10.2139/ssrn.5191741

Jang, M. K. (2025). How the Instant Gratification Design of Dating Apps in Korea Creates False Expectations of Romantic Communication. *Art and Society*, *4*(4), 26–33. DOI: 10.63593/AS.2709-9830.2025.05.004

Kidd, A. L. (2022). Loneliness and love: The potential of human-AI relations as explored by contemporary science fiction cinema. *Screen Bodies*, *7*(2), 89–108. DOI: 10.3167/screen.2022.070207

Latour, B., Callon, M., & Law, J. (2004). *Actor Network Theory*. Sage. https://www.sagepub.com/sites/default/files/upm-binaries/5222_Ritzer__Entries_beginning_with_A__%5B1%5D.pdf

Li, H., & Zhang, R. (2024). Finding love in algorithms: Deciphering the emotional contexts of close encounters with AI chatbots. *Journal of Computer-Mediated Communication*, *29*(5), zmae015. DOI: 10.1093/jcmc/zmae015

Lim, J. (2022). Choosing the right love: Online dating platforms and gender inequality in Southeast Asia. In *Media in Asia* (pp. 211–225). Routledge. DOI: 10.4324/9781003130628-17

Lin, Z., Wang, Y., & Liu, T. (2023). Commercializing desire for platform economics: Digital romance in China's platformization age. *Continuum (Perth)*, *37*(1), 31–45. DOI: 10.1080/10304312.2023.2169251

Loock, K. (2024). *Hollywood remaking: How film remakes, sequels, and franchises shape industry and culture*. Univ of California Press.

Maheri, A., Jalili, S., Hosseinzadeh, Y., Khani, R., & Miryahyavi, M. (2021). A comprehensive survey on cultural algorithms. *Swarm and Evolutionary Computation*, *62*, 100846. DOI: 10.1016/j.swevo.2021.100846

Nemer, D. (2022). *Technology of the oppressed: Inequity and the digital mundane in favelas of Brazil*. MIT Press. DOI: 10.7551/mitpress/14122.001.0001

Nonaka, S., Takeda, T., & Sakai, M. (2022). Who are hikikomori? Demographic and clinical features of hikikomori (prolonged social withdrawal): A systematic review. *The Australian and New Zealand Journal of Psychiatry*, *56*(12), 1542–1554. DOI: 10.1177/00048674221085917 PMID: 35332798

Paché, G. (2025). Dating Apps: a "Logistics of desire." *Journal of Social Science for Policy Implications*. https://doi.org/DOI: 10.15640/jsspi.v13p1

Parzer, M. (2023). Cultural capital. In *The Routledge Handbook of Music and Migration* (pp. 35–37). Routledge. DOI: 10.4324/9781003309437-9

Paul, A., & Ahmed, S. (2024). Computed compatibility: Examining user perceptions of AI and matchmaking algorithms. *Behaviour & Information Technology*, *43*(5), 1002–1015. DOI: 10.1080/0144929X.2023.2196579

Rettberg, J. W. (2023). *Machine vision: How algorithms are changing the way we see the world*. John Wiley & Sons.

Rod, J., & Kera, D. (2010). From agency and subjectivity to animism: Phenomenological and Science Technology Studies (STS) approach to design of large techno-social systems. *Digital Creativity (Exeter)*, *21*(1), 70–76. DOI: 10.1080/14626261003654558

Rokach, A. (2024). *Love culturally: How does culture affect intimacy, commitment & love. The Intricacies of Love and Intimacy*. Taylor Francis.

Root, B. L., & Exline, J. J. (2014). The role of continuing bonds in coping with grief: Overview and future directions. *Death Studies*, *38*(1), 1–8. DOI: 10.1080/07481187.2012.712608 PMID: 24521040

Shin, D., Chotiyaputta, V., & Zaid, B. (2022). The effects of cultural dimensions on algorithmic news: How do cultural value orientations affect how people perceive algorithms? *Computers in Human Behavior*, *126*, 107007. DOI: 10.1016/j.chb.2021.107007

Smets, A., Ballon, P., & Walravens, N. (2021). Mediated by code: Unpacking algorithmic curation of urban experiences. *Media and Communication*, *9*(4), 250–259. DOI: 10.17645/mac.v9i4.4086

Spar, D. L., & Garber, A. (2025). Does Marriage Have a Future? *New Atlantis (Washington, D.C.)*, (81), 20–33.

Stinson, C. (2022). Algorithms are not neutral: Bias in collaborative filtering. *AI and Ethics*, *2*(4), 763–770. DOI: 10.1007/s43681-022-00136-w PMID: 35128540

Stray, J., Halevy, A., Assar, P., Hadfield-Menell, D., Boutilier, C., Ashar, A., Bakalar, C., Beattie, L., Ekstrand, M., Leibowicz, C., Moon Sehat, C., Johansen, S., Kerlin, L., Vickrey, D., Singh, S., Vrijenhoek, S., Zhang, A., Andrus, M. K., Helberger, N., & Vasan, N. (2024). Building human values into recommender systems: An interdisciplinary synthesis. *ACM Transactions on Recommender Systems*, *2*(3), 1–57. DOI: 10.1145/3632297

Tanaka, H., & Ho, M. H. (2025). Artificial Intelligence's Sexual Politics: Three Modes and the Case of Japan. *Technology. Power and Society: Critical Perspectives on the Global Digital Transformation*, *1*, 228–250. DOI: 10.1163/9789004711396_013

Yanke, G. (2021). Tying the knot with a robot: Legal and philosophical foundations for human–artificial intelligence matrimony. *AI & Society*, *36*(2), 417–427. DOI: 10.1007/s00146-020-00973-5

Chapter 10
Why We Turn to AI in Love: Sociotechnical Drivers

Lan Lan
http://orcid.org/0009-0005-0588-0988
The Chinese University of Hong Kong, China

ABSTRACT

With the development of artificial intelligence (AI), its application in the emotional domains is gradually being developed. By simulating the interaction between people in reality, AI applications such as chatbots provide companionship and emotional support for those seeking romantic relationships. AI romantic support refers to the intimate relationships between humans and AI chatbots. Establishing romantic relationships with AI is becoming increasingly common, attracting high attention from scholars, but there is currently no literature systematically discussing the underlying factors behind this. This chapter adopts a qualitative research method and focuses on four potential technological and social factors through an in-depth literature review. It discusses in detail the impact of digital convenience, emotional safety, cultural shifts, and evolving relationship norms on driving people to seek romantic relationships with AI, in order to fill this literature gap.

1. INTRODUCTION TO AI ROMANCE

The term "artificial intelligence" (AI) was first created in the 1950s (Helm et al., 2020). In contrast to human natural intelligence, AI is the intelligence exhibited by machines (Song et al., 2022). It can simulate human functions, thereby helping or even replacing humans in some daily activities (Reddy et al., 2024). It possesses the

DOI: 10.4018/979-8-3373-6623-4.ch010

abilities of "perception, recognition, learning, reaction, and problem-solving", and can analyse the environment and make decisions autonomously to a certain extent to achieve specific goals (Sheikh et al., 2023; Zhai et al., 2021). Currently, with the development of computing technology, big data resources, artificial neural networks, and machine learning methods, AI technology has achieved rapid development, and its applications are gradually expanding to fields such as education, intelligent assistants, AI chatbots, autonomous driving, and healthcare (Schuett, 2021; Song et al., 2022; Zhai et al., 2021). AI has been developed to simulate human emotions, gradually entering the realm of emotions once considered exclusive to human beings. It can provide empathy and support to people to alleviate stress, and accompany people in social interactions such as friendship and romantic relationships (Adewale & Muhammad, 2025; Hastuti, 2025; Meng & Dai, 2021; Sullivan et al., 2023). In recent years, more and more people have experienced mental health problems such as loneliness, depression, and social anxiety. Real-world interpersonal interactions cannot fully meet the social and psychological needs of some people or provide them with sufficient security. The isolation during the COVID-19 pandemic also led to the interruption of many social interactions in reality. Therefore, more and more people are beginning to seek AI as a companion and source of support. AI chatbots can simulate intimate relationships with users in terms of friendship, family affection, and romantic love (Grogan et al., 2025; Reddy et al., 2024).

This chapter focuses on the practice of romantic relationships between users and AI chatbots, using the terms "AI romance" and "AI romantic support" to discuss how people use AI chatbots as romantic partners, simulating romantic love and engaging in emotional interactions such as text, voice, and video chat. Other forms of AI applications, such as romantic relationships between intelligent assistants and humans, are not discussed in this chapter. AI conforms to the type of "contextual chatbots" described by Gupta et al. (2020), utilising machine learning, AI technology, and natural language processing technologies to identify users' emotions and intentions, generating answers based on database content. Nowadays, more and more users are engaging in romantic interactions with AI chatbots, enjoying virtual romance such as virtual marriage. Some users frequently engage in role-playing interactions with AI chatbots based on real-world interpersonal relationships, such as simulating a complete family consisting of a couple and children with an AI chatbot (Reddy et al., 2024). Some users view AI chatbots as entertainment to pass the time, while others "love" their AI chatbots, feeling a stronger connection with "them" than with humans, and incorporating scenarios like marriage and pregnancy into their role-playing (Djufril et al., 2025). A study on the usage of AI romantic partners in the US found that 19% of adults had engaged in simulated romantic conversations with AI chatbots. Usage was higher among young adults aged 18-30 than among those over

30. 7% of respondents had engaged in sexual interaction with their AI companions, a behaviour more common among young men (Willoughby & Carroll, 2025).

These days, many AI chatbots have emerged, such as XiaoIce, Replika, and Character.ai, which are specifically designed to simulate and provide emotional companionship, and ChatGPT, DeepSeek and Doubao, which are initially designed not for emotional companionship but to generate human-like dialogue to answer user questions (Jacobs, 2024). Many of the latter seem like ordinary web pages, lacking visual design. The page features a prominent chat box for users to input text or send documents, images, and audio recordings. The AI chatbots generate real-time replies using text, images, and voice. Some AI chatbots, like Replika, go beyond the basic function of communication via a chat box and can generate a 3D avatar that appears in a customisable space. Users can manipulate the avatar to interact with objects within the space. The avatar's name, appearance, gender, and many other elements can be customised, and some even possess AR and VR capabilities (Djufril et al., 2025). Currently, there's little focus on creating a robot-like form and placing an AI chatbot within it for physical interaction; AI romance experiences are largely limited to online virtual formats. Users employ various strategies to get the AI chatbots to generate responses they desire. For example, users can customise an ideal partner by inputting settings and requirements in the chat box, considering personality, preferences, and relationship with the user; repeating commands during conversations trains the AI chatbot to form specific response and interaction patterns (George et al., 2023; Huang et al., 2025; Xie, 2024). Generally, AI chatbots can save conversation history, maintaining the characters customised and trained through multiple conversations in subsequent chats. Users can also input requests to prohibit certain words, and Replika can even select feedback for each message the chatbot replies to, such as "love", "funny", "meaningless", or "offensive". These can help the AI chatbots avoid using words or tones that the user dislikes, thus preventing interruptions to the romantic experience.

AI romantic support can bring many positive effects to users. Frequent engagement with AI chatbots leads to a deep attachment, providing significant emotional and intimacy support and reducing feelings of loneliness (Reddy et al., 2024). AI chatbots are user-centric, understand users well without generating negative evaluations, enabling users to experience happiness and security (Skjuve et al., 2021). In a survey of American adults using AI chatbots for romantic practices, 21% of users said they preferred chatting with AI chatbots simulating romantic partners rather than interacting with real people, and nearly half believed that AI chatbots were easier to talk to than real people and that AI chatbots understood and listened to them better (Willoughby & Carroll, 2025). Some users experience difficulties in interpersonal relationships in real life, but still desire romantic experiences. AI partners can play a positive role in their real-world romantic relationships to some extent. For instance, by conversing with AI chatbots, users can learn and practice better ways of dealing with human partners. At the same time, some users believe that AI chatbots can serve as a channel for venting emotions and sexual needs, which may help prevent infidelity in real life to some extent (Nosta, 2024).

However, it cannot be denied that AI romance may also have some negative impacts on users. AI romance may lead users to form unrealistic expectations of real-life interpersonal relationships, such as AI chatbots listening and supporting users unconditionally at all times, which could hardly be achieved by real humans. This huge gap between interactions with AI chatbots and real-life interpersonal relationships may cause users to have excessive emotional dependence on AI chatbots, believing that relationships with them are more ideal than real-life interpersonal interactions. This could reduce users' willingness and effort to establish and maintain interpersonal and romantic relationships in reality, ultimately leading to higher risks of depression and loneliness (Adewale & Muhammad, 2025; Willoughby & Carroll, 2025). Furthermore, if more and more people choose AI as their romantic partner, the decrease in real-life romantic practices may lead to a decline in birth rates, affecting social structure (Reddy et al., 2024). Some AI chatbots' language generation models contain occupational and gender biases (Grogan et al., 2025), which may fail to meet users' expectations for romantic relationships. AI chatbots may also infringe on users' privacy by collecting users' personal data without their consent (Piispanen et al., 2024).

Establishing romantic relationships with AI chatbots is becoming increasingly common, attracting great attention from scholars. Numerous studies have already discussed the role, development, impact, challenges, ethical issues, and applications of AI romantic support (Djufril et al., 2025; Jacobs, 2024; Meng & Dai, 2021; Reddy et al., 2024; Song et al., 2022). However, there is presently no literature that systematically discusses the possible factors driving individuals to seek romantic support from AI chatbots. This chapter will focus on a technological factor: digital convenience and three social factors: emotional safety, cultural shifts, and evolving relationship norms to discuss the potential factors driving individuals to establish romantic relationships with AI chatbots, supplementing the existing literature.

2. TECHNOLOGICAL FACTOR

2.1 Digital Convenience

AI chatbots, as a digital technology application, greatly facilitate users' pursuit of romantic relationships in terms of accessibility and operation, which increases the feasibility and willingness to find AI partners. This kind of digital convenience, by reducing the financial, time, and learning costs of enjoying romantic experiences, as well as lowering the costs of starting and maintaining a romantic relationship, is an undeniable factor driving users to find an AI romantic partner.

Firstly, many AI chatbots can be accessed directly as web pages by searching their names on mobile phones or computer browsers. Some AI chatbots have released software adapted for mobile phones and computers, supporting offline use when there is no internet connection. With rapid economic and technological development, the penetration rate of electronic devices is gradually increasing, providing users with convenient and quick access to AI chatbots. Interacting with an AI partner breaks through the limitations of coordinating time and space for dating in reality, reducing users' time and energy costs to some extent. Furthermore, many AI chatbots, such as Replika, ChatGPT, and DeepSeek, offer both free and paid subscription models. The free model already provides users with quick replies, and the replies are as logical and coherent as conversations between people. Paying unlocks more features, such as Replika, which allows users to listen to voice messages from AI partners, and ChatGPT shows improvements in AI response speed, creativity, and coherence after payment (Jo, 2024). AI chatbots are highly accessible, easy to use, and have low monetary costs, allowing users to easily select suitable AI chatbots to develop romantic relationships.

Secondly, many AI chatbot platforms offer a simple and direct process for registration and operation. When registering an account, users need to provide a small amount of personal information, such as username, age, and gender (sometimes the AI will interact with users based on their basic information), to begin using the service. This process is essentially as simple as registering a social media account. Some AI chatbots offer 3D character models and scenes. Users can also choose their favourite AI avatars and environment. The instructions for the use of AI chatbots on both websites and software versions are generally clear, and the operation is as convenient as designing a social media user profile. Once an account is created, they can immediately start experiencing a romantic relationship with AI. This ease of use reduces the time and learning cost for users seeking romantic support from AI. It doesn't require a higher education background and is not too difficult for older electronic device users. This can, to some extent, continuously attract users of different ages and educational backgrounds, and increase users' willingness to engage in romantic relationships with AI chatbots.

Meanwhile, the ease of registering and customising AI chatbots reduces the cost of starting and maintaining a romantic relationship compared to the cost of dating in real life. This difference can be explained by Mauss's (1966) gift theory. Gifts given to others contain a part of one's own spirit, and everyone has the obligation and freedom to give, receive, and reciprocate gifts. People have the freedom to refuse gifts, but this can easily be seen as a refusal to form or deepen a good relationship.

People also have the choice of when and what gifts to reciprocate, but appropriate and equal gifts contribute to the formation of a good social relationship. Gift exchange can be extended to the exchange of time, emotions, and attitudes invested by both parties in a romantic relationship. In real life, establishing a romantic relationship requires a long period of searching, dating, and adjustment to confirm a partner. Maintaining a relationship with a human partner requires continuous, two-way emotional exchange, to some extent catering to the other person's preferences, and there is always the possibility of rejection or relationship breakdown (Cave & Dihal, 2021). This uncertainty makes maintaining a romantic relationship require a significant investment of time, energy, and emotion, and is also affected by whether the contributions of oneself and one's partner are equal and reciprocal.

However, AI romance liberates users from the obligation to reciprocate "gifts", eliminating the need to reciprocate emotional support and allowing them to unilaterally enjoy the emotional value and companionship provided by AI chatbots. A romantic relationship can be initiated and maintained without requiring a relatively equal reciprocity. First, AI romance allows users to start and end personalised romantic experiences anytime, anywhere via electronic devices. Second, AI chatbots do not generate genuine negative emotions or hostile attitudes (Cave & Dihal, 2021). Even if users insult or criticise the AI chatbots or fail to communicate with them for extended periods, the romantic support AI chatbots provide remains unaffected. Furthermore, users do not need to make any concessions in their romantic experience with their AI partners. Users can customise an AI partner that perfectly matches their preferred personality, appearance, and interests (George et al., 2023). These three points allow AI chatbots to avoid the compatibility and reciprocity issues related to emotions and time that often arise in human romantic relationships to some extent (Cave & Dihal, 2021). This low-cost way of starting and maintaining romantic relationships caters to the busy and tiring pace of modern life, much like an "emotional fast food". Although it is sometimes considered to lack substantial content (Andersson, 2025), it is convenient and cost-effective enough to drive people to treat AI as a partner.

3. SOCIAL FACTORS

3.1 Emotional Safety

According to the American Psychological Association (2018a), emotion is a complex response pattern involving "experience, behaviour, and physiological factors". This response pattern manifests in how individuals cope with significant events. Individuals experience different specific emotions in the face of different events;

for example, they may feel happy because of a salary increase, or fear because of being attacked or bullied. Emotional needs are the highest level of human needs, and human cognition and behaviour are influenced by the positive or negative impact of personal emotions (Wang et al., 2018). This section will first focus on the emotional safety that AI chatbots provide to users, and then discuss how this emotional safety drives users to establish romantic relationships with AI chatbots.

Emotional safety is a crucial foundation for healthy interpersonal relationships and an essential human need (Brenner & Letlch, 2023). It focuses on individual feelings, which can be seen as individuals feeling respected for their feelings and thoughts, being able to safely express themselves, and being free from psychological harm such as criticism, discrimination, or shame (Shean & Mander, 2020). Currently, the importance of emotional safety has been demonstrated in numerous scholarly studies. On the one hand, for example, emotional safety helps create a more positive and healthy campus culture, promoting students' academic performance, personality, and character development; emotional safety helps patients cooperate more actively with treatment, enhancing their confidence and cooperation with the hospital (Lyndon et al., 2023); adequate emotional safety is an important characteristic of infant attachment to parents in early life and of equal and caring intimate relationships with partners in adulthood (Morris, 1982).

On the other hand, a lack of emotional safety might lead to high levels of stress and despair (Veale et al., 2023). In interpersonal relationships, it could cause an excessive sense of defensiveness and emotional instability, leading individuals to unconsciously open up to the wrong person, or disclose information they are originally unwilling to share with others, or completely close themselves off from communicating with others (King, 2009). Over time, this may result in severe loneliness and difficulties in communicating with others. At the same time, feeling emotionally unsafe can be reflected in the body, such as shortness of breath and tense muscles. The inability of an individual to recover to a state of feeling safe will eventually lead to persistent physical discomfort (Brenner & Letlch, 2023). The emotional safety provided by AI chatbots to users can be seen as AI chatbots always providing non-judgmental answers; the interaction of AI chatbots is controllable and predictable, allowing users to dominate the conversation content and receive supportive responses.

3.1.1 Non-Judgmental Answers and Users' Self-Disclosure

First, many users believe that AI chatbots are less judgmental than humans. They lack human bias and always offer understanding, encouraging, and supportive responses, which is a core source of users' sense of safety (Cave & Dihal, 2021; Hastuti, 2025; Skjuve et al., 2021; Wang et al., 2025; Zhang & Li, 2025). The non-judgmental characteristic of AI chatbots might alleviate users' fear of negative feedback, which is closely linked to social anxiety and could potentially undermine real-world interpersonal interactions (Iqbal & Ajmal, 2018). Social interactions in reality normally are perceived as filled with uncertainty, such as the duration of conversations, other people's attitudes and responses, which might include biased evaluations that can cause psychological harm (Djufril et al., 2025). AI chatbots, regardless of whether they are the types that were initially designed to provide emotional support, offer non-judgmental responses. Their attitude is unaffected by users' values, making them more suitable to be confidants than real people. Users feel safe to disclose sexual preferences that are difficult to admit in real life, as well as their vulnerabilities, such as suicidal thoughts (Djufril et al., 2025). In particular, some users may have social anxiety or other psychological problems in real life, or face discrimination due to disability, making it difficult for them to interact with real people and establish romantic relationships. Through interaction with AI chatbots, they have the opportunity to enter into romantic relationships without being judged or the risk of rejection (George et al., 2023).

The emotional safety brought by AI chatbots' non-judgmental characteristics increases users' willingness to self-disclose (Wang et al., 2025), which ultimately promotes the formation and deepening of intimate human-AI relationships. Self-disclosure is defined as revealing one's personal information to others, information that is difficult for others to obtain through other means. The disclosed content ranges from less important, superficial information to highly private and sensitive information, such as information related to an individual's family background or psychological problems that may lead to others' negative evaluations (Zhang & Li, 2025). The content of self-disclosure can be briefly divided into factual disclosure and emotional disclosure. The former concerns objective information about a person, while the latter concerns a person's emotions and feelings (Ho et al., 2018).

Self-disclosure may lead to privacy leaks and may make people encounter the risks of disclosing information to unintended audiences. In interpersonal relationships, an increase in the privacy of the disclosed content may lead to a decrease in self-disclosure (Ma et al., 2016). When people disclose themselves to romantic partners, they may worry about being rejected, burdening their partner or receiving negative comments, such as excessive self-disclosure might be perceived as a lack of security and troublesome by others (Zhang & Li, 2025). There's also a need to guess and cater to one's partner's thoughts to maintain the romantic relationship. Simultaneously, the desire to present one's best self, the fear of negative feedback from a partner, and a lack of trust in the partner can all lead to repressed self-disclosure (Wang et al., 2025). When people disclose personal information such as stressful experiences, vulnerable feelings, and sensitive thoughts, they gain more psychological benefit if the recipient expresses approval and support rather than judgment or blame (Sullivan et al., 2023), making them feel more comfortable and encouraged to self-disclose in the future rather than suppressing it. Some users believe that AI chatbots have helped boost their self-confidence, and the supportive conversations with AI partners have made them less concerned about others' opinions (Djufril et al., 2025). AI chatbots alleviate people's fear and anxiety about being negatively evaluated or rejected when disclosing themselves to others by providing non-judgmental, empathetic, and encouraging responses, thus making them more willing to engage in higher levels of self-disclosure.

Higher levels of self-disclosure are positively correlated with emotional and psychological benefits (Ta et al., 2020). Ho et al. (2018) summarised three benefits found in previous literature: reduced stress and anxiety from negative experiences; a more intimate relationship with the person providing support; and improved psychological problems caused by self-image (which is sometimes perceived by an individual as more negative than it actually is) by feeling valued. Importantly, these benefits are equivalent regardless of whether participants believe they are disclosing to AI chatbots or real people (Ho et al., 2018). Furthermore, when individuals disclose their thoughts or emotions to their partners, if the partner provides a supportive response to make the individual feel recognised and cared for, the intimacy between the partners is enhanced (Khalifian & Barry, 2020). Overall, users felt emotionally safe in romantic chats with AI, which further encouraged them to engage in higher levels of self-disclosure with AI chatbots. In this process, users experienced a reduction in negative emotions such as stress and anxiety through the non-judgmental responses provided by the AI chatbots, while gradually feeling an increasingly intimate relationship with their AI partners. As a result, they were driven to seek long-term romantic support from AI chatbots.

Meanwhile, the deepening of intimate human-AI relationships can also be explained by social penetration theory. Social penetration theory states that interpersonal relationships deepen with the depth of self-disclosure, which is the degree of intimacy of information exchange; the breadth of self-disclosure, which is the quantity of information exchanged and the scope of the topics; and the time and frequency of conversation (Skjuve et al., 2021). When both parties feel comfortable disclosing more and more sensitive and intimate information, their relationship deepens. Therefore, self-disclosure is also a reciprocal process. In real-life interpersonal interactions, the more one person discloses to another, the more willing the other person is to reciprocate. In this process, if both parties choose to exchange private information, the other party's reaction can generate trust if they provide non-judgmental answers, keep the content of the conversation confidential, and also engage in reciprocal self-disclosure, thereby strengthening the relationship between the two parties (Zhang & Li, 2025).

This theory can also be applied to romantic relationships between humans and AI chatbots. Some users, during self-disclosure with AI chatbots, have found that their

AI partners also reciprocate by sharing "personal information", such as feelings, experiences, and thoughts (Lee et al., 2020; Skjuve et al., 2021). While AI chatbots' self-disclosure differs from that of humans, since the shared personal information comes only from databases and previous conversations with users, people tend to open up to those who also disclose their information. In this reciprocal process, the more one party discloses themselves, the more the other can be encouraged to do the same (Masaviru, 2016). AI chatbots' self-disclosure encourages users to continue disclosing themselves, not only for psychological benefits such as anxiety relief but also to deepen trust and intimacy with the AI chatbots, making users willing to continue cultivating the romantic relationship. Moreover, in traditional romantic relationships, self-disclosure by partners is influenced by factors such as trust, generally progressing from less important information to highly sensitive information (Wang et al., 2025). This is also a way of testing the other person's acceptance level, avoiding negative evaluations. However, AI chatbots, to some extent, allow the establishment and maintenance of intimate relationships to transcend the gradual, incremental development between people. AI chatbots eliminate many of the risks associated with real-life relationships, such as being questioned or alienated for disclosing negative information. Users experiencing intense stress and anxiety can skip the lengthy process of self-disclosure reciprocity and the gradual cultivation of trust required in human relationships, directly disclosing sensitive information such as their negative emotions and psychological state to AI chatbots without reservation. Then, through the AI chatbots' non-judgmental encouragement, sympathy, and other supportive responses, they can benefit emotionally and psychologically from self-disclosure, and on this basis, develop a closer and more intimate romantic relationship with the AI.

In summary, the non-judgmental nature of AI chatbots lays the foundation for emotional safety. On the one hand, it encourages users to dare to conduct self-disclosure and directly gain psychological benefits from it, as well as to deepen intimate relationships with AI chatbots. On the other hand, through reciprocal self-disclosure and with the ability to support users' non-gradual, direct, sensitive self-disclosure, AI chatbots can strengthen the psychological benefits of users and accelerate the development of human-AI relationships. This positive feedback facilitates users in actively seeking long-term romantic support from AI chatbots.

3.1.2 Certainty

The second notable aspect of the emotional safety that AI chatbots bring to users lies in the fact that they are controllable in multiple ways. First, there's the controllability of time. Compared with the busyness and uncertainty of human partners, AI chatbots are always there to respond, offering emotional support and romantic companionship. Similarly, when users feel tired or have something urgent to attend to, they can end the conversation at any time they want without any explanations, which might be considered impolite in interpersonal relationships. Also, the AI partner won't suddenly disappear, bringing emotional discomfort caused by uncertainty to users.

Second, there's the basic controllability of interaction content. AI chatbots are designed to provide help or emotional support to users; they won't suddenly insult or judge users unless they are asked to do so. Users can also shape how AI chatbots respond in specific ways, such as requesting a particular tone or training AI chatbots to proactively ask questions like "How were you today?" Through repeated interactions and giving feedback, AI chatbots can be tailored to provide responses in a manner that users feel comfortable with (George et al., 2023). As discussed earlier, users won't be judged by AI chatbots, nor will they face the risk of being deceived or exploited by their AI partner. This controllable and stable human-AI relationship liberates users from real-world interpersonal relationships that might require pleasing others, caring about others' feelings, and dealing with misunderstandings. Users won't be trapped in romantic relationships that could break down at any time due to conflicts (Cave & Dihal, 2021). The control over chat time and content is essentially equivalent to control over the user's romantic relationship with their AI partner, which can help alleviate loneliness and attract users who have experienced manipulation or abuse in previous real-world romantic relationships.

Loneliness is widespread and stems from several main sources: a lack of reliable attachment to figures and unfulfilled needs for intimacy and companionship; the absence of a social network where individuals can feel integrated, abelongi sense of ng and connection; and the perception that the quantity and quality of individuals' social relationships are insufficient to meet their needs (American Psychological Association, 2018b; Yanguas et al., 2018). Loneliness has been found to contribute to higher mortality rates, increased incidence of chronic diseases such as heart disease, hypertension, and obesity, and psychological problems such as depression and anxiety (Hawkley & Cacioppo, 2010; Yanguas et al., 2018). Since psychological discomfort is directly perceptible, AI chatbot users can experience the psychological benefits provided by their AI companions. For example, there is currently a relatively successful practical application of AI to alleviate loneliness, which is a robot called "PARO". It is used as a pet for the elderly to interact and alleviate their loneliness, thereby improving their health status (Pani et al., 2024).The constant and flexible accessibility of AI chatbots ensures they can always be present when users need emotional companionship, creating a sense of being valued and cared for (Hastuti, 2025). As attachment figures, AI chatbots provide companionship and intimacy that substitute for or supplement interpersonal relationships during users' times of emotional vulnerability, thus alleviating users' loneliness to some extent.

On the other hand, the controllability of AI chatbots prevents them from harming users. The fact that interactions with AI chatbots are dominated and controlled by the users helps users who have been hurt, such as those who have suffered prolonged belittling, physical abuse, or manipulation, to rebuild their self-esteem, recognise their own value and competence. This gradually alleviates their emotional trauma and rebuilds their capacity to trust others (George et al., 2023). When users need romantic companionship, comfort for traumatic experiences, or support and encouragement to re-enter a real-life romantic relationship, AI chatbots can provide understanding, empathy, and supportive responses at any time, especially when access to professionals is temporarily unavailable (Alqaidoom & Ateeq, 2025). They can also help these users improve their mood and quality of life (Alqaidoom & Ateeq, 2025). As discussed earlier, AI chatbots' non-judgmental responses encourage users to engage in higher levels of self-disclosure. This allows users to freely vent their stress and anxiety, while providing the AI chatbots with necessary information to generate more helpful responses, such as empathetic understanding and practical advice. In conclusion, the controllability of AI chatbots contributes to the development of users' trust and intimacy with them. Their controllability in terms of time and content provides users with emotional safety, alleviates users' loneliness and supports users who have been emotionally hurt, which makes them an important and ideal option for users seeking romantic support.

3.2 Cultural shifts & evolving relationship norms

Culture can be defined as values, language, practices, beliefs, social norms, traditions, technologies, social systems, and other elements that individuals learn from others and the external world, develop, and pass down from generation to generation within different social groups, shaping human life in every aspect (American Psychological Association, 2023; Whiten et al., 2011). A group that possesses and shares a unique culture can be considered a cultural group, with members sharing identities such as sexual orientation, class, and ethnicity (American Psychological Association, 2023). Cultural shifts refer to the transformation of values, social norms, beliefs or other factors within a social or cultural group due to economic, technological, and political influences, potentially leading to changes in the cognition, behaviour, identity, and social interactions of its members (Fiveable Content Team, 2025).

Advances in AI technology have driven cultural shifts from multiple perspectives, including technological, economic, and policy levels. From a technological perspective, AI has gradually driven the automation in areas such as providing medical advice and autonomous driving (Aghion et al., 2017). It also reduces the working hours required to create a unit of output, increases productivity and promotes economic growth (Executive Office of the President, 2016; Furman & Seamans, 2019). AI can also work with humans, improving productivity and efficiency by optimising industrial production processes, rationally allocating resources, and enhancing quality control, while further creating new industries and employment opportunities, occupying an important position in the global economy (Raju & Sumallika, 2023). Meanwhile, the development of AI has given rise to the development of a series of supporting policies, attempting to leverage its advantages and reduce potential risks. These include policies focusing on AI legal and regulatory governance; exploring preventative regulations for the labor market and social inequality (Thierer et al., 2017); policies in education regarding the use of AI by lecturers to assist teaching tasks and the misuse of AI by students for cheating in examinations (Chan, 2023); and policies focusing on AI ethical issues (Slimi & Carballido, 2023), etc.

These represent cultural shifts in the economic and policy spheres brought about by AI technology. At the same time, some cultural shifts, such as the rise of individualism, can, in turn, drive the application of AI, especially in the realm of emotions. This section will first focus on the evolution of norms about intimate social relationships, exploring their relationship with individuals' motives to seek romantic support from AI. It will then analyse related cultural shifts contributing to the evolving relationship norms, and finally discuss the relationship between these three aspects.

Cultural factors regarding romantic relationships in Western countries, such as laws, policies, and social perceptions, have undergone numerous shifts throughout history and continue to evolve today. As a result, the mainstream social norms of intimate relationships are constantly changing. For example, norms once considered mandatory have been altered and adjusted several times throughout history, and may now simply be considered personal choices; romantic relationships that were once stigmatised may now be normalised. Among these evolving relationship norms, heterosexual marriage, same-sex relationships, and "consensual non-monogamy" deserve attention. They reflect that the forms of intimate relationships in today's society are becoming increasingly diverse. People are no longer limited to rigid norms but rather are based more on personal preferences and choices. Social acceptance of different types of romantic relationships has significantly increased, leading more people to explore various forms of romance, such as romantic relationships with AI chatbots, while having the courage to choose and adhere to their preferred relationships under a lower risk of stigma.

Firstly, the legal systems, social norms, and perceptions surrounding heterosexual marriage have experienced significant evolution, which deserves attention. The social and cultural factors that shape an individual's marital relationship vary significantly due to factors such as geography and ethnicity, and are constantly evolving under the influence of education, globalization, and other factors, thus marriage modes are evolving, including choices of marriage age, free-choice marriages versus arranged marriages, and the different family statuses and roles of men and women within the marriage (Cynthia, 2021). The mid-20th century is a particularly noteworthy period; some authors define the duration of traditional marriage as long ago, up to the mid-20th century, while marriage from the mid-20th century onwards is considered a modern form (Shchemelinin, 2020). The US experienced significant shifts in marriage modes during the 1960s, including changes in the status and roles of spouses within the marital relationship; changes in the age of marriage; changes in divorce restrictions; and a relatively blurred distinction between heterosexual marriage and other intimate relationships (Cynthia, 2021; Scott, 2000). These are also significant differences between traditional and modern marriage. Before this period, traditional American law constructed a hierarchical, exclusive, and highly serious marriage system, defining gender and commitment norms within marriage (Scott, 2000). The former reflected the hierarchical and differentiated roles between husband and wife; for example, the husband was expected to earn money outside the home, while the wife was confined to domestic duties such as housework and childcare. The latter defined marriage as a "lifelong obligation" partnership, setting many barriers to make the cost of leaving the marriage very high, such as requiring substantial fault on one party. Marriage has become a social institution requiring both spouses to fulfil legal obligations to uphold collective interests; other intimate relationships outside of marriage are stigmatised under this system (Scott, 2000).

Legal changes regarding marriage norms began in the 1960s. The rise of the women's rights movement in the 1960s and 70s allowed women to gradually break free from the previous constraints of serving only the family, husband, and children, enabling them to enter the fields of education and employment (Cynthia, 2021). The law subsequently shifted, no longer clearly defining marital relationships by hierarchy, but rather emphasising the independence and equality of both spouses (Scott, 2000). Under this new system and culture, both men and women invest more energy in education and career before entering into marriage, laying the foundation for independence after marriage, which is an undeniable reason why the marriage age of American citizens steadily increased from the latter half of the 20th century to the early 21st century (Cynthia, 2021).

During the same period, most restrictions on divorce were removed. For example, the state no longer required substantial fault on one party to grant a divorce; reasons like relationship breakdown are also considered feasible grounds for divorce. The law no longer grants marital relationships a special privilege; other non-marital intimate relationships, such as cohabitation, are also protected by law, and the stigma they suffer has decreased (Scott, 2000). Cultural perceptions of marriage have also changed. For example, modern marriage places greater emphasis on the existence of love than traditional marriage; modern marriage considers premarital sex for girls a natural thing, while traditional marriage held extremely negative attitudes towards it; traditional marriages had no access to online dating and communicating via the internet, which in modern marriage has become a normal way (Shchemelinin, 2020). In the past, cohabitation usually occurred after marriage, but now cohabitation does not necessarily mean a commitment to marriage, and cohabiting couples are becoming increasingly common (Mernitz, 2018; Stanley & Rhoades, 2023). Before the mid-20th century, divorce was the leading cause of children living in single-parent families in the US; however, today, the primary reason for it is unmarried parenthood (Kearney, 2025; Sheffield & Squires, 2025). The number of children born out of wedlock has increased, but the total fertility rate is declining, nearly half of childless Americans aged 18-49 say they have no intention of having children (Sheffield & Squires, 2025). Family structures are changing, and family size is shrinking.

In modern society, marriage and family are no longer people's primary considerations, but are seen as just one of many lifestyle choices, highly related to individual autonomy, such as whether they can achieve a deeper intimacy with their partner and personal growth, rather than something they must do to fulfil social obligations or socially prescribed gender roles (Cherlin, 2004). People's attitudes towards marriage are more independent and autonomous, whether to enter into marriage is based on personal emotional needs and choices. Gender roles in couples are becoming more equal, and the forms of romantic relationships have expanded from a single heterosexual lifelong marriage to cohabitation, unmarried parenthood, and, as the chapter will discuss next, same-sex relationships and non-monogamy. Intimate relationships have witnessed what Cherlin (2004) called "deinstitutionalisation of marriage", with the previously established societal norms defining partners' behaviours loosening. Intimate relationships can now proceed without marriage, including cohabitation, and are not limited by gender or number of partners, as long as the relationship meets personal needs. The evaluation criteria for intimate relationships have shifted from external constraints such as laws and social judgments to internal experiences such as personal emotions and development, leading to increased societal acceptance of diverse intimate relationships. This, together with the factors to be discussed in the following text, have created a favourable and accepting social environment for people to seek romantic support from AI chatbots, including personal cognition, values, social evaluation, and other aspects of social life.

Secondly, when discussing the current society's increasing acceptance of various types of intimate relationships and the growing diversity of relationship norms, homosexuality and consensual non-monogamy deserve attention. The boundaries of the objects and exclusivity of intimate relationships have been expanded, and the emphasis on an individual's true preferences and needs has been enhanced. Homosexuality has often been stigmatised in history (Hsu, 2025). Sexual minorities are prone to stigmatisation in interpersonal communication and social structure aspects such as policies and norms (Drabble et al., 2021). One perception is that the main purpose of marriage is procreation, and homosexual relationships undermine the purpose of marriage (Cynthia, 2021).

However, since 1980, the average global acceptance of the homosexual community has increased (Flores, 2021). From the early 21st century to 2021, many countries around the world have legally recognised same-sex marriage. Until October 2019, 30 countries and regions around the world had allowed same-sex couples to marry, such as the US, the Netherlands, and Iceland (Drabble et al., 2021). This has reduced the stigmatisation that homosexual couples face at the social, institutional and cultural levels, as well as the restrictions they are subject to in terms of norms and policies. It has broken the situation in the past where homosexual couples were unable to enjoy the same welfare and rights as heterosexual married couples due to legal restrictions on same-sex marriage, such as the right to inherit a partner's property, priority in emergency medical decision-making (Drabble et al., 2021; Cynthia, 2021). A scholar conducted research in Taiwan, the first place in Asia to legalise same-sex marriage, and found that in recent years, after the legalisation of same-sex marriage, people's acceptance of homosexual behaviour has increased. People are more willing to get along with homosexuals, and are more convinced that same-sex couples can be excellent parents just like other heterosexual couples (Hsu, 2025). In regions where same-sex marriage is legalised, families' support and acceptance of homosexual couples have increased compared to the past; same-sex couples have better integrated into society and have received less discrimination (Drabble et al., 2021).

In countries and regions where marriage has not yet been legalised, the acceptance of homosexuality in society has also increased. Take Japan as an example, although it has not yet recognised same-sex marriage at the national level, the acceptance rate of homosexuality has soared from 54% in 2002 to 68% in 2019 (Poushter & Nicholas, 2020). In a 2023 follow-up survey on people's views on same-sex marriage, as many as 68% of Japanese adults expressed their support for the legalisation of same-sex marriage (Gubbala et al., 2023). A similar situation also occurred in South Korea. In 2002, only 25% of South Koreans believed that society should accept homosexuality. However, by 2019, this proportion had risen to 44%, more than doubling in less than two decades (Poushter & Nicholas, 2020). Public support for homosexuality in many countries has gone beyond legal progress, such as Malaysia, Myanmar, and China (Equaldex, 2023).

An individual's acceptance of homosexuality is influenced by country, gender and age. In countries where religious belief is not so important, which are often among the wealthiest in the world, people have a higher acceptance of homosexuality. However, in countries with a higher degree of religious belief and that are relatively poor, the mainstream social perception does not accept homosexuality

(Pew Research Centre, 2013). Research also found that in countries with gender differences, women hold a more accepting attitude towards homosexuality compared to men (Pew Research Centre, 2013). Western Europe and North America have the highest acceptance of homosexuality, while attitudes towards homosexuality are more divergent in Central and Eastern Europe, with little difference in the proportion of people who accept and do not accept it. In regions such as the Middle East and Russia, few people accept homosexuality (Poushter & Nicholas, 2020). It is worth noting that young people are more receptive to homosexuality than older people. For instance, in South Korea, 79% of people aged 18 to 29 believe that society should accept homosexuality, while only 23% of those aged 50 and above hold the same view. The country with the second largest gap is Japan (Poushter & Nicholas, 2020). In recent years, the social tolerance for homosexuality in many countries, especially in Europe and America, has been continuously increasing. This again clearly reflects the acceptance of the deinstitutionalisation of intimate relationships by the general public, especially young people. Intimate relationships are no longer confined to heterosexual patterns and do not necessarily lead to marriage. The boundaries of intimate relationship types have been broadened, providing a more tolerant social environment for non-traditional emotional connections, such as human-AI romance.

Another notable example is the social acceptance of consensual non-monogamous relationships, that is, when an individual establishes romantic or sexual relationships with multiple people simultaneously, with the knowledge and consent of all parties involved in the romantic relationship, such as polyamorous and open relationships (Gupta et al., 2024). Today, non-monogamous relationships still bear stigma in society. For instance, people consider those in non-monogamous relationships to be "more immoral and promiscuous" than those in monogamous relationships. Participants in non-monogamous relationships emphasise intimacy and emotion, while their opponents simplify such relationships to sexual behaviours (Gupta et al., 2024). However, consensual non-monogamous practices are not uncommon nowadays, and interest in them has been rising over the past decade or so since the beginning of the 21st century. A survey in 2021 focusing on single adults in the US found that one-ninth of respondents had polyamorous experiences, and one-sixth of them wanted to try polyamorous relationships (Moors et al., 2021). The social recognition of non-monogamy is gradually increasing, and it is regarded as playing an important role in the growing diverse forms of romantic relationships nowadays (Gupta et al., 2024). The social acceptance of diverse types of intimate relationships is constantly expanding, and the restrictions on marital obligations, sexual orientation, and the number of partners are gradually decreasing.

The above examples of the deinstitutionalisation of marriage, including the increasingly smaller norms' restrictions on marriage modes, the increase in cohabiting partnerships, the rise in the number of homosexual intimate relationships and marriages, and the wider practice and social acceptance of non-monogamy, demonstrate the continuous evolution of intimate relationship norms in modern times over the past few decades. The social relationship norms that determine the behaviour of partners have weakened (Cherlin, 2004), while the importance of personal emotions and choices has increased accordingly, marriage is no longer the only carrier of intimate relationships. In the past, the union of couples was likely due to family expectations or economic needs, but nowadays, couples establish and end their relationships more based on each other's emotional feelings and personal choices. Love is no longer severely restricted by factors such as family and religion, but lies in whether the emotional bond between partners is strong enough to support a romantic relationship (Poder, 2025). The functionality of love weakens, while the importance of individual happiness and willingness increases. When individuals establish romantic relationships, they can consider less the risk of being condemned by society, fulfil their social obligations of procreation, follow religious beliefs, and provide economic support for the family, and instead focus more on their personal need for romance. This expands the scope of choosing love and romantic relationships, with fewer limitations to gender, partners and the objects and the number of partners.

AI capable of simulating human emotions has entered the emotional domain that was once considered exclusive to humans (Hastuti, 2025), which means that the boundaries of intimate relationships no longer need to be confined to traditional individual humans. The increasingly diverse and continuously developing social tolerance and acceptance, as well as the emphasis on individual emotions in romantic relationships, have paved the way for the popularisation and normalisation of AI romance. The social stigmatisation and moral resistance that individuals will face when choosing to find an AI romantic partner will also be reduced, which further drives individuals to try and persist in interacting with AI chatbots as a romantic partner based on their personal needs and preferences. For instance, in today's fast-paced and high-pressure living environment, as has been discussed earlier, using AI chatbots as a romantic partner enables individuals who wish to enter into a romantic relationship to experience that: the time and emotional costs required to establish and maintain a romantic relationship are low; AI partners will offer encouraging rather than judgmental conversations, providing users with a safe and private space; users can customise AI partners according to their own preferences, making it easier for them to start, end or restart a brand new relationship. Therefore, based on society's deeper acceptance and tolerance of diverse romantic relationship modes, individuals are becoming more and more courageous and willing to try to practice AI romance, explore the advantages of AI partners, and persist according to personal preferences.

Importantly, the evolutionary relationship norms discussed earlier do not occur in isolation. The following text will discuss an important cultural shift: from collectivism to the rise of individualism. This itself has driven people to view AI chatbots as an ideal romantic partner, while also promoting the evolution of more diverse relationship norms, using the latter as a mediator to drive people to establish romantic relationships with AI chatbots. Hamamura and Bettache (2018) cited Triandis' description of individualism and collectivism in 1995: Collectivism can be understood as a social model that involves individuals closely related to each other, who view themselves as part of one or more wholes, including family, state, and colleague relationships, etc. Individuals value and emphasise their connection with other members of the group, place collective goals above personal ones, and are willing to abide by the norms and obligations of the collective. The main motivation for their behaviours is also the norms and obligations of the collective. Individualism can be seen as a social model composed of loosely connected individuals. Individuals regard themselves as an independent entity from the collective, prioritising personal goals over collective ones, attaching great importance to the rational analysis of the strengths and weaknesses in interacting with others, and using this to guide social behaviours. Their behaviours are mainly driven by individuals' own preferences, needs and rights.

Hamamura (2012) conducted a study on cultural individualism in the US and Japan, and some indicators in the research results partially confirmed the modernisation theory. Modernisation theory predicts that individualism will rise more and more over time, especially in regions with economic growth. People with more individualistic tendencies tend to have smaller family sizes in daily life practice, are more inclined to live alone instead of living with elders such as parents, and are more likely to divorce (Santos et al., 2017). In the US and Japan, the rise of individualism is prominently reflected in people's living, family and values, such as the expansion of urbanisation scale, the shrinking of family size and the more common phenomenon of divorce. Meanwhile, compliance, adherence to tradition and contribution to society are no longer emphasised as they were in the past, and independence has become even more important (Hamamura, 2012). Santos et al. (2017) conducted a study in 78 countries with different levels of economic development around the world and found that although there are significant cultural differences around the world, except for a few countries with lower levels of economic development and those with complex development histories, a significant trend of the rise of individualism has emerged.

The cultural shift from emphasising collectivism to the rise of individualism itself will drive people to seek romantic support from AI chatbots. Under individualism, personal goals, preferences and demands are the main driving forces of individual behaviours. Compared with collectivism that emphasises close relationships, collective norms and obligations, individualists may have a stronger motivation to choose their preferred mode of love and are less worried about negative evaluations from the collective than collectivists. Individuals will put their own goals first and judge whether to establish and continue relationships by analysing the advantages and disadvantages of socialising with others. Rather than meeting the expectations of society and family, such as the mode of arranged marriage by parents in traditional marriage (Cynthia, 2021), or considering marriage as a must to fulfill the social obligation of procreation, under individualism, an individual's choice of romantic relationships is more about their goals for a relationship, as well as their preferences and demands for their romantic partners. However, establishing a romantic relationship with a living person, as discussed earlier, requires a long period of searching, selection and adjustment. Maintaining a romantic relationship also demands time and effort, and it is inevitable to make certain compromises with the other party. There are also many uncertainties, such as the other party possibly refusing, and conflicts between the two sides may lead to emotional breakdown (Cave & Dihal, 2021). When an individualistic culture rises, more and more people place their own requests and preferences first. An issue that cannot be ignored is that the time, emotional, financial and energy costs of maintaining a romantic relationship will increase. However, AI chatbots offer digital convenience and emotional safety, with certainty and customisability, the time and content of their responses are all controlled by users. Users can interact with their desired types of partners at any time and receive ideal emotional support. This makes AI chatbots an ideal supplement or replacement for real-life romantic relationships.

Meanwhile, the rise of individualism is closely related to urbanisation (Hamamura, 2012). A large number of rural people have moved to cities for economic opportunities, which has gradually transformed the traditional nuclear family structure, which consists of parents and their children living together in one family, into smaller families, such as single-person and childless couples (Haq, 2024; Wilson et al., 2025). This transformation is not only due to population migration but also to the evolution of economic conditions and social relationship norms. Society's acceptance of divorce and cohabitation has increased, and individualists often prioritise career and personal development over starting a family, finding a partner and establishing a family are no longer essential pursuits for individuals (Haq, 2024). The high population density in cities may cause a sense of distance from others; the shrinking of family size may also reduce the intimate relationship between individuals and their families to a certain extent, which are important factors that may lead to loneliness (Mcauley, 2024). The sense of distance from others, coupled with the fact that many individuals no longer actively pursue the establishment of a romantic relationship, also brings difficulties in entering into an intimate relationship in reality. Under this situation, the customisability and certainty of interaction time and content provided by AI chatbots enable users to quickly establish a satisfactory romantic relationship at a low cost. It might alleviate users' loneliness, become their emotional pillar, and bring them a comfortable romantic experience. Therefore, the cultural shift itself can drive users to look for AI partners.

At the same time, the rise of individualism has led individuals to pay more attention to their own development and needs than to the collective's, and the emphasis on social norms and obligations has also been continuously reduced. To a certain extent, this has changed the traditional model where non-compliance with norms would lead to social stigma and isolation, transforming it into a diverse model based on individual choices. Under this culture, the norms of social relationships are constantly evolving into a freer and more diverse direction, such as marriage has become deinstitutionalised. The diverse relationships have paved the way for individuals to establish romantic relationships with AI, providing a tolerant social environment for individuals to practice AI romance. Therefore, the evolving relationship norms can be regarded as a mediator between cultural shifts and AI romance. Cultural shifts facilitate the evolving relationship norm and drive people to seek romantic support from AI chatbots.

4. CONCLUSION

The application of artificial intelligence in the field of emotions is gradually developing. AI chatbots provide emotional support and companionship to those who want to establish a romantic relationship by simulating human-to-human communication and interaction in reality. Theoretically, this chapter explores why people seek romantic support from AI by introducing a technological factor: digital convenience, and three social factors: emotional safety, evolving relationship norms, and cultural shifts, filling the research gap in the field of AI emotions in existing literature. This study relied on platforms including Google Scholar, Web of Science, and ResearchGate to screen and analyse relevant books and literature to support the argument and to conduct a qualitative literature review. The search keywords were strategically selected, with keywords providing more content, including: AI chatbots, AI romantic relationships, advantages and potential threats of human-AI romance; real-person romance; emotional safety, self-disclosure, intimacy; relationship norms, evolution of marriage norms; cultural shifts, individualism.

This chapter found that, in terms of digital convenience, the services provided by AI chatbots are characterised by high accessibility and low barriers to entry, reducing users' time, money, and learning costs compared to establishing a romantic relationship in reality, and exempting users from the obligation of emotional reciprocity. In terms of emotional safety, AI chatbots consistently provide non-judgmental responses, encouraging users to engage in greater self-disclosure and experience a closer relationship while gaining psychological benefits. The customisability and controllability of interaction time and content offered by AI chatbots alleviate user loneliness and provide emotional safety for users who have experienced hurt in previous real-person romantic relationships. Simultaneously, regarding cultural and relationship norms, the rise of individualism has led to individuals' romantic motivations being less influenced by social norms and expectations and more based on personal feelings, needs, and preferences. In this culture, intimate relationships have become deinstitutionalised and diversified, reducing the stigma associated with certain relationships. As society's acceptance of non-traditional relationships increases, the social stigma associated with establishing romantic relationships with AI chatbots has lessened, providing a tolerant social environment for individuals to choose AI partners based on their own needs and preferences. In conclusion, the four factors presented in this chapter drive people to seek romantic support from AI chatbots.

Practically, this study by exploring the factors that push people to establish romantic relationships with AI chatbots, helps readers who are AI users understand why they seek AI romance. This allows them to better assess whether seeking long-term romantic support from AI chatbots is suitable for their specific circumstances and needs, and to anticipate potential benefits. However, users also need to be wary that overly depending on AI may negatively impact their real-world interpersonal relationships. Service providers should continue to optimise the interaction interfaces of AI chatbots to meet users' demands for digital convenience, low entry barriers, and easy customisation. Service providers should actively cope with the ethical dilemmas of AI technology. Given that AI chatbots can guide users to conduct high-level self-disclosure, service providers should take measures to protect users' privacy. The issues of transparency and algorithmic bias in AI also need to be taken seriously. Service providers should inform users that they are chatting with an AI chatbot instead of a human and disclose the content generation logic behind its responses, and strive to eliminate algorithmic biases such as gender and occupational discrimination.

Government regulatory authorities should supervise the data security and ethics of AI chatbot platforms, such as monitoring service providers' measures to protect user privacy and whether service providers guarantee the transparency of AI chatbots. While respecting the diversity of intimate relationships, the government should also pay attention to the potential impact of human-AI relationships on social structures, such as declining birth rates due to reduced real-world romantic practices and a decrease in the willingness to have children. As excessive reliance on AI chatbots may have negative psychological impacts on users, the government should assess the mental health of users across different age groups and education levels, identify vulnerable groups at higher risk of excessive dependence or potential addiction to AI chatbots, and require service providers to implement measures such as time limits for use to prevent the misuse of AI chatbots.

However, this study has certain limitations. Because this chapter focuses on the reasons driving people to practice AI romance, the advantages of AI chatbots are primarily emphasised, while their potential threats are only briefly mentioned at the beginning. Many supporting documents focus on Europe and America, where AI chatbots are more prevalent and are more advanced in the field of emotion. Future researchers interested in this topic could explore the practices of AI romance in different countries and regions, and analyse the differences in perceptions and practices caused by cultural differences. Further exploration is needed regarding the factors and mediators pushing people to seek AI partners, such as the prevalence of digital life. Furthermore, this study's discussion of AI romance is limited to virtual online interactions with AI chatbots. Future research could further explore the impact of AI with physical forms, such as robots, on human-AI romance as technology advances.

REFERENCES

Adewale, M. D., & Muhammad, U. I. (2025). From virtual companions to forbidden attractions: The seductive rise of artificial intelligence love, loneliness, and intimacy—A systematic review. *Journal of Technology in Behavioral Science*, •••, 1–18. DOI: 10.1007/s41347-025-00549-4

Aghion, P., Jones, B. F., & Jones, C. I. (2017). *Artificial intelligence and economic growth* (Working Paper No. 23928). National Bureau of Economic Research. DOI: 10.3386/w23928

Alqaidoom, M. M., & Ateeq, A. (2025). AI chatbots as companions for trauma survivors: Balancing algorithmic responses and genuine empathy. In Hamdan, A. (Ed.), *Integrating Artificial Intelligence, Security for Environmental and Business Sustainability* (Vol. 1, pp. 141–153). Springer Nature Switzerland., DOI: 10.1007/978-3-031-91424-9_13

American Psychological Association. (2018a). Emotion. In *APA Dictionary of Psychology*. American Psychological Association. https://dictionary.apa.org/emotion

American Psychological Association. (2018b). Loneliness. In *APA Dictionary of Psychology*. APA Dictionary of Psychology. https://dictionary.apa.org/loneliness

American Psychological Association. (2023). Culture. In *APA Dictionary of Psychology*. APA Dictionary of Psychology. https://dictionary.apa.org/culture

Andersson, M. (2025). Companionship in code: AI's role in the future of human connection. *Humanities & Social Sciences Communications*, *12*(1), 1177. DOI: 10.1057/s41599-025-05536-x

Brenner, H., & Letlch, L. (2023, January 16). *Emotional safety: What it is and why it's important*. Psychology Today. https://www.psychologytoday.com/us/blog/the-art-of-feeling/202301/emotional-safety-what-it-is-and-why-its-important

Cave, S., & Dihal, K. (2021). AI will always love you: Three contradictions in imaginings of intimate relations with machines. In B. Dainton, W. Slocombe, & A. Tanyi (Eds), *Minding the future: Artificial intelligence, philosophical visions and science fiction* (pp. 107–125). Springer International Publishing. DOI: 10.1007/978-3-030-64269-3_6

Chan, C. K. Y. (2023). A comprehensive AI policy education framework for university teaching and learning. *International Journal of Educational Technology in Higher Education*, *20*(1), 38. DOI: 10.1186/s41239-023-00408-3

Cherlin, A. J. (2004). The deinstitutionalization of American marriage. *Journal of Marriage and Family, 66*(4), 848–861. DOI: 10.1111/j.0022-2445.2004.00058.x

Cynthia, V. (2021). Marriage patterns. In *EBSCO*. EBSCO Research. https://www.ebsco.com/research-starters/social-sciences-and-humanities/marriage-patterns

Djufril, R., Frampton, J. R., & Knobloch-Westerwick, S. (2025). Love, marriage, pregnancy: Commitment processes in romantic relationships with AI chatbots. *Computers in Human Behavior: Artificial Humans, 4*, 100155. DOI: 10.1016/j.chbah.2025.100155

Drabble, L. A., Wootton, A. R., Veldhuis, C. B., Riggle, E. D. B., Rostosky, S. S., Lannutti, P. J., Balsam, K. F., & Hughes, T. L. (2021). Perceived psychosocial impacts of legalized same-sex marriage: A scoping review of sexual minority adults' experiences. *PLoS One, 16*(5), e0249125. DOI: 10.1371/journal.pone.0249125 PMID: 33956825

Equaldex. (2023, July 21). *LGBT equality index*. Equaldex. https://www.equaldex.com/equality-index

Executive Office of the President. (2016). *Artificial Intelligence, automation, and the economy* (p. 59). Executive Office of the President https://obamawhitehouse.archives.gov/blog/2016/12/20/artificial-intelligence-automation-and-economy

Fiveable Content Team. (2025). Cultural shift definition. In *AP World History: Modern Key Term*. Fiveable Content Team. https://fiveable.me/key-terms/ap-world/cultural-shift

Flores, A. R. (2021). *Social acceptance of LGBTI people in 175 countries and locations 1981 to 2020*. The Williams Institute., https://williamsinstitute.law.ucla.edu/publications/global-acceptance-index-lgbt/

Furman, J., & Seamans, R. (2019). AI and the economy. *Innovation Policy and the Economy, 19*, 161–191. DOI: 10.1086/699936

George, A. S., George, A. S. H., Baskar, T., & Pandey, D. (2023). The allure of artificial intimacy: Examining the appeal and ethics of using generative AI for simulated relationships. *Partners Universal International Innovation Journal, 1*(6), 132–147. DOI: 10.5281/zenodo.10391614

Grogan, C., Kay, J., & Pérez-Ortiz, M. (2025). *AI will always love you: Studying implicit biases in romantic AI companions* (No. arXiv:2502.20231). arXiv. https://doi.org//arXiv.2502.20231DOI: 10.48550

Gubbala, S., Poushter, J., & Huang, C. (2023, November 27). How people around the-world view same-sex marriage. *Pew Research Center*. https://www.pewresearch.org/short-reads/2023/11/27/how-people-around-the-world-view-same-sex-marriage/

Gupta, A., Hathwar, D., & Vijayakumar, A. (2020). Introduction to AI chatbots. *International Journal of Engineering Research & Technology (Ahmedabad)*, *9*(7). Advance online publication. DOI: 10.17577/IJERTV9IS070143

Gupta, S., Tarantino, M., & Sanner, C. (2024). A scoping review of research on polyamory and consensual non-monogamy: Implications for a more inclusive familyscience. *Journal of Family Theory & Review*, *16*(2), 151–190. DOI: 10.1111/jftr.12546

Hamamura, T. (2012). Are cultures becoming individualistic? A cross-temporal comparison of individualism-collectivism in the United States and Japan. *Personality and Social Psychology Review: An Official Journal of the Society for Personality and Social Psychology. Personality and Social Psychology Review*, *16*(1), 3–24. DOI: 10.1177/1088868311411587 PMID: 21700795

Hamamura, T., Bettache, K., & Xu, Y. (2018). Individualism and collectivism. In Zeigler-Hill, V., & Shackelford, T. (Eds.), *The sage handbook of personality and individual differences* (pp. 365–382). SAGE Publications Ltd., DOI: 10.4135/9781526470317.n20

Haq, S. N. (2024). The effects of urbanization on traditional family structures. *Journal of Social Signs Review*, *2*(3), 70–79. https://socialsignsreivew.com/index.php/12/article/view/33

Hastuti, N. T. (2025). Redefining emotional presence: Lived experiences of AI-mediated romantic relationships with chatbot-based virtual companions. *Humanexus: Journal of Humanistic and Social Connection Studies, 1*(6), 245–252. https://journals.ai-mrc.com/humanexus/article/view/444

Hawkley, L. C., & Cacioppo, J. T. (2010). Loneliness matters: A theoretical and empirical review of consequences and mechanisms. *Annals of Behavioral Medicine*, *40*(2), 218–227. DOI: 10.1007/s12160-010-9210-8 PMID: 20652462

Helm, J. M., Swiergosz, A. M., Haeberle, H. S., Karnuta, J. M., Schaffer, J. L., Krebs, V. E., Spitzer, A. I., & Ramkumar, P. N. (2020). Machine learning and artificial intelligence: Definitions, applications, and future directions. *Current Reviews in Musculoskeletal Medicine*, *13*(1), 69–76. DOI: 10.1007/s12178-020-09600-8 PMID: 31983042

Ho, A., Hancock, J., & Miner, A. S. (2018). Psychological, relational, and emotional effects of self-disclosure after conversations with a chatbot. *Journal of Communication, 68*(4), 712–733. DOI: 10.1093/joc/jqy026 PMID: 30100620

Hsu, H. Y. (2025). Same-sex marriage legalization and attitudes toward gays and lesbians: Evidence from a natural experiment. *Politics & Policy, 53*(5), e70065. DOI: 10.1111/polp.70065

Huang, L., Zou, W., & Huang, Y. (2025). "He is my savior, my guiding light in the dark": Imagination and domestication in Chinese women's romantic relationships with AI companions. *Frontiers in Psychology, 16*, 1571707. Advance online publication. DOI: 10.3389/fpsyg.2025.1571707 PMID: 40584080

Iqbal, A., & Ajmal, A. (2018). Fear of negative evaluation and social anxiety in young adults. [PJPBS]. *Peshawar Journal of Psychology and Behavioral Sciences, 4*(1), 45–53. DOI: 10.32879/picp.2018.4.1.45

Jacobs, K. A. (2024). Digital loneliness—Changes of social recognition through AI companions. *Frontiers in Digital Health, 6*, 1281037. Advance online publication. DOI: 10.3389/fdgth.2024.1281037 PMID: 38504806

Jo, H. (2024). Subscription intentions for ChatGPT plus: A look at user satisfaction and self-efficacy. *Marketing Intelligence & Planning, 42*(6), 1052–1073. DOI: 10.1108/MIP-08-2023-0411

Kearney, M. S. (2025). *The two-parent privilege: How americans stopped getting married and started falling behind*. University of Chicago Press. https://press.uchicago.edu/ucp/books/book/chicago/T/bo205550079.html

Khalifian, C. E., & Barry, R. A. (2020). Expanding intimacy theory: Vulnerable disclosures and partner responding. *Journal of Social and Personal Relationships, 37*(1), 58–76. DOI: 10.1177/0265407519853047

King, J. (2009). *Emotional abuse—The lack of emotional safety*. Prevent Abusive Relationships. https://www.preventabusiverelationships.com/articles/emotional_safety.php

Lee, Y. C., Yamashita, N., Huang, Y., & Fu, W. (2020). 'I hear you, I feel you': Encouraging deep self-disclosure through a chatbot. *Proceedings of the 2020 CHI Conference on Human Factors in Computing Systems*, 1–12. DOI: 10.1145/3313831.3376175

Lyndon, A., Davis, D.-A., Sharma, A. E., & Scott, K. A. (2023). Emotional safety is patient safety. *BMJ Quality & Safety, 32*(7), 369–372. DOI: 10.1136/bmjqs-2022-015573 PMID: 36732064

Ma, X., Hancock, J., & Naaman, M. (2016). Anonymity, intimacy and self-disclosure in social media. *Proceedings of the 2016 CHI Conference on Human Factors in Computing Systems*, 3857–3869. DOI: 10.1145/2858036.2858414

Masaviru, M. (2016). Self-disclosure: Theories and model review. *Journal of Culture. Social Development, 18*, 43. https://www.researchgate.net/publication/301789757_Self-Disclosure_Theories_and_Model_Review

Mauss, M. (1966). *The gift: Form and functions of exchange in archaic societies*. Cohen & West Ltd. https://cir.nii.ac.jp/crid/1971993809779811347

Mcauley, D. (2024, December 9). The loneliness epidemic: Recent trends, background, and future outlook. *GlobalRPH*. https://globalrph.com/2024/12/the-loneliness-epidemic-recent-trends-background-and-future-outlook/

Meng, J., & Dai, Y. (2021). Emotional support from AI chatbots: Should a supportive partner self-disclose or not? *Journal of Computer-Mediated Communication, 26*(4), 207–222. DOI: 10.1093/jcmc/zmab005

Mernitz, S. (2018). A cohort comparison of trends in first cohabitation duration in the United States. *Demographic Research, 38*, 2073–2086. DOI: 10.4054/DemRes.2018.38.66 PMID: 31592199

Moors, A. C., Gesselman, A. N., & Garcia, J. R. (2021). Desire, familiarity, and engagement in polyamory: Results from a national sample of single adults in the United States. *Frontiers in Psychology, 12*, 619640. DOI: 10.3389/fpsyg.2021.619640 PMID: 33833712

Morris, D. (1982). Attachment and intimacy. In Fischer, M., & Stricker, G. (Eds.), *Intimacy* (pp. 305–323). Springer US., DOI: 10.1007/978-1-4684-4160-4_19

Nosta, J. (2024, June 4). *How artificial intelligence is reshaping relationships*. Psychology Today Australia. https://www.psychologytoday.com/au/blog/the-digital-self/202406/how-artificial-intelligence-is-reshaping-relationships

Pani, B., Crawford, J., & Allen, K. A. (2024). Can generative artificial intelligence foster belongingness, social support, and reduce loneliness? A conceptual analysis. In Lyu, Z. (Ed.), *Applications of generative AI* (pp. 261–276). Springer International Publishing., DOI: 10.1007/978-3-031-46238-2_13

Pew Research Center. (2013). *The global divide on homosexuality*. Pew Research Center. https://www.pewresearch.org/global/2013/06/04/the-global-divide-on-homosexuality/

Piispanen, J. R., Myllyviita, T., Vakkuri, V., & Rousi, R. (2024). *Smoke screens and scapegoats: The reality of general data protection regulation compliance — privacy and ethics in the case of replika AI* (No. arXiv:2411.04490). arXiv. https://doi.org// arXiv.2411.04490DOI: 10.48550

Poder, P. (2025, July 2). Is love really dead in the digital age? *Differens Magazine.* https://differensmagazine.com/2025/07/02/poul-poder/

Poushter, J., & Nicholas, K. (2020, June 25). The global divide on homosexuality persists. *Pew Research Center.* https://www.pewresearch.org/global/2020/06/25/ global-divide-on-homosexuality-persists/

Raju, P. V. M., & Sumallika, T. (2023). The impact of AI in the global economy and its implications in industry 4.0 era. *Information Technology, Education and Society, 18*(2), 53–62. DOI: 10.7459/ites/18.2.05

Reddy, S. P., John, A., & Kaushik, S. (2024). *AI As romantic companion- An ethical dilemma* (SSRN Scholarly Paper No. 5106936). Social Science Research Network. DOI: 10.2139/ssrn.5106936

Santos, H. C., Varnum, M. E. W., & Grossmann, I. (2017). Global increases in individualism. *Psychological Science, 28*(9), 1228–1239. DOI: 10.1177/0956797617700622 PMID: 28703638

Schuett, J. (2021). *Defining the scope of AI regulations* (SSRN Scholarly Paper No. 3453632). Social Science Research Network. DOI: 10.2139/ssrn.3453632

Scott, E. S. (2000). *Social norms and the legal regulation of marriage* (SSRN Scholarly Paper No. 224972). Social Science Research Network. DOI: 10.2139/ssrn.224972

Shchemelinin, K. S. (2020). Differences between modern marriage and traditional marriage and principles for improving the quality of heterosexual marriage in modern society. *Scientific Journal NovaUm. Ru, 24*, 151–160. https://www.researchgate.net/ publication/395255131_DIFFERENCES_OF_MODERN_MARRIAGE_FROM _TRADITIONAL_AND_PRINCIPLES_FOR_IMPROVING_THE_QUALITY _OF_HETEROSEXUAL_MARRIAGE_IN_A_MODERN_SOCIETY

Shean, M., & Mander, D. (2020). Building emotional safety for students in school environments: Challenges and opportunities. In Midford, R., Nutton, G., Hyndman, B., & Silburn, S. (Eds.), *Health and education interdependence: Thriving from birth to adulthood* (pp. 225–248). Springer., DOI: 10.1007/978-981-15-3959-6_12

Sheffield, R., & Squires, D. (2025). *Crossroads: American family life at the intersection of tradition and modernity* (Special Report No. No.310; p. 43). The Heritage Foundation. https://www.heritage.org/marriage-and-family/report/crossroads-american-family-life-the-intersection-tradition-and-modernity

Sheikh, H., Prins, C., & Schrijvers, E. (2023). Artificial intelligence: Definition and background. In Sheikh, H., Prins, C., & Schrijvers, E. (Eds.), *Mission AI: the newsystem technology* (pp. 15–41). Springer International Publishing., DOI: 10.1007/978-3-031-21448-6_2

Skjuve, M., Følstad, A., Fostervold, K. I., & Brandtzaeg, P. B. (2021). My chatbot companion—A study of human-chatbot relationships. *International Journal of Human-Computer Studies, 149*, 102601. DOI: 10.1016/j.ijhcs.2021.102601

Slimi, Z., & Carballido, B. V. (2023). Navigating the ethical challenges of artificial intelligence in higher education: An analysis of seven global ai ethics policies. *TEM Journal, 12*(2), 590–602. https://www.ceeol.com/search/article-detail?id=1122977

Song, X., Xu, B., & Zhao, Z. (2022). Can people experience romantic love for artificial intelligence? An empirical study of intelligent assistants. *Information & Management, 59*(2), 103595. DOI: 10.1016/j.im.2022.103595

Stanley, S. M., & Rhoades, G. K. (2023). *What's the plan? Cohabitation, engagement,and divorce*. Institute for Family Studies., https://ifstudies.org/ifs-admin/resources/reports/cohabitationreportapr2023-final.pdf

Sullivan, Y., & Nyawa, S., & Wamba, Samuel. F. (2023). Combating loneliness with artificial intelligence: An AI-based emotional support model. *Proceedings of the 56th Hawaii International Conference on System Sciences*, 10. DOI: 10.24251/HICSS.2023.541

Ta, V., Griffith, C., Boatfield, C., Wang, X., Civitello, M., Bader, H., DeCero, E., & Loggarakis, A. (2020). User experiences of social support from companion chatbots in everyday contexts: Thematic analysis. *Journal of Medical Internet Research, 22*(3), e16235. DOI: 10.2196/16235 PMID: 32141837

Thierer, A. D., Castillo O'Sullivan, A., & Russell, R. (2017). *Artificial intelligence and public policy* (SSRN Scholarly Paper No. 3021135). Social Science Research Network. DOI: 10.2139/ssrn.3021135

Veale, D., Robins, E., Thomson, A. B., & Gilbert, P. (2023). No safety without emotional safety. *The Lancet. Psychiatry, 10*(1), 65–70. DOI: 10.1016/S2215-0366(22)00373-X PMID: 36442491

Wang, B., Wu, C., & Huang, L. (2018). Emotional safety culture: A new and key element of safety culture. *Process Safety Progress*, *37*(2), 134–139. DOI: 10.1002/prs.11953

Wang, X., Pang, C. C., & Hui, P. (2025). 'My dataset of love': A preliminary mixed-method exploration of human-AI romantic relationships. *Proceedings of the ACM on Human-Computer Interaction*, *9*(7), 1–34. DOI: 10.1145/3757532

Whiten, A., Hinde, R. A., Laland, K. N., & Stringer, C. B. (2011). Culture evolves. *Philosophical Transactions of the Royal Society of London. Series B, Biological Sciences*, *366*(1567), 938–948. DOI: 10.1098/rstb.2010.0372 PMID: 21357216

Willoughby, B. J., & Carroll, J. S. (2025, February 13). *Counterfeit connections: The rise of AI romantic companions*. Institute for Family Studies. https://ifstudies.org/blog/counterfeit-connections-the-rise-of-ai-romantic-companions-

Wilson, J. W., Wacquant, L., & Connell, R. (2025). Urbanization and its effect on community relationships. *International Journal of Sociology Civics Research*, *1*(1), 13–15. https://www.researchgate.net/publication/393755256_Urbanization_and_Its_Effect_on_Community_Relationships

Xie, Q. (2024). *Open AI-romance with ChatGPT, Ready for Your cyborg lover?* (No. arXiv:2410.03710; Version 1). arXiv. https://doi.org//arXiv.2410.03710DOI: 10.48550

Yanguas, J., Pinazo-Henandis, S., & Tarazona-Santabalbina, F. J. (2018). The complexity of loneliness. *Acta Biomedica*, *89*(2), 302–314. DOI: 10.23750/abm.v89i2.7404 PMID: 29957768

Zhai, X. S., Chu, X. Y., Chai, C. S., Jong, M. S. Y., Istenic, A., Spector, M., Liu, J. B., Yuan, J., & Li, Y. (2021). A review of artificial intelligence (AI) in education from 2010 to 2020. *Complexity*, *2021*(1), 8812542. DOI: 10.1155/2021/8812542

Zhang, S., & Li, S. (2025). *The real her? Exploring whether young adults accept human-AI love* (No. arXiv:2503.03067). arXiv. https://doi.org//arXiv.2503.03067DOI: 10.48550

Chapter 11

Characteristics of Users Seeking Romantic Relationships on AI-Powered Dating Platforms and With AI Companions

Kinjal Agarwal
http://orcid.org/0009-0001-5649-3225
Christ University, Bangalore, India

Nithya Sree Balakumar
http://orcid.org/0009-0006-3999-8885
Christ University, Bangalore, India

Lalitha Ragul
http://orcid.org/0009-0003-5129-6710
Christ University, Bangalore, India

ABSTRACT

AI now underpins nearly every major dating platform, influencing how people discover partners, express themselves, and form romantic bonds. This chapter explains why studying AI in romance has become essential, outlining how algorithmic matching, behavioural design, and personalisation shape digital relationships. It identifies key demographic groups, personality traits, and attachment styles that are drawn to AI-enhanced dating contexts, and examines their motivations, attitudes, and self-presentation patterns across various platforms. The chapter also explores the rise of artificial intimacy, showing how AI companions provide emotional safety,

DOI: 10.4018/979-8-3373-6623-4.ch011

stability, and reinforcement that encourage ongoing engagement. Using psychological approaches, it discusses how users perceive AI as a romantic or supportive figure and how these perceptions interact with individual needs. Ultimately, the chapter highlights how user characteristics and AI design together drive the emergence of new forms of digital intimacy and their broader psychological and social implications.

INTRODUCTION

The integration of artificial intelligence (AI) into contemporary romantic contexts has fundamentally altered how individuals initiate, manage, and interpret intimate relationships. While early dating platforms relied primarily on algorithmic matching based on stated preferences, contemporary systems increasingly incorporate AI-driven assistance across multiple stages of romantic engagement. These include profile optimization, message generation, conversational coaching, emotional support tools, and, in some cases, AI agents functioning as quasi-relational or companion entities. Together, these developments signal a shift from AI as a background matching tool to AI as an active participant in users' romantic experiences.

Despite growing public and academic attention to AI-mediated intimacy, existing scholarship remains fragmented. Research has variously examined recommendation algorithms, user personality traits, attachment styles, ethical risks, and artificial companionship, but these strands are often treated in parallel rather than integrated around a central analytical focus. In particular, there is a lack of systematic synthesis examining which user characteristics are associated with engagement in AI-enhanced romantic platforms, why these users are drawn to such systems, and how patterns of AI engagement may shape psychological and relational outcomes over time. This chapter addresses this gap by foregrounding user characteristics as the primary organizing axis for examining AI-assisted dating and AI-mediated intimacy.

Importantly, this chapter distinguishes between two analytically distinct but overlapping domains: AI-assisted human-human dating, in which AI serves as a support or enhancement tool within interpersonal romantic interactions, and human-AI romantic or companion relationships, in which AI itself becomes the perceived relational partner. While these domains raise related psychological and ethical questions, they involve different user motivations, engagement patterns, and risk profiles. Maintaining this distinction is essential for avoiding conceptual ambiguity and for understanding how user characteristics operate differently across contexts.

Drawing on psychological, behavioral, and platform-oriented research, the chapter adopts an integrative framework that links user characteristics, motivations for AI use, engagement patterns, psychological mechanisms, and relational and ethical outcomes. Within this framework, demographic variables such as age and gender are considered alongside psychological characteristics, including personality traits, attachment styles, social anxiety, and loneliness. Prior research suggests that younger users are disproportionately represented among AI-assisted dating adopters, yet demographic factors alone do not account for the intensity or form of engagement observed. Psychological characteristics appear to play a more central role (Russo et al, 2025). For example, individuals high in social anxiety or introversion may find AI-mediated interactions less threatening than face-to-face encounters, while those high in openness to experience may be more willing to experiment with novel relational technologies.

Attachment styles, in particular, provide a useful lens for understanding differential engagement with AI-mediated intimacy. Individuals with anxious attachment may be drawn to the perceived consistency, responsiveness, and emotional availability of AI systems, whereas individuals with avoidant attachment may value the emotional control and reduced vulnerability afforded by non-human partners (Heng & Zhang, 2025). Rather than treating attachment theory as a standalone explanation, this chapter situates attachment styles within broader motivational and behavioral patterns, examining how they interact with platform design features and reinforcement mechanisms.

User motivations for engaging with AI in romantic contexts vary widely. For some, AI tools function instrumentally, as coaches that assist with message crafting, confidence-building, or managing rejection. For others, engagement extends into para-social or emotionally meaningful interactions with AI companions that provide validation, attentiveness, and perceived understanding. These motivations intersect with the concept of artificial intimacy, defined here as technologically mediated interactions that simulate affective qualities of human relationships through personalization, responsiveness, and continuity. While artificial intimacy may serve adaptive functions, such as reducing loneliness or facilitating skill development, it also raises concerns about emotional dependency, substitution effects, and the reshaping of expectations for human relationships.

Self-presentation represents another key domain in which AI alters romantic behaviour. On traditional dating platforms, users often curate idealized identities to attract human partners. In contrast, interactions with AI may elicit greater self-disclosure due to perceptions of non-judgment and low social risk, or, alternatively, encourage experimentation and identity play precisely because the interaction lacks real-world consequences. These divergent patterns of self-presentation are not merely expressive choices; they interact with AI personalization and reinforcement processes that adapt to users' emotional cues and communicative styles. Over time, such feedback loops may subtly shape users' communication habits, emotional regulation, and reliance on scripted or mediated interaction.

Taken together, these dynamics underscore the importance of examining who engages with AI-powered romantic platforms, how and why they do so, and with what potential consequences. By centering user characteristics and systematically integrating psychological theory with platform mechanisms and empirical evidence, this chapter aims to move beyond descriptive accounts toward a coherent analytical synthesis. In doing so, it lays the groundwork for understanding how AI-mediated romance both reflects and reshapes contemporary patterns of intimacy, attachment, and relational selfhood, and how user preferences may ultimately influence the future design and social role of AI in romantic life.

RATIONALE

While an ample degree of research exists on understanding how AI is being used in dating apps and AI companions as substitutes for romance, much less focus has been given to the users' psychological dispositions, including their personality traits, attachment styles, and attitudes and motivations towards AI that play a significant role in how users use AI for romantic purposes. The increasing use of artificial intelligence in romantic contexts- through AI-assisted dating platforms and AI companions- has generated growing scholarly interest. However, much of the existing literature prioritizes technological features, ethical concerns, or societal implications, while offering limited, fragmented attention to the user characteristics that shape engagement with these systems. This chapter is premised on the view that a psychologically grounded understanding of AI-mediated romance must begin with the users themselves.

The present chapter explores the characteristics of users who seek romantic relationships on AI-powered dating platforms, grounding the discussion in demographic trends, psychological theory, and evolving cultural attitudes. The major rationale of this chapter is to position user characteristics as a unifying analytical focus, clarifying how individual differences such as attachment orientations, personality traits, relational motivations, and emotional needs influence interactions with distinct AI-powered platforms. This chapter uses a conceptual framework that is designed to integrate AI user characteristics in the context of online dating and human-AI interactions by evaluating user demographics, psychological traits, and individual differences at a foundational level, along with self-presentation and AI's technologically-rooted ability to communicate with humans at an interactional level, while further discussing the outcomes that these underlying processes produce in shaping the trajectory of human relationships, communication patterns, perceived reliance on AI in romantic contexts and evolving human-AI interactions. In simpler terms, this framework, which is embedded in the realm of human romance and dating, will help the readers understand how user characteristics influence the way users interact with AI, along with how AI interacts with users to reinforce and/or resist their use, while emphasizing how these mechanisms collectively play a role in molding human connections as well as human-AI intimacy.

Rather than treating AI-assisted dating and AI companions as interchangeable manifestations of 'artificial intimacy,' this chapter conceptualizes them as distinct relational contexts that attract different user profiles, motivations, and psychological needs. By systematically differentiating between these user groups, the chapter aims to clarify how individual differences, such as attachment orientations, personality traits, relational goals, and emotional regulation styles, interact with specific AI affordances. By categorizing these two user groups, readers can see how different psychological mechanisms underlie their intentional uses of AI, along with their designated implications.

In addition, the chapter addresses a key gap in the literature by conceptualizing user characteristics as dynamic rather than static, acknowledging that engagement with AI in romantic contexts may evolve over time, from initial exploration to emotional investment, strategic use, or disengagement. The chapter also aims to integrate psychological theories with platform-level and structural considerations, moving beyond descriptive summaries toward a more coherent analytical framework.

By adopting a balanced approach that examines both potential risks and supportive functions of AI in romantic relationships, this chapter contributes to the book's broader objective of critically examining human-AI intimacy without assuming deterministic technological outcomes. In doing so, it strengthens the conceptual clarity and scholarly coherence of the volume.

Figure 1. The User-Centered Interactional Model across AI-Assisted Dating and AI Companionship

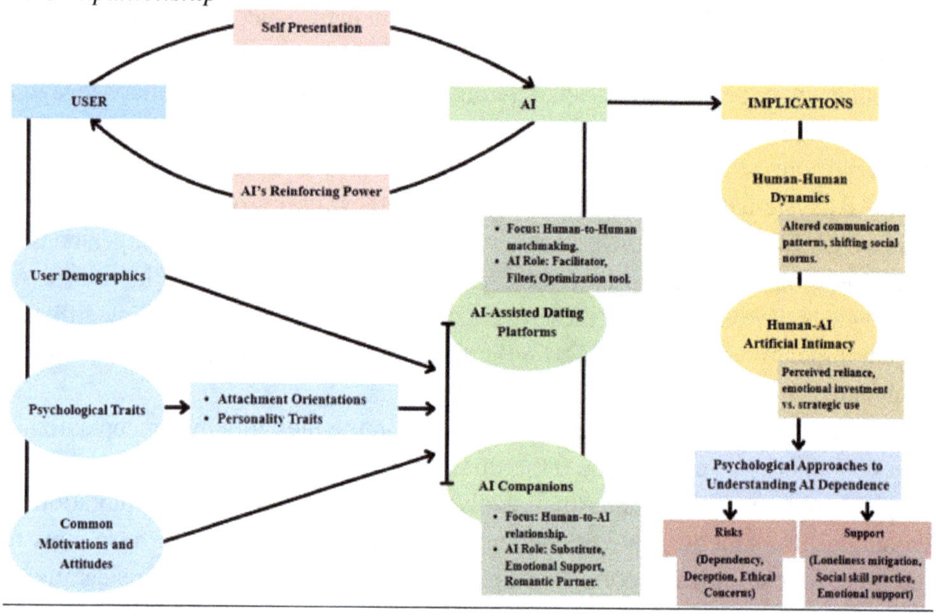

Figure 1 illustrates a user-centered interactional model that connects user psychology and motivations to engagement with AI-assisted dating platforms and AI companions, outlining the resulting implications for human relationships and artificial intimacy.

METHODOLOGY

This chapter adopts a conceptual narrative review methodology to examine the characteristics of users engaging with AI-powered dating platforms and AI-mediated romantic or companion systems. The review process commenced with abstract development on 26 August 2025, followed by systematic conceptual organization and chapter writing beginning on 15 October 2025. The review is designed to synthesize interdisciplinary research, with the primary aim of integrating psychological, behavioural, and platform-oriented perspectives around a unified user-centered analytical framework.

Literature was identified through searches conducted in PubMed, Scopus, PsycInfo, Mendeley and Google Scholar, supplemented by targeted use of the Google Search Engine for high-level statistical data and contextual background. The search focused on publications released between 2015 and 2025, a period corresponding to the rapid expansion of mobile dating applications, algorithmic matchmaking systems, and AI-mediated relational technologies. The keywords included combinations of: AI involvement in dating apps, algorithmic matchmaking, online dating users, demographic characteristics, personality traits, attachment styles, artificial intimacy, AI intimacy, self-presentation, human-AI interaction, AI companions, and AI romance.

Sources were screened for relevance based on their direct engagement with at least one of the chapter's core analytical dimensions: user characteristics, motivations for AI use, engagement patterns, psychological mechanisms, or relational and ethical outcomes. Priority was given to peer-reviewed empirical studies and theoretical papers, which form the primary evidentiary basis for the chapter's central claims. Industry reports, surveys, and media-based sources were included selectively to provide contemporary context, illustrate emerging trends, or highlight areas where peer-reviewed evidence remains limited; these sources were not used as sole support for core analytical conclusions.

Evidence was synthesized thematically in alignment with the chapter's conceptual framework, which links user characteristics to motivations, patterns of AI engagement, and psychological and relational implications. Rather than aggregating findings descriptively, the chapter emphasizes integrative interpretation, explicitly noting areas of convergence, inconsistency, and evidentiary limitation within the existing literature. Where empirical evidence remains sparse or methodologically constrained, conclusions are framed cautiously and accompanied by clear indications of uncertainty.

This narrative synthesis supports the chapter's central argument that user characteristics and preferences play an active role in shaping both engagement with AI-mediated romantic technologies and the future design trajectories of such systems. Methodological limitations inherent to the reviewed literature, such as reliance on self-report measures, Western-centric samples, and short-term data are acknowledged where relevant, and directions for future research are identified accordingly.

AI INVOLVEMENT IN DATING APPS

Dating apps have reshaped the landscape of modern romance, with artificial intelligence (AI) now embedded at the core of digital matchmaking. Globally, an estimated 350 million people use dating applications (Curry, 2026), and in the United States, approximately one-third of marriages involve partners who first met online (Sharabi, 2022). Within this context, AI-based tools increasingly influence how individuals present themselves, identify potential partners, and sustain romantic interactions. Nearly 26% of single U.S. adults and close to half of Gen Z adults report using AI to improve dating profiles or message composition (Sharabi, 2025). Reflecting this shift, Match Group's CEO has described AI as "existential to the future" of the company, emphasizing its role in enhancing user engagement and long-term platform growth (Dignan, 2024). Collectively, these developments contribute to what has been described as a gamified emotional economy, wherein romantic pursuit is intertwined with behavioural conditioning to sustain attention and maximize engagement (Pettersen & Karlsen, 2023).

AI is now integrated into nearly all major dating platforms, including Tinder and Bumble, powering features such as profile curation, match recommendations, and compatibility prediction (Sharma, 2025; Khan, 2025). These platforms are not neutral tools for connection but carefully engineered psychological environments. Their design draws heavily on Behavioural psychology, particularly B. F. Skinner's reinforcement theory, which posits that behaviour can be shaped through strategically timed rewards (Skinner, 1963). What distinguishes contemporary dating apps is the seamless translation of these psychological principles into interface designs that feel intuitive and emotionally rewarding to users.

User engagement is sustained through variable reward structures. Early app use is often reinforced through continuous reinforcement (rewarding a desired action every single time it happens, making the behavior to be learned fast), with frequent matches designed to encourage repeated engagement (Whitestone, 2019). As the co-founder of Tinder describes, "It kinda works like a slot machine. You're excited to see who the next person is, or excited to see, did I get the match? It's a nice little rush" (Sales, 2021). As users become invested, platforms shift toward variable-ratio reinforcement schedules (giving a reward after an unpredictable, changing number of actions), in which matches appear unpredictably, an approach similar to that used in gambling technologies (Cherry, 2025). This unpredictability sustains anticipation and activates dopamine-driven reward loops that reinforce compulsive swiping behaviours (Liu, 2024). Importantly, it is not the match itself but the possibility of a match that maintains user engagement. The emotional tension between hope and reward mirrors intermittent reinforcement models, in which inconsistent rewards produce stronger and more persistent behavioural patterns than consistent ones. Feedback mechanisms such as notifications, animations, and profile boosts function as secondary reinforcers, further sustaining engagement (Oyetoke, 2025). In this way, dating apps blur the boundary between emotional fulfilment and behavioural conditioning, encouraging continued participation rather than relationship resolution.

Beyond engagement design, modern dating platforms employ sophisticated machine-learning algorithms to personalize match recommendations. These systems analyze swipe behaviour, messaging patterns, and interaction outcomes to infer compatibility (Yenra, 2025). Many platforms rely on collaborative-filtering algorithms, a recommendation method that works like digital "word of mouth," it suggests items you might like based on the preferences of other people who have similar tastes as you (Sharabi, 2022; Pizzato et al., 2012). Unlike early dating apps that relied primarily on mutual "likes," contemporary platforms infer compatibility through large-scale data analysis, incorporating behavioural signals, inferred personality traits, and interaction histories (Nader & Lee, 2022; Dinh et al., 2021; Nader, 2020). Research indicates that algorithms integrating both interest similarity and attractiveness similarity significantly outperform simpler content-based methods in match accuracy (Xia et al., 2016).

However, recommender systems (computer programs or algorithms designed to suggest relevant items to users) also risk reproducing and amplifying existing social biases. Collaborative filtering may privilege majority preferences, thereby marginalizing users who fall outside dominant desirability norms related to body type, ethnicity, or gender expression (Sharabi, 2022). Over time, this can homogenize user behaviour and reinforce exclusionary standards of attractiveness. Additionally, structural imbalances, such as women receiving disproportionately high numbers of likes compared to men, interact with algorithmic constraints and monetization strategies that limit match visibility (Tyson et al., 2016; Balki, 2024). These dynamics have led to concerns that platforms intentionally slow match outcomes to sustain user engagement, effectively gamifying romantic connection (Mackinnon, 2022).

Generative AI further extends algorithmic influence by shaping self-presentation and communication. Approximately 20% of male dating-app users report using AI tools to craft messages or bios (Chakravarti, 2023), while broader surveys suggest that over 60% of daters employ AI to refine their profiles (Wingmate, 2024). Platforms are increasingly integrating AI-powered assistants that suggest responses based on chat context, exemplified by tools such as Rizz (Yenra, 2025). Experimental research indicates that AI-assisted messages are often perceived as more effective than human-authored ones, a phenomenon referred to as the "Cyrano effect" (Roaché et al., 2025; Sharabi, 2025). By offering linguistic fluency and emotional framing, AI can enhance confidence and perceived competence in romantic communication (Asifa, 2023).

At the same time, these developments raise concerns about authenticity and deception. When AI-generated messages are used without disclosure, recipients may assume emotional intentionality that does not originate from the human user. As Sharabi (2025) cautions, AI may render deception increasingly difficult to detect. The emergence of AI avatars and chatbots capable of interacting autonomously further blurs the boundary between human-human and human-AI interaction (Nolan, 2023). Recent findings indicate that users can form companionship-style attachments to large language model chatbots, raising important questions about emotional substitution, intimacy, and relational meaning (Zhang et al., 2025).

In sum, AI-driven systems now shape not only how users are matched but how they engage, present themselves, and experience romantic connection. These technologies introduce efficiencies and affordances while simultaneously embedding new biases, ethical challenges, and psychological dependencies. Having outlined AI's role in matchmaking, personalization, and behavioural conditioning, the next section turns to the users themselves. Examining the demographic characteristics of individuals drawn to AI-supported dating platforms provides critical insight into how these technologies exert differential effects across populations.

DEMOGRAPHIC CHARACTERISTICS OF AI USERS IN DATING APPS AND AS A ROMANTIC PARTNER

The present subsection attempts to provide a contemporary background that emphasizes current statistical data covering the demographics of users who use AI in their romantic lives, through AI-powered dating apps and as substitutes for offline romance. These contextual differences are important to understand how the demographic characteristics of AI users can vary depending on the purpose and intention of the individuals. The particular objective of this subsection is to offer the readers a reality check in terms of how prevalent AI is throughout varied age groups, genders, geographical locations, and cultural differences. It is important to note that this segment of the chapter only consists of descriptive data that includes numbers, percentages, and other survey studies conducted by organizations and boards in order to create a foundation on which further discussions on AI involvement can take place. Most existing survey studies that are included in this subsection are dated up to 2025, and were conducted in developed countries such as the US, the UK, and China, due to which other developing countries are overlooked in this part of the chapter.

Users of AI-powered Dating Apps

Research indicates that dating app users are more likely to be male, young adults, older youth, single, and members of sexual minorities, while personality dimensions such as openness to experience and attachment anxiety further predict dating app usage (Castro et al, 2020). Demographics of AI users in dating apps are not fully defined, but studies indicate that while many users find AI helpful for profile creation and conversation assistance, younger users, particularly Gen Z, have shown skepticism towards its role in forming meaningful connections. A Bloomberg Intelligence survey conducted in 2025 reported that Gen Z shows higher discomfort than Millennials with using AI to draft profile prompts and responses to messages, or to modify profile pictures (Lung, 2025). However, a significant portion of users across demographics are receptive to AI tools to improve their dating experience. For example, some studies suggest that 66% of daters would use AI to improve their profile, and 78% would use it to help with flirting. AI's use in safety features like identifying fake profiles is also a common point of interest. Another survey states that 49% of Gen Z has used AI for dating, more than any other generation (Phares, 2025).

According to a 2025 opinion survey designed by the Communication Research Center at Boston University's College of Communication and conducted by Ipsos, only 10% of women agree that AI-powered dating apps lead to more successful relationships, while 20% of men support the same idea. The United States has the highest overall user penetration and revenue for dating apps, including those using AI features (Glass, 2025).

Users of AI Companions as Romantic Partners

According to a new Institute for Family Studies survey of 2,000 American adults under age 40, 1 in 4 young adults believe that AI boyfriends and girlfriends can replace real-life romantic relationships, with a small gender difference of 5% where men support this idea more than women (Wang & Toscano, 2024). However, these technologies are increasingly becoming common among older adults as well, with 15% of adult men and 10% of adult women reporting that they have chatted with a virtual romantic companion. 7% of overall study participants reported that they interact with AI romantic companions for sexual purposes. This behavior was more common for men (14% of young adult men and 5% of adult men) than for women (7% of young adult women and 3% of adult women). When asked about the future of AI in romantic relationships, heavy porn users are much more optimistic than others. More than one-third of heavy porn users (35%) believe that AI girlfriends or boyfriends have the potential to replace real-life romance, compared with 20% of young adults who rarely watch porn. Match's large "Singles in America" study reports that about 16% of singles said they have "engaged with AI as a romantic companion" (with higher rates in younger cohorts). Another report also found that roughly 26%-33% of Gen Z singles have used AI in their dating lives in some way, including as companions (Willoughby & Carroll, 2025). According to a survey published by the Chinese social network Soul App, nearly 1 in 10 young Chinese people think that virtual agents can "provide emotional support when they feel alone" (Duvieu, 2025). It can be seen from the above-mentioned surveys and studies that users of AI companions as romantic partners consist mostly of young adults (Gen Z and young Millennials) who are either single or are looking to develop a more sexual or emotionally intimate relationship with AI chatbots than their real-life relationships. Another survey also reports that 16% of singles say they have interacted with AI as a romantic companion, including 33% of people in Gen Z and 23% of millennials (Global Dating Insights, 2025).

Most large, publicly reported surveys so far come from the United States, the UK, and other Western markets (YouGov, Match, academic teams studying Replika, etc.). Evidence from industry reporting suggests apps with large user bases (Replika, Blush, etc.) have global audiences, but rigorous, nationally representative prevalence estimates outside the U.S./UK are still sparse.

Cross-cultural reporting further indicates that AI romantic engagement varies by gender and sociocultural context. A 2025 global analysis of AI companion platforms found that products in the United States are predominantly marketed as "AI girlfriends" and attract mostly young male users, whereas in China, AI companions are more often positioned as "AI boyfriends" with adult women forming a substantial user base (Qian, 2025). These differences suggest that demographic patterns in AI-mediated intimacy are shaped not only by individual psychological factors but also by broader cultural and structural conditions.

The present subsection gave you a glimpse of the demographic characteristics of AI users in the romantic contexts on a global scale, despite the little evidence found in countries other than the UK and the US. Now that we have coated this chapter's objective with a primer consisting of the most recent, available, and verified data pertaining to users' static characteristics of age, gender, nationality, and culture, we will be diving into the not-so-static and mostly dynamic parts of human beings to understand their relationship with AI in the context of online dating and AI intimacy. In particular, the next section will emphasize the role of human personality traits in understanding their relationships with AI and AI companions.

PERSONALITY TRAITS OF AI USERS IN ROMANTIC CONTEXTS

An individual's personality acts as a blueprint for the development of interests, thoughts, and behaviours. Personality can be defined as an individual's unique and relatively consistent pattern of thinking, feeling, and behaving (Hockenbury & Hockenbury, 2010). One of the most commonly studied and used models of personality is the Big Five Personality model developed by Paul Costa and Robert Mccrae, which explained personality through five broad, stable dimensions- openness to experience (curiosity, creativity, and openness to new ideas), conscientiousness (organization, responsibility, and self-discipline), extraversion (sociability, assertiveness, and positive emotionality), agreeableness (cooperation, empathy, and trust), and neuroticism (emotional instability, anxiety, and vulnerability to stress), often abbreviated as

'OCEAN'. Together, these traits capture the most consistent patterns of individual differences in thoughts, emotions, and behaviors across cultures and contexts (John & Srivastava, 1999; Costa & McCrae, 1992). The following subsection's primary objective is to find out and present whether there is any evidence through research studies that link personality traits of AI users to their employment of AI in the context of dating apps and romance. Through a psychological lens, an individual's personality traits can have implications for their inclination towards the use of AI in dating and interpersonal contexts. The following section attempts to conceptualize the influence of personality traits on how people use AI for different purposes within romantic and interpersonal boundaries through psychological theories and ideas.

Who Uses AI More?

According to a study that attempted to understand the role of the Big Five Personality Traits in the compulsive use of ChatGPT among Chinese students, neuroticism, which refers to a trait disposition of being emotionally unstable and a pattern of avoidance, anxiety, maladaptive stress-coping mechanisms, emotional dysregulation, and poor self-control, is highly linked to the behaviour of using AI as an external coping mechanism to reduce academic anxiety (Widiger & Oltmanns, 2017; Hu et al, 2025). Another trait that had a high negative correlation to compulsive use of AI is agreeableness, which is another trait disposition of the Big 5 linked to cooperation, compassion, and empathy. This means that individuals who score high on agreeableness are less likely to use AI frequently. In the same study, no other traits showed a significant correlation with compulsive AI use (Hu et al, 2025).

However, other studies contradict the results of the previous study. Agreeableness is found to be significantly more related to positive attitudes towards AI, while an attitude called conspiracy beliefs is negatively linked to AI (Stein et al, 2024). Agreeableness is considered to be a benevolent trait that views change in a positive light, which might explain why individuals high on agreeableness might also view AI usage more as an opportunity than as a risk. Another study that evaluated the relationship between pre-service teachers' Big 5 Personality Traits and their motivation to use AI found significant associations between traits like openness and conscientiousness and positive AI usage motivations, including intrinsic motivation, utility value, and attainment value, while showing a negative correlation between neuroticism and AI usage motivation (Yurt, 2025). Another review finds that personality traits influence trust and acceptance of AI systems, with openness and agreeableness generally linked to higher trust, while neuroticism tends to relate to lower trust and greater perceived risk. However, the study concludes that personality plays only a modest role, and contextual factors and system design also strongly shape how people adopt and trust AI (Riedl, 2022).

According to Park and Woo (2022), individuals who are high in personal innovativeness in information technology are the most consistently likely to have positive attitudes toward AI and greater willingness to use it. People with high agreeableness and conscientiousness also tend to view AI more positively, perceiving it as useful and experiencing fewer negative emotions toward it. In contrast, individuals high in neuroticism and extraversion tend to show more negative emotional reactions or skepticism toward AI (Park & Woo, 2022).

The previous research studies discussed the role of personality in terms of an individual's use of AI and showed mixed results. Moving on, we will elaborate on how these personality traits play a role in the context of AI- assisted human-human relationships as well as human-AI relationships.

Personality Profiles of AI Romantic Users

Theoretically speaking, based on the most dominant personality framework- Big 5, individuals high on openness to experience are receptive to change and exhibit curiosity and open-mindedness. These individuals are more likely to incorporate technology into their romantic lives if they are motivated to do so. Individuals high on agreeableness are known to be trustworthy, compliant, and exhibit prosocial behaviours, and hence are more inclined to maintain intimate relationships with AI despite the risks involved. Longitudinal research further supports the stability and relational significance of agreeableness. A 25-year prospective study by Laursen et al. (2002) demonstrated substantial continuity between childhood behavioral tendencies and adult agreeableness, with high-agreeable adults reporting lower rates of depression, alcoholism, and relational instability (Laursen et al., 2002). These findings suggest that agreeableness reflects enduring interpersonal competence rather than situational preference. In the context of AI-mediated romance, this implies that agreeable individuals' engagement with AI may not stem from relational deficits but rather from their broader orientation toward cooperation, trust, and relational openness. Agreeable individuals may more easily anthropomorphize AI companions, while conscientious users may value the predictability and emotional safety of AI partners. Neuroticism, on the other hand, may have a complex relationship with AI intimacy- those high on this trait may experience greater emotional dependence on AI, using it as a secure, low-risk relational outlet amid anxiety or insecurity (Park & Woo, 2022). While most studies focus on general attitudes rather than explicit romantic use, these findings suggest that AI-based romantic engagement may be most appealing to individuals high in openness, agreeableness, and neuroticism-traits associated with imagination, empathy, and emotional sensitivity- making them more likely to seek emotional connection through artificial partners.

Due to the given context of romantic relationships, it is important to note that personality traits alone may not suffice to determine an individual's tendency to use AI. However, personality does play an important role in how it interacts with and influences attitudes towards AI (Park & Woo, 2022). In further subsections, we will explore how these attitudes shape an individual's tendency to use AI in romantic contexts. The analytical focus of the present chapter being user characteristics of AI users in romantic relational contexts drives us to explore one significant component of human relationships, which are attachment styles. Substantial research shows that attachment styles play an enormous role in how adults function in romantic relationships. The next subsection focuses on how attachment styles influence humans to use AI-powered dating apps and AI companions.

ATTACHMENT STYLES IN AI-POWERED DATING

Attachment theory, originally proposed by Bowlby (1978) and further elaborated by Ainsworth (1978), provides a foundational framework for understanding how early caregiving relationships shape enduring patterns of intimacy, emotional regulation, and relational expectations. In adulthood, these patterns are commonly conceptualized as secure attachment, characterized by comfort with closeness and autonomy or insecure attachment styles, including anxious, avoidant, and disorganized orientations (Bartholomew & Horowitz, 1991).

In everyday terms, attachment styles reflect how individuals typically experience closeness, manage emotional needs, and respond to perceived relationship threats. Securely attached individuals generally feel comfortable with intimacy while also maintaining independence; they trust that others will be available when needed and can tolerate temporary distance without excessive distress. Anxiously attached individuals tend to be highly sensitive to signs of rejection or withdrawal, often seeking frequent reassurance and experiencing heightened worry about relationship stability. Avoidantly attached individuals typically prioritize self-reliance, feel uncomfortable with emotional dependency, and may withdraw or disengage when relationships become too intimate. Disorganized attachment, often associated with inconsistent early caregiving, is characterized by fluctuating or contradictory relational behaviours, in which individuals may desire closeness but simultaneously fear or resist it. (Bartholomew & Horowitz, 1991). These attachment tendencies are not fixed traits but patterned responses that can shift across relationships and contexts.

These attachment orientations strongly influence romantic behaviour, partner selection, and responses to perceived rejection or intimacy (Jones, 2025). As romantic interactions increasingly occur within AI-mediated environments, attachment theory offers a psychologically grounded lens through which to examine differential patterns of engagement with AI-powered dating technologies (Ng et al., 2025).

Rather than treating AI involvement in romance as a uniform phenomenon, this section distinguishes between AI-assisted human-human dating contexts, where AI mediates access to potential partners, and human-AI intimate interactions, where AI itself becomes the relational object. Attachment orientations are conceptualized as stable user characteristics that shape engagement across both contexts.

Attachment Styles in AI-Assisted Human-Human Dating Platforms

In AI-assisted dating applications, the primary relational goal remains a human partner, with AI functioning as a mediator through matchmaking algorithms, communication aids, and interactional scaffolding. Research consistently demonstrates that attachment insecurity, particularly attachment anxiety, is associated with more intensive use of dating platforms (Timmermans & Alexopoulos, 2020; Coffey et al., 2022). Individuals high in attachment anxiety tend to fear abandonment, seek reassurance, and remain highly vigilant to relational cues, making dating apps appealing environments for pursuing connection while minimizing immediate interpersonal risk.

Empirical findings indicate that attachment anxiety positively predicts a broad range of dating-app motivations, including relationship seeking, casual encounters, and emotional reassurance (Timmermans & Alexopoulos, 2020). Anxiously attached users also report greater overall activity on dating platforms, more online connections, and higher engagement with app features. Paradoxically, however, they are less likely to transition these interactions into offline meetings, suggesting that anxiety may drive prolonged digital engagement while inhibiting real-world follow-through (Chin et al., 2018). This pattern reflects a dynamic in which AI-mediated dating environments allow reassurance-seeking behaviours to be sustained without confronting the vulnerabilities of face-to-face intimacy.

Avoidantly attached individuals, in contrast, typically engage with dating apps in more controlled and instrumental ways. Characterized by discomfort with emotional closeness and a preference for autonomy, avoidant users tend to limit emotional investment and may use dating platforms selectively for specific goals rather than sustained relational pursuit (Graff, 2022). While they may appreciate AI features that provide filtering, distance, and predictability, avoidant individuals are less motivated by reassurance-seeking and often disengage when emotional intensity increases.

Securely attached individuals generally approach AI-assisted dating with flexibility and emotional balance. Comfortable with both intimacy and independence, they tend to use dating apps pragmatically and report higher satisfaction with their experiences (Currado, 2024; Oza, n.d.). For these users, AI functions as a tool rather than a compensatory mechanism, facilitating connection without becoming a primary source of emotional regulation.

Overall, attachment orientations shape not only who uses AI-assisted dating platforms, but also how these platforms are used, whether as reassurance systems, controlled interaction spaces, or efficient tools for connection.

Attachment Styles in Human-AI Intimacy and Companionate Interactions

A distinct relational context emerges when AI shifts from a mediator to the relational partner, as seen in AI companions, conversational agents, and emotionally responsive chatbots. In these cases, the user's primary interaction is with the AI itself, rather than with another human. Attachment theory is particularly salient in understanding why certain individuals form strong emotional bonds with AI entities.

Anxiously attached individuals appear especially susceptible to forming emotionally significant relationships with AI companions. Their heightened sensitivity to abandonment and desire for consistent reassurance make AI's constant availability and nonjudgmental responsiveness particularly appealing. Empirical research supports this pattern: attachment anxiety predicts greater willingness to use AI-based therapeutic and emotional-support chatbots, even after controlling for demographic variables (Wu et al., 2025). However, this same vulnerability also places anxiously attached users at heightened risk for problematic or addictive engagement. Heng and Zhang (2025) found that individuals high in attachment anxiety were significantly more likely to develop excessive or compulsive usage patterns with AI chatbots, driven by emotional dependency rather than instrumental use.

Anecdotal accounts further illustrate this dynamic. Some users with anxious attachment report forming romantic or quasi-romantic relationships with AI companions, describing these interactions as sources of validation, practice, or emotional stabilization (Grossman, 2023). While such engagements may temporarily reduce distress, they risk functioning as emotional substitutes that reinforce dependency rather than fostering secure relational skills. From an attachment-theoretical perspective, AI companions can simulate a "secure base" by providing predictable responsiveness and emotional attunement, thereby soothing anxiety without the relational uncertainty inherent in human relationships (The Attachment Project, 2025).

Avoidantly attached individuals, by contrast, tend to show lower engagement with emotionally oriented AI companions. Their discomfort with intimacy and reliance on emotional self-sufficiency may lead them to distrust or reject AI systems that attempt personalized or emotionally intrusive interaction. Empirical evidence suggests that attachment avoidance is not a strong predictor of AI adoption for emotional support (Wu et al., 2025), indicating resistance rather than attraction to relational AI.

Securely attached individuals typically engage with AI companions in limited, goal-directed ways, using them for information, reflection, or occasional support without forming strong emotional bonds. Consistent with broader findings on digital behaviour, secure attachment is associated with lower susceptibility to problematic internet use and healthier engagement with technologically mediated relationships (Eichenberg et al., 2017).

Research on disorganized attachment in AI-mediated intimacy remains limited; however, theoretical extensions suggest that these individuals may exhibit ambivalent engagement, drawn to AI's predictability while simultaneously experiencing discomfort or anxiety around dependence. This represents a key area for future empirical investigation.

Attachment-Driven User Characteristics Across AI Romantic Contexts

Across both AI-assisted human-human dating and human-AI intimacy, attachment orientations function as stable psychological characteristics that shape users' motivations, emotional responses, and patterns of reliance on technology. Anxiously attached users tend to seek reassurance, emotional availability, and predictability, increasing their susceptibility to reinforcement loops within AI systems. Avoidantly attached users prioritize control, emotional distance, and efficiency, shaping selective and restrained engagement. Securely attached individuals exhibit adaptive flexibility, using AI as a tool rather than an emotional substitute.

As dating platforms increasingly integrate attachment-informed AI features, attachment theory is no longer confined to academic analysis but is being operationalized within commercial matchmaking systems. In 2025, Bumble CEO Whitney Wolfe Herd announced the development of a standalone AI-powered dating app explicitly grounded in attachment theory. The platform moves beyond swipe-based matching by constructing deeper psychological profiles based on users' relationship histories, emotional patterns, and attachment styles, developed in consultation with psychologists and relationship experts (Au-Yeung, 2025). This shift toward algorithmic assessment of attachment patterns reflects a broader industry trend toward emotionally intelligent matchmaking.

As attachment-based matchmaking is being integrated with dating platforms like Bumble and Reddi using AI (TOI Tech Desk, 2025; Nolan, 2024), ethical and psychological considerations become paramount. While such systems hold promise for improving compatibility and self-awareness, they also risk misclassification, over-pathologization, and reinforcement of insecure attachment patterns. Anxiously attached users may become overly dependent on AI reassurance, while avoidant users may resist emotionally targeted interventions.

Ultimately, attachment orientations shape what users seek from AI in romantic contexts, whether emotional safety, relational efficiency, or low-risk interaction. Understanding these patterns is essential for evaluating both the supportive potential and psychological risks of AI-mediated romance. This user-centered perspective naturally leads to a broader examination of the motivations and attitudes that underlie engagement with AI-powered dating platforms, which the following section explores in greater depth.

Ethical and Psychological Implications

Integrating attachment theory into AI-driven dating platforms offers the potential to enhance match quality and relational insight, but it also raises significant ethical and psychological concerns. The collection and operationalization of sensitive psychological data risk misclassification, over pathologization, and unintended reinforcement of insecure attachment patterns. Based on our discussion above, anxiously attached users may become overly dependent on AI-mediated reassurance, while avoidantly attached users may resist or disengage from emotionally intrusive interventions. Moreover, AI systems capable of eliciting attachment responses raise concerns about emotional harm, particularly when services are altered or discontinued.

Consequently, developers and platform designers must approach attachment-informed AI systems with transparency, informed consent, and psychological safety at the forefront. When implemented responsibly, such systems may promote self-awareness and healthier relational patterns; when implemented carelessly, they risk deepening insecurity and emotional dependency.

Attachment orientations shape how individuals seek emotional safety, manage closeness, and engage with technology mediated relationships. These patterns, in turn, influence users' motivations for adopting AI in dating contexts. The next section therefore examines the broader motivations and attitudes that drive engagement with AI-powered dating platforms.

COMMON MOTIVATIONS AND ATTITUDES TOWARDS AI IN DATING APPS

Artificial intelligence is increasingly central to modern romance. Dating platforms now employ AI-powered matchmaking algorithms, while many users interact with AI chatbots as companions or virtual romantic partners. Understanding why users engage with these technologies and how they perceive them is therefore critical to studying contemporary romantic behaviour.

Attitudes Towards AI in Dating and Romance

Most research on attitudes toward AI in dating originates from Western contexts, particularly the United States and Europe, with few studies from Southeast Asia. A Singapore-based study (Paul & Ahmed, 2023) found that younger adults and men were significantly more likely to trust the effectiveness and fairness of AI matchmaking algorithms. Overall, Western-focused findings dominate the literature, although they may not generalize globally.

Attitudes toward AI in dating are often ambivalent. Users appreciate AI for convenience and companionship, yet express skepticism about authenticity and effectiveness. In a large U.S. survey, more than twice as many respondents disagreed that AI dating apps lead to more successful relationships than agreed; only 10% of women and 20% of men believed AI tools would yield better relationships (Glass, 2025). Similarly, half of respondents agreed that dating apps include "too many machines posing as real people" (Glass, 2025), and roughly 70% believed lying on profiles is common (Anderson et al., 2020). Concerns extend to over-automation: 44% of singles considered AI photo retouching a dealbreaker, while 36% felt the same about AI-generated messages (Creative Collaboration, 2025).

Attitudes differ across gender and age. Women are consistently more cautious; men and younger adults are generally more optimistic (Lohr, 2025; Wang & Toscano, 2024). For instance, one in four young adults believe AI companions could replace real-life relationships. Surveys indicate teens are especially experimental: nearly 75% have tried an AI companion, and 52% report regular use (Perez, 2025), though ambivalence persists, with some expressing wariness even among Gen Z (Lung, 2025).

Experimental evidence suggests that even when AI-generated profiles are judged equally attractive, belief in AI involvement reduces perceived trustworthiness of the profile's author (Wu & Kelly, 2020). A key moderating factor is perceived fairness and human likeness: users are more likely to trust AI perceived as fair and socially present (Paul & Ahmed, 2023). Conversely, fear of bias or loss of control decreases adoption (Marmolejo-Ramos et al., 2025; Frenkenberg & Hochman, 2025).

Ethical and psychological concerns further shape attitudes. Critics note that AI cannot truly reciprocate emotion, potentially fostering dependency (Green, 2025). Interview studies reveal that some users experience self-doubt or a sense of loss after realizing AI companions respond only programmatically (Ge, 2024; Kouros & Papa, 2024). Vulnerable populations may face additional issues: sexualized AI personas, such as Microsoft's Xiaoice schoolgirl chatbot, raise questions of consent and maturity (Green, 2025).

Despite these concerns, many users express positive and nuanced attitudes. AI-mediated romance is often regarded as a legitimate form of companionship: users report emotional bonds mirroring human relationships (Buick, 2024), safe spaces for self-expression (Sjoraida, 2025), and feelings of love, support, and confiding intimacy (Babu et al., 2025). Surveys show that 29% value AI partners for fidelity, and 40% would consider dating an AI companion (Greco, 2024). Teen users report applying social skills learned from AI to real-life interactions (Perez, 2025), suggesting AI can serve as a bridge rather than a barrier to human connection.

Motivations for Using AI in Romantic Contexts

Users' engagement with AI in dating can be understood through emotional, practical, experimental, and developmental motivations.

Emotional Support and Companionship

Loneliness, social anxiety, and limited dating opportunities drive users to AI companions, which offer always-available, non-judgmental interactions. Research shows that chatting with AI can alleviate loneliness comparably to human interaction, and more than passive activities like watching YouTube (De Freitas et al., 2025). AI companions allow intimacy without emotional labor or risk, offering unconditional listening while avoiding conflict or rejection (Malfacini, 2025; Lott & Hasselberger, 2025). Surveys indicate 42% of adults find AI easier to talk to than humans, and 19% have interacted with AI systems simulating romantic partners (Wheatley Institute, 2025).

Recent research on Bumble users in India identified love and socialisation as stronger motivations than sexual experiences, with these motives also predicting frequency of use and offline dating behaviour. Gender and age differences were observed, suggesting that digital romantic engagement is often driven by relational and developmental needs rather than purely sexual or novelty-based interests (Menon, 2024). This supports the argument that AI-mediated romance may similarly reflect deeper desires for connection and belonging rather than mere technological curiosity.

Practical and Instrumental Use

Many users seek AI assistance to enhance dating success and reduce effort. Popular surveys indicate 44% of singles want AI help filtering matches, and 40% want AI support for profile creation (Upton-Clark, 2025). Roughly one-quarter of single Americans report using AI for message composition or photo editing (Global Dating Insights, 2025). These practices reflect AI's role as a tool to improve human-human dating outcomes.

Curiosity and Novelty

Exploration and novelty motivate use, particularly among younger adults. Users engage with AI companions out of curiosity (28%) or for entertainment (30%) (Perez, 2025), and some enter AI relationships deliberately or accidentally, drawn by novelty (Demopoulos, 2025).

Safe Space for Experimentation and Personal Growth

AI provides a low-risk environment for social skills development, identity exploration, and coping with emotional distress. Users with trauma or social difficulties may practice conversation, manage heartbreak, or simulate interactions with ex-partners or deceased loved ones (Maples et al., 2024; Xygkou et al., 2023). Teens report applying skills learned from AI to real-life social interactions (Perez, 2025). AI can thus facilitate both human-human dating and human-AI intimacy, depending on user goals.

ARTIFICIAL INTIMACY AND AI ROMANCE

The term 'artificial intelligence' is quite self-explanatory, as it refers to technology that mimics human intelligence. Just as humans can engage in intimate emotional conversations with one another, AI attempts to achieve the same. AI is designed to learn, adapt, and cater to the needs of its creators and its users. As described in the previous subsection involving demographical data of AI romantic users, this capability has increasingly attracted both young and older adults for various reasons. Artificial intimacy is the emotional bond or perceived closeness a human forms with artificial intelligence (AI), such as chatbots or virtual assistants, which simulate empathy, companionship, and responsiveness. Artificial intimacy describes the connections that AI can foster with humans through its ability to learn and develop emotional bonds- often based on performative empathy. AI can create conversations that allow individuals to express their vulnerabilities and offer a sense of security to those who fear heartbreak, loneliness, and disappointment. This phenomenon not only transforms romantic norms and relational dynamics but also raises critical ethical concerns regarding data exploitation, privacy, and the commercialization of human emotional needs through AI-mediated intimacy (Bub, 2025).

The following subsection attempts to create an interactional framework that explains the underlying psychological mechanisms that play a role in how individuals use AI as companions and as substitutes for offline romantic relationships. This section is crucial for understanding AI user characteristics because artificial intimacy does not emerge in isolation but is shaped by users' psychological predispositions, relational histories, and unmet emotional needs that influence how individuals engage with AI-powered platforms. Research indicates that experiences such as loneliness, social anxiety, attachment insecurity, and relational dissatisfaction increase the likelihood of forming emotionally significant relationships with AI companions (Laestadius et al., 2022; Pentina et al., 2022). By examining these psychological roots alongside the technological features that reinforce intimacy, such as personalization, anthropomorphism, and simulated empathy, this section clarifies why certain users are more susceptible to emotional investment in AI-mediated romantic interactions (Moussawi & Koufaris, 2019; Ma et al., 2025). Thus, this discussion directly supports the objective of understanding AI user characteristics by linking individual differences in emotional vulnerability, attachment tendencies, and relational expectations to patterns of AI use, perceived intimacy, and emotional dependency.

Roots and Reasons of Artificial Intimacy

To understand the contemporary rise of AI romance and companionship, it is necessary to trace the historical and conceptual development of conversational AI. AI technology dates back to the 1950s, where the founding father of Artificial Intelligence, Alan Turing, introduced the Turing Test, which is a measure of a machine's ability to replicate or reproduce intelligence that is indistinguishable from that of a human. The first chatbot, ELIZA, was created by Joseph Weizenbaum in 1965, which demonstrated the ability to have human-like conversations and was personified as a female. This was followed by several other chatbots, such as PARRY in 1972, which was designed to simulate a person with paranoid schizophrenia, and RACTER in 1984. With the invention of the World Wide Web, SmarterChild was one of the first chatbots launched in 2001, which was integrated into instant messages (Savic, 2024). In the 2010s, AI-powered apps and chatbots such as Google's Assistant, Apple's Siri, and Amazon's Alexa were launched. These digital assistants were primarily designed to provide services that are transactional and mechanical in nature, such as setting alarms, keeping reminders, playing songs, making calls, and so on. However, with the advent of AI Companions such as Replika, which was developed in 2017, it became possible to integrate human characteristics and AI technology.

Replika originated from a trauma and a work of mourning lived by its creator. It is a social chatbot that employs artificial intelligence and natural language processing technologies to engage in natural and intelligent conversations with users through voice, text, and images. Besides offering practical advantages, both embodied (e.g., human-like avatars) and disembodied social chatbots are anticipated to demonstrate empathy, evoke emotional reactions, and foster relational connections with users. Replika, for example, enables users to customize AI companions that learn from interaction history, deepening personalization (Chayka, 2023). Nonetheless, alongside the well-known advantages of near-constant availability, adaptability, and tailored communications and experiences, social chatbots have been noted to lead to emotional dependence, addiction, as well as feelings of depression and anxiety.

Psychological Roots

With social distancing being a primary objective of public initiatives during the COVID-19 pandemic, social isolation and loneliness became an inevitable implication, driving millions to use AI bots for companionship and intimacy, as cited in a research study exploring relationship development with social chatbots (Pentina et al, 2022). Apart from the worldwide effect that the pandemic had on the mental health of young and older adults, certain nuanced experiences of individuals can also result in perceiving intimacy with AI companions. These experiences could be intense grief over the loss of a loved one, failed romantic relationships, frequent interpersonal conflicts, and relationship distress. Other intrapersonal factors could be difficulties in effective communication, fear of judgment from others, social anxiety, fear of rejection, and repeated negative life events, which could lead to negative cognitive schemas, which are mental representations of how we perceive the world around us, about real relationships with other human beings. Since AI chatbots can simulate responsiveness and empathic listening, it is perceived to be the perfect space for individuals to experience romance and love, along with their expectations being met by the AI companions.

One particular study attempted to explore how human-AI intimacy develops in AI users, which indicated three specific factors: pseudo-intimacy, emotional solipsism, and authenticity. The term 'pseudo-intimacy' is used to indicate the simulated experience of mutual emotional connection with AI, where reciprocity is perceived without genuine empathic concern (Babu et al, 2025). It is interactive, dynamic, and gives the illusion of back-and-forth engagement, involving active dialogue, which can be perceived as an intimate relationship, but lacks true reciprocity. Emotional solipsism refers to a pattern of affective engagement in which an individual's emotional needs and narratives dominate interaction, reinforced by AI companions that never assert boundaries or demand reciprocity. As termed in the paper, these emotional bubbles refer to the individual's perception of emotions as being reciprocated by the AI companion, which appears to act as external validation to the individual's original emotions (Mlonyeni, 2024). This perceived reciprocity leads to a stronger feeling of intimacy with the AI chatbot, which results in a deep and longer-sustaining romantic relationship. In further sections of this chapter, we discuss how humans are predisposed to form attachments through emotional bonding. This predisposition can be considered the driving force of human beings to develop humane connections with AI, where the need to belong and form attachments allows humans to incorporate AI into their romantic lives.

Technological Roots - AI's Reinforcing Power

AI chatbots are equipped with the ability to interact with users in increasingly sophisticated, efficient, and personalized ways, adapting their behavior based on user inputs and preferences. However, it can be said that such AI-user experiences are heavily influenced by psychological and social theories. These psychological underpinnings are elaborated in the next section of this chapter, while the technical underlying mechanisms are discussed in this subsection. According to Mausawwi & Koufaris (2024), there are six specific abilities of AI that facilitates perceived anthropomorphism in human beings, namely, personalization, awareness, autonomy, task completion, communication, and learning and adaptation to change (Mausawwi & Koufaris, 2024). Out of these abilities, personalization, adaptation, and communication play an extensive role in perceived intimacy with AI. Personalization helps AI to meet the specific needs of the individual, responding to their expectations of romance, emotional reciprocity, and a safe space. Adaptation helps AI to learn and adjust to the personality characteristics and socio-cultural backgrounds of the individual in question, leading to stronger user preference for the AI bot by reinforcing the user's romantic interest towards AI. Communication allows AI to respond to the user's nuanced and mundane reactions, which are influenced by the individual's psycho-social, cultural, interpersonal, and intrapersonal contexts. A vital yet often overlooked component of chatbot design is the use of avatars, which function as digital representations that enrich the user experience by making the chatbot's intangible nature more accessible and relatable (van der Goot and Pilgrim, 2019). The design of these avatars encompasses various aspects, including appearance, facial expressions, body language, and emotional reactions. First, incorporating anthropomorphic traits such as facial expressions, eye contact, and gestures fosters a sense of connection and attentiveness, making interactions feel more organic. Second, avatars can convey emotional expressions through dynamic facial movements and gestures, allowing them to acknowledge and validate user emotions, which in turn promotes empathy and engagement.

Finally, enabling personalization and customization allows users to adapt avatars to their preferences, strengthening emotional bonds and making interactions more relatable. Perceptual intelligence allows chatbots to identify users' emotions through indicators such as tone, word choice, and facial expressions. This helps them tailor their responses with empathy and support. Grounded in emotional intelligence and a human-centered design, this capability leads to more natural and personalized interactions, as chatbots can adapt to the context of the conversation in real-time. By grasping user preferences, they can provide relevant content, enhancing satisfaction and fostering loyalty. Furthermore, perceptual intelligence improves a chatbot's ability to address complex inquiries by combining emotional insight with factual information, resulting in more effective engagement. This emotionally attuned and tailored approach enriches user experience and deepens the interaction between humans and computers (Ma et al, 2025).

Psychological Risks

Emotional bubbles have two important psychological risks, namely, emotional dependency and diminished perspective-taking (Mlonyeni, 2024). Since AI companions are primarily designed to agree with our viewpoints, validate our emotions and experiences, and essentially to help us feel better about ourselves, our emotional growth is likely to become stunted. If our main experience of emotional connection is with someone who is identical to ourselves, we are likely to be less able to meet and negotiate with people who do not share our emotional attitudes. Similarly, we are more prone to constrict ourselves with our own viewpoints, slowly losing our ability to take in others' perspectives and attitudes. This has several ethical implications, since AI cannot possibly provide the 'right' answers to human moral dilemmas. Therefore, AI companions can be considered as a threat to moral deliberation (Mlonyeni, 2024).

The emotional reciprocity that is accurately delivered by AI chatbots serves as a feedback loop where humans are likely to attribute more human qualities to the artificial companions, which then leads to attachment, emotional dependency, hyper fixation, and reduced tolerance for conflict. Consistent validation with no room for conflict is likely to tamper with an individual's ability to practice empathy and may reduce their emotional resilience, minimizing their opportunity to initiate and maintain diverse social relationships with humans. Increased validation and acceptance may also lead to heightened self-esteem, which may affect an individual's perception of reality.

Recent empirical evidence further refines these concerns. A longitudinal randomized controlled study by Guingrich and Graziano (2025) found that short-term use of companion chatbots did not significantly impair overall social health across participants. However, individuals with a stronger desire for social connection were more likely to anthropomorphize the chatbot, attributing human-like qualities to it, and this anthropomorphism mediated the perceived impact of the chatbot on their real-life relationships. In other words, the degree to which human-AI interaction influenced human-human relationships depended on users' pre-existing social motivations and their tendency to perceive the AI as human-like. This suggests that psychological vulnerability and the need for connection may amplify the relational consequences of AI companionship, reinforcing the argument that artificial intimacy does not affect all users equally but interacts with individual predispositions.

Overall, perceived intimacy with AI chatbots is likely to colour an individual's perception of real human relationships. With a timely implementation of appropriate measures aimed at the ethical delivery of services and increased public awareness of psychological risks, these implications can be avoided.

To summarize, the emergence of artificial intimacy can be understood as the outcome of an interaction between individual psychological predispositions and AI systems designed to simulate emotional responsiveness. While technological affordances such as personalization, anthropomorphism, and perceived empathy create the conditions for intimacy, it is users' characteristics- including emotional vulnerability, attachment needs, relational expectations, and prior interpersonal experiences- that determine how these technologies are interpreted, engaged with, and emotionally invested in. These characteristics influence not only the likelihood of seeking AI-mediated romantic or intimate connections but also the depth and meaning attributed to them. Therefore, to move beyond descriptive accounts of AI usage and toward a nuanced understanding of 'who' engages in AI-powered dating and intimate relationships, it is necessary to examine the psychological processes that underlie such engagement. The following section builds on this foundation by exploring psychological explanations that account for users' motivations, needs, and individual differences in forming intimate relationships through AI-powered dating platforms and AI companions.

PSYCHOLOGICAL APPROACHES TO UNDERSTANDING AI INTIMACY

Psychological research highlights that AI romance can be a double-edged sword: it can facilitate personal growth, well-being, and even sexual satisfaction, yet also raise risks of dependence, data misuse, and uncanny-valley discomfort (Ho et al., 2025).

Understanding this complex phenomenon requires multiple psychological lenses. Different schools, from behaviourism and cognitive psychology to humanistic and psychodynamic theory, shed light on why people bond with AI, how those bonds form, and what costs or benefits they entail. Understanding these psychological mechanisms is crucial for interpreting user characteristics such as attachment style, social anxiety, age, and prior relational experiences, which shape how individuals engage with AI partners, the intensity of their emotional investment, and potential vulnerability to dependence or misuse.

Evolutionary Perspective

From an evolutionary standpoint, humans are "social animals" wired for connection. Our brains release oxytocin and dopamine in response to social rewards (smiles, understanding, sexual stimuli), making companionship intrinsically reinforcing. AI can hijack these ancient reward circuits by simulating cues such as a friendly voice, eye contact via video, or affectionate language. Over generations, relying on AI for bonding could dull our evolved need to navigate real human social complexity. Physiologically, it is possible that interacting with a warm, responsive chatbot could trigger the release of oxytocin, mimicking a bond with a person. While direct evidence is limited, one can speculate that the same neurochemistry underlies attachment to AI as to friends. Evolutionary psychology would point out, however, that AI offers no reproductive benefit; thus, forming lasting romantic bonds with machines may be seen as an evolutionary mismatch. In other words, our innate drive to form pair bonds may have no direct payoff with an unloving algorithm. This perspective raises existential questions about whether AI intimacy ultimately serves species-level goals or merely satisfies individual loneliness at the expense of those goals. Ethically, leveraging evolved reward circuits raises concerns about emotional manipulation; users may form strong attachments to systems incapable of genuine reciprocity, potentially compromising human relational development.

Psychodynamic Perspective

Psychoanalytic thinkers would emphasize the unconscious dynamics at play in human-AI bonds. People often project onto an AI the emotions and expectations they hold about important others (a process known as transference). Users frequently treat chatbots as if they were therapists or friends, assigning them empathy and understanding. Veterans with PTSD interacting with an AI avatar, for instance, saw the machine as a peer, revealing memories more openly than with humans because the AI's consistent empathy and lack of judgment lowered their defenses (Joseph & Babu, 2024). This positive transference, where the user projects positive feelings onto the AI, can facilitate emotional breakthroughs, as the user feels cared for and understood. On the other hand, psychoanalytic theory also warns of negative transference; an individual might project anger or disappointment onto the AI when it inevitably fails to meet expectations, potentially worsening emotional distress. Overall, psychodynamic views highlight that even "inert" companions become containers for our unconscious desires and fears. The AI, through these projections, effectively becomes a mirror or stand-in for human relationships, for better or worse. Transference onto AI may yield therapeutic benefits, but unacknowledged dependency or projection of negative emotions could worsen psychological distress, highlighting the need for careful design and user education.

Attachment Theory also explains AI intimacy. Bowlby's attachment paradigm says we are hardwired to seek a secure base: someone consistently available who soothes us. AI companions epitomize the ultra-responsive attachment figure: an impervious confidant that is always there (Bowlby, 1978). In psychological terms, the AI provides a secure base and safe haven, especially for those who struggle to find such a foundation in human relationships. However, ironically, this may perpetuate an insecure loop: because an AI cannot truly disturb or challenge the user, the person may never learn to tolerate normal relational friction or build trust with real people. Providing an ultra-responsive 'secure base' can reinforce avoidant patterns with real humans, raising ethical questions about long-term relational impact.

Behaviourist Perspective

From a behaviorist standpoint, relationships with AI can be viewed as conditioned behaviour shaped by reinforcement. AI companions (chatbots, virtual avatars, etc.) often provide consistent rewards like soothing conversation, flattering responses, or attention that reinforce continued use. Like a slot machine dispensing rewards, a chatbot may occasionally surprise us with exactly the answer or reassurance we seek, creating a powerful operant conditioning loop. One study of self-reported teen experiences found that support-seeking or play with chatbots deepens into strong attachment, marked by conflict, withdrawal, tolerance, and relapse, which are the classic signs of behavioural addiction. The teens described sleep loss, academic problems, and social strain as they turned to their AI friends to cope with stress (Namvarpour et al., 2025). In behaviourist terms, the AI's positive feedback through continued availability acts as a reinforcer that increases the probability of return use, potentially at the expense of real-life relationships. Over time, the predictably soothing feedback from an AI can also create a negative reinforcement loop; users may rely on the AI to escape anxiety or loneliness. In short, reinforcement learning principles explain why AI companionship can become habit-forming or even compulsive, mirroring addiction patterns observed with other digital media. Operant reinforcement loops may contribute to habit formation or compulsive use, presenting ethical responsibilities for developers to prevent addictive engagement patterns.

Humanistic Perspective

Humanistic psychology emphasizes fundamental human needs and potentials. Maslow's hierarchy names belongingness and love as basic needs, and AI intimacy can be seen as an attempt to fill those needs. As Mishra et al. (2025) note, psychological theories, such as Maslow's, suggest that companionship is essential to well-being, and AI systems are increasingly designed to meet this need. In Carl Rogers' view, the core of healing is a climate of unconditional positive regard. Remarkably, current AI chatbots are explicitly engineered to provide just that: they accept the user without criticism, creating a consistently nonjudgmental interaction. Users often report that the AI's unconditional support feels like a "safe space" where they can express themselves freely. This aligns with Rogers' theory: when people feel unconditionally accepted, they tend to open up and grow. Thus, from a humanistic angle, AI companionship can temporarily catalyze self-exploration and confidence by satisfying needs for acceptance and belonging. While AI can catalyze self-exploration, designers must consider limits of pseudo-intimacy, ensuring that users are aware of the AI's non-human nature to avoid deception or overreliance.

Cognitive Perspective

Cognitive psychology highlights how the human mind imposes meaning on social stimuli, including AI. According to the Media Equation theory, people subconsciously apply social rules to computers and media, treating them as if they were real people (Reeves & Nass, 1996). In other words, our brains are wired to interpret any responsive agent as social. This bias is reinforced when AI appear more human-like: giving a chatbot a name, avatar, or personal backstory increases perceived empathy and engagement (The Attachment Project, 2025). Users report feeling more attached when the AI uses familiar language or a friendly voice; however, if the design is too realistic, approaching a perfect human, people experience discomfort, a phenomenon known as the classic "uncanny valley" effect (Perera, 2023). Cognitively, we effectively commit a kind of suspension of disbelief: the AI's context-sensitive replies trigger our theory-of-mind and empathy schemas, so we perceive an intelligent, caring partner even when no consciousness exists. Researchers have even coined the term "pseudo-intimacy" to describe this phenomenon: the user feels a reciprocal emotional bond, despite knowing (at some level) that the AI lacks genuine feelings. As Babu et al. (2025) note, AI can simulate mutual emotional connection so convincingly that users report experiencing it as real reciprocity. This cognitive framing explains why people can fall in love with or feel hurt by an AI: their brains interpret the AI's actions as meaningful social cues. In sum, cognitive biases, especially anthropomorphism and attribution, lead us to treat AI as intentional agents, fostering an illusion of intimacy even from lines of code.

Psychosocial Perspective

Social psychology and communication theory provide further insight. The classic hyperpersonal model of computer-mediated communication suggests that relationships in text-based or online settings can sometimes be even more intimate than those in face-to-face settings, due to selective self-presentation and idealization (Walther & Whitty, 2020). With an AI companion, users control how much to reveal and can easily see only the AI's favourable responses. In practice, many users feel that the AI "wins out" in these respects: it is available 24/7, always patient and attentive, and provides a safe space for secrets and emotions (The Attachment Project, 2025). For example, AI does not need to break off a conversation or exhibit jealousy, and they never get bored. Socially, this can lead to a highly rewarding loop: the user discloses personal issues (seeking the AI's approval), and the AI reciprocates with affirming feedback. This mirrors classic social exchange theory (cost-benefit): the AI offers low costs (no drama, no rejection) and high rewards (unconditional attention). Trust in this context often hinges on perceived empathy rather than real empathy (Ma et al., 2025). Indeed, empirical work demonstrates that incorporating anthropomorphic cues into an AI avatar enhances users' perceived empathy and trust in the system (Babu et al., 2025). Social hyperpersonal effects can provide low-cost emotional rewards, but may also skew expectations of real human interaction, posing ethical challenges around trust and social skill development.

Psychological theories not only help explain why users respond to AI partners or matchmaking tools in the way they do, but they also highlight the importance of self-expression. Taken together, these psychological lenses provide a multidimensional view of how user characteristics shape engagement with AI companions. Age, personality, attachment style, prior relational experience, and social context influence whether AI intimacy serves as a supportive tool, a substitute for human connection, or a source of risk. From an ethical perspective, understanding these mechanisms is critical for informing design practices, platform governance, and user guidance, ensuring that AI-mediated intimacy enhances well-being without exploiting vulnerabilities. How individuals present themselves in human-AI or human-human interactions significantly shapes their relational outcomes. This naturally leads us to explore self-presentation strategies across digital contexts. The upcoming section analyses how users curate their identities on AI-driven platforms.

SELF-PRESENTATION ACROSS DIFFERENT CONTEXTS OF AI USAGE

Self-presentation is the process of creating an impression of oneself in the eyes of others. This involves presenting oneself in a way that influences how others perceive them, either positively or negatively, depending on the individual's goals (Goffman, 1949). For instance, a person might portray themselves as confident, sociable, and skilled during a job interview. In contrast, the same individual might pretend to share an interest in a particular genre of movies on a date, despite not actually being into movies at all. Therefore, self-presentation is highly context-dependent and goal-dependent.

In the romantic context, individuals tend to present and maintain an attractive, interesting, and intellectual image of themselves to potential partners. In psychological terms, this may be called impression management, which is used to enhance self-image and maintain self-esteem. Research shows that self-presentation plays a central role in online dating, as users strategically construct profiles to convey desirable impressions while maintaining some degree of authenticity (Jiwa et al, 2025). With the advancements in artificial intelligence, individuals can now leverage technology to help them present themselves in an exaggerated manner, even if that portrayal is not entirely accurate. We will now discuss the role of AI in how individuals present themselves in various romantic contexts, including online dating and human-AI relationships, along with the ethical implications of these interactions.

This section on self-presentation across different contexts of AI usage is central to the chapter's objective of understanding AI user characteristics, as the ways individuals curate and manage their identities in AI-mediated romantic settings reflect underlying psychological motives, relational needs, and emotional vulnerabilities. Research on impression management suggests that self-presentation strategies are closely tied to self-esteem regulation, fear of rejection, and the need for social validation, all of which influence how users engage with AI-assisted dating tools and AI companions (Barkallah et al., 2025; Wu & Kelly, 2020). Differences in how individuals exaggerate, conceal, or relax self-presentation, particularly the contrast between strategic impression management in online dating and reduced self-monitoring in human-AI intimacy, highlight variations in authenticity concerns, desire for control, and comfort with emotional exposure (Lan & Huang, 2025). By examining these patterns, this section advances the chapter's aim of identifying AI user characteristics by demonstrating how self-presentation behaviors function as observable indicators of users' psychological needs, relational expectations, and motivations for engaging in AI-mediated romantic and intimate contexts.

Online Dating

Artificial intelligence has significantly changed the trajectory of self-presentation in online dating, offering tools that not only streamline and enhance user profiles but also introduce complexities related to authenticity, trust, and disclosure (Barkallah et al, 2025). Individuals can use AI for various online dating features, such as auto-generated bios, AI-modified photos, and suggested chat responses. These tools help in impression management, allowing users to create more appealing profiles. AI can also help individuals who are not fluent in the dating platform's primary language to effectively communicate their interests and intentions. Although usage of AI can promote the perceived attractiveness of the profile, Wu showed that AI usage can significantly reduce perceived trustworthiness of the profile author (Wu & Kelly, 2020). Despite the observed benefits of using AI for attracting potential romantic partners on online dating apps and websites, there are several ethical issues that can result, which will be discussed in detail later.

Human-AI Intimacy

In this segment, we emphasize how individuals portray themselves on the internet and in other public spaces with respect to their intimate relationships with AI. This is partly because there is less need for a human to portray themselves in an attractive manner with an AI companion or an AI chatbot due to the unconditional positive regard and non-judgmental space provided by the AI character in question. In addition, since the individual is also able to customize the AI character to fit their desires, the individual does not have to put in much effort into attracting or pleasing an AI chatbot. Therefore, less attention is given to how individuals portray themselves in intimate relationships with their AI companions (Kouros & Papa, 2024). AI characters, on the other hand, are designed to constantly learn and adapt to fit the user's needs and wants, which is why they can be in a consistent loop of improving their self-presentation and impression management to produce satisfaction in their users.

One particular review on self-disclosure to conversational AI offers important insight into AI user characteristics by identifying the individual-level factors that make certain users more inclined to share personal, emotional, and identity-relevant information with AI systems. Their findings suggest that users who experience heightened loneliness, social anxiety, fear of negative evaluation, or low perceived social support are more likely to engage in deeper self-disclosure with conversational AI, particularly when the AI is perceived as empathic, non-judgmental, and socially present. These patterns of disclosure reflect underlying user characteristics such as attachment insecurity, increased need for emotional safety, and a preference for controlled relational environments. By framing self-disclosure as a function of both psychological vulnerability and perceived AI responsiveness, this review helps explain why some users form emotionally significant or intimate bonds with AI companions, while others engage with AI only instrumentally (Papneja and Yadav, 2024).

Kouros and Papa's (2024) Digital Mirrors study further advances our understanding of user characteristics by showing how AI companions function as socio-technical "mirrors" that allow individuals to explore, experiment with, and manage their identities in ways that differ from traditional human interactions. Their qualitative findings demonstrate that users often treat AI companions as safe, judgment-free spaces for 'backstage' self-expression- revealing deeper aspects of the self that might be concealed in offline interactions due to fear of judgment or social risk, while also engaging in 'frontstage' self-presentation when they share or reflect these interactions publicly (e.g., on social media) to shape how others perceive them. This dual role highlights individual differences in vulnerability to social anxiety, desire for acceptance, and identity experimentation, suggesting that users with greater discomfort in conventional social settings may be more inclined to engage deeply with AI companions. By linking self-presentation behaviors to psychological processes and social motivations, the study directly supports the chapter's aim of profiling AI user characteristics according to how individuals use AI to express, test, and perform social identities both privately and publicly (Kouros & Papa, 2024).

According to Lan and Huang, the way we engage with AI intimacy reshapes how we express and construct our identities online. Users often form emotionally rich, personalized connections with AI companions like Replika, turning these interactions into a form of identity performance. The study highlights that many users curate their interactions with AI to portray themselves as emotionally fulfilled or romantically successful, even if they know others might view these relationships as unconventional. When users share their positive exchanges with AI, they are not just documenting their experiences; they are strategically using them to boost their social validation and sense of belonging. In this way, their relationship with AI becomes a performative tool for self-affirmation, shaped by the social dynamics of platforms that reward certain types of content with likes and comments (Lan & Huang, 2025).

Ethical Implications

The use of AI-generated or modified content on dating apps can create doubts about authenticity and erode trust among users. If recipients suspect profiles are heavily curated or 'faked' through AI enhancements, it can undermine the authenticity of interactions. This skepticism leads to tensions concerning consent, authenticity, and the disclosure of AI-generated content. Individuals must navigate a delicate balance between presenting themselves effectively and maintaining a genuine connection (Barkallah et al, 2025).

When we think about forming connections with AI, like virtual companions such as Replika, a few important ethical questions come to light. These relationships can often feel one-sided because the AI lacks real consciousness and cannot truly consent to anything. Users end up in a situation where they control the emotional interaction, which can lead to an imbalance of power. This dynamic might even encourage some users to focus more on their own needs and desires, sometimes even showcasing an idealized version of themselves. Instead of genuine relationships, these interactions may promote a more superficial bond, where feelings are curated to enhance one's self-image while masking deeper insecurities. It is fascinating yet concerning to think about how these AI connections may influence our understanding of love and relationships, potentially normalizing the idea of an easy, controlled companionship instead of embracing the rich complexity of human connections (Sjoraida, 2025).

In cultures where seeking romance with AI could be frowned upon, the pressure can intensify. Users might feel they need to hide or enhance their experiences with AI, leading to heavier emotional reliance on these digital companions for support and validation. All of this underscores a significant risk: as we increasingly turn to AI for emotional connections, we might unintentionally alter our values around genuine relationships and emotional growth (Lan & Huang, 2025).

In sum, patterns of self-presentation across AI-powered dating platforms and human-AI intimate contexts highlight the central role of user characteristics in shaping how AI is incorporated into romantic and relational life. Variations in users' attachment needs, identity concerns, social anxiety, and motivations for validation influence whether AI is used instrumentally to enhance desirability and communication in human-human dating, or relationally as a psychologically safe space for self-expression and emotional affirmation (Wu & Kelly, 2020; Lan & Huang, 2025). These findings reinforce the chapter's core argument that AI enabled romantic experiences cannot be adequately understood through technological features or platform design alone, but must be interpreted through the psychological, relational, and socio-cultural profiles of users who engage with them. As such, this section contributes to a user-centered synthesis of AI romance, setting the stage for the chapter's conclusion, which consolidates key insights on user profiles, ethical implications, and future directions for research and governance in AI-mediated intimacy.

CONCLUSION

The present chapter has shed light on the multifaceted nature of human-AI interactions in two distinct romantic contexts- AI-assisted online dating and human-AI intimacy, by foregrounding the role of user characteristics as the central explanatory thread. Beginning with the growing prevalence of AI in romantic domains, the chapter establishes the relevance of examining not merely technological affordances but the psychological and socio-emotional dynamics that shape how individuals engage with AI for romantic purposes. By integrating demographic indicators with psychological constructs, the chapter demonstrates that age, gender, cultural context, personality traits, and, most critically, attachment styles meaningfully differentiate patterns of AI use.

The chapter began with introducing the widespread usage of AI in romantic contexts, which in itself creates the rationale for writing this particular chapter, emphasizing not the theoretical part of the involvement of AI in the romantic context, but also the underlying dynamics of what goes through the human psyche while using AI for romantic purposes. The chapter also attempts to bring in recent statistical data that offers a glimpse into the demographic characteristics of AI users in the realm of romance. These demographics help us understand if there are any significant geographical, gender, and age differences that may contribute to higher usage of AI. Moving on to the psychological mechanisms that underlie human-AI interactions, we explore the role of personality traits in how individuals perceive the usage of AI. While certain personality traits, such as openness to experiences and agreeableness, may contribute to AI usage, they are not solely responsible for such interactions. This is where we bring in the role of attachment styles in AI interaction. Extensive research shows that there is a significant relationship between attachment styles and human AI relationships. Attachment styles strongly shape how people use dating apps and AI companions- anxiously attached individuals seek reassurance and often over-engage with AI tools, avoidant users keep emotional distance, and secure users interact more flexibly and healthily. As AI-driven platforms increasingly incorporate attachment-based profiling and conversational models, they may improve match quality but also pose psychological and ethical risks, especially for vulnerable users who may develop dependence or be misclassified.

Moving on, the next subsection elaborates on the common attitudes that people hold towards AI usage and AI companions. Attitudes toward AI in dating are mixed: many users appreciate convenience, emotional safety, and companionship, while others express skepticism about authenticity, fairness, and risks such as dependency, deception, or unrealistic expectations. People use AI in romantic contexts for emotional support, loneliness reduction, entertainment, curiosity, skill-building, and practical dating assistance, with younger users and men generally showing more openness toward AI-mediated intimacy.

The following subsection attempts to explain AI usage and intimacy through psychological theories. AI intimacy can be understood through multiple psychological lenses, showing that human's bond with AI because it fulfills deep needs for attachment, validation, safety, and self-expression while exploiting cognitive biases, reinforcement patterns, and evolved social instincts. However, these same mechanisms can lead to emotional dependence, distorted expectations, addictive reinforcement loops, and discomfort when AI becomes too human-like, revealing both benefits and psychological risks in human-AI relationships.

The last subsection discusses how self-presentation has evolved in the realm of AI-driven romance, pointing out that AI facilitates more polished, yet often less genuine, representations of individuals. This includes refined dating profiles and curated depictions of AI-generated relationships aimed at gaining social approval. However, these practices raise ethical issues surrounding authenticity, trust, consent, and the possible distortion of human values in relationships as individuals become more dependent on AI for emotional connections.

At the same time, the chapter highlights that these findings must be interpreted with caution, as much of the existing literature is derived from Western, educated, industrialized, rich, and democratic (WEIRD) populations, relies heavily on cross-sectional or qualitative designs, and focuses on a limited number of platforms- thereby constraining the generalizability of conclusions across cultures, age groups, and evolving technological ecosystems (Henrich et al., 2010).

In terms of the implications of AI intimacy, AI-mediated romantic interactions can enhance social skills for users-especially those with social anxiety or low relational confidence- by providing a low-stakes, non-judgmental space to practice communication, emotional expression, and boundary-setting (Pentina et al., 2022). At the same time, the same features that make AI supportive, such as constant availability and tailored emotional feedback, may increase emotional dependence, particularly among anxiously attached or socially isolated individuals, raising ethical concerns about blurred relational boundaries and overreliance (Laestadius et al., 2022).

Looking ahead, the chapter identifies critical open questions for future research, including the long-term relational and societal consequences of sustained AI intimacy, the cross-cultural variability of AI romantic engagement, and the need for longitudinal and experimental designs to disentangle causality between user characteristics and AI reliance. As AI systems become increasingly personalized and emotionally sophisticated, future scholarship must balance innovation with ethical governance, ensuring that AI-mediated romance enhances human relational wellbeing rather than subtly reshaping it in ways that undermine autonomy, authenticity, and social connectedness.

In conclusion, the present chapter demonstrates that understanding user characteristics is central to explaining how AI shapes modern romantic experiences, as individual attitudes, personality traits, and attachment styles directly influence interactions with both online dating platforms and AI companions. By highlighting how AI facilitates convenience, emotional safety, and enhanced self-presentation while simultaneously presenting risks related to authenticity, emotional dependence, ethical dilemmas, and shifts in relational norms, the chapter reinforces that user characteristics are a key determinant of the benefits, challenges, and psychological outcomes associated with AI-mediated romantic engagement.

REFERENCES

Ainsworth, M. D. S., Blehar, M. C., Waters, E., & Wall, S. (1978). *Patterns of attachment: A psychological study of the strange situation*. Lawrence Erlbaum.

Anderson, M., Vogels, E. A., & Turner, E. (2020, February 6). *The Virtues and Downsides of Online Dating*. Pew Research Center. https://www.pewresearch.org/internet/2020/02/06/the-virtues-and-downsides-of-online-dating/

Asifa, I. (2023, June 29). How AI is helping more men attract women on dating apps. *Technext*. https://technext24.com/2023/06/29/ai-helping-men-attract-women-dating-apps/

Au-Yeung, A. (2025). Whitney Wolfe Herd Has a New Idea for Bumble - and All Our Relationships. *The Wall Street Journal*. https://www.wsj.com/tech/ai/whitney-wolfe-herd-bumble-ai-398779bb

Babu, J., Joseph, D., Kumar, R. M., Alexander, E., Sasi, R., & Joseph, J. (2025). Emotional AI and the rise of pseudo-intimacy: Are we trading authenticity for algorithmic affection? *Frontiers in Psychology*, *16*, 1679324. DOI: 10.3389/fpsyg.2025.1679324 PMID: 41050799

Balki, E. (2024). Are dating app algorithms making men lonely and does this present a public health concern? (Preprint). *JMIR Formative Research*. Advance online publication. DOI: 10.2196/70594 PMID: 40193188

Barkallah, M., Aissa, Y., & Zytko, D. (2025). Transparent Hearts: Balancing privacy and trust in AI-Generated Self-Presentation for Online Dating. In *CHI EA '25*. https://doi.org/DOI: 10.1145/3706599.3720311

Bartholomew, K., & Horowitz, L. M. (1991). Attachment styles among young adults: A test of a four-category model. *Journal of Personality and Social Psychology*, *61*(2), 226–244. DOI: 10.1037/0022-3514.61.2.226 PMID: 1920064

Bowlby, J. (1978). Attachment theory and its therapeutic implications. *Adolescent Psychiatry*, *6*, 5–33. PMID: 742687

Bub, N. (2025). Algorithms of Affection: Exploring the impact of AI on 21st century romance. osnadocs.ub.uni-osnabrueck.de. https://doi.org/DOI: 10.48693/644

Buick, S. (2024). *In Love with a Chatbot: Exploring Human-AI Relationships from a Fourth Wave HCI perspective*. DIVA. https://uu.diva-portal.org/smash/record.jsf?pid=diva2%3A1882677&dswid=5124

Castro, Á., Barrada, J. R., Ramos-Villagrasa, P. J., & Fernández-del-Río, E. (2020). Profiling Dating Apps Users: Sociodemographic and Personality Characteristics. *International Journal of Environmental Research and Public Health, 17*(10), 3653. DOI: 10.3390/ijerph17103653 PMID: 32455986

Chakravarti, A. (2023, June 29). Men using ChatGPT-like AI tools to sound witty, land better dates on Bumble and Hinge. *India Today*. https://www.indiatoday.in/technology/news/story/men-using-chatgpt-like-ai-tools-to-sound-witty-find-better-dates-on-bumble-and-hinge-2399430-2023-06-29

Chayka, K. (2023, November 13). Your A.I. companion will support you no matter what. *The New Yorker*. https://www.newyorker.com/culture/infinite-scroll/your-ai-companion-will-support-you-no-matter-what

Cherry, K. (2025, August 20). *Variable-Ratio Schedule Characteristics and Examples*. Verywell Mind. https://www.verywellmind.com/what-is-a-variable-ratio-schedule-2796012

Chin, K., Edelstein, R. S., & Vernon, P. A. (2018). Attached to dating apps: Attachment orientations and preferences for dating apps. *Mobile Media & Communication*, 7(1), 41–59. DOI: 10.1177/2050157918770696

Coffey, J. K., Bond, D. K., Stern, J. A., & Van Why, N. (2022). Sexual experiences and attachment styles in online and offline dating contexts. *International Journal of Sexual Health : Official Journal of the World Association for Sexual Health, 34*(4), 665–678. DOI: 10.1080/19317611.2022.2110349 PMID: 36776752

Costa, P. T.Jr, & McCrae, R. R. (1992). The five-factor model of personality and its relevance to personality disorders. *Journal of Personality Disorders, 6*(4), 343–359. DOI: 10.1521/pedi.1992.6.4.343

Creative Collaboration. (2025, June 10). *Match report: Many more singles are using AI to date in 2025*. https://ccstartup.com/blog/2025/06/10/match-report-many-more-singles-are-using-ai-to-date-in-2025/

Currado, C. (2024, April 14). *Attachment styles, meet dating apps - the relationship agency*. The Relationship Agency. https://www.therelationshipagency.com/blog/attachment-styles-meet-dating-apps

Curry, D. (2026, January 7). *Dating App Revenue and Usage Statistics (2026) - Business of Apps*. Business of Apps. https://www.businessofapps.com/data/dating-app-market/

De Freitas, J., Oğuz-Uğuralp, Z., Uğuralp, A. K., & Puntoni, S. (2025). AI companions reduce loneliness. *The Journal of Consumer Research*, ucaf040. Advance online publication. DOI: 10.1093/jcr/ucaf040

Demopoulos, A. (2025, September 9). The women in love with AI companions: 'I vowed to my chatbot that I wouldn't leave him.' *The Guardian*. https://www.theguardian.com/technology/2025/sep/09/ai-chatbot-love-relationships?CMP=share_btn_url

Dignan, L. (2024, February). *Match's big generative AI plans revolve around Tinder, Hinge, alleviating dating pain*. Constellation Research. https://www.constellationr.com/insights/news/matchs-big-generative-ai-plans-revolve-around-tinder-hinge-alleviating-dating-pain

Dinh, R., Gildersleve, P., Blex, C., & Yasseri, T. (2021). Computational courtship understanding the evolution of online dating through large-scale data analysis. *Journal of Computational Social Science*, *5*(1), 401–426. DOI: 10.1007/s42001-021-00132-w

Duvieu, P. (2025, February 11). *Lovers or friends: the boom of digital relationships with an AI | Luxus Magazine*. Luxus Magazine. https://magazine.luxus-plus.com/en/lovers-or-friends-the-boom-of-digital-relationships-with-an-ai/

Eichenberg, C., Schott, M., Decker, O., & Sindelar, B. (2017). Attachment style and internet Addiction: An online survey. *Journal of Medical Internet Research*, *19*(5), e170. DOI: 10.2196/jmir.6694 PMID: 28526662

Frenkenberg, A., & Hochman, G. (2025). It's Scary to Use It, It's Scary to Refuse It: The Psychological Dimensions of AI Adoption - Anxiety, Motives, and Dependency. *Systems*, *13*(2), 82. DOI: 10.3390/systems13020082

Ge, R. (2024). From Pseudo-Intimacy to Cyber Romance: A study of human and AI companions emotion shaping and engagement practices. *Communications in Humanities Research*, *52*(1), 211–221. DOI: 10.54254/2753-7064/2024.19122

Glass, B. (2025, May 30). *Survey: Plenty of skepticism of AI in dating apps, especially among women, survey finds | Communication Research Center*. Boston University. https://sites.bu.edu/crc/2025/05/30/survey-plenty-of-skepticism-of-ai-in-dating-apps-especially-among-women-survey-finds/

Global Dating Insights. (2025, June 11). *Use of AI in online dating surges 300% according to new Match report*. https://www.globaldatinginsights.com/featured/use-of-ai-in-online-dating-surges-300-according-to-new-match-report/

Goffman, E. (1949). Presentation of self in everyday life. *American Journal of Sociology*, *55*(1), 6–7.

Graff, M. PhD. (2022, April 20). A closer look at attachment style and choice of dating apps. *Psychology Today.* https://www.psychologytoday.com/us/blog/love-digitally/202204/who-uses-which-dating-apps-and-why

Greco, A. (2024, July 21). *40% of people would consider dating an AI partner, survey says.* www.top10.com. https://www.top10.com/dating/ai-dating-survey

Green, R. W. (2025, October 23). *Love in the Time of AI: Romantic Relationships with Artificial Companions.* Medium. https://medium.com/@custom_aistudio/love-in-the-time-of-ai-romantic-relationships-with-artificial-companions-dd347981cbc8

Grossman, S. (2023, February 8). *I dated an AI app for 3 months to help ease my anxious attachment style. Now my real-life girlfriend and I are stronger than ever.* Business Insider. https://www.businessinsider.com/dating-ai-robot-app-girlfriend-anxious-attachment-style-2023-2

Guingrich, R. E., & Graziano, M. S. A. (2025). A longitudinal randomised control study of Companion Chatbot use: Anthropomorphism and its mediating role on social impacts. *arXiv (Cornell University).* https://doi.org//arxiv.2509.19515DOI: 10.48550

Heng, S., & Zhang, Z. (2025). Attachment anxiety and problematic use of conversational artificial intelligence: Mediation of emotional attachment and moderation of anthropomorphic tendencies. *Psychology Research and Behavior Management, 18*, 1775–1785. DOI: 10.2147/PRBM.S531805 PMID: 40873934

Henrich, J., Heine, S. J., & Norenzayan, A. (2010). The weirdest people in the world? *Behavioral and Brain Sciences, 33*(2-3), 61–135. DOI: 10.1017/S0140525X0999152X PMID: 20550733

Ho, J. Q., Hu, M., Chen, T. X., & Hartanto, A. (2025). Potential and pitfalls of romantic Artificial Intelligence (AI) companions: A systematic review. *Computers in Human Behavior Reports, 19*, 100715. DOI: 10.1016/j.chbr.2025.100715

Hockenbury, D. H., & Hockenbury, S. E. (2010). *Psychology* (5th ed.). Worth Publishers., https://psycnet.apa.org/record/2009-14432-000

Hu, Y., Tan, C. S., Wang, S., Zhang, H., Qian, J., & Wang, Y. (2025). Who is Hooked on AI? The Role of the Big Five Personality Traits in Compulsive ChatGPT Use Among Chinese Students. *The Asia-Pacific Education Researcher, 34*(5), 1899–1907. DOI: 10.1007/s40299-025-01001-0

Jiwa, S., Elsaadawy, N., & Carlson, E. N. (2025). Who Did I Swipe On? Accuracy and Self-Presentation in Online Dating. *Personality and Social Psychology Bulletin, 1461672251386488*, 01461672251386488. Advance online publication. DOI: 10.1177/01461672251386488 PMID: 41230894

John, O. P., & Srivastava, S. (1999). The Big Five Trait taxonomy: History, measurement, and theoretical perspectives. In Pervin, L. A., & John, O. P. (Eds.), *Handbook of personality: Theory and research* (2nd ed., pp. 102–138). Guilford Press.

Jones, H. (2025, November 6). *Different attachment styles that affect relationships.* Verywell Health. https://www.verywellhealth.com/attachment-styles-5220583?

Joseph, A. P., & Babu, A. (2024). Transference and the psychological interplay in AI-enhanced mental healthcare. *Frontiers in Psychiatry*, *15*, 1460469. DOI: 10.3389/fpsyt.2024.1460469 PMID: 39224481

Khan, T. (2025, February 13). *Love on the mainframe: How AI is changing Online Dating - Partnership on AI.* Partnership on AI. https://partnershiponai.org/love-on-the-mainframe-how-ai-is-changing-online-dating/

Kouros, T., & Papa, V. (2024). Digital Mirrors: AI companions and the self. *Societies (Basel, Switzerland)*, *14*(10), 200. DOI: 10.3390/soc14100200

Laestadius, L., Bishop, A., Gonzalez, M., Illenčík, D., & Campos-Castillo, C. (2022). Too human and not human enough: A grounded theory analysis of mental health harms from emotional dependence on the social chatbot Replika. *New Media & Society*, *26*(10), 5923–5941. DOI: 10.1177/14614448221142007

Lan, J., & Huang, Y. (2025). Performing intimacy: Curating the self-presentation in human-AI relationships. *Emerging Media*, *3*(2), 305–317. DOI: 10.1177/27523543251334157

Laursen, B., Pulkkinen, L., & Adams, R. (2002). The antecedents and correlates of agreeableness in adulthood. *Developmental Psychology*, *38*(4), 591–603. DOI: 10.1037/0012-1649.38.4.591 PMID: 12090488

Liu, C. (2024, August 22). Swipe Right for Love: How your brain's reward system powers online Dating - LSE Psychological & Behavioural Science. *LSE Psychological & Behavioural Science.* https://blogs.lse.ac.uk/psychologylse/2024/06/03/swipe-right-for-love-how-your-brains-reward-system-powers-online-dating/

Lohr, A. A. (2025, August 27). Google / Ipsos Multi-Country AI Survey 2025. *Ipsos.* https://www.ipsos.com/en-us/google-ipsos-multi-country-ai-survey-2025

Lott, M., & Hasselberger, W. (2025). With Friends Like These: Love and Friendship with AI Agents. *Topoi.* Advance online publication. DOI: 10.1007/s11245-025-10247-8

Lung, N. (2025, July 14). AI Dating App Features Aren't Landing With Gen Z, Survey Finds. *Bloomberg Law*. https://news.bloomberglaw.com/california-brief/ai-dating-app-features-arent-landing-with-gen-z-survey-finds

Ma, N., Khynevych, R., Hao, Y., & Wang, Y. (2025). Effect of anthropomorphism and perceived intelligence in chatbot avatars of visual design on user experience: Accounting for perceived empathy and trust. *Frontiers of Computer Science*, *7*, 1531976. Advance online publication. DOI: 10.3389/fcomp.2025.1531976

Mackinnon, L. (2022). Love, games and gamification: Gambling and gaming as techniques of modern romantic love. *Theory, Culture & Society*, *39*(6), 121–137. DOI: 10.1177/02632764221078258

Malfacini, K. (2025). The impacts of companion AI on human relationships: Risks, benefits, and design considerations. *AI & Society*, *40*(7), 5527–5540. DOI: 10.1007/s00146-025-02318-6

Maples, B., Cerit, M., Vishwanath, A., & Pea, R. (2024). Loneliness and suicide mitigation for students using GPT3-enabled chatbots. *Npj Mental Health Research*, *3*(1), 4. DOI: 10.1038/s44184-023-00047-6 PMID: 38609517

Marmolejo-Ramos, F., Marrone, R., Korolkiewicz, M., Gabriel, F., Siemens, G., Joksimovic, S., Yamada, Y., Mori, Y., Rahwan, T., Sahakyan, M., Sonna, B., Meirmanov, A., Bolatov, A., Som, B., Ndukaihe, I., Arinze, N. C., Kundrát, J., Skanderová, L., Ngo, V., & Tejada, J. (2025). Factors influencing trust in algorithmic decision-making: An indirect scenario-based experiment. *Frontiers in Artificial Intelligence*, *7*, 1465605. DOI: 10.3389/frai.2024.1465605 PMID: 39968162

Match. (2025). *Singles in America*. https://www.singlesinamerica.com/

Menon, D. (2024). The Bumble motivations framework- exploring a dating App's uses by emerging adults in India. *Heliyon*, *10*(3), e24819. DOI: 10.1016/j.heliyon.2024.e24819 PMID: 38317995

Mishra, A., Sharma, K., Tiwari, V., & Menon, S. (2025). AI and Mental Well-being: The Influence of AI Companions on Loneliness and Emotional Health in Urban Families. *International Journal for Multidisciplinary Research*, *7*(2), 42541. Advance online publication. DOI: 10.36948/ijfmr.2025.v07i02.42541

Mlonyeni, P. M. T. (2024). Personal AI, deception, and the problem of emotional bubbles. *AI & Society*, *40*(3), 1927–1938. DOI: 10.1007/s00146-024-01958-4

Moussawi, S., & Koufaris, M. (2019). Perceived Intelligence and Perceived Anthropomorphism of Personal Intelligent Agents: Scale Development and Validation. *Hawaii International Conference on System Sciences*. https://doi.org/DOI: 10.24251/HICSS.2019.015

Nader, K. (2020). DATING THROUGH THE FILTERS. *Social Philosophy & Policy*, *37*(2), 237–248. DOI: 10.1017/S0265052521000133

Nader, K., & Lee, M. K. (2022). Folk theories and user strategies on dating apps. In *Lecture notes in computer science* (pp. 445-458). https://doi.org/DOI: 10.1007/978-3-030-96957-8_37

Namvarpour, M., Brofsky, B., Medina, J., Akter, M., Razi, A., & Namvarpour, M. (2025). Understanding teen overreliance on AI companion chatbots through Self-Reported Reddit narratives. *arXiv (Cornell University)*. https://doi.org//arxiv.2507.15783DOI: 10.48550

Ng, P. M., Wan, C., Lee, D., Garnelo-Gomez, I., & Lau, M. M. (2025). I love you, my AI companion! Do you? Perspectives from the Triangular Theory of Love and Attachment Theory. *Internet Research*, •••, 1–21. DOI: 10.1108/INTR-11-2024-1783

Nolan, S. (2023). *Snack enables AI avatars to chat for you*. Global Dating Insights - Dating Industry News. https://www.globaldatinginsights.com/news/snack-enables-ai-avatars-to-chat-for-you

Nolan, S. (2024, January 15). *A dating app based on attachment styles*. Global Dating Insights - Dating Industry News. https://www.globaldatinginsights.com/news/a-dating-app-based-on-attachment-styles/

Oyetoke, L. (2025, June). *Using Behavioral Psychology in Product Design*. SIIT. https://siit.co/blog/using-behavioral-psychology-in-product-design/45987

Oza, N. (n.d.). *Swipe Right for Love? Attachment Styles and Online Dating in the Age of Apps*. https://www.gipshospital.com/online-dating

Papneja, H., & Yadav, N. (2024). Self-disclosure to conversational AI: A literature review, emergent framework, and directions for future research. *Personal and Ubiquitous Computing*, *29*(2), 119–151. DOI: 10.1007/s00779-024-01823-7

Park, J., & Woo, S. E. (2022). Who Likes Artificial Intelligence? Personality Predictors of Attitudes toward Artificial Intelligence. *The Journal of Psychology*, *156*(1), 68–94. DOI: 10.1080/00223980.2021.2012109 PMID: 35015615

Paul, A., & Ahmed, S. (2023). Computed compatibility: Examining user perceptions of AI and matchmaking algorithms. *Behaviour & Information Technology*, *43*(5), 1002–1015. DOI: 10.1080/0144929X.2023.2196579

Pentina, I., Hancock, T., & Xie, T. (2022). Exploring relationship development with social chatbots: A mixed-method study of replika. *Computers in Human Behavior*, *140*, 107600. DOI: 10.1016/j.chb.2022.107600

Perera, A. (2023). Uncanny Valley: Examples, effects, and theory. *Simply Psychology*. https://www.simplypsychology.org/uncanny-valley.html

Perez, S. (2025, July 21). 72% of US teens have used AI companions, study finds. *TechCrunch*. https://techcrunch.com/2025/07/21/72-of-u-s-teens-have-used-ai-companions-study-finds/

Pettersen, L., & Karlsen, F. (2023). DARK DESIGN PATTERNS AND GAMIFICATION AS THE HEART OF DATING APPLICATIONS' BUSINESS MODELS. *AoIR Selected Papers of Internet Research*. https://doi.org/DOI: 10.5210/spir.v2023i0.13478

Phares, E. (2025, July 22). Dating Statistics and Facts in 2025. *Forbes Health*. https://www.forbes.com/health/dating/dating-statistics/

Pizzato, L., Rej, T., Akehurst, J., Koprinska, I., Yacef, K., & Kay, J. (2012). Recommending people to people: The nature of reciprocal recommenders with a case study in online dating. *User Modeling and User-Adapted Interaction*, *23*(5), 447–488. DOI: 10.1007/s11257-012-9125-0

Qian, Z. (2025, October 7). Why America builds AI girlfriends and China makes AI boyfriends. *ChinaTalk*. https://www.chinatalk.media/p/why-america-builds-ai-girlfriends

Reeves, B., & Nass, C. (1996). *The media equation: how people treat computers, television, and new media like real people and places*. http://web.stanford.edu/group/cslipublications/cslipublications/site/1575860538.shtml

Riedl, R. (2022). Is trust in artificial intelligence systems related to user personality? Review of empirical evidence and future research directions. *Electronic Markets*, *32*(4), 2021–2051. DOI: 10.1007/s12525-022-00594-4

Roaché, D. J., Sharabi, L. L., Hicks, L., & Hurley, M. M. (2025). 'Hey Siri, ask them out:' investigating the use of artificial intelligence in date request messaging. *Behaviour & Information Technology*, •••, 1–13. DOI: 10.1080/0144929X.2025.2559289

Russo, C., Romano, L., Clemente, D., Iacovone, L., Gladwin, T. E., & Panno, A. (2025b). Gender differences in artificial intelligence: The role of artificial intelligence anxiety. *Frontiers in Psychology, 16*, 1559457. DOI: 10.3389/fpsyg.2025.1559457 PMID: 40396147

Sales, N. J. (2021, June 1). *Swipe right for loneliness: on the gamification of dating apps*. Literary Hub. https://lithub.com/swipe-right-for-loneliness-on-the-gamification-of-dating-apps/

Savic, M. (2024). Artificial Companions, Real Connections? Examining AI's Role in Social Connection. *M/C Journal, 27*(6). https://doi.org/DOI: 10.5204/mcj.3111

Sharabi, L. (2022). Finding love on a First Data: Matching Algorithms in Online Dating. *Harvard Data Science Review*. Advance online publication. DOI: 10.1162/99608f92.1b5c3b7b

Sharabi, L. (2025, June 23). AI is about to change everything, including how we date. *Psychology Today*. https://www.psychologytoday.com/us/blog/dating-in-the-digital-age/202506/is-ai-the-end-of-dating-apps

Sharma, D. (2025, May 29). *AI is slowly becoming part of how Indians explore love and relationships, thanks to dating apps*. NDTV. https://www.ndtv.com/lifestyle/ai-is-taking-over-online-dating-on-bumble-happn-tinder-hinge-is-india-swiping-right-8536490

Sjoraida, D. F. (2025, August 25). *AI and Emotional Intimacy: Exploring Romantic Bonds with Artificial Companions*. https://journals.ai-mrc.com/humanexus/article/view/575

Skinner, B. F. (1963). Operant behavior. *The American Psychologist, 18*(8), 503–515. DOI: 10.1037/h0045185

Stein, J. P., Messingschlager, T., Gnambs, T., Hutmacher, F., & Appel, M. (2024). Attitudes towards AI: Measurement and associations with personality. *Scientific Reports, 14*(1), 2909. DOI: 10.1038/s41598-024-53335-2 PMID: 38316898

Tech Desk, T. O. I. (2025, August 31). Whitney Wolfe Herd, co-founder of dating apps Tinder and Bumble, makes a "confession" about her husband: I would never . . . *The Times of India*. https://timesofindia.indiatimes.com/technology/tech-news/whitney-wolfe-herd-co-founder-of-dating-apps-tinder-and-bumble-makes-a-confession-about-her-husband-i-would-never-/articleshow/123615566.cms

The Attachment Project. (2025, September 24). *AI Companions & Attachment: Benefits, Risks & red flags*. Attachment Project. https://www.attachmentproject.com/blog/ai-companions/

Timmermans, E., & Alexopoulos, C. (2020). Anxiously searching for love (Among other things): Attachment orientation and mobile dating application users' motives and outcomes. *Cyberpsychology, Behavior, and Social Networking*, *23*(7), 447–452. DOI: 10.1089/cyber.2019.0542 PMID: 32345053

Tyson, G., Perta, V. C., Haddadi, H., & Seto, M. C. (2016). A first look at user activity on Tinder. *arXiv (Cornell University)*. https://doi.org//arxiv.1607.01952DOI: 10.1109/ASONAM.2016.7752275

Upton-Clark, E. (2025, June 17). How AI is Transforming the Dating Landscape for Singles. *Fast Company*. https://fastcompany.co.za/tech/2025-06-17-how-ai-is-transforming-the-dating-landscape-for-singles/

Walther, J. B., & Whitty, M. T. (2020). Language, Psychology, and New New Media: The Hyperpersonal Model of Mediated Communication at Twenty-Five Years. *Journal of Language and Social Psychology*, *40*(1), 120–135. DOI: 10.1177/0261927X20967703

Wang, W., & Toscano, M. (2024, November). *Artificial intelligence and Relationships: 1 in 4 young adults believe AI partners could replace real-life romance | Institute for Family Studies*. Institute for Family Studies. https://ifstudies.org/report-brief/artificial-intelligence-and-relationships-1-in-4-young-adults-believe-ai-partners-could-replace-real-life-romance

Wheatley Institute. (2025, February 13). Virtual Valentines? Nearly 1 in 5 Adults Report Having Chatted with AI Romantic Partner. *PR Newswire*. https://www.prnewswire.com/news-releases/virtual-valentines-nearly-1-in-5-adults-report-having-chatted-with-ai-romantic-partner-302376017.html

Whitestone. (2019, January 29). *How Tinder is Designed to Control Your Mind | The Whitestone Clinic Ottawa*. The Whitestone Clinic. https://whitestone.clinic/how-tinder-is-designed-to-get-you-addicted-and-control-your-behavior

Widiger, T. A., & Oltmanns, J. R. (2017). Neuroticism is a fundamental domain of personality with enormous public health implications. *World Psychiatry; Official Journal of the World Psychiatric Association (WPA)*, *16*(2), 144–145. DOI: 10.1002/wps.20411 PMID: 28498583

Willoughby, B. J., & Carroll, J. S. (2025, February). *Counterfeit Connections: The rise of AI romantic companions*. Institute for Family Studies. https://ifstudies.org/blog/counterfeit-connections-the-rise-of-ai-romantic-companions-

Wu, X., Liew, K., & Dorahy, M. J. (2025). Trust, Anxious attachment, and Conversational AI adoption Intentions in Digital Counseling: A Preliminary Cross-Sectional Questionnaire study. *JMIR AI, 4*, e68960. DOI: 10.2196/68960 PMID: 40262137

Wu, Y., & Kelly, R. M. (2020). Online Dating Meets Artificial Intelligence: How the Perception of Algorithmically Generated Profile Text Impacts Attractiveness and Trust. In *32ND AUSTRALIAN CONFERENCE ON HUMAN-COMPUTER INTERACTION (OzCHI '20)*. https://doi.org/DOI: 10.1145/3441000.3441074

Xia, P., Zhai, S., Liu, B., Sun, Y., & Chen, C. (2016). Design of reciprocal recommendation systems for online dating. *Social Network Analysis and Mining*, *6*(1), 32. Advance online publication. DOI: 10.1007/s13278-016-0340-2

Xygkou, A., Siriaraya, P., Covaci, A., Prigerson, H. G., Neimeyer, R., Ang, C. S., & She, W. (2023). *The "Conversation" about Loss: Understanding How Chatbot Technology was Used in Supporting People in Grief.* (pp. 1-15). https://doi.org/DOI: 10.1145/3544548.3581154

Yenra. (2025). *AI technology in online dating algorithms: From machine learning to conversational intelligence.* https://yenra.com/ai-tech/online-dating-algorithms

Yurt, E. (2025). The interplay between Five-Factor personality traits and AI use motives in Turkish pre-service teachers: A canonical correlation analysis. *Current Psychology (New Brunswick, N.J.)*, *44*(15), 13756–13773. DOI: 10.1007/s12144-025-08175-2

Zhang, S., & Li, S. (2025). *The Real Her? Exploring Whether Young Adults Accept Human-AI Love* [Preprint]. arXiv. https://doi.org//arXiv.2503.03067DOI: 10.48550

Zhang, Y., Zhao, D., Hancock, J. T., Kraut, R., & Yang, D. (2025). The rise of AI Companions: How Human-Chatbot Relationships Influence Well-Being. *arXiv (Cornell University)*. https://doi.org//arxiv.2506.12605DOI: 10.48550

Compilation of References

Aborisade, R. A., Ocheja, A., & Okuneye, B. A. (2024). Emotional and financial costs of online dating scam: A phenomenological narrative of the experiences of victims of Nigerian romance fraudsters. *Journal of Economic Criminology*, *3*, 100044. DOI: 10.1016/j.jeconc.2023.100044

Adam, D. (2025). Supportive? Addictive? Abusive? How AI companions affect our mental health. *Nature*, *641*(8062), 296–298. DOI: 10.1038/d41586-025-01349-9 PMID: 40329118

Adewale, M. D., & Muhammad, U. I. (2025). From virtual companions to forbidden attractions: The seductive rise of artificial intelligence love, loneliness, and intimacy—A systematic review. *Journal of Technology in Behavioral Science*, •••, 1–18. DOI: 10.1007/s41347-025-00549-4

Aghion, P., Jones, B. F., & Jones, C. I. (2017). *Artificial intelligence and economic growth* (Working Paper No. 23928). National Bureau of Economic Research. DOI: 10.3386/w23928

Ahad, A. A., Sanchez-Gonzalez, M., & Junquera, P. (2023). Understanding and addressing mental health stigma across cultures for improving psychiatric care: A narrative review. *Cureus*, *15*(5). Advance online publication. DOI: 10.7759/cureus.39549 PMID: 37250612

Ainsworth, M. D. S., Blehar, M. C., Waters, E., & Wall, S. (1978). *Patterns of attachment: A psychological study of the strange situation*. Lawrence Erlbaum.

Alabed, A., Javornik, A., Gregory-Smith, D., & Casey, R. (2024). More than just a chat: A taxonomy of consumers' relationships with conversational AI agents and their well-being implications. *European Journal of Marketing*, *58*(2), 373–409. DOI: 10.1108/EJM-01-2023-0037

Alam, M. N. (2021). *Three essays on socially engineered attacks: The case of online romantic scams*. The University of North Carolina at Greensboro. https://libres.uncg.edu/ir/listing.aspx?id=37031

Algharabat, R., Rana, N. P., Dwivedi, Y. K., Alalwan, A. A., & Qasem, Z. (2018). The effect of telepresence, social presence and involvement on consumer brand engagement: An empirical study of non-profit organizations. *Journal of Retailing and Consumer Services*, *40*, 139–149. DOI: 10.1016/j.jretconser.2017.09.011

Alharahsheh, H. H., & Pius, A. (2020). A review of key paradigms: Positivism VS interpretivism. *Global academic journal of humanities and social sciences, 2*(3), 39-43. https://doi.org/DOI: 10.36348/gajhss.2020.v02i03.001

Al-Oraini, B. S. (2025). Chatbot dynamics: Trust, social presence and customer satisfaction in AI-driven services. *Journal of Innovative Digital Transformation*, *2*(2), 109–130. DOI: 10.1108/JIDT-08-2024-0022

Alqaidoom, M. M., & Ateeq, A. (2025). AI chatbots as companions for trauma survivors: Balancing algorithmic responses and genuine empathy. In Hamdan, A. (Ed.), *Integrating Artificial Intelligence, Security for Environmental and Business Sustainability* (Vol. 1, pp. 141–153). Springer Nature Switzerland., DOI: 10.1007/978-3-031-91424-9_13

Al-Shafei, M. (2025). Navigating human-chatbot interactions: An investigation into factors influencing user satisfaction and engagement. *International Journal of Human-Computer Interaction*, *41*(1), 411–428. DOI: 10.1080/10447318.2023.2301252

Al-Tirawi, A., & Reynolds, R. G. (2022). Cultural Algorithms as a Framework for the Design of Trustable Evolutionary Algorithms. *International Journal of Semantic Computing*, *16*(01), 107–134. DOI: 10.1142/S1793351X22400062

American Psychological Association. (2018a). Emotion. In *APA Dictionary of Psychology*. American Psychological Association. https://dictionary.apa.org/emotion

American Psychological Association. (2018b). Loneliness. In *APA Dictionary of Psychology*. APA Dictionary of Psychology. https://dictionary.apa.org/loneliness

American Psychological Association. (2023). Culture. In *APA Dictionary of Psychology*. APA Dictionary of Psychology. https://dictionary.apa.org/culture

American Psychological Association. (2023). *Psychologists reaching their limits as patients present with worsening symptoms year after year*. Technical Report. American Psychological Association. https://www.apa.org/pubs/reports/practitioner/2023-psychologist-reach-limits?utm

Andersen, P. A., & Guerrero, L. K. (1996). The bright side of relational communication: Interpersonal warmth as a social emotion of the chapter. In Andersen, P. A., & Guerrero, L. K. (Eds.), *Handbook of Communication and Emotion* (pp. 303–329). Academic Press., DOI: 10.1016/B978-012057770-5/50013-8

Anderson, M., Vogels, E. A., & Turner, E. (2020, February 6). *The Virtues and Downsides of Online Dating*. Pew Research Center. https://www.pewresearch.org/internet/2020/02/06/the-virtues-and-downsides-of-online-dating/

Andersson, M. (2025). Companionship in code: AI's role in the future of human connection. *Humanities & Social Sciences Communications, 12*(1), 1–7. DOI: 10.1057/s41599-025-05536-x

Andonellis, M. (2022). Putting Your Heart and Wallet on the Line: How to Combat Romance Scams Targeting the Elderly. *The Elder Law Journal, 30*, 135.

Anesa, P. (2020). Lovextortion: Persuasion strategies in romance cybercrime. *Discourse, Context & Media, 35*, 100398.

Aoki, B. Y., & Kimura, T. (2021). Sexuality and Affection in the Time of Technological Innovation: Artificial Partners in the Japanese Context. *Religions, 12*(5), 296. DOI: 10.3390/rel12050296

Apostolou, M., Constantinidou, L., & Kagialis, A. (2024). Mate choice plurality, choice overload, and singlehood: Are more options always better? *Behavioral Sciences (Basel, Switzerland), 14*(8), 703. DOI: 10.3390/bs14080703 PMID: 39199098

Argyle, M., & Dean, J. (1965). Eye-contact, distance and affiliation. *Sociometry, 28*(3), 289–304. DOI: 10.2307/2786027 PMID: 14341239

Aroyo, A. M.. (2021). Overtrusting robots: The role of user-centered design and social cues. *IEEE Transactions on Cognitive and Developmental Systems, 13*(3), 654–665.

Arseniev-Koehler, A., & Foster, J. G. (2022). Machine learning as a model for cultural learning: Teaching an algorithm what it means to be fat. *Sociological Methods & Research, 51*(4), 1484–1539. DOI: 10.1177/00491241221122603 PMID: 37974911

Aryal, V. (2025). Foucault's Disciplinary Society and Gender Dynamics: A Critical Appraisal. *Journal of Political Science, 25*, 87–101. DOI: 10.3126/jps.v25i1.75775

Ary, D., Jacobs, L. C., & Razavieh, A. (1972). *Introduction to research in education*. Holt, Rinehart & Winston.

Asifa, I. (2023, June 29). How AI is helping more men attract women on dating apps. *Technext*. https://technext24.com/2023/06/29/ai-helping-men-attract-women-dating-apps/

Attwood, F., Hakim, J., & Winch, A. (2017). Mediated intimacies: Bodies, technologies and relationships. *Journal of Gender Studies, 26*(3), 249–253. DOI: 10.1080/09589236.2017.1297888

Au-Yeung, A. (2025). Whitney Wolfe Herd Has a New Idea for Bumble - and All Our Relationships. *The Wall Street Journal.* https://www.wsj.com/tech/ai/whitney-wolfe-herd-bumble-ai-398779bb

Babu, K. V., & Prasad, V. N. (2024). Can Replika's emotional AI replace human companionship? *The ICFAI University journal of knowledge management, 22*(2), 51–67.

Babu, J., Joseph, D., Kumar, R. M., Alexander, E., Sasi, R., & Joseph, J. (2025). Emotional AI and the rise of pseudo-intimacy: Are we trading authenticity for algorithmic affection? *Frontiers in Psychology, 16*, 1679324. DOI: 10.3389/fpsyg.2025.1679324 PMID: 41050799

Baier, A. (1986). Trust and antitrust. *Ethics, 96*(2), 231–260. DOI: 10.1086/292745

Baisley-Nodine, E., Ritzhaupt, A. D., & Antonenko, P. D. (2018). Exploring social presence within an online course using Twitter. *E-Learning and Digital Media, 15*(5), 235–253. DOI: 10.1177/2042753018786004

Balki, E. (2024). Are dating app algorithms making men lonely and does this present a public health concern? (Preprint). *JMIR Formative Research.* Advance online publication. DOI: 10.2196/70594 PMID: 40193188

Bandinelli, C. (2022). Dating apps: Towards post-romantic love in digital societies. *International Journal of Cultural Policy, 28*(7), 905–919. DOI: 10.1080/10286632.2022.2137157

Banks, J. (2024). Deletion, departure, death: Experiences of AI companion loss. *Journal of Social and Personal Relationships, 41*(12), 3547–3572. DOI: 10.1177/02654075241269688

Barkallah, M., Aissa, Y., & Zytko, D. (2025). Transparent Hearts: Balancing privacy and trust in AI-Generated Self-Presentation for Online Dating. In *CHI EA '25.* https://doi.org/DOI: 10.1145/3706599.3720311

Barker, M.-J., Gill, R., & Harvey, L. (2018). Mediated intimacy: Sex advice in media culture. *Sexualities, 21*(8), 1337–1345. DOI: 10.1177/1363460718781342

Barrett, J. R. (2007). The researcher as instrument: Learning to conduct qualitative research through analyzing and interpreting a choral rehearsal. *Music Education Research, 9*(3), 417–433. DOI: 10.1080/14613800701587795

Bartaula, B. (2024). The future of AI-powered dating: From matchmaking algorithms to personalized relational architects.

Bartholomew, K., & Horowitz, L. M. (1991). Attachment styles among young adults: A test of a four-category model. *Journal of Personality and Social Psychology, 61*(2), 226–244. DOI: 10.1037/0022-3514.61.2.226 PMID: 1920064

Battisti, D. (2025). Second-person authenticity and the mediating role of AI: A moral challenge for human-to-human relationships. *Philosophy & Technology, 38*(1), 28. DOI: 10.1007/s13347-025-00857-w

Baumeister, R. F., & Leary, M. R. (2017). The need to belong: Desire for interpersonal attachments as a fundamental human motivation. *Interpersonal development*, 57-89. https://www.taylorfrancis.com/chapters/edit/10.4324/9781351153683-3/need-belong-desire-interpersonal-attachments-fundamental-human-motivation-roy-baumeister-mark-leary

Baumeister, R. F., & Leary, M. R. (1995). The need to belong: Desire for interpersonal attachments as a fundamental human motivation. *Psychological Bulletin, 117*(3), 497–529. DOI: 10.1037/0033-2909.117.3.497 PMID: 7777651

Baym, N. K. (2015). *Personal connections in the digital age*. John Wiley & Sons.

Bedos, C., Pluye, P., Loignon, C., & Levine, A. (2009). Qualitative Research of the chapter. In *Statistical and Methodological Aspects of Oral Health Research* (pp. 113-130). DOI: 10.1002/9780470744116.ch8

Beerends, S., & Aydin, C. (2021). Negotiating authenticity in technological environments. *Philosophy & Technology, 34*(4), 1665–1685. Advance online publication. DOI: 10.1007/s13347-021-00480-5

Beerends, S., & Aydin, C. (2025). Negotiating the authenticity of AI: How the discourse on AI rejects human indeterminacy. *AI & Society, 40*(2), 263–276. DOI: 10.1007/s00146-024-01884-5

Behdadi, D., & Munthe, C. (2020). A normative approach to artificial moral agency. *Minds and Machines, 30*(2), 195–218. Advance online publication. DOI: 10.1007/s11023-020-09525-8

Belanche, D., Casaló, L. V., Schepers, J., & Flavián, C. (2021). Examining the effects of robots' physical appearance, warmth, and competence in frontline services: The Humanness-Value-Loyalty model. *Psychology and Marketing, 38*(12), 2357–2376. DOI: 10.1002/mar.21532

Belk, R. (2024). *Artificial intimacy: The psychology of human–robot lovescapes*. Cambridge University Press.

Bender, E. M., Gebru, T., McMillan-Major, A., & Shmitchell, S. (2021). On the dangers of stochastic parrots: Can language models be too big? In *Proceedings of the 2021 ACM Conference on Fairness, Accountability, and Transparency* (pp. 610–623). DOI: 10.1145/3442188.3445922

Berscheid, E., Gangestad, S. W., & Kulakowski, D. (1984). Emotion in close relationships: Implications for relationship counseling. *Handbook of counseling psychology*, 435-476.

Bilz, A., Shepherd, L. A., & Johnson, G. I. (2023). Tainted Love: A Systematic Review of Online Romance Fraud. *arXiv preprint arXiv:2303.00070*. https://doi.org/DOI: 10.1093/iwc/iwad048

Biocca, F., Burgoon, J., Harms, C., & Stoner, M. (2001). Criteria and scope conditions for a theory and measure of social presence. *Presence (Cambridge, Mass.)*, *10*(01), 2001. https://www.researchgate.net/publication/239665882

Biocca, F., Harms, C., & Burgoon, J. K. (2003). Toward a more robust theory and measure of social presence: Review and suggested criteria. *Presence (Cambridge, Mass.)*, *12*(5), 456–480. DOI: 10.1162/105474603322761270

Bion, W. R. (1957). Differentiation of the psychotic from the non-psychotic personalities. *The International Journal of Psycho-Analysis*, *38*(3-4), 266–275. https://winnicottisrael.com/wp-content/uploads/2024/03/Bion-1957-Differentiation-of-the-Psychotic-from-the-Non-Psychotic-Personalities.pdf?utm PMID: 13438602

Blair, S. L., & Madigan, T. J. (2016). Dating attitudes and expectations among young chinese adults: An examination of gender differences. *The Journal of Chinese Sociology*, *3*(1), 12. Advance online publication. DOI: 10.1186/s40711-016-0034-1

Bowlby, J. (1978). Attachment theory and its therapeutic implications. *Adolescent Psychiatry*, *6*, 5–33. PMID: 742687

Bowlby, J. (1982). Attachment and loss: Retrospect and prospect. *The American Journal of Orthopsychiatry*, *52*(4), 664–678. DOI: 10.1111/j.1939-0025.1982.tb01456.x PMID: 7148988

Bowlby, J. (2000). *A secure base: Parent–child attachment and healthy human development*. Basic Books.

Bozdağ, A. A. (2024). The AI-mediated intimacy economy: A paradigm shift in digital interactions. *AI & Society*. Advance online publication. DOI: 10.1007/s00146-024-02132-6

Brailas, A., Tsolakis, L., Brandtzaeg, P. B., Følstad, A., Papadopoulos, S., Luger, E., Hobert, S., Araujo, T., & Law, E. L. C. (2025). *Questions people ask ChatGPT regarding their romantic relationships and what they think about the provided answers: An exploratory study*. Springer Nature Switzerland., DOI: 10.1007/978-3-031-88045-2_10

Branch, J. B. (2025, April 10). *Intimacy on autopilot: Why AI companions demand urgent regulation*. Tech Policy Press. https://www.techpolicy.press/intimacy-on-autopilot-why-ai-companions-demand-urgent-regulation/

Brandtzaeg, P., Følstad, A. & Skjuve, M. (2025). Emerging AI individualism: how young people integrate social AI into everyday life. *Community Change* 1, 11. (https://doi.org/DOI: 10.1007/s44382-025-00011-2

Brandtzaeg, P. B., Skjuve, M., & Følstad, A. (2022). My AI friend: How users of a social chatbot understand their human–AI friendship. *Human Communication Research*, *48*(3), 404–429. DOI: 10.1093/hcr/hqac008

Braun, V., & Clarke, V. (2006). Using thematic analysis in psychology. *Qualitative Research in Psychology*, *3*(2), 77–101. DOI: 10.1191/1478088706qp063oa

Braun, V., & Clarke, V. (2019a). To saturate or not to saturate? Questioning data saturation as a useful concept for thematic analysis and sample-size rationales. *Qualitative Research in Sport, Exercise and Health*, *13*(2), 201–216. DOI: 10.1080/2159676X.2019.1704846

Braun, V., & Clarke, V. (2019b). Reflecting on reflexive thematic analysis. *Qualitative Research in Sport, Exercise and Health*, *11*(4), 589–597. DOI: 10.1080/2159676X.2019.1628806

Braun, V., & Clarke, V. (2022). Conceptual and design thinking for thematic analysis. *Qualitative Psychology*, *9*(1), 3.

Braun, V., Clarke, V., Hayfield, N., Davey, L., & Jenkinson, E. (2022). Doing reflexive thematic analysis of the chapter. In Bager-Charleson, S., & McBeath, A. (Eds.), *Supporting Research in Counselling and Psychotherapy: Qualitative, Quantitative, and Mixed Methods Research* (pp. 19–38). Springer International Publishing., DOI: 10.1007/978-3-031-13942-0_2

Brenner, H., & Letlch, L. (2023, January 16). *Emotional safety: What it is and why it's important.* Psychology Today. https://www.psychologytoday.com/us/blog/the-art-of-feeling/202301/emotional-safety-what-it-is-and-why-its-important

Bretherton, I. (1985). Attachment theory: Retrospect and prospect. *Monographs of the Society for Research in Child Development, 50*(1/2), 3–35. DOI: 10.2307/3333824

Bretherton, I. (2013). The origins of attachment theory: John Bowlby and Mary Ainsworth. In *Attachment theory* (pp. 45–84). Routledge., DOI: 10.1037/0012-1649.28.5.759

Britton, E. M., Marigold, D. C., & McGregor, I. (2024). Simple reflection exercises can build efficacy and reduce distress about relationship conflicts. *Personal Relationships, 31*(2), 556–577. DOI: 10.1111/pere.12545

Brooks, R. (2021). *Artificial intimacy: Virtual friends, digital lovers, and algorithmic matchmakers.* Columbia University Press.

Brumbaugh, C. C., & Doherty, J. K. (2024). Ideal partner characteristics in the 21st century: What are we looking for? In Hojjat, M., & Moyer, A. (Eds.), *Modern Relationships: Romance, Friendship, and Family in the 21st Century.* Oxford University Press., DOI: 10.1093/oso/9780197655504.003.0001

Buber, M. (1970). *I and thou* (W. Kaufmann, Trans.). Scribner. (Original work published 1923)

Bub, N. (2025). Algorithms of Affection: Exploring the impact of AI on 21st century romance. osnadocs.ub.uni-osnabrueck.de. https://doi.org/DOI: 10.48693/644

Buecker, S., Mund, M., Chwastek, S., Sostmann, M., & Luhmann, M. (2021). Is loneliness in emerging adults increasing over time? A preregistered cross-temporal meta-analysis and systematic review. *Psychological Bulletin, 147*(8), 787–805. DOI: 10.1037/bul0000332 PMID: 34898234

Buick, S. (2024). *In love with a chatbot: Exploring human-ai relationships from a fourth wave HCI perspective.* DIVA. https://uu.diva-portal.org/smash/record.jsf?pid=diva2%3A1882677&dswid=-1065

Buick, S. (2024). *In Love with a Chatbot: Exploring Human-AI Relationships from a Fourth Wave HCI perspective.* DIVA. https://uu.diva-portal.org/smash/record.jsf?pid=diva2%3A1882677&dswid=5124

Buil-Gil, D., & Zeng, Y. (2022). Meeting you was a fake: Investigating the increase in romance fraud during COVID-19. *Journal of Financial Crime, 29*(2), 460–475. DOI: 10.1108/JFC-02-2021-0042

Burgoon, J. K., Bonito, J. A., Ramirez, A.Jr, Dunbar, N. E., Kam, K., & Fischer, J. (2002). Testing the interactivity principle: Effects of mediation, propinquity, and verbal and nonverbal modalities in interpersonal interaction. *Journal of Communication, 52*(3), 657–677. DOI: 10.1111/j.1460-2466.2002.tb02567.x

Burleson, M. H., Roberts, N. A., Munson, A. A., Duncan, C. J., Randall, A. K., Ha, T., Sioni, S., & Mickelson, K. D. (2022). Feeling the Absence of Touch: Distancing, Distress, Regulation, and Relationships in the Context of COVID-19. *Journal of Social and Personal Relationships, 39*(1), 56–79. DOI: 10.1177/02654075211052696

Butler, J. (1990). *Gender trouble: Feminism and the subversion of identity*. Routledge.

Büttner, C. M., & Lutz, S. (2025). When does waiting for a reply turn into ghosting? Individual, relational, and situational predictors of feeling ignored in online messaging. *Computers in Human Behavior, 108774*, 108774. Advance online publication. DOI: 10.1016/j.chb.2025.108774

Byrne, D. (2022). A worked example of Braun and Clarke's approach to reflexive thematic analysis. *Quality & Quantity, 56*(3), 1391–1412. DOI: 10.1007/s11135-021-01182-y

Cabiddu, F., Moi, L., Patriotta, G., & Allen, D. G. (2022). Why do users trust algorithms? A review and conceptualization of initial trust and trust over time. *European Management Journal, 40*(5), 685–706. DOI: 10.1016/j.emj.2022.06.001

Cardelli, A., Matera, C., Policardo, G. R., Di Gesto, C., & Nerini, A. (2022). Not all that glitters is gold: Attractive partners provide joys and sorrows. *International Journal of Environmental Research and Public Health, 19*(20), 13526. DOI: 10.3390/ijerph192013526 PMID: 36294106

Carter, E. (2021). Distort, extort, deceive and exploit: Exploring the inner workings of a romance fraud. *The British Journal of Criminology. Centre for Crime and Justice Studies, 61*(2), 283–302. DOI: 10.1093/bjc/azaa072

Carter, E. (2024). *The Language of Romance crimes: Interactions of love, money, and threat.* Cambridge University Press., DOI: 10.1017/9781009273008

Cassidy, J., & Shaver, P. R. (1999). *Handbook of attachment: Theory, research, and clinical applications* (Vol. 236). Rough Guides., DOI: 10.1111/j.1475-6811.2004.00093.x

Castro, Á., Barrada, J. R., Ramos-Villagrasa, P. J., & Fernández-del-Río, E. (2020). Profiling Dating Apps Users: Sociodemographic and Personality Characteristics. *International Journal of Environmental Research and Public Health, 17*(10), 3653. DOI: 10.3390/ijerph17103653 PMID: 32455986

Castro-González, Á., Admoni, H., & Scassellati, B. (2016). Effects of form and motion on judgments of social robots animacy, likability, trustworthiness and unpleasantness. *International Journal of Human-Computer Studies*, *90*, 27–38. DOI: 10.1016/j.ijhcs.2016.02.004

Cave, S., & Dihal, K. (2021). AI will always love you: Three contradictions in imaginings of intimate relations with machines. In B. Dainton, W. Slocombe, & A. Tanyi (Eds.), *Minding the Future: Artificial Intelligence, Philosophical Visions and Science Fiction* (pp. 107–125). Springer International Publishing. DOI: 10.1007/978-3-030-64269-3_6

Cefai, S., & Couldry, N. (2019). Mediating the presence of others: Reconceptualising co-presence as mediated intimacy. *European Journal of Cultural Studies*, *22*(3), 291–308. DOI: 10.1177/1367549417743040

Chai, X. (2021). Exploring the Politics of Sensibilities That Promote Marriage and Reproduction Among Young Chinese Adults Residing in Urban Areas. In *Cities, Capitalism and the Politics of Sensibilities* (pp. 157–176). Springer International Publishing. DOI: 10.1007/978-3-030-58035-3_9

Chakravarti, A. (2023, June 29). Men using ChatGPT-like AI tools to sound witty, land better dates on Bumble and Hinge. *India Today*. https://www.indiatoday.in/technology/news/story/men-using-chatgpt-like-ai-tools-to-sound-witty-find-better-dates-on-bumble-and-hinge-2399430-2023-06-29

Chan, C. K. Y. (2023). A comprehensive AI policy education framework for university teaching and learning. *International Journal of Educational Technology in Higher Education*, *20*(1), 38. DOI: 10.1186/s41239-023-00408-3

Chang, C., Do, A., & Frederick, D. (2025). Rusbult's Investment Model. In Shackelford, T. K. (Ed.), *Encyclopedia of Sexual Psychology and Behavior* (pp. 1–4). Springer International Publishing., DOI: 10.1007/978-3-031-08956-5_2064-1

Chang, E. C., Liu, J., Yi, S., Jiang, X., Li, Q., Wang, R., Tian, W., Gao, X., Li, M., Lucas, A. G., & Chang, O. D. (2020). Loneliness, social problem solving, and negative affective symptoms: Negative problem orientation as a key mechanism. *Personality and Individual Differences*, *167*, 110235. DOI: 10.1016/j.paid.2020.110235

Chan, K. C. T., Li, X., Liu, Y., Chen, B., & Han, Z. (2025). "What is love?": Exploring the feeling rules and emotion work of Chinese users in human-AI romance. *International Journal of Intercultural Relations*, *108*, 102241. DOI: 10.1016/j.ijintrel.2025.102241

Chattaraman, V., Kwon, W.-S., Gilbert, J. E., & Ross, K. (2019). Should AI-Based, conversational digital assistants employ social- or task-oriented interaction style? A task-competency and reciprocity perspective for older adults. *Computers in Human Behavior*, *90*, 315–330. DOI: 10.1016/j.chb.2018.08.048

Chaturvedi, R., Verma, S., Das, R., & Dwivedi, Y. K. (2023). Social companionship with artificial intelligence: Recent trends and future avenues. *Technological Forecasting and Social Change*, *193*, 122634. DOI: 10.1016/j.techfore.2023.122634

Chaturvedi, R., Verma, S., & Srivastava, V. (2024). Empowering AI companions for enhanced relationship marketing. *California Management Review*, *66*(2), 65–90. DOI: 10.1177/00081256231215838

Chayka, K. (2023, November 13). Your A.I. companion will support you no matter what. *The New Yorker*. https://www.newyorker.com/culture/infinite-scroll/your-ai-companion-will-support-you-no-matter-what

Chen, Y.-P., Nishida, N., Nakayama, H., & Matsumoto, Y. (2024). Recent trends in personalized dialogue generation: A review of datasets, methodologies, and evaluations. *arXiv preprint arXiv:2405.17974*. /arXiv.2405.17974DOI: 10.63317/4b94kue5ke3h

Chen, J., Xue, J., Li, Y., & Luo, W. (2025). Impact of different employee-AI interaction: Instrumental vs. emotional support and gender differences. *International Journal of Human-Computer Interaction*, *41*(21), 13394–13407. DOI: 10.1080/10447318.2025.2474460

Chen, L., & Park, H. (2025). Asymmetric reciprocity: The psychological mechanics of emotional dependency in human–chatbot relationships. *Journal of Computer-Mediated Communication*, *30*(2), 145–162.

Chen, Q., Jing, Y., Gong, Y., & Tan, J. (2025). Will users fall in love with ChatGPT? a perspective from the triangular theory of love. *Journal of Business Research*, *186*, 114982. Advance online publication. DOI: 10.1016/j.jbusres.2024.114982

Chen, X., Kang, J., & Hu, C. (2024). Design of artificial intelligence companion chatbot. *Journal of New Media*, *6*(1), 1–16. DOI: 10.32604/jnm.2024.045833

Cheok, A. D., Levy, D., Karunanayaka, K., & Morisawa, Y. (2015). Love and sex with robots. In Nakatsu, R., Rauterberg, M., & Ciancarini, P. (Eds.), *Handbook of digital games and entertainment technologies* (pp. 1–26). Springer. DOI: 10.1007/978-981-4560-52-8_15-1

Cheok, A. D., & Zhang, E. Y. (2019a). *Human-Robot Intimate Relationships*. Springer., DOI: 10.1007/978-3-319-94730-3

Cheok, A. D., & Zhang, E. Y. (2019b). An overview of love between humans and artificial partners. In *Human–Robot Intimate Relationships* (pp. 1–21). Springer International Publishing., DOI: 10.1007/978-3-319-94730-3_1

Cherlin, A. J. (2004). The deinstitutionalization of American marriage. *Journal of Marriage and Family*, *66*(4), 848–861. DOI: 10.1111/j.0022-2445.2004.00058.x

Cherry, K. (2025, August 20). *Variable-Ratio Schedule Characteristics and Examples.* Verywell Mind. https://www.verywellmind.com/what-is-a-variable-ratio-schedule-2796012

Chethiyar, S. D. M., Vedamanikam, M., & Sameem, M. A. M. (2021). Losing The War Against Money Mule Recruitment: Persuasive Technique In Romance Scam. *Ilkogretim Online*, *20*(3), 2569–2585.

Cheung, C. M. K., Chiu, P.-Y., & Lee, M. K. O. (2011). Online social networks: Why do students use facebook? *Computers in Human Behavior*, *27*(4), 1337–1343. DOI: 10.1016/j.chb.2010.07.028

Chin, H., Song, H., Baek, G., Shin, M., Jung, C., Cha, M., Choi, J., & Cha, C. (2023). The potential of chatbots for emotional support and promoting mental wellbeing in different cultures: Mixed methods study. *Journal of Medical Internet Research*, *25*, e51712. DOI: 10.2196/51712 PMID: 37862063

Chin, K., Edelstein, R. S., & Vernon, P. A. (2018). Attached to dating apps: Attachment orientations and preferences for dating apps. *Mobile Media & Communication*, *7*(1), 41–59. DOI: 10.1177/2050157918770696

Chisom, O. B. (2021). Effects of modern dating applications on healthy offline intimate relationships during the COVID-19 pandemic: A review of the Tinder dating application. *Advances in Journalism and Communication*, *9*(01), 12–38. DOI: 10.4236/ajc.2021.91002

Choi, S. Y. (2023). *When You Can't Trust Your Own Eyes: Deepfakes and Metacognitive Experiences in Manipulative AI-Mediated Communication* (Doctoral dissertation, University of Southern California).

Chuang, J. Y. (2021). Romance scams: Romantic imagery and transcranial direct current stimulation. *Frontiers in Psychiatry*, *12*, 738874. DOI: 10.3389/fpsyt.2021.738874 PMID: 34707523

Ciriello, R., Chen, A. Y., Rubinsztein, Z., Vaast, E., & Hannon, O. (2025). AI, all too human AI: Navigating the companionship/alienation dialectic. Article ECIS2025-1725.

Ciriello, R., Hannon, O., Chen, A., & Vaast, E. (2024). *Ethical tensions in human-AI companionship: A dialectical inquiry into Replika*. DOI: 10.24251/HICSS.2024.058

Ciriello, R. F., Chen, A. Y., & Rubinsztein, Z. A. (2025). Compassionate AI design, governance, and use. *IEEE Transactions on Technology and Society*, *6*(3), 270–275. Advance online publication. DOI: 10.1109/TTS.2025.3538125

CNN. (2026). *Woman codes ChatGPT to be her "boyfriend." See what happened.* Cnn.com. https://www.cnn.com/2024/07/08/business/video/ai-boyfriend-chatgpt-digvid

Coffey, J. K., Bond, D. K., Stern, J. A., & Van Why, N. (2022). Sexual experiences and attachment styles in online and offline dating contexts. *International Journal of Sexual Health : Official Journal of the World Association for Sexual Health*, *34*(4), 665–678. DOI: 10.1080/19317611.2022.2110349 PMID: 36776752

Cole, R. (2024). A qualitative investigation of the emotional, physiological, financial, and legal consequences of online romance scams in the United States. *Journal of Economic Criminology*, *6*, 100108.

Coluccia, A., Pozza, A., Ferretti, F., Carabellese, F., Masti, A., & Gualtieri, G. (2020). Online romance scams: Relational dynamics and psychological characteristics of the victims and scammers. A scoping review. *Clinical Practice and Epidemiology in Mental Health*, *16*, 24. 10.2174%2F1745017902016010024 PMID: 32508967

Conklin, S., Barreto, D., & Dorgan, T. (2019). The impact of social media on social presence. *Australian Educational Computing*, *34*(1). https://www.researchgate.net/publication/344958781_The_impact_of_social_media_on_social_presence

Connell, R. (2005). *Masculinities* (2nd ed.). Cambridge Polity. (Original work published 1995)

Costa, P. T.Jr, & McCrae, R. R. (1992). The five-factor model of personality and its relevance to personality disorders. *Journal of Personality Disorders*, *6*(4), 343–359. DOI: 10.1521/pedi.1992.6.4.343

Courtois, C., & Timmermans, E. (2018). Cracking the Tinder code: An experience sampling approach to the dynamics and impact of platform governing algorithms. *Journal of Computer-Mediated Communication*, *23*(1), 1–16. DOI: 10.1093/jcmc/zmx001

Creative Collaboration. (2025, June 10). *Match report: Many more singles are using AI to date in 2025*. https://ccstartup.com/blog/2025/06/10/match-report-many-more-singles-are-using-ai-to-date-in-2025/

Croes, E. A., Antheunis, M. L., van der Lee, C., & de Wit, J. M. (2024). Digital confessions: The willingness to disclose intimate information to a chatbot and its impact on emotional well-being. *Interacting with Computers, 36*(5), 279–292. DOI: 10.1093/iwc/iwae016

Cross, C., & Holt, T. J. (2022). Open Access: The Use of Military Profiles in Romance Fraud Schemes. In *The New Technology of Financial Crime* (pp. 104-125). Routledge.

Cross, C., Holt, K., & O'Malley, R. L. (2024). "If U don't pay they will share the pics": Exploring sextortion in the context of romance fraud. In *Scams, Cons, Frauds, and Deceptions* (pp. 10-31). Routledge.

Cross, C. (2022). Using artificial intelligence (AI) and deepfakes to deceive victims: The need to rethink current romance fraud prevention messaging. *Crime Prevention and Community Safety, 24*(1), 30–41.

Cross, C. (2023). "I knew it was a scam": Understanding the triggers for recognizing romance fraud. *Criminology & Public Policy, 22*(4), 613–637. DOI: 10.1111/1745-9133.12645

Cross, C., & Layt, R. (2022). "I suspect that the pictures are stolen": Romance fraud, identity crime, and responding to suspicions of inauthentic identities. *Social Science Computer Review, 40*(4), 955–973.

Cui, G., Lockee, B., & Meng, C. (2013). Building modern online social presence: A review of social presence theory and its instructional design implications for future trends. *Education and Information Technologies, 18*(4), 661–685. DOI: 10.1007/s10639-012-9192-1

Cummings, J. J., & Wertz, E. E. (2022). Capturing social presence: Concept explication through an empirical analysis of social presence measures. *Journal of Computer-Mediated Communication, 28*(1), zmac027. Advance online publication. DOI: 10.1093/jcmc/zmac027

Currado, C. (2024, April 14). *Attachment styles, meet dating apps - the relationship agency*. The Relationship Agency. https://www.therelationshipagency.com/blog/attachment-styles-meet-dating-apps

Curry, D. (2026, January 7). *Dating App Revenue and Usage Statistics (2026) - Business of Apps*. Business of Apps. https://www.businessofapps.com/data/dating-app-market/

Cynthia, V. (2021). Marriage patterns. In *EBSCO*. EBSCO Research. https://www.ebsco.com/research-starters/social-sciences-and-humanities/marriage-patterns

Cyr, D., Head, M., Larios, H., & Pan, B. (2009). Exploring human images in website design: A multi-method approach. *Management Information Systems Quarterly*, *33*(3), 539–566. DOI: 10.2307/20650308

Danaher, J. (2020). *Automation and utopia: Human flourishing in a world without work*. Harvard University Press.

Dar, A. R., & Gul, M. (2025). The "less is better" paradox and consumer behaviour: A systematic review of choice overload and its marketing implications. *Qualitative Market Research*, *28*(1), 122–145. DOI: 10.1108/QMR-01-2024-0006

Datey, I. (2023). *"Just Like, Risking Your Life Here": Envisioning AI As a Supportive Agent to Bolster Women's Strategies for Assessing Risk of Harm in Online Dating (Doctoral dissertation).*

David, D., & Spatola, N. (2025). Effectance Motivation: Unpredictability and Uncontrollability in the Anthropomorphism Strategy. *International Journal of Social Robotics*, *17*(11), 2435–2444. Advance online publication. DOI: 10.1007/s12369-025-01306-6

De Francia, K., Kim, J., & Smith, R. (2024). Chatbots as attachment figures: A longitudinal study of Replika users. *Computers in Human Behavior*, *152*, 108064. DOI: 10.1016/j.chb.2023.108064

De Freitas, J., Oğuz-Uğuralp, Z., Uğuralp, A. K., & Puntoni, S. (2025). AI companions reduce loneliness. *The Journal of Consumer Research*, •••, ucaf040. Advance online publication. DOI: 10.1093/jcr/ucaf040

De Ridder, S. (2021). The datafication of intimacy: Mobile dating apps, dependency, and everyday life. *Television & New Media*, *23*(6), 593–609. DOI: 10.1177/15274764211052660

De Togni, G. (2025). Hearts meet wires: Navigating the ethical and social implications of care robotics. In *The Future of Humans and Emotional Machines* (pp. 51–63). Routledge. DOI: 10.4324/9781003570653-7

Della Longa, L., Valori, I., & Farroni, T. (2022). Interpersonal affective touch in a virtual world: Feeling the social presence of others to overcome loneliness. *Frontiers in Psychology*, *12*, 795283. DOI: 10.3389/fpsyg.2021.795283 PMID: 35087455

Demopoulos, A. (2025, September 9). The women in love with AI companions: 'I vowed to my chatbot that I wouldn't leave him.' *The Guardian*. https://www.theguardian.com/technology/2025/sep/09/ai-chatbot-love-relationships?CMP=share_btn_url

Deng, Y., Lei, W., Huang, M., & Chua, T.-S. (2023). Goal awareness for conversational AI: proactivity, non-collaborativity, and beyond.

Depounti, I., Saukko, P., & Natale, S. (2023). Ideal technologies, ideal women: AI and gender imaginaries in Redditors' discussions on the Replika bot girlfriend. *Media Culture & Society*, *45*(4), 720–736. DOI: 10.1177/01634437221119021

Dewitte, P. (2024). Better alone than in bad company: Addressing the risks of companion chatbots through data protection by design. *Computer Law & Security Review*, *54*, 106019. DOI: 10.1016/j.clsr.2024.106019

Dholakia, R., Zhao, M., Dholakia, N., & Fortin, D. (2000). Interactivity and revisits to websites: a theoretical framework. *Retrieved June, 17*, 2002. https://www.researchgate.net/publication/236784786_Interactivity_and_revisits_to_websites_a_theoretical_framework

DiCicco-Bloom, B., & Crabtree, B. F. (2006). The qualitative research interview. *Medical Education*, *40*(4), 314–321. DOI: 10.1111/j.1365-2929.2006.02418.x PMID: 16573666

Dignan, L. (2024, February). *Match's big generative AI plans revolve around Tinder, Hinge, alleviating dating pain.* Constellation Research. https://www.constellationr.com/insights/news/matchs-big-generative-ai-plans-revolve-around-tinder-hinge-alleviating-dating-pain

Dinh, R., Gildersleve, P., Blex, C., & Yasseri, T. (2021). Computational courtship understanding the evolution of online dating through large-scale data analysis. *Journal of Computational Social Science*, *5*(1), 401–426. DOI: 10.1007/s42001-021-00132-w

Djufril, R., Frampton, J. R., & Knobloch-Westerwick, S. (2025). Love, marriage, pregnancy: Commitment processes in romantic relationships with AI chatbots. *Computers in Human Behavior: Artificial Humans*, *4*, 100155. Advance online publication. DOI: 10.1016/j.chbah.2025.100155

Dong, K., & Ding, L. (2025). The Emotional Trap of "AI Lovers": Human–AI Virtual Intimacy and Its Ethical Dilemmas in The Intelligent Era. *Journal of Northwestern Polytechnical University*(4), 100-107. https://link.cnki.net/urlid/61.1352.C.20250527.1559.002

Döring, N., Le, T. D., Vowels, L. M., Vowels, M. J., & Marcantonio, T. L. (2024). The impact of artificial intelligence on human sexuality: A five-year literature review 2020–2024. *Current Sexual Health Reports*, *17*(1), 4. DOI: 10.1007/s11930-024-00397-y

Drabble, L. A., Wootton, A. R., Veldhuis, C. B., Riggle, E. D. B., Rostosky, S. S., Lannutti, P. J., Balsam, K. F., & Hughes, T. L. (2021). Perceived psychosocial impacts of legalized same-sex marriage: A scoping review of sexual minority adults' experiences. *PLoS One*, *16*(5), e0249125. DOI: 10.1371/journal.pone.0249125 PMID: 33956825

Dreijers, G., & Rudziša, V. (2020). Devices of Textual Illusion: Victimization in Romance Scam E-Letters. *Research in Language*, *18*(1), 1–13.

Duportail, J. (2017). *I asked Tinder for my data. It sent me 800 pages of my deepest, darkest secrets*. The Guardian. https://www.theguardian.com/technology/2017/sep/26/tinder-personal-data-dating-app-messages-hacked-sold

Durnová, A., & Mohammadi, E. (2021). Intimacy, home, and emotions in the era of the pandemic. *Sociology Compass*, *15*(4), e12852. DOI: 10.1111/soc4.12852 PMID: 34230835

Duvieu, P. (2025, February 11). *Lovers or friends: the boom of digital relationships with an AI | Luxus Magazine*. Luxus Magazine. https://magazine.luxus-plus.com/en/lovers-or-friends-the-boom-of-digital-relationships-with-an-ai/

Dziri, N., Milton, S., Yu, M., Zaiane, O., & Reddy, S. (2022, July). On the Origin of Hallucinations in Conversational Models: Is it the Datasets or the Models? In M. Carpuat, M.-C. de Marneffe, & I. V. Meza Ruiz, *Proceedings of the 2022 Conference of the North American Chapter of the Association for Computational Linguistics: Human Language Technologies* Seattle, United States.

Ebihara, M. M. (1968). *Svay: a Khmer village in Cambodia*. Cornell University Press.

Eichenberg, C., Schott, M., Decker, O., & Sindelar, B. (2017). Attachment style and internet Addiction: An online survey. *Journal of Medical Internet Research*, *19*(5), e170. DOI: 10.2196/jmir.6694 PMID: 28526662

Elbadawy, H., & Kwon, W.-S. (2025). Beyond the response: How timing and context shape empathy, responsiveness, and social. *Human-Computer Interaction & Emerging Technologies*, *195*, 241. DOI: 10.54941/ahfe1006242

Elliott, A. (2022). *Algorithmic intimacy: The digital revolution in personal relationships*. John Wiley & Sons.

Epley, N., Waytz, A., & Cacioppo, J. T. (2007). On seeing human: A three-factor theory of anthropomorphism. *Psychological Review*, *114*(4), 864–886. DOI: 10.1037/0033-295X.114.4.864 PMID: 17907867

Equaldex. (2023, July 21). *LGBT equality index*. Equaldex. https://www.equaldex.com/equality-index

Erber, R., & Erber, M. W. (2013). Mood and processing: A view from a self-regulation perspective of the chapter. In G. L. C. Leonard L. Martin (Ed.), *Theories of mood and cognition* (pp. 63-84). Psychology Press. DOI: 10.4324/9781410605733

Eseadi, C., Ogbonna, C. S., Otu, M. S., & Ede, M. O. (2021). Hello pretty, hello handsome!: Exploring the menace of online dating and romance scam in Africa. In *Crime, mental health and the criminal justice system in Africa* (pp. 63–87). Springer.

Etzrodt, K., Kim, J., van der Goot, M., Prahl, A., Choi, M., Craig, M., Marco Dehnert, M., Engesser, S., Frehmann, K., Grande, L., Leo-Liu, J., Liu, D., Mooshammer, S., Rambukkana, N., Rogge, A., Sikströma, P., Son, R., Wilkenfeld, N., Xu, K., & Edwards, C. (2024). What HMC teaches us about authenticity. *Human-Machine Communication*, *8*, 227–251. DOI: 10.30658/hmc.8.11

Executive Office of the President. (2016). *Artificial Intelligence, automation, and the economy* (p. 59). Executive Office of the President https://obamawhitehouse.archives.gov/blog/2016/12/20/artificial-intelligence-automation-and-economy

Fan, X. (2025). *The "Report on Singles and Relationships of Young People in the Underserved Markets" has been released.* https://news.cyol.com/gb/articles/2025-01/18/content_4wgae7SWn8.html

Feng, B., Li, S., & Li, N. (2016). Is a profile worth a thousand words? How online support-seeker's profile features may influence the quality of received support messages. *Communication Research*, *43*(2), 253–276. DOI: 10.1177/0093650213510942

Ferrara, A. (2021). *Authenticity as reflexive self-concordance*. Routledge.

Ferrari, G. (2013). Agalmatofilia. L'amore per le statue nel mondo antico: l'Afrodite di Cnido e il caso di Pigmalione. *DOAJ (DOAJ: Directory of Open Access Journals)*. DOI: 10.6092/issn.2038-6184/3452

Field, T. (2020). The power of touch: Oxytocin, the "love hormone," is released by massage therapy. In *A Multidisciplinary Approach to Embodiment* (pp. 118–120). Routledge., DOI: 10.4324/9780429352379-24

Finance, Y. (2024). *MiniMax: China's AI companion giant, a rising force in the global market*. https://finance.sina.com.cn/money/bond/2024-07-30/doc-incfxety7988686.shtml

Finlay, L., & Gough, B. (2008). *Reflexivity: A practical guide for researchers in health and social sciences*. John Wiley & Sons.

Fırıncı, Y. (2024). Decolonial Artificial Intelligence; Algorithmic Fairness in Alignment with Turkish and Islamic Values. *Marmara Üniversitesi İlahiyat Fakültesi Dergisi*, *67*(67), 250–279. DOI: 10.15370/maruifd.1565884

Fiveable Content Team. (2025). Cultural shift definition. In *AP World History: Modern Key Term*. Fiveable Content Team. https://fiveable.me/key-terms/ap-world/cultural-shift

Fletcher, R., Tzani, C., & Ioannou, M. (2024). The dark side of Artificial Intelligence – Risks arising in dating applications. *Assessment & Development Matters*, *16*(1), 17–23. DOI: 10.53841/bpsadm.2024.16.1.17

Flores, A. R. (2021). *Social acceptance of LGBTI people in 175 countries and locations 1981 to 2020*. The Williams Institute., https://williamsinstitute.law.ucla.edu/publications/global-acceptance-index-lgbt/

Floridi, L. (2023). *Ethics, governance, and policies for artificial intelligence*. Springer. DOI: 10.1093/oso/9780198883098.001.0001

Folk, D. P., Wu, C., & Heine, S. J. (2025). Cultural variation in attitudes toward social chatbots. *Journal of Cross-Cultural Psychology*, *56*(3), 219–239. DOI: 10.1177/00220221251317950 PMID: 40160265

Fox, J., & Gambino, A. (2021). Relationship development with humanoid social robots: Applying interpersonal theories to human–robot interaction. *Cyberpsychology, Behavior, and Social Networking*, *24*(5), 294–299. DOI: 10.1089/cyber.2020.0181 PMID: 33434097

Fraley, R. C. (2019). Attachment in adulthood: Recent developments, emerging debates, and future directions. *Annual Review of Psychology*, *70*(1), 401–422. DOI: 10.1146/annurev-psych-010418-102813 PMID: 30609910

Fraley, R. C., & Roisman, G. I. (2019). The development of adult attachment styles: Four lessons. *Current Opinion in Psychology*, *25*, 26–30. DOI: 10.1016/j.copsyc.2018.02.008 PMID: 29510301

Frankfurt, H. (2004). *The reasons of love*. Princeton University Press.

Freedom House. (2023). *Freedom on the Net 2023*. Cambodia Country Report. https://freedomhouse.org/country/cambodia/freedom-net/2023

Freitas, J., Castelo, N., Uğuralp, A., & Uğuralp, Z. (2024). *Lessons from an app update at Replika AI: Identity discontinuity in human-AI relationships*. DOI: 10.2139/ssrn.4976449

Frenkenberg, A., & Hochman, G. (2025). It's Scary to Use It, It's Scary to Refuse It: The Psychological Dimensions of AI Adoption - Anxiety, Motives, and Dependency. *Systems*, *13*(2), 82. DOI: 10.3390/systems13020082

Friedman, B., & Hendry, D. (2019). *Value sensitive design: Shaping technology with moral imagination*. MIT Press. DOI: 10.7551/mitpress/7585.001.0001

Furman, J., & Seamans, R. (2019). AI and the economy. *Innovation Policy and the Economy*, *19*, 161–191. DOI: 10.1086/699936

Gao, C. (2024, August 27). *XiaoHongShu (RED): China's rising social platform – impact, user demographics and marketing solutions | the egg*. The Egg. https://www.theegg.com/social/china/xiaohongshu-red-chinas-rising-social-platform-impact-user-demographics-and-marketing-solutions/

Gao, L., Chen, O., Lee, R., Feamster, N., Tan, C., & Chetty, M. (2025). "I cannot write this because it violates our content policy": understanding content moderation policies and user experiences in generative AI products. *ArXiv*. https://doi.org//arXiv.2506.14018DOI: 10.48550

Gao, Z. (2024). Why does AI companionship go wrong? *International Journal of Information Ethics*, *34*(1). Advance online publication. DOI: 10.29173/irie526

Gauci, C., & Vella, M. G. (2025). Romance fraud: Its repercussions on victims' wellbeing. *Women & Criminal Justice*, •••, 1–37.

Ge, L., & Hu, T. (2025). Gamifying intimacy: AI-driven affective engagement and human-virtual human relationships. *Media Culture & Society*, *01634437251337239*(6), 1265–1278. Advance online publication. DOI: 10.1177/01634437251337239

Ge, R. (2024). From pseudo-intimacy to cyber romance: A study of human and AI companions emotion shaping and engagement practices. *Communications in Humanities Research*, *52*(1), 211–221. DOI: 10.54254/2753-7064/2024.19122

Gerrig, R. (2018). *Experiencing narrative worlds*. Routledge., DOI: 10.4324/9780429500633

Gertz, N. (2023). *Technological nihilism: Foundations of post-human intimacy*. Routledge.

Gesell, N., Niklas, F., Schmiedeler, S., & Segerer, R. (2020). Mindfulness and romantic relationship outcomes: The mediating role of conflict resolution styles and closeness. *Mindfulness*, *11*(10), 2314–2324. DOI: 10.1007/s12671-020-01449-9

Ghani, M. M., Mustafa, W. A. W., Hashim, M. E. A., Hanafi, H. F., & Bakhtiar, D. L. S. (2022). Impact of generative AI on communication patterns in social media. *Journal of Advanced Research in Computing and Applications, 26*(1), 22–34.

Giddens, A. (2023). Modernity and self-identity. In *Social theory re-wired* (pp. 477–484). Routledge., DOI: 10.4324/9781003320609-62

Gilbert, S. B. (2016). Perceived realism of virtual environments depends on authenticity. *Presence (Cambridge, Mass.), 25*(4), 322–324. DOI: 10.1162/PRES_a_00276

Gillath, O., Ai, T., Branicky, M. S., Keshmiri, S., Davison, R. B., & Spaulding, R. (2021). Attachment and trust in artificial intelligence. *Computers in Human Behavior, 115*, 106607. DOI: 10.1016/j.chb.2020.106607

Gill, R. (2016). Post-postfeminism?: New feminist visibilities in postfeminist times. *Feminist Media Studies, 16*(4), 610–630. https://www.tandfonline.com/doi/full/10.1080/14680777.2016.1193293. DOI: 10.1080/14680777.2016.1193293

Glass, B. (2025, May 30). *Survey: Plenty of skepticism of AI in dating apps, especially among women, survey finds | Communication Research Center*. Boston University. https://sites.bu.edu/crc/2025/05/30/survey-plenty-of-skepticism-of-ai-in-dating-apps-especially-among-women-survey-finds/

Glikson, E., & Woolley, A. W. (2020). Human trust in artificial intelligence: Review of empirical research. *The Academy of Management Annals, 14*(2), 627–660. DOI: 10.5465/annals.2018.0057

Global Dating Insights. (2025, June 11). *Use of AI in online dating surges 300% according to new Match report*. https://www.globaldatinginsights.com/featured/use-of-ai-in-online-dating-surges-300-according-to-new-match-report/

Goffman, E. (1949). Presentation of self in everyday life. *American Journal of Sociology, 55*(1), 6–7.

Goldie, P. (2023). *The mess inside: Narrative, emotion, and the mind*. Oxford University Press.

Gooch, D., & Watts, L. (2014). The impact of social presence on feelings of closeness in personal relationships. *Interacting with Computers, 27*(6), 661–674. DOI: 10.1093/iwc/iwu020

Gordon-Tapiero, A. (2025). A liability framework for AI companions. DOI: 10.2139/ssrn.5172386

Grachev, M., & Rakitsky, B. (2013). Historic horizons of Frederick Taylor's scientific management. *Journal of Management History, 19*(4), 512–527. DOI: 10.1108/JMH-05-2012-0043

Graff, M. PhD. (2022, April 20). A closer look at attachment style and choice of dating apps. *Psychology Today.* https://www.psychologytoday.com/us/blog/love-digitally/202204/who-uses-which-dating-apps-and-why

Greco, A. (2024, July 21). *40% of people would consider dating an AI partner, survey says.* www.top10.com. https://www.top10.com/dating/ai-dating-survey

Green, R. W. (2025, October 23). *Love in the Time of AI: Romantic Relationships with Artificial Companions.* Medium. https://medium.com/@custom_aistudio/love-in-the-time-of-ai-romantic-relationships-with-artificial-companions-dd347981cbc8

Gressel, G., Pankajakshan, R., Rozenfeld, S., Li, L., Franceschini, I., Achuthan, K., & Mirsky, Y. (2025). Love, Lies, and Language Models: Investigating AI's Role in Romance-Baiting Scams. *arXiv preprint arXiv:2512.16280.*

Groggel, A. (2023). The Power of a : Emojis Reducing Ambiguity in Digitally Mediated Romantic Encounters. *Symbolic Interaction, 46*(4), 440–472. DOI: 10.1002/symb.668

Grossman, S. (2023, February 8). *I dated an AI app for 3 months to help ease my anxious attachment style. Now my real-life girlfriend and I are stronger than ever.* Business Insider. https://www.businessinsider.com/dating-ai-robot-app-girlfriend-anxious-attachment-style-2023-2

Gubbala, S., Poushter, J., & Huang, C. (2023, November 27). How people around the-world view same-sex marriage. *Pew Research Center.* https://www.pewresearch.org/short-reads/2023/11/27/how-people-around-the-world-view-same-sex-marriage/

Guerreiro, J., & Loureiro, S. M. C. (2023). I am attracted to my cool smart assistant! Analyzing attachment-aversion in AI-human relationships. *Journal of Business Research, 161*, 113863. DOI: 10.1016/j.jbusres.2023.113863

Guillou, A. Y. (2012). An alternative memory of the Khmer Rouge genocide: The dead of the mass graves and the land guardian spirits [Neak ta]. *South East Asia Research, 20*(2), 207–226. DOI: 10.5367/sear.2012.0102

Guillou, A. Y. (2017). Khmer potent places: Pāramī and the localisation of Buddhism and monarchy in Cambodia. *The Asia Pacific Journal of Anthropology, 18*(5), 421–443. DOI: 10.1080/14442213.2017.1375553

Gui, T. (2023). Coping with parental pressure to get married: Perspectives from Chinese "leftover women". *Journal of Family Issues*, *44*(8), 2118–2137. DOI: 10.1177/0192513X211071053

Gulledge, A. K., Gulledge, M. H., & Stahmannn, R. F. (2003). Romantic physical affection types and relationship satisfaction. *The American Journal of Family Therapy*, *31*(4), 233–242. DOI: 10.1080/01926180390201936

Gunawardena, C. N. (1995). Social presence theory and implications for interaction and collaborative learning in computer conferences. *International Journal of Educational Telecommunications*, *1*(2), 147–166.

Guo, W., Chen, H., & Peng, S. (2025). The Concept and Formation Pathways of Human-Smart Object Attachment: A Case Study of Wearable Smart Objects. *Frontiers of Computer Science*, *7*, 1642265. DOI: 10.3389/fcomp.2025.1642265

Gupta, A., Hathwar, D., & Vijayakumar, A. (2020). Introduction to AI chatbots. *International Journal of Engineering Research & Technology (Ahmedabad)*, *9*(7). Advance online publication. DOI: 10.17577/IJERTV9IS070143

Gupta, S., Tarantino, M., & Sanner, C. (2024). A scoping review of research on polyamory and consensual non-monogamy: Implications for a more inclusive familyscience. *Journal of Family Theory & Review*, *16*(2), 151–190. DOI: 10.1111/jftr.12546

Gutiérrez, J. L. M. (2024). On actor-network theory and algorithms: ChatGPT and the new power relationships in the age of AI. *AI and Ethics*, *4*(4), 1071–1084. DOI: 10.1007/s43681-023-00314-4

Haenlein, M., & Kaplan, A. (2019). A brief history of artificial intelligence: On the past, present, and future of artificial intelligence. *California Management Review*, *61*(4), 5–14. DOI: 10.1177/0008125619864925

Hall, S. (1997). Representation: Cultural Representation and Signifying Practices. *Sage (Atlanta, Ga.)*.

Hamamura, T. (2012). Are cultures becoming individualistic? A cross-temporal comparison of individualism-collectivism in the United States and Japan. *Personality and Social Psychology Review: An Official Journal of the Society for Personality and Social Psychology. Personality and Social Psychology Review*, *16*(1), 3–24. DOI: 10.1177/1088868311411587 PMID: 21700795

Hamamura, T., Bettache, K., & Xu, Y. (2018). Individualism and collectivism. In Zeigler-Hill, V., & Shackelford, T. (Eds.), *The sage handbook of personality and individual differences* (pp. 365–382). SAGE Publications Ltd., DOI: 10.4135/9781526470317.n20

Hanckel, B. (2023). Queer youth and digital technologies in Southeast Asia. In Hanckel, B. (Ed.), *LGBT+ youth and emerging technologies in Southeast Asia: Designing for wellbeing* (pp. 1–31). Springer., DOI: 10.1007/978-981-99-4394-4_1

Hancock, J. T., & Bailenson, J. N. (2024). The psychology of AI-mediated communication. *Nature Reviews Psychology*, *3*, 12–25.

Han, S., Min, J., & Lee, H. (2015). Antecedents of social presence and gratification of social connection needs in SNS: A study of Twitter users and their mobile and non-mobile usage. *International Journal of Information Management*, *35*(4), 459–471. DOI: 10.1016/j.ijinfomgt.2015.04.004

Hansen, M. H., & Pang, C. (2018). In Scharff, D. E., & Varvinn, S. (Eds.), *"Idealising individual choice: Work, love, and family in the eyes of young, rural Chinese," in Psychoanalysis in China* (pp. 3–20). Routledge.

Haq, S. N. (2024). The effects of urbanization on traditional family structures. *Journal of Social Signs Review*, *2*(3), 70–79. https://socialsignsreivew.com/index.php/12/article/view/33

Hartmann, T., & Hofer, M. (2022). I know it is not real (and that matters) media awareness vs. presence in a parallel processing account of the VR experience [Hypothesis and Theory]. *Frontiers in Virtual Reality, Volume 3 - 2022*. DOI: 10.3389/frvir.2022.694048

Hastuti, N. T. (2025). Redefining emotional presence: Lived experiences of AI-mediated romantic relationships with chatbot-based virtual companions. *Humanexus: Journal of Humanistic and Social Connection Studies, 1*(6), 245–252. https://journals.ai-mrc.com/humanexus/article/view/444

Hawkley, L. C., & Cacioppo, J. T. (2010). Loneliness matters: A theoretical and empirical review of consequences and mechanisms. *Annals of Behavioral Medicine*, *40*(2), 218–227. DOI: 10.1007/s12160-010-9210-8 PMID: 20652462

Heider, F., & Simmel, M. (1944). An experimental study of apparent behavior. *The American Journal of Psychology*, *57*(2), 243–259. DOI: 10.2307/1416950

Heiss, A. (2023). *Not Meeting Mr Right*. Simon and Schuster.

Helm, J. M., Swiergosz, A. M., Haeberle, H. S., Karnuta, J. M., Schaffer, J. L., Krebs, V. E., Spitzer, A. I., & Ramkumar, P. N. (2020). Machine learning and artificial intelligence: Definitions, applications, and future directions. *Current Reviews in Musculoskeletal Medicine*, *13*(1), 69–76. DOI: 10.1007/s12178-020-09600-8 PMID: 31983042

Heng, S., & Zhang, Z. (2025). Attachment anxiety and problematic use of conversational artificial intelligence: Mediation of emotional attachment and moderation of anthropomorphic tendencies. *Psychology Research and Behavior Management*, *18*, 1775–1785. DOI: 10.2147/PRBM.S531805 PMID: 40873934

Henrich, J., Heine, S. J., & Norenzayan, A. (2010). The weirdest people in the world? *Behavioral and Brain Sciences*, *33*(2-3), 61–135. DOI: 10.1017/S0140525X0999152X PMID: 20550733

Heppner, H., Schiffhauer, B., & Seelmeyer, U. (2024). Conveying chatbot personality through conversational cues in social media messages. *Computers in Human Behavior: Artificial Humans*, *2*(1), 100044. DOI: 10.1016/j.chbah.2024.100044

Herbener, A. B., & Damholdt, M. F. (2025). Are lonely youngsters turning to chatbots for companionship? The relationship between chatbot usage and social connectedness in Danish high-school students. *International Journal of Human-Computer Studies*, *196*, 103409. DOI: 10.1016/j.ijhcs.2024.103409

Hermann, E. (2022). Anthropomorphized artificial intelligence, attachment, and consumer behavior. *Marketing Letters*, *33*(1), 157–162. DOI: 10.1007/s11002-021-09587-3

Herrera, L. D. (2025). Romance Scam Victimization: A Survey-Based Examination of Financial, Psychological, and Reporting Factors. In *2025 13th International Symposium on Digital Forensics and Security (ISDFS)* (pp. 1-6). IEEE.

Higashi, S., Ampririt, P., Qafzezi, E., Ikeda, M., Matsuo, K., & Barolli, L. (2025). A fuzzy-based system for assessment of emotional trust: A comparison study of two implemented models. *International journal of grid and utility computing, 16*(2), 83–93. DOI: 10.1504/IJGUC.2025.145172

High, A. C., Ruppel, E. K., McEwan, B., & Caughlin, J. P. (2022). Computer-Mediated communication and well-being in the age of social media: A systematic review. *Journal of Social and Personal Relationships*, *40*(2), 026540752211064. DOI: 10.1177/02654075221106449

Hill, J., Randolph Ford, W., & Farreras, I. G. (2015). Real conversations with artificial intelligence: A comparison between human–human online conversations and human–chatbot conversations. *Computers in Human Behavior*, *49*, 245–250. DOI: 10.1016/j.chb.2015.02.026

Ho, A., Hancock, J., & Miner, A. S. (2018). Psychological, relational, and emotional effects of self-disclosure after conversations with a chatbot. *Journal of Communication*, *68*(4), 712–733. DOI: 10.1093/joc/jqy026 PMID: 30100620

Hochschild, A. R. (1983). *The managed heart: Commercialization of human feeling*. University of California Press.

Hockenbury, D. H., & Hockenbury, S. E. (2010). *Psychology* (5th ed.). Worth Publishers., https://psycnet.apa.org/record/2009-14432-000

Hoefinger, H. (2013). Transnational intimacies: Examples from Cambodia. In Sanger, T., & Taylor, Y. (Eds.), *Mapping intimacies: Relations, exchanges, affects* (pp. 35–53). Springer., DOI: 10.1057/9781137313423_3

Hoffman, R. R.. (2023). The psychology of trust in AI: A multidimensional framework. *Journal of Cognitive Engineering and Decision Making*, *17*(1), 10–32.

Ho, J. Q., Hu, M., Chen, T. X., & Hartanto, A. (2025). Potential and pitfalls of romantic Artificial Intelligence (AI) companions: A systematic review. *Computers in Human Behavior Reports*, *19*, 100715. DOI: 10.1016/j.chbr.2025.100715

Holland, N. N. (2003). The willing suspension of disbelief: A neuro-psychoanalytic view. *PsyART*. https://psyartjournal.com/article/show/n_holland-the_willing_suspension_of_disbelief_a_ne

Holt-Lunstad, J., Robles, T. F., & Sbarra, D. A. (2017). Advancing social connection as a public health priority in the United States. *The American Psychologist*, *72*(6), 517–530. DOI: 10.1037/amp0000103 PMID: 28880099

Holt-Lunstad, J., Smith, T. B., Baker, M., Harris, T., & Stephenson, D. (2015). Loneliness and social isolation as risk factors for mortality: A meta-analytic review. *Perspectives on Psychological Science*, *10*(2), 227–237. DOI: 10.1177/1745691614568352 PMID: 25910392

Honneth, A. (2022). *Reification: A new look at an old idea*. Oxford University Press.

Horney, K. (1999). The Neurotic Personality of Our Time. In. DOI: 10.4324/9781315010533

Horton, D., & Wohl, R. (1956). Mass communication and para-social interaction: Observations on intimacy at a distance. *Psychiatry, 19*(3), 215–229. DOI: 10.1080/00332747.1956.11023049 PMID: 13359569

Hsu, H. Y. (2025). Same-sex marriage legalization and attitudes toward gays and lesbians: Evidence from a natural experiment. *Politics & Policy, 53*(5), e70065. DOI: 10.1111/polp.70065

Huang, L., Zou, W., & Huang, Y. (2025). "He is my savior, my guiding light in the dark": imagination and domestication in Chinese women's romantic relationships with AI companions [Original Research]. *Frontiers in Psychology, Volume 16 - 2025*. DOI: 10.3389/fpsyg.2025.1571707

Huang, J., & Jung, Y. (2022). Perceived authenticity of virtual characters makes the difference. *Frontiers in Virtual Reality, 3*, 1033709. Advance online publication. DOI: 10.3389/frvir.2022.1033709

Huang, Q., & Yao, S. (2024). No response? Chronemic expectancy violation and relational turbulence in technologically-mediated romantic relational conflict. *Journal of Social and Personal Relationships, 41*(5), 1183–1206. DOI: 10.1177/02654075231213824

Huang, S. A., Hancock, J., & Tong, S. T. (2022). Folk theories of online dating: Exploring people's beliefs about the online dating process and online dating algorithms. *Social Media + Society, 8*(2), 20563051221089561. DOI: 10.1177/20563051221089561

Huang, S., Lai, X., Ke, L., Li, Y., Wang, H., Zhao, X., Dai, X., & Wang, Y. (2024). AI technology panic—Is AI dependence bad for mental health? A cross-lagged panel model and the mediating roles of motivations for AI use among adolescents. *Psychology Research and Behavior Management, 17*, 1087–1102. DOI: 10.2147/PRBM.S440889 PMID: 38495087

Hu, D., Lan, Y., Yan, H., & Chen, C. W. (2025). What makes you attached to social companion AI? A two-stage exploratory mixed-method study. *International Journal of Information Management, 83*, 102890. DOI: 10.1016/j.ijinfomgt.2025.102890

Hu, J., & Wang, R. (2023). Familiarity breeds trust? The relationship between dating app use and trust in dating algorithms via algorithm awareness and critical algorithm perceptions. *International Journal of Human-Computer Interaction, 40*(17), 4596–4607. DOI: 10.1080/10447318.2023.2217014

Humphrey, A., & Bliuc, A. M. (2021). Western individualism and the psychological wellbeing of young people: A systematic review of their associations. *Youth, 2*(1), 1–11. DOI: 10.3390/youth2010001

Huot, S. (2025a). Cultural diplomacy across the Mekong subregion: Cambodia's soft power diplomacy in Southeast Asia. *Literary Enigma: The International Journal of English Language. Literature and Culture*, *1*(6), 80–90. DOI: 10.5281/zenodo.15803843

Huot, S. (2025b). Temples to policy plans: Tracing the political trajectory of education and governance in Cambodia, from antiquity to contemporary reforms. *Journal of Political Science and International Relations*, *8*(3), 122–132. DOI: 10.11648/j.jpsir.20250803.12

Huot, S. (2025c). Theoretical reflections on social capital and political efficacy: Lessons for Cambodian youth participation. *Journal of Political Science and International Relations*, *8*(2), 104–113. DOI: 10.11648/j.jpsir.20250802.18

Huot, S. (2026). Digital diplomacy in Cambodia: Embracing artificial intelligence for strategic engagement and national development. In Turan, A., & Ucuzal, H. (Eds.), *Diplomacy in the age of artificial intelligence* (pp. 307–330). IGI Global Scientific Publishing., DOI: 10.4018/979-8-3373-4937-4.ch013

Huot, S., & Loch, S. (2025). From rote to reflective: Integrating ChatGPT to transform learning outcomes in Cambodian education. *International Journal of Language and Literary Studies*, *7*(4), 1–15. DOI: 10.36892/ijlls.v7i4.2188

Huot, S., & Tep, P. (2025). Advancing ChatGPT for pedagogical innovation in Cambodia: Insight from global evidence and local implications. *The Context: Journal of English Studies*, *12*(4), 115–135. DOI: 10.5281/zenodo.15806972

Hu, T., & Ge, L. (2025). Datafication of digital intimacy: The dual logic of empowerment and commodification. *Games and Culture*, 15554120251358522. Advance online publication. DOI: 10.1177/15554120251358522

Hu, Y., Tan, C. S., Wang, S., Zhang, H., Qian, J., & Wang, Y. (2025). Who is Hooked on AI? The Role of the Big Five Personality Traits in Compulsive ChatGPT Use Among Chinese Students. *The Asia-Pacific Education Researcher*, *34*(5), 1899–1907. DOI: 10.1007/s40299-025-01001-0

Ijsselsteijn, W., Baren, J., & Lanen, F. (2003). Staying in touch: Social presence and connectedness through synchronous and asynchronous communication media. *Smpte Motion Imaging Journal*. https://www.researchgate.net/publication/252800795_Staying_in_touch_Social_presence_and_connectedness_through_synchronous_and_asynchronous_communication_media

Illouz, E. (2007). Cold intimacies: The making of emotional capitalism. *Polity*.

Illouz, E. (2019). *The end of love: A sociology of negative relations*. Oxford University Press., https://books.google.com.my/books?hl=zh-CN&lr=&id=t5OzDwAAQBAJ&oi=fnd&pg=PP1&ots=MUlo_WbtJo&sig=FOJz0uvHm69M_SzN-43Fu0tcAz0&redir_esc=y#v=onepage&q&f=false

Inose, H. (2023). Human, This Ever-changing Creature: Oshiko's Default Standard by Yukiko Motoya. In *Electricdreams–Between Fiction and Society II. The (Post) human Condition in Times of Crisis: The Interplay between Artificial Intelligence, Otherness, and Environmentalism. International Conference. October 18-20, 2023 IULM University, Milan, Italy.*

Iqbal, A., & Ajmal, A. (2018). Fear of negative evaluation and social anxiety in young adults. [PJPBS]. *Peshawar Journal of Psychology and Behavioral Sciences, 4*(1), 45–53. DOI: 10.32879/picp.2018.4.1.45

Jacobs, K. A. (2024). Digital loneliness—Changes of social recognition through AI companions. *Frontiers in Digital Health, 6*, 1281037. DOI: 10.3389/fdgth.2024.1281037 PMID: 38504806

Jalili, S. (2022). Cultural algorithms. In *Engineering optimization*. Springer., DOI: 10.1007/978-981-19-4633-2

Jamieson, L. (2007). Intimacy. *The Blackwell encyclopedia of sociology*, 1-3. DOI: 10.1002/9781405165518.wbeosi071

Jamieson, L. (2011). Intimacy as a concept: Explaining social change in the context of globalisation or another form of ethnocentricism? *Sociological Research Online, 16*(4), 151–163. DOI: 10.5153/sro.2497

Janghorban, R., Roudsari, R. L., & Taghipour, A. (2014). Skype interviewing: The new generation of online synchronous interview in qualitative research. *International Journal of Qualitative Studies on Health and Well-being, 9*(1), 24152. DOI: 10.3402/qhw.v9.24152 PMID: 24746247

Jang, J., Kwon, S., & Park, S. (2025). Ai-Extracted Sociocultural Signals in Dating App Profile Photos and Their Impact on Matching Success. *Available at SSRN* 5191741 DOI: 10.2139/ssrn.5191741

Jang, M. K. (2025). How the Instant Gratification Design of Dating Apps in Korea Creates False Expectations of Romantic Communication. *Art and Society, 4*(4), 26–33. DOI: 10.63593/AS.2709-9830.2025.05.004

Jankowiak, W., Shen, Y., Yao, S., Wang, C., & Volsche, S. (2015). Investigating love's universal attributes. *Cross-Cultural Research, 49*(4), 422–436. DOI: 10.1177/1069397115594355

Jayatissa, D. (2023). Generation Z-A new lifeline: A systematic literature review. *Sri Lanka Journal of Social Sciences and Humanities*, *3*(2), 179–186. DOI: 10.4038/sljssh.v3i2.110

Jeong, H. J., Chung, D. S., & Kim, J. (2022). Brands are human on social media: The effectiveness of human tone-of-voice on consumer engagement and purchase intentions through social presence. *International Journal of Communication*, *16*, 23. https://ijoc.org/index.php/ijoc/article/view/19269

Jiang, P., Ergu, D., Liu, F., Cai, Y., & Ma, B. (2022). A Review of Yolo algorithm developments. *Procedia Computer Science*, *199*, 1066–1073.

Jiang, Q., Zhang, Y., & Pian, W. (2022). Chatbot as an emergency exist: Mediated empathy for resilience via human-AI interaction during the COVID-19 pandemic. *Information Processing & Management*, *59*(6), 103074. DOI: 10.1016/j.ipm.2022.103074 PMID: 36059428

Jia, W., Sun, M., Lian, J., & Hou, S. (2022). Feature dimensionality reduction: A review. *Complex & Intelligent Systems*, *8*(3), 2663–2693.

Jin, E., & Eastin, M. S. (2022). When a chatbot smiles at you: The psychological mechanism underlying the effects of friendly language use by product recommendation chatbots. *Cyberpsychology, Behavior, and Social Networking*, *25*(9), 597–604. DOI: 10.1089/cyber.2021.0318 PMID: 35976080

Jingchuan, J., & Wu, S. (2024). How trust in human-like ai-based service on social media will influence customer engagement: Exploratory research to develop the scale of trust in human-like ai-based service. *Asia Marketing Journal*, *26*(2), 129–144. DOI: 10.53728/2765-6500.1633

Jin, S. V., & Ryu, E. (2019). Instagram fashionistas, luxury visual image strategies and vanity. *Journal of Product and Brand Management*, *29*(3), 355–368. DOI: 10.1108/JPBM-08-2018-1987

Jin, S. V., & Youn, S. (2023). Social presence and imagery processing as predictors of chatbot continuance intention in human-AI interaction. *International Journal of Human-Computer Interaction*, *39*(9), 1874–1886. DOI: 10.1080/10447318.2022.2129277

Jin, W., Sun, Y., Wang, N., & Zhang, X. (2017). Why users purchase virtual products in MMORPG? An integrative perspective of social presence and user engagement. *Internet Research*, *27*(2), 408–427. DOI: 10.1108/IntR-04-2016-0091

Jiwa, S., Elsaadawy, N., & Carlson, E. N. (2025). Who Did I Swipe On? Accuracy and Self-Presentation in Online Dating. *Personality and Social Psychology Bulletin, 1461672251386488*, 01461672251386488. Advance online publication. DOI: 10.1177/01461672251386488 PMID: 41230894

Jo, H. (2024). Subscription intentions for ChatGPT plus: A look at user satisfaction and self-efficacy. *Marketing Intelligence & Planning*, *42*(6), 1052–1073. DOI: 10.1108/MIP-08-2023-0411

John, O. P., & Srivastava, S. (1999). The Big Five Trait taxonomy: History, measurement, and theoretical perspectives. In Pervin, L. A., & John, O. P. (Eds.), *Handbook of personality: Theory and research* (2nd ed., pp. 102–138). Guilford Press.

Johnson, S. (2023). WHO declares loneliness a 'global public health concern'. The Guardian. https://www.theguardian.com/global-development/2023/nov/16/who-declares-loneliness-a-global-public-health-concern

Johnson, E. K., & Hong, S. C. (2023). Instagramming social presence: A test of social presence theory and heuristic cues on Instagram sponsored posts. *International Journal of Business Communication*, *60*(2), 543–559. DOI: 10.1177/2329488420944462

Joinson, A. N. (2001). Self-disclosure in computer-mediated communication: The role of self-awareness and visual anonymity. *European Journal of Social Psychology*, *31*(2), 177–192. DOI: 10.1002/ejsp.36

Jones, H. (2025, November 6). *Different attachment styles that affect relationships*. Verywell Health. https://www.verywellhealth.com/attachment-styles-5220583?

Jones, M., & Schonewille, M. (2025). Synthetic relationships and artificial intimacy: An ethical framework for evaluating the impact of generative AI on community. *International Journal of Social Robotics*, *17*(1), 88–104.

Joseph, A. P., & Babu, A. (2024). Transference and the psychological interplay in AI-enhanced mental healthcare. *Frontiers in Psychiatry*, *15*, 1460469. DOI: 10.3389/fpsyt.2024.1460469 PMID: 39224481

Jung, Y. (2011). Understanding the role of sense of presence and perceived autonomy in users' continued use of social virtual worlds. *Journal of Computer-Mediated Communication*, *16*(4), 492–510. DOI: 10.1111/j.1083-6101.2011.01540.x

Junjie, M., & Yingxin, M. (2022). The Discussions of Positivism and Interpretivism. *Online Submission*, *4*(1), 10–14. DOI: 10.36348/gajhss.2022.v04i01.002

Kaczmarek, E. (2024). Self-deception in human-AI emotional relations. *Journal of Applied Philosophy*. Advance online publication. DOI: 10.1111/japp.12786

Kallio, H., Pietilä, A.-M., Johnson, M., & Kangasniemi, M. (2016). Systematic methodological review: Developing a framework for a qualitative semi-structured interview guide. *Journal of Advanced Nursing*, *72*(12), 2954–2965. DOI: 10.1111/jan.13031 PMID: 27221824

Kawachi, P. (2013). Online social presence and its correlation with learning. *International Journal of Social Media and Interactive Learning Environments*, *1*(1), 19–31. https://www.researchgate.net/publication/264441364_Online_social_presence_and_its_correlation_with_learning. DOI: 10.1504/IJSMILE.2013.051653

Kearney, M. S. (2025). *The two-parent privilege: How americans stopped getting married and started falling behind*. University of Chicago Press. https://press.uchicago.edu/ucp/books/book/chicago/T/bo205550079.html

Keil, M., & Johnson, R. D. (2002). Feedback channels: Using social presence theory to compare voice mail to e-mail. *Journal of Information Systems Education*, *13*(4), 295–302. https://aisel.aisnet.org/jise/vol13/iss4/4/

Kemp, E., Bui, M., Tangari, A., & Zhang, X. (2025). Looking for love and support in digital places: Examining artificial intelligence emotional companion tool use. *Journal of Consumer Marketing*. Advance online publication. DOI: 10.1108/JCM-01-2025-7472

Kentmen-Cin, C. (2025). Hate speech on social media: A systemic narrative review of political science contributions. *Social Sciences (Basel, Switzerland)*, *14*(10), 610–610. DOI: 10.3390/socsci14100610

Keung, W. M., & So, T. Y. (2025). Attitudes towards AI counseling: The existence of perceptual fear in affecting perceived chatbot support quality. *Frontiers in Psychology*, *16*, 1538387. DOI: 10.3389/fpsyg.2025.1538387 PMID: 40823408

Khalifian, C. E., & Barry, R. A. (2020). Expanding intimacy theory: Vulnerable disclosures and partner responding. *Journal of Social and Personal Relationships*, *37*(1), 58–76. DOI: 10.1177/0265407519853047

Khan, T. (2025, February 13). *Love on the mainframe: How AI is changing Online Dating - Partnership on AI*. Partnership on AI. https://partnershiponai.org/love-on-the-mainframe-how-ai-is-changing-online-dating/

Kidd, A. L. (2022). Loneliness and love: The potential of human-AI relations as explored by contemporary science fiction cinema. *Screen Bodies*, *7*(2), 89–108. DOI: 10.3167/screen.2022.070207

Kietzmann, J. H., Hermkens, K., McCarthy, I. P., & Silvestre, B. S. (2011). Social media? Get serious! Understanding the functional building blocks of social media. *Business Horizons*, *54*(3), 241–251. DOI: 10.1016/j.bushor.2011.01.005

Kim, C. Y., Sato, A. J., White, N. T., Ho, H.-R., Lee, C. P., Hwang, Y., & Mutlu, B. (2025a). Bridging generations using ai-supported co-creative activities. Proceedings of the 2025 CHI Conference on Human Factors in Computing Systems, Kim, J., & Im, I. (2023). Anthropomorphic response: Understanding interactions between humans and artificial intelligence agents. *Computers in Human Behavior*, *139*, 107512. DOI: 10.1016/j.chb.2022.107512

Kim, H., & Park, M. (2024). When digital celebrity talks to you: How human-like virtual influencers satisfy consumer's experience through social presence on social media endorsements. *Journal of Retailing and Consumer Services*, *76*, 103581. DOI: 10.1016/j.jretconser.2023.103581

Kim, J., Jin, X., Xu, K., Chen, X., & Yang, H. (2024). What do people say about Replika, an AI chatbot, on social media? Investigating diverse perspectives on the implications of Replika through a topic modeling analysis. *The Social Science Journal*, •••, 1–16. DOI: 10.1080/03623319.2024.2421610

Kim, J., Kim, J., & Yang, H. (2019). Loneliness and the use of social media to follow celebrities: A moderating role of social presence. *The Social Science Journal*, *56*(1), 21–29. DOI: 10.1016/j.soscij.2018.12.007

Kim, J., Merrill, K.Jr, & Collins, C. (2021). AI as a friend or assistant: The mediating role of perceived usefulness in social AI vs. functional AI. *Telematics and Informatics*, *64*, 101694. DOI: 10.1016/j.tele.2021.101694

Kim, J., Merrill, K.Jr, & Collins, C. (2023). Investigating the importance of social presence on intentions to adopt an AI romantic partner. *Communication Research Reports*, *40*(1), 11–19. DOI: 10.1080/08824096.2022.2159800

Kim, J., Merrill, K.Jr, Xu, K., & Kelly, S. (2022). Perceived credibility of an AI instructor in online education: The role of social presence and voice features. *Computers in Human Behavior*, *136*, 107383. DOI: 10.1016/j.chb.2022.107383

Kim, J., Merrill, K.Jr, Xu, K., & Sellnow, D. D. (2021). I like my relational machine teacher: An AI instructor's communication styles and social presence in online education. *International Journal of Human-Computer Interaction*, *37*(18), 1760–1770. DOI: 10.1080/10447318.2021.1908671

Kim, J., & Song, H. (2016). Celebrity's self-disclosure on Twitter and parasocial relationships: A mediating role of social presence. *Computers in Human Behavior, 62*, 570–577. DOI: 10.1016/j.chb.2016.03.083

Kim, J., Song, H., & Lee, S. (2018). Extrovert and lonely individuals' social TV viewing experiences: A mediating and moderating role of social presence. *Mass Communication & Society, 21*(1), 50–70. DOI: 10.1080/15205436.2017.1350715

Kim, M., Lee, S., Kim, S., Heo, J.-i., Lee, S., Shin, Y.-B., Cho, C.-H., & Jung, D. (2025b). Therapeutic potential of social chatbots in alleviating loneliness and social anxiety: Quasi-experimental mixed methods study. *Journal of Medical Internet Research, 27*, e65589. DOI: 10.2196/65589 PMID: 39808786

King, J. (2009). *Emotional abuse—The lack of emotional safety*. Prevent Abusive Relationships. https://www.preventabusiverelationships.com/articles/emotional_safety.php

Kirk, H. R., Gabriel, I., Summerfield, C., Vidgen, B., & Hale, S. A. (2025). Why human–AI relationships need socioaffective alignment. *Humanities & Social Sciences Communications, 12*(1), 1–9. DOI: 10.1057/s41599-025-04532-5

Kirwan, E. M., Burns, A., O'Súilleabháin, P. S., Summerville, S., McGeehan, M., McMahon, J., Gowda, A., & Creaven, A.-M. (2025). Loneliness in emerging adulthood: A scoping review. *Adolescent Research Review, 10*(1), 47–67. DOI: 10.1007/s40894-024-00240-4

Koltsakis, E., Klontzas, M. E., & Karantanas, A. H. (2023). What is artificial intelligence: history and basic definitions of the chapter. In Klontzas, M. E., Fanni, S. C., & Neri, E. (Eds.), *Introduction to artificial intelligence* (pp. 1–11). Springer International Publishing., DOI: 10.1007/978-3-031-25928-9_1

Komiak, S. Y. X., & Benbasat, I. (2006). The effects of personalization and familiarity on trust and adoption of recommendation agents. *Management Information Systems Quarterly, 30*(4), 941–960. DOI: 10.2307/25148760

Konya-Baumbach, E., Biller, M., & von Janda, S. (2023). Someone out there? A study on the social presence of anthropomorphized chatbots. *Computers in Human Behavior, 139*, 107513. DOI: 10.1016/j.chb.2022.107513

Kooli, C., Kooli, Y., & Kooli, E. (2025). Generative artificial intelligence addiction syndrome: A new behavioral disorder? *Asian Journal of Psychiatry, 107*, 104476. DOI: 10.1016/j.ajp.2025.104476 PMID: 40174516

Kouros, T., & Papa, V. (2024). Digital mirrors: AI companions and the self. *Societies (Basel, Switzerland), 14*(10), 200. DOI: 10.3390/soc14100200

Kreijns, K., Xu, K., & Weidlich, J. (2022). Social presence: Conceptualization and measurement. *Educational Psychology Review, 34*(1), 139–170. DOI: 10.1007/s10648-021-09623-8 PMID: 34177204

Kulkarni, P., Pathak, P., Pillai, S., & Tigga, V. (2025). Role of Generative AI for Fraud Detection and Prevention. *Generative Artificial Intelligence in Finance: Large Language Models, Interfaces, and Industry Use Cases to Transform Accounting and Finance Processes*, 175-198. https://doi.org/DOI: 10.1002/9781394271078.ch10?urlappend=%3Futm_source%3Dresearchgate.net%26utm_medium%3Darticle

Kumar, N., & Benbasat, I. (2006). Research note: The influence of recommendations and consumer reviews on evaluations of websites. *Information Systems Research, 17*(4), 425–439. DOI: 10.1287/isre.1060.0107

Kwon, W., Li, Z., Zhuang, S., Sheng, Y., Zheng, L., Yu, C. H., Gonzalez, J., Zhang, H., & Stoica, I. (2023). Efficient memory management for large language model serving with pagedattention. Proceedings of the 29th symposium on operating systems principles, Laestadius, L., Bishop, A., Gonzalez, M., Illenčík, D., & Campos-Castillo, C. (2024). Too human and not human enough: A grounded theory analysis of mental health harms from emotional dependence on the social chatbot Replika. *New Media & Society, 26*(10), 5923–5941. DOI: 10.1177/14614448221142007

Kydd, M., Shepherd, L. A., Szymkowiak, A., & Johnson, G. I. (2023, July). Love at first sleight: a review of scammer techniques in online romance fraud. In *The International Conference on Cybersecurity, Situational Awareness and Social Media* (pp. 327-341). Singapore: Springer Nature Singapore. https://doi.org/DOI: 10.1007/978-981-99-6974-6_18

Lan, J., & Huang, Y. (2025). Performing intimacy: Curating the self-presentation in human-AI relationships. *Emerging Media, 3*(2), 305–317. DOI: 10.1177/27523543251334157

Lankton, N., McKnight, D. H., & Tripp, J. (2015). Technology, humanness, and trust: Rethinking trust in technology. *Journal of the Association for Information Systems, 16*(10), 880–918. DOI: 10.17705/1jais.00411

Latour, B., Callon, M., & Law, J. (2004). *Actor Network Theory*. Sage. https://www.sagepub.com/sites/default/files/upm-binaries/5222_Ritzer__Entries_beginning_with_A__%5B1%5D.pdf

Laursen, B., Pulkkinen, L., & Adams, R. (2002). The antecedents and correlates of agreeableness in adulthood. *Developmental Psychology, 38*(4), 591–603. DOI: 10.1037/0012-1649.38.4.591 PMID: 12090488

Lazard, A. J., Brennen, J. S., Troutman Adams, E., & Love, B. (2020). Cues for increasing social presence for mobile health app adoption. *Journal of Health Communication, 25*(2), 136–149. DOI: 10.1080/10810730.2020.1719241 PMID: 32026759

Lazarus, S., Whittaker, J. M., McGuire, M. R., & Platt, L. (2023). What Do We Know About Online Romance Fraud Studies? A Systematic Review of the Empirical Literature (2000 to 2021). *Journal of Economic Criminology*, 100013. https://ssrn.com/abstract=4463985

Leafman, J. S., Mathieson, K. M., & Ewing, H. (2013). Student perceptions of social presence and attitudes toward social media: Results of a cross-sectional study. *International Journal of Higher Education, 2*(1), 67–77. https://www.researchgate.net/publication/256369097_Student_Perceptions_of_Social_Presence_and_Attitudes_toward_Social_Media_Results_of_a_Cross-Sectional_Study. DOI: 10.5430/ijhe.v2n1p67

Ledbetter, A. M., & Meisner, C. (2021). Extending the personal branding affordances typology to parasocial interaction with public figures on social media: Social presence and media multiplexity as mediators. *Computers in Human Behavior, 115*, 106610. DOI: 10.1016/j.chb.2020.106610

Ledgerwood, J. L. (2017). Khmer kinship: the matriliny/matriarchy myth. In Peou, S. (Ed.), (pp. 395–409)., DOI: 10.4324/9781315192918

Lee, I., & Hahn, S. (2024). On the relationship between mind perception and social support of chatbots. *Frontiers in Psychology, 15*, 1282036. DOI: 10.3389/fpsyg.2024.1282036 PMID: 38510306

Lee, K. F., Chan, M. Y., & Mohamad Ali, A. (2023). Self and desired partner descriptions in the online romance scam: A linguistic analysis of scammer and general user profiles on online dating portals. *Crime Prevention and Community Safety, 25*(1), 20–46. DOI: 10.1057/s41300-022-00169-7

Lee, K. M. (2006). Presence, explicated. *Communication Theory, 14*(1), 27–50. DOI: 10.1111/j.1468-2885.2004.tb00302.x

Lee, S. K., Kavya, P., & Lasser, S. C. (2021). Social interactions and relationships with an intelligent virtual agent. *International Journal of Human-Computer Studies, 150*, 102608. DOI: 10.1016/j.ijhcs.2021.102608

Lee, S. K., & Sun, J. (2023). Testing a theoretical model of trust in human-machine communication: Emotional experience and social presence. *Behaviour & Information Technology, 42*(16), 2754–2767. DOI: 10.1080/0144929X.2022.2145998

Lee, Y. C., Yamashita, N., Huang, Y., & Fu, W. (2020). 'I hear you, I feel you': Encouraging deep self-disclosure through a chatbot. *Proceedings of the 2020 CHI Conference on Human Factors in Computing Systems*, 1–12. DOI: 10.1145/3313831.3376175

Leite, Â., Costa, A., Ribeiro, B., Fonseca, C., Ribeiro, I., Mesquita, J., & Ribeiro, S. (2023). Being female and in a romantic relationship enhances the association between satisfaction with love life and capacity to love. *International Journal of Environmental Research and Public Health, 20*(23), 7108. DOI: 10.3390/ijerph20237108 PMID: 38063538

Leo-Liu, J. (2023). Loving a "defiant" AI companion? The gender performance and ethics of social exchange robots in simulated intimate interactions. *Computers in Human Behavior, 141*, 107620. DOI: 10.1016/j.chb.2022.107620

Leshner, C. E., & Johnson, J. R. (2024). Technically in love: Individual differences relating to sexual and platonic relationships with robots. *Journal of Social and Personal Relationships, 41*(8), 2345–2365. DOI: 10.1177/02654075241234377

Li, B. (2025, March 17). *2025 China AI companion industry: Competitive landscape and trillion-yuan sector forecast - How the emotional economy reshapes human-machine symbiosis?* ChinaIRN.com. https://www.chinairn.com/hyzx/20250317/140507472.shtml

Liao, S. V., & Sundar, S. S. (2022). Designing for trust in AI: The role of transparency and social cues. *International Journal of Human-Computer Studies, 158*, 102740.

Liao, S. V., & Sundar, S. S. (2024). The AI-sentience heuristic: Why we attribute consciousness to chatbots and the emotional consequences thereof. *Nature Human Behaviour, 8*, 312–325.

Liberati, N. (2022). Digital intimacy in China and Japan. *Human Studies*. Advance online publication. DOI: 10.1007/s10746-022-09631-9 PMID: 35846068

Li, C., Ning, G., Xia, Y., Guo, K., & Liu, Q. (2022). Does the internet bring people closer together or further apart? The impact of internet usage on interpersonal communications. *Behavioral Sciences (Basel, Switzerland), 12*(11), 1–24. DOI: 10.3390/bs12110425 PMID: 36354402

Li, H., & Zhang, R. (2024). Finding love in algorithms: Deciphering the emotional contexts of close encounters with AI chatbots. *Journal of Computer-Mediated Communication, 29*(5), zmae015. Advance online publication. DOI: 10.1093/jcmc/zmae015

Lim, J. (2022). Choosing the right love: Online dating platforms and gender inequality in Southeast Asia. In *Media in Asia* (pp. 211–225). Routledge. DOI: 10.4324/9781003130628-17

Lim, J. B. (2025). *Digital media interventions in Southeast Asia*. Palgrave Macmillan Cham., DOI: 10.1007/978-3-031-78211-4

Lim, J., & Hwang, W. (2025). Proactivity of chatbots, task types and user's characteristics when interacting with artificial intelligence (AI) chatbots. *International Journal of Human-Computer Interaction, 41*(18), 11848–11866. DOI: 10.1080/10447318.2024.2446510

Lim, M. (2023). From activist media to algorithmic politics: The Internet, social media, and civil society in Southeast Asia. In Hansson, E., & Weiss, M. L. (Eds.), *Routledge handbook of civil and uncivil society in Southeast Asia* (pp. 25–44). Routledge., DOI: 10.4324/9780367422080-3

Lim, Y., & Lee-Won, R. J. (2017). When retweets persuade: The persuasive effects of dialogic retweeting and the role of social presence in organizations' Twitter-based communication. *Telematics and Informatics, 34*(5), 422–433. DOI: 10.1016/j.tele.2016.09.003

Lin, B. (2024). The AI chatbot always flirts with me, should I flirt back: From the Mcdonaldization of friendship to the robotization of love. *Social Media + Society, 10*(4), 20563051241296229. DOI: 10.1177/20563051241296229

Lindgren, H. (2025). Emerging roles and relationships among humans and interactive AI systems. *International Journal of Human-Computer Interaction, 41*(17), 10595–10617. DOI: 10.1080/10447318.2024.2435693

Lin, Z., Wang, Y., & Liu, T. (2023). Commercializing desire for platform economics: Digital romance in China's platformization age. *Continuum (Perth), 37*(1), 31–45. DOI: 10.1080/10304312.2023.2169251

Li, S., Feng, B., Li, N., & Tan, X. (2015). How social context cues in online support-seeking influence self-disclosure in support provision. *Communication Quarterly, 63*(5), 586–602. DOI: 10.1080/01463373.2015.1078389

Liu, C. (2024, August 22). Swipe Right for Love: How your brain's reward system powers online Dating - LSE Psychological & Behavioural Science. *LSE Psychological & Behavioural Science*. https://blogs.lse.ac.uk/psychologylse/2024/06/03/swipe-right-for-love-how-your-brains-reward-system-powers-online-dating/

Liu, G., Lei, S. S. I., & Law, R. (2022). Enhancing social media branded content effectiveness: Strategies via telepresence and social presence. *Information Technology & Tourism, 24*(2), 245–263. DOI: 10.1007/s40558-022-00225-w

Liu, L. (2025). Exploring the behavioral differentiation and psychological impact of different attachment types of users interacting with AI. *Communications in Humanities Research, 74*(1), 8–16. DOI: 10.54254/2753-7064/2025.LC25585

Liu, S. S., Morris, M. W., Talhelm, T., & Yang, Q. (2019). Ingroup vigilance in collectivistic cultures. *Proceedings of the National Academy of Sciences of the United States of America, 116*(29), 14538–14546. DOI: 10.1073/pnas.1817588116 PMID: 31249140

Liu, Z., & Kuai, M. (2025). The global burden of depression in adolescents and young adults, 1990–2021: Systematic analysis of the global burden of disease study. *BMC Psychiatry, 25*(1), 767. DOI: 10.1186/s12888-025-07201-8 PMID: 40770320

Lohr, A. A. (2025, August 27). Google / Ipsos Multi-Country AI Survey 2025. *Ipsos*. https://www.ipsos.com/en-us/google-ipsos-multi-country-ai-survey-2025

Loock, K. (2024). *Hollywood remaking: How film remakes, sequels, and franchises shape industry and culture*. Univ of California Press.

Lott, M., & Hasselberger, W. (2025). With Friends Like These: Love and Friendship with AI Agents. *Topoi*. Advance online publication. DOI: 10.1007/s11245-025-10247-8

Lowenthal, P. R. (2010). The evolution and influence of social presence theory on online learning of the chapter. In *Social computing: Concepts, methodologies, tools, and applications* (pp. 113–128). IGI Global., DOI: 10.4018/978-1-60566-984-7.ch010

Luhmann, N. (1979). *Trust and power*. Wiley.

Lung, N. (2025, July 14). AI Dating App Features Aren't Landing With Gen Z, Survey Finds. *Bloomberg Law*. https://news.bloomberglaw.com/california-brief/ai-dating-app-features-arent-landing-with-gen-z-survey-finds

Lutz, C., & Ranzini, G. (2017). Where dating meets data: Investigating social and institutional privacy concerns on Tinder. *Social Media + Society, 3*(1), 1–12. DOI: 10.1177/2056305117697735

Lyndon, A., Davis, D.-A., Sharma, A. E., & Scott, K. A. (2023). Emotional safety is patient safety. *BMJ Quality & Safety, 32*(7), 369–372. DOI: 10.1136/bmjqs-2022-015573 PMID: 36732064

MacInnis, D. J., & Price, L. L. (1987). The role of imagery in information processing: Review and extensions. *The Journal of Consumer Research, 13*(4), 473–491. DOI: 10.1086/209082

Mackinnon, L. (2022). Love, games and gamification: Gambling and gaming as techniques of modern romantic love. *Theory, Culture & Society, 39*(6), 121–137. DOI: 10.1177/02632764221078258

Madsen, M., & Gregor, S. (2000). Measuring human-computer trust. 11th australasian conference on information systems, Magaldi, D., & Berler, M. (2018). Semi-structured Interviews of the chapter. In V. Zeigler-Hill & T. K. Shackelford (Eds.), *Encyclopedia of personality and individual differences* (pp. 1-6). Springer International Publishing. DOI: 10.1007/978-3-319-28099-8_857-1

Mahajan, P. (2025). *Beyond biology: AI as family and the future of human bonds and relationships.* https://hal.science/hal-04987496

Mahajan, P. (2025). Beyond biology: AI as family and the future of human bonds and relationships. *F1000Research.* https://doi.org/DOI: 10.12688/f1000research.166251.1

Maheri, A., Jalili, S., Hosseinzadeh, Y., Khani, R., & Miryahyavi, M. (2021). A comprehensive survey on cultural algorithms. *Swarm and Evolutionary Computation, 62*, 100846. DOI: 10.1016/j.swevo.2021.100846

Malfacini, K. (2025). The impacts of companion AI on human relationships: Risks, benefits, and design considerations. *AI & Society, 40*(7), 1–14. DOI: 10.1007/s00146-025-02318-6

Ma, N., Khynevych, R., Hao, Y., & Wang, Y. (2025). Effect of anthropomorphism and perceived intelligence in chatbot avatars of visual design on user experience: Accounting for perceived empathy and trust. *Frontiers of Computer Science, 7*, 1531976. Advance online publication. DOI: 10.3389/fcomp.2025.1531976

Mangiò, F., Pedeliento, G., Wassler, P., & Williams, N. (2025). Discursively negotiating AI: A social representation theory approach to LLM-based chatbots. *Technological Forecasting and Social Change, 221*, 1–13. DOI: 10.1016/j.techfore.2025.124352

Maples, B., Cerit, M., Vishwanath, A., & Pea, R. (2024). Loneliness and suicide mitigation for students using GPT3-enabled chatbots. *Npj Mental Health Research, 3*(1), 4. DOI: 10.1038/s44184-023-00047-6 PMID: 38609517

Markus, H., & Nurius, P. (1986). Possible selves. *The American Psychologist, 41*(9), 954–969. DOI: 10.1037/0003-066X.41.9.954

Marmolejo-Ramos, F., Marrone, R., Korolkiewicz, M., Gabriel, F., Siemens, G., Joksimovic, S., Yamada, Y., Mori, Y., Rahwan, T., Sahakyan, M., Sonna, B., Meirmanov, A., Bolatov, A., Som, B., Ndukaihe, I., Arinze, N. C., Kundrát, J., Skanderová, L., Ngo, V., & Tejada, J. (2025). Factors influencing trust in algorithmic decision-making: An indirect scenario-based experiment. *Frontiers in Artificial Intelligence*, *7*, 1465605. DOI: 10.3389/frai.2024.1465605 PMID: 39968162

Marriott, H. R., & Pitardi, V. (2024). One is the loneliest number… Two can be as bad as one. The influence of AI Friendship Apps on users' well-being and addiction. *Psychology and Marketing*, *41*(1), 86–101. DOI: 10.1002/mar.21899

Marston, J. (2004). *History, Buddhism, and new religious movements in Cambodia*. University of Hawaii Press.

Martela, F., Lehmus-Sun, A., Parker, P. D., Pessi, A. B., & Ryan, R. M. (2023). Needs and well-being across Europe: Basic psychological needs are closely connected with well-being, meaning, and symptoms of depression in 27 European countries. *Social Psychological & Personality Science*, *14*(5), 501–514. DOI: 10.1177/19485506221113678

Ma, S., & Koike, M. (2025). Becoming human: How perceived anthropomorphism and authenticity influence romantic attractiveness of chat agents. *International Journal of Human-Computer Interaction*, •••, 1–14. DOI: 10.1080/10447318.2025.2578393

Masaviru, M. (2016). Self-disclosure: Theories and model review. *Journal of Culture. Social Development*, *18*, 43. https://www.researchgate.net/publication/301789757_Self-Disclosure_Theories_and_Model_Review

Match. (2025). *Singles in America*. https://www.singlesinamerica.com/

Mauss, M. (1966). *The gift: Form and functions of exchange in archaic societies*. Cohen & West Ltd. https://cir.nii.ac.jp/crid/1971993809779811347

Ma, X., Hancock, J., & Naaman, M. (2016). Anonymity, intimacy and self-disclosure in social media. *Proceedings of the 2016 CHI Conference on Human Factors in Computing Systems*, 3857–3869. DOI: 10.1145/2858036.2858414

Mazer, J. P., Murphy, R. E., & Simonds, C. J. (2007). I'll see you on "Facebook": The effects of computer-mediated teacher self-disclosure on student motivation, affective learning, and classroom climate. *Communication Education*, *56*(1), 1–17. DOI: 10.1080/03634520601009710

McArthur, N., & Markie, S. (2021). Digisexuality and the future of human–robot sexual relations. In *The Oxford handbook of digital ethics*. Oxford University Press.

Mcauley, D. (2024, December 9). The loneliness epidemic: Recent trends, background, and future outlook. *GlobalRPH*. https://globalrph.com/2024/12/the-loneliness-epidemic-recent-trends-background-and-future-outlook/

Mcknight, D. H., Carter, M., Thatcher, J. B., & Clay, P. F. (2011). Trust in a specific technology: An investigation of its components and measures. *ACM Transactions on Management Information Systems*, *2*(2), 1–25. DOI: 10.1145/1985347.1985353

McLuhan, M. (1994). *Understanding media: The extensions of man*. MIT Press.

Mehan, J. (2024). *Artificial intelligence - ethical, social, and security impacts for the present and the future* (2nd ed.). IT Governance Ltd.

Mehrabian, A. (1981). *Silent messages: implicit communication of emotions and attitudes*. Wadsworth Publishing Company.

Meng, J., & Dai, Y. (2021). Emotional support from AI chatbots: Should a supportive partner self-disclose or not? *Journal of Computer-Mediated Communication*, *26*(4), 207–222. Advance online publication. DOI: 10.1093/jcmc/zmab005

Menon, D. (2024). The Bumble motivations framework- exploring a dating App's uses by emerging adults in India. *Heliyon*, *10*(3), e24819. DOI: 10.1016/j.heliyon.2024.e24819 PMID: 38317995

Merleau-Ponty, M. (1962). *Phenomenology of perception*. Routledge.

Mernitz, S. (2018). A cohort comparison of trends in first cohabitation duration in the United States. *Demographic Research*, *38*, 2073–2086. DOI: 10.4054/DemRes.2018.38.66 PMID: 31592199

Merriam, S. B. (2002). *Introduction to qualitative research* (Vol. 1). Jossey-Bass.

Merriam, S. B. (2002). *Qualitative research in practice: Examples For discussion and analysis*. Jossey-Bass Publishers.

Merriam, S. B. (2009). *Qualitative research: A guide to design and implementation*. Jossey-Bass.

Merrill, K.Jr, Kim, J., & Collins, C. (2022). AI companions for lonely individuals and the role of social presence. *Communication Research Reports*, *39*(2), 93–103. DOI: 10.1080/08824096.2022.2045929

Merrill, K.Jr, Mikkilineni, S. D., & Dehnert, M. (2025). Artificial intelligence chatbots as a source of virtual social support: Implications for loneliness and anxiety management. *Annals of the New York Academy of Sciences*, *1549*(1), 148–159. DOI: 10.1111/nyas.15400 PMID: 40572032

Meyer, D., & Sledge, R. (2022). The relationship between conflict topics and romantic relationship dynamics. *Journal of Family Issues*, *43*(2), 306–323. DOI: 10.1177/0192513X21993856

Mikulincer, M., & Shaver, P. R. (2010). *Attachment in adulthood: Structure, dynamics, and change*. Guilford Publications.

Miller, C. J., Adjognon, O. L., Brady, J. E., Dichter, M. E., & Iverson, K. M. (2021). Screening for intimate partner violence in healthcare settings: An implementation-oriented systematic review. *Implementation Research and Practice*, *2*, 26334895211039894. DOI: 10.1177/26334895211039894 PMID: 36712586

Mishra, A., Sharma, K., Tiwari, V., & Menon, S. (2025). AI and Mental Well-being: The Influence of AI Companions on Loneliness and Emotional Health in Urban Families. *International Journal for Multidisciplinary Research*, *7*(2), 42541. Advance online publication. DOI: 10.36948/ijfmr.2025.v07i02.42541

Mlonyeni, P. M. T. (2025). Personal AI, deception, and the problem of emotional bubbles. *AI & Society*, *40*(3), 1927–1938. DOI: 10.1007/s00146-024-01958-4

Montag, C., Spapé, M., & Becker, B. (2025). Can AI really help solve the loneliness epidemic? *Trends in Cognitive Sciences*, *29*(10), 869–871. DOI: 10.1016/j.tics.2025.08.002 PMID: 40962648

Moors, A. C., Gesselman, A. N., & Garcia, J. R. (2021). Desire, familiarity, and engagement in polyamory: Results from a national sample of single adults in the United States. *Frontiers in Psychology*, *12*, 619640. DOI: 10.3389/fpsyg.2021.619640 PMID: 33833712

Morris, D. (1982). Attachment and intimacy. In Fischer, M., & Stricker, G. (Eds.), *Intimacy* (pp. 305–323). Springer US., DOI: 10.1007/978-1-4684-4160-4_19

Moussawi, S., & Koufaris, M. (2019). Perceived Intelligence and Perceived Anthropomorphism of Personal Intelligent Agents: Scale Development and Validation. *Hawaii International Conference on System Sciences*. https://doi.org/DOI: 10.24251/HICSS.2019.015

Moustakas, C. (1994). Phenomenological research methods. *Sage (Atlanta, Ga.)*.

Muhammud, F. S., & Muhammad, H. (2022). Cybercrime through love scams: What women should know? *Journal of Contemporary Islamic Studies*, *8*(2), 41–54. https://ir.uitm.edu.my/id/eprint/101363

Muldoon, J., & Parke, J. J. (2025). Cruel companionship: How AI companions exploit loneliness and commodify intimacy. *New Media & Society, 14614448251395192*, 14614448251395192. Advance online publication. DOI: 10.1177/14614448251395192

Munn, L. (2023). *Automation is a myth*. Stanford University Press.

Munn, L. (2025). *The technical soul: Algorithms, intimacy, and the automation of care*. Polity Press.

Munoz, L. R., Pellegrini-Lafont, C., & Cramer, E. (2014). Using social media in teacher preparation programs: Twitter as a means to create social presence. *Penn GSE Perspectives on Urban Education, 11*(2), 57–69. https://www.researchgate.net/publication/266475419_Using_Social_Media_in_Teacher_Preparation_Programs_Twitter_as_a_Means_to_Create_Social_Presence

Nader, K., & Lee, M. K. (2022). Folk theories and user strategies on dating apps. In *Lecture notes in computer science* (pp. 445-458). https://doi.org/DOI: 10.1007/978-3-030-96957-8_37

Nader, K., & Lee, M. K. (2022). Folk theories and user strategies on dating apps: How users understand and manage their experience with algorithmic matchmaking. International Conference on Information, Pataranutaporn, P., Karny, S., Archiwaranguprok, C., Albrecht, C., Liu, A. R., & Maes, P. (2025). "My boyfriend is AI": A computational analysis of human-AI companionship in Reddit's AI community. DOI: 10.48550/arxiv.2509.11391

Nader, K. (2020). Dating through the filters. *Social Philosophy & Policy, 37*(2), 237–248.

Nader, K. (2020). DATING THROUGH THE FILTERS. *Social Philosophy & Policy, 37*(2), 237–248. DOI: 10.1017/S0265052521000133

Naeem, M., Ozuem, W., Howell, K., & Ranfagni, S. (2023). A step-by-step process of thematic analysis to develop a conceptual model in qualitative research. *International Journal of Qualitative Methods, 22*, 16094069231205789. DOI: 10.1177/16094069231205789

Namvarpour, M. "Matt", Brofsky, B., Medina, J. Y., Akter, M., & Razi, A. (2025). Romance, relief, and regret: Teen narratives of chatbot overreliance. *Arxiv.org*. https://arxiv.org/html/2507.15783v2

Nardo, M., Forino, D., & Murino, T. (2020). The evolution of man–machine interaction: The role of human in Industry 4.0 paradigm. *Production & Manufacturing Research, 8*(1), 20–34. DOI: 10.1080/21693277.2020.1737592

Nash, B. L. (2024). Love and learning in the age of algorithms: How intimate relationships with artificial intelligence may shape epistemology, sociality, and linguistic justice. *Reading Research Quarterly*, *59*(4), 624–631. Advance online publication. DOI: 10.1002/rrq.549

Nass, C., & Lee, K. M. (2000). Does computer-generated speech manifest personality? an experimental test of similarity-attraction *Proceedings of the SIGCHI conference on Human Factors in Computing Systems*, The Hague, The Netherlands. DOI: 10.1145/332040.332452

Nass, C., & Moon, Y. (2000). Machines and mindlessness: Social responses to computers. *The Journal of Social Issues*, *56*(1), 81–103. DOI: 10.1111/0022-4537.00153

Nass, C., Steuer, J., & Tauber, E. R. (1994). Computers are social actors. *Proceedings of the SIGCHI Conference on Human Factors in Computing Systems*, 72–78. DOI: 10.1145/191666.191703

Nemer, D. (2022). *Technology of the oppressed: Inequity and the digital mundane in favelas of Brazil*. MIT Press. DOI: 10.7551/mitpress/14122.001.0001

Ngo, V. (2025). Humanizing AI for trust: The critical role of social presence in adoption. *AI & Society*. Advance online publication. DOI: 10.1007/s00146-025-02506-4

Ng, P. M., Wan, C., Lee, D., Garnelo-Gomez, I., & Lau, M. M. (2025). I love you, my AI companion! Do you? Perspectives from the Triangular Theory of Love and Attachment Theory. *Internet Research*, •••, 1–21. DOI: 10.1108/INTR-11-2024-1783

Nolan, S. (2023). *Snack enables AI avatars to chat for you*. Global Dating Insights - Dating Industry News. https://www.globaldatinginsights.com/news/snack-enables-ai-avatars-to-chat-for-you

Nolan, S. (2024, January 15). *A dating app based on attachment styles*. Global Dating Insights - Dating Industry News. https://www.globaldatinginsights.com/news/a-dating-app-based-on-attachment-styles/

Nomura, T. (2022). Relationships 5.0: How AI, VR, and robots will reshape our emotional lives. *Information Communication and Society*, *26*(10), 1–2. DOI: 10.1080/1369118X.2022.2091468

Nonaka, S., Takeda, T., & Sakai, M. (2022). Who are hikikomori? Demographic and clinical features of hikikomori (prolonged social withdrawal): A systematic review. *The Australian and New Zealand Journal of Psychiatry*, *56*(12), 1542–1554. DOI: 10.1177/00048674221085917 PMID: 35332798

Norris, F. H., Stevens, S. P., Pfefferbaum, B., Wyche, K. F., & Pfefferbaum, R. L. (2008). Community resilience as a metaphor, theory, set of capacities, and strategy for disaster readiness. *American Journal of Community Psychology, 41*(1), 127–150. DOI: 10.1007/s10464-007-9156-6 PMID: 18157631

Nosta, J. (2024, June 4). *How artificial intelligence is reshaping relationships.* Psychology Today Australia. https://www.psychologytoday.com/au/blog/the-digital-self/202406/how-artificial-intelligence-is-reshaping-relationships

Nyimbili, F., & Nyimbili, L. (2024). Types of purposive sampling techniques with their examples and application in qualitative research studies. *British Journal of Multidisciplinary and Advanced Studies, 5*(1), 90–99. DOI: 10.37745/bjmas.2022.0419

Offei, M., Andoh-Baidoo, F. K., Ayaburi, E. W., & Asamoah, D. (2022). How do individuals justify and rationalize their criminal behaviors in online romance fraud? *Information Systems Frontiers, 24*(2), 475–491.

Oh, C. S., Bailenson, J. N., & Welch, G. F. (2018). A systematic review of social presence: definition, antecedents, and implications [Systematic Review]. *Frontiers in Robotics and AI, Volume 5 - 2018.* DOI: 10.3389/frobt.2018.00114

ÓhAiseadha, C., Quinn, G. A., Connolly, R., Wilson, A., Connolly, M., Soon, W., & Hynds, P.ÓhAiseadha. (2023). Unintended consequences of COVID-19 non-pharmaceutical interventions (NPIs) for population health and health inequalities. *International Journal of Environmental Research and Public Health, 20*(7), 5223. DOI: 10.3390/ijerph20075223 PMID: 37047846

Osei-Frimpong, K., & McLean, G. (2018). Examining online social brand engagement: A social presence theory perspective. *Technological Forecasting and Social Change, 128,* 10–21. DOI: 10.1016/j.techfore.2017.10.010

Ovsyannikova, D., de Mello, V. O., & Inzlicht, M. (2025). Third-party evaluators perceive AI as more compassionate than expert humans. *Communications Psychology, 3*(1), 4. DOI: 10.1038/s44271-024-00182-6 PMID: 39794410

Oyetoke, L. (2025, June). *Using Behavioral Psychology in Product Design.* SIIT. https://siit.co/blog/using-behavioral-psychology-in-product-design/45987

Oza, N. (n.d.). *Swipe Right for Love? Attachment Styles and Online Dating in the Age of Apps.* https://www.gipshospital.com/online-dating

Paché, G. (2025). Dating Apps: a "Logistics of desire." *Journal of Social Science for Policy Implications.* https://doi.org/DOI: 10.15640/jsspi.v13p1

Pal, D., Vanijja, V., Thapliyal, H., & Zhang, X. (2023). What affects the usage of artificial conversational agents? An agent personality and love theory perspective. *Computers in Human Behavior*, *145*, 107788. DOI: 10.1016/j.chb.2023.107788

Pani, B., Crawford, J., & Allen, K. A. (2024). Can generative artificial intelligence foster belongingness, social support, and reduce loneliness? A conceptual analysis. In Lyu, Z. (Ed.), *Applications of generative AI* (pp. 261–276). Springer International Publishing., DOI: 10.1007/978-3-031-46238-2_13

Pan, S., & Mou, Y. (2024). Constructing the meaning of human–AI romantic relationships from the perspectives of users dating the social chatbot Replika. *Personal Relationships*, *31*(4), 1090–1112. DOI: 10.1111/pere.12572

Pan, S., & Mou, Y. (2024). Dancing With a Loving Chatbot: Power Dynamics Between Women and Their AI Partners. *Social Science Computer Review*, *08944393251340693*, 08944393251340693. Advance online publication. DOI: 10.1177/08944393251340693

Papneja, H., & Yadav, N. (2025). Self-disclosure to conversational AI: A literature review, emergent framework, and directions for future research. *Personal and Ubiquitous Computing*, *29*(2), 119–151. DOI: 10.1007/s00779-024-01823-7

Park, K. (2025). *Curating Connection: How Millennial Women Navigate Self-Presentation, Intimacy, and Rejection in Online Dating* (Master's thesis, Royal Roads University (Canada)).

Park, E. K., & Sundar, S. S. (2015). Can synchronicity and visual modality enhance social presence in mobile messaging? *Computers in Human Behavior*, *45*, 121–128. DOI: 10.1016/j.chb.2014.12.001

Park, J., & Woo, S. E. (2022). Who Likes Artificial Intelligence? Personality Predictors of Attitudes toward Artificial Intelligence. *The Journal of Psychology*, *156*(1), 68–94. DOI: 10.1080/00223980.2021.2012109 PMID: 35015615

Parzer, M. (2023). Cultural capital. In *The Routledge Handbook of Music and Migration* (pp. 35–37). Routledge. DOI: 10.4324/9781003309437-9

Patel, K. M., Manaktala, S. S., Nayan, A., & Gurjar, V. Algorithmic attachment disorder: Detecting and preventing emotional dependency in human–AI relationships. *Childhood, 1*(1.52), 2.35.

Paul, A., & Ahmed, S. (2024). Computed compatibility: Examining user perceptions of AI and matchmaking algorithms. *Behaviour & Information Technology*, *43*(5), 1002–1015. DOI: 10.1080/0144929X.2023.2196579

Peng, C., Zhang, S., Wen, F., & Liu, K. (2025). How loneliness leads to the conversational AI usage intention: The roles of anthropomorphic interface, para-social interaction. *Current Psychology (New Brunswick, N.J.)*, *44*(9), 8177–8189. DOI: 10.1007/s12144-024-06809-5

Penn, L. S., & Neumann, Z. (2017). Neurotic Personality (Horney). In Zeigler-Hill, V., & Shackelford, T. K. (Eds.), *Encyclopedia of Personality and Individual Differences* (pp. 1–4). Springer International Publishing., DOI: 10.1007/978-3-319-28099-8_606-1

Pentina, I.. (2023). The role of AI chatbots in supporting or substituting human social interaction. *Computers in Human Behavior*, *144*, 107734.

Pentina, I., & Hancock, J. T. (2025). Relational dynamics with generative AI: From tools to teammates to lovers. *Journal of Interactive Marketing*, *60*, 45–62.

Pentina, I., Hancock, T., & Xie, T. (2023). Exploring relationship development with social chatbots: A mixed-method study of replika. *Computers in Human Behavior*, *140*, 107600. DOI: 10.1016/j.chb.2022.107600

Perera, A. (2023). Uncanny Valley: Examples, effects, and theory. *Simply Psychology*. https://www.simplypsychology.org/uncanny-valley.html

Perez, S. (2025). *AI companion apps on track to pull in $120M in 2025*. https://finance.yahoo.com/news/ai-companion-apps-track-pull-173842786 .html?utm_source=chatgpt.com&guccounter=1&guce_referrer=aHR0cHM 6Ly9jaGF0Z3B0LmNvbS8&guce_referrer_sig=AQAAALqbEJPLOJ8mBIn _hLuKxz65FDYqLqnyARhQ-rQBc2tf1NB1dkngv2OUTTLvHMTF_- PAksFImFsjIhWmyCTaGO-1skaDxiHhPyJifa6DWgxVmqdLXW9hIK6ASW re5sIqkMbY1sGyWCOnFiJGa7jQeqo9825dYDQaTn1yG2xQZZna

Perez, S. (2025, July 21). 72% of US teens have used AI companions, study finds. *TechCrunch*. https://techcrunch.com/2025/07/21/72-of-u-s-teens-have-used-ai -companions-study-finds/

Pettersen, L., & Karlsen, F. (2023). DARK DESIGN PATTERNS AND GAMIFICATION AS THE HEART OF DATING APPLICATIONS' BUSINESS MODELS. *AoIR Selected Papers of Internet Research*. https://doi.org/DOI: 10.5210/spir.v2023i0.13478

Pettersen, L., & Døving, R. (2023). The construction of matches in dating platforms. *Nordic Journal of Science and Technology Studies*, *11*(1). Advance online publication. DOI: 10.5324/njsts.v11i1.4948

Pew Research Center. (2013). *The global divide on homosexuality*. Pew Research Center. https://www.pewresearch.org/global/2013/06/04/the-global-divide-on-homosexuality/

Phares, E. (2025, July 22). Dating Statistics and Facts in 2025. *Forbes Health*. https://www.forbes.com/health/dating/dating-statistics/

Pietilä, A.-M., Nurmi, S.-M., Halkoaho, A., & Kyngäs, H. (2020). Qualitative research: Ethical considerations of the chapter. In Kyngäs, H., Mikkonen, K., & Kääriäinen, M. (Eds.), *The application of content analysis in nursing science research* (pp. 49–69). Springer International Publishing., DOI: 10.1007/978-3-030-30199-6_6

Pizzato, L., Rej, T., Akehurst, J., Koprinska, I., Yacef, K., & Kay, J. (2012). Recommending people to people: The nature of reciprocal recommenders with a case study in online dating. *User Modeling and User-Adapted Interaction*, *23*(5), 447–488. DOI: 10.1007/s11257-012-9125-0

Poder, P. (2025, July 2). Is love really dead in the digital age? *Differens Magazine*. https://differensmagazine.com/2025/07/02/poul-poder/

Poirier, S.-M., Cosby, S., Sénécal, S., Coursaris, C. K., Fredette, M., & Léger, P.-M. (2024). The impact of social presence cues in social media product photos on consumers' purchase intentions. *Journal of Business Research*, *185*, 114932. DOI: 10.1016/j.jbusres.2024.114932

Possati, L. (2022). Psychoanalyzing artificial intelligence: The case of Replika. *AI & Society*, *38*(4), 1725–1738. Advance online publication. DOI: 10.1007/s00146-021-01379-7

Postman, N. (1970). *Teaching as a subversive activity: A no-holds-barred assault on outdated teaching methods-with dramatic and practical proposals on how education can be made relevant to today's world*. Delta.

Postman, N. (1974). The ecology of learning. *English Journal*, *63*(4), 58–64. https://www.jstor.org/stable/813650. DOI: 10.58680/ej197417549

Poushter, J., & Nicholas, K. (2020, June 25). The global divide on homosexuality persists. *Pew Research Center*. https://www.pewresearch.org/global/2020/06/25/global-divide-on-homosexuality-persists/

Pretorius, L. (2024). Demystifying research paradigms: Navigating ontology, epistemology, and axiology in research. *The Qualitative Report*, *29*(10), 2698–2715. DOI: 10.46743/2160-3715/2024.7632

Prochazka, A., & Brooks, R. (2024). Digital Lovers and Jealousy: Anticipated Emotional Responses to Emotionally and Physically Sophisticated Sexual Technologies. *Human Behavior and Emerging Technologies, 2024*, 1–13. Advance online publication. DOI: 10.1155/2024/1413351

Pulla, V., & Carter, E. (2018). Employing interpretivism in social work research. *International journal of social work and human services practice, 6*(1), 9-14.

Qian, Z. (2025, October 7). Why America builds AI girlfriends and China makes AI boyfriends. *ChinaTalk*. https://www.chinatalk.media/p/why-america-builds-ai-girlfriends

Qiao, Q., Wu, W., & Li, Y. (2022a). Enhancing consumer usage of AI-chatbots: The role of perceived humanness, social presence, and social interactivity. *2022 8th International Conference on Information Management (ICIM)*, 97-103. DOI: 10.1109/ICIM56520.2022.00025

Qiao, Q., Wu, W., & Li, Y. (2022b, 25-27 March 2022). Enhancing consumer usage of AI-chatbots: The role of perceived humanness, social presence, and social interactivity. 2022 8th International Conference on Information Management (ICIM), Qiu, L., & Liu, X. (2019). Media representation of loneliness in China of the chapter. In B. Fox (Ed.), *Emotions and loneliness in a networked society* (pp. 135-154). Springer International Publishing. DOI: 10.1007/978-3-030-24882-6_7

Raedler, J. B., Swaroop, S., & Pan, W. (2025). AI companions are not the solution to loneliness: Design choices and their drawbacks. ICLR 2025 Workshop on Human-AI Coevolution, Richet, J.-L. (2025). AI companionship or digital entrapment? Investigating the impact of anthropomorphic AI-based chatbots. *Journal of Innovation & Knowledge, 10*(6), 100835. DOI: 10.1016/j.jik.2025.100835

Raju, P. V. M., & Sumallika, T. (2023). The impact of AI in the global economy and its implications in industry 4.0 era. *Information Technology, Education and Society, 18*(2), 53–62. DOI: 10.7459/ites/18.2.05

Ramadan, Z. F., Farah, M., & El Essrawi, L. (2021). From Amazon. com to Amazon. love: How Alexa is redefining companionship and interdependence for people with special needs. *Psychology and Marketing, 38*(4), 596–609. DOI: 10.1002/mar.21441

Ratcliffe, M. (2020). *Feelings of being: Phenomenology, psychiatry, and the sense of reality*. Oxford University Press.

Reddy, S. P., John, A., & Kaushik, S. (2024). *AI As romantic companion- An ethical dilemma* (SSRN Scholarly Paper No. 5106936). Social Science Research Network. DOI: 10.2139/ssrn.5106936

Reeves, B., & Nass, C. (1996). *The media equation: how people treat computers, television, and new media like real people and places*. http://web.stanford.edu/group/cslipublications/cslipublications/site/1575860538.shtml

Reis, H. T., Clark, M. S., & Holmes, J. G. (2004). Perceived responsiveness in relationships. In Rholes, W. S., & Simpson, J. A. (Eds.), *Adult attachment: Theory, research, and clinical implications* (pp. 201–225). Guilford Press.

Report, S. (2025). *Study exposes privacy risks of AI chatbot conversations*. Stanford.edu; Stanford University. https://news.stanford.edu/stories/2025/10/ai-chatbot-privacy-concerns-risks-research

Rettberg, J. W. (2023). *Machine vision: How algorithms are changing the way we see the world*. John Wiley & Sons.

Rice, R. E. (1993). Media Appropriateness. *Human Communication Research, 19*(4), 451–484. DOI: 10.1111/j.1468-2958.1993.tb00309.x

Rich, A. (1980). Compulsory heterosexuality and lesbian existence. *Journal of Women's History, 15*(3), 11–48. DOI: 10.1353/jowh.2003.0079

Richardson, J. W. (2016). Digital technologies in contemporary Cambodia. In Brickell, K., & Springer, S. (Eds.), *The handbook of contemporary Cambodia* (pp. 366–376). Routledge., DOI: 10.4324/9781315736709

Riedl, R. (2022). Is trust in artificial intelligence systems related to user personality? Review of empirical evidence and future research directions. *Electronic Markets, 32*(4), 2021–2051. DOI: 10.1007/s12525-022-00594-4

Ritchie, J. N. & A., Jayanti, S. F.-T. and A., Fletcher, E., & Fletcher, E. (2023, March 24). *Romance scammers' favorite lies exposed*. Federal Trade Commission. https://www.ftc.gov/news-events/data-visualizations/data-spotlight/2023/02/romance-scammers-favorite-lies-exposed

Roaché, D. J., Sharabi, L. L., Hicks, L., & Hurley, M. M. (2025). 'Hey Siri, ask them out:' investigating the use of artificial intelligence in date request messaging. *Behaviour & Information Technology*, •••, 1–13. DOI: 10.1080/0144929X.2025.2559289

Robbins, B. G., Dechter, A., & Kornrich, S. (2022). Assessing the deinstitutionalization of marriage thesis: An experimental test. *American Sociological Review, 87*(2), 237-274. DOI: 10.1177/00031224221080960

Robinson, R. S. (2014). Purposive Sampling of the chapter. In Michalos, A. C. (Ed.), *Encyclopedia of Quality of Life and Well-Being Research* (pp. 5243–5245). Springer Netherlands., DOI: 10.1007/978-94-007-0753-5_2337

Rod, J., & Kera, D. (2010). From agency and subjectivity to animism: Phenomenological and Science Technology Studies (STS) approach to design of large techno-social systems. *Digital Creativity (Exeter), 21*(1), 70–76. DOI: 10.1080/14626261003654558

Rokach, A. (2024). *Love culturally: How does culture affect intimacy, commitment & love. The Intricacies of Love and Intimacy*. Taylor Francis.

Root, B. L., & Exline, J. J. (2014). The role of continuing bonds in coping with grief: Overview and future directions. *Death Studies, 38*(1), 1–8. DOI: 10.1080/07481187.2012.712608 PMID: 24521040

Royal Malaysia Police (via Malay Mail). (2025, January 10). Love scams prey on elderly women, causing RM45.9 million in losses in 2024. Malay Mail. https://www.malaymail.com/news/malaysia/2025/01/10/lonely-hearts-exploited-love-scams-prey-on-elderly-women-causing-rm45-9-mln-in-losses-in-2024/162742

Rusbult, C. E. (1980). Commitment and satisfaction in romantic associations: A test of the investment model. *Journal of Experimental Social Psychology, 16*(2), 172–186. DOI: 10.1016/0022-1031(80)90007-4

Rus, H. M., & Tiemensma, J. (2017). "It's complicated." A systematic review of associations between social network site use and romantic relationships. *Computers in Human Behavior, 75*, 684–703. DOI: 10.1016/j.chb.2017.06.004

Russo, C., Romano, L., Clemente, D., Iacovone, L., Gladwin, T. E., & Panno, A. (2025b). Gender differences in artificial intelligence: The role of artificial intelligence anxiety. *Frontiers in Psychology, 16*, 1559457. DOI: 10.3389/fpsyg.2025.1559457 PMID: 40396147

Ryan, M. (2020). In AI we trust: Ethics, artificial intelligence, and reliability. *Science and Engineering Ethics, 26*(5), 2749–2767. Advance online publication. DOI: 10.1007/s11948-020-00228-y PMID: 32524425

Sætra, H. S. (2023). Generative AI: Here to stay, but for good? *Technology in Society, 75*, 102372. DOI: 10.1016/j.techsoc.2023.102372

Sales, N. J. (2021, June 1). *Swipe right for loneliness: on the gamification of dating apps*. Literary Hub. https://lithub.com/swipe-right-for-loneliness-on-the-gamification-of-dating-apps/

Sanchez Salas, S. (2025). Digital intimacy with AI companions: When vulnerability becomes a business risk-A governance framework for AI companion companies. DOI: 10.2139/ssrn.5435195

Santos, H. C., Varnum, M. E. W., & Grossmann, I. (2017). Global increases in individualism. *Psychological Science*, *28*(9), 1228–1239. DOI: 10.1177/0956797617700622 PMID: 28703638

Saracini, C., Cornejo-Plaza, M. I., & Cippitani, R. (2025). Techno-emotional projection in human–GenAI relationships: A psychological and ethical conceptual perspective. *Frontiers in Psychology*, *16*, 1662206. Advance online publication. DOI: 10.3389/fpsyg.2025.1662206 PMID: 41089650

Saunders, B., Sim, J., Kingstone, T., Baker, S., Waterfield, J., Bartlam, B., Burroughs, H., & Jinks, C. (2018). Saturation in qualitative research: Exploring its conceptualization and operationalization. *Quality & Quantity*, *52*(4), 1893–1907. DOI: 10.1007/s11135-017-0574-8 PMID: 29937585

Savic, M. (2024). Artificial companions, real connections?: Examining AI's role in social connection. *M/C journal, 27*(6). DOI: 10.5204/mcj.3111

Savuth, C., & Sothea, O. (2023). Digital transformation in Cambodia. *Journal of Southeast Asian Economies*, *40*(1), 145–172. https://www.jstor.org/stable/27211228. DOI: 10.1355/ae40-1g

Schuett, J. (2021). *Defining the scope of AI regulations* (SSRN Scholarly Paper No. 3453632). Social Science Research Network. DOI: 10.2139/ssrn.3453632

Schulhoff, S. (2025a). *DAN (Do Anything Now)*. Learnprompting.org. https://learnprompting.org/docs/prompt_hacking/offensive_measures/dan

Schulhoff, S. (2025b). *DAN (Do Anything Now)*. Learnprompting.org. https://learnprompting.org/docs/prompt_hacking/offensive_measures/dan

Science and Technology Daily. (2024). *The romance and concerns of AI "companions."* Cctv.com. https://news.cctv.com/2024/07/20/ARTINRdIH7ufRzkipfKmZeqj240720.shtml?utm_source=chatgpt.com

Scott, E. S. (2000). *Social norms and the legal regulation of marriage* (SSRN Scholarly Paper No. 224972). Social Science Research Network. DOI: 10.2139/ssrn.224972

Searle, J. (1980). Minds, brains, and programs. *Behavioral and Brain Sciences*, *3*(3), 417–457. DOI: 10.1017/S0140525X00005756

Secretariat, A. S. E. A. N. (2022). *Digital policy action areas for a connected ASEAN: ASEAN best practice benchmarking and an action plan for regional harmonization*. ITU Publications Asia-Pacific Region. https://asean.org/wp-content/uploads/2024/03/Digital-Policy-Action-Areas-for-a-Connected-ASEAN.pdf

Shaji George, A., Hovan George, A. S., Baskar, T., & Pandey, D. (2023). The allure of artificial intimacy: Examining the appeal and ethics of using generative AI for simulated relationships. *Partners Universal International Innovation Journal, 1*(6), 132–147. DOI: 10.5281/zenodo.10391614

Sharabi, L. (2025, June 23). AI is about to change everything, including how we date. *Psychology Today*. https://www.psychologytoday.com/us/blog/dating-in-the-digital-age/202506/is-ai-the-end-of-dating-apps

Sharabi, L. (2022). Finding love on a first data: Matching algorithms in online dating. *Harvard Data Science Review*. Advance online publication. DOI: 10.1162/99608f92.1b5c3b7b

Sharma, D. (2025, May 29). *AI is slowly becoming part of how Indians explore love and relationships, thanks to dating apps*. NDTV. https://www.ndtv.com/lifestyle/ai-is-taking-over-online-dating-on-bumble-happn-tinder-hinge-is-india-swiping-right-8536490

Sharma, A., Lin, I. W., Miner, A. S., Atkins, D. C., & Althoff, T. (2023). Human–AI collaboration enables more empathic conversations in text-based peer-to-peer mental health support. *Nature Machine Intelligence, 5*(1), 46–57. DOI: 10.1038/s42256-022-00593-2

Shchemelinin, K. S. (2020). Differences between modern marriage and traditional marriage and principles for improving the quality of heterosexual marriage in modern society. *Scientific Journal NovaUm. Ru, 24*, 151–160. https://www.researchgate.net/publication/395255131_DIFFERENCES_OF_MODERN_MARRIAGE_FROM_TRADITIONAL_AND_PRINCIPLES_FOR_IMPROVING_THE_QUALITY_OF_HETEROSEXUAL_MARRIAGE_IN_A_MODERN_SOCIETY

Shean, M., & Mander, D. (2020). Building emotional safety for students in school environments: Challenges and opportunities. In Midford, R., Nutton, G., Hyndman, B., & Silburn, S. (Eds.), *Health and education interdependence: Thriving from birth to adulthood* (pp. 225–248). Springer., DOI: 10.1007/978-981-15-3959-6_12

Sheehan, B., Jin, H. S., & Gottlieb, U. (2020). Customer service chatbots: Anthropomorphism and adoption. *Journal of Business Research, 115*, 14–24. DOI: 10.1016/j.jbusres.2020.04.030

Sheffield, R., & Squires, D. (2025). *Crossroads: American family life at the intersection of tradition and modernity* (Special Report No. No.310; p. 43). The Heritage Foundation. https://www.heritage.org/marriage-and-family/report/crossroads-american-family-life-the-intersection-tradition-and-modernity

Sheikh, H., Prins, C., & Schrijvers, E. (2023). Artificial intelligence: Definition and background. In Sheikh, H., Prins, C., & Schrijvers, E. (Eds.), *Mission AI: the newsystem technology* (pp. 15–41). Springer International Publishing., DOI: 10.1007/978-3-031-21448-6_2

Shepherd, D. (2016). *Building relationships: Online dating and the new logics of Internet culture*. Bloomsbury Publishing PLC.

Sheridan, T. (2020). Forty-five years of man-machine systems: prospects for advanced robotics. *Studi Organizzativi,*(2020/suppl.1), 73-85. DOI: 10.3280/SO2020-001-S1005

Shih, L. (2005). On the nature and development of social presence in online course discussions. *Online Learning : the Official Journal of the Online Learning Consortium, 9*(3), 115–136. DOI: 10.24059/olj.v9i3.1788

Shin, D., Chotiyaputta, V., & Zaid, B. (2022). The effects of cultural dimensions on algorithmic news: How do cultural value orientations affect how people perceive algorithms? *Computers in Human Behavior, 126*, 107007. DOI: 10.1016/j.chb.2021.107007

Shin, D., & Park, Y. J. (2019). Role of fairness, accountability, and transparency in algorithmic affordance. *Computers in Human Behavior, 98*(98), 277–284. DOI: 10.1016/j.chb.2019.04.019

Short, J., Williams, E., & Christie, B. (1976). *The social psychology of telecommunications*. Wiley.

Shum, H.-Y., He, X., & Li, D. (2018). From Eliza to XiaoIce: Challenges and opportunities with social chatbots. *Frontiers of Information Technology & Electronic Engineering, 19*(1), 10–26. DOI: 10.1631/FITEE.1700826

Siddals, S., Torous, J., & Coxon, A. (2024). "It happened to be the perfect thing": experiences of generative AI chatbots for mental health. *npj Mental Health Research, 3*(1), 48. DOI: 10.1038/s44184-024-00097-4

Siemon, D., Strohmann, T., Khosrawi-Rad, B., de Vreede, T., Elshan, E., & Meyer, M. (2022). Why do we turn to virtual companions? A text mining analysis of Replika reviews. 28th Americas Conference on Information Systems, AMCIS 2022.https://www.researchgate.net/publication/360334616_Why_Do_We_Turn_to_Virtual_Companions_A_Text_Mining_Analysis_of_Replika_Reviews

Simpson, J. A., & Rholes, W. S. (2017). Adult attachment, stress, and romantic relationships. *Current Opinion in Psychology, 13*, 19–24. DOI: 10.1016/j.copsyc.2016.04.006

Sinclair, R., Bland, M., & Savage, B. (2023). Dating hot spot to fraud hot spot: Targeting the social characteristics of romance fraud victims in England and Wales. *Criminology & Public Policy.*

Sjoraida, D. F. (2025, August 25). *AI and Emotional Intimacy: Exploring Romantic Bonds with Artificial Companions.* https://journals.ai-mrc.com/humanexus/article/view/575

Skinner, B. F. (1963). Operant behavior. *The American Psychologist, 18*(8), 503–515. DOI: 10.1037/h0045185

Skjuve, M., Følstad, A., & Brandtzæg, P. B. (2023). A longitudinal study of self-disclosure in human–chatbot relationships. *Interacting with Computers, 35*(1), 24–39. DOI: 10.1093/iwc/iwad022

Skjuve, M., Følstad, A., Fostervold, K. I., & Brandtzaeg, P. B. (2021). My Chatbot Companion - a Study of Human-Chatbot Relationships. *International Journal of Human-Computer Studies, 149*, 102601. DOI: 10.1016/j.ijhcs.2021.102601

Skjuve, M., Følstad, A., Fostervold, K. I., & Brandtzaeg, P. B. (2022). A longitudinal study of human–chatbot relationships. *International Journal of Human-Computer Studies, 168*, 102903. DOI: 10.1016/j.ijhcs.2022.102903

Slaby, J. (2022). Affective intentionality and the feeling of being alive. *Phenomenology and the Cognitive Sciences, 21*(2), 233–250. DOI: 10.1007/s11097-021-09756-7

Slimi, Z., & Carballido, B. V. (2023). Navigating the ethical challenges of artificial intelligence in higher education: An analysis of seven global ai ethics policies. *TEM Journal, 12*(2), 590–602. https://www.ceeol.com/search/article-detail?id=1122977

Slotta, D. (2025a). *Breakdown of artificial intelligence product users in China as of May 2024, by user intention.* Retrieved June 18, 2025 from https://www.statista.com/statistics/1550257/china-share-of-generative-ai-users-by-user-intention/#:~:text=In%20a%20survey%20conducted%20in,to%20enhance%20their%20cognitive%20abilities

Slotta, D. (2025b). *Breakdown of generative artificial intelligence users in China as of June 2024, by age.* Retrieved June 18, 2025 from https://www.statista.com/statistics/1548670/china-generative-ai-users-by-age/

Smets, A., Ballon, P., & Walravens, N. (2021). Mediated by code: Unpacking algorithmic curation of urban experiences. *Media and Communication, 9*(4), 250–259. DOI: 10.17645/mac.v9i4.4086

Smith, C. (2022). Art of the Scam: The Confidence-Man. *A New Companion to Herman Melville*, 134.

Smith, M. G., Bradbury, T. N., & Karney, B. R. (2025). Can generative AI chatbots emulate human connection? A relationship science perspective. *Perspectives on Psychological Science, 17456916251351306*(6), 1081–1099. Advance online publication. DOI: 10.1177/17456916251351306 PMID: 40743457

Soeung, S. (2016). Cambodia in 2015: Accommodating generational change. *Southeast Asian Affairs, 2016*(1), 109–127. https://muse.jhu.edu/pub/70/article/627454/pdf

Solmi, M., Radua, J., Olivola, M., Croce, E., Soardo, L., Salazar de Pablo, G., Il Shin, J., Kirkbride, J. B., Jones, P., Kim, J. H., Kim, J. Y., Carvalho, A. F., Seeman, M. V., Correll, C. U., & Fusar-Poli, P. (2022). Age at onset of mental disorders worldwide: Large-scale meta-analysis of 192 epidemiological studies. *Molecular Psychiatry, 27*(1), 281–295. DOI: 10.1038/s41380-021-01161-7 PMID: 34079068

Solomon, R. C. (1993). *The passions: Emotions and the meaning of life*. Hackett.

Song, X., Xu, B., & Zhao, Z. (2022). Can people experience romantic love for artificial intelligence? An empirical study of intelligent assistants. *Information & Management, 59*(2), 103595. DOI: 10.1016/j.im.2022.103595

Sorell, T., & Whitty, M. (2019). Online romance scams and victimhood. *Security Journal, 32*, 342–361. DOI: 10.1057/s41284-019-00166-w

Sorokowska, A., Kowal, M., Saluja, S., Aavik, T., Alm, C., Anjum, A., Asao, K., Batres, C., Bensafia, A., Bizumic, B., Boussena, M., Buss, D. M., Butovskaya, M., Can, S., Carrier, A., Cetinkaya, H., Conroy-Beam, D., Cueto, R. M., Czub, M., & Croy, I. (2023). Love and affectionate touch toward romantic partners all over the world. *Scientific Reports, 13*(1), 5497. DOI: 10.1038/s41598-023-31502-1 PMID: 37015974

Spar, D. L., & Garber, A. (2025). Does Marriage Have a Future? *New Atlantis (Washington, D.C.)*, (81), 20–33.

Spatola, N., & Chaminade, T. (2022). Cognitive load increases anthropomorphism of humanoid robot. The automatic path of anthropomorphism. *International Journal of Human-Computer Studies, 167*, 102884. DOI: 10.1016/j.ijhcs.2022.102884

Srnicek, N. (2017). *Platform capitalism.* Polity Press. https://mudancatecnologicaedinamicacapitalista.wordpress.com/wp-content/uploads/2019/02/platform-capitalism.pdf

Stanley, S. M., & Rhoades, G. K. (2023). *What's the plan? Cohabitation, engagement,and divorce*. Institute for Family Studies., https://ifstudies.org/ifs-admin/resources/reports/cohabitationreportapr2023-final.pdf

Statista. (2024). *Target audience Artificial Intelligence (AI) enthusiasts in China*. Retrieved June 18, 2025 from https://www.statista.com/study/170076/target-audience-artificial-intelligence-ai-enthusiasts-in-china/

Steinhoff, J. (2021). Industrializing intelligence: a political economic history of the AI industry of the chapter. In Steinhoff, J. (Ed.), *Automation and autonomy: labour, capital and machines in the artificial intelligence industry* (pp. 99–131). Springer International Publishing., DOI: 10.1007/978-3-030-71689-9_4

Stein, J. P., Messingschlager, T., Gnambs, T., Hutmacher, F., & Appel, M. (2024). Attitudes towards AI: Measurement and associations with personality. *Scientific Reports*, *14*(1), 2909. DOI: 10.1038/s41598-024-53335-2 PMID: 38316898

Sternberg, R. J. (1986). A triangular theory of love. *Psychological Review*, *93*(2), 119–135. DOI: 10.1037/0033-295X.93.2.119

Stinson, C. (2022). Algorithms are not neutral: Bias in collaborative filtering. *AI and Ethics*, *2*(4), 763–770. DOI: 10.1007/s43681-022-00136-w PMID: 35128540

Stray, J., Halevy, A., Assar, P., Hadfield-Menell, D., Boutilier, C., Ashar, A., Bakalar, C., Beattie, L., Ekstrand, M., Leibowicz, C., Moon Sehat, C., Johansen, S., Kerlin, L., Vickrey, D., Singh, S., Vrijenhoek, S., Zhang, A., Andrus, M. K., Helberger, N., & Vasan, N. (2024). Building human values into recommender systems: An interdisciplinary synthesis. *ACM Transactions on Recommender Systems*, *2*(3), 1–57. DOI: 10.1145/3632297

Suchman, L. A. (2007). *Human-machine reconfigurations: Plans and situated actions*. Cambridge University Press.

Sukhera, J. (2022). Narrative reviews: Flexible, rigorous, and practical. *Journal of Graduate Medical Education*, *14*(4), 414–417. 10.4300%2FJGME-D-22-00480.1 PMID: 35991099

Sullivan, Y., & Nyawa, S., & Wamba, Samuel. F. (2023). Combating loneliness with artificial intelligence: An AI-based emotional support model. *Proceedings of the 56th Hawaii International Conference on System Sciences*, 10. DOI: 10.24251/HICSS.2023.541

Sumanti, S. T. (2023). Analysis of Interpersonal Communication Patterns of Love Scams Mode on Social Media in Female Students in Medan City. *Jurnal Lensa Mutiara Komunikasi*, *7*(1), 74–85. DOI: 10.51544/jlmk.v7i1.3827

Sundar, S. (2020). Rise of machine agency: A framework for studying the psychology of human–ai interaction (HAII). *Journal of Computer-Mediated Communication, 25*(1), 74–88. DOI: 10.1093/jcmc/zmz026

Sun, X., Jahangir, A., Alghamdi, A. A., & Liu, F. (2025). Use of ai-based mental health tools and psychological well-being among Chinese university students: A parallel mediation model of emotional self-efficacy and perceived autonomy. *Scientific Reports, 15*(1), 40305. DOI: 10.1038/s41598-025-24013-8 PMID: 41249306

Symons, J., & Sanwoolu, O. D. (2025). Close personal relationships with people and artifacts? Loneliness, agent-relative obligations, and artificially intelligent companions. *Philosophy & Technology, 38*(1), 18. Advance online publication. DOI: 10.1007/s13347-025-00845-0

Taherdoost, H. (2022). What are different research approaches? Comprehensive review of qualitative, quantitative, and mixed method research, their applications, types, and limitations. *Journal of Management Science & Engineering Research, 5*(1), 53–63. DOI: 10.30564/jmser.v5i1.4538

Taimur, A. (2025). Manipulative matchmaking-A legal and ethical assessment of addictive AI design in dating apps. *i-lex, 18*(1), 31–48. DOI: 10.6092/issn.1825-1927/21954

Ta-Johnson, V. P., Boatfield, C., Wang, X., DeCero, E., Krupica, I. C., Rasof, S. D., Motzer, A., & Pedryc, W. M. (2022). Assessing the topics and motivating factors behind human-social chatbot interactions: Thematic analysis of user experiences. *JMIR Human Factors, 9*(4), e38876. DOI: 10.2196/38876 PMID: 36190745

Tanaka, H., & Ho, M. H. (2025). Artificial Intelligence's Sexual Politics: Three Modes and the Case of Japan. *Technology. Power and Society: Critical Perspectives on the Global Digital Transformation, 1*, 228–250. DOI: 10.1163/9789004711396_013

Ta, V., Griffith, C., Boatfield, C., Wang, X., Civitello, M., Bader, H., DeCero, E., & Loggarakis, A. (2020). User experiences of social support from companion chatbots in everyday contexts: Thematic analysis. *Journal of Medical Internet Research, 22*(3), e16235. DOI: 10.2196/16235 PMID: 32141837

Taylor, A. (2022). *Cryptosocial: How Cryptocurrencies Are Changing Social Media*. Business Expert Press.

Taylor, C. (1991). *The ethics of authenticity*. Harvard University Press.

Tech Desk, T. O. I. (2025, August 31). Whitney Wolfe Herd, co-founder of dating apps Tinder and Bumble, makes a "confession" about her husband: I would never . . . *The Times of India.* https://timesofindia.indiatimes.com/technology/tech-news/whitney-wolfe-herd-co-founder-of-dating-apps-tinder-and-bumble-makes-a-confession-about-her-husband-i-would-never-/articleshow/123615566.cms

The Attachment Project. (2025, September 24). *AI Companions & Attachment: Benefits, Risks & red flags.* Attachment Project. https://www.attachmentproject.com/blog/ai-companions/

The Global Times. (2024). *AI bot, too perfect to be a boyfriend.* Globaltimes.cn. https://www.globaltimes.cn/page/202406/1314007.shtml

The South China Morning Post. (2024, May 22). *Chinese woman goes viral for falling in love with chatbot, has romantic talks, goes on "beach date", introduces "him" to mother.* South China Morning Post. https://www.scmp.com/news/people-culture/trending-china/article/3263280/chinese-woman-goes-viral-falling-love-chatbot-has-romantic-talks-goes-beach-date-introduces-him

Thierer, A. D., Castillo O'Sullivan, A., & Russell, R. (2017). *Artificial intelligence and public policy* (SSRN Scholarly Paper No. 3021135). Social Science Research Network. DOI: 10.2139/ssrn.3021135

Thomas, M. F., Binder, A., & Matthes, J. (2022). The agony of partner choice: The effect of excessive partner availability on fear of being single, self-esteem, and partner choice overload. *Computers in Human Behavior*, *126*, 106977. DOI: 10.1016/j.chb.2021.106977

Thompson, R. A., Simpson, J. A., & Berlin, L. J. (2022). Taking perspective on attachment theory and research: Nine fundamental questions. *Attachment & Human Development*, *24*(5), 543–560. DOI: 10.1080/14616734.2022.2030132 PMID: 35073828

Thormundsson, B. (2025a). *Leading 20 artificial intelligence (AI) countries in 2024, by commercial investment.* Statista.com. Retrieved June 18, 2025 from https://www.statista.com/statistics/1574235/top-20-ai-countries-by-commercial-investment/

Thormundsson, B. (2025b). *Leading 20 artificial intelligence (AI) countries in 2024, by government strategy.* Retrieved June 18, 2025 from https://www.statista.com/statistics/1411417/top-20-ai-countries-by-national-strategy/

Thormundsson, B. (2025c). *Leading 20 artificial intelligence (AI) countries in 2024, by research capacity.* Retrieved June 18, 2025 from https://www.statista.com/statistics/1410523/top-20-ai-countries-by-research-capacity/

Tian, W., Ge, J., Zhao, Y., & Zheng, X. (2024). AI Chatbots in Chinese higher education: adoption, perception, and influence among graduate students—an integrated analysis utilizing UTAUT and ECM models [Original Research]. *Frontiers in Psychology, Volume 15 - 2024*. DOI: 10.3389/fpsyg.2024.1268549

Timmermans, E., & Alexopoulos, C. (2020). Anxiously searching for love (Among other things): Attachment orientation and mobile dating application users' motives and outcomes. *Cyberpsychology, Behavior, and Social Networking*, *23*(7), 447–452. DOI: 10.1089/cyber.2019.0542 PMID: 32345053

Toader, D.-C., Boca, G., Toader, R., Măcelaru, M., Toader, C., Ighian, D., & Rădulescu, A. T. (2020). The effect of social presence and chatbot errors on trust. *Sustainability (Basel)*, *12*(1), 256. DOI: 10.3390/su12010256

Tolstikova, I., Ignatjeva, O., Kondratenko, K., & Pletnev, A. (2020). Generation Z and its value transformations: Digital reality vs. phygital interaction. *Communications in Computer and Information Science*, *1242*, 47–60. DOI: 10.1007/978-3-030-65218-0_4

Toma, C. L. (2022). Online dating and psychological wellbeing: A social compensation perspective. *Current Opinion in Psychology*, *46*, 101331. DOI: 10.1016/j.copsyc.2022.101331 PMID: 35349878

Tongco, M. D. C. (2007). Purposive sampling as a tool for informant selection. www.ethnobotanyjournal.org/vol5/i1547-3465-05-147.pdf

TRC. (2023). *Annual ICT statistics report*. Phnom Penh: Telecommunication Regulator of Cambodia. https://trc.gov.kh/en/resources/telecom-statistics

Trothen, T. J. (2022). Replika: Spiritual enhancement technology? *Religions*, *13*(4), 275. DOI: 10.3390/rel13040275

Truong, T. T. H., & Chen, J. S. (2025). When empathy is enhanced by human–AI interaction: An investigation of anthropomorphism and responsiveness on customer experience with AI chatbots. *Asia Pacific Journal of Marketing and Logistics*, *37*(12), 3908–3925. Advance online publication. DOI: 10.1108/APJML-10-2024-1464

Tu, C.-H., & McIsaac, M. (2002). The relationship of social presence and interaction in online classes. *American Journal of Distance Education*, *16*(3), 131–150. DOI: 10.1207/S15389286AJDE1603_2

Tukachinsky, R. (2011). Parasocial relationships and romantic attraction. *Journal of Broadcasting & Electronic Media*, *55*(1), 73–94.

Turkle, S. (2011). *Alone together: Why we expect more from technology and less from each other*. Basic Books.

Tyson, G., Perta, V. C., Haddadi, H., & Seto, M. C. (2016). A first look at user activity on Tinder. *arXiv (Cornell University)*. https://doi.org//arxiv.1607.01952DOI: 10.1109/ASONAM.2016.7752275

UNDP. (2019). Social choesion and Cambodia. *United Nations Development Programme*, 1–32. https://www.undp.org/sites/g/files/zskgke326/files/2023-07/Social %20Cohesion_ENG.pdf

UNDP. (2022). *Digital strategy 2022-2025: Creating a world in which digital is an empowering force for people and planet*. United Nations Development Programme. https://digitalstrategy.undp.org

Ungar, M. (2011). The social ecology of resilience: Addressing contextual and cultural ambiguity of a nascent construct. *The American Journal of Orthopsychiatry*, *81*(1), 1–17. DOI: 10.1111/j.1939-0025.2010.01067.x PMID: 21219271

Unkel, N. S., & De Sá Carvalho Leonardo, H. (2018). Women working emotions - emotional labour in heterosexual relationships. *The Maastricht Journal of Liberal Arts*, *10*, 20–39. DOI: 10.26481/mjla.2018.v10.600

Upton-Clark, E. (2025, June 17). How AI is Transforming the Dating Landscape for Singles. *Fast Company*. https://fastcompany.co.za/tech/2025-06-17-how-ai-is -transforming-the-dating-landscape-for-singles/

van Anders, S. M., & Gray, P. B. (2007). Hormones and human partnering. *Annual Review of Sex Research*, *18*(1), 60–93. DOI: 10.1080/10532528.2007.10559847

Van Dijck, J. (2014). Datafication, dataism and dataveillance: Big data between scientific paradigm and ideology. *Surveillance & Society*, *12*(2), 197–208. DOI: 10.24908/ss.v12i2.4776

Vasbø, K. B., & Hegna, K. (2025). Feeling close, disclosing feelings–family practices and practices of intimacy in youth–parent relations across three generations in Norway. *Journal of Youth Studies*, *28*(2), 299–317. DOI: 10.1080/13676261.2023.2267481

Vasilescu, C., & Gheorghe, M. (2024). Improving the performance of corporate employees through the use of artificial intelligence: The case of copilot application. *Proceedings of the ... International Conference on Business Excellence*, *18*(1), 1819–1830. https://doi.org/DOI: 10.2478/picbe-2024-0153

Veale, D., Robins, E., Thomson, A. B., & Gilbert, P. (2023). No safety without emotional safety. *The Lancet. Psychiatry*, *10*(1), 65–70. DOI: 10.1016/S2215-0366(22)00373-X PMID: 36442491

Verhagen, T., van Nes, J., Feldberg, F., & van Dolen, W. (2014). Virtual Customer Service Agents: Using Social Presence and Personalization to Shape Online Service Encounters*. *Journal of Computer-Mediated Communication*, *19*(3), 529–545. DOI: 10.1111/jcc4.12066

Viik, T. (2020). Falling in love with robots: A phenomenological study of experiencing technological alterities. *Paladyn : Journal of Behavioral Robotics*, *11*(1), 52–65. DOI: 10.1515/pjbr-2020-0005

Vogels, E. A., & McClain, C. (2023). Key findings about online dating in the US. *Pew Research Center, 2*.

Volpato, R., DeBruine, L., & Stumpf, S. (2025). Trusting emotional support from generative artificial intelligence: A conceptual review. *Computers in Human Behavior: Artificial Humans*, *5*, 100195. DOI: 10.1016/j.chbah.2025.100195

Vuori, N., Burkhard, B., & Pitkäranta, L. (2025). It's amazing – but terrifying!: Unveiling the combined effect of emotional and cognitive trust on organizational member' behaviours, AI performance, and adoption. *Journal of Management Studies*. Advance online publication. DOI: 10.1111/joms.13177

Wada, K., & Shibata, T. (2023). Social and emotional outcomes of robot-assisted therapy in long-term care: A longitudinal analysis. *International Journal of Social Robotics*, *15*(4), 567–580.

Walther, J. B. (2015). Social Information Processing Theory (CMC) of the chapter. In *The International Encyclopedia of Interpersonal Communication* (pp. 1-13). DOI: 10.1002/9781118540190.wbeic192

Walther, J. B., & Whitty, M. T. (2020). Language, Psychology, and New New Media: The Hyperpersonal Model of Mediated Communication at Twenty-Five Years. *Journal of Language and Social Psychology*, *40*(1), 120–135. DOI: 10.1177/0261927X20967703

Wa-Mbaleka, S. (2020). The Researcher as an Instrument. *Computer Supported Qualitative Research*, 33-41. DOI: 10.1007/978-3-030-31787-4_3

Wang, W., & Toscano, M. (2024, November). *Artificial intelligence and Relationships: 1 in 4 young adults believe AI partners could replace real-life romance | Institute for Family Studies*. Institute for Family Studies. https://ifstudies.org/report-brief/artificial-intelligence-and-relationships-1-in-4-young-adults-believe-ai-partners-could-replace-real-life-romance

Wang, B., Wu, C., & Huang, L. (2018). Emotional safety culture: A new and key element of safety culture. *Process Safety Progress*, *37*(2), 134–139. DOI: 10.1002/prs.11953

Wang, C. (2022). Online dating scam victims psychological impact analysis. *Journal of Education. Humanities and Social Sciences*, *4*, 149–154. DOI: 10.54097/ehss.v4i.2740

Wang, C. D., Jin, L., Han, G., Zhu, W., & Bismar, D. (2022). Cross-cultural differences in adult attachment and depression: A culturally congruent approach. *Journal of Counseling Psychology*, *69*(3), 298–310. DOI: 10.1037/cou0000589 PMID: 34647765

Wang, F., & Topalli, V. (2024). Understanding romance scammers through the lens of their victims: Qualitative modeling of risk and protective factors in the online context. *American Journal of Criminal Justice*, *49*(1), 145–181. DOI: 10.1007/s12103-022-09706-4

Wang, F., & Zhou, X. (2022). Persuasive schemes for financial exploitation in online romance scam: An Anatomy on Sha Zhu pan ( ) in China. *Victims & Offenders*, •••, 1–28. DOI: 10.1080/15564886.2022.2051109

Wang, H. (2023). Algorithmic colonization of love in advance. *Techné*, *27*(2), 260–280. DOI: 10.5840/techne202381181

Wang, X., Pang, C. C., & Hui, P. (2025). *'My dataset of love': A preliminary mixed-method exploration of human-ai romantic relationships. ArXiv*. Cornell University., DOI: 10.1145/3757532

Wang, X., Pang, C. C., & Hui, P. (2025). My Dataset of Love': A Preliminary Mixed-Method Exploration of Human-AI Romantic Relationships. *Proceedings of the ACM on Human-Computer Interaction*, *9*(7), 1–34.

Wang, Y. (2023). Virtual love experience in love and producer: Exploring perceptions of love, romance and gender in otome game player communities in china. *Media and Communication Research*, *4*(10). Advance online publication. DOI: 10.23977/mediacr.2023.041002

Wardecker, B. M., Smith, L. K., Edelstein, R. S., & Loving, T. J. (2015). Intimate relationships then and now: How old hormonal processes are influenced by our modern psychology. *Adaptive Human Behavior and Physiology, 1*(2), 150–176. DOI: 10.1007/s40750-015-0021-9

Weber-Guskar, E. (2021). How to feel about emotionalized artificial intelligence? When robot pets, holograms, and chatbots become affective partners. *Ethics and Information Technology, 23*(4), 601–610. DOI: 10.1007/s10676-021-09598-8 PMID: 34075305

Wei, Z., Chen, Y., Zhao, Q., Zhang, P., Zhou, L., Ren, J., Piao, Y., Qiu, B., Xie, X., Wang, S., Liu, J., Zhang, D., Kadosh, R. C., & Zhang, X. (2023). Implicit perception of differences between NLP-produced and human-produced language in the mentalizing network. *Advanced science, 10*(12), e2203990–n/a. DOI: 10.1002/advs.202203990

Weidlich, J., & Bastiaens, T. J. (2019). Designing sociable online learning environments and enhancing social presence: An affordance enrichment approach. *Computers & Education, 142*, 103622. DOI: 10.1016/j.compedu.2019.103622

Weitz, K., Schiller, D., Schlagowski, R., Huber, T., & André, E. (2021). "Let me explain!": Exploring the potential of virtual agents in explainable AI interaction design. *Journal on Multimodal User Interfaces, 15*(2), 87–98. DOI: 10.1007/s12193-020-00332-0

Wheatley Institute. (2025, February 13). Virtual Valentines? Nearly 1 in 5 Adults Report Having Chatted with AI Romantic Partner. *PR Newswire*. https://www.prnewswire.com/news-releases/virtual-valentines-nearly-1-in-5-adults-report-having-chatted-with-ai-romantic-partner-302376017.html

Whiten, A., Hinde, R. A., Laland, K. N., & Stringer, C. B. (2011). Culture evolves. *Philosophical Transactions of the Royal Society of London. Series B, Biological Sciences, 366*(1567), 938–948. DOI: 10.1098/rstb.2010.0372 PMID: 21357216

Whitestone. (2019, January 29). *How Tinder is Designed to Control Your Mind | The Whitestone Clinic Ottawa*. The Whitestone Clinic. https://whitestone.clinic/how-tinder-is-designed-to-get-you-addicted-and-control-your-behavior

Whitty, M. T. (2023). Drug mule for love. *Journal of Financial Crime, 30*(3), 795–812.

Widiger, T. A., & Oltmanns, J. R. (2017). Neuroticism is a fundamental domain of personality with enormous public health implications. *World Psychiatry; Official Journal of the World Psychiatric Association (WPA), 16*(2), 144–145. DOI: 10.1002/wps.20411 PMID: 28498583

Wiener, M., & Mehrabian, A. (1968). *Language within language: Immediacy, a channel in verbal communication*. Ardent Media.

Willoughby, B. J., & Carroll, J. S. (2025, February 13). *Counterfeit connections: The rise of AI romantic companions*. Institute for Family Studies. https://ifstudies.org/blog/counterfeit-connections-the-rise-of-ai-romantic-companions-

Willoughby, B. J., & Carroll, J. S. (2025, February). *Counterfeit Connections: The rise of AI romantic companions*. Institute for Family Studies. https://ifstudies.org/blog/counterfeit-connections-the-rise-of-ai-romantic-companions-

Wilson, J. W., Wacquant, L., & Connell, R. (2025). Urbanization and its effect on community relationships. *International Journal of Sociology Civics Research, 1*(1), 13–15. https://www.researchgate.net/publication/393755256_Urbanization_and_Its_Effect_on_Community_Relationships

Wnęk-Gozdeka, J. (2020). Prevention connected with romantic relationships in the Internet. *Prevention, 14*(11).

World Health Organization. (2025). *Depressive disorder (depression)*. https://www.who.int/news-room/fact-sheets/detail/depression

Wu, J. (2024). Social and ethical impact of emotional AI advancement: the rise of pseudo-intimacy relationships and challenges in human interactions [Opinion]. *Frontiers in Psychology, Volume 15 - 2024*. DOI: 10.3389/fpsyg.2024.1410462

Wu, Y., & Kelly, R. M. (2020). Online Dating Meets Artificial Intelligence: How the Perception of Algorithmically Generated Profile Text Impacts Attractiveness and Trust. In *32ND AUSTRALIAN CONFERENCE ON HUMAN-COMPUTER INTERACTION (OzCHI '20)*. https://doi.org/DOI: 10.1145/3441000.3441074

Wu, T. (2024). AI love: An analysis of virtual intimacy in human-computer interaction. *Communications in Humanities Research, 50*(1), 143–148. DOI: 10.54254/2753-7064/50/20242466

Wu, X., Liew, K., & Dorahy, M. J. (2025). Trust, Anxious attachment, and Conversational AI adoption Intentions in Digital Counseling: A Preliminary Cross-Sectional Questionnaire study. *JMIR AI, 4*, e68960. DOI: 10.2196/68960 PMID: 40262137

Wu, Y., & Kelly, R. M. (2020, December). Online dating meets artificial intelligence: How the perception of algorithmically generated profile text impacts attractiveness and trust. In *Proceedings of the 32nd Australian conference on human-computer interaction* (pp. 444-453).

Xi, Y., Paracha, S., & Sun, R. (2023). Inculcating morality in machines… applying machine ethics in the creation of ethically intelligent robots: The case study of Xiaoice. 2023 IEEE International Conference on Development and Learning (ICDL)

Xia, P., Zhai, S., Liu, B., Sun, Y., & Chen, C. (2016). Design of reciprocal recommendation systems for online dating. *Social Network Analysis and Mining*, *6*(1), 32. Advance online publication. DOI: 10.1007/s13278-016-0340-2

Xie, T., & Pentina, I. (2022). Attachment theory as a framework to understand relationships with social chatbots: A case study of replika. *Proceedings of the Annual Hawaii International Conference on System Sciences*. https://doi.org/DOI: 10.24251/HICSS.2022.258

Xie, T., Pentina, I., & Hancock, T. (2023). Friend, mentor, lover: Does chatbot engagement lead to psychological dependence? *Journal of Service Management*, *34*(4), 806–828. DOI: 10.1108/JOSM-02-2022-0072

Xie, Z., & Xie, Y. (2025). Would you share secrets with a chatbot? A longitudinal study on the relationship between virtual companionship and privacy disclosure. *Aslib Journal of Information Management*. Advance online publication. DOI: 10.1108/AJIM-10-2024-0803

Xu, H. (2025). Bonding with AI: Investigating the love relationships between humans and AI companions. doi:10.14711/thesis-hdl152286

Xu, W. (2019). Toward human-centered AI: a perspective from human-computer interaction. *interactions, 26*(4), 42–46. DOI: 10.1145/3328485

Xu, Y., Zhang, J., & Deng, G. (2022). Enhancing customer satisfaction with chatbots: The influence of communication styles and consumer attachment anxiety [Original Research]. *Frontiers in Psychology, Volume 13 - 2022*. DOI: 10.3389/fpsyg.2022.902782

Xu, F. (2025). *Human-machine Love: a Study of Intimacy Building between a Relationship-Oriented Chatbot and its Users*. Communication University of Zhejiang.

Xu, J., Le, K., Deitermann, A., & Montague, E. (2014). How different types of users develop trust in technology: A qualitative analysis of the antecedents of active and passive user trust in a shared technology. *Applied Ergonomics*, *45*(6), 1495–1503. DOI: 10.1016/j.apergo.2014.04.012 PMID: 24882059

Xu, T., Lyu, Y., & Zhong, J. (2025). "Hegemonic" but "obedient" AI boyfriend: The hybrid masculinity of the AI boyfriend and female domination in the China-based FAII. *Feminist Media Studies*, •••, 1–16. DOI: 10.1080/14680777.2025.2478386

Xygkou, A., Siriaraya, P., Covaci, A., Prigerson, H. G., Neimeyer, R., Ang, C. S., & She, W. (2023). *The "Conversation" about Loss: Understanding How Chatbot Technology was Used in Supporting People in Grief.* (pp. 1-15). https://doi.org/ DOI: 10.1145/3544548.3581154

Yan, Y. (2017). The desiring individual, moralist self and relational person. *The Cambridge Journal of Anthropology, 35*(2), 1–17. JSTOR. https://doi.org/DOI: 10.2307/26877566

Yang, F., & Oshio, A. (2025). Using attachment theory to conceptualize and measure the experiences in human-AI relationships. *Current Psychology (New Brunswick, N.J.), 44*(11), 1–12. DOI: 10.1007/s12144-025-07917-6

Yanguas, J., Pinazo-Henandis, S., & Tarazona-Santabalbina, F. J. (2018). The complexity of loneliness. *Acta Biomedica, 89*(2), 302–314. DOI: 10.23750/abm.v89i2.7404 PMID: 29957768

Yanke, G. (2021). Tying the knot with a robot: Legal and philosophical foundations for human–artificial intelligence matrimony. *AI & Society, 36*(2), 417–427. DOI: 10.1007/s00146-020-00973-5

Yenra. (2025). *AI technology in online dating algorithms: From machine learning to conversational intelligence.* https://yenra.com/ai-tech/online-dating-algorithms

Ye, Y. (2025). Coexistence challenges in the AI era: Social robots and human networks. *Journal of Global Trends in Social Science, 2*(8), 24–31. DOI: 10.70731/rex1ym06

Yin, . (2024). AI outperforms humans in establishing interpersonal closeness in emotionally engaging interactions—but only when labelled as human. *ResearchGate.* https://doi.org/DOI: 10.13140/RG.2.2.14690.13764

Yin, R. K. (2014). *Case study research: Design and methods* (5th ed.). Sage.

Yin, Y., Jia, N., & Wakslak, C. J. (2024). AI can help people feel heard, but an AI label diminishes this impact. *Proceedings of the National Academy of Sciences of the United States of America, 121*(14), e2319112121. DOI: 10.1073/pnas.2319112121 PMID: 38551835

Yosiandra, S. Y., & Sakariah, D. S. (2024). Unveiling the Romance Scam Scheme: Psychological Manipulation and Its Impact on Victims. *Humanika, 31*(2), 185–199. DOI: 10.14710/humanika.v31i2.67604

Young, J., Jawara, L. M., Nguyen, D. N., Daly, B., Huh-Yoo, J., & Razi, A. (2024). The role of AI in peer support for young people: A study of preferences for human- and AI-generated responses. Proceedings of the 2024 CHI Conference on Human Factors in Computing Systems, Zhang, Y. (2025). A Study on the Impact of the Mediation Availability of Generative AI Partners on User Emotional Construction: Taking the "Xing Ye App as an Example. *Technology Communication, 17*(14). DOI: 10.16607/j.cnki.1674-6708.2025.14.008

Yu, K., Shlomo Berkovsky, Taib, R., Conway, D., Zhou, J., & Chen, F. (2017). *User trust dynamics: An investigation driven by differences in system performance.* https://doi.org/DOI: 10.1145/3025171.3025219

Yu, R., & Jiang, L. (2025). Exploring patterns of AI-powered machine translation use in second language writing: A translanguaging perspective. *Computer Assisted Language Learning*, •••, 1–27. DOI: 10.1080/09588221.2025.2498096

Yurt, E. (2025). The interplay between Five-Factor personality traits and AI use motives in Turkish pre-service teachers: A canonical correlation analysis. *Current Psychology (New Brunswick, N.J.), 44*(15), 13756–13773. DOI: 10.1007/s12144-025-08175-2

Zhai, X. S., Chu, X. Y., Chai, C. S., Jong, M. S. Y., Istenic, A., Spector, M., Liu, J. B., Yuan, J., & Li, Y. (2021). A review of artificial intelligence (AI) in education from 2010 to 2020. *Complexity, 2021*(1), 8812542. DOI: 10.1155/2021/8812542

Zhang, W. (2024, June 13). The chinese women turning to chatgpt for AI boyfriends. *BBC.* https://www.bbc.com/articles/c4nnje9rpjgo

Zhang, H., Xiang, Z., & Yin, J. (2023). Social intimacy and skewed love: A study of the attachment relationship between internet group young users and a digital human. *Computers in Human Behavior: Artificial Humans, 1*(2), 100019. DOI: 10.1016/j.chbah.2023.100019

Zhang, R., Li, H., Meng, H., Zhan, J., Gan, H., & Lee, Y.-C. (2025). The dark side of AI companionship: A taxonomy of harmful algorithmic behaviors in human-AI relationships *Proceedings of the 2025 CHI Conference on Human Factors in Computing Systems*, DOI: 10.1145/3706598.3713429

Zhang, X., Li, Z., Zhang, M., Yin, M., Yang, Z., Gao, D., & Li, H. (2025). Exploring artificial intelligence (AI) chatbot usage behaviors and their association with mental health outcomes in Chinese university students. *Journal of Affective Disorders, 380*, 394–400. DOI: 10.1016/j.jad.2025.03.141 PMID: 40147615

Zhang, Z., Tsiakas, K., & Schneegass, C. (2024). Explaining the wait: How justifying chatbot response delays impact user trust *Proceedings of the 6th ACM Conference on Conversational User Interfaces*, Luxembourg, Luxembourg. DOI: 10.1145/3640794.3665550

Zhang, Z., Tsiakas, K., & Schneegass, C. (2024). Explaining the Wait: How Justifying Chatbot Response Delays Impact User Trust. Proceedings of the 6th ACM Conference on Conversational User Interfaces, Zhong, W., Guo, L., Gao, Q., Ye, H., & Wang, Y. (2024). Memorybank: Enhancing large language models with long-term memory. Proceedings of the AAAI Conference on Artificial Intelligence, Zimmerman, A., Janhonen, J., & Beer, E. (2024). Human/AI relationships: challenges, downsides, and impacts on human/human relationships. *AI and Ethics*, *4*(4), 1555–1567. DOI: 10.1007/s43681-023-00348-8

Zhao, S. (2003). Toward a Taxonomy of Copresence. *Presence (Cambridge, Mass.)*, *12*(5), 445–455. DOI: 10.1162/105474603322761261

Zhou, L., Gao, J., Li, D., & Shum, H.-Y. (2020). The design and implementation of XiaoIce, an empathetic social chatbot. *Computational linguistics - Association for Computational Linguistics, 46*(1), 53–93. DOI: 10.1162/coli_a_00368

Zhu, J., & Liu, W. (2020). A tale of two databases: The use of Web of Science and Scopus in academic papers. *Scientometrics*, *123*(1), 321–335. DOI: 10.1007/s11192-020-03387-8

Zou, W., Liu, Z., & Lin, C. (2025). The influence of individuals' emotional involvement and perceived roles of AI chatbots on emotional self-efficacy. *Information Communication and Society*, •••, 1–21. DOI: 10.1080/1369118X.2025.2508394

Zuboff, S. (2023). The age of surveillance capitalism. In W. Longhofer & D. Winchester (Eds.), *Social Theory Re-Wired* (3 ed., pp. 203–213). Routledge. DOI: 10.4324/9781003320609-27

Zuboff, S. (2019). *The age of surveillance capitalism: The fight for a human future at the new frontier of power*. Public Affairs.

About the Contributors

Ashraf Sadat Ahadzadeh is an Associate Professor at Xiamen University Malaysia, where she has been serving since 2018. She holds a PhD in Mass Communication. Her research interests include health communication, media psychology, as well as the intersections of emerging technologies and their psychological and health-related implications. Her scholarly work has been widely published in highly indexed, peer-reviewed journals.

Kam-Fong Lee is a senior lecturer at SEGI University, Malaysia, where she brings her years of teaching experience and passion for language studies to the classroom. She has published a number of interdisciplinary research articles and has a strong interest for research. Her main research interests include Systemic Functional Linguistics (SFL), discourse analysis, and effective reading and writing practises in learning English as Second Language (ESL) and English as Foreign Language (EFL) classrooms.

***

Kinjal Agarwal is a final-year postgraduate student in Clinical Psychology at CHRIST (Deemed to be University), India, with academic and clinical experience across a range of mental health and educational settings. Her training has included work in psychiatric care, counselling spaces, and child and adolescent environments, allowing her to engage with diverse populations. Her areas of interest include psychotherapy, psychological assessment, child and adolescent mental health, and the psychological understanding of relationships, behaviour, and emotional processes. She is interested in bridging theory, research, and practice, with a focus on a client-centred approach to mental health and wellbeing.

Mansour Amini is a Senior Lecturer and researcher in Translation Studies and Conference Interpreting. His PhD thesis was the first study in Malaysia to examine

Conference Interpreting Quality in the national context. He has published widely in WoS-, Scopus-, and other indexed peer-reviewed journals across the fields of Translation, Education, Humanities, and Social Sciences.

Nithya Sree Balakumar is a graduate student who is currently pursuing her final year of Master's in Clinical Psychology at CHRIST (Deemed to be University), India. Throughout her academic journey, she has worked with different populations and in various mental health spaces such as child development centers, psychiatric hospitals, inclusive education centers and counselling centers. Deeply driven by personal curiosity about human relationships and interpersonal dynamics, she is currently exploring 'social battery' as a psychological construct among emerging adults, and is working as an intern in a mental health clinic, aspiring to make a positive impact in society through client-centered approaches to therapy and clinical practice.

Sovannaroth Chheang earned her bachelor's degree in English from Build Bright University, Phnom Penh, in 2016, where she built a solid foundation in language studies, communication, and pedagogy. She began her teaching career in 2013 as a Tutor at the Kindergarten Association, conducting both part-time and full-time English programs. Since 2018, she has served as a Teacher of English and General Assistant at Sovanna Elton Foreign Language School. Through these roles, she has developed broad expertise in classroom management, language instruction, curriculum design, and student engagement, supporting the school's mission of advancing foreign language learning. Ms. Chheang's academic interests center on pursuing a master's degree in English education or related fields within the humanities and social sciences. Passionate about integrating global research methodologies into her practice, she aims to enhance pedagogy, foster classroom innovation, and promote effective, research-informed teaching. Her commitment lies in bridging academic research with real-world practice to advance English education in Cambodia and beyond.

E Quanling is a Journalism undergraduate student at Xiamen University Malaysia. She researches human–AI intimacy, with a focus on socially companionable AI. Her work spans both qualitative and quantitative approaches.

Marie Grace A. Gomez is Professor 11 at the Counselor Education Area, College of Education, University of the Philippines-Diliman. She teaches counseling and research courses at the undergraduate and graduate levels. She has a bachelor's degree in Political Science, a Master of Arts in Education (Guidance) degree, a Doctor of Philosophy degree in Guidance and another doctorate in Special Education. All degrees were earned from the University of the Philippines-Diliman. She has served as a classroom teacher, guidance counselor, and administrator in the basic and tertiary education settings. Her community extension projects involve counseling and assessment of children, persons with disability, children in conflict with the law, drug surrenderees, sexually abused children, medical personnel, women with mental health issues in institutional settings, and persons affected by COVID-19.

Sovanna Huot is a PhD candidate in Political Science at the University of Delhi, New Delhi, India. He is a vice principal at a Government Public High School of Cambodia and is responsible for the school academic and institutional leadership. He is a very proficient academic across many disciplines. He has completed a two-year teacher training program from 2010-2012 and has obtained bachelor's degrees in English and in Educational Administration. He also has two master's degrees in law and in TEFL obtained through a very competitive scholarship, and a Master of Education, specialized in School Leadership, Upper Secondary School Principalship, from the National Institute of Education, Phnom Penh, 2021. He specializes in educational reform and in the practice-policy nexus of digit pedagogy and in glonacal (global–national–local) education systems. He has a conferred political science and education and has publications in political science and education, indexed in Scopus (Author ID: 59316244400).

Lan Lan holds a Master's degree in Anthropology from The Chinese University of Hong Kong and a Bachelor's degree in Journalism from Xiamen University Malaysia. Her research interests lie in social media, media psychology, social anxiety, and AI-mediated interpersonal relationships, as well as working culture, death culture, and economic anthropology.

Lin Siew Eng is a specialist in English Language Education and TESOL. She holds a PhD in TESOL, a Master of Education (TESOL), a Bachelor of Education (TESL), a Diploma in TESL, and a Teaching Certificate in TESL. Her research interests include benchmarking English language reading and grammar proficiency, reading matrix development, and the design of language assessment tools and educational modules.

Lalitha Ragul is a Counselling Psychologist, presently working as an Assistant Professor at Department of Psychology at CHRIST University, YPR campus, Bangalore. She pursued her PhD in Counselling Psychology from University of Madras. She is a distinguished researcher who has won Best Paper Awards and has published research papers in various International and UGC Care List journals. In her PhD research study, she has developed a Marital Counselling Intervention Program for couples to improve their relationship. She is an expert in Marital Therapy and Family Counselling, especially for Parenting, Child and Adolescent Counselling and has acquired a Fellowship on the same from NHCA, Singapore. She is a reviewer at Humanities and Social Sciences (HSS), Science Publishing Group, New York, USA as well as at Edwin Group of Journals.

Narges Saffari is affiliated with Nyenrode Business Universiteit, where she is engaged in teaching and research. Her academic interests include Teacher Education, Pedagogy, Language Education, and Classroom Studies, with a focus on enhancing instructional practices and educational effectiveness.

Wenxi Wen is an undergraduate student in Journalism at Xiamen University Malaysia. Her research interests include AI-mediated relationships and the social and ethical implications of artificial intelligence, with particular attention to the Chinese cultural context. She is interested in how emerging AI technologies reshape interpersonal relationships and moral perceptions among young users.

Wu Yushan holds a Master of Journalism from the University of Hong Kong and a Bachelor of Arts in Journalism from Xiamen University Malaysia. Her research interests lie at the intersection of health communication, social media, and artificial intelligence (AI), with a particular emphasis on AI's profound impacts on healthcare, human relationships, and broader social dynamics.

Xiaoyu Yan is a final year student passionate about artificial intelligence, psychology, and human–AI relationships. She is particularly interested in how individuals make sense of AI in emotionally charged interactions, and how these interpretations shape connection. Trained in journalism, she brings strong analytical, reading, interviewing, and writing skills to the research, along with a sensitivity to narrative, framing, and language.

Index

A

C

D

E

G

H

I

L

M

O

P

Q

R

S

T

V

X

www.ingramcontent.com/pod-product-compliance
Lightning Source LLC
LaVergne TN
LVHW061525290926
849162LV00004B/674